1970   1980   1990   2000   2010

Liberal ascendancy
(1965–1978)

"Deficits to surplus"
(1979–1999)

Republican Era
(1995– 2006)

Divided
Government
(2007–2009)

Unified
Government
(2009–2011)

Divided
Government
(2011–)

Kennedy/
Johnson
(1961–1969)

Nixon
(1969–1974)

Ford
(1974–1977)

Carter
(1977–1981)

Reagan
(1981–1989)

G. H.W. Bush
(1989–1993)

Clinton
(1993–2001)

G. W. Bush
(2001– 2009)

Obama
(2009–)

Electronic
voting,
House
(1973)

Computers
on Capitol
Hill
(1975)

Televised
House
(1979)

Televised
Senate
(1986)

Senators' first
Web pages
(1993)

Members' blogs

"Reform Era"
(power dispersed)
(1970–1975)

Special caucuses grow
Thomas
"Tip" O'Neill
(1977–1987)

Leadership
strengthened
Jim Wright
(1987–1989)

GOP Speakers

Newt Gingrich
(1995–1998)

Dennis Hastert
(1999–2007)

Democratic
Control
Nancy Pelosi
(2007– 2011)

John A.
Boehner
(2011–)

Medicare
Modernization Act
(2003)

American
Recovery and
Reinvestment
Act (2009)

National Environmental
Policy Act (1969)

Ethics in
Government Act
(1978)

Americans with
Disabilities Act
(1991)

Welfare
reform
(1996)

No Child Left
Behind Act
(2001)

Patient Protection and
Affordable Care Act (2010)/
Financial Regulatory
Reform (2010)

Buckley v.
Valeo
(1976)

I.N.S. v. Chadha
(1983)

U.S. Term Limits
v. Thornton
(1995)

Hamdan v.
Rumsfeld (2006)

Citizens
United v. FEC (2010)

Legislative
Reorganization Act of
1970

Gramm-Rudman-Hollings
(1985, 1987)

Reform period
(1993–1995)

Intelligence reform
(2004)

Congressional Budget Act
(1974)

Budget Enforcement Act
(1990)

Homeland Security
Department
(2002)

Honest Leadership and
Open Government Act
(2007)

Watergate
break-in
(1972)

Church
Committee
(1975)

Nixon impeachment,
resignation
(1974)

9/11 Intelligence
Commission
(2004)

EPA
regulatory
reform
hearings
(2011)

War Powers Resolution
(1973)

Iran-contra scandal
(1986)

Clinton scandal,
impeachment
(1998–1999)

Iraq Study Group
(2006)

"Cold War"
(1945–1991)

Berlin Wall falls (1989)

Terrorist attacks (2001)

Afghanistan and
Pakistan
(2009–)

Libya
Air Strikes
(2011)

Afghanistan War (2001–)
Iraq War
(2003–)

Vietnam War
(1965–1974)

Persian Gulf War
(1991)

1970   1980   1990   2000   2010

PRAISE FOR *CONGRESS AND ITS MEMBERS*

"I always assign *Congress and Its Members* because it provides the most comprehensive assessment of Congress and the individuals and groups within and outside of the institution. Each volume is meticulously researched, timely, and accessible to students who appreciate the text's balance between statistical data and in-depth, member-specific cases. I highly recommend *Congress and Its Members* for anyone interested in understanding Congress and its central role in American politics.

"I am delighted to sing the praises of *Congress and Its Members*. It is simply an outstanding text."

—Rosalyn Cooperman, *University of Mary Washington*

"*Congress and Its Members* stands out among textbooks on the topic. Its substantive coverage is comprehensive, ranging from campaigns and elections to committee politics, floor procedure, and inter-branch relations. It reflects the best recent scholarship about Congress. And the authors do a great job of integrating up-to-date illustrations and examples. The book is a superb vehicle for getting undergraduate students interested in the legislative process."

—C. Lawrence Evans, *College of William & Mary*

"Organized around the simple, but incisive, theme of the 'two Congresses,' *Congress and Its Members* provides students with a valuable framework for understanding lawmaking and representation in Congress. Just as successful members of Congress must balance the competing demands of the institution and their constituents back home, Davidson, Oleszek, and Lee masterfully balance the historical with the contemporary, the theoretical with the practical, and the sophisticated with the accessible."

—Vincent G. Moscardelli, *University of Connecticut*

"*Congress and Its Members* is a classic. Its authors have written a book that combines analytic depth and up to date coverage of the latest congressional controversies. The text is great for students and scholars alike."

—Eric Smith, *University of California, Santa Barbara*

"In an age when it is easy to be cynical about politics and Congress's standing with the public continues to plummet, *Congress and Its Members* challenges its readers to understand the complexities and contradictions faced by legislators and Congress as an institution. The authors engage both students and scholars by combining discussions of the latest political controversies with historical and theoretical analyses that engage readers of all backgrounds."

—Michele Swers, *Georgetown University*

"This is a book I have used with great success, not only with an advanced class of college students, but which I have recommended to curious Americans and foreign visitors alike who want to learn more about how Congress really works in easy-to-understand, non-technical language. The contemporary examples used to bring the modern Congress to life are worth the price of admission alone."

—Donald R. Wolfensberger, Director, The Congress Project,
Woodrow Wilson International Center for Scholars

_F__our Pivotal Events in Congressional History._ British troops burn the Capitol and capture Washington, D.C., in 1814 (top left). Inflamed sectional passions caused violence on the Senate floor in 1856 (top right): An enraged Rep. Preston Brooks (S.C.), right, raises his cane against an unsuspecting Sen. Charles Sumner (Mass.). Laurence M. Keitt, a fellow South Carolinian, (center), raises his cane and holds a pistol behind his back to keep other northerners from interfering. In the televised Army-McCarthy hearings of 1954 (bottom), Sen. Joseph McCarthy (R-Wis.) is chastened by U.S. Army counsel Joseph Welsh (left) during the Senate inquiry into McCarthy's reckless charges about communists in government. "At long last, sir, have you no sense of decency?" Welsh exclaimed after McCarthy attacked one of the lawyer's young aides. The dramatic exchange was a turning point in McCarthy's career; eventually he was censured by his Senate colleagues. Finally (center), Senate Majority Leader Lyndon B. Johnson (D-Texas) gives "the treatment"—prolonged persuasion at very close range—to Sen. Theodore Francis Green (D-R.I.).

THIRTEENTH EDITION

Congress and Its Members

Roger H. Davidson
University of Maryland

Walter J. Oleszek
Congressional Research Service

Frances E. Lee
University of Maryland

Los Angeles | London | New Delhi
Singapore | Washington DC

CQ Press
2300 N Street, NW, Suite 800
Washington, DC 20037

Phone: 202-729-1900; toll-free, 1-866-4CQ-PRESS (1-866-427-7737)

Web: www.cqpress.com

Cover design: Matthew Simmons, www.MyselfIncluded.com
Composition: C&M Digitals (P) Ltd.

♾ The paper used in this publication exceeds the requirements of the American National Standard for Information Sciences—Permanence of Paper for Printed Library Materials, ANSI Z39.48-1992.

Printed and bound in the United States of America

15   14   13   12   11   1   2   3   4   5

ISBN: 978-1-60871-642-5
ISSN: 1539-1779

FOR *Nancy; Douglas, Victoria, Elizabeth, Thomas, James, Alexander; Chris, Theo, Emily, and Olivia*

—R.H.D.

FOR *Janet, Mark, and Eric*

—W.J.O.

FOR *Emery and Beverly*

—F.E.L.

Roger H. Davidson is professor emeritus of government and politics at the University of Maryland, and has served as visiting professor of political science at the University of California, Santa Barbara. He is a Fellow of the National Academy of Public Administration. During the 1970s, he served on the staffs of reform efforts in both the House (Bolling-Martin Committee) and the Senate (Stevenson-Brock Committee). For the 2001–2002 academic year, he served as the John Marshall Chair in political science at the University of Debrecen, Hungary. His books include *Remaking Congress: Change and Stability in the 1990s,* co-edited with James A. Thurber (1995), and *Understanding the Presidency,* 6th ed., co-edited with James P. Pfiffner (2011). Davidson is co-editor with Donald C. Bacon and Morton Keller of *The Encyclopedia of the United States Congress* (1995).

Walter J. Oleszek is a senior specialist in the legislative process at the Congressional Research Service. He has served as either a full-time professional staff aide or consultant to every major House and Senate congressional reorganization effort beginning with passage of the Legislative Reorganization Act of 1970. In 1993 he served as Policy Director of the Joint Committee on the Organization of Congress. A longtime adjunct faculty member at American University, Oleszek is a frequent lecturer to various academic, governmental, and business groups. He is the author or co-author of several books, including *Congressional Procedures and the Policy Process,* 8th ed. (2011), and *Congress under Fire: Reform Politics and the Republican Majority,* with C. Lawrence Evans (1997).

Frances E. Lee is professor of government and politics at the University of Maryland. She has been a Research Fellow at the Brookings Institution and an APSA Congressional Fellow. She is the author of *Beyond Ideology: Politics, Principles, and Partisanship in the U.S. Senate* (2009), which received the Richard F. Fenno Jr. Prize for the best book on legislative politics in 2010 and the D.B. Hardeman Prize for the best book on the U.S. Congress published in 2009. She is also co-author, with Bruce I. Oppenheimer, of *Sizing Up the Senate: The Unequal Consequences of Equal Representation* (1999). Her articles have appeared in *American Political Science Review, Journal of Politics, Legislative Studies Quarterly,* and *American Journal of Political Science,* among others.

BRIEF CONTENTS

CONTENTS

Reference Materials

TABLES, FIGURES, AND BOXES

Boxes

PREFACE

As authors of the thirteenth edition of a book that first appeared in 1981, we are perforce believers in the maxim that in politics six months is a long time and four years practically a lifetime. Events of recent years surely bear out this wisdom.

The roller-coaster performances of the U.S. legislative and executive branches form the backdrop for our discussion. In the almost seven decades since the end of World War II, nearly every president has endured declines in public support during his tenure in office. Three of them—Gerald R. Ford, Jimmy Carter, and George H. W. Bush, were denied a second term. At some point, nearly all faced a Congress controlled wholly or in part by the opposition party. Indeed, only John F. Kennedy, Lyndon B. Johnson, and Jimmy Carter had the luxury of working solely with their own Capitol Hill majority. Yet Johnson pulled out of his 1968 reelection race because of public rancor over the Vietnam War; Carter lost his reelection bid in 1980 to Ronald Reagan.

More recently, George W. Bush's support plummeted amid vocal opposition from Democrats and independents, and even factions within his own Republican ranks. Disapproval of the administration—especially over the Iraq war and the failure to cope with the devastation of Hurricane Katrina in 2005—led to election losses in 2006 and 2008. Democrats controlled both chambers of Congress from 2007 to 2011.

The remarkable rise of first-term Illinois senator Barack Obama underscores the unpredictability of politics. No one rated him a front-runner in the 2008 presidential race, but his campaign—innovatively designed, skillfully managed, and lavishly financed—won him the Democratic nomination over New York senator Hillary Clinton, which was then followed by his defeat of Republican senator John McCain of Arizona. But Obama found the spectre of national and global economic collapse taking precedence over his ambitious "change" agenda. Although financial collapse was avoided and the severe recession stabilized, the economic recovery was too sluggish to help the millions of job seekers. At midterm, Obama's overall job rating sank below 50 percent. Disheartened by the nation's economy, voters in 2010 gave control of the House to the GOP and squeezed the Democrats' hold on the Senate to a fragile margin: 53–47, counting two independents who caucus with the Democrats.

The precarious fortunes of recent presidents and congressional majorities are a reminder of the pervasive pluralism of the American political system, with its diverse viewpoints and interests. Presidents and congressional leaders see their mandates sooner or later bump against the founders' intricate "auxiliary precautions" for preventing majorities from winning quick or total victories. Not the least of the system's attributes is what we call the "two-Congresses" dilemma: Congress is both a conduit for localized interests and a maker of national policy.

In this edition, we discuss new developments and fresh research findings on nearly every aspect of Congress. The wartime context—thus far embracing two wars, reconstruction efforts in Afghanistan and Iraq, and efforts in Libya and against terrorists worldwide—places extreme pressures on Congress. Deliberative legislative processes may seem out of place when people demand immediate, concerted actions. But hasty responses are invariably regretted, and sober reflections demand legislative oversight and remediation.

Strength of partisanship and party leaders is the chief characteristic of today's Capitol Hill. Congress is a vortex of so-called permanent campaigns, in which electioneering goals and techniques are routinely interlocked with the process and content of lawmaking. We record shifts in party leaders and their rank-and-file members, the committee system, floor procedures, and the Capitol Hill community. Adaptive relationships with presidents, bureaucrats, and the courts illustrate Congress's centrality to the entire federal government apparatus.

Amid all these global and political changes are the underlying constants in Congress's character and behavior. Most important is the dual nature of Congress as a collection of career-minded politicians, and also as a forum for shaping and refining national policy. We employ the two-Congresses theme to explain the details of congressional life as well as the scholarly findings about legislators' behavior. Colorful personalities and practical examples illustrate the enduring topics essential for understanding Capitol Hill. We strive to describe recent events and trends precisely and perceptively; more important, we try to place these developments in the broader historical and conceptual frameworks needed for understanding how Congress and its members function.

These are troubling times for those of us who believe in representative democracy. True, Congress has, with varying levels of success, absorbed astonishing changes in its membership, partisan control, structural and procedural arrangements, and policy agendas. Yet Congress has all too often retreated from its constitutional mandate to initiate national policy and oversee government operations. Its prerogatives are under siege from executive decision makers, federal judges, and elite opinion makers, who constantly belittle its capacities, ignore its authority, and evade its scrutiny. Yet lawmakers themselves are to blame for yielding too often to the initiatives of others, for failing to ask hard questions, for reinforcing disdain of the institution, and for substituting partisan allegiance for independent judgment and critical thinking. Yes, today's Congress all too often falls short of the Founders' vision that it is the "first branch of government"—for reasons that this book explains.

This edition, like its predecessors, is written for general readers seeking an introduction to the modern Congress as well as for college or university students taking courses on the legislative process or national policy making.

We try to present accurate, timely, and readable information, along with thoughtful and influential insights from scholars and practitioners alike. Although wrapped around our core theme, the book's chapters are long on analysis. We make no apologies for this. Lawmaking is an arduous, complicated business that demands special skills; those who would understand it must master its details and nuances. At the same time, we hope to convey the energy and excitement of the place. After all, our journalist friends are right: Capitol Hill is the best beat in town.

ACKNOWLEDGMENTS

We have incurred more debts to friends and fellow scholars than we could ever recount. We thank especially our colleagues at the Congressional Research Service and elsewhere: Richard Beth, Ida Brudnick, Curtis Copeland, Royce Crocker, Christopher Davis, C. Lawrence Evans, Louis Fisher, Sam Garrett, Richard Grimmett, Valerie Heitshusen, William Heniff Jr., Henry Hogue, Frederick Kaiser, Robert Keith, Michael Koempel, Emery Lee, Megan Lynch, Jennifer Manning, Betsy Palmer, Steve Rutkus, Elizabeth Rybicki, James Saturno, Wendy Schiller, Judy Schneider, Barbara Schwemle, Stephen W. Stathis, Michele Swers, Sean M. Theriault, Kenneth Thomas, Jim Thurber, and Donald Wolfensberger. The views and interpretations expressed in this book are in no way attributable to the Congressional Research Service.

We also wish to thank Eric Schickler, University of California, Berkeley, for his comprehensive, insightful review of our last edition. His comments and suggestions provoked us to consider new questions and revisit enduring ones, and helped us to shape the current edition.

Our friends at CQ Press deserve special appreciation. Brenda Carter, director of the college division, has inspired and prodded us over the last nine editions. Charisse Kiino, our editor, capably reviewed the book's overall structure and helped us tighten this edition. Sabra Bissette Ledent and Nancy Loh offered skilled and probing editorial assistance. Belinda Josey supervised the book's production. And we thank Adena Boghos for providing photo research.

Our deep appreciation for our families, for their love and support, cannot be fully expressed in words. As a measure of our affection, this book is dedicated to them.

—Roger H. Davidson
Santa Barbara, California

—Walter J. Oleszek
Fairfax, Virginia

—Frances E. Lee
Washington, D.C.

June 2011

THIRTEENTH EDITION

Congress and Its Members

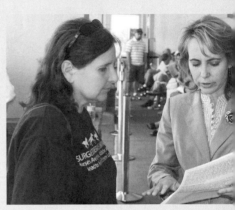

Dual Duties. Rep. Gabrielle Giffords's "Congress on Your Corner" sign (top left) announcing her fateful Tucson event for meeting constituents on January 8, 2011. The arrival of the Arizona Democrat is awaited by her constituents (top right). Rep. Giffords (middle right) discusses a constituent's problem. A year earlier, she testified before the House Budget Committee (bottom left). The congresswoman gives space shuttle astronauts Akihiko Hoshide of Japan and commander Mark Kelly, her husband, a tour of the Capitol (bottom right).

The Two Congresses

On January 8, 2011, a Saturday morning, Democratic representative Gabrielle Giffords was engaged in congressional work in a Safeway parking lot in Tucson, Arizona. She was conducting one of her frequent "Congress on Your Corner" events at which she met and talked with her constituents. By 10 a.m. everything was set up—that is, a couple of tables with handouts and roped posts to allow people to walk one by one to meet the congresswoman. The first person to come up was an Army Reservist who wanted to show Giffords his commendation from Iraq. Next, a couple chatted with her. Then federal district judge John M. Roll, who had just come from Mass, thanked Giffords for her help on a judicial matter.

What happened next was described by Ron Barber, the lawmaker's district director: "It's a bit of a blur, but I saw a man with a gun come into our little exit. He came in that area, between the two tables. His gun was drawn, and I saw him shoot the congresswoman. Almost right away, he shot me, and I went down."[1] The assailant's spray of bullets was deadly: six people died, including Judge Roll and the young man who planned the event, Gabe Zimmerman, Giffords's director of community outreach. Another fourteen were wounded, including the congresswoman and Barber, her district director. The tragic event for a time made Gabby Giffords, who survived the shooting, one of the nation's best-known House members.

A third-generation Arizonan, Giffords has deep roots in the Eighth Congressional District, with its thorny local issues and divided loyalties. She grew up in Tucson, riding horses and racing motorcycles competitively. Before entering politics, she ran a Tucson tire business started by her father.[2] Her political independence reflects her hometown. "We are . . . a very diverse community in so many ways—socio-economically, ethnically, religiously," a close friend explained. "Tucson, above all, has had to learn to compromise and to be compassionate and responsive to people, mostly because of their differences. That is part of Gabby's upbringing. She's not going to take the strict party message."[3] Although her congressional record tends to reflect her Democratic Party's stance, she cultivates her independence.

Before Giffords's election in 2006, her Eighth District seat had been held by a Republican. With most of Tucson's Latino population located in a neighboring constituency, the district leans Republican in presidential voting, albeit with a large share of independent voters. "I've got a very tough district," observed Giffords, "a district that voted for President [George W.] Bush twice; a district that did not support Barack Obama in the primary or the general election; and right now, I'm just focused on my job."[4]

The greatest challenge of Representative Giffords's second term was health care reform, the leading domestic agenda item of President Obama's first two years in office. At town hall meetings during the summer of 2009, Giffords faced large raucous crowds demanding that she explain her position on the legislation.[5] Her district appearances were trailed by angry reform opponents. Meanwhile, her district office was vandalized, and at another "Congress on Your Corner" event, one attendee dropped a gun from his pocket. After Giffords voted in favor of the legislation, a Tucson Tea Party leader flatly pronounced, "Giffords is toast."[6]

Another of Giffords's tasks was to address her constituents' concerns about illegal immigration. Spread over the entire southeastern part of the state, the district has a hundred-mile border with Mexico. The immigration issue was a flash point in March 2010 following the brutal murder of Robert N. Krenz Jr., a member of one of the oldest ranching families in southeastern Arizona. Found dead on his ranch after radioing to his brother that he was aiding someone he believed to be an illegal immigrant, police suspected that Krenz was shot by a Mexican drug trafficker.[7] "This was our BP oil spill," Giffords said of the local outcry.[8] She successfully pressed the Obama administration for 1,200 more National Guard troops to help secure the border in the wake of the murder.[9]

Giffords also was managing constituency turmoil about immigration checkpoints. Although Arizona's Eighth District was the only border district without a permanent checkpoint to apprehend smugglers, constituents worried about the safety of a proposed checkpoint in a populated area, disliked the traffic disruptions, and resented its placement deep in state territory. Giffords convened a community work group on the issue and held a series of public forums at which constituents offered alternative ideas and voiced objections. Her group then presented a report to the Border Patrol, and the agency then revised its plans to conform with local preferences.[10]

Local conservative activists and Republicans expected to defeat Giffords in 2010. She faced fierce Republican opposition in a district rated as a "pure tossup" by election experts Charlie Cook and Stuart Rothenberg. With such a challenge, it was no surprise that Giffords raised more campaign money than any other Arizona lawmaker, made 340 appearances in her district in her first term, and in 2007 sent out more franked mail than other any House member.[11] In the 2010 general election, running against a six-foot, eight-inch U.S. Marine combat veteran with rock star appeal, she pulled out a victory margin of just over 1 percent of the votes cast.[12]

Giffords's experiences illustrate the themes in this book. The work of Congress is conducted not only on Capitol Hill but also in states and districts hundreds or thousands of miles away. In a swing district, Giffords has had to balance her party's positions with constituency sentiment. She has sought to build a reputation for pragmatism and bipartisanship. When she first took her seat in Congress, she joined the Blue Dog caucus of centrist Democrats. She has also cultivated an independent image with her roll-call voting record, despite supporting her party on high-profile issues such as health care reform and the 2009 economic stimulus. She stood against the majority of her party in opposing the popular "Cash for Clunkers" program, the auto bailout, and appropriations earmarks. When asked about Giffords's relationship with Democratic Party leaders, her communications director bristled: "Congresswoman Giffords does not vote 'for' or 'against' leadership. The men and women of Arizona's 8th Congressional District sent her to the House of Representatives to represent them and be their advocate. That's what she does with each and every vote she casts."[13]

With extraordinary good fortune, Representative Giffords was rushed immediately after the shooting to a world-class trauma center (that she had supported as a state legislator). There, she quickly underwent brain surgery. With quality care, she recovered enough to be transferred to a rehabilitation hospital in Houston, Texas, where her husband, an astronaut, was stationed. Her future role in Congress is uncertain, but her staff soldiers on to represent her to the district and the public.[14]

THE DUAL NATURE OF CONGRESS

Gabrielle Giffords's representational dilemmas underscore the dual nature of Congress.[*] Like all members, Giffords inhabits two very different but closely linked worlds. As a representative of a district deeply concerned about federal immigration policy, Giffords needs to prove that she can be an effective local advocate—that she understands her constituents' needs and will act on their behalf. At the same time, Giffords also endeavors to be a national policy maker. An advocate of solar power, she successfully spearheaded legislation providing new federal funding for solar energy research and a solar energy tax cut.[15] She also had to vote on controversial national issues that deeply divided her district such as health care reform, cap-and-trade carbon regulations, and the $700 billion bailout of the U.S. financial markets. Giffords's various goals and activities highlight the dual character of the national legislature—Congress as a lawmaking institution and Congress as an assembly of local representatives.

---

[*]NOTE TO OUR READERS: Long before the tragic events of January 8, 2011, we had decided to illustrate our two-Congresses theme with the work of Rep. Gabrielle Giffords and her challenges of lawmaking and representing her district, which lies some 2,700 miles from the nation's capital. Those events, and the intense press coverage that followed, made our case even more compelling.

In this sense, there are two Congresses. One is the Congress of textbooks, of "how a bill becomes a law." It is Congress acting as a collegial body, performing constitutional duties, and debating legislative issues that affect the entire nation. This Congress is a fascinating arena in which all the forces of American political life converge—presidents, cabinet members, career bureaucrats, activists, lobbyists, policy wonks, military leaders, and ambitious political entrepreneurs of every stripe. This Congress is more than a collection of its members at any given time. It is a mature institution with a complex network of rules, organizations, and traditions. Norms mark the boundaries of the legislative playing field and define the rules of the game. Individual members generally must accept Congress on its own terms and conform to its established ways of doing things.

A second Congress also exists, and it is every bit as important as the Congress portrayed in textbooks. This is the representative assembly of 541 individuals (100 senators, 435 representatives, 5 delegates, and 1 resident commissioner). This Congress includes men and women of many different ages, backgrounds, and routes to office, all doing what is necessary to maintain political support in their local constituencies. Their electoral fortunes depend less on what Congress produces as a national institution than on the policy positions they take individually and the local ties they build and maintain. "As locally elected officials who make national policy," observes Paul S. Herrnson, "members of Congress almost lead double lives."[16]

The two Congresses are in many ways separated by a wide gulf. The complex, often insular world of Capitol Hill is far removed from most constituencies, in perspective and outlook, as well as in miles. Lawmaking and representing are separate tasks, and members of Congress recognize them as such. Yet these two Congresses are bound together. What affects one affects the other—sooner or later.

Legislators' Tasks

The duality between institutional and individual duties permeates legislators' daily activities and roles. As Speaker Sam Rayburn, D-Texas, once remarked: "A congressman has two constituencies—he has his constituents at home, and his colleagues here in the House. To serve his constituents at home, he must also serve his colleagues here in the House."[17]

No problem vexes members more than that of juggling constituency and legislative tasks. The pull of constituency business is relentless. To maintain their local connections, Congress schedules lengthy recesses, termed "district work periods," and many short Tuesday-to-Thursday legislative weeks. "I can tell you based on my experience that the number of days Congress spends in Washington should not be correlated with the quality of the work that is accomplished. . . . I can also tell you that time spent in our districts is not 'time off,'" observed Rep. Rob Bishop, R-Utah. "There is much more to effective representation than just voting in Washington."[18] On average, between 2000 and 2011 Congress was in session for less than 40 percent of the calendar year. Members largely spent the rest of their time at home in their constituencies. Even when members are in Washington, one study found that they spend less than half of their time on lawmaking duties on the floor of the House or in committee.[19]

Reelection is the paramount operational goal of members of Congress. As a former representative put it, "All members of Congress have a primary interest in getting reelected. Some members have no other interest."[20] After all, politicians must win elections before they can achieve any long-range political goals. "[Reelection] has to be the *proximate* goal of everyone, the goal that must be achieved over and over if other ends are to be entertained," David R. Mayhew observed in *Congress: The Electoral Connection.*[21]

Individual legislators vary in how they balance the twin roles of legislator and representative. Some legislators devote more time and resources to lawmaking, while others focus almost entirely on constituency tending. With their longer terms, some senators stress voter outreach and fence mending during the year or two before reelection and focus on legislative activities at other times. Yet senatorial contests normally are more competitive and costlier than House races, and many senators now run for reelection all the time—like most of their House colleagues.[22] Across the board, most senators and representatives would like to devote more time to lawmaking and other Capitol Hill duties instead of to constituency demands, according to the results of a congressionally sponsored survey of members.[23]

Popular Images

The notion of two Congresses also conforms to the average citizen's perceptions. Opinion studies reveal that people view the U.S. Congress differently from the way they see their individual senators and representatives. Congress as an institution is perceived primarily as a lawmaking body. It is judged mainly on the basis of citizens' overall attitudes toward politics, policy processes, and the state of the Union. Do people like the way things are going, or not? Do they feel that Congress is carrying out its duties equitably and efficiently? Are they optimistic or pessimistic about the nation's future? Do they subscribe to Mark Twain's cynical view that Congress is "a distinctly native criminal class"?

In contrast with their expectations of Congress as a whole, citizens view their own legislators largely as agents of local concerns. People judge individual legislators by yardsticks such as service to the district, communication with constituents, and home style (the way officeholders present themselves in their districts or states). In judging their senators or representatives, voters are more likely to ponder questions such as: Is the legislator trustworthy? Does the legislator communicate well with the state (or district) by answering mail promptly and offering timely help to constituents? Does the legislator listen to the state (or district) and its concerns?[24]

The public's divergent expectations of Congress and its members send conflicting signals to senators and representatives. Congress as a whole is judged by the processes it uses and the policies it adopts (or fails to adopt), however vaguely voters understand them.[25] But individual legislators are regularly elected and returned to office because of their personal qualities, the positions they take, and constituency service. In response to this incongruity, some officeholders adopt a strategy of opening as much space as possible between themselves and those other politicians back in Washington—even sometimes their own party's leaders.

The Constitutional Basis

Congress's dual nature—the dichotomy between its lawmaking and representative functions—is dictated by the U.S. Constitution. Congress's mandate to write the nation's laws is found in Article I of the Constitution. By contrast, Congress's representational functions are not specified in the Constitution; rather, these duties flow from the constitutional provisions for electing senators and House members.

It is no accident that the Constitution's drafters devoted the first article to establishing the legislature and enumerating most of the government's powers. Familiar with the British Parliament's prolonged struggles with the Crown, the authors assumed the legislature would be the chief policy-making body and the bulwark against arbitrary executives. "In republican government, the legislative authority necessarily predominates," observed James Madison in *The Federalist Papers.*[26]

Although in the ensuing years the initiative for policy making has shifted many times between the legislative and executive branches, the U.S. Congress remains virtually the only national assembly in the world that drafts in detail the laws it passes instead of simply debating and ratifying measures prepared by the government in power.

The House of Representatives was intended to be the most representative element of the U.S. government. Representatives are elected directly by the people for two-year terms to ensure that they do not stray too far from popular opinion. As Madison explained, the House should have "an immediate dependence on, and an intimate sympathy with, the people."[27] For most members of the House, this two-year cycle means nonstop campaigning, visiting, and looking after constituents.

The Senate was originally one step removed from popular voting: state legislatures selected senators. Some of the Constitution's Framers hoped the Senate would temper the popular passions expressed in the House. But they were ultimately overruled in favor of a Senate that, like the House, directly expresses the people's voice. In 1913 the Seventeenth Amendment to the Constitution was adopted, providing for direct popular election of senators. Although elected for six-year terms, senators must stay in close touch with the electorate. Like their House colleagues, senators typically regard themselves as constituency servants. Most have transformed their office staffs into veritable cottage industries for generating publicity and handling constituents' inquiries.

Thus the Constitution and subsequent historical developments affirm Congress's dual functions of lawmaker and representative assembly. Although the roles are tightly bound together, they nonetheless impose separate duties and functions.

Back to Burke

On November 3, 1774, in Bristol, England, the British statesman and philosopher Edmund Burke set forth in a speech the dual character of a national legislature. The constituent-oriented parliament, or Congress, he described as

> a Congress of ambassadors from different and hostile interests, which interests each must maintain, as an agent and advocate, against other agents and advocates.

The parliament of substantive lawmaking he portrayed in different terms. It was

> a deliberative assembly of one nation, with one interest, that of the whole—where not local purposes, not local prejudices, ought to guide, but the general good, resulting from the general reason of the whole.[28]

Burke preferred the second concept and did not hesitate to let his voters know it. He would give local opinion a hearing, but his judgment and conscience would prevail in all cases. "Your faithful friend, your devoted servant, I shall be to the end of my life," he declared; "a flatterer you do not wish for."[29]

Burke's Bristol speech is an enduring statement of the dilemma legislators face in balancing their two roles. Burke was a brilliant lawmaker. (He even sympathized with the cause of the American colonists.) But, as might be said today, he suffered from an inept home style. His candor earned him no thanks from his constituents, who turned him out of office at the first opportunity.

Burke's dilemma applies equally on this side of the Atlantic. American voters tend to prefer their lawmakers to be delegates who listen carefully to constituents and follow their guidance. For example, during an encounter in Borger, Texas, an irate Baptist minister shouted at then-representative Bill Sarpalius, D-Texas, "We didn't send you to Washington to make intelligent decisions. We sent you to represent us."[30] Sarpalius was later defeated for reelection.

Representing local constituents is not the whole story, of course. Burke's idea that legislators are trustees of the nation's common good is still extolled. In a 1995 decision, U.S. Supreme Court justice John Paul Stevens noted that, once elected, members of Congress become "servants of the people of the United States. They are not merely delegates appointed by separate, sovereign states; they occupy offices that are integral and essential components of a single national Government."[31]

Many talented individuals seek public office, often forgoing more lucrative opportunities in the private sector precisely because they believe strongly in a vision of what government should do and how it should do it. For such legislators, winning office is simply a means to a larger end. It is reasonable to assume that elected officials "make an honest effort to achieve good public policy."[32]

Burke posed the tension between the two Congresses so vividly that we have adopted his language to describe the conceptual distinction that forms the crux of this book. From Burke, we have also drawn the titles for Part II, "A Congress of Ambassadors," and Part III, "A Deliberative Assembly of One Nation." Every member of Congress sooner or later must come to terms with Burke's dichotomy; citizens and voters will have to form their own answers.

THE TWO CONGRESSES IN COMPARATIVE CONTEXT

A look around the world reveals that most democracies differ from the United States in how they elect legislators. Members of Congress are selected by means of the oldest form of democratic representation involving elections: a plurality vote within geographic constituencies. By contrast, most other advanced democracies elect legislative representatives under systems of proportional representation (PR), a more recent innovation in democratic institutions. Many varieties of PR are in use, but compared with the U.S. electoral system, these systems tend to tie legislators more closely to their political parties than to local constituencies. In this way, PR systems somewhat alleviate the difficult trade-offs that members of Congress face as they attempt to balance national lawmaking with attention to local constituencies.

PR systems rest on the basic principle that the number of seats a political party wins in the legislature should be proportional to the level of support it receives from voters. If a political party wins 40 percent of the vote overall, then it should receive about 40 percent of the seats. In other words, these systems explicitly assume that political parties are more important than geographic locales to voters' values and political interests.[33] Most commonly in these systems, the parties put lists of candidates before the electorate. The number of a party's candidates to be seated in the legislature from those lists then depends on the percentage of voters supporting that party in legislative elections. To a greater extent than is true of members of the U.S. Congress, candidates elected in PR systems thus serve as representatives of their party's policy goals and ideological commitments.

Legislators in PR systems face fewer dilemmas about how to balance local constituency politics with national party platforms. Indeed, some PR systems, such as those in Israel and the Netherlands, do not tie representatives to local geographic constituencies at all; legislators represent the entire nation. Other countries, such as Austria and Sweden, elect multiple representatives from regional districts. Such districts are not captured by a single party on a winner-take-all basis (this is the system used in the United States—each constituency has only one representative). Districts in which more than one political party enjoys a meaningful level of voter support will elect representatives from more than one party, with each legislator representing those voters who supported his or her party. Some countries, such as Italy, Germany, and New Zealand, use a mixed system, with some representatives elected in individual geographic constituencies and others drawn from party lists to ensure proportionality. In all cases, citizens and legislators alike recognize that the system is primarily designed to ensure that voters' party preferences are proportionally represented.

Members of the U.S. Congress, by contrast, officially represent all residents of their geographic constituency, a difficult task. The constituents grouped together within congressional districts often have little in common. Indeed, constituencies can be very diverse in terms of race, class, ethnicity, religion, economic interests, and urbanization. The largest states are microcosms of the nation. Some constituencies are narrowly divided in terms of partisanship and ideology, forcing representatives to cope with continual local controversy about their stances on national issues. Other constituencies, such as Gabrielle Giffords's Eighth District of Arizona, present a member with the challenge of representing constituents who lean toward the opposing party.

In attempting to represent their whole state or district, some House members and senators attempt a "lowest common denominator" form of representation, de-emphasizing their party affiliation and their opinions on controversial national issues. Instead, they advertise their personal accessibility to constituents and focus on narrow, localized concerns.[34] This strategy is most appealing to members representing swing or cross-pressured districts. But, to an important extent, the U.S. system of representation encourages a focus on parochial matters among lawmakers generally. All members see themselves, at least to some degree, as attorneys for their constituencies.

Even though the U.S. system of representation does not recognize the importance of political parties in the way that PR systems do, members of Congress have nevertheless become more closely tied to their parties since the 1970s. Lawmakers vote with their parties on controversial issues far more reliably than they did in the 1950s and 1960s. The sources of this increased partisanship are many, but it has corresponded with an increasing partisan-ideological polarization in the activist base of both political parties. "The American public has become more consistent and polarized in its policy preferences over the past several decades," writes Alan I. Abramowitz, "and this increase in consistency and polarization has been concentrated among the most politically engaged citizens."[35] At the same time, the politically engaged public has also sorted itself into more ideologically coherent political parties, with fewer liberals identifying with the Republican Party and fewer conservatives identifying with the Democratic Party.[36] Consequently, relatively few voters split their tickets today by voting for one party's presidential candidate and another party's congressional candidate. These trends have reduced the cross-pressures that members face as they attempt to balance their roles as constituency representatives and national policy makers. More members are able to cooperate with their national party leaders without endangering the support of an electoral majority in their constituency. At the same time, a body of members responding to this more polarized activist base may have a harder time engaging in genuine deliberation and crafting workable legislative compromises.

All members must constantly cultivate the local roots of their power as national legislators. Yet Congress is one body, not two. The same members who must forge national legislation in committee and on the floor must rush to catch planes back to their districts, where they are plunged into a different world of local problems and personalities. The same candidates who sell themselves at shopping centers also shape the federal budget or military weapons systems in the nation's capital. The unique character of Congress arises directly from its dual role as a representative assembly and a lawmaking body.

DIVERGENT VIEWS OF CONGRESS

Congress is subject to intense scrutiny, as the huge array of books, monographs, blogs, and articles devoted to it attest. Many of its features make Congress an especially favorite object of scholarly attention. For one thing, it is relatively open and accessible. And so it can be approached by traditional means—journalistic stories, case studies, normative assessments, and historical accounts. It is also amenable to the analytic techniques of social science. Indeed, the availability of quantitative indicators of congressional work (floor votes, for example) permits elaborate statistical analyses. Its rule-governed processes allow it to be studied with increasingly sophisticated formal models. And Congress is, above all, a fascinating place—the very best location from which to view the varied actors in the American political drama.

Writers of an interpretive book on the U.S. Congress thus can draw on a multitude of sources, an embarrassment of riches. In fact, studies of Congress constitute a vast literature. This is a mixed blessing because all this information must be integrated into a coherent whole. Moreover, the scholarly writing is often highly detailed, technical, and theoretical. We have tried to put such material into perspective, make it accessible to all interested readers, and use illustrative examples wherever possible.

Meanwhile, a gaping chasm exists between this rich scholarly literature and the caricature of Congress prevalent in the popular culture. Humorists from Mark Twain and Will Rogers to Jay Leno, Stephen Colbert, and Jon Stewart have found Congress an inexhaustible source of raw material. Citizens tend to share this disdain toward the legislative branch—especially at moments of furor over, say, congressional pay raises or ethics scandals or difficult legislative fights such as that over the 2009 economic stimulus package. When they are at home with constituents, legislators themselves often reinforce Congress's poor image by portraying themselves as escapees from the funny farm on

Capitol Hill. As Richard F. Fenno puts it, members "run *for* Congress by running *against* Congress."[37]

The picture of Congress conveyed by the media is scarcely more flattering. Journalistic hit-and-run specialists perpetuate a cartoon-like stereotype of Congress as "a place where good ideas go to die in a maelstrom of bureaucratic hedging and rank favor-trading."[38] News magazines, editorial writers, comedians, and nightly news broadcasts regularly portray Congress as an irresponsible and somewhat disreputable gang resembling Woodrow Wilson's caustic description of the House as "a disintegrated mass of jarring elements."[39]

To comprehend how the two Congresses function—both the institution and individual members—popular stereotypes must be abandoned and the complex realities examined. Citizens' ambivalence toward the popular branch of government—which, by the way, goes back to the beginnings of the Republic—says something about the milieu in which public policy is made. We believe we know our subject well enough to appreciate Congress's foibles and understand why it works the way it does. Yet we try to maintain a professional—yes, scholarly—distance from it.

According to an old saying, two things should never be viewed up close: making sausages and making laws. Despite this warning, we urge readers to take a serious look at the workings of Congress and form their own opinions about Congress's effectiveness. Some may recoil from what they discover. Numerous flaws can be identified in members' personal or public behavior, in their priorities and incentive structures, and in lawmaking processes generally. Recent Congresses especially have displayed troubling tendencies, including rushed legislation, extreme partisanship, minimal executive oversight, and abdication of legislative power to the executive branch.[40]

Yet careful observers will also discover much behavior in Congress that is purposeful and principled, many policies that are reasonable and workable. We invite students and colleagues to examine with us what Congress does, and why, and ponder its values and its prospects.

Changing Gender Demography on Capitol Hill. Former Speaker "Uncle Joe" Cannon, R-Ill., the last of the strong post–Civil War House leaders, gets a shave from his barber (top). Challenging male domination on Capitol Hill, the women of the 71st Congress (1929–1931) pose on the Capitol steps (center). In 2009 (bottom), the Congressional Women's Caucus gathers in the White House's East Room to witness President Obama signing legislation creating a White House Council on Women and Girls.

Evolution of the
Modern Congress

The first Congress met in New York City, the seat of government, in the spring of 1789. Business was delayed until April 1 when a majority of the fifty-nine House members finally arrived to make a quorum. Members then chose Frederick A. C. Muhlenberg of Pennsylvania as Speaker of the House. Five days later, the Senate achieved its first quorum, although its presiding officer, Vice President John Adams, did not arrive for another two weeks.

New York City was then a bustling port on the southern tip of Manhattan Island. Congress met in Federal Hall at the corner of Broad and Wall Streets. The House of Representatives occupied a large chamber on the first floor and the Senate a more intimate chamber upstairs. The new chief executive, George Washington, was still en route from his plantation, Mount Vernon, in Virginia; his trip had become a triumphal procession with crowds and celebrations at every stop. To most of his countrymen, Washington—austere, dignified, the soul of propriety—embodied a government that otherwise was no more than a plan on paper.

The two houses of Congress did not wait for Washington's arrival. The House began debating tariffs, a perennial legislative topic. In the Senate, Vice President Adams, a brilliant but self-important man, prodded his colleagues to decide on proper titles for addressing the president and himself. Adams was dubbed "His Rotundity" by a colleague who thought the whole discussion absurd.

On inaugural day, April 30, Adams was still worrying about how to address the president when the representatives, led by Speaker Muhlenberg, burst into the Senate chamber and seated themselves. Meanwhile, a special committee was dispatched to escort Washington to the chamber for the ceremony. The swearing-in was conducted on an outside balcony in front of thousands of assembled citizens.[1] Then the nervous Washington reentered the Senate chamber and haltingly read his inaugural address. After the speech, everyone adjourned to nearby St. Paul's Chapel for a special prayer service. Thus the U.S. Congress became part of a functioning government.[2]

ANTECEDENTS OF CONGRESS

The legislative branch of the new government was untried and unknown, searching for procedures and precedents. And yet it grew out of a rich history of development—stretching back more than five hundred years in Great Britain and no less than a century and a half in North America. If the architects of the U.S. Constitution of 1787 were unsure how well their new design would work, they had firm ideas about what they intended.

The English Heritage

The evolution of representative institutions on a national scale began in medieval Europe. Monarchs gained power over large territories where inhabitants were divided into social groupings, called "estates of the realm"—among them, the nobility, clergy, landed gentry, and town officials. The monarchs brought together the leaders of these estates, not to create representative government but to fill the royal coffers.

These assemblies later came to be called parliaments, from the French *parler*, "to speak." Historians and political scientists have identified four distinct stages in the evolution of the assemblies of estates into the representative legislatures of today. The first stage saw the assemblies representing the various estates gathering merely to vote taxes for the royal treasury; they engaged in little discussion. During the second stage, these tax-voting bodies evolved into bodies that presented the king with petitions for redressing grievances. In the third stage, by a gradual process that culminated in the revolutions of the seventeenth and eighteenth centuries, parliaments wrested lawmaking and tax-levying powers from the king. In the fourth and final stage, during the nineteenth and twentieth centuries, parliamentary representation expanded beyond the older privileged groups to embrace all adult men and women.[3]

By the time the New World colonies were founded in the 1600s, the struggle for parliamentary rights was well advanced into the third stage, at least in England. Bloody conflicts, culminating in the beheading of Charles I in 1649 and the dethroning of James II in the Glorious Revolution of 1688, established parliamentary influence over the Crown.

Out of the struggles between the Crown and Parliament flowed a remarkable body of political and philosophic writings. By the eighteenth century, works by James Harrington (1611–1677), John Locke (1632–1704), William Blackstone (1723–1780), and the Frenchman Baron de Montesquieu (1689–1755) were the common heritage of educated leaders in North America as well as in Europe.

The Colonial Experience

European settlers in the New World brought this tradition of representative government with them. As early as 1619, the thousand or so Virginia colonists elected twenty-two burgesses, or delegates, to a General Assembly. In 1630 the Massachusetts Bay Company established itself as the governing body for the

Bay Colony, subject to annual elections. The other colonies, some of them virtually self-governing, followed suit.

Representative government took firm root in the colonies. The broad expanse of ocean shielding America from its European masters fostered self-reliance and autonomy on the part of the colonial assemblies. Claiming prerogatives similar to those of the British House of Commons, these assemblies exercised the full range of lawmaking powers—levying taxes, issuing money, and providing for colonial defense. Legislation could be vetoed by colonial governors (appointed by the Crown in the eight royal colonies); but the governors, cut off from the home government and dependent on local assemblies for revenues and even for their own salaries, usually preferred to reach agreement with the locals. Royal vetoes could emanate from London, but these took time and were infrequent.[4]

Other elements nourished the growth of democratic institutions. Many of the colonists were free-spirited dissidents set on resisting traditional forms of authority, especially that of the Crown. Their self-confidence was bolstered by the readily available land, harsh frontier life, and—by the eighteenth century—a robust economy. The town meeting form of government in New England and the separatists' church assemblies helped cultivate habits of self-government. Newspapers, unfettered by royal licenses or government taxes, stimulated lively exchanges of opinions.

When Britain decided in the 1760s, following the ruinous French and Indian War, to tighten its rein on the American colonies, it met with stubborn opposition. Colonists asked: Why don't we enjoy the same rights as Englishmen? Why aren't our colonial assemblies legitimate governments, with authority derived from popular elections? As British enactments grew increasingly unpopular, along with the governors who tried to enforce them, the locally based legislatures took up the cause of their constituents.

The colonists especially resented the Stamp Act of 1765, which provoked delegates from nine colonies to meet in New York City. There, the Stamp Act Congress adopted a fourteen-point *Declaration of Rights and Grievances*—mainly written by John Dickinson, who called himself a Pennsylvania farmer but who had studied law in London. The Stamp Act was later repealed. But new import duties levied in 1767 brought inflated customs receipts that enabled the Crown to begin directly paying the salaries of royal governors and other officials, thereby freeing those officials from the influence of colonial assemblies. The crisis worsened in the winter of 1773–1774, when a group of colonists staged a revolt, the Boston Tea Party, to protest the taxes imposed by the Tea Act. In retaliation, the House of Commons closed the port of Boston and passed a series of so-called Intolerable Acts, further tightening royal control.

National representative assemblies in America were born on September 5, 1774, when the First Continental Congress convened in Philadelphia. Every colony except Georgia sent delegates—a varied group that included peaceable souls loyal to the Crown, moderates such as Pennsylvania's Dickinson, and firebrands such as Samuel Adams and Paul Revere. Gradually, anti-British sentiment congealed, and Congress passed a series of declarations and resolutions (each colony casting one vote) amounting to a declaration of war against the mother country.[5] After Congress adjourned on October 22, King George III declared that the colonies were "now in a state of rebellion; blows must decide whether they are to be subject to this country or independent."[6]

If the First Continental Congress gave colonists a taste of collective decision making, the Second Continental Congress proclaimed their independence from Britain. When this second Congress convened on May 10, 1775, many colonists still believed war might be avoided. A petition to King George asking for "happy and permanent reconciliation" was even approved. The British responded by proclaiming a state of rebellion and launching efforts to crush it. Sentiment in the colonies swung increasingly toward independence, and by the middle of 1776 Congress was debating Thomas Jefferson's draft resolution that "these united colonies are, and of right ought to be, free and independent states."[7]

The two Continental Congresses gave birth to national politics in America. Riding the wave of patriotism unleashed by the British actions of 1773–1774, the Congresses succeeded in pushing the sentiments of leaders and much of the general public toward confrontation and away from reconciliation with the mother country. They did so by defining issues one by one and by reaching compromises acceptable to both moderates and radicals—no small accomplishment. Shared legislative experience, in other words, moved the delegates to the threshold of independence. Their achievement was all the more remarkable in light of what historian Jack N. Rakove describes as the "peculiar status" of the Continental Congress, "an extra-legal body whose authority would obviously depend on its ability to maintain a broad range of support."[8]

More than five years of bloody conflict ensued before the colonies won their independence. Meanwhile, the former colonies hastened to form new governments and draft constitutions. Unlike the English constitution, these charters were written documents. All included some sort of bill of rights, and all paid lip service to the doctrine of separating powers among legislative, executive, and judicial branches of government. But past conflicts with the Crown and the royal governors had instilled a fear of all forms of executive authority. So nearly all the constitutions gave the bulk of powers to their legislatures, effectively creating what one historian termed "legislative omnipotence."[9]

The national government was likewise, as James Sterling Young put it, "born with a legislative body and no head."[10] Strictly speaking, no national executive existed between 1776 and 1789—the years of the Revolutionary War and the Articles of Confederation (adopted in 1781). On its own, Congress struggled to wage war against the world's most powerful nation, enlist diplomatic allies, and manage internal affairs. As the war progressed and legislative direction proved unwieldy, Congress tended to delegate authority to its own committees and to permanent (executive) agencies. Strictly military affairs were placed in the hands of Commander in Chief

George Washington, who at the war's end returned his commission to Congress in a public ceremony. Considering the obstacles it faced, congressional government was far from a failure. Yet the mounting inability of the all-powerful legislative bodies, state and national, to deal with the postwar problems spurred demands for change.

At the state level, Massachusetts and New York rewrote their constitutions, adding provisions for stronger executives. At the national level, the Confederation's frailty led many to advocate what Alexander Hamilton called a more "energetic" government—one with enough authority to implement laws, control currency, levy taxes, dispose of war debts, and, if necessary, put down rebellion. Legislative prerogatives, Hamilton and others argued, should be counterbalanced with a vigorous, independent executive.

In this spirit, delegates from the states convened in Philadelphia on May 25, 1787, intending to strengthen the Articles of Confederation. Instead, they drew up a wholly new governmental charter.

CONGRESS IN THE CONSTITUTION

The structure and powers of Congress formed the core of the Constitutional Convention's deliberations. The delegates broadly agreed that a stronger central government was needed.[11] But the fifty-five delegates who met in the summer of 1787 in Philadelphia were deeply divided on issues of representation, and more than three months passed before they completed their work. The plan, agreed on and signed on September 17, 1787, was a bundle of compromises. In structuring the representational system, divergent interests—those of large and small states, land-locked states and those with ports, northern and southern (that is, slave-holding) states—had to be placated. The final result was an energetic central government that could function independently of the states, but with power limited to specific purposes and divided among three branches.

Powers of Congress

The federal government's powers are shared by three separate branches: legislative, executive, and judicial. Separation of powers was not a new idea. Philosophers revered by the Framers of the Constitution, including Harrington, Locke, and especially Montesquieu, had advocated the principle. But the U.S. Constitution's elaborate system of checks and balances is considered one of its most innovative features. The failure of the Articles of Confederation to separate governmental functions was widely regarded as a serious defect, as were the all-powerful legislatures created by the first state constitutions. Thus the Framers sought to create a federal government that would avoid the excesses and instabilities that had marked policy making at both the national and state levels.

Article I of the Constitution embraces many provisions to buttress congressional authority and independence. Legislators have unfettered authority to organize the chambers as they see fit and are accorded latitude in performing their duties. To prevent intimidation, they cannot be arrested during sessions or while traveling to and from sessions (except for treason, felony, or breach of the peace). In their deliberations, members enjoy immunity from any punitive action: For their speech and debate, "they shall not be questioned in any other place" (Article I, section 6).

Despite their worries over all-powerful legislatures, the Framers laid down an expansive mandate for the new Congress. Mindful of the achievements of New World assemblies, not to mention the British Parliament's struggles with the Crown, the Framers viewed the legislature as the chief repository of the government's powers. Locke had observed that "the legislative is not only the supreme power, but is sacred and unalterable in the hands where the community have placed it."[12] Locke's doctrine found expression in Article I, section 8, which enumerates Congress's impressive array of powers and sets out virtually the entire scope of governmental authority as the eighteenth-century Founders understood it. This portion of the Constitution clearly envisions a vigorous legislature as the engine of a powerful government.

Raising and spending money for governmental purposes lie at the heart of Congress's prerogatives. The "power of the purse" was historically the lever by which parliaments gained bargaining advantages over kings and queens. The Constitution's authors, well aware of this lever, gave Congress full powers over taxing and spending.

Financing the government is carried out under Congress's broad mandate to "lay and collect taxes, duties, imposts and excises, to pay the debts and provide for the common defense and general welfare of the United States" (Article I, section 8). Although this wording covered almost all known forms of taxation, there were limitations. Taxes had to be uniform throughout the country; duties could not be levied on goods traveling between states; and "capitation or other direct" taxes were prohibited, unless levied according to population (Article I, section 9). This last provision proved troublesome when the U.S. Supreme Court held in 1895 (*Pollock v. Farmers' Loan and Trust Co.*) that it applied to taxes on incomes. To overcome this obstacle, the Sixteenth Amendment, ratified eighteen years later, explicitly conferred on Congress the power to levy income taxes.

Congressional power over government spending is no less sweeping. Congress is to provide for the "common defense and general welfare" of the country (Article I, section 8). Furthermore, "[n]o money shall be drawn from the Treasury, but in consequence of appropriations made by law" (Article I, Section 9). This funding provision is one of the legislature's most potent weapons in overseeing the executive branch.

Congress possesses broad powers to promote the nation's economic well-being and political security. It has the power to regulate interstate and foreign commerce, which it has used to regulate not only trade, but also transportation, communications, and such disparate subjects as civil rights and violent crime. The exact limits of the commerce power have been the subject of numerous political and legal battles. Most recently, questions about the scope of the commerce power have formed the basis of several legal challenges to the 2010 Patient Protection and Affordable Care Act. Congress may also coin money, incur debts, establish post offices, build post roads, issue patents and copyrights, provide for the armed forces, and call forth the militia to repel invasions or suppress rebellions.

Although the three branches supposedly are coequal, the legislature is empowered to define the structure and duties of the other two. The Constitution mentions executive departments and officers, but it does not specify their organization or functions, aside from those of the president. Thus the design of the executive branch, including cabinet departments and other agencies, is spelled out in laws passed by Congress and signed by the president.

The judiciary, too, is a statutory creation. The Constitution provides for a federal judicial system consisting of a Supreme Court and "such inferior courts as the Congress may from time to time ordain and establish" (Article III, section 1). Congress determines the number of justices on the Supreme Court, and the number and types of lower federal courts. The outer limits of the federal courts' jurisdiction are delineated in Article III, but Congress must also define their jurisdictions through statute. (It is worth noting that Congress has never extended the federal courts' jurisdiction as far as the Constitution would presumably allow.) Moreover, the Supreme Court's appellate jurisdiction is subject to "such exceptions" and "such regulations as the Congress shall make" (Article III, section 2).

Congress can also limit the federal courts' discretion in ways other than altering their jurisdiction. Mandatory minimum sentences imposed by statute, for example, limit judges' discretion in imposing prison sentences.

Congress's powers within the federal system were greatly enlarged by the Civil War amendments—the Thirteenth (ratified in 1865), Fourteenth (ratified in 1868), and Fifteenth (ratified in 1870). The Radical Republicans, who had supported the war and controlled Congress in its aftermath, feared that former Confederate states would ignore the rights of former slaves—the cause over which the war had ultimately been waged. The Civil War amendments were primarily intended to ensure that former slaves would have the rights to vote, to be accorded due process, and to receive equal protection of the laws. In particular, the language of the Fourteenth Amendment was cast broadly, referring to "all persons," rather than only to "former slaves." These amendments also authorized Congress to enforce these rights with "appropriate legislation." In so doing, these amendments (and subsequent legislation) greatly expanded the federal government's role relative to the states. Over time, the Civil War amendments effectively nationalized the key rights of citizenship throughout the United States. Through a long series of Court rulings, state governments were eventually required to respect many of the Bill of Rights guarantees that originally applied only to the federal government.

Congress can also be an active partner in foreign relations and national defense. It has the power to declare war, ratify treaties, raise and support armies, provide and maintain a navy, and make rules governing the military forces—including those governing "captures on land and water." Finally, Congress is vested with the power "to make all laws which shall be necessary and proper for carrying into execution the foregoing powers" (Article I, section 8).

Limits on Legislative Power

The very act of enumerating these powers was intended to limit government, for by implication those powers not listed were prohibited. The Tenth Amendment reserves to the states or to the people all those powers neither delegated nor prohibited by the Constitution. This guarantee has long been a rallying point for those who take exception to particular federal policies or who wish broadly to curtail federal powers.

Eight specific limitations on Congress's powers are noted in Article I, section 9. The most important bans are against bills of attainder, which pronounce a particular individual guilty of a crime without trial or conviction and impose a sentence, and ex post facto laws, which make an action a crime after it has been committed or otherwise alter the legal consequences of some past action. Such laws are traditional tools of authoritarian regimes.

The original Constitution contained no bill of rights. Pressed by opponents during the ratification debate, supporters of the Constitution promised early enactment of amendments to remedy this omission. The resulting ten amendments, drawn up by the First Congress (James Madison was their main author) and ratified December 15, 1791, are a basic charter of liberties that limit the reach of government. The First Amendment prohibits Congress from establishing a national religion, preventing the free exercise of religion, or abridging the freedoms of speech, press, peaceable assembly, and petition. Other amendments secure the rights of personal property and fair trials and prohibit arbitrary arrest, questioning, or punishment.

Rights not enumerated in the Bill of Rights are not necessarily denied (Ninth Amendment). In fact, subsequent amendments, legislative enactments, judicial rulings, and states' actions have enlarged citizens' rights to include the rights of citizenship, of voting, of privacy, and of "equal protection of the laws."

Separate Branches, Shared Powers

The Constitution not only lists Congress's powers but also sets them apart from those of the other two branches. Senators and representatives, while in office, are prohibited from serving in other federal posts; those who serve in such posts are, in turn, forbidden from serving in Congress (Article I, section 6). This restriction forecloses any form of parliamentary government in which leading members of the dominant party or coalition form a cabinet to direct the ministries and other executive agencies.

Because the branches are separated, some people presume that their powers should be isolated as well. In practice, however, governmental powers are interwoven, even though the branches are separate. Madison explained that the Constitution created not a system of separate institutions performing separate functions but separate institutions that share functions, so that "these depart-ments be so far connected and blended as to give each a constitutional control over the others."[13]

Historically, presidents, Congress, and the courts have reached accommo-dations to exercise the powers they share. As Justice Joseph Story once wrote, the authors of the Constitution sought to "prove that rigid adherence to [sepa-ration of powers] in all cases would be subversive to the efficiency of govern-ment and result in the destruction of the public liberties." Justice Robert Jackson noted in 1952 that "while the Constitution diffuses power the better to secure liberty, it also contemplates that practice will integrate the dispersed powers into a workable government."[14]

Legislative-Executive Interdependence. Each branch of American govern-ment needs cooperation from its counterparts. Although the Constitution vests Congress with "all legislative powers," these powers cannot be exercised without the involvement of the president and the courts. This same interde-pendency applies to executive and judicial powers.

The president is a key figure in lawmaking. According to Article II, the president "shall from time to time give to the Congress information on the state of the Union, and recommend to their consideration such measures as he shall judge necessary and expedient." Although Congress is not required to consider the president's legislative initiatives, the president's State of the Union address profoundly shapes the nation's political agenda. In the modern era, Congress has "enacted in some form roughly six in ten presidential initia-tives."[15] The Constitution also grants the president the power to convene one or both houses of Congress in a special session.

The president's ability to veto congressional enactments influences both the outcome and content of legislation. After a bill or resolution has passed both houses of Congress and has been delivered to the White House, the president must sign it or return it within ten days (excluding Sundays). Overruling a presidential veto requires a two-thirds vote in each house. Presidential review might seem to be an all-or-nothing affair. In the words of George Washington, a president "must approve all the parts of a bill, or reject it in toto." Veto messages, however, often suggest revisions that would make the measure more likely to win the president's approval. Furthermore, veto threats allow the president to intervene earlier in the legislative process by letting members of Congress know in advance what measures or provisions will or will not receive presidential support. Considering the extreme difficulty of overriding a president's veto, members of Congress know that White House support for legislation is almost always necessary and so will often incorporate presidential preferences into early drafts of legislation.

Carrying out laws is the duty of the president, who is directed by the Constitution to "take care that the laws be faithfully executed" (Article II, section 3). To this end, as chief executive the president has the power to appoint "officers of the United States." However, the president's appointment power is limited by the requirement to obtain the Senate's advice and consent for nominees, which has been interpreted as requiring a majority vote in the Senate. The president's executive power is further constrained by Congress's role in establishing and overseeing executive departments and agencies. Because these agencies are subject to Congress's broad-ranging influence, modern presidents have struggled to force them to march to a common cadence.

Even in the realms of diplomacy and national defense—the traditional domains of royal prerogative—the Constitution apportions powers between the executive and legislative branches. Following tradition, presidents are given wide discretion in such matters. They appoint ambassadors and other envoys, negotiate treaties, and command the country's armed forces. However, like other high-ranking presidential appointees, ambassadors and envoys must be approved by the Senate. Treaties do not become the law of the land until they are ratified by a two-thirds vote of the Senate. Although the president may dispatch troops by means of executive order, only Congress may formally declare war. Even in time of war, Congress still wields formidable powers if it chooses to employ them. Congress can refuse to provide continued funding for military actions, engage in vigorous oversight of the executive branch's military operations, and influence public opinion regarding the president's leadership.[16]

Impeachment. Congress has the power to impeach and remove the president, the vice president, and other "civil officers of the United States" for serious breaches of the public trust: treason, bribery, or "other high crimes and misdemeanors." The House of Representatives has the sole authority to draw up and adopt (by majority vote) articles of impeachment, which are specific charges that the individual has engaged in one of the named forms of misconduct. The Senate is the final judge of whether to convict on any of the articles of impeachment. A two-thirds majority is required to remove the individual from office, or to remove and also bar the individual from any future "offices of public trust."

Three attributes of impeachment fix it within the separation of powers framework. First, it is exclusively the domain of Congress. (The chief justice of the United States presides over Senate trials of the president, but rulings by the chief justice may be overturned by majority vote.) The two chambers are also free to devise their own procedures for reaching their decisions.[17]

Second, impeachment is essentially political in character. The structure may appear judicial—with the House resembling a grand jury and the Senate a trial court—but lawmakers decide whether and how to proceed, which evidence to consider, and even what constitutes an impeachable offense. Treason is defined by the Constitution and bribery is defined by statute, but the words "high crimes and misdemeanors" are open to interpretation. They are usually defined (in Alexander Hamilton's words) as "abuse or violation of some public trust"—on-the-job offenses against the state, the political order, or the society at large.[18] According to this definition, they could be either more or less than garden variety criminal offenses. Both presidential impeachment trials

(Andrew Johnson, 1868; Bill Clinton, 1998–1999) were fiercely partisan affairs, in which combatants disputed not only the facts but also the appropriate grounds for impeachment.

Finally, impeachment is a clumsy instrument for punishing officials for the gravest of offenses. Congress has many lesser ways of reining in wayward officials. As for presidents and vice presidents, their terms are already limited. Although impeachments are often threatened, only sixteen Senate trials have taken place, and only eight individuals have been convicted. Significantly, all eight who were removed from office were judges—who, unlike executive officers, enjoy open-ended terms of office.[19]

Interbranch "No-Fly Zones." Although the constitutional system requires that the separate branches share powers, each branch normally honors the integrity of the others' internal operations. Communications between the president and his advisers are mostly (though not entirely) exempt from legislative or judicial review under the doctrine of "executive privilege."

Similarly, Article I places congressional organization and procedures beyond the scrutiny of the other branches. In 2006 House leaders of both parties protested when Federal Bureau of Investigation (FBI) agents staged a Saturday night raid on the office of Rep. William J. Jefferson, D-La., who was under investigation for accepting illegal payments for supporting certain legislation. Jefferson filed suit in federal court challenging the constitutionality of the search, and the courts agreed that the FBI's search violated the Constitution's Speech and Debate clause.[20] The case established a precedent that members of Congress be provided advance notice and the right to review materials before the execution of a search warrant on their congressional offices.

Judicial Review

The third of the separated branches, the judiciary, takes a leading role in interpreting laws and determining their constitutionality. Whether the Framers anticipated this function of judicial review is open to question. Perhaps they expected each branch to reach its own judgments on constitutional questions, especially those pertaining to its own powers. Whatever the original intent, Chief Justice John Marshall soon preempted the other two branches with his Supreme Court's unanimous assertion of judicial review in *Marbury v. Madison* (1803). Judicial review involves both interpretation and judgment. First, "it is emphatically the province and duty of the judicial department to say what the law is." Second, the Supreme Court has the duty of weighing laws against the Constitution, the "supreme law of the land," and invalidating those that are inconsistent—in *Marbury,* a minor provision of the Judiciary Act of 1789.[21]

Despite the *Marbury* precedent, Congress—not the Court—was the primary forum for weighty constitutional debates until the Civil War. Before 1860, only one other law (the Missouri Compromise of 1820) had been declared unconstitutional by the Court (in *Dred Scott v. Sandford,* 1857). Since the Civil War, and especially since the 1960s, the Court has been more aggressive in interpreting and judging congressional handiwork. For the record, the Supreme Court has invalidated 164 congressional statutes in whole or in part—the vast majority of these during the twentieth century.[22] This count does not include lower-court holdings that have not been reviewed by the Supreme Court. Nor does it include laws whose validity has been impaired because a similar law was struck down.

Who Is the Final Arbiter? Congress's two most common reactions to judicial review of its enactments are not responding at all (in 38 percent of cases, 1954–1997) or amending the statute to comply with the Court's holding (in 36 percent of cases).[23] Other responses are repealing the law, repealing the law to pass new legislation, or even seeking a constitutional amendment.

Reconstruction laws and constitutional amendments after the Civil War explicitly nullified the Court's 1857 holding in *Dred Scott v. Sandford*.[24] More recently, a great deal of legislative activity has followed the Supreme Court's ruling in *Citizens United* v. *Federal Election Commission* (2010),[25] a 5–4 decision that held that the First Amendment protects corporate, union, and nonprofit funding of independent political speech. Even though legislation has not yet been passed in response to *Citizens United*, it is clear that many members of Congress want to find ways to undo or mitigate the Court's holding in this case.

In some cases, Congress reacts to Supreme Court rulings by simply ignoring them. For example, even though legislative veto provisions were largely outlawed by the Court's decision in *Immigration and Naturalization Service v. Chadha* (1983),[26] Congress continues to enact them, and administrators nevertheless feel obliged to honor them out of political prudence.

The Supreme Court does not necessarily have the last word in saying what the law is. Its interpretations of laws may be questioned and even reversed. One study found that 121 of the Court's interpretive decisions were overridden between 1967 and 1990, an average of ten per Congress. The author of the study concluded that "congressional committees in fact carefully monitor Supreme Court decisions." Congress was most apt to override decisions of a closely divided Court, decisions that relied on the law's plain meaning, and decisions that clashed with positions taken by federal, state, and local governments.[27]

Nor are the courts the sole judges of what is or is not constitutional. Courts routinely accept customs and practices developed by the other two branches. Likewise, they usually decline to decide sensitive political questions within the province of Congress and the executive.

In summary, the courts play a leading but not exclusive role in interpreting laws and the regulations implementing them. When Congress passes a law, the policy-making process has just begun. Courts and administrative agencies then assume the task of refining the policy, but they do so under Congress's watchful eye. "What is 'final' at one stage of our political development," Louis Fisher observes, "may be reopened at some later date, leading to revisions, fresh interpretations, and reversals of Court doctrines. Through this never-ending dialogue, all three branches are able to expose weaknesses, hold excesses in check, and gradually forge a consensus on constitutional issues."[28]

Bicameralism

Although "the Congress" is discussed as if it were a single entity, Congress is divided internally into two very different, virtually autonomous chambers—that is, it is bicameral. Following the pattern that originated with the British Parliament and was then imitated by most of the states, the Constitution created a bicameral legislature. If tradition recommended the two-house formula, the politics of the early Republic commanded it. The larger states that were home to more people preferred population-based representation, but the smaller states insisted on retaining the equal representation they enjoyed under the Articles of Confederation.

The first branch—as the House was called by Framer James Madison and Gouverneur Morris, among others—rests on the idea that the legislature should represent "the many," the people of the United States. As George Mason, another Framer, put it, the House "was to be the grand depository of the democratic principles of the government."[29]

By contrast, the composition of the Senate reflected the Framers' concerns about controlling excessive popular pressures. Senators were chosen by the state legislatures and not by popular vote. The Senate—which, in theory, would be insulated—would curb the excesses of popular government. "The use of the Senate," explained Madison, "is to consist in its proceeding with more coolness, with more system, and with more wisdom, than the popular branch."[30]

Senate behavior did not necessarily match up with the Framers' theories, however. Even though senators were chosen by state legislatures, they were not insulated from democratic pressures. To be selected, Senate candidates "had to cultivate local party officials in different parts of the state and appeal directly to constituents in order to bolster their electoral chances."[31] Once in office, senators voiced their state's dominant economic interests. They also sponsored private bills for pensions and other relief for individual constituents, doled out federal patronage, and sought committee assignments that would enable them to bring home their state's share of federal money. Recent research has shown that senators selected by state legislators were not substantially different from modern, directly elected senators.[32]

Historical evolution finally overran the Framers' intentions. Direct election of senators was ushered in with the Seventeenth Amendment, ratified in 1913. A by-product of the Progressive movement, the new arrangement was designed to broaden citizens' participation and blunt the power of shadowy special interests such as party bosses and business trusts. Thus the Senate became directly subject to popular will.

Bicameralism is the most obvious organizational feature of the U.S. Congress. Each chamber has distinct processes for handling legislation. According to the Constitution, each house sets its own rules, keeps a journal of its proceedings, and serves as final judge of its members' elections and qualifications. In addition, the Constitution assigns unique duties to each of the two chambers. The Senate ratifies treaties and approves presidential appointments. The House must originate all revenue measures; by tradition, it also originates appropriations bills.

The two houses jealously guard their prerogatives and resist intrusions by the other body. Despite claims that one or the other chamber is more important—for example, that the Senate has more prestige or that the House pays more attention to legislative details—the two houses staunchly defend their equal places. On Capitol Hill, there is no "upper" or "lower" chamber.

INSTITUTIONAL EVOLUTION

Written constitutions go only a short way toward explaining how real-life governmental institutions work. On many questions such documents are inevitably silent or ambiguous. Important issues of both power and process emerge and develop only in the course of later events. Political institutions continually change under pressures from public demands, shifting political contexts, and the policy and electoral goals of officeholders.

Congress has evolved dramatically over time. "Reconstitutive change" is what Elaine K. Swift calls instances of "rapid, marked, and enduring shift[s] in the fundamental dimensions of the institution."[33] During one such period—1809–1829—Swift argues, the Senate was transformed from an elitist, insulated "American House of Lords" into an active, powerful institution whose debates stirred the public and attracted the most talented politicians of the time. Major reform efforts in Congress have also periodically resulted in bold new departures in process and structure.

Yet much of Congress's institutional development has occurred gradually. Early on, Congress had little formal structure. When the first Congress convened, there were no standing committees. Deliberation about policy issues occurred directly on the floors of the House and Senate, where any interested members could participate. After chamber-wide debate had taken place on a broad issue, members would create temporary ad hoc committees to draft bills. The early Congress also had no formal party leadership organization.[34] Prior to the 1830s, the Federalist and Republican coalitions that existed in Congress were "no more than proto-parties."[35] There was almost no professional staff. Even by 1891, only 142 clerks, 62 for the House and 80 for the Senate, were on hand to serve members of Congress. Many senators and all representatives handled their own correspondence. Compared to the present, the early Congress was informal, fluid, and unstructured.

Today's Congress is a mature institution characterized by complex internal structures and procedures. It is led by a well-defined party apparatus, with each party organized according to its established rules and headed by a hierarchy of leaders and whips, elected and appointed. Party organization extends to policy committees, campaign committees, research committees, and numerous task forces. Minority and majority party leaders command considerable resources in terms of budgets and staff. Taken together, they employ some four hundred staff aides, and the various party committees employ about an equal number.[36]

The contemporary Congress also has an elaborate committee system bolstered by a vast body of rules and precedents regulating committee jurisdictions and operations.[37] In the 112th Congress (2011–2013), the Senate has sixteen standing committees and the House has twenty. But these committees are only the tip of the iceberg. House committees have about one hundred subcommittees; Senate committees, nearly seventy subcommittees. Four joint House-Senate committees have been retained. All this adds up to some two hundred work groups, plus an abundance of informal caucuses.

In addition, every member heads up a well-staffed personal office with employees to handle mail and phone calls, appointments, policy research, speechwriting, and constituent service. Employing nearly thirty thousand staff members who are housed in nearly a dozen Capitol Hill buildings, Congress now sustains a distinct Washington subculture.

A basic concept scholars use to analyze the development of Congress's growth and adaptation is *institutionalization.* Political scientist Nelson W. Polsby applied this concept to track the institution's professionalization of the legislative career; its increasing organizational complexity—the growth of more component parts (committees, subcommittees, caucuses, leadership organizations) within the institution; and its elaboration and observance of formal rules governing its internal business.[38] Scholars have identified some important factors that have driven institutional development. Among these are legislative workload, institutional size, conflict with the executive branch, and members' partisan interests.

Workload

Congress's workload—once limited in scope, small in volume, and simple in content—has burgeoned since 1789. Today's Congress grapples with many issues that were once considered entirely outside the purview of governmental activity or were left to states or localities. From eight to ten thousand bills and joint resolutions are introduced in the span of each two-year Congress; from four to eight hundred of them are enacted into law. By most measures—hours in session, committee meetings, floor votes—the congressional workload doubled between the 1950s and the late 1970s. Legislative business expanded in scope and complexity as well as in sheer volume. The average public bill of the late 1940s was two and a half pages long; by the late 1990s it ran to more than eighteen pages.[39]

Changes in workload have been an important driver of institutional change over the course of congressional history. Many of the earliest committees were established to help Congress manage a growing volume of constituent requests. "Congress was confronted with thousands of petitions requesting benefits of various sorts," writes Eric Schickler. Committees such as Claims, Pensions, and Public Lands "facilitated the processing of such requests."[40] Similarly, the creation and, occasionally, the abolition of committees parallel shifting perceptions of public problems. As novel policy problems arose, new committees were added.[41] The House, for example, established Commerce and Manufactures in 1795, Public Lands in 1805, Freedmen's Affairs in 1866, Roads in 1913, Science and Astronautics in 1958, Standards of Official Conduct in 1967, Small Business in 1975, and Homeland Security in 2005. An extensive system of committees allows the contemporary Congress to benefit from a division of labor as it strives to manage a far-reaching governmental agenda and the press of public business.

Congress's growing workload does not come only from outside the institution. From the earliest days to the present, members themselves have contributed to their collective burden. Seeking to make names for themselves, members champion causes, deliver speeches on various subjects, offer floor amendments, refer matters to committees for consideration, and engage in much policy entrepreneurship. All these activities raise the congressional workload.

At regular intervals over congressional history, the crush of business, combined with a widespread sense that Congress is unable to manage its responsibilities, prompts members to experiment with institutional reforms.[42] Under workload pressure, Congress has repeatedly adopted measures to streamline procedures and to limit the participation of individual members. Such reforms are ongoing, with congressional innovators devising new "unorthodox" procedures to cope with the workload challenges of today.[43]

The Size of Congress

Like workload, the size of a legislative institution profoundly affects its work. From a study of fifty-five legislatures worldwide, Andrew J. Taylor found that "legislators in large chambers are willing to trade away procedural rights for centralized procedures [in order to] prevent gridlock and cut the costs of forging cooperation."[44] Legislatures with more members face greater problems of agenda control and time management, unless they adopt mechanisms to manage the participation of their members. The U.S. Congress has grown dramatically over time, and this growth has created pressure for institutional adaptation.

Looking at the government of 1789 through modern lenses, one is struck by the relatively small circles of people involved. The House of Representatives, that "impetuous council," was composed of sixty-five members—when all of them showed up. The aristocratic Senate boasted only twenty-six members, two from each of the thirteen original states.

As new states were added, the Senate grew, from thirty-two senators in 1800 to sixty-two in 1850, ninety by 1900, and one hundred today. (Since 1912 only the states of Alaska and Hawaii have been added to the Union.)

For much of the nation's history, the House grew alongside the nation's population. The House membership was raised to 104 after the first census, and it steadily enlarged throughout the nineteenth century. The 1910 census, which counted 92 million people, led to a final expansion to 435 members.

After the 1920 census, Congress declined to enlarge the House further. And that is the way things stand to this day.

Growth impelled House members to empower strong leaders, to rely on committees, to impose strict limits on floor debate, and to devise elaborate ways of channeling the flow of floor business. It is no accident that strong leaders emerged during the periods the House experienced the most rapid growth. After the initial growth spurt in the first two decades of the Republic, vigorous leadership appeared in the person of Henry Clay (1811–1814, 1815–1820, and 1823–1825). Similarly, the post–Civil War expansion of the House was met with an era of forceful Speakers that lasted from the 1870s until 1910.

In the smaller and more intimate Senate, vigorous leadership has been the exception rather than the rule. The relative informality of Senate procedures and the long-cherished right of unlimited debate testify to the looser reins of leadership. Compared with the House's complex rules and voluminous precedents, the Senate's rules are relatively brief and simple. Informal negotiations among senators interested in a given measure prevail on most matters. Although too large for its members to draw their chairs around the fireplace on a chilly winter morning—as they did in the early years—the Senate today retains a clubby atmosphere that the House lacks.

Conflict with the Executive Branch

Conflict with the president is a perennial impetus for institutional reform. When Congress cannot collaborate effectively with the executive branch to develop policy, members seek out ways to increase their capacity for independent action. During such confrontations, Congress creates new institutions and procedures that often endure long beyond the specific contexts that gave rise to them.

One of the most important standing House committees, Ways and Means, was first established to provide a source of financial information independent of the controversial and divisive Treasury secretary at the time, Alexander Hamilton. "Members understood that the alternative to a standing committee would be continued reliance on Hamilton and his department for information about such issues as tariffs and economic development," observes Eric Schickler.[45]

Similarly, the landmark Legislative Reorganization Act of 1946 was adopted amidst members' growing concerns about congressional power. Following the massive growth of the administrative state during the New Deal and World War II, members feared that Congress could simply no longer compete with the executive branch. Reformers saw "a reorganized Congress as a way to redress the imbalance of power that had developed between the branches."[46] The act streamlined the legislative process by dramatically reducing the number of committees and regularizing their jurisdictions. Sen. Owen Brewster, R-Maine, argued at the time that the reforms were necessary "to retain any semblance of the ancient division of functions under our constitution."[47] The act was adopted by a sizable bipartisan majority, with both

Republicans and Democrats expressing hope that reform would strengthen Congress's power and prestige.

Another major institutional innovation, Congress's budget process, was fashioned in an environment of intense interbranch warfare between President Richard Nixon and a Democratic Congress.[48] President Nixon's unprecedented assertion of authority to withhold funds that Congress had appropriated was a major stimulus for passage of the Congressional Budget and Impoundment Control Act of 1974. Without the power of the purse, Sen. John Tunney, D-Calif., remarked, "we may as well go out of business."[49] However, the act addressed an array of structural issues that went far beyond the particulars of the dispute over the president's impoundment powers. It established a new internal congressional budget process, new budget committees in both chambers, and a new congressional agency, the nonpartisan Congressional Budget Office (CBO). The goal was to allow Congress to formulate on its own a comprehensive national budget, backed by appropriate estimates and forecasts, without relying on the president's budget or the executive branch's Office of Management and Budget.

In *Federalist* No. 51 Madison justified the Constitution as a system to "divide and arrange the several offices in such a manner as that each may be a check on the other." Congress's institutional development bears the indelible stamp of this checking and balancing, as Congress has repeatedly reformed itself to meet challenges from the executive branch.

Partisan Interests

Political parties had no place in the original constitutional blueprint. However, no account of institutional development in Congress can ignore their vital role. Everything about the organization and operation of Congress is shaped by political parties. Indeed, the first thing a visitor to the House or Senate chamber notices is that the seats or desks are divided along partisan lines— Democrats to the left facing the dais, Republicans to the right. Although today's congressional parties are remarkably cohesive and energetic, their importance is by no means confined to the present day. The goals and capacities of the political parties have been a major engine of change throughout congressional history.

Parties began to develop in Congress during the first presidential administration. When Treasury secretary Alexander Hamilton unveiled his financial program in 1790, a genuine partisan spirit swept Capitol Hill. The Federalists, with Hamilton as their intellectual leader, espoused energetic government to deal forcefully with national problems and foster economic growth. The rival Republicans, who looked to Thomas Jefferson and James Madison for leadership, rallied opponents of Federalist policies and championed local autonomy, a weaker national government, and programs favoring rural, lower-class, or debtor interests. By 1794 Sen. John Taylor of Virginia could write:

The existence of two parties in Congress is apparent. The fact is disclosed almost upon every important question. Whether the subject be foreign or domestic—relative to war or peace—navigation or commerce—the magnetism of opposite views draws them wide as the poles asunder.[50]

Parties flourished in the years following the Civil War. Regional conflicts, along with economic upheavals produced by rapid industrialization, nurtured partisan differences. The Civil War and World War I mark the boundaries of the first era of militant partisanship on Capitol Hill and in the country at large. At the grassroots level, the parties were divided along class, occupational, and regional lines. Grassroots party organizations were massive and militant. Strong Speakers tamed the unruly House, and a coterie of statewide party bosses dominated the Senate. However, even after this partisan era, parties never became irrelevant. During periods of party weakness after the demise of the strong Speakership (1910) and direct election of senators (1913), the parties were still able to organize the Congress.[51] The Speaker of the House has always been the leader of the majority party. House and Senate members receive and retain their committee assignments through their parties. Likewise, senior members of the majority party chair all the standing committees of Congress.

The political parties have profoundly influenced the development of the legislative process. Party politics has impelled the development of floor procedure, members' parliamentary rights, leaders' prerogatives, and agenda control devices. The rules of the legislative process at any given time are, in Sarah A. Binder's words, a "result of hard-nosed partisan battles—fought, of course, under a particular set of inherited institutional rules."[52]

A watershed moment in the development of the House of Representatives, the adoption of Reed's Rules in 1890, offers one of the clearest examples of partisan influence on institutional procedure. Prior to 1890, the minority party in the House of Representatives possessed an arsenal of dilatory tactics to obstruct the majority party's agenda. Reed's Rules, named for then-House Speaker Thomas Brackett Reed, R-Maine, revolutionized House procedure by granting the Speaker secure control over the order of business and strictly curbing the minority party's ability to obstruct the majority party's floor agenda. Republicans, the majority party, fought for the adoption of Reed's Rules over strong opposition from the Democrats. At that time, Republicans had just won unified party control of the government for the first time in more than a decade, and they had an ambitious and controversial agenda. Knowing that Democrats would use their resources to obstruct their agenda, Republicans changed the rules of the House to permit majority party control over the institution, a fact of life in the House of Representatives ever since. In procedural terms, Reed's Rules permanently transformed the House of Representatives.

The circumstances surrounding the adoption of Reed's Rules offers a blueprint for many partisan rules changes over the course of House history. Based on a study of all procedural rules changes that benefited the majority party at the expense of the minority party between 1789 and 1990, Binder finds that "crucial procedural choices have been shaped not by members' collective concerns about the institution, but by calculations of partisan advantage."[53] When cohesive in their policy preferences but narrow enough that the minority party's resistance could obstruct their agenda, majority parties will be inclined to alter the institution's rules to ensure the passage of their agenda. They are especially likely to adopt this approach when the minority party makes aggressive use of its procedural powers of obstruction.

Members' Individual Interests

Institutional development has been driven by more than members' partisan and institutional goals; members also have individual goals. As individuals, members want to build a reputation as effective lawmakers and representatives. To do so, they must be able to point to achievements of their own. When congressional rules or structures inhibit their ability to do so, pressure builds for institutional reform.

In addition to its value as an institutional division of labor, the elaborate committee system in Congress serves members' individual political needs and policy goals. Because of the multitude of leadership positions created by the numerous committees and subcommittees, nearly every member has an opportunity to make an individual contribution. "Whatever else it may be, the quest for specialization in Congress is a quest for credit," observes David R. Mayhew. "Every member can aspire to occupy a part of at least one piece of policy turf small enough that he can claim personal responsibility for some of the things that happen on it."[54]

The congressional reforms of the 1970s are one example of the ways in which members' individual goals have affected institutional development. Over that decade, the two chambers extensively reworked their committee systems through a series of measures designed to allow more input from rank-and-file members. The streamlined committee systems put in place after the Legislative Reorganization Act of 1946 offered relatively few committee leadership positions, and those were gained on the basis of seniority. Every committee was led by its longest-serving members, who retained their positions until death, defeat, or retirement. The large classes of new members elected in the 1970s, feeling thwarted by this system, began to press for change.[55] Out of this ferment emerged a variety of reforms that opened up new opportunities for junior members. Among these reforms, the seniority system was weakened as committee chairs were forced to stand for election in their party caucus, making them accountable to the party's rank and file.

The persistence of Senate rules that permit unlimited debate is another example of the ways in which individual goals shape institutional rules.[56]

Despite the many frustrations unlimited debate has caused for Senate majority parties over the years, senators have been unwilling to embrace changes that would allow for simple majority rule. Senators realize that a great part of their own institutional power derives from their ability to take advantage of unlimited debate to block votes on matters that have majority support. Senate leaders are forced to negotiate with senators who obstruct Senate action via unlimited debate.

Reforms that would make it possible for a Senate majority to force a vote have long been in the interest of the Senate's majority party. But such reforms come at a direct, substantial cost to senators' individual power. Not surprisingly, senators have proven very reluctant to trade off so much of their individual influence in favor of collective party goals. Although a number of Democratic senators pressed for reform of Senate procedure at the start of the 112th Congress, none of their proposed reforms would go so far as to turn the Senate into an institution in which a simple majority can bring debate to a close. Even after the minority Republicans' forceful and highly effective obstruction of Democratic priorities during the 111th Congress, not even Senate Democrats were eager to exchange many of their individual prerogatives for more effective majority party rule.

Like everything else about Congress, the institution's rules and procedures can only be fully understood in the context of the two Congresses. Members want rules and processes to serve them as individual lawmakers and representatives, as well as to facilitate the functioning of the legislature as a whole.

Changing pressure on the institution, congressional-executive conflicts, partisan agendas, and members' individual goals have all been important drivers of Congress's institutional development. Indeed, significant reforms are almost always the result of several of these forces simultaneously buffeting the institution. In his broad-ranging survey of forty-two major institutional innovations, Schickler finds that institutional reforms are typically brought about through "common carriers," reform initiatives that are at once supported by several different groups of legislators for different sets of reasons.[57] The Legislative Reorganization Act of 1946, for example, was espoused by many legislators who wanted to enhance the power and effectiveness of the legislative branch, but it was also supported by members who valued the new pay and pension benefits included in the legislation.[58] Similarly, many members favored the 1970s reforms reducing the power of committee chairs because they wanted access to more policy turf of their own. Many liberal members backed the reforms because they wanted to reduce the influence of the disproportionately conservative committee chairs.[59]

Because the same reforms are so often backed for several different reasons, no single theory can explain congressional change. According to Schickler, "legislative institutions are historical composites, full of tensions and contradictions."[60] Furthermore, reforms inevitably fall short of their sponsors' objectives. Instead of achieving stable, effective arrangements, reforms frequently produce "a set of institutions that often work at cross-purposes."[61] Also, innovations usually have unanticipated consequences, which may lead to yet another round of reform. In broadest terms, change is always a product of the dual Congress—driven by both electoral and institutional goals.

EVOLUTION OF THE LEGISLATOR'S JOB

What is it like to be a member of Congress? The legislator's job, like the institution of Congress, has evolved since 1789. During the early Congresses, being a senator or representative was a part-time occupation. Few members regarded congressional service as a career, and according to most accounts the rewards were slim. Since then, lawmakers' exposure to constituents' demands and their career expectations have changed dramatically. Electoral units, too, have grown very large. With the nation's population estimated at some 309 million citizens, the average House constituency after the 2010 reapportionment will consist of more than 710,000 people, and the average state of more than six million.

The Congressional Career

During its early years, Congress was an institution composed of transients. The nation's capital was an unsightly place, and its culture was provincial. Members remained in Washington only a few months, spending their unpleasant sojourns in boardinghouses. "While there were a few for whom the Hill was more than a way station in the pursuit of a career," notes James Sterling Young, "affiliation with the congressional community tended to be brief."[62]

The early Congresses failed to command the loyalty needed to keep members in office. Congressional service was regarded more as odious duty than as rewarding work. "My dear friend," wrote a North Carolina representative to his constituents in 1796, "there is nothing in this service, exclusive of the confidence and gratitude of my constituents, worth the sacrifice. . . . Having secured this, I could freely give place to any fellow citizen, that others too might obtain the consolation due to faithful service."[63] Of the ninety-four senators who served between 1789 and 1801, thirty-three resigned before completing their terms, only six to take other federal posts.[64] In the House, almost 6 percent of all early nineteenth-century members resigned during each Congress. Citizen legislators, not professional politicians, characterized that era.

Careerism mounted toward the end of the nineteenth century. As late as the 1870s, more than half the House members at any given time were freshmen, and the mean length of service was barely two terms. By the end of the century, however, the proportion of newcomers had fallen to 30 percent, and average House tenure had reached three terms, or six years. About the same time, senators' mean term of service topped seven years, in excess of one full term.[65]

TABLE 2-1 **Length of Service in House and Senate, 1789–2013**				

	Congress			
Chamber and terms	1st–56th (1789–1901)	57th–103d (1901–1995)	104th–111th (1995–2011)	112th (2011–2013)
House				
One (up to 2 years)	44.0%	23.3%	13.3%	21.6%
Two to six (3–12 years)	53.4	49.7	53.3	41.4
Seven or more (12+ years)	2.6	27.0	33.4	37.0
Mean number of terms[1]	2.1	4.8	5.5	4.9
Senate				
One (up to 6 years)	65.6%	45.6%	32.8%	42.0%
Two (7–12 years)	23.4	22.4	26.8	21.0
Three or more (12+ years)	11.0	32.0	40.4	37.0
Mean number of terms[1]	1.5	2.2	2.6	1.9

Sources: Adapted from David C. Huckabee, *Length of Service for Representatives and Senators: 1st–103d Congresses*, Congressional Research Service Report No. 95-426GOV, March 27, 1995. Authors' calculations for the 104th through 111th Congresses. See also Mildred Amer, *Average Years of Service for Members of the Senate and House of Representatives, First–109th Congresses*, Congressional Research Service Report RL32648, November 9, 2005.

[1] Figures are derived from the total number of terms claimed by members whether or not those terms were served out. For example, members in their initial year of service are counted as having one full term, and so on. Thus the figures cannot be equated precisely with years of service.

Today, the average senator has served more than eleven years, the average House member nearly ten. Table 2-1 shows changes since 1789 in the percentages of new and veteran members and the mean number of terms claimed by incumbents. In both the House and Senate, members' average length of service has increased over time, and the proportion of first-termers is substantially lower than it was during the first two hundred years of the nation's history.

Rising careerism has a number of causes. The increase in one-party states and districts following the Civil War, and especially after the partisan realignment of 1896, enabled repeated reelection of a dominant party's candidates— Democrats in the core cities and the South, Republicans in the Midwest and the rural Northeast. Members themselves also began to find congressional service more rewarding. The growth of national government during the twentieth century enhanced the excitement and glamour of the Washington political scene, especially when compared with state or local renown.

The prerogatives accorded to seniority further rewarded lengthy service. Beginning in the late nineteenth century in the Senate and in the early twentieth century in the House, members with the longest tenure in office began to dominate positions of power in Congress. However, seniority norms have seen significant challenges since the 1990s. After taking over the House in 1995, Republican leaders passed over several senior members in naming committee chairs. At the same time, the GOP Conference also limited chairs' terms to six years—a provision again enforced when Republicans selected committee chairs after reclaiming a House majority in the 2010 elections.[66] Although seniority is no longer the unquestioned norm it once was, extended service generally remains a prerequisite for top party and committee posts. The benefits accruing to seniority continue to compound the returns on long service in the contemporary Congress.

Professionalization

During the Republic's early days, lawmaking was not a full-time occupation. As President John F. Kennedy was fond of remarking, the Clays, Calhouns, and Websters of the nineteenth century could afford to devote a whole generation or more to debating and refining the few great controversies at hand. Rep. Joseph W. Martin, R-Mass., who entered the House in 1925 and went on to become Speaker (1947–1949, 1953–1955), described the leisurely atmosphere of earlier days and the workload changes during his service:

> From one end of a session to another Congress would scarcely have three or four issues of consequence besides appropriations bills. And the issues themselves were fundamentally simpler than those that surge in upon us today in such a torrent that the individual member cannot analyze all of them adequately before he is compelled to vote. In my early years in Congress the main issues were few enough so that almost any conscientious member could with application make himself a quasi-expert at least. In the complexity and volume of today's legislation, however, most members have to trust somebody else's word or the recommendation of a committee. Nowadays bills, which thirty years ago would have been thrashed out for hours or days, go through in ten minutes.[67]

The most pressing issue considered by the Foreign Affairs Committee during one session, Martin related, was a $20,000 authorization for an international poultry show in Tulsa, Oklahoma.

For most of its history, Congress was a part-time institution. Well into the twentieth century, Congress remained in session for only nine of every twenty-four months; the members spent the rest of their time at home attending to private business. As Representative Martin related,

The installation of air conditioning in the 1930s did more, I believe, than cool the Capitol: it prolonged the session. The members were no longer in such a hurry to flee Washington in July. The southerners especially had no place else to go that was half as comfortable.[68]

In recent decades, legislative business has kept the House and Senate almost perpetually in session—punctuated by constituency work periods. The average senator or representative works an eleven-hour day when Congress is in session.[69] Members of the contemporary Congress are—and must be— full-time professional politicians.

Constituency Demands

Since the beginning, American legislators have been expected to remain close to their voters. Early representatives reported to their constituents through circular letters, communications passed around throughout their districts.[70] In an era of limited government, however, there was less constituent errand running. "It was a pretty nice job that a member of Congress had in those days," recalled Rep. Robert Ramspeck, D-Ga. (1929–1945), describing the Washington of 1911, when he came to take a staff job:

> At that time the government affected the people directly in only a minor way. It was an entirely different job from the job we have to do today. It was primarily a legislative job, as the Constitution intended it to be.[71]

In those days, a member's business on behalf of constituents was confined mainly to awarding rural mail routes, arranging for Spanish War pensions, sending out free seed, and only occasionally explaining legislation. At most, a single clerk was required to handle correspondence. Members from one-party areas often did little personal constituency work. It was said that Democratic Speaker John Nance Garner, who entered the House in 1903 and ended his career as vice president (1933–1941), "for thirty years did not canvass his [south Texas] district and franked no speeches home."[72] His major constituency outreach consisted of the barbecues he gave at his home in Uvalde, Texas.

This unhurried pace has long since vanished. Reflecting on his forty years on Capitol Hill, Representative Martin remarked on the dramatic upsurge of constituent awareness:

> Today the federal government is far more complex, as is every phase of national life. People have to turn to their Representative for aid. I used to think ten letters a day was a big batch; now I get several hundred a day. In earlier times, constituents didn't know their Congressman's views. With better communications, their knowledge has increased along with their expectations of what he must know.[73]

Even people of Martin's era (he left the House in 1967) would be astonished at the volume of constituency work now handled by House and Senate offices. The advent of new communications technologies has increased the volume of congressional mail by an order of magnitude. In 1997, the last year before e-mail use became widespread, members of Congress received 30.5 million pieces of posted mail; by 2007 the volume of mail, e-mail included, had surged to 491 million pieces.[74] Not only are constituents more numerous than ever before, but they are also better educated, served by faster communication and transportation, and mobilized by lobby organizations. Public opinion surveys reveal that voters expect legislators to dispense federal services and to communicate frequently with the home folks. Even though the more flagrant forms of pork-barrel politics are denounced, constituents' demands are unlikely to ebb in the future.

CONCLUSION

Although the Founders understood the guiding principles of representative assemblies, they could not have foreseen what sort of institution they had created. They wrote into the Constitution legislative powers as they understood them and left the details to future generations.

Just as physical anthropologists believe the earth's history is marked by periods of intense, even cataclysmic, change—punctuated equilibrium—so historians of Congress have identified several eras of intensive institutional change, such as the advent of Reed's Rules or the early nineteenth-century transformation of the Senate described by Elaine Swift. But institutional change is not necessarily dramatic. Incremental changes of one kind or another are also always unfolding.

Over time, as a result of changes large and small, Congress became the mature institution of today. The contemporary Congress bristles with norms and traditions, rules and procedures, committees and subcommittees. In short, the modern Congress is highly institutionalized. How different it is from the First Congress, personified by fussy John Adams worrying about what forms of address to use.

The institutionalization of the contemporary Congress must be taken into account by anyone who seeks to understand it today. Capitol Hill newcomers—even those who vow to shake things up—confront not an unformed, pliable institution but also an established, traditional one that must be approached largely on its own terms. This institutionalization has a number of important consequences, some good and some bad.

Institutionalization enables Congress to cope with its extensive workload. A division of labor, primarily through standing committees, permits the two houses to process a wide variety of issues simultaneously. In tandem with staff resources, this specialization allows Congress to compete with the executive branch in absorbing information and applying expertise to public issues.

The division of labor also serves the personal and political diversity of Congress. At the same time, careerism encourages legislators to develop skills and expertise in specific areas.

The danger of institutionalization is organizational rigidity. Institutions that are too rigid can frustrate policy making, especially in periods of rapid social or political change. Structures that are too complex can tie people in knots, producing inaction, delays, and confusion. Despite its size and complexity, however, today's Congress continues to adapt and change.

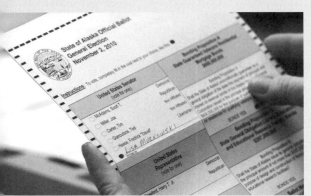

***E**lectoral Process.* Census Bureau worker conducts a personal interview, 2010 (top left). Voting at a polling place in San Jose, Calif. (top right). A Fairbanks, Alaska, poll worker checks a voter's write-in vote for Lisa Murkowski, who lost the GOP primary but whose visibility won her a rare write-in victory to retain her U.S. Senate seat, 2010 (middle left). Pizzeria owner Bobby Schilling, a Tea Party conservative, won his House seat in a normally Democratic district (bottom left). New senator Rand Paul, R-Ky., takes his oath of office in the Old Senate chamber as his wife and family look on. Vice President Joseph R. Biden Jr., officiates (bottom right).

chapter 3

Going for It: Recruitment and Candidacy

On the first day of the 112th Congress in January 2011, one of the largest freshmen classes in two decades assembled to take the oath of office. Among the sixteen new senators (13R, 3D) were an ophthalmologist, a plastics manufacturer, a former U.S. trade representative, a former governor and state attorney general, and five former House members. Among the ninety-six new House members (87R, 9D) were an airline pilot, a former FBI special agent, two surgeons, a professor, a former professional football player, a roofing contractor, an auctioneer, a car dealership owner, a nurse, a banker, a radio talk show host, and many state and local lawmakers.

How did these people get to Congress? This question has no simple answer. In the broadest sense, all legislators are products of recruitment—the social and political process through which people achieve leadership posts. Recruitment is a key to the effective functioning of all institutions, including legislatures. Ideally, the recruitment process should secure the ablest individuals to lead their community, a subject addressed in the first great book about politics, Plato's *Republic.* Sociologists, however, have long observed that recruitment reflects a society's class structure, with the most privileged disproportionately represented in the power structure. Contemporary political scientists, whatever their normative concerns, have charted the paths that individuals travel to gain positions in Congress and other institutions of government.

Any recruitment process has both formal and informal elements. For Congress, the formal elements include the Constitution and state and federal laws governing nominations and elections. Equally important are the informal, often unwritten, rules of the game. Ambitions, skills, and resources favor certain aspirants over others; popular moods and attitudes—which are changeable—induce citizens to support some candidates and reject others. Taken together, such elements add up to a series of filters or screens. The recruitment process is a mix of rules, probabilities, chance events, and timing. Its biases, both overt and hidden, affect the day-to-day operation of the House and Senate, not to mention the quality of representation and decision making.

FORMAL RULES OF THE GAME

The formal gateways to congressional office are wide. There are only three constitutional qualifications for holding congressional office: age (twenty-five years of age for the House, thirty for the Senate); citizenship (seven years for the House, nine years for the Senate); and residency (in the state from which the officeholder is elected).

These qualifications cannot be augmented by the states or by Congress. As the Supreme Court established in a 1995 case concerning term limits,[1] these qualifications can be changed only through constitutional amendment. By the early 1990s, twenty-three states had adopted restrictions on the number of terms their members of Congress could serve. Speaking for the Court as it struck down these term limits in 1995, Justice John Paul Stevens wrote: "Allowing individual States to adopt their own qualifications for congressional service would be inconsistent with the Framers' vision of a uniform National Legislature representing the people of the United States."

Notably, the drafters of the Constitution considered but rejected term limits. According to *The Federalist Papers,* the Framers left reelection of senators and representatives unrestricted because they did not wish to limit electors' choices. They regarded officeholders' desire for reelection as a powerful incentive for faithful service. Gouverneur Morris (speaking of the presidency) called the opportunity of reelection "the great motive to good behavior." In addition, the Framers valued the expertise that experienced lawmakers—much like the Framers themselves—could bring to legislative deliberations.

The residency requirement is traditionally stricter in practice than the Constitution prescribes. Voters tend to prefer candidates with long-standing ties to their states or districts and to shun outsiders who move into a state primarily to seek public office (so-called carpetbaggers). Nevertheless, Americans' geographical mobility has swollen the "carpetbagger caucus" on Capitol Hill. About a third of the members of both chambers in recent Congresses were born outside the states they represent. Especially in the more populous, faster-growing areas, shrewd candidates can overcome objections to their outsider status. Barely a year after he settled in Arizona, Republican John McCain, a career navy officer and six-year prisoner of war in North Vietnam, beat three established politicians for a congressional nomination. He stifled carpetbagging charges by explaining that, as the son of a navy officer and one himself, he had never been able to put down roots: "The longest place I ever lived was Hanoi."

Senate Apportionment

At the 1789 Constitutional Convention, the delegates from small states demanded equal representation in the Senate as the price for their support of the Constitution. This arrangement is virtually unamendable, because Article V assures that no state can be deprived of its equal voice in the Senate without its own consent. As a result, the Senate is the one legislative body in the nation in which "one person, one vote" emphatically does not apply. By this standard, the Senate is one of the most malapportioned legislatures in the democratic world.[2] As one scholar has noted, "The nine largest states are home to 51 percent of the population but elect only 18 percent of the Senate; the twenty-six smallest states control 52 percent of the Senate but hold only 18 percent of the population."[3]

These figures confirm that, over time, the Senate's representative character has been undermined by widening disparities in state population. After the first census in 1790, the spread between the most populous state (Virginia) and the least populous one (Delaware) was nineteen to one. Today, the spread between the most populous state (California) and the least populous state (Wyoming) is fifty-three to one.

Populous states complain that they are shortchanged in the federal bargain. Compared with lightly populated states, they contribute more revenue and receive fewer benefits.[4] Based on a a recent study using polling, electoral, and demographic data, John D. Griffin concludes that the Senate's malapportionment "has increasingly come to underweight the preferences of ideological liberals, Democrats, African Americans, and Latinos."[5] Reflecting on such inequities, the late senator Daniel Patrick Moynihan, D-N.Y. (1977–2001), warned that "sometime in the twenty-first century the United States is going to have to address the question of apportionment in the Senate."[6]

House Apportionment

The 435 House seats are apportioned among the states by population, with districts averaging more than 710,000 people each. This apportionment process excludes the five delegates (American Samoa, the District of Columbia, Guam, the Virgin Islands, and the Northern Mariana Islands) and one resident commissioner (Puerto Rico). These nonapportioned seats represent populations ranging from 66,432 (American Samoa) to 3.7 million (Puerto Rico).

Role of the Census. To allocate House seats among the states, the Constitution requires a census of the population every ten years. Once the census figures are gathered by the Commerce Department's Census Bureau, House apportionment is derived by a mathematical formula called the method of equal proportions.[7] However, reapportionment does not fully guarantee equality of district population, because of two additional requirements: (1) every state must receive one House member, and (2) congressional districts cannot cross state lines.[8] After the 2010 apportionment, for example, the entire state of Montana, with one representative-at-large for nearly a million people, was the nation's most populous district. Neighboring Wyoming, with slightly over half a million represented by its single seat, was the least populous.

Because the size of the House has remained fixed since 1911, one state's gain means another state's loss.[9] This reality provoked sharp controversy in the aftermath of the 1920 census. For the first time ever, the results indicated that more Americans lived in urban than in rural areas. With the nation's cities and

FIGURE 3-1 **House Apportionment in the 112th Congress**

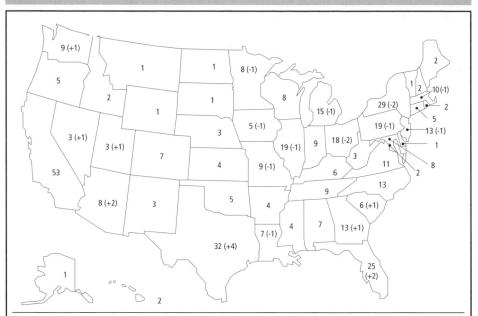

Source: "Apportionment Population and Number of Representatives, By State: 2010 Census," Census Bureau, U.S. Department of Commerce, December 21, 2010, http://2010.census.gov/news/pdf/apport2010_table1.pdf.

Note: Entries show the total number of House seats held by each state. Numbers in parentheses show the seats each state will gain or lose under the post-2010 reapportionment.

rural towns sharply at odds over the burning issue of the enforcement of Prohibition, the power struggle over representation was so intractable that Congress failed to pass a reapportionment bill after the 1920 census.[10] Finally, in 1929 a law was enacted that "established a permanent system for apportioning the 435 House seats following each census."[11] Thus the reapportionment of House seats occurred after the 1930 census and every census since (Figure 3-1).

For some decades now, older industrial and farm states of the Northeast and Midwest have lost ground to fast-growing states in the South and West— the declining Rust Belt versus the booming Sun Belt. After the 1940 census, states in the East and Midwest commanded 58 percent of all House seats, compared with 42 percent for states in the South and West. With the 2000 census, the ratio was exactly reversed. Over two generations, then, "a huge shift in political power" occurred between the geographic regions.[12] The trend continued with the results of the 2010 census, after which the northeastern and midwestern states once again lost seats to the Sun Belt. Most dramatically, Texas and Florida increased their congressional representation by four and two seats, respectively, while Ohio and New York each lost two seats. Redistricting is likely to be particularly contentious in the states losing congressional representation. But the census also reveals how populations have shifted within states, and congressional districts must be revised to take account of these changes. States with two or more House seats will have to engage in the often-contentious redistricting process before the November 2012 elections.

Census Politics. The Constitution describes the decennial census as an "actual enumeration" of persons (Article I, section 2). The Fourteenth Amendment adds: "Representatives shall be apportioned among the several States according to their respective numbers, counting the whole number of persons in each State, excluding Indians not taxed." Because population figures determine seats and affect power, including each state's share of the Electoral College vote for president and vice president, controversy surrounds nearly every aspect of apportionment and districting.

First, counting such a large and diverse population is logistically and methodologically daunting. Certain hard-to-contact groups—transients, the homeless, renters, immigrants (legal or not), children, and poorer people generally—elude census takers and are undercounted. College students or others temporarily living away from home are sometimes double-counted (an overcount, in effect).[13] The so-called "tri-caucus" in the House—the Black Caucus, the Hispanic Caucus, and the Asian Caucus—has long been concerned about getting accurate counts of hard-to-reach minorities, and they lobbied for adequate resources to conduct an accurate head count for the 2010 census.[14]

Second, the issue of statistical sampling has been a subject of considerable controversy. For the 2000 census, the Census Bureau had planned to use statistical sampling to augment their traditional methods for counting people to minimize the undercount of minority populations. But, because minorities tend to vote Democratic, congressional Republicans feared "that sampling would overestimate minority populations and thereby cause Republicans to lose seats to Democrats."[15] Legal challenges to the sampling plan eventually ended up in the Supreme Court, which held that sampling could not be used to apportion seats among the states, but kept open the possibility that it could be used for other purposes, such as the redistricting of House seats within a state.[16]

Third, the immigration issue adds yet another dimension to census politics. Because the Fourteenth Amendment refers to "persons" rather than "citizens," states with large numbers of undocumented immigrants (such as California, Arizona, and Texas) gain House seats at the expense of states with fewer undocumented immigrants (such as Michigan and Pennsylvania). "It's one thing if we lose seats simply because of population loss," complained Rep. Candice Miller, R-Mich., "but it's another thing if we lose this seat because of illegal immigration, and that's exactly what is happening."[17] In addition, Latinos are the fastest-growing group in the United States because of both immigration and higher birthrates, which will translate eventually into increasing numbers of Latinos in the House of Representatives.

DISTRICTING IN THE HOUSE

Redistricting is fundamentally a state responsibility, but the federal courts increasingly govern the process. Congressional districting is regulated by two federal statutes. The first is a 1967 statute that mandates that all states entitled to more than one seat create districts, each represented by a single member. At-large or multimember districts are prohibited. The second statute is the Voting Rights Act of 1965, which requires that districts not dilute the representation of racial minorities. In addition to interpreting these statutes, the courts have construed the Constitution to require that districts be nearly equal in population, a standard that they rigorously enforce.

Redistricting is a fiercely political process that affects the fortunes of many people—state legislators, governors, incumbent House members, the congressional leadership, lobbyists, and the leaders of racial and ethnic groups.[18] To insulate the process from politics, a handful of states have turned the job over to some form of independent commission.[19] In most states, however, redistricting is carried out by the legislature, with the governor able to approve or veto the plan. Political considerations of all kinds affect redistricting. In California, where Democrats controlled the state in 2001, the party was buffeted by clashing interests: nervous incumbents who sought safer reelection margins; term-limited state legislators with their sights set on Washington, D.C.; minority groups demanding more representation (especially Latinos, who account for much of the state's population growth); and national party leaders counting on California to help Democrats win a House majority.

In the redistricting wars no weapons are left sheathed. Both political parties pour money into state legislative and gubernatorial elections and into post-census lobbying efforts so they can control the mapmaking process. The shift of only a few seats in a state legislature can thereby determine not only which party dominates its congressional delegation, but potentially which party achieves majority control of the House itself. Republicans, for example, gained large advantages over the redrawing of House district boundaries with their victories in the 2010 elections: "Republicans hold the governor's mansion and both chambers of the state legislature—the three legs of the redistricting process—in at least 17 states, which are projected to contain 196 of the House's 435 districts," four times as many seats as Democrats will be able to redraw.[20] As a GOP consultant said about his role in drawing House seats, "As a mapmaker, I can have more of an impact on an election than a campaign, than a candidate."[21]

If a state's politicians become deadlocked on redistricting, or if they fail to observe legal guidelines, judges may finish the job—sometimes awarding victory to parties that lost out earlier in the political fracas. Both parties engage in "forum shopping," seeking the court friendliest to their side. Republicans during both Bush administrations could rely on the Justice Department and a federal bench composed of mostly GOP appointees. State courts also become engaged in these battles. The Supreme Court has ruled that normally state courts should be preferred over federal courts in redistricting cases.[22]

Because congressional seats are political prizes, districting is a tool by which politicians seek partisan, factional, and even personal advantage. Two perennial problems of districting are malapportionment and gerrymandering.

Malapportionment

Before 1964, districts of grossly unequal populations often existed side by side in the same state. As metropolitan areas grew in population, rurally dominated legislatures simply refused to redistrict, holding on to power regardless of population movements and demographic trends—the "silent gerrymander." The courts were slow to venture into this "political thicket." By the 1960s, however, the problem of unequal representation was crying out for resolution.[23]

In a series of landmark rulings in the 1960s, the Supreme Court held that districting schemes that fell short of standards of equality violated the Constitution. In *Reynolds v. Sims* (1964), the Court ruled that the Fourteenth Amendment's equal protection clause requires that all state legislative seats be apportioned "substantially on population." That same year, the Court also applied the "one person, one vote" principle to the U.S. House of Representatives. An Atlantan who served in the Georgia senate, James P. Wesberry Jr., charged that the state's congressional districting violated the equal protection clause of the Constitution. The Supreme Court upheld his challenge in *Wesberry v. Sanders* (1964), but it based its decision not on the Fourteenth Amendment but on Article I, section 2, of the Constitution, which directs that House representatives be apportioned among the states according to their respective numbers and chosen by the people of the several states. This language, argued Justice Hugo Black, means that "as nearly as is practicable, one person's vote in a congressional election is to be worth as much as another's."

How much equality of population is "practicable" within the states? The Supreme Court has adopted rigid mathematical equality as the underlying standard. In a 1983 case (*Karcher v. Daggett*), a 5–4 majority voided a New Jersey plan in which districts varied by no more than one-seventh of 1 percent. "Adopting any standard other than population equality would subtly erode the Constitution's ideal of equal representation," wrote Justice William J. Brennan for the majority.[24]

Other goals must sometimes be sacrificed to achieve population equality. It is often not feasible to follow other economic, social, or geographic boundaries in drawing districts of equal population in more populous states. The congressional district, therefore, tends to be an artificial creation, often bearing little relationship to real communities of interest—economic, geographic, or political. "The main casualty of the tortuous redistricting process now under way," remarked journalist Alan Ehrenhalt, "is the erosion of geographical community—of place—as the basis of political representation."[25]

Gerrymandering

The term *gerrymander* refers to district line-drawing that purposefully maximizes seats for one party or voting bloc. The gerrymander takes its name

· BOX 3-1 **Origins of the Gerrymander**

The practice of "gerrymandering"—the excessive manipulation of the shape of a legislative district to benefit certain persons or groups—is probably as old as the Republic, but the name for the practice originated in 1812.

In that year, the Massachusetts legislature carved out of Essex County a district that historian John Fiske described as having a "dragon-like contour." When the painter Gilbert Stuart saw the misshapen district, he penciled in a head, wings, and claws and exclaimed, "That will do for a salamander!" to which editor Benjamin Russell replied, "Better say a Gerrymander"—after Elbridge Gerry, then-governor of Massachusetts.

By the 1990s, the term had broadened to include the modern-day practice of drawing maps to benefit racial and ethnic groups. In the past, the term was applied largely to districts drawn to benefit incumbents or political parties.

Source: CQ's Guide to Congress, 5th edition, Vol. III (Washington, DC: CQ Press, 2007).

from Gov. Elbridge Gerry of Massachusetts, who in 1812 created a peculiar salamander-shaped district north of Boston to benefit his Democratic Party (see Box 3-1). Gerrymandering is used not only to gain partisan advantage but also to shape the political prospects of incumbents, particular aspiring politicians, or racial or ethnic groups. For most of its history, Congress has regarded gerrymandering as part of the spoils of partisan warfare.

Two common gerrymandering techniques are cracking and packing.[26] Cracking splits a party's or a group's strength between two or more districts, thereby diluting its voting leverage. A Republican cracking strategy, for example, might call for dividing a Democratic-leaning university town across two districts, combining each with the surrounding Republican-leaning rural areas, ensuring that Democrats will have difficulty winning either seat. A packing strategy draws districts dominated by voters of one party or group. Obviously, packing will likely make a district safe for a particular party, group, or incumbent. But it is also a way to waste votes. If a party's or ethnic group's voters are systematically concentrated in a small number of districts, it will win those seats with more votes than it needs, reducing its chances of winning nearby seats.

Today, gerrymandering is much more easily carried out than in the past. Using computer technology and software, knowledgeable individuals and groups can use census and other data to match people's voting patterns where they live, even street by street. Political leaders are able to consider various alternative plans until they identify a redistricting map that achieves their objectives.

Partisan Gerrymandering. The most common form of gerrymandering is aimed at partisan advantage. This type of gerrymandering occurs in states in which one political party controls the process. A noteworthy and unusual example involved the Texas legislature after the 2002 elections. Texas Republicans—controlling both legislative chambers and the state house for the first time since Reconstruction—pushed through a new districting plan even though an earlier post-census districting scheme was already in place. When the plan—masterminded by U.S. House majority leader Tom DeLay of Texas—was used for the 2004 balloting, the GOP gained five seats, four of them from defeated Democratic incumbents. Subsequently, the U.S. Supreme Court upheld the 2003 Texas redistricting scheme by a 7–2 margin (*League of United Latin American Citizens v. Perry*, 2006).[27] Despite finding that the Texas GOP appeared to have acted "with the sole purpose of achieving a Republican majority," Justice Anthony M. Kennedy—speaking for the Court—found that the case did not provide a "workable test" for deciding "how much partisan dominance is too much."

On the issue of partisan gerrymandering, the Supreme Court, like Congress, has largely chosen to look the other way. In a 1986 case involving Indiana state legislative districts, a Court majority held that gerrymandering was a justiciable issue—that is, it could be properly raised in court (*Davis v. Bandemer*).[28] If the gerrymandering were substantial, long-standing, and truly harmful to a political minority, it could violate the Constitution's equal protection clause. At the same time, the Court's majority was not convinced that the Indiana gerrymander met those tests. Indeed, the Court has never overturned a districting scheme on the grounds of partisan gerrymandering. Despite a number of cases dealing with the issue, the Court has neglected to set out any standard for distinguishing permissible from impermissible partisan gerrymandering.[29]

Many pundits and politicians complain that the prevalence of partisan gerrymandering inhibits the construction of cross-party coalitions. As Rep. John Tanner, D-Tenn., stated:

> When Members come here from these [partisan] districts that have been gerrymandered, they have little incentive really to work across party lines in order to reach solutions. As a matter of fact, they have a disincentive because if their district is skewed so heavily one way or the other, then the election is really in the party primaries, where . . . the highly charged partisans, either Democrat or Republican, [dominate]. And so if one comes here wanting to work across the aisle, one has to watch one's back, because the highly charged partisans don't like that.[30]

Scholarly research, however, has not provided much support for the claim that gerrymandering is an important cause of party polarization in Congress. Political scientist Sean M. Theriault reports that redistricting is responsible for between 10 and 20 percent of the party polarization that has occurred.[31] Other scholars dispute even this relatively modest effect. A study by Nolan McCarty, Keith T. Poole, and Howard Rosenthal concludes that gerrymandering has not contributed to the rise of partisanship to any meaningful extent: "Polarization is not primarily a phenomenon of how voters are sorted into districts. It is mainly the consequence of the different ways Democrats and Republicans would represent the same districts."[32]

Pro-Incumbent Gerrymandering. Bipartisan or "sweetheart" gerrymanders are those with lines drawn to protect incumbents. These gerrymanders are often by-products of divided party control—either between the two chambers of the legislature or between the legislature and the governor. In the wake of the 2000 census, the dominant parties in several populous states—California, Illinois, Michigan, and New York—chose to hoard their existing assets. In New York, which lost two seats in the reapportionment, two pairs of incumbents (one from each party) were thrown into the same districts, and the remaining twenty-seven districts were drawn for incumbents. "Neither party [wanted] to lose its hard-won gains," election analyst Rhodes Cook explained.[33]

In California, home of 12 percent of all House members, the ascendant Democrats opted to play it safe and claim only the added seat awarded by the 2000 census. The redrawn map eliminated one swing district in Los Angeles County (when its Republican incumbent retired) to craft a new Latino district, created a new GOP seat in the Central Valley, and shored up several swing district members. Under this incumbent-friendly districting plan, only one California congressional incumbent was defeated over the course of the five election cycles between 2002 and 2010.[34]

Political analysts are almost as divided as judges in assessing the consequences of gerrymandering. Some commentators blame incumbent-protective line-drawing for producing noncompetitive elections.[35] However, the prevalence of partisan gerrymandering (parties' efforts to boost their number of seats) helps to counteract the pattern. When parties seek to maximize the number of seats they can win, they cannot afford to create many entirely "safe" seats without wasting votes.[36]

The competitiveness of congressional elections is almost certainly shaped more by demography than by gerrymandering. "The problem is not who draws the legislative lines, it's where people live," notes one observer.[37] As Bruce Oppenheimer of Vanderbilt University explains, "Democrats tend to live next to Democrats. Republicans tend to live next to Republicans."[38] The state of California illustrates this insight. California has a deep political fault line readily visible on electoral maps: Democratic voters tend to cluster in the populous and mainly coastal counties, whereas Republicans are strongest in the inland counties. Creating truly competitive districts would mean linking together disparate coastal and inland communities—an exercise that could itself require extensive gerrymandering. Marked geographic patterns in voting like these are by no means peculiar to California.

Combating partisan and incumbent-friendly districting has nevertheless become a reformist cause. "The reason that people push for taking this out of the hands of the Legislature is there is really an inherent conflict of interest here where politicians are getting to custom-design which voters they want in their districts," as one reform advocate explained.[39] A number of reform initiatives were considered in the lead-up to the 2010 census, with Florida and California reformers having the most success. After several previous failed attempts, Californians finally passed a proposition creating an independent commission to draw congressional districts.[40] Florida voters also adopted amendments to their state constitution that will require legislators to draw lines that do not favor incumbents and are contiguous and compact. Whether such remedies can address the root causes of safe districts is another matter.

Majority-Minority Districts

Another form of gerrymandering involves the districting of racial minorities. After the Fifteenth Amendment was ratified to grant former slaves the right to vote, southern states adopted a variety of measures to thwart implementation of the law. One of those was the racial gerrymander—that is, "the deliberate and arbitrary distortion of district boundaries for racial purposes."[41] In the 1870s, for example, Mississippi opponents of Reconstruction concentrated the bulk of their state's black population in a long, narrow congressional district running along the Mississippi River, leaving five other districts with white majorities. Meanwhile, Alabama lawmakers scattered black voters over six different congressional districts to dilute their influence.[42] In other words, blacks were systematically "packed" into or "cracked" across congressional districts in order to weaken their electoral influence. In addition to racial gerrymandering, a variety of tools, such as literacy tests and poll taxes were employed over time to disenfranchise black voters across the South, largely denying them the right to participate in elections until the civil rights reforms of the 1960s.

The Voting Rights Act (VRA) of 1965 is arguably the most effective civil rights law ever enacted. It did away with the whole panoply of legal impediments erected to limit minority electoral participation. Section 2 of the VRA abolished all voting qualifications or prerequisites that had stood in the way of the franchise. In addition, sixteen states (mainly southern) that historically had discriminated against minorities were required (under the VRA's Section 5) to "pre-clear" with either the U.S. District Court for the District of Columbia or the U.S. attorney general any changes in election rules to ensure that those changes would not deny or abridge the right to vote on account of race or color. Officials announced that changes to election rules would only be pre-cleared if they would not lead to "a retrogression in the position of racial minorities."[43] For districting, this requirement means that changes must not lessen the likelihood that minorities will be elected. Amendments to the VRA in 1982 strengthened the legislation, establishing that a state's redistricting plan or other changes to its electoral laws could be overturned if they had racially discriminatory effects, even if it was impossible to prove that state officials had intended to discriminate.

As states and the Department of Justice attempted to implement the amended VRA after the 1990 census, congressional district lines were drawn to help minorities elect candidates of their choice, unlike in previous eras when districts had been manipulated to limit minority influence. Indeed, states began to deliberately create "majority-minority" districts to enhance the probability that minorities would be elected to Congress. A National Conference of State Legislatures report describes the effect:

> As states drew the [post-1990] plans, they discovered that the Justice Department had little concern that majority-minority districts be compact. In some cases, the department refused to pre-clear a plan unless the state "maximized" the number of majority-minority districts by drawing them wherever pockets of minority population could be strung together. As the plans were redrawn to obtain pre-clearance, some districts took on bizarre shapes that caused them to be labeled "racial gerrymanders."[44]

During this time, fifteen new majority African American districts were created, thirteen of them in the South (for a total of thirty-two nationwide, seventeen in the South), and nine new majority Latino districts (totaling twenty). Many of these districts were so oddly shaped that they made Governor Gerry's 1812 creation look amateurish by comparison.

The Supreme Court Enters the Quagmire. Some of these newly created majority-minority districts were later attacked in federal court. Plaintiffs charged that the districts violated white voters' Fourteenth Amendment right to equal protection of the law. The legal battles that resulted progressively deepened the Court's involvement in congressional districting. In a long series of complex, sometimes contradictory cases in this area, the Court has attempted to balance two competing values: first, the Fourteenth Amendment's requirement that states not discriminate on the basis of race, and, second, the VRA's protection against racial discrimination in the electoral process.

At the center of the controversy was North Carolina's shoestring Twelfth District, which remained under a legal cloud after four remappings (see Figure 3-2). As first drawn, this district was 160 miles long, in many places no wider than a two-lane highway, winding back and forth to capture pockets of black voters. Examining the North Carolina map, Justice Sandra Day O'Connor questioned "districting so highly irregular that, on its face, it rationally cannot be understood as anything other than an effort to segregate voters . . . on the basis of race."[45] In the 1993 case reviewing the North Carolina districting scheme (*Shaw v. Reno*), a narrowly divided Supreme Court recognized a claim of "racial gerrymandering" and held that districts could be challenged under the Fourteenth Amendment's equal protection clause.

In cases dealing with racial gerrymandering, the Court has indicated that it will apply a standard of "strict scrutiny" to any district in which race was the "predominant factor" in its creation.[46] To prove racial predominance, it must be shown that "the legislature subordinated to racial considerations traditional race-neutral districting principles, including but not limited to compactness, contiguity, and respect for political subdivisions of communities defined by actual shared interests."[47]

"Strict scrutiny" sets a very high bar that requires a state to demonstrate that its districting plan is, in the language of the legal test, "narrowly tailored to achieve a compelling state interest." For a districting scheme to survive this test, states must show that the challenged districts were drawn specifically to satisfy the requirements of Sections 2 or 5 of the VRA. According to the Court's reading of Section 2, a districting scheme is not narrowly tailored to avoid discrimination when there is not a population of minority voters "sufficiently large and geographically compact to constitute a majority in a single-member district."[48] As a consequence, majority-minority districts that are not "reasonably compact" have been unable to withstand strict scrutiny.[49] According to the Court's reading of Section 5 of the VRA, the requirement is "non-retrogression," meaning that a new districting scheme must not cause fewer minority representatives to be elected than before.[50] Most districting schemes subjected to the strict scrutiny standard have been overturned.[51]

Subsequent cases have clarified the law, although considerable uncertainty remains about precisely what majority-minority districting schemes will stand or fall upon judicial review. One important clarification is that racial gerry-mandering claims will fail unless race was the "predominant factor" in the creation of the district.[52] Writing for the Court in *Easley v. Cromartie* (2001), Justice Clarence Thomas declared:

> A jurisdiction may engage in constitutional political gerrymandering, even if it so happens that the most loyal Democrats happen to be black Democrats and even if the state were conscious of that fact.[53]

A racial gerrymandering challenge will not be upheld even if race was a factor in the districting but it was not the predominant factor.[54]

FIGURE 3-2 **Racial Gerrymandering in the 1990s and 2000s: North Carolina's First and Twelfth Congressional Districts**

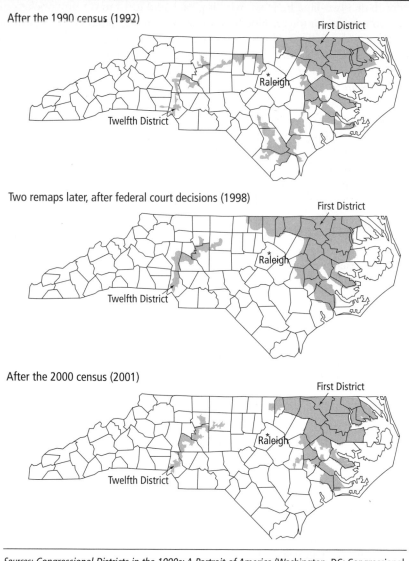

After the 1990 census (1992)

First District

Raleigh

Twelfth District

Two remaps later, after federal court decisions (1998)

First District

Raleigh

Twelfth District

After the 2000 census (2001)

First District

Raleigh

Twelfth District

Sources: *Congressional Districts in the 1990s: A Portrait of America* (Washington, DC: Congressional Quarterly, 1993), 548; *Congressional Districts in the 2000s: A Portrait of America* (Washington, DC: CQ Press, 2003), 673.

Note: North Carolina's First and Twelfth Congressional Districts were drawn to give the state its first black representatives in ninety-three years. First elected in 1992, the two African American representatives were subsequently reelected. After the First District representative retired in 2003, she was replaced by another African American.

In the end, the key question is whether the Supreme Court will provide clear guidelines as to what racial (even partisan) redistricting the Constitution will permit. In the quest for a workable standard, the justices have adopted a version of Justice Potter Stewart's 1964 test for defining obscenity: "I know it when I see it." And in view of the closeness of its past decisions on majority-minority districts—nearly every major case on this question has turned on a 5–4 vote—the Court could again shift its direction as its membership changes. Race-conscious districting will surely be contested well beyond 2010. As a North Carolina state senator quipped, "If the Lord God Almighty threw down lightning bolts and carved plans into the side of Mount Mitchell, and we adopted them, there would still be challenges to redistricting under every legal theory devised."[55]

Consequences of Majority-Minority Districts. Proponents of majority-minority districts view them as "the political equivalent to the ethnically homogeneous neighborhood," in the words of law professor Lani Guinier. "They are a safe haven for members of that group, a bit of turf that one ethnic grouping controls, a place where their voice is pre-eminent."[56] The growing numbers of majority-minority districts have unquestionably made the House of Representatives more racially and ethnically diverse. Most minority legislators are elected in districts where minority groups make up the majority of the population. Indeed, a recent study confirms that a district's racial composition is by far the most important factor in determining the race of the representative it elects: "Race-conscious redistricting and the creation of effective minority districts remain the basis upon which most African American and Latino officials gain election."[57] Over time, representatives of majority-minority districts have built up a great deal of seniority and institutional clout within the Democratic Party in the House.

Nevertheless, the creation of majority-minority districts, comes at some cost to minority voters. Concentrating minorities into districts where they constitute a majority can also waste their votes by producing outsized electoral majorities for the winning candidates. It simultaneously "bleaches" surrounding nonminority districts, as minority voters, along with whatever leverage they have, are drained away to create majority-minority districts. Even if the share of minority officeholders rises, "the number of white legislators who have any political need to respond to minority concerns goes down as their minority constituents are peeled off to form the new black and Hispanic districts."[58]

There is evidence that racial redistricting has contributed to the Democratic Party's southern meltdown since the 1990s.[59] Concentrating minority (mostly Democratic) voters in safe (mainly urban) districts strengthened the GOP in outlying suburban and rural areas. The combination of African Americans, who wanted more representation in the House, and Republicans, who supported that goal because it served their political purposes, has been dubbed an "unholy alliance."[60] Scholar David Lublin has described the outcome as a "paradox of representation" in which packed districts yielded more minority lawmakers but also led to a more conservative House that reduced minorities' leverage and influence over legislative outcomes.[61]

Many doubt that packing districts is the best way to advance minorities' interests. Another strategy for enhancing the political influence of minorities is to maintain substantial minorities of racial and ethnic voters, say 40 percent or so, in a larger number of districts (so-called influence districts) to expand the ranks of officeholders responsive to minority needs.[62] In the wake of the 2000 census, many Democrats concluded that racial gerrymandering had hurt their party and set about unpacking some of the minority districts. "For 20 years I've been arguing against the stacking of black voters in districts that has the overall effect of diluting the voting strength of black people," pointed out Rep. James E. Clyburn, D-S.C. "It's better to maintain a 35 to 40 percent black district where [blacks] would have a tremendous influence on elections. I don't think you need 75 percent in order for a black to be elected. That's kind of insulting to me."[63]

BECOMING A CANDIDATE

Very few of those who are eligible for Congress vie for a seat. Candidates who meet the legal qualifications must weigh a variety of considerations—some practical and rational, others personal and emotional. Candidacy decisions are often the pivotal moments in the entire recruitment process, although students of politics have only recently given them the attention they deserve. "The decision to run obviously structures everything else that goes on in the primary process," writes political scientist L. Sandy Maisel. "Who runs, who does not run, how many candidates run. These questions set the stage for the campaigns themselves."[64]

Called or Chosen?

From their Jacksonian heyday in the 1830s to the decline of big-city machines in the 1960s, local party organizations customarily enlisted and sponsored candidates. When these organizations withered, the initiative passed to the candidates themselves: self-starters who pulled their own bandwagons. "The boys in the back room aren't going to decide who stays in this race," one representative remarked. "There are no boys anymore."[65] "The skills that work in American politics at this point in history," writes Alan Ehrenhalt, "are those of entrepreneurship. At all levels of the political system, from local boards and councils up to and including the presidency, it is unusual for parties to nominate people. People nominate themselves."[66]

Congressional aspirants, however, quickly encounter national networks of party committees and their allied interest groups. At the heart of these networks are the two major parties' House and Senate campaign committees, now active in nearly all phases of congressional elections.[67] They seek out and encourage promising candidates at the local level, sometimes even taking sides to help ensure their nomination. Once nominated, candidates receive help for nearly every phase of the campaign, from fund raising to finding seasoned campaign managers to researching the backgrounds of their opponents. Filing deadlines must be met, backers lined up, and financing sought. Candidates may feel free to keep their national party at arm's length, but few nonincumbents can turn their backs on party sponsorship.

During the recruiting season (beginning in early 2011 for the 2012 contests, for example), the leaders and campaign committee staffs of the two major parties "reach out across the country in search of political talent. Like college football coaching staffs in hot pursuit of high-school prospects, they are putting together the lineups of the future."[68] Prospects can expect calls from the president, former presidents, governors, high-profile financial backers, and other notables. The run-ups to recent elections all began with fierce recruiting seasons, as both parties sought lineups that could win House and Senate majorities.

Not all recruiting takes place on the road. Open seats—those in newly created districts or those in which incumbents have died or retired—are less secure. To the extent they can, then, party leaders try to discourage their incumbent colleagues from retiring.

A few nonparty groups also sponsor congressional candidates. The leading small business lobby, the National Federation of Independent Business (NFIB), has been a major contributor to the GOP cause. In the mid-1990s, the NFIB began to pick potential candidates from its own membership, train them, and help them run for office. "We're trying to develop a farm team for down the road," explained the federation's national political director, "so we can work in more of a proactive instead of a reactive way," fielding, not just endorsing, candidates who support the small business agenda.[69] Other organizations with strong grassroots networks now pursue a similar course.

Most would-be officeholders seek advancement within the two major parties, which boast not only the brand loyalties of a huge majority of voters but also extensive financial and logistical resources. Still, independents and minorparty candidates enter congressional contests. Some twenty-three party labels, for example, appeared on ballots somewhere in 2008. Seldom do these contenders win a sizable number of votes, but they do provide alternatives where only one major party fields a candidate. Only two independents served in Congress in 2011: Vermont senator Bernard Sanders, a self-styled "democratic socialist," and Connecticut senator Joseph I. Lieberman, who announced that he would retire in 2012.

Amateurs and Professionals

How do would-be candidates, whether self-starters or recruited by party leaders, make up their minds to run? The answer often depends on whether the individual is a political amateur or a professional.

Amateurs. Amateur candidates are defined by their lack of previous political experience. Despite inexperience and nonexistent name recognition, many amateurs run for Congress. A few run to bring a specific issue to public attention and are less interested in winning than in advancing their cause. Most amateurs are what David T. Canon calls "hopeless amateurs"—people with little or no chance of winning.[70] Nevertheless, political amateurs regularly compete, and almost every congressional election brings a few amateurs to Capitol Hill. Indeed, the freshman class of 2010 has the largest number of political amateurs of any class since 1944.[71]

Amateurs are more willing than experienced politicians to make a long-shot bid for office. They are frequently the only candidates who will take on seemingly invulnerable incumbents. Amateurs often find that an uncompetitive primary offers their only chance to win a major-party nomination. More attractive political opportunities will generally entice more politically experienced competitors. "I think his chances have gone from absolutely out of the question to extremely remote," remarked the wife of one hopeless contender. "But he's learning a lot, and I think he has enjoyed it."[72] Many such amateurs nevertheless indulge in self-delusion about their prospects. Maisel, a political scientist who wrote candidly about his own unsuccessful congressional primary campaign, described politicians as possessing an "incredible ability to delude themselves about their own chances."[73]

One group of amateurs, however, sometimes proves to be the exception—those with highly visible nonpolitical careers. Astronauts, war heroes, entertainers, and athletes are in big demand as candidates. Local or statewide television personalities also make attractive contenders. In 2000 Republican Tom Osborne captured 80 percent of the vote in Nebraska's open Third District even though he wholly lacked political experience. Everyone in the state knew him as the longtime football coach of the University of Nebraska Cornhuskers.[74] Al Franken's status as a nationally known comedian, writer, and commentator helped to launch his political career as a candidate in 2008 for Minnesota's U.S. Senate seat.

Professionals. Professionals are more cautious than amateurs about the races they enter. Those who seek to make a career in politics must consider carefully not just whether to run for a particular political office but when to do so. Political careerists often have more to lose than an amateur from an unsuccessful bid for office, because entering one race often means foregoing the office they already hold. An experienced state legislator is unlikely to gamble a safe seat in the state house or senate on a remote chance that he or she might defeat a popular congressional incumbent. Such a candidate will wait for a better opening, when an incumbent retires or is clearly vulnerable. Similarly, a sitting House member will usually wait for an open seat or an exceptional opportunity before attempting to move up to the Senate. In the end, such decisions hinge on "the not-so-simple calculus of winning."[75]

Strategic contenders weigh the chances of getting the party's nomination in view of the party's ideological bent, leadership, and nominating procedures. They also consider what it will cost to succeed. If there is an incumbent, they identify the incumbent's weaknesses. And they take a look at the broader political environment, including the condition of the economy, the president's standing, and public dissatisfaction with the status quo. They then evaluate their own personal strengths and weaknesses in campaigning, voter appeal, and fund raising,

Most successful congressional candidates are professionals—seasoned politicians—before they run for Congress. Grassroots organizations and movements are a breeding ground for candidates—for example, environmental activists in the 1970s, religious conservatives in the 1990s, antiwar activists during the George W. Bush presidency, and Tea Party activists after 2008. But more often, elective office is the immediate springboard: mayors, district attorneys, or state legislators for the House; and governors, lieutenant governors, and attorneys general—who have already faced a statewide electorate—for the Senate. House members, especially from smaller states, are also strategically positioned to run for the Senate. A majority of senators in the 112th Congress had "moved up" from the House.

The circle of people pondering a candidacy (the challenger pool) may be large or small, depending on the office and the circumstances.[76] Any number of elected officials—state legislators (especially if subject to term limits), county officers, mayors, city council members, even governors—are weighing a race for Congress at any given time. "The people who have been successful in the political world are people who know when to strike at the right time," remarked a veteran state legislator contemplating a run against an incumbent House member.[77]

Finding Quality Candidates

Candidate quality and campaign strength are critical factors in many battles for congressional seats.[78] A party's success in November hinges on its efforts during the recruitment season. Often races turn on bids that are not made. An election outcome frequently becomes a fait accompli when a strong potential candidate chooses not to run.

According to Maisel and his colleagues, candidate quality is measured in strategic resources and personal attributes.[79] Quality candidates are skilled in presenting themselves as candidates and are attractive to voters. Previous experience in public office—and the accompanying visibility and credibility—is one of the most important attributes of a quality candidate. Simply having a familiar political name can also be a ticket to candidacy. Fame or notoriety can sometimes overcome lack of relevant background or experience. Other characteristics of quality candidates include physical appearance, personality, speaking ability, and a talent for organizing or motivating others. Fund-raising ability or potential is essential as well. Overall, likely candidates have ambition and a keen desire for public life, both of which will help them to succeed in their attempt to gain public office.[80]

Stamina is also important. No matter how talented, principled, or well funded, aspirants for public office must be ready, physically and emotionally, to face the rigors of campaigning. They must be willing to hit the road nonstop, meet new people, attend gatherings, sell themselves, ask for money, and endure verbal abuse—all the while appearing to enjoy it. "People who do not like to knock on strangers' doors or who find it tedious to repeat the same 30-second introduction thousands of times," explains Alan Ehrenhalt, "are at a severe disadvantage in running for office."[81]

The Incumbency Factor. Of all the inducements for launching a candidacy, the odds of winning stand at the top. A clearly winnable seat seldom lacks for eager quality candidates. Open seats—those without an incumbent running—are especially attractive. As a result, open-seat races are more likely to be competitive and to shift party control than those with an incumbent. Party strategists thus concentrate on these races.

In most House and Senate contests, however, incumbents will be running, and most of them will be reelected. As Gary C. Jacobson writes, "Nearly everything pertaining to candidates and campaigns for Congress is profoundly influenced by whether the candidate is an incumbent, challenging an incumbent, or pursuing an open seat."[82] Perhaps less forcibly, the same could be said of the Senate. Since World War II, on average 93.3 percent of all incumbent representatives and 81.5 percent of all incumbent senators running for reelection have been returned to office.

Because any savvy politician contemplating a bid for Congress recognizes the difficulty of defeating an incumbent, incumbents frequently face only low-quality opponents. Challengers are often weak fund-raisers, poorly qualified, and unknown to voters. Party leaders often struggle to even find candidates willing to run against some incumbents. In 2010 twenty-seven incumbent House members and one senator ran for reelection unopposed. Similarly, Democrats had great difficulty finding a challenger for Sen. Richard Burr, R-N.C. With his relatively low approval ratings and poor visibility for an incumbent, Democrats perceived Burr as one of their best pick-up opportunities in 2010. But one after another, high-profile Democrats declined to run against him. "It's clear that experienced Democratic officials on the ground in North Carolina have a much different view of this race than party officials in Washington," observed a spokesman for the National Republican Senatorial Committee.[83] From the perspective of local Democrats, the prospects of winning were simply not favorable enough to attract much interest in the race.

An incumbent's most effective electoral strategy is to scare off serious opposition. "If an incumbent can convince potentially formidable opponents and people who control campaign resources that he or she is invincible," says Jacobson, "he or she is very likely to avoid a serious challenge and so will be invincible—as long as the impression lasts."[84] Any sign of weakness is likely to encourage opponents in the next election.[85] For that reason, incumbents try to sustain wide electoral margins, show unbroken strength, keep up constituency ties, and build giant war chests of reelection money.

Incumbents are not invincible, however, even if their high reelection rates make them seem so. Indeed, in view of the prevalence of strategic retirement—the tendency of incumbents to retire when they perceive themselves to be politically vulnerable—reelection rates are a somewhat misleading indicator of incumbent safety. Incumbents keep close tabs on political developments in their constituencies, and many would prefer to retire rather than suffer the rebuke of voters. These strategic considerations lurk behind many incumbents' retirements, even when they cite other reasons for their decisions. In 2010, for example, Democratic senators Byron Dorgan of South Dakota and Evan Bayh of Indiana both opted to retire rather than face the voters of their Republican-leaning states in a political climate so unfavorable to Democrats. In short, the chances of success are equally important for incumbents as for challengers when considering future career options.[86]

No-Shows. High-caliber potential candidates apparently abound in America's communities—even in minority-party circles within noncompetitive districts.[87] But all too often these individuals prefer to remain on the sidelines. The road to public office is increasingly arduous and costly. And the odds are often long, especially when running against a dominant party or an entrenched incumbent. Therefore, quality challengers often fail to step forward. Poor-quality challengers raise less money and are less successful than the handful of blue-ribbon contenders. This dynamic depresses competition in congressional elections across the board.

Raising the money needed to run an effective race is a major deterrent to would-be candidates. This stumbling block was cited twice as often as any other factor by the potential contenders in the two hundred electoral districts surveyed by Maisel and Walter J. Stone.[88] Other candidates reject campaigns because of the high costs for their personal lives, incomes, careers, and families. The benefits side of the ledger may not outweigh the costs of gaining and holding public office. Rep. Thomas M. Davis III, R-Va., a former House GOP campaign chair who chose not to seek reelection in 2008, describes the main selling point:

> We'd get them here under the Capitol dome, have their wife take a picture, have the Speaker of the House tell how important they'll be. You're not selling the lifestyle. You're not selling the salary. You're selling relevance.[89]

All too often, prospective candidates decide that their destinies lie elsewhere—in state or local politics, in nonprofit community service, or in family and profession.

Women are especially likely to forego opportunities to run for political office, even when they have been highly successful in the professions that usually precede public office. Research by political scientists Jennifer L. Lawless and Richard L. Fox has revealed that prominent female lawyers, businesspeople, educators, and political activists are less likely than similarly situated males to see themselves as good candidates for political office.[90] U.S. political institutions are more male-dominated than those in most other advanced democracies, but the cause appears to lie more with the calculations of prospective candidates than with voters. Women are not less likely than men to win races they enter, but they are less likely to consider a candidacy in the first place. In part, this difference reflects the fact that party leaders, elected officials, and advocacy groups are less likely to recruit women to run. But it also reflects broader societal norms and socialization processes that make it more difficult for women to promote themselves and seek political leadership positions.

NOMINATING POLITICS

Nominating procedures, set forth in state laws and conditioned by party customs, further shape the potential pool of candidates. Historically, these procedures have expanded to ever wider circles of participants—a development that has diminished the power of party leaders and thrust more initiative upon the candidates themselves. In most states, the direct primary—allowing party voters to choose their party's nominees—is the formal mechanism for selecting congressional candidates.

Rules of the Nominating Game

Every state has election laws that provide for primary elections for House and Senate candidates, but these laws vary widely.[91] The critical question is who should be permitted to vote in a party's primary. The states have adopted varying answers. Party leaders naturally prefer strict rules that reward party loyalty, discourage outsider candidates, and maximize their own influence on the outcome. States with strong party traditions therefore tend to have closed primaries. This arrangement, found in twenty-six states, requires voters to declare party affiliation in order to vote in the primary. (Their affiliation is considered permanent until they take steps to change it.) In open primaries, conducted in twenty states, voters can vote in the primary of either party (but not in both) simply by requesting the party's ballot at the polling place.

Few primaries are competitive races. Primary winners typically prevail in lopsided victories, and incumbents are almost always renominated. According to a recent study, only about 1 percent of incumbents in the postwar period were defeated in a primary.[92] Nominations for open-seat races are virtually certain to feature contested primaries. "If a district party is without an incumbent, and has a fighting chance in November," Harvey L. Schantz writes, "there is a strong possibility of a public contest for the U.S. House nomination."[93] But even including primaries for open seats, the typical primary winner's share is more than 60 percent of the vote.[94]

Parties and Nominations

Despite the prevalence of primaries, party organizations at all levels are hardly without leverage in nominations. Although party organizations do not play a formal role in the primary process in the majority of states, in nine states parties have conventions that influence candidates' access to the primary ballot.[95] More important, party organizations influence nominations indirectly—by contacting promising prospects, linking them with campaign contributors, endorsing them, and assisting in other ways.

Parties are centrally involved in candidate recruitment. Of the hundreds of prospective candidates identified in recent canvassing, about two out of five had been contacted by one or more party organizations—local, state, or national.[96] Parties are most active in districts regarded as winnable, and the people they seek out are the "usual suspects"—officeholders, prominent figures, and the wealthy.[97] The obvious candidate also may be someone who has run for the seat before. For example, fifty-seven House races in 2010 were rematches of the same candidates from a previous election.[98]

Party leaders tend to be pragmatists—above all, bent on finding winners. Thus Democrats deliberately embarked on a strategy in 2006 and 2008 to recruit antiabortion, pro–gun rights candidates in conservative areas such as the South. In 2008, for example, the staunchly antiabortion mayor of Montgomery, Alabama, Bobby Bright, received extensive financial assistance from the national party.[99] (Bright was elected, but then was defeated for reelection in November 2010.) Republican leaders, too, lean toward moderates over extremists in swing states or districts. Sometimes, however, leaders simply prefer to wait and see which primary contender emerges victorious. "There's some arrogance in always thinking you know who the right nominee is," said Rep. Tom Cole of Oklahoma, the GOP's campaign chair for 2008. "Sometimes these candidates have to be produced locally and the process has to play out."[100]

Intraparty rivalries often mark nominating contests. In 2010 intraparty conflicts led to primary or convention defeats for three sitting senators and four incumbent House members. Most remarkably, Sen. Lisa Murkowski, R-Alaska, was defeated for renomination in the GOP primary by challenger Joe Miller, but then went on to wage a successful write-in candidacy for reelection to become only the second senator ever elected in this manner. The Tea Party movement fueled an unusually high level of internal contention within the Republican Party in 2009 and 2010. Candidates endorsed by the Tea Party unseated eighteen-year veteran senator Bob Bennett, R-Utah, and three-term incumbent representative Bob Inglis, R-S.C. Although the Tea Party activated disaffected Republicans voters and helped the party retake control of the House of Representatives,[101] its role in the primaries harmed Republican chances in the Senate. Republicans would have stood a better chance of winning the Senate contests in Nevada, Colorado, and Delaware if Tea Party activists had not defeated more centrist candidates for the party's nomination.

Sizing Up the Primary System

The direct primary was one of the reforms adopted early in the twentieth century to overcome corrupt, boss-dominated nominating conventions. It has permitted more participation in selecting candidates, and yet primaries normally attract a narrower segment of voters than do general elections (except in one-party areas, where primaries dictate the outcomes). In recent years, primary contests have drawn less than 20 percent of eligible voters—or less than half the number who voted in the general elections.[102] Less publicized than general elections, primaries tend to attract voters who are somewhat older, wealthier, better educated, more politically aware, and more ideologically committed than the electorate as a whole.[103]

Primaries also have hampered the political parties by encouraging would-be officeholders to appeal directly to the public and construct support networks apart from the party machinery. Still, leaders strive to influence who enters their primaries and who wins them. Displaying impressive resilience and adaptability, party organizations at all levels have recast themselves into organizations "'in service' to [their] candidates and officeholders but not in control of them."[104]

Finally, primaries are a costly way of choosing candidates. Unless candidates begin with overwhelming advantages (such as incumbency), they must mount virtually the same kind of campaign in the primary that they must repeat later in the general election.

CONCLUSION

The rules of the game that narrow the potential field of congressional contenders can be thought of as a series of gates, each narrower than the one before. First are the constitutional qualifications for holding office. Far more restrictive are the personal attributes associated with a successful public career. Next are the complex rules of apportionment and districting. Beyond these are the nominating procedures (usually primaries). These successive gates sharply reduce the number of people who are likely to become real contenders.

Equally important, individuals must make up their own minds about running for the House or Senate. Such choices embrace a range of considerations—many personal and emotional but all based on some estimate of the likely benefits and costs of the candidacy. This winnowing process presents voters with a limited choice on election day: two, occasionally more, preselected (or self-selected) candidates. From this tiny circle, senators and representatives are chosen.

Winners and losers: Oshkosh, Wisconsin, businessman Ron Johnson and his wife celebrate his GOP primary victory in September 2010 (top). Johnson went on to defeat three-term Democratic senator Russ Feingold, seen conceding on election night, November 2 (middle). Senate majority leader Harry Reid, D-Nev., shakes hands with GOP candidate Sharron Angle (bottom) after a debate moderated by Las Vegas PBS reporter Mitch Fox. Reid won the closely fought race.

Making It:
The Electoral Game

Businessman Ron Johnson had never given a political speech before. On a cold Saturday in October 2009, hundreds of people were assembled in the parking lot in front of the Winnebago County courthouse in Oshkosh, Wisconsin, for a TEA (Taxed Enough Already) Party rally.[1] He was not the event's headline speaker (that was Samuel Joseph Wurzelbacher, who became famous as "Joe the Plumber" during the 2008 presidential campaign). Owner of an Oshkosh plastics company, Johnson had been asked to speak briefly about government regulation of business. But when he mounted the podium, he gave instead an impassioned speech about a life-changing experience twenty-seven years earlier when his daughter had been born with a heart defect. He described how his daughter's life had been saved by a state-of-the-art surgical procedure. "What that experience taught me, is that the United States has the finest health-care system in the world. . . . [M]y daughter had a chance at a full life because my wife and I had the freedom to seek out the most advanced surgical treatment at the time."[2] Pivoting to the debate over health care reform, Johnson then "let loose with an attack on the demonization of doctors and, more broadly, the mortal threat to American exceptionalism."[3]

Johnson's speech struck a chord in his audience, several of whom urged him to run for office. Shortly afterward, a local conservative talk radio host read a lengthy excerpt of his speech on the air. Word spread among conservative activists around the state.[4] In Wisconsin, the speech had the effect of putting Johnson "on the political map."[5] Though reluctant at first, Johnson began to consider running for office. When Congress passed the Patient Protection and Affordable Care Act several months later, Johnson decided to run for the U.S. Senate: "That was the final straw," he said. The legislation is "the greatest assault on our freedom in my lifetime."[6] A mere two months later, Johnson easily won the endorsement of the Wisconsin Republican Party's convention for the race, despite facing better-known and well-funded opponents who had been in the race longer.[7] He went on to win a lopsided victory in the statewide primary for the Republican Senate nomination.

Johnson's Democratic opponent in November was eighteen-year veteran senator Russ D. Feingold. No ordinary politician, Feingold had a record of political independence, legislative accomplishments, and close ties with constituency groups throughout Wisconsin. An energetic campaigner, Feingold held seventy-two town hall meetings throughout the state in 2010, more than any other senator.[8] He raised more than $20 million for his campaign.[9] Additional funds and help streamed from outside organizations. The progressive advocacy group MoveOn.org made reelecting Feingold its top 2010 priority; it organized teams of volunteers and tapped its membership for donations. Even so, Feingold had to contend with the stormy political climate that would bring down hundreds of Democrats across the country at all levels of government. Indeed, the turn against the Democratic Party was sharper in Wisconsin than anywhere else, with one poll showing that President Barack Obama's approval rating had fallen faster in Wisconsin than in any other state.[10]

Despite being new to politics, Johnson had some formidable assets. His political inexperience helped him capture the prevailing anti-Washington mood. Johnson bragged that he had never set foot in Washington, D.C., before the campaign.[11] His business background helped persuade many voters concerned about Wisconsin's high unemployment rate that he knew how to create jobs.[12] Finally, Johnson's deep pockets as a millionaire business owner allowed him to underwrite his own campaign. Pouring $8.2 million of his own money into the race, he personally supplied over half of the cost of his $14.8 million campaign.[13]

The contest would prove to be the most expensive Senate race in Wisconsin history.[14] Johnson crisscrossed the state, slamming Feingold for his support of health care reform and for increasing the national debt. On television, he ran biographical ads portraying himself as "just a guy from Oshkosh" who would bring common sense to Washington.[15] Although Johnson made some controversial comments early in the campaign—for example, referring to "sunspots" as the cause of global warming and to Social Security as a "Ponzi scheme"—he ran a cautious campaign that largely avoided missteps.[16] On election day, Johnson prevailed with 52 percent of the vote to Feingold's 47 percent.

Idiosyncratic as it may be in many respects, the Wisconsin Senate battle illustrates several elements of congressional elections. It highlights how even seemingly secure incumbents can become vulnerable when voters are deeply dissatisfied with the status quo. It points to the importance of campaigns, especially candidates' abilities to find the right message to respond to voters' concerns. Finally, it exemplifies how national party politics reverberates down to local races.

CAMPAIGN STRATEGIES

Campaigns are volatile mixtures of personal contacts, fund raising, speechmaking, advertising, and symbolic appeals. As acts of communication, campaigns are designed to convey messages to potential voters. The overriding goal is to win over a plurality of those who cast ballots on election day.

Asking the Right Questions

Whether incumbents or challengers, candidates for Congress strive to map out a successful campaign strategy. To that end, each potential candidate must consider: What sort of constituency do I seek to represent? Are my name, face, and career familiar to voters? What resources—money, group support, volunteers—can I attract? What leaders and groups are pivotal to a winning campaign? What issues are uppermost in potential voters' minds? How can I reach those voters most effectively? When should my campaign begin, and how should it be paced? And, perhaps most important, what are my chances for victory? The answers to such questions define the campaign strategy.

The constituency itself shapes a candidate's campaign strategy. In populous states, Senate aspirants must appeal to diverse economic and social groups scattered over wide areas and many media markets. In fast-growing states, even Senate incumbents must introduce themselves to new voters who have arrived since the last election. Only small-state Senate candidates are able to know their constituents as well as House candidates know theirs. But unlike states, House districts often fit within no natural geographic community, media market, or existing political division.[17] In such situations, candidates and their managers must find the most suitable forums, media outlets, and organizations to reach voters who may have little in common except being enclosed within the same district boundaries.

Because incumbents are typically hard to defeat, the incumbent's decision to seek reelection colors the entire electoral undertaking. The partisan leanings of the electorate are also critical. The dominant party's candidates stress party loyalty, underscore long-standing partisan values, and sponsor get-out-the-vote (GOTV) drives, because high voter turnout usually aids their cause. Minority-party campaigns highlight personalities, downplay partisan differences, and exploit factional splits within the majority party, perhaps by invoking "wedge issues" designed to pry voters away from their usual party home.

Finally, the perceptions and attitudes of voters must be reflected in campaign planning. Through surveys, focus groups, or old-fashioned informal pulse taking, strategists take account of what is on voters' minds and what, if anything, they know or think about the candidate. Well-known candidates try to capitalize on their visibility; lesser-known ones run ads that repeat their names over and over again. Candidates with a reputation for openness and geniality highlight those qualities in ads. Those who are more introverted (yes, there are such politicians) stress experience and competence. Candidates who are young emphasize their vigor, energy, new ideas, and independence. Candidates who have made tough, unpopular decisions are touted as courageous leaders.

Candidates' appearances, speeches, advertising, and appeals are designed to exploit changing voter preferences. In the wake of scandals, honesty and openness are on display. In 2010 Republican challengers successfully capitalized on the public's dissatisfaction with a sluggish economy, Washington politics as usual, and the policies adopted under unified Democratic control during the first two years of the Obama presidency.

Choosing the Message

The average citizen is barraged with media messages of all kinds—an hour of television commercials per day, among other things. The candidate's overarching challenge is to project an image through this cacophony of media appeals, including those from other candidates. "The only way to cut through this communication clutter," a political marketing executive points out, "is to adopt the strategy proven effective by successful businesses. Create a brand. And manage the message with discipline and impact."[18] In other words, forge a message that will stand out from all the competing messages in the media marketplace.

A candidate's message is usually distilled into a single theme or slogan that is repeated on radio, TV, billboards, and in campaign literature. "A good message . . . is a credible statement that can be summed up in a few sentences and frequently ends with a kicker slogan. . . . In most races, messages define campaigns."[19]

Strategists use these messages to frame the campaign: to set the election's agenda—not by changing people's attitudes, but by shifting their attention to issues that favor their candidate or diminish the opponent. "There's only three or four plots," explained Carter Eskew, a Democratic consultant. "Plots for incumbents are Representative X is different from the rest; X can deliver; X stands with you. And the perennial plot for challengers is (fill in the blank) years are long enough; it's time for a change."[20]

As challengers seek lines of attack, officeholders often find that incumbency has its liabilities. An extensive public record gives enterprising opponents many potential openings to exploit. Past votes or positions may be highlighted to discredit the officeholder, sometimes fairly and sometimes unfairly. Incumbents may be shackled to unpopular issues, such as a growing federal deficit, Medicare premium hikes, unresolved wars, economic crises, or unpopular presidents. Sometimes incumbents become complacent and take voters' support for granted, a major political mistake. One campaign consultant summed up the lesson of such races: "You have to earn that support every two years. A lot of members of Congress forget how to run."[21]

CAMPAIGN RESOURCES

Even the best campaign strategy will fail if the candidate cannot muster the resources necessary to implement it. The chief resources in congressional elections are money and organization.

"Money is the mother's milk of politics," declared California's legendary Assembly Speaker Jess Unruh. Money is not everything in politics, but many candidates falter for lack of it, and nearly all expend valuable time and energy struggling to get it. Every candidate, writes Paul S. Herrnson, wages not one but two campaigns—a campaign for resources (the so-called money primary) that precedes, and underwrites, the more visible campaign for votes.[22]

Campaigns in the United States are very costly. In the 2009–2010 electoral cycle, congressional candidates raised $1.1 billion and spent most of it. The average winning Senate race cost $7 million. Winning House contests averaged $1.4 million.[23] Thirty years ago (when modern record keeping began), no House candidate spent half that much.[24] Even controlling for inflation, expenditures for congressional campaigns have more than doubled over the last thirty years.

No mystery surrounds these skyrocketing costs. Population growth and new campaign technologies—electronic media, polling, and consultants of all kinds—account for much of the increase. To be sure, old-fashioned campaigns based on armies of volunteers canvassing door-to-door can be effective in some contests. But candidates raise as much money as they can for good reason.

Table 4-1 gives some sense of the time commitment involved in fund raising. According to the results of this time management study of the 1998 campaign of Democratic representative Brian Baird of Washington, fund raising

TABLE 4-1   **See How He Ran: Candidate Brian Baird's Time Budget, July–October 1998**

Activity	Hours and minutes spent[1]	Percentage of time
Fundraising call time	397:30	32
Other fundraising	36:00	3
Meeting with individuals, groups, politicians	146:00	12
Public events	96:00	8
Meeting with media	31:00	2
Voter contact	89:15	7
Meeting with staff	58:45	5
Travel	203:15	16
Personal time	201:30	16
Total hours	1,259:15	101[2]
Average hours per day	10:12	

Sources: Baird for Congress Campaign, 1998; and James A. Thurber and Carolyn Long, "Brian Baird's 'Ring of Fire': The Quest for Funds and Votes in Washington's Third District," in *The Battle for Congress,* ed. James A. Thurber (Washington, D.C.: Brookings Institution, 2001), 188.

[1] Excludes the three days of campaigning in November: 33 hours, 15 minutes, mostly in voter contact.

[2] Does not add to 100 percent because of rounding.

consumed by far the largest block of time. More than one-third of his time was spent raising the $1.3 million he needed to win his open seat. Most of those hours he sat in a tiny room he called his bunker, wearing a headset and phoning potential contributors. Many of his meetings with individuals, groups, and other politicians also involved fund raising. Not surprisingly, candidates often find fund raising odious and demeaning. "I'd rather wrestle a gorilla than ask anybody for another fifty cents," grumbled John Glenn, D-Ohio, as he retired after twenty-four years in the Senate.[25]

Regulations on Fund Raising

The regulation of campaign finance in the United States is a complicated subject for at least two reasons. First, Congress's regulatory efforts have led to a proliferation of entities, many with the sole purpose of raising and spending money in political campaigns, each with its own rules and regulations. Political action committees (PACs), for example, are an artifact of campaign finance law. Under federal law, corporations and labor unions cannot contribute directly to political candidates, but they are permitted to establish PACs to raise funds from their shareholders, employees, or members and then make campaign contributions. Because of limits on what PACs can do, however, interest groups have sought out other ways to influence elections—so-called 527s, 501(c)(3)s, and so on. Each of these is also subject to regulations.

Second, campaign finance in the United States is complicated because it has become a matter of constitutional law. In the landmark case of *Buckley v. Valeo* (1976),[26] the Supreme Court held that campaign contributions and spending are free speech protected by the First Amendment of the Constitution. The Court ruled that Congress may legitimately regulate contributions—to prevent corruption or the appearance of corruption—but that campaign spending largely cannot be regulated.

Congressional candidates may raise funds from four sources: individual contributors, PACs, party committees, and themselves and their families. More than half of the money raised by House and Senate candidates comes from individuals. In the 2009–2010 election cycle, a congressional candidate (or the candidate's campaign committee) could receive up to $2,400 from each individual contributor for each election (primary, general, run-off). Individual contributions of more than $200 must identify the contributor's name and employer, and this information is reported to the Federal Election Commission, the federal agency charged with regulating campaign finance. An individual contributor's overall contribution to federal candidates for the entire cycle was capped at $45,600.

PACs may also contribute directly to congressional candidates. Under current regulations, multicandidate PACs are defined as those registered for more than six months, having fifty or more contributors, and making contributions to five or more candidates for federal office. In the 2009–2010 election cycle, multicandidate PACs could contribute up to $5,000 to a congressional candidate (or the candidate's campaign committee) for each election. For PACs not meeting the definition of multicandidate PACs, contributions to congressional candidates were capped at $2,400 per election. Neither type of PAC is subject to an overall cap on contributions for the election cycle.

PACs have grown in numbers and clout since the campaign finance reforms of the 1970s. At the end of 1974, there were 608 PACs. By 2008 there were more than 4,600. In dollar terms, PACs contributed $8.5 million to House and Senate candidates in 1972. In the 2009–2010 election cycle, their contributions topped $420 million. PAC contributions are especially significant in House races. They accounted for almost a third of House candidates' receipts in 2010 but less than a seventh for Senate candidates.

In the 2009–2010 election cycle, party committees—national, state, congressional, and local—could contribute up to $5,000 per election to congressional candidates. National party committees could not exceed a total of $42,600 to any Senate candidate per campaign. As these amounts make clear, party funds cannot begin to cover the costs of campaigns today. Party organizations of all types account for a relatively small portion of individual candidates' funding. More significant are the parties' coordinated and independent expenditures (these are discussed later in this chapter under "The Parallel Campaigns").

A fourth source of campaign money for congressional candidates is the candidate's own funds. Candidates and their families may spend as much of their own money in a campaign as they wish. Under *Buckley v. Valeo,* such campaign spending cannot be limited. Thus, Wisconsin's successful Senate candidate Ron Johnson was able to contribute heavily to his own campaign. Self-financing is no guarantee of success, however. In the 2010 elections, extraordinary sums were personally invested by Senate candidates Linda McMahon in Connecticut ($46.6 million), Jeff Greene in Florida ($24 million) and Carly Fiorina in California ($5.5 million)—and they all lost.[27]

Incumbents vs. Challengers

Although incumbents need less money than do challengers, they receive more—a double-barreled financial advantage (see Figure 4-1). Incumbents are both better known than challengers and enjoy government-subsidized ways of reaching constituents. Nevertheless, incumbents are able to raise substantially more money. In 2010 House incumbents raised $1.5 million on average to defend their seats—nearly six times what their opponents could muster. Senate incumbents outpaced their challengers by an even wider margin in 2010, raising on average 11.9 times more than their opponents.[28]

Challengers' first hurdle is to raise enough money to make their names and faces known to voters. Because they start from such a low baseline of name recognition, challengers' campaign dollars tend to be more cost-effective than incumbents'. Nevertheless, they must raise a great deal of money to defeat an incumbent. As Gary C. Jacobson points out, "The minimum price tag for a competitive House campaign under average conditions today is probably [around] $800,000; sixty-two of the sixty-four challengers who defeated incumbents from 1996 through 2006 spent more than that amount."[29]

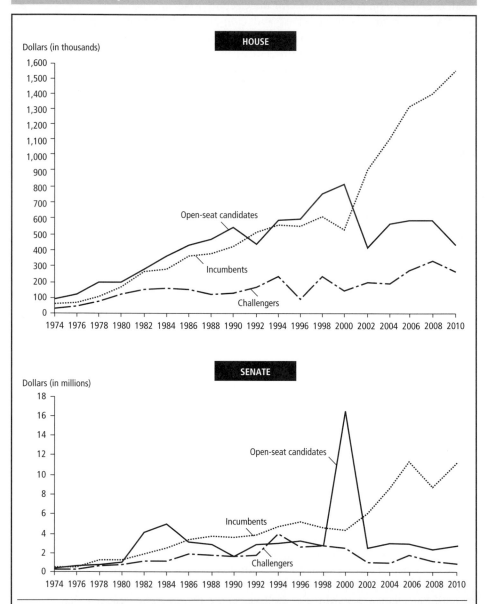

FIGURE 4-1   **Average Campaign Expenditures for Incumbents, Challengers, and Open-Seat Candidates: House and Senate, 1974–2010**

HOUSE

Dollars (in thousands)

Open-seat candidates

Incumbents

Challengers

1974 1976 1978 1980 1982 1984 1986 1988 1990 1992 1994 1996 1998 2000 2002 2004 2006 2008 2010

SENATE

Dollars (in millions)

Open-seat candidates

Incumbents

Challengers

1974 1976 1978 1980 1982 1984 1986 1988 1990 1992 1994 1996 1998 2000 2002 2004 2006 2008 2010

Sources: Federal Election Commission (FEC) figures for campaigns through 2000 are compiled in Norman J. Ornstein, Thomas E. Mann, and Michael J. Malbin, *Vital Statistics on Congress 2001–2002* (Washington, DC: AEI Press, 2002), 87–98. Figures through 2010, also derived from the FEC, are found at Center for Responsive Politics, "Election Overview, Incumbent Advantage," www.opensecrets.org.

Incumbents of both parties are so much better able to raise money than challengers because contributors see them as better investments. Most money donated to congressional campaigns is aimed at cultivating closer relationships with people in positions of power. Donors know that incumbents usually win reelection. And so donors concerned about access to powerful officeholders do not usually waste their money on challengers, even when those challengers might be more appealing in their policy stances or party affiliation. Indeed, "access-oriented" giving follows the shifts in party control of Congress, as donors curry favor with committee chairs and other leaders regardless of party. Challengers obviously cannot attract this type of campaign donation, which gives incumbents a substantial fund-raising advantage.

Challengers have a difficult time convincing donors that they have any reasonable chance of winning. In this arena as in so many others, nothing succeeds like success. "Failure to raise enough money creates a vicious spiral," explains political analyst Thomas B. Edsall. "Some donors become reluctant to invest their cash, and then state and national parties are less likely to target . . . party building and get out the vote drives in those races."[30]

When challengers are successful in raising money, they typically find that the funds make a significant difference in their electoral chances. Generally speaking, the more a challenger spends, the more votes that challenger is likely to attract.[31] The same is not true of incumbents. In fact, for incumbents there is actually a negative correlation between campaign expenditures and electoral success. Vulnerable incumbents tend to greatly step up their fund raising. As Jacobson points out, "Incumbents can raise whatever they think they need."[32] Endangered incumbents thus raise prodigious sums as they seek to hold onto their seats. Meanwhile, safe incumbents—especially senior members who infrequently face significant electoral challenges—raise and spend much less. Despite the negative correlation, incumbents are unquestionably better off with more campaign money than less. But incumbents' success or failure is less tied to their fund-raising totals than challengers'.

Many incumbents raise and spend far more than is necessary. Incumbents' overspending is frequently motivated by a sense of uncertainty and risk. "Because of uncertainty," Jacobson explains, "members tend to exaggerate electoral threats and overreact to them. They are inspired by worst-case scenarios— what would they have to do to win if everything went wrong?—rather than objective probabilities."[33]

Not all incumbent fund raising is actually aimed at the race at hand. Incumbents often have strategic purposes for fund raising beyond campaign finance. Preemptive fund raising is aimed at dissuading serious opponents. "If you look like a 900-pound gorilla, people won't want to take you on," remarked a GOP campaign aide.[34] Some members, especially those with party leadership ambitions, raise money so they can impress colleagues by distributing funds to needier candidates. Sometimes established incumbents deliberately overspend in pursuit of decisive electoral victories that might establish their claims for higher office.

Allocating Resources

As exercises in communication, campaigns are driven by the need to find a cost-effective way of reaching citizens and getting them to vote. Candidates and their managers face many different trade-offs as they make decisions about allocating resources, depending on the context.

As a rule, statewide Senate races are mass media contests with messages conveyed mainly through radio and television. Costs are especially high in densely populated states with large metropolitan media markets. Senate candidates typically spend far more on media advertising and fund raising than do their House counterparts, who spend more on traditional means of voter contact.

Despite its astronomical costs, television advertising is popular because candidates believe it works. Almost all households in the United States own at least one television, and the average adult watches three and a half to four hours of television a day.[35] Candidates also tailor their use of media to their political circumstances. Confident incumbents can channel their money into telephone, Internet and e-mail, or door-to-door appeals that direct their messages to activists, partisans, and supporters. Lesser-known candidates must turn to broad-scale media, such as television, radio, newsletters, and billboards, to promote name recognition.

Candidates also have to make decisions about their pace of spending. Especially useful is early money—that is, having funds on hand to organize a campaign at the outset. EMILY's List—Early Money Is Like Yeast ("It makes the 'dough' rise")—a group begun in 1985, was formed on this premise. This group collects (bundles) individuals' donations for Democratic women candidates who support abortion rights. The Republican counterpart is Women in the Senate and House (WISH).

Late blitz money also can turn the tide, although money alone rarely makes the difference at the end of a race. In the final weeks of a hard-fought race, both sides are trying to reach undecided voters. "You've got to move that 10 or 15 percent, many of whom are not paying much attention," a Democratic consultant explained. "Unfortunately, the way to do that is with negative or comparative ads."[36] Late in a competitive race, opponents frantically attack and—despite the scant time—counterattack.

Another question of timing involves candidates facing tough contests in both the primary and general elections. In this situation, candidates lacking personal wealth find themselves in an especially vexing dilemma. Should they ration their outflow of funds and risk losing the primary, or should they wage an expensive primary campaign and risk running out of money later on?

Organizing the Campaign

Implementing a campaign strategy is the job of the candidates and their organizations. Waging a campaign is not for the fainthearted. Take the case of psychology professor Brian Baird, the Democrat mentioned earlier who won Washington's Third District (comprising Olympia and southwest Washington State) seat in 1998. Having lost to the incumbent by a mere 887 votes two years earlier, Baird vowed to run full tilt the second time (see Table 4-1). As a result, he spent almost all of his waking hours campaigning during the peak months (July–October)—more than ten hours a day for 123 days. Travel consumed many valuable hours in his average-sized district.

Few localities today boast tight party organizations. In some strong party areas, voter contact is the job of ward, precinct, and block captains. Candidates in some such areas still dispense "walking-around money" to encourage precinct captains to get out the vote and provide small financial rewards for voting. But in most places today the traditional local parties have been replaced by hybrid organizations that partner with state and national parties and their allied interest groups.

When they can pay the price, today's candidates purchase campaign services from political consulting firms, most of them operating within partisan networks. According to an independent survey of the 2004 federal election cycle, political candidates, national parties, and advocacy (527) groups paid nearly $1.8 billion to some six hundred professional consultants—half of their total campaign spending. Two-thirds of that money went to media consultants.[37] Some firms offer a wide array of services; others specialize in polling, direct mail, phone banks, advertising, purchasing media time, coordinating volunteer efforts, fund raising, or financial management and accounting. Despite the hype they often receive, consultants by themselves rarely turn a campaign around. At best, they can make the most of a candidate's resources and help combat opponents' attacks. They cannot compensate for an unskilled or lazy candidate or for a candidate's staff that does not follow through on details.

CAMPAIGN TECHNIQUES

Campaigns are designed to convey the candidates' messages to people who will lend support and vote in the election. Campaigns are not necessarily directed at all voters. Often narrower groups are targeted—most notably, the political parties' core supporters.

The Air War: Media and Other Mass Appeals

Candidates reach the largest numbers of voters by running broadcast ads and making televised appearances. Television is the broadest spectrum medium, and its costs eat up the bulk of most campaign budgets.

Candidates obviously cannot fully control their media coverage. Some of the most effective appeals—news coverage and endorsements, for example— are determined by persons other than the candidate. Because journalists can raise unwanted or hostile questions, many politicians seek out the friendlier environments of talk shows hosted by nonjournalists. Even more congenial are appeals the candidates themselves buy and pay for—newsletters, websites, media ads, and direct mail. The drawback is that self-promotion is seen as less credible than information from independent sources.

Nearly two-thirds of all voters receive campaign news from television—network, cable, or local. Forty percent turn to the Internet as their primary campaign news source, and 31 percent rely on newspapers.[38] And yet local news programming largely ignores congressional campaign coverage. In the weeks preceding the 2004 elections, for example, 92 percent of the scheduled half-hour local news programs in eleven select media markets offered no coverage at all of local candidates' races, including U.S. House races. In the ten markets with statewide Senate races, the "blackout rate" was 94 percent.[39] Most candidates must therefore pay to reach the voters. Campaign advertising costs in the 2010 congressional races were estimated at $735 million—a 61 percent increase over 2008. It was "a record breaking year."[40]

Positive Themes. Most campaign themes call for promotions that evoke positive responses from citizens. Positive ads present candidates in warm, human terms to which citizens can relate. Skillfully done, TV ads can be very effective in bringing home the candidates' themes. A case in point was the series of brilliant, funny—and inexpensive—television ads that helped a little-known Wisconsin state legislator, Russ Feingold, win the Democratic primary, defeat a two-term incumbent senator, and then go on to serve three terms in the U.S. Senate (1993–2011). As his opponents battered each other with negative ads, Feingold ran clever, personal spots describing himself as the "underdog candidate." One showed Elvis, alive and endorsing Feingold. Another showed Feingold walking through his modest home, opening up a closet and saying, "No skeletons."

One of the best positive ads in 2010 was run by Feingold's successful Republican challenger, Ron Johnson. In one ad, Johnson appears before a whiteboard tallying up the total number of lawyers (57), manufacturers (0), and accountants (1) in the U.S. Senate. Based on the tally, Johnson remarks, "It's no wonder we're losing jobs and piling up debt." He continues: "I'm not a politician; I'm an accountant and a manufacturer. I know how to balance a budget, and I do know how to create jobs. Now that's something we can really use." With simple, clean visuals and a clear message, the ad powerfully conveyed Johnson's strongest pitch as a candidate.[41]

Some media appeals are coordinated with field operations. Trolling for the student vote in Madison, Wisconsin, Democratic candidate Tammy Baldwin, ran what her staff called the "Bucky" ad (for "Bucky Badger," the University of Wisconsin mascot) on MTV and youth-oriented shows. The ad said that "there is one candidate who understands our issues" and ended with a pitch to get out and vote, with a phone number and Baldwin's website. Every time the ad ran, all the phone lines at headquarters would light up.[42]

Negative Themes. Candidates also deploy campaign resources against their opponents. Contrast ads distinguish the candidate from the opponent on the grounds of policy and experience, and attack ads strike at the opponent's record or personal character. Republican representative Leonard Lance's 2008 winning bid for an open seat in New Jersey's Seventh District offers an example of an effective contrast ad. The ad featured a series of "man on the street"–style shots, showing male and female voters of different ages and races, each saying "Linda Stender is a Spender." The ad's tone was high-spirited, with bright colors and punctuated by a cash register sound. One voter is even shown cracking up in laughter as he attempts the line. The repetition, combined with the rhyme on his opponent's name, memorably conveyed the central contrast Lance sought to draw in his campaign.

Negative campaign themes are often the result of opposition research (called "oppo" by campaigners). Its purpose is "to get the skinny on the client's opponents and, if all goes well, expose them as hypocrites, liars, thieves, or just plain unsavory characters."[43] Both national parties and many campaigns invest in opposition research. Because challengers are usually less known than incumbents, they are more vulnerable to attacks and unflattering personal revelations.

Though not technically a campaign ad, the "push poll" is another negative campaign technique. These are not actual polls designed to elicit public attitudes, but instead advocacy phone calls with questions aimed at changing voters' opinions. The caller divulges negative information—often false or misleading—in the hope of pulling the voter away from the opponent and toward the candidate paying for the call.

Negative ads are common in modern campaigning because politicians believe they work. This strategy was forcefully described by Rep. Tom Cole, R-Okla., in a memo to his House colleagues: "Define your opponent immediately and unrelentingly. Do not let up—keep the tough ads running right up to election day. Don't make the mistake of pulling your ads in favor of a positive rotation the last weekend."[44]

Recent experiments by two noted communications researchers tend to confirm the power of negative ads. Such ads, these scholars found, lift voters' information levels, even if the information conveyed is distorted or trivial. Although neither positive nor negative ads have much effect on strong partisans, negative ads can work powerfully on citizens who have little information to begin with and on those with little or no party allegiance.[45] Many researchers take a benign view of such ads. "We should not necessarily see negative ads as a harmful part of our electoral system," argues Kenneth Goldstein, head of the University of Wisconsin's political advertising project. "They are much more likely [than positive ads] to be about policy, to use supporting information, and to be reliable. Few negative ads are on personal issues."[46] One study of 189 different Senate campaigns found that "negative campaigning generally *mobilizes,* rather than *de*mobilizes, the electorate."[47]

Like other forms of product promotion, political ads often stretch or distort the truth. Sometimes the disinformation is so blatant that the term *dirty tricks* applies. This tactic includes not only spreading falsehoods but also using doctored photographs or faking news reports or news headlines.

One of the most controversial attack ads in the 2010 campaign was aired by Democratic candidate Jack Conway in his unsuccessful attempt to defeat Republican Rand Paul for the open Senate seat in Kentucky. The ad asserted that when Paul was a student at Baylor University he was "a member of a secret society that called the Holy Bible 'a hoax,'" and the society "was banned for mocking Christianity and Christ." The ad also asked, "Why did Rand Paul once tie a woman up and tell her to bow down before a false idol and say his god was Aqua Buddha?"[48] The subject matter of the ad was obviously inflammatory, particularly in Kentucky, one of the most religious states in the country.[49]

Victims of such tactics have some means of defense, even when attacks are leveled close to election day. The campaign can promptly air response ads or accuse the offender of mudslinging. During a candidate debate, for example, Rand Paul repeatedly called on Jack Conway to apologize. In the end, many analysts felt that Conway's ad backfired, undermining his support among independents and even among Democrats. "Backlash [over the ad] may have sunk Conway's campaign for good," reported PPP, a Democratic-leaning polling firm.[50]

Formal complaints can sometimes persuade opponents to disavow attack ads or local broadcasters to pull them off the air. Media outlets find themselves in the unwanted role of arbitrating between contending candidates. The legal situation is murky. Courts have held that candidates have a right to buy ads even if their content is challenged, but broadcasters are not legally required to air ads.[51] As one deterrent to smear tactics, the Bipartisan Campaign Reform Act (BCRA) of 2002 requires that candidates personally appear and vouch for their advertisements.

Evolving Mass Media. The old-fashioned media—newspapers, radio, and television networks—are on the decline. The newspaper business in the United States, in particular, appears to be in crisis. Even before the 2007–2009 recession, newspapers around the country had cut staff and closed bureaus in an effort to remain economically viable. This evolution is partly a result of generational replacement: whereas two-thirds to three-quarters of the oldest age cohorts are daily newspaper readers, only about 20 percent of the youngest cohorts are.[52] A similar generational trend has been seen in network news viewership. By contrast, the Internet is becoming an increasingly important news source. A study by the Pew Research Center reported a 130 percent increase in Internet usage for campaign news between 2004 and 2008, with the shift most pronounced among young people.[53]

Web outlets are thus far unregulated. In 2006 the Federal Elections Commission (FEC) decided to treat the Internet "as a unique and evolving mode of mass communication and political speech that warrants a restrained regulatory approach."[54] Critics of the hands-off approach point out that web political messages can be costly to produce, and are sometimes far edgier than would be permitted in traditional media outlets. At the least, the public has an interest in learning who instigates these messages, who prepares them, and who pays for them.[55]

Still, the variety and seeming spontaneity of the web intrigue many political analysts. One observer of the web scene calls it "word of mouth on steroids." Although campaign organizations use the medium, the knowledge and skill to make compelling videos—like those unleashed on YouTube and other outlets for and against the 2008 presidential contenders—have "moved out of campaign headquarters" and into the hands of private citizens.

In this decentralized and diverse media environment, campaigns increasingly display what political scientist Darrell West describes as the law of diminishing returns. "It becomes difficult to break through the clutter," he observes, "and at this point there is a lot of clutter out there."[56]

The Ground War: Pressing the Flesh and Other Forms of Close Contact

Direct appeals to voters through personal appearances by candidates or their surrogates—at shopping centers, factory gates, or even door to door—are part of every campaign. In his successful 1948 Senate campaign, Lyndon B. Johnson swooped out of the sky in a helicopter to visit small Texas towns, grandly pitching his Stetson from the chopper for a bold entrance; an aide was assigned to retrieve the hat for use at the next stop.[57] Other candidates, preferring to stay closer to the ground, stage walking tours or other events to attract attention. Few elected officials get by without doing a great deal of what is inelegantly called "pressing the flesh."

Contemporary politicians have rediscovered the virtues of retail as opposed to wholesale campaigning. As political reporter David S. Broder put it, "More and more political strategists are coming to believe that the high-tech tools that have dominated campaigns for the past four decades—TV spots, mass mailings and professionally staffed phone banks—are far less effective than the old-fashioned way of turning out the vote."[58]

An obvious advantage of so-called shoe leather campaigning is cost, at least when compared with mass media appeals. "Door-to-door canvassing is the tactic of choice among candidates and campaigns that are short on cash," explain Yale political scientists Donald P. Green and Alan S. Gerber. "Precinct walking is often described as the weapon of underdogs."[59] Former representative Dan Glickman, D-Kan. (1977–1995), describes his first House campaign as a thirty-one-year-old challenger facing a long-term incumbent:

> I walked door-to-door to 35,000 homes over an eight-month period.
> I walked from 10:30 a.m. to 2 p.m. and again from 5:30 to 8 p.m. I lost
> 35 pounds and learned to be very realistic about dogs. I met a woman
> my father had lent $100 or $150 to 30 years before. She embraced me
> and said, "You saved us." I won by three percentage points.[60]

Face-to-face campaigning is obligatory in smaller communities, where people expect politicians to show up at festivals, parades, or annual county fairs. "If you ain't seen at the county fair, you're preached about on Sunday," remarked a politician as he led his party's Senate candidate around the hog and sheep barns in Ada, Oklahoma.[61] In small states, first-name relationships are often valued. Of Vermont's voters, political scientist Garrison Nelson remarks, "They want to know you." The state's Independent senator, Bernard Sanders, distributes bumper stickers that simply say, "Bernie."[62] In Bristol, on Rhode Island's coast, the Fourth of July parade—the oldest in the country—is "the first and perhaps biggest event of the campaign season."[63]

One-on-one campaigning is physically and emotionally challenging, and the payoff is often elusive. At best, canvassers reach only about 30 percent of an area's voters, cautions campaign specialist Ron Faucheux.[64] Only about 60 percent of the people will be home, and the person who comes to the door may represent only half of the household's eligible voters. To reach more voters per visit, candidates seek out shopping malls, organized groups, fairs, or rallies.

Getting Out the Vote. GOTV drives are focused on making sure constituents are registered and getting voters to the polls. Such tasks (staffing phone banks or canvassing), which can be farmed out for a price, are most effective when carried out by someone who can connect with the potential voter. According to Green and Gerber, face-to-face canvassing raises turnout by seven to twelve percentage points and in the end is more cost-effective than alternative media–based campaigns.[65]

Recognizing the importance of personalized voter contact, both parties have developed sophisticated GOTV operations. Each now relies on "microtargeting" to reach sympathetic voters. This approach employs computer models to exploit a wide array of data, such as the groups to which people belong or the magazines they read, to identify potential voters and the issues that are important to them. "Microtargeting has become so widespread that it is now used by all House and Senate candidates, on both sides, in state legislative races, and in some cases, all the way down the ballot to local school board elections."[66]

In addition, many groups are prepared to finance their own field operations in support of favored candidates. In this sense, the parties' GOTV efforts are just part of a broader campaign waged by their allied groups. For example, "in most states union members will be contacted between fourteen and twenty-four times by other union members in some fashion," the AFL-CIO's political director reported in 2002.[67] In 2008 labor unions spent more than $300 million in their efforts to organize and mobilize voters on behalf of Democratic candidates.[68] For their part, Republicans depend on a wide array of pro-life, evangelical, and socially conservative organizations to undertake GOTV drives for their candidates.

THE PARALLEL CAMPAIGNS

The scene is a hospital operating room; the patient is surrounded by surgeons and nurses. One surgeon in a voice of astonished concern exclaims, "Oh my." A nurse asks, "Colitis?" Another nurse asks, "Hepatitis?" A third, "Diverticulitis?" The surgeon replies, "No, I'm afraid it's Dina Titus. Taxes up the yingyang. Her tax policy is killing us." The target of this television ad was 2008 Democratic

House challenger Dina Titus, a former political science professor at University of Nevada–Las Vegas and one-term representative for Nevada's Third Congressional District (2009–2011). The ad was paid for by Freedom's Watch, a lobbying group bankrolled by wealthy conservatives, notably billionaire developer Sheldon Adeson.

An important story in recent congressional campaigns is the role played by organizations such as Freedom's Watch—that is, big spenders in congressional elections that are not formally affiliated with either the candidates or the parties. Campaigns no longer resemble boxing matches between two combatants. They have become free-for-alls in which multiple combatants throw punches and land roundhouse kicks. Candidates compete not only against their opponents and their parties, but also against scores of groups that join the fray. Hundreds of such organizations engage in congressional campaigning, most of them favoring one major political party. Groups interested in congressional elections have every reason to mount such efforts. The legal limits on what individuals can contribute to candidates mean that a single individual can have only a very limited effect by donating directly to candidates. But donors can give unrestricted amounts to advocacy organizations that, in turn, can make unlimited expenditures on campaign and policy ads.

Independent groups are also less constrained by spending limits than political parties. Since passage of the BCRA, contributions to the parties have been subjected to caps, though higher ones than permitted as direct contributions to the candidates themselves.[69] In the 2009–2010 election cycle, the national parties, including House and Senate campaign committees, raised and spent nearly $2.4 billion. This is a staggering figure in view of the fact that since passage of the Bipartisan Campaign Reform Act of 2002 the parties have been prohibited from taking unlimited donations from individuals and groups. (Before the reform, so-called soft money—funds unregulated by the Federal Election Commission and donated to party committees but not designated for a specific candidate or purpose—was not subject to caps.) Parties may use such funds to pay for services requested by a candidate such as polling, advertisements, and media time. These "coordinated expenditures" are subject to limits set by the FEC. But party committees can also sponsor their own campaigns, run media ads, and underwrite get-out-the-vote drives—that is, make independent expenditures that have no formal connection to candidates' own efforts. Parties' independent expenditures are not subject to limits.

Independent expenditures by advocacy groups allow large donors to escape the contribution limits on donations to parties and candidates. Recent elections have seen a proliferation of such groups. There are several types, each typically identified by the sections of the Internal Revenue Code that govern their structure and activities. Tax-exempt 527s, for example, must register with the Internal Revenue Service (IRS) and disclose expenses and contributors. Subject to those requirements, they may raise unlimited funds from individuals, labor unions, and corporations. In the 2009–2010 election cycle, 527s raised about $440 million.

Just as contributions to such groups are unlimited, so too are their expenditures, as long as they are made independently of candidates. Until 2010, corporations, nonprofits, and labor unions could not spend funds out of their general treasuries for pro-candidate advertisements. Then the Supreme Court, in *Citizens United v. FEC* (2010), struck down that limitation as a form of censorship of protected political speech. The five-justice majority concluded that only the prevention of *quid pro quo* corruption, or its appearance, could justify such a restriction on the freedom of speech. The long-standing prohibition against direct corporate contributions to candidates had rested on such a justification. The Court held that independent expenditures do not give rise to an appearance of *quid pro quo* corruption, even if they suggest influence or access. In the majority opinion, Justice Anthony Kennedy stressed, "The appearance of influence or access . . . will not cause the electorate to lose faith in our democracy. By definition, an independent expenditure is political speech presented to the electorate that is not coordinated with a candidate."[70]

The Court held, however, that such independent expenditures were subject to the disclaimer and disclosure imposed by the BCRA. Thus advertisements would have to identify their sponsor organizations, and independent expenditures in excess of $10,000 would have to be reported to the FEC, along with the names of contributors of more than $1,000. In the Court's opinion, Justice Kennedy theorized, "A campaign finance system that pairs corporate independent expenditures with effective disclosure has not existed before today. . . . With the advent of the Internet, prompt disclosure of expenditures can provide shareholders and citizens with the information needed to hold corporations and elected officials accountable."[71]

The disclosure requirements in the BCRA, however, do not afford the kind of information about many of these advocacy groups that Justice Kennedy assumed would be available. Under the current FEC interpretation of the BCRA, a contribution of $1,000 or more to a group making an electioneering communication—that is, a pro-candidate advertisement in close proximity to an election—is reportable only if the contributor designated it to be used for a particular electioneering communication.[72] In other words, a contributor may avoid disclosure by not designating a contribution for any particular advertisement.

Certain types of groups are not subject to disclosure laws at all. The 2010 midterm elections saw the emergence of groups organized under section 501(c)(4) of the Internal Revenue Code.[73] These groups are generally civic organizations, with no more than half of their activities classed as political. Karl Rove's Crossroads Grassroots Policy Strategies, for example, organized as a 501(c)(4), spent $17.1 million in the 2010 midterms, including more than $4 million to defeat Democratic Senate candidate Alexi Giannoulias in Illinois.[74] The U.S. Chamber of Commerce, which is organized as a 501(c)(6), refuses to identify its donors, even as it spent $33 million dollars in the 2010 midterms, mostly to support Republican candidates.[75]

The 2010 election cycle made it clear that many big-dollar contributors prefer to remain anonymous. Corporations and their officers have an economic incentive not to anger consumers by taking public stands in favor of particular parties or candidates. Target's CEO, for example, drew a backlash against his company after it was revealed that he contributed $150,000 to support a candidate hostile to gay rights.[76]

As one former FEC commissioner put it, then, "the money's flowing."[77] And not only is the money flowing, but flowing into new and unprecedented channels. In the wake of *Citizens United,* the D.C. Circuit Court of Appeals held in *Speechnow.org v. Federal Election Commission*[78] that PACs organized only to make independent expenditures—and not to make contributions directly to candidates—are not subject to contribution limits imposed by federal law. Thus the "Super PAC"—able to receive unlimited contributions from individuals, labor unions, and corporations—was born.

When the last major campaign finance reform law (BCRA) was enacted in 2002, skeptics had argued that the new law would do little to halt the overall flow of money into political campaigns. "This law will not remove one dime from politics," predicted Sen. Mitch McConnell, R-Ky., the leading GOP opponent of the measure. McConnell's skepticism has certainly been borne out, both by innovations in campaign finance and by Supreme Court rulings limiting the scope of regulatory restrictions. In the end, campaign finance laws have failed to limit the influence of money in politics. Big money is alive and well in U.S. elections.

WHO VOTES?

Although Congress is supposed to be the people's branch of government, only around half of voting-age citizens normally take part in House elections. In the 2010 House elections just 40.7 percent of the voting-age population, or VAP (all eligible residents age eighteen and over), participated.[79]

As Figure 4-2 indicates, turnout varies according to whether the election is held in a presidential or a midterm year. Midterm races lack the intense publicity and stimulus to vote provided by presidential contests. Since the 1930s, turnout in midterm congressional elections has averaged about 12 percent below that of the preceding presidential election. In the presidential election of 2008, voter turnout was 61.6 percent.[80] By contrast, in the midterm elections of 2006 the turnout was only 40.8 percent. Midterm electorates include more people who are interested in politics, and—not unrelated—who are also more affluent and better educated.[81] Voter turnout in congressional races fails to match that of presidential elections—even in presidential election years.

Reasons for Not Voting

Political analysts disagree over the reasons for the anemic voting levels in the United States, which are near the bottom among established democratic countries. Several explanations—not all of them compatible—have been suggested.[82]

FIGURE 4-2   **Turnout in Presidential and Congressional Elections, 1946-2010**

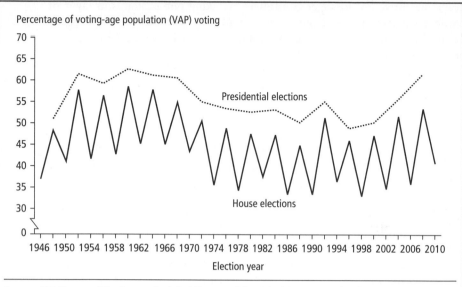

Sources: *U.S. Bureau of the Census, Statistical Abstract of the United States: 2001* (Washington D.C.: U.S. Government Printing Office, 2001), table 418; Michael P. McDonald, "Voter Turnout in the 2010 Midterm Election," *The Forum* 8 (4): art. 8.

One explanation for nonvoting is simply demographic. Groups with low voting rates, such as young people, African Americans, and Latinos, have been growing as a share of the U.S. population. Young people (ages eighteen through twenty-nine) are traditional no-shows, perhaps because they have fewer of the life experiences (mortgages, taxes, school-age children, community ties) that propel older people toward activism. Four out of ten young people have not registered to vote (three times greater than those aged fifty and older).[83] Turnout among young Americans in the 2010 midterms was estimated at 20.4 percent, slightly lower than the 23.5 percent in the 2006 midterms.[84]

A second explanation stresses legal barriers to voting. Only about 70 percent of the VAP are registered to vote. Many democracies automatically register all adults; some even require that people vote. By contrast, U.S. citizens must take the initiative to register and vote. The National Voter Registration Act of 1993 (the so-called Motor Voter law) aimed to increase citizens' access to voter registration by, among other things, requiring states to offer voter registration as an option when citizens apply for a driver's license. Registration of eligible voters soon rose about 3.8 percent nationwide, but voting levels failed to climb—especially among the young and the poor, the targets of the measure.[85]

Other disincentives can be blamed on electoral arrangements. U.S. citizens are asked to vote far more often than voters in parliamentary regimes; and elections are held on weekdays, not on the weekend or national holidays. A number of states and localities, however, have modernized their election procedures, making it easier to register and vote. Absentee balloting and vote-by-mail have become more common. Some states permit ballots to be submitted over a period of time. Oregon citizens may even vote by telephone.

Biased or careless election administration can also turn away voters or lead to a miscount of their ballots as uncovered in voting scandals in Florida (2000) and Ohio (2004). Local election practices often weigh most heavily on minority or socioeconomically disadvantaged citizens, who are more likely to encounter insufficient numbers of poll workers, antiquated or badly designed voting machines, and longer lines. In many states, lawmakers have raised further barriers through voter ID requirements—such as photo IDs or proof-of-citizenship papers.[86] Although passed under the pretext of combating "voter fraud," these are in fact partisan measures intended "to depress voter turnout in minority and poor communities."[87] In 2008 the Supreme Court upheld the strictest such law, Indiana's 2005 statute that requires all voters to present a valid government ID.[88]

A third explanation for low voter turnout is citizen disaffection. Noncompetitive elections, poor candidates, and contentious or negative campaigning are thought to keep people away from the polling booths. Apathy and cynicism are, to be sure, part of the picture. Surveys sponsored by Harvard University's *Vanishing Voters* project found that four out of ten nonvoters in 2000 claimed to care little about politics and public affairs. A quarter was dismayed or confused by the barrage of campaign messages. And another quarter was simply angry or cynical about politics.[89]

Finally, even conceding all these disincentives, the level of nonvoting is frequently exaggerated. In calculating turnout, many scholars fail to take into account the large number of voting-age residents who are not eligible to vote. Three sizable and growing segments of the population are not entitled to vote and must be excluded when properly calculating turnout: (1) jailed felons (two million) are barred from voting in all but two states; (2) ex-felons (1.4 million) are barred from voting in fourteen states; and undocumented aliens (twelve million or more) may not vote anywhere. According to Samuel L. Popkin and Michael P. McDonald, failure to take account of these ineligible residents artificially depresses the turnout rate. Recalculating the VAP for elections between World War II and 2000, they estimated turnout ranging from 52.7 to 60.6 percent—still nothing to be proud of, but "a lot less dismal than is generally believed."[90]

Biases of Voting

Although voting is the simplest and most accessible form of political involvement, it is still biased in favor of people at the higher rungs of the social and generational ladders—those who are older, more affluent, better educated, and more in touch with political events. Eight in ten people whose annual incomes exceed $50,000 vote in a typical election. This is twice the voting rate of the poor, defined as people with annual incomes of less than $15,000.

Alternative forms of political participation are even more sharply biased. For example, giving money is mainly an elite activity. According to a study by Sidney Verba and his colleagues, 35 percent of all political money flowed from the 4 percent of people making more than $125,000 a year. Poor people, who were 19 percent of the sample, made only 2 percent of political donations.[91]

HOW VOTERS DECIDE

What induces voters to cast their ballots for one candidate and not another? As a general rule, voters reach their decisions on the basis of party loyalty. But candidate assessments and salient issues also figure into voters' decisions. The relative strength of these elements varies over time and among specific races.

Although American voters are often uninformed or indifferent about political issues and candidates, they employ what is called low-information rationality, or gut reasoning, to make voting booth decisions. As Samuel Popkin explains, people "triangulate and validate their opinions in conversations with people they trust and according to the opinions of national figures whose judgments and positions they have come to know."[92] Thus voters work through imperfect information to make choices that will often roughly approximate the choices they would have made with more perfect information.

Party Loyalties

Party identification is the single most powerful factor in determining voters' choices. And it remains the strongest single correlate of voting in congressional elections. In recent elections, at least nine in every ten Democrats and Republicans voted for their parties' nominees. Independents tend to split their votes more evenly between the parties. In 2006 they veered toward Democratic candidates by a three-to-two margin.[93] In 2008 they preferred Obama to John McCain by six percentage points.[94] But in 2010 independents preferred Republican to Democratic candidates by 19 percentage points.[95]

According to surveys, most people who claim to be independents are in fact closet partisans who lean toward one party or the other. These independent leaners—about a quarter of the total electorate—hold attitudes similar to those of partisans. Not only do they favor one party over the other, but they also share many (though not necessarily all) of the party's values and will vote for the party's candidates—if they vote at all.

Only a small percentage of citizens (5–10 percent) are true independents; they are unpredictable, however, and have dismal turnout rates. "I would encourage candidates not to play to them," advises David Magleby of Brigham Young University, "because they tend to jump on bandwagons, to follow tides. You're better off [working] on getting your weak partisans and your leaners."[96]

Partisan Resurgence. Today's voters are as loyal to their professed party identification as they have ever been.[97] Few voters who identify as either Republicans or Democrats defect from their party when they cast votes in particular congressional races. However, today's high level of party loyalty is a notable shift from the 1970s and 1980s.

Between 1950 and 1980, partisan loyalty declined among the American electorate, with voters identifying with one party and often supporting candidates from the other party. These weakened party ties led to an epidemic of split-ticket voting—that is, voters supporting one party's presidential candidate and the opposition party's congressional candidate. Between 1952 and 1988, the number of voters who reported in surveys that they split their ticket between presidential and House candidates rose from 12 percent to 25 percent. Those who split their ballots between different parties' House and Senate candidates grew from 9 percent to 27 percent.[98]

Most of these ticket splitters, it turned out, were in the throes of moving from one party to another. White southern conservatives made up a large share of ticket-splitters during this era. Targeted by the GOP's so-called southern strategy, these voters were attracted to presidential candidates such as Barry Goldwater, Richard Nixon, and Ronald Reagan. But southern conservatives kept backing Democrats in congressional and state races because strong Republican candidates often were unwilling to challenge entrenched incumbents, because the Democratic Party put up conservative candidates, and because long-serving Democrats won the "personal vote" of constituents by delivering more benefits back home through their party's control of legislative chambers. The same phenomenon occurred to a lesser degree in the Northeast, where voters were drawn to the Democrats' national policies and candidates, but continued to support moderate to liberal Republican representatives or senators.[99]

Recent party realignment has brought party affiliation into sync with policy and ideological preferences. Although the process extended over many years, the long Republican courtship of southern conservatives was consummated in 1994. Merle Black of Emory University estimates that more than 80 percent of white conservatives in the South are Republicans; only 10 percent are Democrats.[100] A parallel trend, no less dramatic, has been the Democratic Party's absorption of GOP moderates and liberals. Finding acceptable candidates up and down the ballot, these voters have less need to pick and choose— hence revived partisanship and dwindling split tickets.

In short, the bulge in split-ticket voting was a by-product of gradual partisan realignment. Over the last five presidential elections, ticket splitting has plummeted to less than 10 percent—exactly the same level it was fifty years ago. The number of congressional districts voting for one party's presidential candidate and the other party's House candidate fell as well. In 2008 less than 19 percent of House members won in districts carried by the opposite party's presidential candidate.

Midterm and Presidential Election Years. Politicians have long talked about coattails: how House and Senate candidates could be pulled into office by the strength of a popular presidential candidate. The idea is that successful presidential candidates will entice new voters not just for themselves, but for their whole party.

In presidential election years, the party that wins the presidency typically does increase its numbers in Congress. As shown in Table 4-2, the winning presidential candidate's party gains on average 15.5 seats in the House and 2.2 seats in the Senate. Boosts for the president's congressional party were considerably more modest in recent election years than they were in the 1930s and 1940s. George H. W. Bush, Bill Clinton, and George W. Bush all began their presidencies with some congressional seat losses for their party. Nevertheless, political scientists who have analyzed the influence of presidential candidates on the outcome of congressional elections have found that "nontrivial coattail effects have been discernible in recent elections."[101] Ronald Reagan, for example, boosted his party's congressional votes by 2–3 percent in 1980 and 5 percent in 1984.[102] In 1996 President Clinton's reelection added about 2.6 percentage points to Democrats' House and Senate totals. President Obama began his presidency with the largest increases in his party's numbers in Congress for any president since Reagan in 1980.

The president's party normally suffers significant reversals in the midterm congressional elections. In fact, the president's party has lost seats in thirty-two of the thirty-five midterm elections since 1860. "This is not quite the certainty of 'death and taxes,' but it is about as dependable as things get in politics," observes political scientist James E. Campbell.[103] As evident in Table 4-3, since 1934 the presidential party has lost an average of 28 House seats and 3.6 Senate seats in midterm elections.

The "midterm law" was broken on only three occasions. Democrats gained four seats in the House and held their own in the Senate in 1998, in the midst of President Clinton's impeachment proceedings. Although voters deplored Clinton's personal behavior, his job ratings remained robust; Republicans were rebuked for insisting on impeaching him. Four years later, President Bush's GOP gained eight House and one Senate seat, no doubt because of the post-9/11 rally effect. The only other anomaly occurred in 1934, when President Franklin D. Roosevelt's popularity strengthened the Democrats' grip on both chambers. Set in historical context, the 2010 election results were an anomaly only in that the loss by the president's party was so huge. It was the largest seat gain by an out-party in a midterm since 1938.

One theory that endeavors to explain this pattern is known as "surge and decline." This theory posits that the visibility and excitement of a winning presidential campaign attract intermittent voters who tend to support the president's party in down-ticket races. When these presidential candidates are not on the ballot, the shrunken electorate of midterm years contains fewer supporters of the president's party—that is, a presidential surge, swollen by less motivated voters attracted by presidential campaigns, is followed two years later by a decline as intermittent voters drop out of the electorate. But other studies suggest that midterm voters are no more or less partisan than those in

TABLE 4-2	**Seats in Congress Gained or Lost by the President's Party in Presidential Election Years, 1932–2008**

		Seats gained or lost	
Year	President	House	Senate
1932	Franklin D. Roosevelt (D)	+90	+9
1936	Roosevelt (D)	+12	+7
1940	Roosevelt (D)	+7	−3
1944	Roosevelt (D)	+24	−2
1948	Harry S. Truman (D)	+75	+9
1952	Dwight D. Eisenhower (R)	+22	+1
1956	Eisenhower (R)	−2	−1
1960	John F. Kennedy (D)	−22	+2
1964	Lyndon B. Johnson (D)	+37	+1
1968	Richard M. Nixon (R)	+5	+6
1972	Nixon (R)	+12	−2
1976	Jimmy Carter (D)	+1	0
1980	Ronald Reagan (R)	+34	+12
1984	Reagan (R)	+14	−2
1988	George H. W. Bush (R)	−2	0
1992	Bill Clinton (D)	−10	0
1996	Clinton (D)	−9	−2
2000	George W. Bush (R)	−3	−4
2004	Bush (R)	+3	+4
2008	Barack Obama (D)	+21	+8
Average seats gained (20 elections)		+15.5	+2.2

Source: Compiled by the authors.

presidential years and share most of their demographic characteristics.[104] Another problem with the theory is that, no matter the circumstances, the president's party typically loses more seats at the midterm than it gains during a presidential year.

A second theory argues that midterm elections serve in part as a referendum on the president's popularity and performance in office during the previous two years.[105] Voters may hold the president's party responsible for economic reverses, unpopular policies, or military ventures.

TABLE 4-3   **Midterm Fortunes of Presidential Parties, 1934–2010**

Year	President	Seats gained or lost House	Senate
1934	Franklin D. Roosevelt (D)	+9	+10
1938	Roosevelt (D)	−71	−6
1942	Roosevelt (D)	−45	−9
1946	Roosevelt and Harry S. Truman (D)	−55	−12
1950	Truman (D)	−29	−6
1954	Dwight D. Eisenhower (R)	−18	−1
1958	Eisenhower (R)	−47	−13
1962	John F. Kennedy (D)	−5	+3
1966	Lyndon B. Johnson (D)	−47	−4
1970	Richard M. Nixon (R)	−12	+3
1974	Nixon and Gerald R. Ford (R)	−48	−5
1978	Jimmy Carter (D)	−15	−3
1982	Ronald Reagan (R)	−26	+1
1986	Reagan (R)	−5	−8
1990	George H. W. Bush (R)	−7	−1
1994	Bill Clinton (D)	−54	−10
1998	Clinton (D)	+4	0
2002	George W. Bush (R)	+8	+1
2006	Bush (R)	−31	−6
2010	Obama (D)	−63	−6
Average seats lost (20 elections)		−27.8	−3.6

Sources: CQ Press Electronic Library, *Vital Statistics on American Politics Online Edition*, table 1-17. Originally published in Harold W. Stanley and Richard G. Niemi, eds., *Vital Statistics on American Politics, 2009–2010* (Washington, DC: CQ Press, 2009). Each entry is the difference between the number of seats held by the president's party at the start of Congress after the midterm election and the number of seats held by that party at the start of Congress after the preceding general election. Special elections that shifted partisan seat totals between elections are not noted.

A third theory emphasizes voters' preferences for "balance." By favoring the out-party at midterm, voters can pull policy back toward the ideological center.[106] Voter behavior may not be driven so much by dissatisfaction with the president as by the desire to check potential presidential excesses. This may seem like an overly sophisticated calculation for the average voter, but even if only a relatively small portion of the electorate follows this logic it can have a sizable impact on electoral outcomes. Balance theory helps explain why the shift against the president's party in midterm elections is typically larger than one would expect based on presidents' (usually favorable) approval ratings or based on the "surge and decline" thesis.[107]

All three schools of thought—"surge and decline," referendum theory, and balance theory—can shed light on such dramatic midterm outcomes as the Democrats' 1974 post-Watergate bonus of forty-eight representatives and five senators, the Democrats' retaking of House and Senate majorities in 2006, and the Republicans' gain of sixty-three representatives and six senators in 2010.

The Appeal of Candidates

"My theory on politics is ultimately that people vote for the person they like most," declared former senator David Pryor, D-Ark. (1979–1997).[108] Apart from partisan loyalties, the appeal of given candidates is the strongest force in congressional voting. Not surprisingly, candidate appeal normally tilts toward incumbents. When voters abandon their party to vote for House or Senate candidates, they usually vote for incumbents.

Incumbency Advantage. Incumbents rarely lose their bids for reelection, as is evident in Table 4-4. Incumbent reelection rates have always been robust. Even in the 2010 watershed election, incumbent winners still included 85 percent of all representatives and 83 percent of all senators who ran for reelection. Comparable percentages from 2006, a year when Democrats retook control of Congress from the Republicans, were 94 percent and 79 percent. Changes in party control of seats are attributable as much to winning seats opened up by retirements as to defeating incumbents.

Defeating a House incumbent is an uphill struggle, absent a scandal or misstep. Senate challengers—more often than not well known and generously financed—have a stronger chance of unseating incumbents than do those seeking House seats. Nevertheless, more than four out of five Senate incumbents win the contests they enter.

Why are incumbents so formidable? Incumbents' success rates go well beyond what one should expect based on the partisan character of their constituencies. In other words, incumbents often win by wide margins in constituencies that are closely divided between Republicans and Democrats. This phenomenon has led scholars to ask whether the sheer fact of incumbency itself offers advantages. Do candidates fare better running as incumbents than they would running as nonincumbents.[109]

To measure this advantage, scholars often look to the "sophomore surge" and the "retirement slump." The sophomore surge refers to the average gain in vote share by candidates running for reelection for the first time, compared with their performance in their first election. The retirement slump is the average drop in a party's vote share when an incumbent retires and the seat opens up. Scholars then average these two calculations into a single index, known as the "slurge," which is often used to measure the overall incumbency advantage. According to this measure, contemporary incumbents enjoy about a six

TABLE 4-4 **Reelection Rates in the House and Senate, by Decade, 1950s–2008, plus 2010**

Decade	House					Senate				
	Sought reelection	Faced no opponent	Lost primary	General election	Percent reelected	Sought reelection	Faced no opponent	Lost primary	General election	Percent reelected
1950s	402	85	6	25	93.2%	30	4	1	6	77.3%
1960s	404	52	8	26	91.5	32	1	2	4	80.8
1970s	389	57	2	23	92.3	27	1	2	6	67.7
1980s	403	67	13	15	95.7	29	1	0	3	88.0
1990s	385	36	8	18	93.6	26	0	0	3	87.4
2000–2008	394	43	3	16	95.1	28	1	0	4	89.1
2010	398	27	4	54	85.4	26	1	3	2	83.3

Sources: CQ Weekly Report, April 5, 1980, 908; November 8, 1980, 3302, 3320–3321; July 31, 1982, 1870; November 6, 1982, 2781; November 10, 1984, 2897, 2901; November 12, 1988, 3264, 3270; November 10, 1990, 3796–3805; November 7, 1992, 3557–3564, 3570–3576; November 12, 1994, 329ff; February 15, 1997, 447–455; November 7, 1998, 3027–3035; November 11, 2000, 2694–2706; December 14, 2002, 3289–3297; November 6, 2004, 2653–2660; November 13, 2006, 3068–3075; November 10, 2008, 3043–3052; November 8, 2010, 2618–1627.

Note: Statistics for each decade are election-year averages for the five elections conducted under that decade's apportionment of House districts. For example, the 1950s include the five elections 1952 through 1960. "Percent reelected" takes into account both primary and general election defeats. "Faced no opponent" means no major-party opponent. Figures for 2000–2008 are derived from the 2002, 2004, 2006, and 2008 elections.

percentage point increase in their share of the vote simply by virtue of being incumbents.[110] Incumbency appears to confer powerful benefits.

Political scientists have launched a veritable cottage industry to explain incumbency advantage. Certainly, one key factor is incumbents' campaign fund-raising advantages, which were described earlier (see "Incumbents vs. Challengers"). It is also no secret that incumbents have many methods of gathering support—through speeches, press coverage, newsletters, staff assistance, and constituent service. Incumbents' popularity depends in large part on their success in shaping information that constituents receive about them and their performance—through advertising, credit claiming, and position taking.[111]

The unequal visibility of candidates is thus an important source of incumbency advantage. In National Election Study (NES) surveys spanning almost thirty years, nearly all respondents were able to recognize the names of, and offer opinions about, their Senate and House incumbents running for reelection (means of 97 percent and 92 percent, respectively). Senate challengers were recognized and rated by 77 percent of the respondents, House challengers by only 53 percent.[112]

Voters also report having high levels of contact with House and Senate incumbents. The more contact voters have with their legislators, the more positive their evaluations are likely to be. According to NES surveys, at least nine out of ten voters said they had some form of contact with their representative. A fifth of them reported having met the lawmaker in person. Many constituents receive mail from their representatives or read about them in newspapers. Virtually all voters reported some contacts with their senators, mostly through mailings, TV appearances, or other media coverage.

Incumbents achieve these high levels of visibility and constituency contact in part because of their perquisites of office. The typical House member receives staff, office, and travel allocations valued at between $2 and $3 million over a two-year term; senators, with six-year terms, command between $17 and $27 million in resources. Everyone concedes the value of incumbents' perquisites, but scholars differ on how much they affect electoral success. One view is that incumbents exploit their resources to ensure reelection, seizing on their ability to assist constituents in dealing with the bureaucracy to build electoral credit. Others counter that legislators are simply responding to constituents' demands, aided by advances in communication technology. Still others question whether incumbents' resources are directly translatable into votes.[113]

Senate and House. The factors contributing to incumbency advantage help explain why senators are more vulnerable at the polls than their House counterparts. First, Senate challengers are far more conspicuous than House challengers. Senate contests are more widely reported by the media, and challengers can gain almost as much exposure as incumbents. Media coverage of House races is more fragmentary than that of Senate races, throwing more weight to incumbents' techniques of contacting voters.

Second, senators cannot manipulate voter contacts as much as representatives do. Voters get their information about Senate races largely through the organized media, which senators do not control. Representatives gain exposure through focused means—personal appearances, mailings, and newsletters—which they fashion to their own advantage. "Somewhat ironically," observes Michael J. Robinson, "powerful senators are less able to control their images than 'invisible' House members."[114]

Among senators, constituency size is also a crucial variable in elections. Small-state senators in many respects resemble representatives. Compared with their large-state colleagues, they are more visible, more accessible, and more able to raise the campaign money they need. But they are not electorally safer because their challengers, too, have an easier time mounting their campaigns and gaining visibility.[115]

Strategic Politicians. A very important and frequently underrated factor contributing to incumbent reelection success is simply the quality of candidates who typically run against incumbents. Jacobson surely captures the normal state of affairs when he observes that "most incumbents face obscure, politically inexperienced opponents whose resources fall far short of what is necessary to mount a formidable campaign."[116] As discussed in Chapter 3, it is often difficult to recruit strong candidates to run against incumbents. Incumbents are reelected at high rates not just because of the advantages they have over challengers in terms of funding and visibility, but simply because they are often far more skilled and more experienced as politicians than their opponents.

Incumbency advantage has a self-fulfilling aspect, because good potential challengers will typically perceive the long odds of defeating an incumbent and therefore choose not to enter the race. Incumbents prevail because the system of candidate recruitment throughout the United States often fails to offer voters viable alternatives.

Issue Voting

Issue preferences and even ideological beliefs figure prominently in voters' decisions. Even if most Americans devote only modest attention to political affairs, a significant number of voters are attuned to issues and base their choices on a specific issue or cluster of issues. Not a few elections turn on those margins.

Congressional Party Platforms. Partisans care deeply about the issues with which their parties are linked. In studying the 1998 House elections, Owen G. Abbe and his colleagues found that "voters are more likely to support candidates whom they deem competent on their issues." They concluded that "party leaders and individual candidates must campaign on a well-defined agenda for party-owned issues to have an impact."[117]

At least since the mid-1970s, congressional parties have forged campaign platforms. The most notable example was the GOP's "Contract with America," the brainchild of then-representative Newt Gingrich of Georgia.[118] The contract was a set of ten proposals that candidates promised to bring to the House floor if Republicans won a majority in the 1994 midterm elections. The proposals included such popular items as a balanced-budget amendment, a presidential line-item veto, term limits for lawmakers, and tax cuts. Similarly, more than a year before the 2006 balloting, House Democrats, led by the minority leader, Nancy Pelosi of California, came up with another list of initiatives known as the "Six for '06" platform. It embraced such universally supported goals as national security, energy independence, and economic strength. In the lead-up to the 2010 elections, congressional Republicans embraced a platform called the "Pledge to America." It included such proposals as a $100 billion cut in 2011 spending, an end to tax hikes, and curbs on new federal regulations.[119]

Issues and Partisanship. Voters' responses to political issues show up in the different patterns of choice displayed by demographic groups (see Figure 4-3). Americans sort themselves out politically according to their age, sex, income, education, race or ethnicity, region, and even by frequency of attendance at religious services.

A demographic snapshot of the two parties' voters would start at the much-discussed gender gap, the difference in voting between men and women. Women lean toward Democratic candidates, men toward Republicans. The gender gap appears in virtually all recent contests. As pollster Celinda Lake remarked, "You'll get [a gender gap] in a race for dogcatcher in Montana, if it's a Republican against a Democrat."[120] The gender gap was seven percentage points in 2008 and 2010 and has been as much as ten percentage points in other recent elections. The explanation for the gender gap probably lies in differing responses to political and social issues. Men are generally more favorable toward military expenditures, tough anticrime laws, and restrictions on welfare recipients and immigrants. Women respond more positively than men to social programs such as government-sponsored health benefits, job training, child care, and assistance to needy families.[121]

A host of similar patterns is found among congressional voters. "There's a family gap, a generation gap, a gender gap," said GOP pollster Neil Newhouse of the fissures among the voting population.[122] Many of the patterns are familiar. The Republicans attract upper-income and conservative voters; the Democrats engage lower-income and liberal voters. The Republicans draw upon married people, whites, regular churchgoers, gun owners, and small business owners; the Democrats attract singles and young people, African Americans, Hispanics, Jews, the secular, and occasional churchgoers. Such loyalties are built on issues and themes adopted by parties and candidates over the years.

Issues and Campaigns. Legislators and their advisers are highly sensitive to voters' expected reactions to stands on issues. Much energy is devoted to framing positions, communicating them (sometimes in deliberately vague language), and assessing their effect. Moreover, every professional politician can relate cases in which issues tipped an election one way or another. Frequently cited is the electoral influence of single-interest groups. Some citizens vote according to a single issue they regard as paramount such as gun control,

FIGURE 4-3   Who Were the Voters in 2010?

Group Percentage of voters		2010 For Democrat		For Republican
	Total vote	45		52
48	Men	41		55
52	Women	48		49
77	White	37		60
11	Black	89		9
8	Hispanic/Latino	60		38
2	Asian	58		40
12	Under 30 years	55		42
24	30–44 years	46		50
43	45–59 years	45		53
21	60 years and older	38		59
3	Not a high school graduate	57		36
17	High school graduate	46		52
28	College incomplete	43		53
51	College graduate	45		53
21	East	54		44
25	Midwest	44		53
31	South	37		61
23	West	49		48
44	White Protestant	28		69
25	White fundamentalist	19		77
23	Catholic	44		54
2	Jewish	—		—
17	Union household	61		37
—	Under $15,000	—		—
17	$15,000–29,999	57		40
19	$30,000–49,999	51		46
21	$50,000–74,999	45		51
42	Over $75,000	41		58
35	Democratic	91		7
29	Independent	37		56
35	Republican	5		94
20	Liberal	90		8
38	Moderate	55		42
42	Conservative	13		84

Source: Adapted from Harold W. Stanley and Richard G. Niemi, *Vital Statistics on American Politics, 2011–2012* (Washington, D.C.: CQ Press, 2011), table 3-8.

Notes: Percentages based on Democratic, Republican, and other (not shown) votes. Data based on questionnaires completed by voters leaving polling places around the nation on election day, 2010.

abortion, or gay marriage. Even if few in numbers, such voters can decide close contests. For that reason, legislators often shrink from taking positions on hot-button issues such as these.

Public policy issues also have powerful indirect effects on election outcomes. Issues motivate "opinion leaders," voters who can influence support far beyond their single vote. Issues are carefully monitored by organized interests, which can channel or withhold funds, publicity, and volunteer workers for the candidate's cause. Legislators devote time and attention to promoting and explaining issues to attentive publics because it pays for them to do so.

ELECTION OUTCOMES

The two Congresses are manifested throughout congressional elections. House and Senate contests are waged one by one on local turf, but always against a backdrop of national events, issues, and partisan alignments. The involvement of national party entities and their allied interest groups has imposed a greater degree of national coordination on congressional campaigns, especially those in marginal states and districts. The resulting fusion of local and national forces shapes the content and results of congressional elections.

Party Balance

Despite the oft-claimed independence of candidates and voters, virtually all races are run under either the Democratic or Republican Party label, fought on playing fields tilted toward one party or the other, and aimed mainly at loyalists who are likely to turn out for their parties' candidates.

Shifting Majorities. In many respects, the overall partisan outcome of the 2010 contests was fixed months and even years before the actual balloting. Because it was a midterm election, the president's party was almost certain to lose seats. In addition, because of their extensive gains in the 2006 and 2008 elections, Democrats held many seats in Republican-leaning territory. In political science parlance, Democrats were heavily "exposed" going into 2010 in that the party claimed many seats above its norm of recent decades.[123] Democrats knew well in advance that they faced a tough election cycle, recognizing that forty-seven Democratic incumbents would be defending House districts that had been carried by both Bush in 2004 and McCain in 2008, while only six Republicans held seats that had been carried by both John Kerry and Obama.[124] To compound the Democrats' difficulties, the 2010 elections took place in economic conditions—a weak recovery following a deep recession—that would be very unfavorable for any party in power. Finally, low presidential approval ratings would also be a drag on the party's performance, as reactions to the president typically do influence the congressional fortunes of the president's party. Structural factors such as these cannot fully explain the outcome (Republican gains exceeded most political science forecasts[125]), but they remain important in understanding congressional elections.

Either the Democrats or the Republicans have controlled Congress since 1855 (see Appendix A for a list of the partisan majorities in the House and Senate since 1901). Between 1896 and 1920, the two parties had approximately equal numbers of partisans in the electorate, but lower participation rates in Democratic areas favored the Republicans. The GOP's relative position improved further after 1920, when women received the vote.

The New Deal realignment of the 1930s shifted the balance to the Democrats. For many years after that, the Democrats were virtually a perennial majority and the Republicans a permanent minority on Capitol Hill. Between 1932 and 1994, the Republicans controlled both chambers simultaneously for only four years (1947–1949, 1953–1955). Democratic sweeps in 1958, 1964, and 1974 padded their majorities. Republicans found the Democratic dominance in Congress hard to overcome, even in years when voters strongly backed Republican presidential candidates. Democrats were able to maintain their majorities as long-serving incumbents effectively exploited their positions of influence and their ability to steer government benefits back home.

In recent decades, however, no party has been able to take control of Congress for granted. Since Republicans won control of the Senate in 1980, neither party has been secure in its control of that chamber. Similarly, control of the House has been a far more open question since the Republican victory of 1994 than during the long years of Democratic dominance. Even while Republicans clung to their post-1994 majority in the House for the next decade, Democrats steadily gained seats throughout the 1990s, and Republicans' control of the chamber progressively narrowed. In 2006 Democrats returned to majority status in both the House and the Senate. They then expanded these margins of control in the 2008 elections. In 2010, however, all the House Democratic gains of 2006 and 2008 were wiped out. Republicans retook House control (242–193), gaining their largest majority in that chamber in sixty-four years. Even so, no analyst believes that the era of intense two-party competition for control of Congress has yet come to an end.

Regional Patterns. Recent elections have cemented long-term shifts in the two parties' power bases. Historically, the Grand Old Party was dominant in the populous states of the Northeast and Midwest. "The Democracy," by contrast, owned the solid South from the Civil War era through the 1970s, as well as the large urban political machines. Today, many of the old patterns are precisely reversed, with the Republican Party dominant in the South and the Democratic Party ascendant in the Northeast.[126] The tectonic plates of political alliances move slowly, but they sometimes produce changes of earthquake proportions.

The 1994 earthquake signaled the Republicans' conquest of the South. For the first time in history, the GOP claimed a majority of the South's seats. The party's grip on the region continued to tighten in subsequent election cycles. Republicans now hold 68 percent of House seats and 72 percent of Senate seats belonging to the eleven states of the Confederacy. The modern-day GOP is the party of choice for conservative white southerners and unquestionably their true philosophical home.

Regionally, the South, the Great Plains, and the Mountain West form the backbone of the congressional GOP. Almost 40 percent of the Republican Conference in both chambers is now from the South, even though that region accounts for only a quarter of the Senate and a third of House districts. In its other regional bastions, the Great Plains and the Mountain West, Republicans claim 64 percent of senators and 71 percent of House districts. Taken together, these regions account for approximately half of the GOP's House majority and two-thirds of its Senate contingent. The Great Lakes states constitute a competitive region, with Republicans controlling 54 percent of its House seats and 50 percent of its Senate seats.

Democrats are strongest on the coastal edges of the national map—the Northeast, the Mid-Atlantic, and the West Coast. The eleven states of New England and the mid-Atlantic are overwhelmingly Democratic (though some have lost population and thus House seats). In these states—all of which were in the Democratic Party's presidential column in 2004 and 2008—the party claims 67 percent of House seats and 77 percent of Senate seats. The GOP holds only two out of twenty-two House seats and four out of twelve Senate seats in New England. Similarly, Democrats dominate the country's western-most coast. All four Pacific Rim states (excluding Alaska) were won by Democratic candidates in the last three presidential elections. Democrats control forty-five of the region's sixty-nine House seats and all eight of its Senate seats.

Looking beyond such regional patterns, the two parties tend to represent different kinds of districts. Democratic strength lies in cities, inner suburbs, and majority-minority districts, including those in the South and Midwest. Republicans dominate rural, small town, and exurban areas. Meanwhile, Democratic voters are more packed together in the districts held by Democrats than are Republican voters in the districts held by their party, which means that Democratic candidates tend to win by larger majorities than Republican winners normally do. Put another way, more Democratic votes are wasted (that is, inefficiently distributed across congressional districts), giving the GOP a structural advantage.[127]

Polarized Parties, Polarized Voters? Underlying this geographic distribution is what might be called a cultural divide between the two parties. Democrats tend to represent urban areas, where most voters favor social welfare spending and environmental and other business regulations. Urban voters also tend to take a more tolerant view of the diversity of racial, ethnic, and sexual identities. Republicans tend to be traditionalists—economic and cultural conservatives who promote businesses large and small, advocate certain religious causes, and generously support military expenditures. Such long-standing issue commitments flatly contradict anyone who claims that there is scant difference between the two parties.

How pervasive are these partisan differences within the electorate? Political elites—candidates, officeholders, activists, and strong party identifiers—have long been found at the extremes of the ideological spectrum: Democrats to the left, Republicans to the right.[128] Such activists do not represent the majority of citizens, average voters, or even average party identifiers. Most voters identify as either "moderate" or refuse to use any ideological term to describe themselves.[129] Rank-and-file party identifiers have, however, become more ideologically polarized than in the past.[130] Many, after all, respond to the rising amount of ideological rhetoric in the contemporary political arena, including that dispensed by congressional representatives and biased cable, Internet, and other partisan communications. Moreover, these loyal voters are ardently wooed by parties and candidates, both of whom seek reliable supporters (rather than waverers) to turn out at the polls.

Party Alignment and Realignment

Historically, political upheavals have shifted party control in the House or Senate with decisive results. Political scientists and journalists often talk of "critical elections" or "critical periods" in which one party yields preeminence to another, or major voting groups alter the shape of the parties' coalitions, or both. Such watershed eras include the Civil War, the turbulent 1890s, the New Deal of the 1930s, and the Republican revolution of 1994. Each of these upheavals brought to Capitol Hill new lawmakers, new voting patterns, and new legislative priorities.[131]

Between the civil rights upheavals of the 1960s and the mid-1990s, the congressional party system went through a gradual transformation that realigned the parties on ideological lines and brought them into competitive balance. The Republican Party achieved ideological consistency by co-opting southern and rural conservatives and by shedding most of its moderate wing, especially members from the northeastern, Mid-Atlantic, and Pacific Rim states. In losing most of the South to Republicans, the Democrats also became more ideologically coherent. Long split by divisions between conservative southerners and northern liberals, the Democratic Party of the 1990s was smaller than in the past, but considerably more unified.

Realignments of the party system are only apparent in hindsight. It now seems clear that the Democratic majorities of the 110th and 111th Congresses (2007–2011) were not grounded in any long-term shifts of voter alliances. Political scientist James Campbell views the post-2010 Republican House majority as a "return to the normal party balance of recent decades," reflecting the temperament of the United States as a center-right country.[132] Indeed, Republicans may enjoy an enduring congressional majority post-2010, especially in view of the hurdles to defeating incumbents. It is likely, though, that they will have difficulty retaining many of their new holdings. After all, sixty House Republicans in the 112th Congress (2011–2012) represent districts that Obama carried. If so, today's party system will remain in the same tight competitive balance characteristic of the 1990s.

Turnover and Representation

Reelection rates should not be confused with turnover rates. Even in years when few members are turned out of office by the voters, many leave Capitol Hill voluntarily—to retire, to run for another office, or to follow other pursuits. In other words, the natural process of membership change is continuous. When the new Congress convened in January 2011, almost half of senators and representatives had served less than a decade. Sixteen senators and ninety-six representatives were newcomers.

For Congress to be a responsive institution, constant turnover of members is essential—whether by steady increments or by watershed elections. Even when few lawmakers are turned out of office, all of them are keenly aware of the threat of defeat. Most take steps to prevent that eventuality by continually monitoring constituents' needs and opinions through personal visits and polls. But are voters' views accurately reflected by the representatives they elect to Congress? This question is not easily answered. Popular control of policy makers is not the same thing as popular control of policies. Constituents' views are not precisely mirrored by legislators' voting behavior or by the laws passed by the legislature.

CONCLUSION

What links voters' attitudes and members' voting on issues? In the 1960s, Warren E. Miller and Donald E. Stokes found that constituency attitudes correlated differently depending on the kind of policy.[133] In foreign affairs, constituents' attitudes and legislators' votes exhibited a negative correlation; in social and economic welfare issues the correlation was moderate; in civil rights issues the correlation was very high. In other words, in at least one and possibly two major policy areas the linkage was weak enough to cast some doubt on constituency control.

Political scientists explain the absence of strong linkages by noting how difficult it is to meet all the conditions needed for popular control of policies. Voters would have to identify the candidates' positions on issues, and they would have to vote by referring to those positions. Differences among candidates would have to be transparent, and winners would have to vote in accord with their pre-election attitudes. These conditions are not routinely met. Candidates' stands are not always clear, and candidates do not invariably differentiate themselves on issues.

Nevertheless, winning candidates learn from their campaign experiences, even from issues raised by their opponents. *Issue uptake* is the term coined by political scientist Tracy Sulkin to describe this effect. From her study of the issue agendas of 473 House and Senate campaigns and the winners' subsequent legislative activity, she demonstrates that the victors embrace many of their opponents' campaign themes when they return to Capitol Hill. "Congressional campaigns have a clear legacy in the content of legislators' agendas," she writes, "influencing the areas in which they choose to be active and the intensity with which they pursue these activities."[134] Legislative responsiveness is best thought of as a process:

> It begins in campaigns as candidates learn about the salience of issues and their strengths and weaknesses on them; continues throughout winning legislators' terms in office, influencing not just how they vote but also the content of legislation they introduce, cosponsor, and speak about on the floor; goes on to inform their career decisions and future electoral prospects; and leaves a tangible trace on public policy outputs.[135]

If ideological or attitudinal links between voters and their representatives are rough and variable, actual contacts between constituents and individual legislators are numerous and palpable. Much of lawmakers' time and effort while in office is devoted to responding to the folks back home. Constituency politics are ever present in the daily lives of senators and representatives. The two Congresses are distinct, but inextricably linked.

L *awmakers on the Hill and at Home* (top left): Sen. Max Baucus, D-Mont., shovel dirt as part of his "work days" program at highway construction site north of Kalispel Montana. On Capitol Hill (bottom left), as cha of the Senate Finance Committee—her appearing with ranking Republican Charle Grassley, Iowa, (standing to the right)—Baucu played a key role in shaping health-care reform legislation, a primary goal of President Obam. And two lawmakers elected in 2008 reach ou to their constituents: (top right) Rep. Lyn Jenkins, R-Kan., talks with voters in Valley Fall Kansas, while Rep. Aaron Schock, R-Ill., meet with constituents at a Peoria restaurar (bottom right).

chapter 5

Being There: Hill Styles and Home Styles

"We are Americans; we're different from Canada, we're different than the United Kingdom," explained Sen. Max Baucus, D-Mont. "We have to come up with a uniquely American solution."[1] Baucus was leading a discussion on health care issues at St. Peter's Hospital in Helena, Montana's state capital, in the sort of town hall meeting that members of Congress regularly hold around the country. But Baucus was no ordinary member of Congress seeking his constituents' views on health care. As chair of the Senate's powerful Finance Committee, Baucus was a central congressional player in the Obama administration's overhaul of the nation's health insurance system.

It is safe to say that Max Baucus is no household name. A low-profile senator from one of the nation's least populated states, Baucus is nevertheless "arguably the most consequential legislator in America."[2] A considerable share of the most significant legislation of recent years bears Baucus's mark. The health care reform proposal forged under his leadership was, in most key respects, the legislation that President Barack Obama eventually signed. Years earlier, while in the minority party in 2001, Baucus shepherded President George W. Bush's $1.35 trillion tax cut through the chamber.[3] In 2003 Baucus was one of only two Democrats permitted in the room during conference committee negotiations over landmark legislation creating a new federal prescription drug benefit program for seniors.[4] Baucus's reputation as a lawmaker is matched only by his reputation for constituency service. On his desk stands a plaque that reads, "Montana comes first." Indeed, Baucus grants open access to Montanans: "He still takes all phone calls from constituents, unscreened."[5] And he is renowned for his ability to bring federal dollars to Montana. Dubbed a "high plains grifter" by the *Washington Post*,[6] Baucus has coaxed federal help for his state, including its roads, farmers, ranchers, and doctors. More broadly, the shape of national policy is indelibly influenced by the concerns of Baucus's local constituency. To win endorsement of Baucus's Finance Committee, trade legislation must take into account Montana's beef producers.[7] Health legislation must make special provision for rural providers.[8]

Baucus's political success has not always come easy. Representing a state that has voted Republican in nine of the last ten presidential elections, Baucus has faced some tough electoral challenges, and so he takes nothing for granted. To stay in close touch with constituents, he schedules regular "work days," working a full day alongside Montanans in various jobs and professions. And he consistently raises large sums for his reelection efforts long before the identity of his challenger is known.

Local champion and national leader, Max Baucus personifies the two Congresses. All members live and work in these two worlds: one on Capitol Hill and the other back home in their states and districts.

HILL STYLES

Congress is a body of transplanted locals who naturally speak up for their constituents. A majority of representatives in one survey agreed with the statement "I seldom have to sound out my constituents because I think so much like them that I know how to react to almost any proposal."[9] However, the ability of Congress to reflect the nation's large and varied population is affected by the diversity of its membership. There is no substitute for having a member of one's own group in a position of influence, and many groups do not receive representation commensurate with their presence in the population.

Who Are the Legislators?

Elections, as Aristotle first observed, are essentially oligarchic affairs that involve few active participants. The active participants are self-starters and risk-takers willing to seek an electoral "contract" for two or six years with no guarantee of renewal. In addition, by almost any measure senators and representatives constitute an economic and social elite. They are well educated. They come from prestigious occupations. The pay of senators and representatives ($174,000 in 2011) alone puts them in the top 1 percent of the nation's wage earners, but many members also have earned or inherited considerable wealth. In 2009 nearly three-quarters of senators and 44 percent of House members were millionaires.[10]

The elite character of the congressional membership raises questions of representation. One central purpose of a representative body is to bring together diverse individuals to deliberate on public policy. When the diversity of viewpoints is systematically limited, important interests and concerns within society are likely to be overlooked or undervalued. As John Stuart Mill argued a century and a half ago, "In the absence of its natural defenders, the interest of the omitted is always in danger of being overlooked."[11]

To meet Mill's standards for representation, must Congress closely mirror the demographics of the populace? Hannah Finichel Pitkin distinguishes between two types of representation: *descriptive* and *substantive*.[12] "Descriptive representation" refers to whether a legislature's membership reflects the diversity of backgrounds and interests in society. "Substantive representation" occurs when legislators consciously act as agents for constituents and their interests—an activity legislators can perform regardless of their personal background or group memberships. For example, legislators can voice farmers' concerns even if they have never plowed a field. Whites can champion equal opportunities for minorities. Few Asian Americans serve in Congress, but their proportion in a district affects representatives' support of issues advocated by that group.[13]

Although descriptive representation and substantive representation are conceptually distinct, a wide range of empirical research has found that they are intertwined in the real world. The social identity of legislators affects representation in myriad ways. Representatives' racial, ethnic, and gender identities shape their priorities, positions, and legislative styles.[14] Whether constituents and representatives share a common identity has also been shown to affect trust and patterns of contact between them.[15]

Education and Occupation. By every measure, Congress is a highly educated body. When the 112th Congress convened in January 2011, 92 percent of House members and 99 percent of senators held university degrees. Two-thirds had graduate degrees. Twenty-four had medical degrees.

Historically, law and politics have been closely linked in the United States. A humorist once quipped that the U.S. government "of laws and not men" is really "of lawyers and not men." And indeed at the beginning of the 112th Congress, 167 representatives and 55 senators were law school graduates.[16]

That so many members have law degrees does not necessarily mean that they possess extensive experience in the practice of law. "They are not, by and large, successful lawyers who left thriving partnerships to run for public office," observes Alan Ehrenhalt, "Rather, they are political activists with law degrees."[17] Legal training develops skills that are useful in gaining and holding public office, such as verbalization, advocacy, and negotiation. A law degree also serves as a stepping-stone into public service at many levels. Lawyers monopolize elected law enforcement and judicial posts, two main pathways to Congress. Hill staffers are often expected to have law degrees, and many members of Congress start out on Capitol Hill as staff aides. The 112th Congress is home to at least 105 former congressional staffers.

The historical dominance of lawyers on Capitol Hill has nevertheless declined in recent decades. Lawyers are now outnumbered by members from other careers. Today's Congress is filled with professional public servants or, in common parlance, "career politicians." The 112th Congress includes thirty-nine former mayors, eleven former governors, nine former lieutenant governors, ten former judges, one former cabinet secretary, and a former secretary of the navy. Nearly half of senators (forty-nine) are former House members.

Many members of Congress have served in the military, though the veterans' ranks have thinned over time. After World War II, returning veterans surged into Congress. Among them were Reps. John F. Kennedy, D-Mass.; Richard M. Nixon, R-Calif.; Gerald R. Ford, R-Mich.; and Bob Dole, R-Kan. By the 1970s, more than seven of ten members were veterans. As World War II faded from view and draftees were replaced by a volunteer force, fewer veterans were elected. Just under a quarter of the members of the 112th Congress have served in the military.[18]

Today's media-centered campaigns have spawned a few celebrity legislators. Several astronauts, including Sen. Bill Nelson, D Fla., have served. Name recognition from his career as a writer and performer on *Saturday Night Live* helped launch the political career of Sen. Al Franken, D-Minn.

Many occupations are, and always have been, drastically underrepresented in Congress. Low-status occupations—including farm labor, service trades, manual and skilled labor, and domestic service—are rare on Capitol Hill. Not a few members, however, held menial jobs at some point in their lives. For example, at a hearing on Social Security taxes for household help Rep. Carrie P. Meek, D-Fla. (1993–2003), a granddaughter of slaves, brought her own vivid experiences to the proceedings. "I was once a domestic worker," she told her colleagues. "My mother was a domestic worker. All my sisters were domestic workers."[19] Such perspectives are valuable for congressional representation and deliberation.

Race. African Americans, who make up 13.5 percent of the nation's population, account for 8.1 percent of the membership of the House of Representatives. There are no African American senators. In 2011, forty-four African Americans (including two delegates) served in the House; forty-two were Democrats. Although their representation in Congress does not reflect the proportion of African Americans in the nation's population, black legislators have gained seniority and congressional influence over time.[20]

Other minorities are more severely underrepresented. Latinos make up 15 percent of the U.S. population but only 5.7 percent of the members on Capitol Hill. Of the thirty-one Latino representatives and two senators, most are Mexican Americans, six are Cuban Americans, and five are of Puerto Rican descent. Twenty-one are Democrats and eight are Republicans. Asians and Pacific Islanders claim eleven representatives and two senators—all but one of them Democrats. There is one Native American, a House Republican.

The growing presence of racial minorities in Congress has had beneficial effects on representational bonds with minority communities. African Americans represented by black lawmakers, for example, tend to know more about their representatives and hold them in higher esteem.[21] "Even controlling for party affiliation," Katherine Tate's survey of black constituents found, "black legislators received significantly higher ratings on average than their white counterparts."[22] Another study showed that constituents of the same race as the incumbent were 27 percent more likely than constituents of other races to recognize the name of their representative.[23]

A growing scholarly literature also suggests that descriptive representation on Capitol Hill yields substantive benefits for minority communities. Black legislators are more active on issues of importance to their constituents of color—that is, they are more likely than their white colleagues to introduce bills on subjects of special concern to black Americans.[24] Based on systematic studies of legislative activity, Katrina Gamble and Michael Minta find that, on policy issues of special interest to African Americans, black members were more active than white members in attending committee meetings, voting, offering amendments, and participating in deliberations.[25]

Gender. Neither chamber accurately reflects the nation in terms of gender. Congress historically has been a male bastion. In international comparisons, it still is: the United States ranks seventy-first worldwide in the proportion of women serving in the national legislature.[26] Diversity has developed slowly.

Unable to vote nationally until 1920, women have always been underrepresented in Congress. Beginning in 1917 with Rep. Jeannette Rankin, R-Mont., the presence of women in Congress has grown very slowly. A near record number of women serve in the 112th Congress—seventy-five representatives (eighteen of them in the California delegation) and seventeen senators (two each from California, Maine, and Washington).[27] More than two-thirds are Democrats. Among them, Nancy Pelosi, D-Calif., serves as House Democratic leader and was the first woman to serve as Speaker of the House (2007–2011).

The advent of a critical mass of women has changed Congress. Policy concerns once labeled "women's issues"—which in truth affect everyone—are now receiving a respectful hearing. Gender discrimination, women's health, and issues involving the balance between family and workplace have begun to be seriously addressed. Rep. Nita M. Lowey, D-N.Y., whose mother died of breast cancer, pressed for increased funding for research on the disease. During a debate over family leave policy, Sen. Patty Murray, D-Wash., recalled having to quit a secretarial job sixteen years earlier when she was pregnant with her first child. "When a person in this body gets up and speaks from personal experience, it changes the whole nature of the debate," observed Sen. Chris Dodd, D-Conn.[28] Referring to the women serving in the Senate, Senator Murray declared, "We've made it okay for men to talk about these [women's] issues, too."[29] Political science research offers systematic confirmation that the presence of women has had notable effects on Congress. Women legislators are more likely than men to introduce, sponsor, and press for bills of special concern to women and children.[30]

Only a handful of women members are mothers of school-age children. They face special challenges, but their presence on the Hill undoubtedly enriches representation. "If we are supposed to be 'the people's House,' we need to look like America," contends Rep. Shelley Berkley, D-Nev. "Mothers with kids at home understand what other women deal with across the country."[31] "Having kids is very relevant for a member of Congress," says former representative Pat Schroeder, D-Colo. (1973–1997), whose children were young when she arrived on Capitol Hill."[32]

Women legislators today are active far beyond the so-called women's issues. For example, Sen. Susan Collins, R-Maine, steered a complex intelligence reform bill through fierce turf battles while chairing the Senate Homeland Security and Governmental Affairs Committee in 2004.[33] Another challenge that women lawmakers face is that voters tend to view them as less competent on military and security issues.[34] According to Michele Swers, to counter voters' stereotypes of female politicians in the post-9/11 environment, women legislators are expanding their activity and visibility on defense issues, particularly on homeland security matters.[35]

Sexual Orientation. Gays and lesbians passed a milestone in 1998 when Tammy Baldwin, D-Wis., became the first lesbian representative whose sexual orientation was known before her initial election. (Other congressional gays and lesbians revealed their sexuality or were outed after they had served for some time; some remain in the closet.) Baldwin did not shy away from the issue. Her campaign slogan was "A different kind of candidate." Baldwin is one of four openly gay members of the 112th Congress.[36]

As with other types of social identity, electing gay and lesbian representatives matters for the group's representation. Indeed, one recent study found that the presence of lesbian and gay elected officials was the single most important factor affecting local adoption of domestic partner benefits.[37] Still, as Rep. Barney Frank, D-Mass., has pointed out, the hardest part of running as a gay man is "convincing voters that you will not disproportionately focus on that minority's issues."[38]

Religion. Nearly all members of Congress cite a specific religious affiliation. By comparison, about 16 percent of Americans do not identify with any particular faith; indeed, the fastest-growing category in recent surveys of American religion is "unaffiliated."[39] Protestants collectively make up a majority of the 112th Congress, but about a quarter of House and Senate members are Roman Catholics, the largest single religious denomination. Jews account for 7 percent. The 112th Congress also includes fifteen Mormons, three Buddhists, and two Muslims.

Age and Tenure. When the 112th Congress convened in 2011, the average age of members was among the highest in history: 56.7 for representatives, 62.2 for senators.[40] Tenure as well as age has risen since the early days. "Few die, and none retire," it was said as the twentieth century began. Today, the average member of Congress has served for approximately a decade.[41]

Age and tenure levels fluctuate over time. Periods of relatively low turnover (the 1980s, for example) are punctuated by dramatic changings of the guard. The 2010 election was one such moment. Fully 21 percent of the House and 15 percent of the Senate are freshmen in the 112th Congress. Similar turnovers occurred in the 1970s and the 1990s, involving both senior and junior members of Congress.[42] Electoral defeats play some role, but the majority of members leave voluntarily. Of course, many departing members retire just because they anticipate electoral difficulty.[43]

A certain balance between new blood and stable membership is undoubtedly optimal for legislative bodies. Rapid turnover—the early 1990s and 2006–2010, for example—can sharpen generational conflict. Many newly elected members indulge in Congress-bashing in their campaigns and want to shake up the institution, and not a few of them shun the idea of making a career of public service. The anti-establishment attitudes of members of the newly founded Tea Party caucuses on Capitol Hill are not unusual among large classes of relative newcomers. Reflecting on these troublesome freshmen, former Senate majority leader Trent Lott, R-Miss., said, "As soon as they get here, we need to co-opt them."[44] If past is prologue, many will eventually settle into the established power structure on Capitol Hill.

Equal Representation of States. The equal voice that all states have in the Senate is a central feature of congressional representation. The Senate's divergence from a population-based representation affects the welfare of many social and economic groups. It enlarges the voice of farmers, ranchers, mining interests, and users of federal lands—all groups that have far more presence in the less populous states than in the nation as a whole. At the same time, racial and ethnic minorities—already underrepresented in Congress relative to their share of the nation's population—are further disadvantaged by the Senate's makeup.[45] The nation's populous states are more racially and ethnically diverse than its less populous ones, and so one effect of Senate representation is to boost the voting power of the predominantly white residents of lightly populated states and to confer less voting power on the more racially diverse residents of populous states.[46]

Equal state representation in the Senate has other meaningful effects as well. Bonds between senators and their constituents are closer and more personalized in less populous states than in more populous ones.[47] And when Congress makes decisions about distributing federal dollars, less populous states receive more benefits than they pay in taxes, whereas populous states provide more revenue but receive fewer returns. Small-population states are advantaged across most federal spending programs, with the effect most pronounced on the types of programs over which Congress maintains tightest control.[48]

Collective Representation. Representation does not always follow state or district boundaries. It occurs when citizens feel they are served by any member of Congress, not just their local member. Congressional representation is, as Robert Weissberg put it, "collective," not just "dyadic."[49] In other words, representation involves more than the interactions between individual members and the residents of their geographic constituencies. Citizens can feel a sense of connection to Congress when the body as a whole includes members who speak for them. When someone from an ethnic or racial minority background goes to Congress, it is often a matter of pride for an entire identity group. Such legislators speak for people like them throughout the nation.[50]

Many constituencies are represented in the same way. One member who suffers from epilepsy defends job rights for other sufferers of the disease; another whose grandson was born prematurely champions funds for medical research into birth defects; members who are openly gay speak out for the rights of homosexuals everywhere. Such causes are close to members' hearts, even though they may pay scant political dividends. Legislators' backgrounds, religious beliefs, social identities, and experiences all shape their views and priorities. Political scientist Barry C. Burden refers to such influences as "the personal roots of representation," and he argues that analysts must take them into account to understand legislators' policy activism in Congress.[51]

Congressional Roles

Members of Congress, as Richard F. Fenno Jr. explains, spend their lives "moving between two contexts, Washington and home, and between two activities, governing and campaigning."[52] The two contexts and the two activities are continuously interwoven. How members govern is deeply affected by their constituency roots and their campaign experiences. In turn, their Capitol Hill activities affect all their subsequent contacts with people back home. As members carry out their representational functions, it is possible to distinguish three roles undertaken to some degree by most members of Congress: legislator, constituency servant, and partisan.

Legislator. The rules, procedures, and traditions of the House and Senate impose many constraints on members' behavior. To be effective, new members must learn their way through the institutional maze. Legislators therefore stress the formal aspects of Capitol Hill duties and routines: legislative work, investigation, and committee specialization. Charles E. Schumer, D-N.Y., an elected official for most of his life (he was elected to the state assembly at age twenty-three and served nine terms in the U.S. House), explained his commitment as a professional legislator during his successful 1998 Senate campaign:

> I love to legislate. Taking an idea—often not original with me— shaping it, molding it. Building a coalition of people who might not completely agree with it. Passing it and making the country a little bit of a better place. I love doing that.[53]

Legislators pursue information and expertise on issues, not only because of their personal interest in public policy but also because it sways others in the chamber. To influence other members, a legislator must be perceived as credible and knowledgeable—in other words, someone worth listening to.

The legislator's role often dovetails with that of representing constituents. Most members seek committee assignments that will serve the needs of their states or districts. One House member related why he sought a seat on the committee handling flood control and water resource development. "The interests of my district dictated my field of specialization," he explained, "but the decision to specialize in some legislative field is automatic for the member who wants to exercise any influence."[54]

Members soon learn the norms, or folkways, that expedite legislative productivity. Examining the post–World War II Senate, Donald R. Matthews identified folkways that restrained and channeled members' legislative activity. Senators were encouraged to serve an apprenticeship, deferring to elders in their early years; to concentrate on Senate work instead of on gaining publicity; to specialize in issues within their committees or affecting their home states; and to extend reciprocity to colleagues—that is, provide willing assistance with the expectation that it will be repaid in kind one day.[55]

These folkways have faded in importance in the contemporary Senate, though they have not entirely disappeared. Barbara Sinclair's major reassessment of senators' Hill styles concluded that the restrained activism of the 1950s

Senate had given way to unrestrained activism in the contemporary era.[56] New senators now actively take part in most aspects of the chamber's work, ignoring the apprenticeship norm. Many senators, especially those with an eye on the White House, work tirelessly to attract national publicity and personal attention. Committee specialization, although still common, is less rigid than it once was. Senators now have many overlapping committee assignments and are expected to express views on a wide range of issues.

The House relies more on formal channels of power than on informal norms. From interviews, however, Herbert B. Asher uncovered some key House norms.[57] Among them are the beliefs that the important work of the House should be done in committees, and that members should specialize in the issues before their committees. Members should be prepared to bargain and trade votes. Members should learn the procedural rules of the chamber. They should not personally criticize a colleague on the House floor.

As in the Senate, House norms of earlier eras have weakened. New members, impatient to make their mark, assert themselves more quickly, aided by party leaders who worry about getting the freshmen reelected. Leadership comes earlier to members than it used to. Specialization remains more compelling in the House than in the Senate, but many members branch out into unrelated issues. No longer are committees the sole forums for influencing legislation. Many of today's members, more partisan and ideologically driven than their predecessors, shun norms such as reciprocity and compromise. One of the most striking recent violations of civility norms occurred during the highly contentious spring of 2010. While staunchly pro-life Rep. Bart Stupak, D-Mich., was announcing his support for health care reform legislation on the House floor, another House member interrupted him by shouting out "Baby killer!"[58]

Constituency Servant. As constituency servants, members of Congress attempt to give voice to local citizens' concerns, solve problems constituents encounter with federal programs, and ensure that their states and districts receive a fair share of federal dollars. Often the task is performed by legislators and their staffs as casework—individual cases triggered by constituent letters or visits. Even though mostly delegated to staff aides, this is a chore that weighs heavily on members. A House member expressed the philosophy of most legislators like this:

> Constituent work: that's something I feel very strongly about. The American people, with the growth of the bureaucracy, feel nobody cares. The only conduit a taxpayer has with the government is a congressional office.[59]

Sometimes, members stress constituency service to gain breathing room for legislative stands that stray from district norms.

Research has shown that developing a reputation as working hard on behalf of constituents in these ways makes a positive difference for legislators' careers. In a recent study, political scientists David C. W. Parker and Craig

Goodman find that "a constituent-service reputation generates the most positive notice among citizens . . . [while] policy expertise appears to be less valuable to, or less noticed by, constituents."[60] Along these lines, procuring pork-barrel projects for local constituencies tends to improve representatives' name recognition back home,[61] reduce their likelihood of facing a strong challenger,[62] and enhance vulnerable members' reelection chances.[63] Even while many members rail against pork-barrel spending in other people's areas, they recognize that their constituents still expect them to bring home the bacon. An Arkansas lobbyist tells the story of going to visit one of his state's Republican members known for his anti-pork speeches. "I know you're anti-pork," the lobbyist began, "but I have to tell you about our needs and how to position yourself." "What do you mean?" the representative retorted. "As far as I can tell, it's not pork if it's for Arkansas."[64]

Members have especially strong incentives to perform the constituency servant role whenever Congress considers government programs with highly visible local benefits, such as highway or mass transit grants, water projects, and homeland security contracts. Members seek many other local benefits beyond earmarks—for example, favorable regulatory rules or trade concessions for local industries.[65]

Partisan. Members of Congress are elected not just as individual representatives, but as members of a political party. Nearly every member of Congress formally affiliates with one of the two major parties, and even the few members elected as independents organize with one of the two parties to receive their committee assignments. Party affiliation is more than a mere label for most members. Members work with and for their parties, and their partisan ties and activities have a pervasive effect on congressional elections, representation, and legislation.

Members have a personal stake in the collective fate of their parties. Whether their party commands a majority of seats in the House or Senate affects their power in the chamber and their ability to achieve personal legislative goals. The majority party elects leaders with agenda-setting responsibilities and controls the chairmanships of all committees and subcommittees in the two chambers. In addition, members know that voters' feelings about the parties will affect their own electoral chances. Former Republican senator Lincoln Chafee of Rhode Island (currently governor of that state) lost his seat in 2006, despite high personal approval ratings, in large part because of his party's unpopularity in Rhode Island. "I give the voters credit," he said. "They made the connection between electing even popular Republicans at the cost of leaving the Senate in the hands of a leadership they had learned to mistrust."[66]

Many members hold posts within their congressional parties. Legislative party organizations are extensive, with whips, deputy whips, regional whips, and a variety of task forces. Elections for party positions are often hotly contested. As discussed in more detail in Chapter 6, members who hold or seek party positions dedicate significant effort to party causes. They do favors for fellow partisans and exhort them to vote the party position. They seek to impress leaders and other party members with their prodigious fund raising and campaigning on behalf of their party's candidates.[67]

Even those members who do not serve as party officers attend and participate in the party caucus. In the contemporary Congress, the House and Senate caucuses of both parties meet at least weekly. Members engage in internal party communications and party message development. They stage press conferences, reach out to sympathetic groups and opinion leaders, and coordinate floor speeches as they seek to shape media coverage to partisan advantage.[68] In short, partisan activities today place significant demands on legislators' time and energy. Not only do members seek to enact good policy as legislators and advance local concerns as constituency servants, but they also are partisans, heavily invested in the collective fortunes of their parties.

How Do Legislators Spend Their Time?

For senators and representatives, time is their most precious commodity, and lack of it is their most frequent complaint about their jobs.[69] Allocating time requires exceedingly tough personal and political choices.

For a breakdown of how members' time is spent, see Table 5-1. According to a 1993 congressional survey, members' daily priorities are roughly as follows: (1) meeting on legislative issues with constituents, either at home or in Washington; (2) attending committee meetings; (3) meeting with government officials and lobbyists; (4) studying pending legislation or discussing legislation with other members or staff; (5) working with informal caucus groups of colleagues; (6) attending floor debates or watching them on television; (7) doing nonlegislative work (casework) for constituents; (8) managing personal office operations and staffs; (9) raising funds; (10) working with party leaders to build legislative coalitions; (11) overseeing how agencies are carrying out laws or policies; and (12) making appearances on legislation outside the state or district.[70] Staff members usually prepare daily schedules for members of Congress to consult as they whirl through a busy day on Capitol Hill. A handful of lawmakers post their schedules on their websites. "I just wanted to give people an opportunity to see who I meet with," explained Sen. Jon Tester, D-Mont.[71]

Scheduling is complicated by the large number of formal work groups—mainly committees and subcommittees, but also joint, party, and ad hoc panels. The average senator sits on three full committees and seven subcommittees; representatives average two committees and four subcommittees. With so many assignments, lawmakers are hard-pressed to control their crowded schedules. Committee quorums are difficult to achieve, and members' attention is often focused elsewhere. All too often working sessions are composed of the chair, the ranking minority member, perhaps one or two interested colleagues, and staff aides. House rules tightening quorum requirements only made scheduling problems worse.[72]

Repeated floor votes, which lawmakers fear missing, are another time-consuming duty. In a typical Congress, more than a thousand recorded votes

TABLE 5-1 **Activities of Members of Congress: Actual and Ideal**

| | Members actually spending time | | | | Members preferring |
Activity	Great deal	Moderate amount	A little	Almost none	to spend more time
Representation					
Meet with citizens in state or district	68%	30%	1%	0%	17%
Meet in Washington, D.C., with constituents	45	50	5	0	17
Manage office	6	45	39	10	13
Raise funds for next campaign, for others, for party	6	33	45	16	7
Lawmaking					
Attend committee hearings, markups, other meetings	48	46	6	0	43
Meet in Washington on legislative issues	37	56	6	0	31
Study, read, discuss pending legislation	25	56	17	2	78
Work with informal caucuses	8	43	36	13	25
Attend floor debate, follow it on television	7	37	44	12	59
Work with party leaders to build coalitions	6	33	43	18	42
Oversee how agencies are carrying out policies and programs	5	22	43	29	53
Give speeches about legislation outside state or district	5	23	49	23	16

Source: U.S. Congress, Joint Committee on the Organization of Congress, *Organization of the Congress, Final Report,* H. Rep. 103–413, 103d Cong., 1st sess., December 1993, 2:231–232, 275–287.

Note: A total of 161 members of Congress (136 representatives, 25 senators) responded to this survey, conducted in early 1993 under the auspices of the Joint Committee on the Organization of Congress. This series of questions elicited responses from 152 to 155 members.

may be taken in the House chamber and perhaps six hundred in the Senate. "We're like automatons," one senator complained. "We spend our time walking in tunnels to go to the floor to vote."[73] "Rep. Debbie Wasserman-Schultz, D-Fla., shuns the House gym, explaining, "I get my exercise running around the Capitol."[74]

Lawmakers' daily schedules in Washington are "long, fragmented, and unpredictable," according to a study based on time logs kept by senators' appointment secretaries.[75] "In Congress you are a total juggler," recalls former representative Pat Schroeder. "You have always got seventeen things pulling on your sleeve."[76] Members' schedules are splintered into so many tiny fragments that effective pursuit of lawmaking, oversight, and constituent service is hampered. According to a management study of several senators' offices, an event occurs every five minutes, on average, to which the senator or the chief aide must respond personally.[77] Often members have scant notice that their presence is required at a meeting or a hearing. Carefully developed schedules can be disrupted by changes in meeting hours, by unforeseen events, or by sessions that run longer than expected. (After the terrorist attacks on the United States in September 2001, members were issued "smart phones" so they could keep track of schedules and developments.)

Political scientists may claim that Congress runs in harmony with members' needs, but the members know otherwise. In a survey of 114 House and Senate members, "inefficiency" was the thing that most surprised them about Congress (45 percent gave this response).[78] "[Congress] is a good job for someone with no family, no life of their own, no desire to do anything but get up, go to work, and live and die by their own press releases," quipped former representative Fred Grandy, an Iowa Republican who left Congress in 1995. "It is a great job for deviant human beings."[79]

Nearly half the respondents in a 1987 survey agreed that they had "no personal time after work"; a third said they had "no time for family."[80] Congress largely adheres to a Tuesday-to-Thursday schedule that gives members some opportunity to spend time back home with families, although constituency business consumes a great deal of members' time when Congress is not in session.

The dilemma legislators face in allocating their time is far more than a matter of scheduling; it is a case of conflicting role expectations. Look again at Table 5-1, where lawmakers' activities are arrayed to illustrate the tensions inherent in the two Congresses, from the representative Congress (at the top of the list) to the legislative Congress (at the bottom). More members want to devote extra time to legislative duties than would choose to spend more time on constituency and political chores. According to the survey, 43 percent of members on average would like to spend more time on the legislative tasks, whereas on average only 14 percent of them would give more time to the representative activities.[81] The two Congresses pull members in different directions. As a retiring House committee chairman remarked:

> One problem is that you're damned if you do and damned if you don't. If you do your work here, you're accused of neglecting your district. And if you spend too much time in your district, you're accused of neglecting your work here.[82]

The Shape of the Washington Career

Once a short-term activity, congressional service has become a career. Accompanying this careerism, or longevity, is a distinctive pattern of Washington activity: the longer members remain in office, the more they sponsor bills, deliver floor speeches, and offer amendments. Despite the democratizing trends of the reform era (1960s and 1970s), senior lawmakers continue to take the lead in legislative activities.[83]

Long tenure also tends to pull members toward legislative specialization. Settling into their committee slots, members gain expertise in a distinct policy field and spend their time managing legislation and conducting oversight in that field. Seniority tends to boost legislative achievement. Veterans usually enjoy significantly more success than do freshmen in getting their bills passed.

The link between members' service and their effectiveness reflects the indispensable role careerists play in the legislative process. As John R. Hibbing observed:

> Senior members are the heart and soul of the legislative side of congressional service. Relatively junior members can be given a subcommittee chairmanship, but it is not nearly so easy to give them an active, focused legislative agenda and the political savvy to enact it. Some things take time and experience, and successful participation in the legislative process appears to be one of those things.[84]

The wisdom of this statement is repeatedly borne out. One recent study drawing on the uniquely detailed data available for the North Carolina General Assembly reports that legislators' "effectiveness rises sharply with tenure," and "there is no evidence that effectiveness eventually declines with tenure, even out to nine terms."[85] The study concludes that "the increased effectiveness [of senior legislators] is due to the acquisition of specific human capital, most likely through learning-by-doing."[86] A comprehensive study of U.S. House members' abilities to get their bills past significant stages in the legislative process reports that "as members become more senior they become more efficient at arranging deals with key office-holders."[87] Newcomers bring with them zeal, energy, and fresh approaches. And yet many of them lack patience, bargaining skills, institutional memory, and respect for the lawmaking process.

LOOKING HOMEWARD

Not all of a representative's or a senator's duties lie in Washington, D.C. Legislators not only fashion policy for the nation's welfare, but they also act as emissaries from their home states or districts.

Independent Judgment or Constituency Opinion?

Although found in virtually every political system, representation is the hallmark of democratic regimes dedicated to sharing power among citizens. In small communities, decisions can be reached by face-to-face discussions, but in populous societies such personalized consultation is impossible. Thus, according to democratic theory, citizens can exert control by choosing "fiduciary agents" who will then deliberate on legislation just as their principals, the voters, would do if they could be on hand themselves.[88] But in attempting to serve as a faithful agent for constituents, legislators are faced with a central dilemma of representation: whether to take actions that are popular with constituents or to do what the legislator believes is in their best interest. As Pitkin explains,

> The representative must act in such a way that, although he is independent, and his constituents are capable of action and judgment, no conflict arises between them. He must act in their interest, and this means he must not normally come into conflict with their wishes.[89]

Recent opinion surveys seem to echo Pitkin's formulation. As one analyst puts it, "The public seems to want elected officials to internalize the majority's values and then try to assess how those values come to bear on an issue." No less than 85 percent agreed with the following statement: "The goal of Congress should be to make the decisions that a majority of Americans would make if they had the information and time to think things over that Congress has."[90]

For Burke, a legislator must do more than register prevailing constituency opinion. Legislators must instead use their superior information about policy, their broader perspective, and their personal judgment in making decisions. This conception of the legislator as a Burkean trustee has always had its admirers. Speaking to a group of newly elected House members, Rep. Henry J. Hyde, R-Ill. (1974–2007), voiced the Burkean ideal:

> If you are here simply as a tote board registering the current state of opinion in your district, you are not going to serve either your constituents or the Congress well. You must take, at times, a national view, even if you risk the displeasure of your neighbors and friends back home. If you don't know the principle, or the policy, for which you are willing to lose your office, then you are going to do damage here.[91]

Nearly every member can point to conscience votes cast on deeply felt issues. A few, such as Rep. Mike Synar, D-Okla. (1979–1995), compile a contrarian record, challenging voters to admire their independence if not their policies. Synar was an unabashed liberal Democrat from a state that now elects mostly conservative Republicans. "I want to be a U.S. congressman from Oklahoma, not an Oklahoman congressman," Synar declared when he arrived in the capital.[92] If turned out of office by hostile sentiment (as Synar later was), the Burkean can at least hope for history's vindication.

Electoral realities always imperil the Burkean ideal, just as Burke himself was ousted from office for his candor. Today's voters similarly prefer instructed delegates rather than lawmakers who exercise too much independent judgment.

In practice, legislators assume different representational styles according to the occasion. They ponder factors such as the nation's welfare, their personal convictions, and constituency opinions. "The weight assigned to each factor," writes Thomas E. Cavanagh, "varies according to the nature of the issue at hand, the availability of the information necessary for a decision, and the intensity of preference of the people concerned about the issue."[93]

Members of Congress are challenged to explain their choices to constituents—no matter how many or how few people truly care about the matter.[94] The anticipated need to explain oneself shapes a member's decisions and is part of the dilemma of choice. A cynical saying among lawmakers asserts that "a vote on anything [is] a wrong vote if you cannot explain it in a 30-second TV ad."[95]

What Are Constituencies?

Senators and representatives cannot respond equally to all the people within a given state or district. A subset of their constituents elected them, and so they interact more with supporters than with opponents. The constituencies that legislators see as they campaign or vote are quite different from the boundaries found on maps. Fenno describes a "nest" of constituencies, ranging from the widest (geographic constituency) to the narrowest (personal constituency), which is made up of supporters, loyalists, and intimates.[96]

Geographic and Demographic Constituencies. The average House district today numbers more than 710,000 people. As for senators, fourteen represent states with only one House district; the rest represent multidistrict states with as many as 37 million people.[97] Such constituencies differ sharply from one another. More than half (57 percent) of the people in Manhattan's Upper East Side (New York's Fourteenth District) have college degrees compared with only 6 percent in California's central valley (Twentieth District). Median family income ranges from $92,000 (New Jersey's Eleventh District, Morris County) to less than $21,000 in New York's Sixteenth District in the South Bronx, where 40 percent of the families live in poverty.[98] Such disparities among districts shape their representatives' outlooks.

There are also political "microclimates." Democrat Nydia M. Velázquez's Twelfth District in New York begins in a Hispanic area of Brooklyn, jumps across the East River to take in Manhattan's Chinatown, Little Italy, and its Lower East Side, and then doubles back again to encompass neighborhoods in northern Brooklyn and Queens. Republican Mary Bono Mack's sprawling Forty-fifth District in southern California embraces the smog-ridden suburbs east of Riverside, the irrigated farmland of the Coachella Valley, and the wealthy desert oases of Palm Springs and Palm Desert. Even these geographical distinctions grossly simplify the complex and subtle ethnic, economic, and social mixture of these communities.

Demographically, constituencies may be homogeneous or heterogeneous.[99] Some constituencies, even a few whole states, remain uniform and one-dimensional—mostly wheat farmers or urban ghetto dwellers or small-town citizens. Because of rising population, economic complexity, and educational levels, however, virtually all constituencies, House as well as Senate, have become more heterogeneous than they used to be. The more diverse a constituency, the more challenging is the representative's task.

Another attribute of constituencies is electoral balance, especially as manifested in the incumbent's reelection chances. Heterogeneous districts tend to be more competitive than uniform ones. Incumbents predictably prefer safe districts—that is, those with a high proportion of groups leaning toward their party. Not only do safe districts favor reelection, but they also imply that voters will be easier to please.[100]

Truly competitive districts are not the norm, especially in the House of Representatives. The 2010 elections were extraordinarily competitive by recent standards. In the last month leading up to the elections, analysts at the Cook Political Report estimated that eighty-seven House seats were either toss-ups or merely leaning toward one political party. "This [was] an unprecedented number in recent history," writes *New York Times* blogger Nate Silver, noting that this year's number of competitive races was roughly twice as high as the average for the past six cycles."[101] Despite this, the majority of incumbents won handily: 60 percent of House victors won by twenty percentage points or more, and twenty-seven faced no challenger at all. Even in the highly competitive 2010 elections, less than 30 percent of House districts were truly competitive.

As Table 5-2 shows, competitiveness varies over time. Senate seats are more likely to be closely contested than House races, but many senators, including most of those up for reelection in 2010, still win in a walk.

Whatever the numbers might show, few incumbents regard themselves as truly safe. The threat of losing an election is very real. Most lawmakers have a close call at some time in their congressional careers, and many of them eventually suffer defeat.[102] In addition to the incumbents who went down to defeat in 2010, a number of others—including five senators and some forty-nine House members—survived while receiving what might be called warning signs from the home folks. Incumbents thus worry not only about winning or losing but also about their margins of safety. Downturns in normal electoral support narrow the member's comfort zone in the job, may invite challengers in future years, and could block chances for further advancement.[103]

Political and Personal Constituencies. As candidates or incumbents analyze their electoral base, three narrower constituencies can be discerned: supporters (the reelection constituency), loyalists (the primary constituency), and intimates (the personal constituency).[104] Supporters are expected to vote for the candidate on election day, but some do not. Candidates and their advisers constantly monitor these voters, reassessing precinct-level political demography—registration figures, survey data, and recent electoral trends. The more elections incumbents have survived, the more precisely they can identify supporters. Areas and groups with the biggest payoffs are usually targeted.

Loyalists are the politician's staunchest supporters. They may be from pre-electoral ventures—civil rights, environmental, or Tea Party activists, for example. They may hail from religious or ethnic groups, or political or civic clubs. They may be friends and neighbors. Whatever their source, they are willing volunteers who can be counted on to lend a hand in reelection campaigns.

Candidates dare not ignore these loyalists. A favorite story of House Speaker Thomas P. "Tip" O'Neill Jr., D-Mass. (1953–1987), emerged from his first campaign for city council (at which he failed). A neighbor told him,

TABLE 5-2 House and Senate Margins of Victory, 1974–2010

Chamber and election year	Percentage of vote				Number of seats
	Under 55	55–59.9	60 plus	Unopposed	
House					
1974	24	16	46	14	435
1976	17	14	56	12	435
1978	17	14	53	16	435
1980	18	14	60	8	435
1982	16	16	63	6	435
1984	12	13	61	14	435
1986	9	10	64	17	435
1988	6	9	67	18	435
1990	11	16	58	15	435
1992	20	18	58	3	435
1994	22	17	52	9	435
1996	22	18	57	3	435
1998	10	17	63	10	435
2000	18	12	56	14	435
2002	10	10	70	10	435
2004	7	14	64	15	435
2006	15	14	62	9	435
2008	14	16	57	12	435
2010	24	16	54	6	435
Senate					
1974	41	18	35	6	34
1976	30	33	30	6	33
1978	24	33	36	6	33
1980	58	18	21	3	34
1982	30	27	43	—	33
1984	18	21	58	3	33
1986	38	15	47	—	34
1988	33	15	52	—	33
1990	26	11	49	14	34
1992	34	34	32	—	35
1994	32	34	34	—	35
1996	59	18	24	—	34
1998	29	9	62	—	34
2000	29	15	55	—	34
2002	32	18	46	4	34
2004	32	15	50	3	34
2006	24	21	55	—	33
2008	26	20	51	3	35
2010	32	27	38	3	37

Sources: *CQ Weekly* and authors' calculations.

Note: Percentages may not add to 100 because of rounding. "Unopposed" includes districts or states where only one major-party candidate was on the ballot.

"Tom, I'm going to vote for you even though you didn't ask me." "Mrs. O'Brien," replied a surprised O'Neill, "I've lived across the street from you for 18 years. I shovel your walk in the winter. I cut your grass in the summer. I didn't think I had to ask you for your vote." To this the lady replied, "Tom, I want you to know something: people like to be asked."[105] Expressions of gratitude are equally important. The elder George Bush reportedly "always carried a box of note cards with him on the campaign trail and penned a personal note immediately following each event to the volunteers and hosts."[106]

Even entrenched officeholders worry about keeping their core supporters energized. Loyalists are a politician's defenders in times of adversity. "There's a big difference between the people who are for you and the people who are excitedly for you," an Iowa politician told Fenno, "between those who will vote if they feel like it and those for whom the only election is [your] election. You need as many of that group as you can get."[107]

Intimates are close friends who supply political advice and emotional support. They may be members of the candidate's family, trusted staff members, political mentors, or individuals who shared decisive experiences early in the candidate's career. The setting and the players differ from state to state and from district to district. Tip O'Neill's inner circle was made up of the "boys" of Barry's Corner, a local clubhouse in Cambridge, Massachusetts, whose families O'Neill had known intimately over more than fifty years of political life. When Rep. David E. Price, D-N.C., first decided to run for Congress, he relied on what he called the "Wednesday night group," which he described as "an inner circle without whom the effort would never have gotten off the ground."[108] Such intimates play an indispensable role. Beyond their enthusiastic support, they provide unvarnished advice on political matters and serve as sounding boards for ideas and strategies.

Home Styles

Legislators evolve distinctive ways of presenting themselves and their records to their constituents—what Fenno calls their home styles. These styles are exhibited in members' personal appearances, mailings, newsletters, press releases, telephone conversations, radio and television spots, and websites. Little is known about how home styles coalesce, but they are linked to members' personalities, backgrounds, constituency features, and resources. The ways members interact with constituents have a powerful effect on their electoral success. As Fenno notes, "It is the style, not the issue content, that counts most in the reelection constituency."[109]

Presentation of Self. A successful home style will elicit trust—constituents' faith that legislators are what they claim to be and will do what they promise.[110] Winning voters' trust does not happen overnight; it takes time, persistence, and consistency. Members must establish their qualification for office—that is, the belief that they are capable of handling the job. Members also strive to convey identification, the impression that legislators resemble their constituents, and empathy, the sense that legislators understand constituents' problems and care about them.

Because of the variations among legislators and constituencies, the use of many different home styles can effectively build the trust relationship. The legendary Speaker "Mr. Sam" Rayburn represented his East Texas district for nearly fifty years (1913–1961) as a plain dirt farmer. Once he was back in his hometown of Bonham, his drawl thickened; his tailored suits were exchanged for khakis, an old shirt, and a slouch hat; and he traveled not in the Speaker's limousine, but in a well-dented pickup truck. His biographer relates:

> If Rayburn ever chewed tobacco in Washington, a long-time aide could not recall it, but in Bonham he always seemed to have a plug in his cheek. He made certain always to spit in the fireplace at his home when constituents were visiting, so that if nothing else, they would take away the idea that Mr. Sam was just a plain fellow.[111]

The aim of a member's home style is to become "one of us" in constituents' estimation. Accomplishing this is a "difficult feat—far more difficult than establishing a reputation as a fine constituency servant or policy expert."[112]

Today's legislators are no less inventive in fashioning home styles. Representative A's direct style features face-to-face contacts with people in his primary constituency. He rarely mentions issues because most people in his district agree on them. Representative B, a popular local athlete, uses national defense issues to symbolize his oneness with a district supportive of the military. Representative C displays himself as a verbal, issue-oriented activist, an outsider ill at ease with conventional politicians. Senator D, articulate and personable, comes across as "a mom in tennis shoes." The repertoire of home styles is virtually limitless.

Voters are likely to remember style long after they forget issue statements or voting records. Even so, legislators know full well that they must explain their decisions to others.[113]

Explaining Washington Activity. Explaining is an integral part of decision making. In home district forums, constituents expect members to be able to describe, interpret, and justify their actions. If they do not agree with the member's conclusions, they may at least respect the decision-making style.

Although few incumbents fear that a single vote can defeat them, all realize that voters' disenchantment with their record can be fatal—more so in these days of Internet communications when lobby groups publicize voting records. Although local news media coverage of Congress is often uncritical, it can promote political accountability. A recent study by political scientist Brian J. Fogarty reveals that local media devote more time and resources to monitoring representatives who are "out of step" with their district's presidential vote than those who are perceived to be in step. Such members face additional media scrutiny and must therefore account for their Washington decisions more frequently.[114]

Members stockpile reasons for virtually every position they take, often more than are needed. Facing especially thorny choices (for example, on aid to

Wall Street firms, Social Security reform, or the war in Iraq), they might follow a middle-of-the-road route. More often, they huddle under the umbrella of their party's line. Whatever course they choose, they will find that inconsistency is mentally and politically costly. Contrary to the popular stereotype of politicians speaking out of both sides of their mouths, members give much the same account of themselves regardless of the group they are talking to.

Constituency Careers. Constituency bonds evolve over the course of a lawmaker's career. Constituency careers have at least two recognizable stages: expansionism and protectionism. In the first stage, the member builds a reelection constituency by solidifying the help of hard-core supporters and reaching out to attract additional blocs of support. Aggressive efforts to reach out to new voters—exploiting the perquisites of incumbency, such as fund raising and an election year avalanche of messages to constituents—account for the "sophomore surge," in which newcomers typically boost their margin in their first reelection bid. In the second stage, the member stops expanding the base, content with protecting support already won. Once established, a successful home style is rarely altered.

Certain developments, however, can lead to a change in a member's home style. One is demographic change in the constituency, as population movement or redistricting force a member to confront unfamiliar voters or territory. A second cause is a strategic reaction, such as when a fresh challenger or a novel issue threatens established voting patterns. Because coalitions may shift over time, members and their advisers pore over the results of the most recent election (and available survey results).

Finally, home styles may change with new personal goals and ambitions. Achieving positions of power in Washington can divert a member's attention from home state business. Family responsibilities or the need to improve one's financial situation may also lead to a shift in priorities. Faced with new aspirations or shifting constituency demands, some members decide to retire. Others struggle ineffectively and are defeated. Still others survive by rejuvenating their constituency base.

OFFICE OF THE MEMBER INC.

Home style includes the way a member answers day-to-day questions: How much attention should I devote to state or district needs? How much time should I spend in the state or district? How should I keep in touch with my constituents? How should I deploy staff aides to handle constituents' concerns?

Road Tripping

During the nineteenth century, legislators spent most of their time at home, traveling to Washington only when Congress was in session. However, after World War II (and the advent of both air travel from home and air-conditioning on Capitol Hill), congressional sessions lengthened until they spanned most of the year.

By the 1970s, both houses had adopted parallel schedules of sessions punctuated with district work periods (House) or nonlegislative periods (Senate). At the same time, members were permitted more paid trips to states or districts. Today, senators and representatives are allowed as many trips home as they want, subject to the limits of their official expense allowances. Many members (even those from the West Coast) go home every weekend.

Today's home styles thus entail frequent commutes. Although travel has increased for all members, the more time-consuming the trips home, the less often they are made. When their families remain at home, members are more inclined to return regularly. Most members stay closer to their districts as election day approaches.[115]

Seniority is also a factor. Senior members tend to make fewer trips to their districts than do junior members, perhaps reflecting junior members' greater attentiveness to their districts or senior members' greater Washington responsibilities. Finally, members' decisions to retire voluntarily are usually accompanied by large drops in trips home.

Constituency Casework

"All God's chillun got problems," exclaimed Rep. Billy Matthews, D-Fla. (1953–1967), as he pondered mail from his constituents.[116] In the early days, lawmakers lacked staff aides and wrote personally to executive agencies for help in matters such as pension or land claims and appointments to military academies. The Legislative Reorganization Act of 1946 provided de facto authority for hiring caseworkers, first in Senate offices and later in the House.

What are these cases all about? As respondents in a nationwide survey reported, the most frequent reason for contacting a member's office (16 percent of all cases) is to express views or obtain information on legislative issues. Requests for help in finding government jobs form the next largest category, followed by cases dealing with government services such as Social Security, veterans' benefits, or unemployment compensation. Military cases (for example, transfers, discharges, personal hardships) are numerous, as are tax, legal, and immigration problems. Constituents often ask for government publications. And there are requests for flags that have flown over the U.S. Capitol.

Many citizen appeals, moreover, betray a hazy understanding of the officeholder's duties. Rep. Luis V. Gutierrez, D-Ill. (1993–2009), reported being barraged with all manner of complaints and requests when he shopped in his North Side Chicago neighborhood. Examples of what he has heard are: "They haven't picked up my trash!" (the city's job). "Can you get my son a scholarship to the state university?" (a state matter). Or "I can't pay my child support" (personal). Rep. Gutierrez's personal favorite was: "I own property in Puerto Rico and someone is blocking my driveway."[117]

Cases arrive in legislators' offices by letter, phone, e-mail, fax, or in person at district or mobile offices. All representatives and senators now have e-mail addresses and websites with contact information. Occasionally, members themselves pick up cases from talking to constituents. Indeed, many hold office hours in their districts for this purpose. When a constituent's request is received, it is usually acknowledged promptly by a letter that either fills the request or promises that an answer will be forthcoming.

Keeping up with incoming communications is a priority for all congressional offices. If the constituent's request requires contacting a federal agency, caseworkers communicate by e-mail, phone, letter, or buckslip (a preprinted referral form).[118] Usually, the contact in the executive agency is a liaison officer, although some caseworkers prefer to deal directly with line officers or regional officials. Once the problem has been conveyed, it is a matter of time before a decision is reached and a reply forwarded to the congressional office. The reply is then sent along to the constituent, perhaps with a cover letter signed by the member. If the agency's reply is deemed faulty, the caseworker may challenge it and ask for reconsideration; in some cases the member may personally intervene to lend weight to the appeal.

The volume of casework varies from state to state and from district to district. In both chambers, senior legislators receive proportionately more casework requests than do junior members.[119] Perhaps senior members are considered more powerful and better equipped to resolve constituents' problems. Legislators themselves certainly cultivate this image. Demographic variation can affect casework volume. Some types of citizens simply are more likely than others to have contact with government agencies.

Comparing senators and representatives, Frances E. Lee and Bruce I. Oppenheimer found that casework loads are affected by constituency size.[120] In smaller states, House members and senators appear equally accessible, and these senators have contact levels that mirror House members'. Indeed, senators representing the smallest states often have casework loads that exceed those of House members, because their greater institutional clout make them even more attractive to small-state residents than their House members. By contrast, large-state senators are perceived as more distant, so constituents in those states are more likely to turn to their House members for casework requests.

From all accounts, casework pays off in citizen support for individual legislators. In one National Election Study (NES) survey, 17 percent of all adults reported that they or members of their families had requested help from their own representatives. Eighty-five percent said they were satisfied with the response they received.[121] "Casework is all profit," contends Morris P. Fiorina. Unlike the positions members take on issues, casework wins friends without alienating anyone. But casework benefits do not entirely supplant issue positions or party loyalties.

Some criticize constituency casework as unfair or biased in practice. Citizens may not enjoy equal access to senators' or representatives' offices. Political supporters or cronies may receive favored treatment at others' expense. But in the great bulk of cases, help is universally dispensed.

Personal Staff

Legislators head sizable office enterprises that reflect their two-Congresses responsibilities within the institution and toward their constituents. Staff members assist with legislative and constituency duties. Constituent representation is deemed so essential that when a member dies, resigns, or is incapacitated, the staff normally remains on the job (supervised by the secretary of the Senate or the clerk of the House, as the case may be).

Each House member is entitled to an annual member representational account (MRA) that ranges from $1.4 to $1.7 million annually. From this account, members pay the salaries of no more than eighteen full-time and four part-time employees. The average House member's full-time staff actually numbers about fifteen. Representatives also are entitled to an annual office allowance, which is used for travel, telecommunications, district office rental, office equipment, stationery, computer services, and mail.[122]

Senators' personal staffs range in size from thirteen to seventy-one; the average is from thirty to thirty-five full-time employees. Unlike the House, the Senate places no limits on the number of staff a senator may employ. A senator's office expense account depends on factors such as the state's population and its distance from Washington, D.C.

Members' offices always seem crowded and overburdened, but freezes on staff size have been partially offset by computerization, shifting work to state and district offices, and use of volunteers. Congressional offices depend heavily on unpaid help, mainly college-age interns. On average, each House and Senate office uses about nine interns every year (see Appendix B for information on internships).

Staff Organization. No two congressional offices are exactly alike. Each is shaped by the personality, interests, constituency, and politics of the individual legislator. State and district needs also influence staff composition. A senator from a farm state likely will employ at least one specialist in agricultural problems; an urban representative might hire a consumer affairs or housing expert. Traditions are important. If a legislator's predecessor had an enviable reputation for a certain kind of service, the new incumbent will dare not let it lapse.

The member's institutional position also affects staff organization. Committee and subcommittee chairmen have committee staff at their disposal. Members without such aides rely heavily on personal staff for their committee work.

Staff Functions. Most personal aides in the House and Senate are young, well educated, and transient. Senate and House aides have served on average less than four years in their posts. Their salaries, although somewhat above the average for full-time workers in the United States, fall well below those for comparably educated workers.[123]

The mix of personal staff functions is decided by each member. Most hire administrative assistants (AAs), legislative assistants (LAs), caseworkers, and press aides, as well as a few people from the home state or district. AAs supervise the office and impart political and legislative advice. Often they function as the legislator's alter ego, negotiating with colleagues, constituents, and lobbyists. LAs work with members in committees, draft bills, write speeches, suggest policy initiatives, analyze legislation, and prepare position papers. They also monitor committee sessions that the member is unable to attend.

To emphasize personal contacts, many members have moved casework staff to their home districts or states. Virtually all House and Senate members have home district offices. Some members have as many as five or six such offices. Field offices have lower staff salaries, cheaper rents, and less overhead. They also are more accessible to constituents, local and state officials, and regional federal officers. Members' district staffs fill the role once performed by local party workers, and simultaneously enhance members' reelection prospects.

This organizational division reflects the fundamental duality of legislative roles. Legislative functions are centered on Capitol Hill, whereas constituency functions are based in field offices. In other words, "Office of the Member, Inc." is increasingly split into headquarters and branch divisions—with the Capitol Hill office dealing with legislative duties and the state or district office dealing with constituents.

Because members' resources—offices, staffs, and allowances—are funded by the taxpayers, they are restricted to the conduct of official business. "Any campaign work by staff members must be done outside the congressional office, and without using any congressional office resources," states a 2006 House ethics memorandum.[124] This distinction may seem cloudy; after all, members' offices are suffused with electoral concerns, and what constitutes "campaign activity" is unclear. During the campaign season, certain aides go on leave and transfer to the campaign organization's payroll.

MEMBERS AND THE MEDIA

Office allowances in both chambers amply support lawmakers' unceasing struggle for media attention. A member's office bears some resemblance to the communications division of a medium-size business. Nearly every day, stacks of printed matter and electronic messages are released for wide distribution. In addition to turning out press releases, newsletters, and individual and mass mailings, members communicate through telephone, interviews, radio and TV programs, e-mail and text messages, official and personal websites, and even through Internet social networking services. Most of the time, these publicity barrages are aimed not at the national media but at individuals and media outlets back in the home state or district.

Direct Mail

The traditional cornerstone of congressional publicity is the franking privilege—the right of members to send out mail at no cost with their signature (the frank) instead of a stamp. This practice, which dates from the First Continental Congress in 1775, is intended to facilitate official communication between elected officials and the people they represent (a rationale accepted by federal courts in upholding the practice). In recent times, members found that aggressive use of the frank could aid reelection. Rep. Bill Frenzel, R-Minn. (1971–1991), noted that both parties teach newcomers three rules for getting reelected: "Use the frank. Use the frank. Use the frank."[125]

Critics point out that franked mail is largely unsolicited and politically motivated. The fact that outgoing mail costs are much higher in election years than in nonelection years seems to bear that criticism out. Most items are mass mailings, not individual letters. Mass mailings are either general-purpose newsletters blanketing home states or districts or special messages targeted to certain categories of voters. Recipients are urged to share their views or contact local offices for help. Sometimes, the newsletter may feature an opinion poll asking for citizens' views on selected issues. Whatever the results, the underlying message is that the legislator cares what folks back home think.

Current law forbids franked mail that is "unrelated to the official business, activities, and duties of members." It also bars the frank for a "matter which specifically solicits political support for the sender or any other person or any political party." In addition, chamber rules forbid mass mailings (five hundred or more pieces) sixty days (Senate) or ninety days (House) before a primary, runoff, or general election. In the two months before the beginning of each cutoff period, streams of U.S. Postal Service trucks are seen pulling away from the loading docks of the congressional office buildings.

Congress has placed caps on newsletters and on total outgoing mail—one piece for each address in the state for senators, three pieces for each address in the district for representatives. Rules governing newsletters curb their advertising features such as personal references to or photographs of the member. Recent reforms reversed the upward spiral of congressional mail costs.[126]

Although it can still be abused, the franking privilege is essential to sustain communications between lawmakers and their constituents. A former chairman of a House oversight commission posed the issue like this: "How do you write rules and regulations that distinguish between a thoughtful discussion of some important public issue and a self-promoting thing with the photograph of a member on every other page?"[127]

The advent of e-mail poses the problem of whether, or how, the much-debated franking restrictions should apply. The Senate has generally applied the franking rules to electronic mail. The House, however, has declined to adopt such strict rules.

Americans increasingly rely on the Internet for news. It is no wonder, then, that lawmakers have rapidly set up websites and even blogs.[128] Most (but not all) sites feature the member's biography, committee assignments, and votes on major issues. Capitol Hill websites exhibit variety in their content, usability, and interactivity.[129] Some members' websites include streaming audio or video of members' speeches or appearances on news programs. Few of them include such potentially sensitive information as the member's financial disclosure reports, travel spending, and meetings with lobbyists.

Members are quick to embrace new communication technologies. Many members now make use of social networking services such as Facebook and Twitter. Reporting on lawmakers using their BlackBerries throughout President Barack Obama's first address to a joint session of Congress, *Washington Post* journalist Dana Milbank joked, "It's bad enough that Americans are paralyzed by economic jitters. Now the president has to deal with lawmakers paralyzed by Twitter."[130]

Feeding the Local Press

News outlets in North America are decentralized and dispersed. These include daily and weekly newspapers, radio and TV stations, and cable systems. Virtually all these media outlets are locally based, centered on local issues, and funded by local advertising.

Most local media outlets have inadequate resources for covering what their congressional delegations are doing in the nation's capital. In fact, very few have their own Washington reporters. Most rely on syndicated or chain services that rarely follow individual members consistently. "If they report national news it is usually because it involves local personalities, affects local outcomes, or relates directly to local concerns," stated a Senate report.[131]

Relations with the press receive close attention from members. Most legislators have at least one staffer who serves as a press aide; some have two or three. Their job is to generate coverage highlighting the member's work. Executive agencies often help by letting incumbents announce federal grants or contracts awarded in the state or district. Even if the member had nothing to do with procuring the funds, the press statement proclaims, "Senator So-and-So announced today that a federal contract has been awarded to XYZ Company in Jonesville." Many offices also prepare weekly or biweekly columns that small-town newspapers can reprint under the lawmaker's byline.

The House, the Senate, and the four Capitol Hill parties (House and Senate Republicans and Democrats) have fully equipped studios and satellite links where audio or video programs or excerpted statements (called actualities) can be produced for a fraction of the commercial cost.[132] Some incumbents produce regular programs that are picked up by local radio or television outlets. More often, these outlets insert brief audio or TV clips on current issues into regular news broadcasts—to give the impression that their reporters have gone out and obtained the story. Members also create their own news reports and beam them directly to hometown stations, often without ever talking to a reporter. With direct satellite feeds to local stations, members regularly go "live at five" before local audiences.

Like printed communications, radio and TV broadcasts pose ethical questions. House and Senate recording studios are supposed to be used only for communicating about legislation and other policy issues, but the distinction between legitimate constituent outreach and political advertising remains blurred. (The studios run by the parties have no such limits.) Some radio and television news editors have qualms about using members' programs. "It's just this side of self-serving," said one television editor of the biweekly "Alaska Delegation Report."[133] Others claim to see little difference between these electronic communications and old-fashioned press releases. Local editors and producers still have to decide whether to use the material, edit it, or toss it.

Local Press Boosterism?

With a few notable exceptions, local media convey little information about their representatives. Most stories are uncritically positive: only 6 percent of the news stories compiled by R. Douglas Arnold cited anyone who criticized the incumbent's performance.[134] As a result of this pervasive positive tilt, when members successfully cultivate local coverage, they are more likely to win reelection.[135]

In the eyes of home district media outlets, incumbents simply fare splendidly. Michael J. Robinson cited the case of "Congressman Press," a midlevel House member, untouched by scandal, who had an average press operation. Drawing on 144 press releases from his office over the course of a year, his local paper ran 120 stories featuring or mentioning him. "On average, every other week, Congressman Press was featured in a story virtually written in his own office."[136]

Even when local stories are not drawn from press releases, they tend to be respectful if not downright laudatory.[137] Broadcast media are even more benign than print media. As one legislator said, "TV people need thirty seconds of sound and video at the airport when I arrive—that's all they want."[138] Most local reporters for radio and TV are on general assignment and do little preparation for interviews. Their primary goal is to get the newsmaker on tape.

Local radio and television's weakness for congressionally initiated communications magnifies the advantages incumbents enjoy. ABC-TV correspondent Cokie Roberts concludes, "The emergence of local TV has made some members media stars in the home towns and, I would argue, done more to protect incumbency than any franking privilege or newsletter ever could, simply because television is a more pervasive medium than print."[139] A recent study reports a strong link between the expansion of local television stations across the country and the rise of incumbency advantage in the post-1960s era.[140]

Reports on Congress from the national press corps are far more critical than those from local news organizations. Following the canons of investigative journalism, many national reporters are on the lookout for scandals or evidence of wrongdoing. The national press reports primarily on the institution of Congress, whereas the local press focuses mostly on local senators and representatives. Individual members tend to be reported on far more favorably than the institution. The content and quality of press coverage in local and national media underscore the differences between the two Congresses. Congress as collective policy maker, covered mainly by the national press, appears in a different light from the politicians who make up the Congress, covered mainly by local news outlets.

CONCLUSION

How members of Congress manage the two Congresses dilemma is reflected in their daily tasks on Capitol Hill and in their home states or districts. Election is a prerequisite to congressional service. Legislators allocate much of their time and energy, and even more of their staff and office resources, to the care and cultivation of voters. Their Hill styles and home styles are adopted with this end in mind.

Yet senators and representatives do not live by reelection alone. Many bemoan the need for constant campaigning. "What drives me nuts about this place is that, when I came here, it used to be that you had at least a year after you were elected where you could get the people's business done before the next election intruded," complained veteran legislator David Obey, D-Wis. (1969–2011). "Now the way politics has been nationalized, the election intrudes every day."[141] For those who remain in office, reelection is not usually viewed as an end in itself, but as a lever for pursuing other goals—policymaking or career advancement. Fenno once remarked to a member that "sometimes it must be hard to connect what you do here with what you do in Washington," "Oh no," the lawmaker replied, "I do what I do here so I can do what I want to do there."[142]

***P**arty Leaders:* Former House Speaker Nancy Pelosi, D-Calif., hands the gavel to the new Speaker, John A. Boehner, R-Ohio (top left), on January 5, 2011, the first day of the 112th Congress. House minority whip Steny H. Hoyer, D-Md., and minority leader Pelosi walk with President Obama to a Democratic Party caucus on the fiscal 2011 budget (top right). Senate Republican minority leader Mitch McConnell, R-Ky., speaks to the press after a Republican issues meeting (middle right). The House GOP leadership team (bottom)—Speaker Boehner, Chief Whip Kevin McCarthy, Calif., and Majority Leader Eric Cantor, Va.—leave the White House, where they discussed government spending and job creation.

Leaders and
Parties in Congress

On January 5, 2011, the new Speaker of the House, John A. Boehner, R-Ohio, smiled as he received the gavel from outgoing Speaker Nancy Pelosi, D-Calif. Jubilant Republicans thundered their applause in a House chamber filled with representatives and their children, grandchildren, and other family members. "I now pass this gavel and the sacred trust that goes with it to the new speaker," said Pelosi, "God bless you, Speaker Boehner."[1]

Although Boehner had worked hard to bring about this transition of power, he does not take credit for it. "What I got out of the election is not so much that we won but they lost," he says.[2] Boehner attributes the outcome to public rejection of unified Democratic rule and to a popular movement loosely organized under the Tea Party banner. Nevertheless, Boehner was highly effective in capitalizing on these broader forces. He tirelessly raised money for Republican candidates, contributing more than $44 million to their campaigns, and appeared at more than 170 events around the country to assist GOP campaigns.[3] In the meantime, he adopted the tough, uncompromising rhetoric of the Tea Party movement, famously shouting "Hell, no" on the House floor while declaring his opposition to the Obama administration's health care reform. And he cannily advised his Republican colleagues to reach out to Tea Party activists. "I urge you to get in touch with these efforts and connect with them," he said to a meeting of the House Republican Conference in 2009. "The people participating in these protests will be the soldiers for our cause a year from now."[4]

Having won the majority, Boehner leads a much larger, more diverse party. Every political leader finds it more difficult to govern than to oppose, but the political environment of the 112th Congress presents special challenges. With divided government and hard questions on the political agenda—such as government retrenchment, fiscal balance, and the debt limit—Boehner must find solutions that can command the support of his party in the House and simultaneously win approval by the Senate and, in most cases, the administration.

The complexity of this legislative task was immediately evident during the consideration of H.R. 1, an omnibus appropriations measure needed to fund ongoing government operations through the rest of the 2011 fiscal year. The spending plan that Boehner and other House leaders originally crafted was flatly rejected by their own party colleagues, who declared the proposal insufficient to fulfill their campaign pledge to cut $100 billion from federal programs.[5] The historic class of eighty-seven Republican freshmen, eager for sweeping change, was not prepared to settle for less than they had promised. "I came out of the private sector, a life that I enjoyed," said newcomer House member Steve Southerland, R-Fla. "I wasn't running for a job. I was running . . . to produce results."[6] When leaders brought a revised bill to the floor, a raucous floor fight broke out. Over the course of five days of floor debate, the new leaders were defeated on a number of amendments and were forced by the party rank and file to accept cuts beyond those they had initially proposed.

The open, free-wheeling debate on H.R. 1 followed Boehner's public declaration that he would lead the chamber in a more open, participatory fashion than other recent House Speakers. On the first day of the new Congress, Boehner gained approval of a set of revisions to House rules to make the body operate "with greater openness, deliberation, and efficiency."[7] The new rules require legislation to be available for other members to review for three calendar days before a vote. They also mandate that committees quickly post information about legislative proposals to be considered, as well as the outcomes of votes and any amendments adopted. Such revisions address many of Boehner's criticisms of his predecessor. But they also reflect the reality of a large group of enthusiastic newcomers in the Republican Party who have no intention of being shut out of power. As former House Speaker Newt Gingrich observed, "None of these folks are coming in saying, 'Mommy, may I?'"[8] Along the same lines, GOP strategist Frank Luntz quipped, Boehner has "some very ornery folks to deal with."[9]

Building electoral majorities, managing internal party politics, and presiding over the House and its internal rules are among the Speaker's wide-ranging duties. These tasks must be carried out with careful attention to the two Congresses. Leaders must facilitate lawmaking, while at the same time attending to party members' representational ties with their constituents. Of his fellow partisans, Boehner says, "You've got to give them room to grow. You've got to give them room to be rebellious from time to time. If you tighten down the pressure cooker too much, it's going to explode."[10] Making national policy means finding ways of persuading members who represent different constituencies, regions, ideologies, values, and interests to support legislation that addresses national concerns. "The only thing that counts is 218 votes, and nothing else is real," a House leader declares. "You have to be able [to attract a majority of the House] to pass a bill."[11]

Implicit in this party leader's statement is recognition that mobilizing winning coalitions is not easy. Party leaders encounter what scholars call a "collective action" dilemma.[12] How can leaders mobilize a majority to pass legislation for the collective or public good when it is in the self-interest of lawmakers to reject the difficult trade-offs that are frequently required? Moreover, lawmakers can free ride on the efforts of their colleagues, while simultaneously claiming credit and receiving benefits from a bill's enactment. If there are too many free riders, little lawmaking will get done.

Congressional leaders resolve the collective action problem in two main ways: devising sufficient incentives (political, policy, or procedural, for example) to attract majority support, and coordinating the work of the bill's champions to win desired objectives. Leadership in legislatures, then, "can be seen as having been instituted to ameliorate the problems of collective action," writes political scientist Barbara Sinclair. "Party leaders are . . . agents of the members who select them."[13]

Taking account of the two Congresses requires party leaders to assume roles both inside and outside the institution. In their inside role, party leaders formulate national policy agendas and use their procedural and organizational authority to advance them. In their outside role, party leaders articulate and publicize issue agendas designed to galvanize partisan support and swing voters. They help recruit candidates for Congress and assist in their campaigns. Leaders also serve as the party's link to the president, the press, the public, and the party faithful. "I see us all in this together," said former House Speaker Dennis Hastert, R-Ill., of his party's relationship to President George W. Bush. "It is important for us to go and run a good campaign for our own survival and that's good for the president. If the president does well and he gets people excited positively, that helps us. There is a cumulative effect here."[14]

The leaders' inside and outside roles are interwoven. In today's era of ideological polarization and intense electoral competition, the line between campaigning and governing has all but disappeared. Locked in a permanent campaign, leaders try to generate public momentum to either force legislative action on party priorities or create issues to take to the voters in the next election. "The reality is, to get something done in this town you've got to deal with the policy and the politics," explained representative Rob Portman, R-Ohio.[15]

Congress is a partisan body—that is, legislative organization is partisan organization. The majority party in the House and Senate controls not only the top leadership posts and each chamber's agenda, but also the chairmanships and majorities on committees and subcommittees.

THE SPEAKER OF THE HOUSE

House rules permit a determined majority to achieve its policy objectives, but it was not always so. Before 1890, intense battles were fought over the majority party's right to govern and the minority party's right to have input. The minority party was able to use a variety of stalling tactics to prevent action in the pre– and post–Civil War House.[16] In the 1890s, however, Republican Speaker Thomas "Czar" Reed of Maine finally broke the minority's capacity to frustrate House decision making. The House adopted new rules (the famous Reed Rules) to facilitate majority rule and action. An 1890 House rule, which remains in effect today, states: "No dilatory motion shall be entertained by the

Speaker." No other congressional leader possesses the visibility and authority of the Speaker. "Because the Speakership is the only leadership position in Congress whose existence and method of selection is mandated by the Constitution," writes political scientist Matthew N. Green, "the office possesses considerable prestige."[17] Although the Constitution does not require the Speaker to be a House member, all of them have been. Under the Presidential Succession Act of 1947, the Speaker is next in line behind the vice president to succeed to the presidency.

The office of Speaker combines procedural and political prerogatives with policy and partisan leadership. Speakers preside over the House, meaning that they rule on points of order, announce the results of votes, refer legislation to committees, name lawmakers to serve on conference committees and select committees, and maintain order and decorum in the House chamber. In addition to these procedural prerogatives, they exercise important political powers. They set the House's agenda of activities, control the Rules Committee, chair or influence the decisions of their party's committee assignment panel, bestow or withhold various rewards, coordinate policy making with Senate counterparts, and, in this age of television and Internet communications, expound party and House positions to the public at large. In practice, Speakers today seldom actually preside over the House because they focus so much attention on external activities such as campaigning for party members, fund raising, and message development.

Speakers are formally elected by the members of the House. Today's Speakers have served long careers in the House, over which they have built relationships with fellow members and risen through the ranks of their party. Before 1899, however, it was not uncommon for Speakers to have only a few years of service as representatives. Henry Clay of Kentucky was elected to the speakership on November 4, 1811—his first day in the House. Speakers elected since 1899 have served, on average, more than twenty years before their election to the post. Both Boehner and Pelosi had served twenty years before becoming Speaker.

Once in office, Speakers traditionally have been reelected as long as their party has controlled the House. Members typically vote for the speakership along straight party lines. Not since 1923 has there been a floor battle over the speakership, because one party has always enjoyed a clear majority. As chief parliamentary officer and leader of the majority party (see Figure 6-1), the Speaker enjoys unique powers in scheduling floor business and in recognizing members during sessions. Occasionally, Speakers will relinquish the gavel to join in the floor debate. Recent Speakers, including Hastert and Pelosi, often voted on issues before the House.[18]

The Speaker is also in charge of administrative matters. The current administrative structure was established after Speaker Newt Gingrich took office in 1994. Gingrich's reforms abolished administrative units, streamlined and modernized management, undertook an independent audit of the accounting systems, and assigned responsibility to a new chief administrative

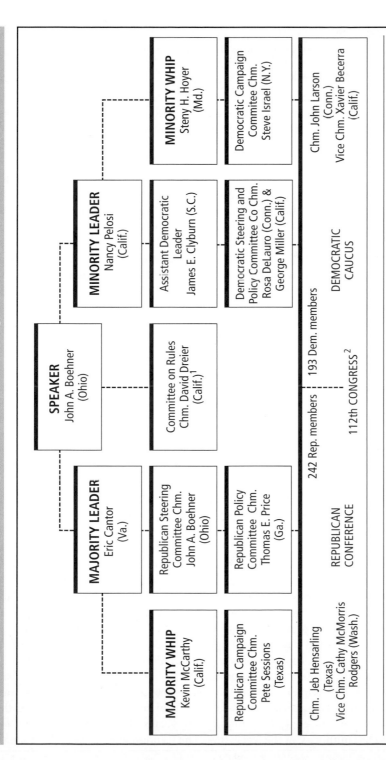

FIGURE 6-1 Organization of the House of Representatives, 112th Congress, 2011–2013

SPEAKER
John A. Boehner
(Ohio)

Committee on Rules
Chm. David Dreier
(Calif.)[1]

MAJORITY LEADER
Eric Cantor
(Va.)

Republican Steering
Committee Chm.
John A. Boehner
(Ohio)

Republican Policy
Committee Chm.
Thomas E. Price
(Ga.)

REPUBLICAN
CONFERENCE

MAJORITY WHIP
Kevin McCarthy
(Calif.)

Republican Campaign
Committee Chm.
Pete Sessions
(Texas)

Chm. Jeb Hensarling
(Texas)
Vice Chm. Cathy McMorris
Rodgers (Wash.)

242 Rep. members

112th CONGRESS[2]

MINORITY LEADER
Nancy Pelosi
(Calif.)

Assistant Democratic
Leader
James E. Clyburn (S.C.)

Democratic Steering and
Policy Committee Co Chm.
Rosa DeLauro (Conn.) &
George Miller (Calif.)

DEMOCRATIC
CAUCUS

MINORITY WHIP
Steny H. Hoyer
(Md.)

Democratic Campaign
Committee Chm.
Steve Israel (N.Y.)

Chm. John Larson
(Conn.)
Vice Chm. Xavier Becerra
(Calif.)

193 Dem. members

[1] Although not strictly a party panel, the Rules Committee in modern times functions largely as an arm of the majority leadership.

[2] The number of representatives as of January 2011.

officer—elected by the House at the start of each Congress—for running the House's administrative operations in a professional manner.[19]

Eclipse of the Speaker

Speakers gradually accrued power over the course of the Republic's first 120 years. By 1910 Speaker Joseph G. Cannon, R-Ill., was dominating the House. He assigned members to committees, appointed and removed committee chairs, referred bills to committee, regulated the flow of bills to the House floor as chair of the Rules Committee, and controlled floor debate. Taken individually, Cannon's powers were little different from those of his immediate predecessors, but taken together and exercised to their limits, they bordered on dictatorial. The result was a revolt. Progressive Republicans joined with discontented minority Democrats to reduce the Speaker's authority.

The House forced Cannon to step down from the Rules Committee in 1910 and required the House to elect the committee's members. The next year, when Democrats took control of the House, the new Speaker, James B. "Champ" Clark of Missouri, was denied the authority to make committee assignments, and his power of recognition was curtailed. The speakership then went into long-term eclipse as power flowed briefly to party caucuses and then to the committee chairs.

Over time after the 1910 revolt, committees became more powerful relative to party leaders. Power in Congress was diffused among a relatively small number of committee chairs who were often called the "dukes" or "barons" of Capitol Hill. These chairs rose to power by means of a nearly inviolable seniority system, in which each committee's longest serving majority party member served as chair until death, resignation, or retirement. This system tended to elevate to top committee posts the long-serving conservative southern Democrats from safe seats, a process that often yielded committee chairs who were out of step with the preferences of party leaders.

Working from a more constricted office, Speakers after Cannon exhibited various leadership styles that reflected their personalities, the historical context in which they operated, and the extent of conflict both within their party and the chamber as a whole. The longest-serving Speaker in history, Democrat Sam Rayburn of Texas (1940–1947, 1949–1953, 1955–1961), functioned largely as a broker or mediator, negotiating with and persuading the powerful chairs to report out legislation supported by the Democratic majority. Rayburn used his personal prestige as well as his long political experience and immense parliamentary skills to provide coherence for a decentralized chamber. As he explained, "The old day of pounding on the desk and giving people hell is gone. A man's got to lead by persuasion and kindness and the best reason—that's the only way he can lead people."[20]

The relationship between these two centers of institutional power—committee and party—provides a useful analytical framework for assessing the extent of centralized (party dominance) versus decentralized (committee autonomy) authority in the legislature. The Cannon era was plainly a time of party power. Over much of the twentieth century, the balance of power tilted toward committee leaders—with the seniority principle governing the selection of House and Senate committee chairmen. Today, although committees and their leaders remain powerful, party leaders are more pivotal in influencing action on the major issues of the day. Meanwhile, both power centers can be fettered by a majority vote of the chamber's membership.

Revival of the Speakership

The distribution of power in the House of Representatives changed fundamentally during the 1970s. Activist, liberal lawmakers elected during the Vietnam War and the Watergate era found themselves frustrated by the conservative tilt of the committee barons. This liberal bloc joined forces with other longtime members disgruntled with the status quo to curb the power of committee chairs. These reformist Democrats took a two-pronged approach toward transforming the distribution of power in the House.

First, the reformers sought to limit the ability of committee chairs to act independently. And, after years of agitation, they succeeded in making chairs more accountable to their party. Rather than allowing them to hold their chairmanships regardless of their adherence to their party's agenda, new party rules adopted in 1973 required that committee chairs be elected by secret ballot of the Democratic Caucus. Committee chairs were also obligated to share power with subcommittee chairs.

Second, the reformers strengthened the hand of the party leadership. The Speaker, for example, gained the right to name all the majority party members of the Rules Committee, including the chair. The Speaker was also permitted to refer measures to more than one committee. By the late 1970s, however, the majority Democrats recognized that dispersing power to more subcommittees had hampered their ability to accomplish policy and political goals. Accordingly, rank-and-file Democrats encouraged their party leaders to use their new powers to overcome institutional fragmentation and to curb the minority Republicans' ability to obstruct action on the floor.

Although the reforms enhanced party leaders' powers, Speakers did not exploit them to the fullest immediately. Instead, power was gradually centralized in the majority party leadership over many subsequent Congresses. Longtime Speaker Thomas P. "Tip" O'Neill Jr. (D-Mass., 1977–1987) strengthened the office by drawing Democratic rank-and-file members into the leadership orbit, expanding the whip structure, and creating leadership task forces to allow them input on party priorities.[21]

O'Neill's successor, Speaker Jim Wright (1987–1989), pushed the prerogatives of the office further. Whereas O'Neill had strived for consensus, Wright laid out an agenda and then worked diligently—by himself, if necessary—to mobilize support. "The Congress," declared Wright, "should not simply react, passively, to recommendations from the president but should come forward with initiatives of its own."[22] His unyielding personal style and knack for making "minority status more painful," as one House GOP leader put it, embittered

Republicans (and even some of his own party).[23] Wright's tenure in office ended in the wake of ethics charges successfully initiated against him by an energetic up-and-coming Republican whip, Newt Gingrich.

The selection of Wright's successor, Majority Leader Thomas S. Foley, D-Wash., seemed to indicate a return to a weaker speakership. Speaker Foley (1989–1995) had a reputation for being a judicious, low-key, and consensus-oriented leader, and his initial objectives were to restore civility and bipartisan cooperation. Although Republicans found Foley easier to deal with than Wright, they soon lamented the Speaker's willingness to use procedural rules to frustrate GOP objectives. Foley began to make far more extensive use of the Rules Committee to shape the floor agenda and restrict amending opportunities. In a departure from his predecessors, Foley favored the use of restrictive rules to govern the consideration of most legislation.[24]

The Contemporary Speaker. Speaker Newt Gingrich, R-Ga., took the office of Speaker to new heights. In the lead-up to the 1994 elections, Gingrich had spearheaded a ten-point party platform called "The Contract with America." Almost all House Republican candidates pledged to act on every item in the platform within the first hundred days of the 104th Congress if their party won a majority. Gingrich was widely credited for the GOP's sweeping victory in the 1994 elections: "[Gingrich is] the one responsible for leading the Republican Party out of the wilderness of the minority to the promised land of the majority," said one GOP House member.[25]

Gingrich was a strikingly effective Speaker, although his power waned over time. In the immediate aftermath of the Republicans' taking control of the House, GOP lawmakers observed a parliamentary model of governance marching in lockstep with their "prime minister." Everything in the ten-point contract except term limits for lawmakers passed the House within a hundred days. Gingrich also adopted a wide array of institutional changes that centralized power in his office. He curbed the independence of committees by personally selecting committee members and chairs who would strongly support his agenda—and, when necessary, he ignored seniority in the process. In addition, he required the GOP members of the Appropriations Committee to sign a written pledge that they would heed the leadership's directives for spending reductions. During his speakership, he often bypassed committees entirely by establishing leadership task forces to process legislation. Most significant, he changed the House rules to impose a six-year term limit on all committee and subcommittee chairs, so that no chair could accumulate enough influence to challenge the central party leaders. In short, party power dominated committee power.

Gingrich's power declined toward the end of his speakership. Two extended face-offs with President Bill Clinton in late 1995 and early 1996 resulted in highly unpopular shutdowns of ongoing government operations, for which the public blamed the Republicans, not President Clinton.[26] In 1996, after President Clinton was reelected, Gingrich faced ethics charges of his own. Two weeks after Gingrich's reelection as Speaker, the House voted 395–28 to reprimand and fine him for ethical misconduct related to inaccurate financial information he had given the House Ethics Committee. Weakened, Gingrich no longer dominated the House as he once did. Indeed, in the summer of 1997 a small group of junior hard-line conservatives hatched an abortive plot to remove him from the speakership. When the 1998 midterm results came in, Republicans were shell-shocked at their poor showing, and many blamed Gingrich for the losses. He then left the speakership and resigned from the House.

Gingrich's successor as Speaker, Dennis Hastert, R-Ill. (1999–2007), played a less visible role outside the House, but inside the institution he was no less powerful than Gingrich. The longest-serving GOP Speaker, Hastert exercised "top-down" command of the House and followed a partisan governing strategy on party-preferred measures. "The job of the Speaker," he said, "is not to expedite legislation that runs counter to the wishes of the majority of his majority."[27] Hastert maintained a modest public profile, sharing his national spokesman's role with other Republicans: "I don't think I have to be [at] the head of every news release or press conference, and on every Sunday talk show," he mused.[28] At the same time, he consolidated power in a trio of leaders—himself, the majority leader (Tom DeLay, Texas), and the majority whip (Roy Blunt, Mo.).

Hastert and his leadership team were not reluctant to direct rank-and-file members or committee chairs to toe the line on issues important to the party. For example, during a GOP conference meeting, Veterans' Affairs chair Christopher H. Smith of New Jersey criticized the Republicans' budget resolution and the White House's spending proposals for veterans. Speaker Hastert "got up and shut him down," said a witness to the tongue-lashing. "I've never seen anything like that. It was scathing."[29] When Smith refused to curb his advocacy of more spending for veterans, GOP leaders removed Smith as Veterans' chair and even from the committee itself.

The trend toward centralization of power in the Speaker's office was not reversed under Hastert's successor, Nancy Pelosi. Her elevation to the speakership was historic in that she was the first woman to rise so high in American politics, but her tenure in office was typical of recent Speakers. Following the Gingrich model, Pelosi imposed message discipline on her colleagues as they showcased a "Six for '06" agenda during the 2006 campaign. The agenda highlighted popular initiatives such as reducing prescription drug costs and student loan interest rates, eliminating tax subsidies for oil and gas companies, implementing the recommendations of the 9/11 Commission, and enacting ethics and lobbying reforms. All these initiatives were adopted within the promised hundred legislative hours after the Democrats took control of the new Congress.[30] Like Gingrich, Pelosi maintained a high national profile. For their part, Republicans turned Pelosi's visibility into a Democratic Party liability, just as Democrats had done with Gingrich during his speakership. By consistently portraying her as an ideologically extreme "San Francisco Democrat," Republicans undermined Pelosi's public image. As Rep. Patrick McHenry, R-N.C., explained, "Our goal is to bring down approval numbers for Pelosi and for House Democrats. That will take repetition. This is a marathon, not a sprint."[31]

Speaker Pelosi's leadership style largely tracked the "top-down," centralized model of her two immediate predecessors, Gingrich and Hastert. Despite having criticized the Republican majority's restrictions on open debate and full committee consideration of bills, Pelosi employed similar limitations on committees and inputs from the minority party. "After months of promising bipartisanship and a return to the regular order," complained Rep. Jack Kingston, R-Ga., "Pelosi's first act was to cut off all amendments and bypass all of her own committees, in a rush to meet an arbitrary and meaningless [hundred-hour] deadline."[32] Under Pelosi's leadership, committee chairs enjoyed a somewhat more prominent role, but this shift did not entail a more decentralized process in which committees enjoyed free rein. Instead, legislation was often worked out in an ad hoc manner behind closed doors in leadership offices.[33] A wide-ranging Brookings Institution report on congressional operations and policy making in the 110th Congress (2007–2009) concluded that "a pattern of tighter, more centralized control—which began more than two decades ago under Democratic rule and then intensified under Republican majorities, especially after the 2000 election—continues unabated."[34]

Although the current Speaker, John Boehner, has indicated an intention to lead the House in a more inclusive manner than his recent predecessors, there is no early indication that the balance of House power will flow back in the direction of committee chairs. Even as minority leader, Boehner demonstrated a willingness to bring ranking members to account when they acted in ways harmful to the party. For example, when Joe L. Barton, R-Texas, ranking member of the Energy Committee, apologized to BP's CEO for President Barack Obama's "$20 billion shakedown" of the company to cover damages from the 2010 Gulf oil spill, Boehner quickly summoned Barton to demand a public retraction.[35] After becoming Speaker, Boehner signaled that he will ensure that committee executive oversight activities are carried out in a way that will serve the leadership's broader interests.[36] Still, the new diversity within the Republican Party will present challenges for centralized leadership in the 112th Congress. The party's large freshman class, as a former leadership aide observed, "is not going to be deferential to the leadership, so it's going to be much harder to be like Moses and demand fealty."[37]

The Speaker's Influence: Style and Context

Congressional analysts disagree about the extent to which congressional leaders can influence policy outcomes. Compared with legislative party leaders in many other democracies, party leaders in Congress unquestionably have fewer tools to induce party loyalty among lawmakers. Nevertheless, congressional leaders enjoy more institutional authority at some times than at others (see Box 6-1 for a brief summary of the principal scholarly theories of congressional leadership). In general, political scientists stress context over personal style as the main factor affecting the Speaker's institutional clout.

BOX 6-1 **Theories of Congressional Leadership**

Political scientists have developed different theories to explain why congressional leaders appear to be stronger during some eras than others. The most prominent is called conditional party government.[1] A competing theory—the pivotal voter theory—suggests that the influence of party leaders is marginal with respect to their ability to shift policy outcomes away from what a majority of the chamber prefers toward the policy preferences of the majority party.[2]

Proponents of each theory view party leaders as agents of their principals—their rank-and-file partisans. Members want their party leaders to help them accomplish their fundamental goals: getting reelected, making good policy, and gaining—or maintaining—power in the House or Senate. A correspondence in leader-member views means that party leaders will work to advance the majority preferences of the rank-and-file. After all, party leaders hold their positions at the sufferance of their partisan colleagues, and they usually want to be reelected to those leadership posts.

Conditional Party Government Theory

◄ The power of congressional leaders hinges on the degree of homogeneity within the majority party concerning policy and on the extent of interparty conflict between Democrats and Republicans.

◄ With both conditions in play, rank-and-file party members are supportive of changes that strengthen their party leaders, such as the Speaker. Thus, a cohesive majority party can pass legislation without any support from the minority party.

◄ Conversely, when parties' policy goals are fragmented, partisan lawmakers have little incentive to give their leaders more authority. They may use their power against the political and policy interests of many in the rank-and-file.

Pivotal Voter Theory

◄ Suggests that policy outcomes on the floor rarely diverge from what is acceptable to the pivotal voter—the member who casts the 218th vote in the House.

◄ Rarely does everyone in the majority party support a particular policy. Why, then, should majority members change their policy views to back a party position with which they disagree? Instead, they will join with members of the other party to form the winning coalition. According to this theory, these pivotal voters determine chamber outcomes.

◄ If each party is internally united in its policy preferences, as the conditional party government theory states, there will be no difference between what the majority party wants and what the chamber membership will agree to.

◄ Simply observing party leaders engaged in frenetic activity—often seeking pivotal votes—does not mean they can skew legislative outcomes beyond what is acceptable to a majority of the entire membership.

---

[1] See, for example, John H. Aldrich and David W. Rohde, "The Transition to Republican Rule in the House: Implications for Theories of Congressional Politics," *Political Science Quarterly* 112 (Winter 1997–1998): 541–567.
[2] See Keith Krehbiel, *Pivotal Politics: A Theory of U.S. Lawmaking* (Chicago: University of Chicago Press, 1998).

Personal style refers to the skills, abilities, and qualities of the Speaker, such as intelligence, talent for coalition building, or political acumen. It also refers to a leader's willingness to utilize the full range of his or her parliamentary prerogatives, to pressure colleagues to vote a certain way, and to advance policy positions independent of consensus within their party.

Context refers to the House's external and internal environment. External elements include whether the Speaker's party controls the White House, the public's demand for legislation, the complexity of national problems, the popularity of the president, and the partisan leanings of the voting public. Internal elements that condition the Speaker's influence are the size and cohesiveness of the majority party, the diffusion of power among members, and the autonomy of committees.

The policy views of rank-and-file party members are one of the most important elements of a leader's context. A prominent scholarly theory, known as conditional party government, suggests that if partisans share common policy views and confront an opposition party with sharply different policy preferences, then these dual conditions favor strong centralized leadership. Rank-and-file partisans will empower their party leaders to advance an agenda that nearly all of them support. According to the two leading proponents of this theory:

> These two considerations—preference homogeneity [or policy agreement within parties] and preference conflict [or policy disagreement between parties]—together form the "condition" in the theory of conditional party government. As these increase, the theory predicts that party members will be progressively more willing to create strong powers for leaders and to support the exercise of those powers in specific instances. But when diversity grows within parties, or the differences between parties are reduced, members will be reluctant to grant greater powers to leaders. This is the central prediction of [conditional party government].[38]

The theory of conditional party government illuminates the role of the Speaker at different times in House history. Speaker Sam Rayburn's role as cautious broker and negotiator, for example, makes sense in light of fractures within the Democratic Party during the 1950s. During Rayburn's era—and for many years afterward—congressional Democrats were deeply divided between their northern and southern wings. For a century after the Civil War, the "Solid South" almost always elected Democrats to Congress. Southern Democrats tended to be more conservative than their northern colleagues on a number of significant political issues, particularly civil rights and labor regulations (such as minimum wage laws, union organizing, and business-labor relations). On such matters, southern Democrats often allied themselves with Republicans in a voting pattern known as the conservative coalition. Recognizing these divisions, Rayburn had to lead cautiously. Just bringing the Democratic Caucus together could be politically explosive, and so Rayburn rarely convened the caucus.[39] Instead, Rayburn dealt with members on a personalized, individual basis. According to the theory of conditional party government, Rayburn's style of leadership was not merely a personal stylistic choice, it was also a way of coping with intractable conflict within the party. Under such conditions, rank-and-file Democrats simply would not trust their Speaker with expansive procedural and political powers.

By the same token, the conditional party government perspective views the forceful leadership of Gingrich, Hastert, Pelosi, and Boehner in light of changes in the political context. Since the 1960s, regional realignments have created far more ideological consensus *within* each of the two congressional parties, and considerably less ideological agreement *between* the two parties than existed during the 1950s and 1960s. After the enfranchisement of southern African Americans in the 1960s, the Democratic Party in the South began to elect Democrats (such as John Lewis of Georgia) who were more responsive to African American constituents and more ideologically compatible with their party colleagues from the rest of the country. Meanwhile, conservative southern voters—mainly whites—gradually moved into the Republican Party. Because the South is now largely in the GOP camp, today's Democratic Party mostly lacks the deep regional divisions that characterized the earlier era. Constituency change in the North reinforced this ideological homogenization of the parties. Liberal "Rockefeller Republicans" have largely disappeared in the Northeast, and the conservative coalition is no longer an important voting bloc in Congress. As a result of these constituency changes, the two parties are more internally coherent in their policy preferences.

This new context helps explain the assertive styles of recent Speakers. The rank-and-file members of both parties are more willing to trust their leaders with institutional authority. For example, contemporary Speakers of both parties have been given more influence over committee assignments, allowing them to appoint like-minded members to coveted committees. By stacking important committees with loyal partisans, a Speaker raises the likelihood that they will report legislation that the Speaker favors. Individual members also recognize that they owe their committee assignments in part to the Speaker. Given the greater willingness of members to tolerate hierarchical leadership, recent Speakers have been able to dictate to committee chairs, advance party agendas, and take procedural actions to hamstring the minority party. Their personal talents have been augmented by formal and informal procedural changes that have raised the likelihood that their objectives would be realized.

Leadership, however, is by no means entirely determined by the congressional context. "Leadership in Congress occurs within an institutional context that imposes limits," writes Randall Strahan, "but some leaders take advantage of those opportunities and others do not. Leadership involves not only the conditions that make leadership possible but also the choice of the leader to act."[40] Adroit and forceful Speakers can lead by molding circumstances and seizing opportunities favoring their own objectives.[41] In short,

Speakers' personal capacities allow them to exercise that elusive quality called leadership—that is, an ability to persuade others to follow even when they disagree with their leaders' views. For example, a committee chair during the Contract with America period explained why he voted for a Gingrich-advocated policy that he opposed: "At times like these many of us subordinate our preferences to the greater good of the team."[42] Context and style interact in dynamic ways that are hard to untangle.

House Floor Leaders

The Speaker's principal deputy—the majority leader—is the party's floor leader. As former majority leader Tom DeLay, R-Texas, said of his relationship with Speaker Hastert, "I see it that Hastert is the chairman of the board and I am the chief executive officer."[43] Elected every two years by secret ballot of the party caucus, the floor leader is not to be confused with a floor manager. Floor managers—usually two for each bill and frequently the chair and ranking minority member of the committee that reported the bill—are appointed to steer particular bills to a final decision.

The House majority leader is usually an experienced legislator. Two recent examples—Tom DeLay (2003–2005) and Steny Hoyer, D-Md. (2007–2011)—illustrate this point. When Tom DeLay assumed the post of majority leader, he had served in the House for eighteen years and had already established himself as perhaps the most effective party whip in the House's history and, aside from Gingrich, the chamber's most influential Republican. Nicknamed "The Hammer" by colleagues for his combative style, DeLay was an accomplished vote counter and enforcer, a shrewd campaign and legislative strategist, an aggressive fund-raiser, and a skillful coordinator of the party's connections to lobbyists.

A more centrist and less partisan majority leader than DeLay or Pelosi, Hoyer was known in the 110th and 111th Congresses for his ability to work well with majority and minority members. Comfortable in front of the cameras, he also excelled at fund raising and campaigning for his partisan colleagues. After the 2010 elections in which Republicans took over the House, Hoyer moved from the position of majority leader to minority whip.

The current majority leader, Eric Cantor, R-Va., rose to the post fairly quickly; he was elected to Congress in 2000, only ten years before taking on that position. His elevation to top leadership reflects his skill as party whip in bridging divergent elements in the Republican Conference, as well as his energetic, forward-looking approach to getting House Republicans to embrace new communications technologies to reach supportive groups beyond Capitol Hill.[44]

House and party rules are largely silent about the majority leader's duties. By tradition, the primary duties are to serve as principal strategist and spokesperson for the party and to monitor the House floor. By modern custom, neither the Speaker nor the Democratic or Republican floor leader chairs committees.[45] The majority and minority leaders, as well as the Speaker, may serve on formal or informal task forces or panels. For example, the Speaker and minority leader are ex officio members of the Permanent Select Intelligence Committee.

The majority leader helps to plan the daily, weekly, and annual legislative agendas. To do so, Cantor must consult with a wide array of players. He meets regularly with the committee chairs to discuss their schedule of activities, review pertinent legislative issues, and coordinate chamber action with the party's floor managers. He also gauges sentiment on legislation among rank-and-file members and urges them to support or reject measures. As one majority leader said, "The Majority Leader has prime responsibility for the day-to-day working of the House, the schedule, working with the committees to keep an eye out for what bills are coming, getting them scheduled, getting the work of the House done, making the place function correctly." He added that the majority leader must also "articulate to the outside world" what his or her party stands for and is trying to do.[46]

The minority leader is the floor leader of the loyal opposition. Like the majority leader, the minority leader promotes unity among party colleagues, monitors the progress of bills through committees and subcommittees, and forges coalitions in support of proposals. However, the minority leader is more often in a reactive position, criticizing the majority party's initiatives and developing alternatives to them. Bertrand Snell, R-N.Y., minority leader from 1931 to 1939, described the duties:

> He is spokesman for his party and enunciates its policies. He is required to be alert and vigilant in defense of the minority's rights. It is his function and duty to criticize constructively the policies and program of the majority, and to this end employ parliamentary tactics and give close attention to all proposed legislation.[47]

Former Speaker Nancy Pelosi is minority leader in the 112th Congress, "the first sitting speaker to move across the hall to the minority leader's office since 1955."[48] Most members of the Democratic Caucus decided to keep Pelosi, a seasoned leader, rather than go with a newcomer. Her prodigious fund raising—$246 million for Democratic candidates since joining the elected party leadership as whip in 2002—established a track record that many members were reluctant to question.[49] There was also no question about her effectiveness in holding the party together to achieve remarkable legislative victories. Even so, she faced a rebellion from a sizable contingent who questioned whether she should remain the public face of the party, particularly in view of her low national approval ratings. The vote retaining Pelosi as Democratic leader divided the caucus 129–68, with the token opposition candidacy of conservative Blue Dog Democrat Heath Shuler, D-N.C., garnering more votes than expected.[50]

The minority leader must forge party unity by managing internal conflicts and resolving intraparty disagreements. Perhaps the most important job of the minority leader is to craft a strategy to win back majority control of the House.

In this respect, the minority leader must decide whether to cooperate with or to confront the majority party. By working with the majority, the minority party can often influence legislation more to its followers' liking. However, cooperation entails supporting the majority party's legislation on the floor—an often unpleasant task.

A minority party can instead pursue a strategy of confrontation. By consistently offering an alternative vision on issues of the day, the minority party can build the case for its return to power. In the 111th Congress, then-minority leader Boehner signaled that House Republicans would focus more on confrontation than on cooperation. "I have been trying to get my Republican colleagues to understand that we are not in the legislative business," Boehner remarked at a lunch with reporters.[51] There is no set formula for how to win back majority control of the House, because many of the electoral and political forces and events that influence majority status are beyond party leaders' control.[52] A strategy of uniform opposition is less likely to be successful for House Democrats under Pelosi in the 112th Congress because of the more complex political environment in which the Senate and the presidency remain in Democratic control.

House Whips

Another top elective party post is that of chief whip. As the term implies, the duties of the whip and the whip's team of deputies and regional whips are to encourage party discipline, count votes, and, in general, mobilize winning coalitions in behalf of partisan priorities. To do so, the chief whip serves as a liaison between the party's rank-and-file membership and its leaders. The whip assembles and communicates political and policy intelligence, assigns deputy whips to take the "temperature" of the various factional groups within the party, and polls members.

Accurate vote counting is a whip's most important skill. When Kevin McCarthy, R-Calif., the new House Republican majority whip, asked veteran former whips for advice, they told him, "You need to know your count, and you don't share your count."[53] Members' voting predilections on important procedural and substantive issues are typically classified as "yea," "leaning yea," "undecided," "leaning no," and "no." Former majority whip James Clyburn, D-S.C., used a fishing metaphor to explain his procedure for forging winning coalitions:

> When it comes to working with the Democratic Caucus I have to fish in a lot of ponds. I go fishing with the Blue Dogs [fiscally conservative Democrats]. I go fishing with the New Dems [moderate Democrats]. I go fishing with the Hispanics and I go fishing with the Asian Pacific Islanders, trying to cobble together the 218 votes I need.[54]

(When Democrats lost the majority, they created a new third-ranking leadership position, assistant leader, to keep Clyburn in the leadership, while also retaining former majority leader Steny Hoyer as minority whip.[55])

First elected to the House in 2006, McCarthy's rise to top leadership in the 112th Congress as majority whip has been quick. Despite the short time frame, he has already distinguished himself as lead author of the House Republican "Pledge to America," a party platform document for the 2010 elections. In addition, he is one of the coauthors (along with Paul Ryan from Wisconsin and Eric Cantor) of *Young Guns,* a small-government manifesto designed to raise the authors' profile as young, reform-minded Republican leaders.[56] McCarthy's effectiveness as whip is enhanced by his ability to avoid being too closely associated with any one faction in his party. "Moderates think he's a moderate. Conservatives think he's a conservative," says Tony Strickland, a former Republican colleague of McCarthy's in the California Assembly.[57]

In recent years, both parties have expanded their whip teams. The whip team meets regularly to discuss issues and strategy. The larger the whip team, the larger is the number of members involved in leadership decision making and the more incentives they have to back their top leaders. As a former GOP majority whip stated, with a sixty-person GOP whip organization, it is feasible "to reach everybody in the [Republican] Conference and deliver their votes when it counts."[58] A larger whip team also ensures leadership representation for important party groups and broadens the party's appeal to outside constituencies. In a conference with 242 members, an extended whip team allows a division of labor as well. "Grunt work is subcontracted out to whip team members," such as Rep. Jeff Denham, R-Calif., and Rep. Devin Nunes, R-Calif. "Each is typically assigned two or three House colleagues. . . . [W]hip team members take cards from the GOP cloakroom, approach their assigned colleagues and check the appropriate box on the card reflecting the lawmaker's intentions."[59]

Each party's whip prepares notices advising members of the daily and weekly floor schedule, with updates as warranted. They identify, for example, the time when the House will convene, the measures to be considered each legislative day, and when the last vote for the week is expected. Information about the House schedule is available on the websites of the majority and minority whips as well as the House majority leader.

LEADERS OF THE SENATE

Unlike the House, today's Senate is an institution that tolerates and even promotes individualism. Candidate-centered elections, the proliferation of policy- and ideology oriented interest groups, the large role of money in campaigns, the staff resources available to every senator, and senators' need to seek news media coverage are among the factors that have led to today's individualistic Senate. Senators cherish and assert their independence, which intensifies the challenges faced by those elected to lead them. Unlike their House counterparts, Senate leaders lack institutional prerogatives and rules designed to facilitate majority rule, and so must rely heavily on personal skills and negotiation with colleagues of both parties.

Presiding Officers

The House majority's highest elected leader, the Speaker, has the authority to preside over the House. By contrast, the Senate's majority leader, the majority party's highest leader, almost never presides in the Senate chamber.

The Senate has three kinds of presiding officers. First, the constitutional president of the Senate is the vice president of the United States (see Figure 6-2). Except for ceremonial occasions, the vice president seldom presides over Senate sessions, and can vote only to break—not make—a tie. When votes on major issues are expected to be close, party leaders make sure that the vice president is presiding so that he can break the tie.

Second, the Constitution provides for a president pro tempore to preside in the vice president's absence. In modern practice, this constitutional officer is the majority party senator with the longest continuous service. Sen. Daniel K. Inouye, D-Hawaii, is president pro tempore of the Democratic-controlled Senate of the 112th Congress (2011–2013). By passing a simple resolution, the Senate sometimes appoints a deputy president pro tempore. This majority party official presides over the Senate in the absence of the vice president and president pro tempore.

Third, a dozen or so senators of the majority party, typically junior members, serve approximately one-hour stints each day as the presiding officer. The opportunity to preside helps newcomers become familiar with Senate rules and procedures.

Floor Leaders

The majority leader is the head of the majority party in the Senate, its leader on the floor, and the leader of the Senate. Similarly, the minority leader heads the Senate's minority party (today, minority leaders prefer to be called "Republican leader" or "Democratic leader," as the case may be). The majority and minority leaders are elected biennially by secret ballot of their party colleagues. Neither position is mentioned in the Constitution; they are relatively recent creations that date from the early 1900s.

Emergence of the Floor Leader. Historically, the Senate has always had leaders, but no single senator exercised central management of the legislative process in the fashion of today's floor leader. During the Senate's first century or so—especially in the 1790s and early 1800s, when there was no system of permanent standing committees or organized senatorial parties—leadership flowed from the personal talents and abilities of individual legislators. The small size of the early Senate promoted an informal and personal style of leadership.

Throughout the nineteenth century, scores of prominent senators were called "leaders" by scholars and other observers. Some were sectional or factional leaders; others headed important committees (by the mid- to late 1840s committees and their chairs were centers of power); and still others (such as Henry Clay, John C. Calhoun, and Daniel Webster) exercised wide influence

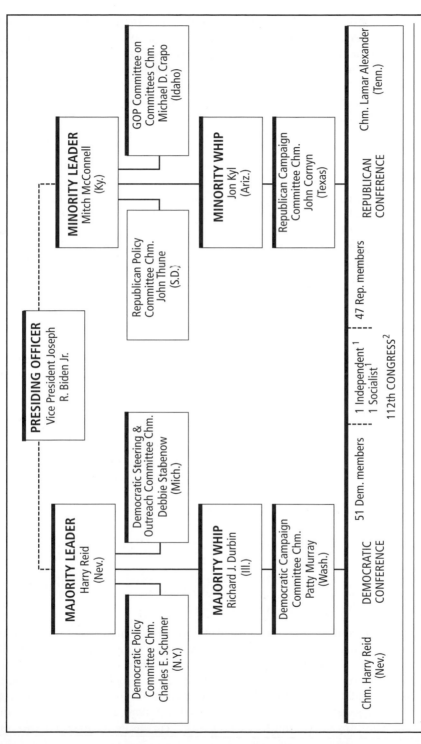

FIGURE 6-2 Organization of the Senate, 112th Congress, 2011–2013

PRESIDING OFFICER
Vice President Joseph R. Biden Jr.

MAJORITY LEADER
Harry Reid
(Nev.)

Democratic Policy Committee Chm. Charles E. Schumer (N.Y.)

Democratic Steering & Outreach Committee Chm. Debbie Stabenow (Mich.)

MAJORITY WHIP
Richard J. Durbin
(Ill.)

Democratic Campaign Committee Chm. Patty Murray (Wash.)

Chm. Harry Reid (Nev.)   DEMOCRATIC CONFERENCE

51 Dem. members

1 Independent[1]
1 Socialist[1]
112th CONGRESS[2]

MINORITY LEADER
Mitch McConnell
(Ky.)

Republican Policy Committee Chm. John Thune (S.D.)

GOP Committee on Committees Chm. Michael D. Crapo (Idaho)

MINORITY WHIP
Jon Kyl
(Ariz.)

Republican Campaign Committee Chm. John Cornyn (Texas)

Chm. Lamar Alexander (Tenn.)

REPUBLICAN CONFERENCE

47 Rep. members

[1] Both align with Democrats.

[2] As of February 2011.

because of their special political, oratorical, or intellectual gifts. Even as late as 1885, however, Woodrow Wilson could write, "No one is *the Senator*. No one exercises the special trust of acknowledged leadership."[60]

By the turn of the twentieth century, the political landscape had changed. Party structures and leaders emerged as clearly identifiable forces for organizing and managing the Senate's proceedings. This important development occurred, according to a historian of the Senate, because of the influx of a "new breed" of senators who valued party unity and "the machinery of [party] organization," especially the party caucus.[61] Soon, those senators who chaired their respective party caucuses acquired levers of authority over senatorial affairs. They chaired important party panels, shaped the Senate's agenda of business, and mobilized party majorities behind important issues. By 1913 the position of majority leader had informally emerged out of the caucus chairmanship.[62]

Not until Lyndon B. Johnson (LBJ) became majority leader in 1955 was the post transformed into one of great authority and prestige.[63] Considered by many analysts to be the most influential majority leader ever, the Texas Democrat had an extensive network of trusted aides and colleagues who gave him better information about more issues than any other senator. Opposition party control of the White House under President Dwight D. Eisenhower gave the aggressive Johnson the luxury of choosing which policies to support and which strategies to employ to get them enacted. Armed with a pragmatic outlook, domineering style, and arm-twisting abilities, Johnson became the premier vote-gatherer in the Senate. The majority leader's awesome display of face-to-face persuasion was called the "Johnson Treatment":

> The Treatment could last ten minutes or four hours. It came, enveloping its target, at the LBJ Ranch swimming pool, in one of LBJ's offices, in the Senate cloakroom, on the floor of the Senate itself. Its tone could be supplication, accusation, cajolery, exuberance, scorn, tears, complaint, the hint of threat. It was all of these together. It ran the gamut of human emotions. Its velocity was breathtaking, and it was all in one direction. Interjections from the target were rare. Johnson anticipated them before they could be spoken. He moved in close, his face a scant millimeter from his target, his eyes widening and narrowing, and his eyebrows rising and falling. From his pockets poured clippings, memos, statistics. Mimicry, humor, and the genius of analogy made The Treatment an almost hypnotic experience and rendered the target stunned and helpless.[64]

Buttressing Johnson was an inner club, a bipartisan group of senior senators. A particularly important ally within this inner club was Richard B. Russell of Georgia. The leader of southern Democrats and a lawmaker of immense influence, Russell endorsed Johnson as Democratic leader. (The Russell Senate Office Building on Capitol Hill is named after the Georgia senator.) The club, observers said, wielded the real power in the Senate through its control of chairmanships and committee assignments.[65] Furthermore, unwritten rules of behavior (for example, junior members should be seen and not heard) encouraged new senators to defer to the establishment.

Today's majority leaders encounter a Senate that is much different from the one led by Johnson. Gone is the seniority-ruled, club-like, relatively closed Senate of old. It was ended largely by three key developments: the influx of independent-minded and activist senators who wanted and expected to be major policy participants; internal senatorial changes that promoted egalitarianism such as the provision of staff resources to all members; and external developments in the broader political environment (such as the twenty-four-hour news cycle).

Together, these developments led to an individualistic Senate where leaders are expected to serve members' personal needs and advance their individual agendas. As former majority leader Robert C. Byrd, D-W.Va. (1977–1981, 1987–1989), once remarked about the egalitarian, individualistic, and C-SPAN-covered Senate: "Circumstances don't permit the Lyndon Johnson style. What I am saying is that times and things have changed. Younger Senators come into the Senate. They are more independent. The 'establishment' is a bad word. Each wants to do his 'own thing.'"[66] Similarly, the current majority leader, Harry Reid, D-Nev., says:

> I don't dictate how people vote. If it's an important vote, I try to tell them how important it is to the Senate, the country, the president.... But I'm not very good at twisting arms. I try to be more verbal and non-threatening. So there are going to be . . . a number of opportunities for people who have different opinions not to vote the way that I think they should. But that's the way it is. I hold no grudges.[67]

Limits on Today's Leadership: Individualism and Partisanship. If individualism characterizes the post-Johnson Senate, another development has added to leaders' difficulties in managing and processing the Senate's business: escalating partisanship. Unlike in the House, having a strong and cohesive party does not necessarily enable a Senate majority leader to govern. As discussed in more detail in Chapter 8, the Senate's rules do not permit the majority party leadership to set the agenda without input from the minority party. The majority leader must negotiate with the minority leader in scheduling legislation for floor consideration. To lead the Senate successfully, then, Senate leaders must achieve considerably more cross-party consensus than is necessary in the House.

As in the House, the two Senate parties have become, in the words of journalist David S. Broder, "more cohesive internally and further apart from each other philosophically."[68] Or as Sen. Orrin G. Hatch, R-Utah, put it, "Today, most Democrats are far left; most Republicans are to the right; and there are very few in between."[69] The wide differences between the parties are grounded not only in members' personal policy preferences but also in the two parties' electoral interests, as each party seeks to establish clear reasons for voters to prefer it to the opposition.[70] Groups allied with the parties contribute to the widening divide. The two Congresses are very much in evidence as Democratic senators champion policies favored by their core national constituencies (such as environmentalists, gays, minorities, and union members), and Republican lawmakers do the same for their constituency base (such as the religious right, the Tea Party, business owners, gun owners, and antiabortion advocates).

By any measure, party conflict is at a historic high for the modern Senate. One indicator of this heightened partisanship is the large number of party-line votes (a majority of Democrats facing off against a majority of Republicans). In the 1970s, only 39 percent of Senate roll-call votes divided a majority of Republicans from a majority of Democrats. In 2010, almost four out of every five Senate roll-call votes, 78.6 percent, divided the parties.[71] Even more striking is the growth in cohesion—call it discipline or philosophical agreement—within both party caucuses. In the 1970s, the average senator backed the party position 65 percent of the time on partisan roll calls. In the 1980s, average partisan loyalty rose to 73 percent, and in the 1990s to 81 percent. In 2010 it was 90 percent.[72]

What all this means for the majority leader is extraordinary difficulty in achieving the consensus needed to enact legislation and approve nominations. Any senator, regardless of party, has awesome parliamentary powers to stymie action, which puts a premium on the leader's skill in negotiating and deal making. Lacking formidable leadership tools to exert tight control over chamber proceedings, Senate leaders rely heavily on patience, perseverance, personal ties, and, on occasion, procedural hardball to move legislation. If one or more senators engages in a filibuster (extended debate) on a matter, the majority leader faces an even higher hurdle: acquiring the sixty votes needed to force debate to a close (that is, to invoke a procedure called cloture) so that the Senate can vote on the measure or matter. As a former majority leader reminisced:

> It's a tough job [being majority leader], and it has gotten tougher and tougher. Part of it is that now you don't need 50 votes—you've got to have 60 votes. The filibuster and cloture used to be used occasionally for big issues. [In more recent years], it has become an instrument used on almost every bill. You can have 51 votes, you can have 55 votes, but if you don't get 60 votes, [the bill] can die. And it is very hard to dredge up 60 votes.[73]

Dredging up sixty votes is especially taxing in the context of the chamber's heightened partisanship. When the minority leader organizes a partisan filibuster, a majority leader with fewer than fifty-nine fellow partisans will have to persuade members of the opposing party to vote against their own party leader in order to end debate—a tall order. In the Senate of the 112th Congress, with a party division of 53–47, Democrats need to find at least seven Republicans willing to buck their party on a procedural question in order to obtain cloture on a partisan issue.

Current majority leader Harry Reid frequently finds it impossible to push legislation past the procedural hurdles erected by the Senate minority. A former

Golden Gloves boxer, he is, by all accounts, a blunt, tough, and savvy leader. "He's very shrewd and effective," points out Sen. John Ensign, R-Nev. "Behind the scenes he is tenacious."[74] Despite his leadership skills and extensive legislative experience, Reid says, "The biggest challenge I have is results. If you have more than half [in the Senate], that doesn't mean you are going to win. You need to have multiple instances where you can create different coalitions to get to 60."[75] Part of Reid's game plan for achieving results is "a highly centralized leadership operation" with floor strategy and message operations managed from his office.[76] He promotes partisan cohesion by keeping note cards in a breast pocket of his jacket "on which he records favors asked and promises made."[77] In addition, Reid enjoys a good working relationship with the Republican leader. Nevertheless, many measures that cleared the Democratic majority House in the Democratic-controlled 111th Congress (2009–2011) failed to pass the Senate.

Minority Leader. The Senate minority leader consults continually with the majority leader, because the Senate usually operates by consensus. Republican leader Mitch McConnell from Kentucky has said that he's "very fond" of Majority Leader Reid. "I think he wants to get solutions to problems, and so do I."[78] Getting things done in the Senate almost always requires cooperation across party lines. In addition, the minority leader acts as his party's representative in any dealings with the president. When the minority leader is a member of the president's party, he or she has the traditional duties of pushing the administration's program and responding to partisan criticisms of the president. When a member of the opposite party, the minority leader has to calculate when to cooperate with and when to confront the president.

McConnell meets regularly with Senate Republicans to build party consensus, craft policy alternatives, and devise tactics to block or modify Democratic initiatives. He also works with his House counterpart to coordinate strategy and to develop and communicate a party agenda. As Sen. Lamar Alexander, Tenn., said of his leader, "Mitch McConnell's strength is he knows the Senate and understands it is almost entirely based on personal relationships. Most successful leaders' strategy is silent, but he has a very good understanding of where each of us is, and he works with us privately."[79]

McConnell has also made it clear that the only way the Senate can function is on a bipartisan basis with legislation containing provisions that appeal to Republicans. During the closely divided 110th Congress, he remarked that there is nothing Democrats "can do without some degree of cooperation from a very robust forty-nine-vote minority."[80]

At the same time, the minority leader is also always striving to win back control of the Senate. In pursuit of that goal, it is often useful for a minority leader to shun compromise, which tends to blur the differences between the parties, in order to present clear alternatives to voters. McConnell made much use of this approach during the unified Democratic government of the 111th Congress (2009–2011). Reflecting on the party's strategy on health care reform, the budget, and economic stimulus, McConnell observed, "It was absolutely critical that everybody be together because if the proponents of the bill were able to say it was bipartisan, it tended to convey to the public that this is O.K., they must have figured it out. It's either bipartisan or it isn't."[81] The approach achieved many of its desired effects: it excited the Republican base, intensified media controversy, defined party lines, and weakened public confidence in President Obama and the Democratic congressional leadership. Of the strategy's success, McConnell said, "I think the reason my members are feeling really good is they believe that the reward for playing team ball this year was the reversal of the political environment and the possibility that we will have a bigger team next year."[82]

Party Whips. The Senate's whip system carries out functions similar to those of the House, such as counting noses before crucial votes, monitoring floor activity, and fostering party consensus. Richard J. Durbin of Illinois is the majority whip of the Senate of the 112th Congress, the Democrats' second-in-command. He heads a whip structure that includes a chief deputy whip and four deputy whips. Durbin and Reid complement each other. Reid excels at knowing the procedural "nuts and bolts" of the Senate. Durbin, also quite knowledgeable about procedures, is "very good at taking issues and making them resonate with the public, and he is good on the [Senate] floor and at message" development.[83] As Sen. Patty Murray, D-Wash., has noted, "He puts issues we're dealing with in real American language. I think he's really a good face for our party."[84]

The Senate's minority whip is Jon Kyl, R-Ariz. Elected to the post in 2007 after Democrats won control of the Senate, Kyl does not face the majority leader's difficulties of moving a legislative agenda through the Senate. Nevertheless, his tasks are similar to those of the majority whip. He serves as one of the public faces of the GOP, articulating its positions on the Sunday morning political talk shows and in other public venues. In the meantime, he works to build consensus around party positions and initiatives, and he identifies effective communicators within his party to take the lead on issues. Indeed, his skill at tapping effective advocates for partisan causes was among the reasons *Time* selected him as one of "America's 10 Best Senators" in 2006.[85]

SELECTION OF LEADERS

Before the opening of each new Congress, senators and representatives elect their top leaders by secret ballot in their party caucuses. Although the whole House votes for the Speaker, the election is pro forma. With straight-party voting—the modern unspoken rule on this and other organizational matters—the majority party has always elected the Speaker.

Candidates for party leadership positions usually wage elaborate campaigns to win support from their partisan colleagues, with some launching websites to support their candidacy. Jack Kingston, R-Ga., launched a "video blog outlining his credentials" in his unsuccessful attempt to be the House GOP conference chair.[86] Occasionally, last-minute entrants successfully bid for leadership positions. But whether brief or lengthy, campaigns for party leadership positions are intense. Members understand that a party leadership post can be a "career launching pad either within the [Congress] or outside it."[87]

The two House parties have historically treated their hierarchies differently: the Democrats view it as a kind of a ladder, and the Republicans view it as a slippery slope. Democrats have tended to elevate their next-in-line officer—from whip to majority (or minority) leader to Speaker—as vacancies occur. Republicans have a history of pushing people off the leadership track because of turmoil in their ranks. For example, in 1959 Charles A. Halleck of Illinois ousted Joseph W. Martin Jr. of Massachusetts as the GOP leader. In 1965 Gerald R. Ford of Michigan turned the tables on Halleck. In 1980 John J. Rhodes of Arizona was persuaded by his colleagues to step down as party leader. And in 1994 Robert H. Michel of Illinois retired in the face of Gingrich's stated intention to challenge him. Four years later, Gingrich resigned the speakership, having lost the support of many House Republicans. Republican leadership succession, however, has been more regularized in the post-Gingrich period.

Both House and Senate leaders are generally chosen from the mainstream of their respective parties. As political scientist David Truman observed as long ago as 1959, party leaders tend to be "middlemen" in their parties—in ideological terms, from neither the far left nor the right fringes.[88] A recent study by Stephen Jessee and Neil Malhotra examining all open leadership contests over the past one hundred years determined that leaders tend to be closer to their party's ideological median than would happen by chance, but also that Democratic leaders tend to come from the left of the party median and Republican leaders from the right of the party median.[89] It also appears that these patterns develop at the candidate emergence stage of the selection process, meaning that candidates with these profiles are more likely to seek leadership positions in the first place.

Seniority in Congress is one of many criteria that influence the election of party leaders. Other considerations are geographical balance within the leadership; parliamentary expertise; competency in organizational matters; skill in forging winning coalitions; fund-raising prowess; communication skills; sensitivity to the mood of the membership; and personal attributes such as intelligence, fairness, persuasiveness, political shrewdness, and media savvy.

Although serving as a party leader in the House is typically a full-time position, every party leader in the Senate sits on one or more committees. The smaller size of the Senate allows leaders to participate in committee work while discharging their leadership duties. In the Senate of the 112th Congress, for example, Reid, McConnell, Durbin, and Kyl each serve on standing committees.

LEADERSHIP ACTIVITIES

House and Senate leaders have basically the same job: to bring coherence, direction, and efficiency to their legislative body. Leadership duties can be broadly described as institutional maintenance (ensuring that Congress and its members perform their lawmaking and oversight duties and preserving Congress's reputation and integrity) and party maintenance (crafting winning coalitions among partisan colleagues and providing assistance to their members).[90] These two tasks are often blended, as leaders perform their institutional tasks in ways that simultaneously serve the purposes of party maintenance. Nevertheless, congressional leaders have responsibilities for the basic functioning of Congress that transcend party politics.

Institutional Tasks

From an institutional perspective, party leaders have various obligations. To help them carry out these diverse responsibilities, their chamber gives them extra staff resources.

Organizing the Chamber. Party leaders select the top administrative officers of both houses of Congress such as the clerk of the House and the secretary of the Senate. These officers are important for the day-to-day functioning of the chambers even if they are invisible to the public. Party leaders also oversee committee jurisdictional revisions and revise congressional rules. Speaker Gingrich backed the abolition of three standing committees in 1995, and Speaker Hastert supported a major recodification of House rules in 1999, the first since 1880. In 2007 Speaker Pelosi endorsed House adoption of new ethics and lobbying rules.

Scheduling Floor Business. "The power of the Speaker of the House is the power of scheduling," Speaker O'Neill once declared.[91] Or, as Newt Gingrich put it, "When you are Speaker you get to set the agenda. [Y]ou get to decide what legislation is up."[92] After consulting with committee leaders, interested members, the president, and others, House and Senate party leaders decide what, when, how, and in which order measures should come up for debate. Setting the chamber's agenda and schedule—determining what each chamber will debate—is perhaps the single most important prerogative of the Speaker and Senate majority leader. Scheduling legislation is a basic task that must be managed for the institution to function at all, but leaders also act strategically in their party's interests as they make these decisions.

Once a bill is scheduled for action, the job of the leaders is to see that members vote—a task more difficult than merely herding bodies into the chamber. Party leaders may seek out certain members to speak on an issue because their endorsement can persuade other legislators to support it. Or they may delay action until the bill's sponsors are present. "The leadership must have the right members at the right place at the right time," said Byrd when he was the Senate majority whip.[93] Although leaders generally seek to influence members of their own party and chamber, they also try to win cooperation from the other chamber and from the opposition party.

Leaders' scheduling prerogatives mold policy outcomes; the point at which bills reach the floor can seal their fate. A week's delay in scheduling a controversial White House initiative, for example, may give the president, lobbying groups, and others additional time to muster votes for the proposal. Depending on the circumstances, delay may also afford the opposition an opportunity to mobilize their forces.

Legislative business is also scheduled with forthcoming elections in mind. Measures are postponed to avoid an electorally embarrassing defeat, or they may be brought to the floor to satisfy groups allied with the party. What better time to take up legislation revamping the Internal Revenue Service than on or around April 15, the filing deadline for federal income taxes? Reflecting the two Congresses, both parties use the floor as an election platform to raise issues that appeal to their outside partisans. After passing measures advocated by its electoral base, a party can say, "Look what we did for you." Conversely, a party that fails to pass a measure can say to its bedrock supporters, "Look what we tried to do."

Consulting the President. A traditional duty of party leaders is to meet with the president to discuss the administration's goals and to convey legislative sentiment about what the executive branch is doing or not doing. Although presidents spend more time dealing with leaders of their own party in Congress, they also consult with opposition leaders.

Party Tasks

From a party perspective, congressional party leaders have a number of formal and informal responsibilities. Each party's rules formally specify certain functions and responsibilities for their leaders. Parliamentary precedents and chamber rules assign additional duties to party leaders. Party leaders have also assumed a wide range of duties on an informal basis.

Organizing the Party. Congressional leaders help to organize their party by selecting partisan colleagues for standing committees, revising party rules, choosing other party leaders, and appointing party committees. A couple of examples illustrate the point. Senate Republicans' rules authorize their leader, Senator McConnell, to appoint party colleagues to certain committees. In the House, Speaker Boehner ensured that many freshmen in the 112th Congress received plum committee assignments.[94] To reward Sen. Charles Schumer, D-N.Y., for his stellar work in helping Democrats win back majority control of the Senate, Senator Reid "installed him in a newly created leadership post— vice chairman of the Democratic Conference."[95] Later, when the chairmanship of the Democratic Policy Committee (DPC) opened up with the retirement of Sen. Byron Dorgan, D-N.D., Schumer was selected DPC chair.

Promoting Party Unity. Another leadership responsibility is to encourage party unity in Congress on priority legislation. Sen. Everett Dirksen, R-Ill. (minority leader, 1959–1969), used social gatherings to accomplish this goal:

> Dirksen brought party members together in a series of social affairs. He held cocktail parties at a Washington country club, inviting all Republican senators and sometimes their wives too. These were calculated by Dirksen to improve party harmony and to build a friendly feeling for himself with the Republican senators.[96]

Party leaders' efforts to foster party cohesion go far beyond extending social invitations. Leaders perform many services for their party rank and file that build goodwill and a sense of common purpose. They schedule members' bills, provide them with timely political information, advise them on electoral issues, visit with their constituents, help them obtain good committee assignments, and work with them to forge policy agendas. "You really have to make people feel part of the process, and I guess it is a little bit like a shepherd," remarked a Senate Democratic leader. "You really want to keep as much as you can the flock together, and that takes different approaches with different people."[97] Periodically, leaders organize partisan retreats where members discuss party and policy goals, consider specific legislative initiatives, air differences, and resolve disputes.

Party leaders do not have to rely solely on their powers of persuasion. Informal political networks and access to strategic information give them an edge in influencing colleagues:

> Because members will respond more candidly to leadership polls than to lobbyist or White House polls, [leaders] have perhaps the most important information in a legislative struggle—information on where the votes are and (sometimes) what it will take to win certain people over.[98]

Top leaders also can bestow or withhold a variety of tangible and intangible rewards such as naming legislators to special or select committees, influencing assignments to standing committees, aiding reelection campaigns, and smoothing access to the White House or executive agencies.

Publicizing Party Views. Leaders are expected to publicize their party's policies and achievements. They give speeches in various forums, appear on radio and television talk shows, write newspaper and journal articles, hold press conferences, organize town meetings around the country, and establish websites that highlight party issues and images. Leaders are also expected to develop public relations strategies to neutralize the opposition's arguments and proposals.[99] The advocacy role has increased in importance in recent years, in part because of the twenty-four-hour news cycle. "We've created a situation," noted a scholar, "where the real way you drive the legislative process is by influencing public opinion, rather than by trading for votes."[100]

Party leaders also provide members with talking points for meetings with journalists or constituents. Parties often create communications teams that meet regularly to discuss message development and delivery and to recommend their more telegenic members to present party positions. "We're focused on making sure we deliver the [party] message both here in Washington and out in the hinterlands," said a chair of the Senate Republican Conference.[101]

Providing Campaign Assistance. Leaders must be energetic campaigners and fund-raisers on behalf of their partisan colleagues. They help party candidates raise campaign funds. They establish their own leadership political action committees (PACs) to solicit contributions and donate to candidates of their party. They direct campaign dollars to groups running issue ads in the months leading up to the November elections. They travel widely to campaign for incumbents and challengers from their party. They encourage outside groups to contribute to the party's electoral efforts. They also help vulnerable colleagues gain a higher profile by giving them a lead role on a major issue or by creating working groups to provide members running for reelection with greater public exposure.[102]

Members anticipating a run for a leadership post distribute campaign funds as standard operating practice. According to one account, "It seems that the job of fundraiser is becoming more important to senators' expectations of what a majority leader should do. The candidates [for this leadership position] thus are not trying to buy votes so much as to demonstrate how well they can fulfill that role."[103] In both the House and the Senate, the ability to raise funds for colleagues is an increasingly important criterion for judging prospective party leaders.[104] Leaders stand at the intersection of the two Congresses—the representative assembly, where money is needed to join, and the lawmaking body, where power calls the shots.

PARTY CAUCUSES, COMMITTEES, AND INFORMAL GROUPS

House and Senate leaders operate in diverse institutional settings. In the larger, more impersonal House, majority party leaders sometimes ignore the wishes of the minority party. But this seldom happens in the Senate, where leaders must cope with the extensive rights of individual senators and the minority party. Despite these differences between the House and the Senate, parties in the two chambers are organized into the same three components: caucuses, committees, and informal party groups.

Party Caucuses

The organization of all partisans in a chamber is called the conference or (in the case of House Democrats) the caucus. Party conferences or caucuses elect leaders, approve committee assignments, provide members with services, debate party and legislative rules and policies, appoint task forces or issue teams, develop themes to keep members on message, enable members to vent their frustrations, and discuss outreach programs that appeal to voters. In an explanation that applies equally well to both parties and chambers, a senior House Democrat said:

> The caucus is the place where a great deal of freewheeling debate over an issue takes place and where sometimes a consensus develops. Most of the discussions, although they have taken place at leadership meetings and at chairmen's meetings and in whips' meetings, have ended up in the broader forum of the caucus where every member of the

Democratic party participates. You don't take a vote, but you try to develop a consensus and make concessions where they're necessary and develop the strongest possible position that can be supported by the maximum number of Democrats [105]

In brief, party caucuses are useful forums where party members and leaders can assess sentiment on substantive or procedural issues and forge party unity. On rare occasions, party caucuses consider whether to strip particular members of their committee seniority or to oust committee leaders. Sometimes presidents attend their party's House or Senate caucus to rally the troops, as President Obama did just before the House of Representatives voted on health care reform in 2010.[106]

Party Committees

Each of the four congressional parties—Senate and House Democrats, Senate and House Republicans—establishes committees to serve partisan needs and objectives (see Table 6-1). Three of the four parties on Capitol Hill have policy committees, for example.[107]

Party committees do not make policy, but they do provide advice on scheduling, study substantive and political issues, distribute policy papers, track votes on issues, and discuss and implement party policy. Their influence has varied over the years, assuming greater importance when the party does not control the White House and thus needs policy and oversight assistance. Byron Dorgan, chair of the Senate Democratic Policy Committee, directed the panel to conduct extensive oversight activities during President George W. Bush's tenure, including investigations of government contracting in Iraq and Afghanistan, the implementation of the Medicare prescription drug policy, and gas prices, among other topics.[108] The two Senate and House GOP policy committees maintain websites that party members and staff can access at any time for information. Other important party panels are the campaign committees (discussed in Chapter 3) and the committee assignment committees (discussed in Chapter 7).

Informal Party Groups

In addition to party committees, a variety of informal partisan groups operate on Capitol Hill. House and Senate leaders employ party task forces to devise policy alternatives, formulate strategy, and coordinate floor action. Although informal groups on Capitol Hill numbered about three hundred in the 111th Congress, most are not explicitly partisan. Instead, many have a policy focus—such as boating, steel, mining, soybeans, rural health, electricity, automobiles, children, bicycles, or the Internet—and promote public awareness of related issues, sometimes favoring specific policies. Among party groups in the House are the conservative Republican Study Committee, the Tea Party Caucus, the centrist New Democrat Coalition, and the fiscally conservative Blue Dog Democrats. Some of these informal House groups, such as the Republican Study Committee and the 30-Something Caucus (moderate to liberal Democrats), regularly reserve time at the end of the

TABLE 6-1 **Party Committees in the Senate and House**	
Committee	Function
Senate Democratic	
Policy	Considers party positions on specific measures and assists the party leader in scheduling bills
Steering and Outreach	Assigns Democrats to committees and coordinates policy, legislative, and message issues for the Democratic Conference
Campaign	Works to elect Democrats to the Senate
Senate Republican	
Policy	Provides summaries of GOP positions on specific issues; researches procedural and substantive issues; drafts policy alternatives
Committee on Committees	Assigns Republicans to committees
Campaign	Works to elect Republicans to the Senate
House Democratic	
Steering	Assists the leadership and Democratic Caucus in establishing, implementing, researching, and communicating party priorities; assigns Democrats to committees
Campaign	Aids in electing Democrats to the House
House Republican	
Policy	Considers majority party proposals and works for consensus among Republican members
Steering	Assigns Republicans to standing committees
Campaign	Seeks to elect Republicans to the House

Note: The official names of the parties' campaign committees are as follows: Democratic Senatorial Campaign Committee, National Republican Senatorial Committee, Democratic Congressional Campaign Committee, and National Republican Congressional Committee.

legislative day to spotlight their party's priorities and successes and to criticize the other party.

PARTY CONTINUITY AND CHANGE

Several features of the contemporary party system on Capitol Hill stand out: the intensity of party conflict, the persistence of the two-party system, and the advent of new coalition-building practices.

Intense Party Conflict

By any test one can use, the four Capitol Hill party groups are flourishing. The organizational elements are healthy and active, their leaders are increasingly prominent, and their party voting is at very high levels. The congressional parties are assisted by well-staffed, professional party units.

The strength of today's parties has definite virtues. For one, it enables voters to better comprehend the divergent views, values, and principles of the two parties, and it may even encourage voter turnout. "Confrontation fits our strategy," said Richard B. "Dick" Cheney when he was in the House (1979–1989). "Polarization often has very beneficial results. If everything is handled through compromise and conciliation, if there are no real issues dividing us from Democrats, why should the country change and make us the majority?"[109]

Nevertheless, compromise is a traditional hallmark of legislative decision making. The intensity and extent of partisan conflict in the contemporary Congress raise questions about the body's ability to engage in meaningful bipartisan deliberation and mutual accommodation. Partisan polarization is decried by observers and members alike. In today's House, the two parties are not "just opponents or rivals now. [They] are enemies, with every fight being zero-sum," exclaimed a senior GOP lawmaker. "Compromise is seen as weakness by many of your constituents, and by all your potential opponents in the next primary."[110]

The call for bipartisanship is an oft-heard refrain on Capitol Hill—but an elusive goal. President Obama campaigned on a promise to "turn the page" on the bitter party politics that had characterized the Bush presidency. But his first major initiative, an economic stimulus package, elicited an almost purely partisan response in Congress. No House Republican and only three Senate Republicans supported the president's package.[111] Similarly, just before the opening of the 110th Congress, Senate majority leader Reid convened a closed-door meeting of all senators.[112] Its purpose was to infuse a spirit of bipartisanship in the working relationships between the two parties. A few weeks later, the Senate was in gridlock as the two parties bitterly clashed over how to debate a measure disapproving of President Bush's deployment of more troops to Iraq.[113] Following the same pattern, Speaker Pelosi promised that Democrats would run the House in an open and fair manner and allow Republicans the opportunity to offer their alternative amendments. Six weeks later, a newspaper headline proclaimed, "In Majority, Democrats Run Hill Much as GOP Did."[114]

The partisan rancor got so bad in the House in the mid-1990s (Speaker Gingrich and Minority Leader Richard A. Gephardt, a Democrat from Missouri, refused to speak to each other for a year) that a bipartisan group of lawmakers organized a weekend retreat in 1997 for all members and their families. The so-called civility retreat was designed to allow members of the two parties to get to know each other better and to facilitate greater bipartisanship in resolving the nation's problems. However, only marginal improvements, if any, flowed from this event. The three other civility retreats held in March 1999, March 2001, and March 2003 produced similar results. No further civility retreats have been held.

Episodes of sharp partisanship occur even in the more sedate Senate, in part because so many House members have been elected to that body. In recent Congresses, nearly half of senators have served in the House. Many bring to the Senate the hard-edged partisanship that they learned in the House.[115] As Sen. Olympia J. Snowe, R-Maine, observed, "The whole Congress has become far more polarized and partisan so it makes it difficult to reach bipartisan agreements. The more significant the issue, the more partisan it becomes."[116]

The Two-Party System

The Democratic and Republican Parties have dominated American politics and Congress since the mid–nineteenth century. Scholars have advanced various theories for the dualistic national politics of a country as diverse as the United States. Plurality elections in single-member congressional districts encouraged the creation and maintenance of two major parties. Under the winner-takes-all principle, the person who wins the most votes in a state or district is elected to the Senate or House. This principle discourages the formation of third parties. Some also trace the origins of the national two-party system to early conflicts between Federalists (advocates of a strong national government) and Antifederalists (advocates of limited national government). This dualism continued in subsequent splits: North versus South, East versus West, agricultural versus financial interests, and rural versus urban areas.[117] In addition, many states have laws that make it difficult to create new parties. Constitutional, political, and legal arrangements all contribute to the existence and maintenance of the two-party system.

Whatever mix of causes produced the two-party system, one thing is clear: few third-party or independent legislators have been elected to Congress during the last century. The high-water mark was the Sixty-third Congress (1913–1915), which had one Progressive senator and nineteen representatives elected as Progressives, Progressive-Republicans, or independents. Since World War II, only a handful of lawmakers have been elected from minor parties or as independents.[118] Most of these legislators have converted to one of the major parties or have voted with them on procedural and substantive matters. The 112th Congress has only two independent lawmakers, each of whom affiliates with the Democratic Party: socialist senator Bernie Sanders of Vermont and former Democratic senator Joseph I. Lieberman of Connecticut. Third-party or independent members participate in Democratic or Republican affairs by invitation only.

Advances in Coalition Building

In Capitol Hill's highly competitive environment, party leaders are constantly searching for new ways to get the legislative results they want. Fierce competition has prompted continual innovation in media, legislative, and public relations strategies.

Media Strategies. Party leaders understand that media strategies—that is, the use of the press, television, radio, polls, the Internet, speeches, and so on— are essential to advance or block legislation. They form issue teams, message groups, "war rooms," or theme teams to orchestrate, organize, and coordinate political events and communications strategies that promote the party's message to the general public. No longer is the inside game—working behind the scenes to line up votes—sufficient to pass major legislation.

Also necessary is the outside game—influencing public opinion, coordinating with advocacy groups, and creating grassroots support for policy initiatives. Today, both parties use the media to complement their parliamentary strategies in order to raise issues, define and frame priorities, and respond to partisan criticisms. Both congressional parties understand the importance of words as political weapons. GOP consultants found, for example, that characterizing the tax on inheritances as the "death tax"—and having GOP officeholders repeat it again and again over several years—aroused public ire against the tax. This sentiment was instrumental in the temporary repeal of the estate tax as part of President Bush's successful 2001 tax cut plan. Republicans continue to advocate for the permanent demise of the "death tax."

President Obama can use his bully pulpit to advance Democratic initiatives, but congressional Republicans have no single messenger who can focus the nation's attention. As a result, Republicans have embraced a wide array of communications techniques to shape national debate. Meanwhile, they have augmented the number of leadership staff handling new media, communications, and grassroots outreach. "Our effort will work to help build dynamic multilayered, outside-the-Beltway coalitions that will help the Republican Conference explain the value of our policies and the impact they will have on the American people," predicted Jeff Burton, the coalitions director for then-minority whip Cantor.[119] Republican leaders hold press conferences, appear on diverse media outlets, organize town meetings, prepare talking points for the press (and their own members), develop party themes, participate in Web forums and blogs, write newspaper editorials, circulate data and statistics, organize policy forums, and engage in a variety of other activities to promote their legislative agenda to the public and to challenge Democratic initiatives.

Omnibus Bills. A phenomenon of modern lawmaking is the rise of megabills—legislation that is hundreds or thousands of pages in length encompassing disparate policy topics. Many of Congress's most significant recent policy departures have been enacted through omnibus bills.

Joining several bills in a single package can help leaders garner support. In such megabills, sweeteners can be added to woo supporters, and provisions that could not win majority support in stand-alone bills can be tucked out of sight. Bundling popular programs with painful spending cuts limits the number of difficult votes lawmakers must cast and provides them with political cover. Members can explain to angry constituents or groups that they had to support the indivisible whole because its discrete parts were not open to separate votes. Leaders, however, must be wary of the reverse concern that a megabill can attract a coalition of minorities with the votes needed to reject the measure.

Megabills can also strengthen Congress's leverage with the executive branch. Measures that a president might veto if presented separately can be folded into megabills and signed in that fashion.

Party leaders command the resources and authority to influence the packaging process. "Omnibus bills place a huge amount of power in the hands of a few key leaders and their staffs," pointed out one House member.[120] Rank-and-file members look to party leaders to formulate a package acceptable to at least a majority of members. Nevertheless, these megabills often arouse lawmakers' suspicions and complaints. "These omnibus bills . . . are abominations," one member complained. "No one member of Congress has a chance to read much of them, let alone understand them, before they are voted on."[121]

Strategic Planning and Coordination. On major policy and political issues, strategic planning and coordination are crucial to the leadership's ability to mobilize successful coalitions. House and Senate leaders meet regularly with their partisan allies to craft their plans and to formulate effective public relations strategies. For example, party leaders employ defensive messages as a way to protect their members from political attack, known as the "inoculation strategy." The objective is to appropriate the other party's popular issues by blurring the distinctions between congressional Democrats and Republicans. For example, on an immigration reform issue, Democrats called their package the Latino and Immigrant Fairness Act, and Republicans dubbed their initiative the Legal Immigration Family Equity Act.[122]

Both parties, too, focus attention on how to win the battle of ideas in Congress and the broader electorate. In the aftermath of their 2006 electoral defeat, Senate Republicans began working to "brand" the GOP nationally as the "reform party"—ironically stressing some of the themes that had won them the majority in 1994: limited government, fiscal restraint, and elimination of wasteful programs and expenditures. The recent publication of *Young Guns* is an attempt to lay claim to a similar reform image for a new generation of House leaders.[123] "In my view," said Senate GOP leader McConnell, "minority status isn't our biggest cause for concern. In the long run, the public's perception of the Republican Party is more dangerous."[124]

CONCLUSION

Congressional parties have elaborate organizations, and their leaders fulfill a multiplicity of roles and duties. As Sen. Robert Byrd explained when he held that post, the Senate majority performs many duties: "He facilitates, he constructs, he programs, he schedules, he takes an active part in the development of legislation, he steps in at crucial moments on the floor, offers amendments, speaks on behalf of legislation and helps to shape the outcome of the legislation."[125] And yet typically party leaders cannot command their colleagues. Their leadership rests chiefly on their skill in giving others reasons to follow them.

The party system organizes Congress. The committee system, however, shapes the measures Congress acts on. These two systems are often in conflict. The first emphasizes aggregation, the second fragmentation. Party leaders struggle to manage an institution that disperses policy-making authority to so many working groups. In short, leaders provide the centripetal force to offset committees' centrifugal influence.

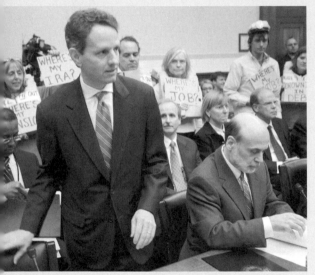

***C**ommitte Hearings and Mark-ups.* Rep. Fre
Upton, R-Mich., House Energy Committee cha
(top left), testifies before the Rules Committee
favor of his panel's bill to repeal the Patie
Protection and Affordable Care Act. He is flanke
by colleagues Steve King, R-Iowa, and John Klin
R-Minn. (Top right), House Appropriations cha
David R. Obey (D-Wis.) consults with the commi
tee's staff director and deputy during markup of th
fiscal 2007 supplemental appropriations bi
(Center), Treasury Secretary Timothy F. Geithne
standing at left, and Federal Reserve Chairman Be
S. Bernanke, seated, prepare to testify before th
House Banking Committee. (Bottom), Committe
aides sort through amendments during a break
the House Energy and Commerce Committee
markup of a 2009 bill designed to reduce gree
house gases.

chapter 7

Committees:
Workshops of Congress

Congress's committees serve two broad purposes: individual and institutional. Individually, lawmakers are able to use their committee assignments to benefit their constituents. "As far as I can see, there is really only one basic reason to be on a public works committee," admitted a House member. "Intellectual stimulation" is not it. "Most of all, I want to be able to bring home projects to my district."[1] At the start of the 112th Congress (2011–2013), no less than twenty House GOP freshmen lawmakers won assignment to the Transportation and Infrastructure Committee, in part because the panel's agenda (highways, mass transit, and water projects) addresses investments that can bring jobs and economic growth to their districts. Legislators know that their letters and telephone calls to the pertinent agency officials can influence the funding of member-proposed federal projects. They also fully understand the connection between their committee assignments and their reelection potential.

Committees also enable legislators to utilize or develop expertise in areas that interest them. A former teacher, for example, may seek assignment to the committee overseeing education policy. And some panels, such as the tax and appropriations committees, enable members to wield personal influence among their colleagues. For much of congressional history, members sought out the House Appropriations Committee, explained a GOP leader, because "instantaneously . . . they have a host of new friends, and we all know why": that panel controls the distribution of discretionary federal money.[2]

However, the GOP takeover of the House after the November 2010 midterm elections produced a cultural shift on the panel. Public dismay over escalating deficits and debt spawned an anti-spending fervor among the panel's GOP members. Budget-cutting fiscal hawks were recruited to the panel. Their mission was to practice the "politics of subtraction" by cutting or terminating agencies or programs. The Appropriations Committee "has been a favor factory for years; now it is going to be [an anti-spending] slaughterhouse," declared Rep. Jeff Flake, R-Ariz., a longtime critic of the favor factory and a newly elected appropriator.[3]

Some Republicans declined appointment to the committee. "We sent a sheet around, people gave us their preferences, and there weren't that many members that chose to serve on the Appropriations Committee," said Speaker John Boehner, R-Ohio.[4] They recognized the potential perils of the two Congresses: members could be challenged electorally either by conservative and Tea Party supporters for not cutting enough or by constituents angry at spending cuts to favorite programs. Still, it is worth underscoring that appropriators remain powerful even in a cost-cutting climate. They are strategically positioned to determine which agencies and programs will be cut and which could obtain increases over the previous year's level.

Institutionally, committees are the centers of policy making, oversight of federal agencies, and public education (largely through the hearings they hold). By dividing their membership into a number of "little legislatures," the House and Senate are able to consider dozens of proposed laws simultaneously.[5] Without committees, a legislative body of 100 senators and 441 House members[6] could not handle biennially the roughly 10,000 bills and nearly 100,000 nominations, a national budget of nearly $4 trillion, and a limitless array of controversial issues. Although floor actions often refine legislation, committees are the means by which Congress sifts through an otherwise impossible jumble of bills, proposals, and issues.

Congressional committees serve another important institutional function in the political system: they act as safety valves—that is, they are outlets for national debates and controversies. Military and economic challenges, demographic shifts, trade agreements, global environmental concerns, the drug war, the social dislocations caused by technological advances, and the rising cost of health care place enormous strains on the political system. As forums for public debates, congressional committees help to vent, absorb, and perhaps resolve these strains. The safety valve function also gives citizens a greater sense of participation in national decision making and helps educate members about public problems.

At times, the individual and institutional purposes of the committee system come into conflict. Because members tend to gravitate to committees for constituency or career reasons, they are not the most impartial judges of the policies they authorize. "It's one of the weaknesses of the system that those attracted to a committee like Agriculture are those whose constituents benefit from farm programs," acknowledged Sen. Charles E. Schumer, D-N. Y. "And so they're going to support those programs and they're not going to want to cut them, even the ones that are wasteful."[7]

THE PURPOSES OF COMMITTEES

Senator's Schumer's comment highlights an ongoing debate about the development and fundamental purposes of the committee system. To explain the organizational logic of legislatures and the behavior of their committees, scholars have advanced the distributional, informational, and party hypotheses.

The *distributional* hypothesis suggests that legislatures create committees to give lawmakers policy influence in areas critical to their reelection. Members seek committee assignments to "bring home the bacon" (public goods and services) to their constituents. Because lawmakers self-select these kinds of committees, the committees become filled with what scholars call preference outliers—members whose homogeneous preferences for benefits to their constituents put them out of step with the heterogeneous views of the membership as a whole. Chamber majorities, in brief, may need to restrain overreaching committees by rejecting or amending their recommended actions.[8]

The *informational* hypothesis proposes that legislative bodies establish committees to provide lawmakers with the specialized expertise required to make informed judgments in a complex world. Furthermore, the division of labor under the committee system augments Congress's role in relation to the executive branch. Instead of being composed primarily of preference outliers, committees under this model will consist of a diverse membership with wide-ranging perspectives. The basic goal of committees, then, is to formulate policies that resolve national problems.[9]

The *party* hypothesis views committees as agents of their party caucuses. According to this perspective, committee members are expected to support their party's programs or, at minimum, not advance policies opposed by a majority of their own party.

Each of these hypotheses captures an aspect of the committee system. Lawmakers are concerned with local issues of immediate concern to constituents, but every district and state are also affected by broad national concerns— the condition of the economy and the environment, for example. Certain issues may lend themselves on occasion more to the distributional than to the informational or party theory of policy making.

Because good public policy may be impeded by the parochial orientations of individual members, Congress has a small number of control, or centralizing, committees that promote institutional and policy integration over committee and programmatic particularism. For example, each house has a Budget Committee, which proposes limits on how much Congress can spend on designated functional areas.[10] However committees are characterized, they concentrate on the policy and oversight activities of individual lawmakers.

EVOLUTION OF THE COMMITTEE SYSTEM

Committees in the early Congresses were generally temporary panels created for specific tasks. Proposals were considered on the House or Senate floor and then were referred to specially created panels that worked out the details—the reverse order of today's system. The Senate, for example, would "debate a subject at length on the floor and, after the majority's desires had been crystallized, might appoint a committee to put those desires into bill form."[11] About 350 ad hoc committees were formed during the Third Congress (1793–1795) alone.[12] The parent chamber closely controlled these temporary committees. It assigned them clear-cut tasks, required them to report back favorably or unfavorably, and dissolved them when they had completed their work.

By about 1816, the Senate—and the House a bit later—had developed a system of permanent, or standing, committees, some of which are still in existence. Standing committees, as historian DeAlva Stanwood Alexander explained, were better suited than ad hoc groups to cope with the larger membership and wider scope of congressional business. Another scholar, George H. Haynes, pointed out that the "needless inconvenience of the frequent choice of select committees" taxed congressional patience. Lawmakers recognized that debating bills one at a time before the whole chamber was an inefficient way of processing Congress's legislative business. Perhaps, too, legislators turned to standing committees as counterweights to presidential influence in setting the legislative agenda.[13] Permanent committees changed the way Congress made policy and allocated authority. The House and Senate now reviewed and voted on recommendations made by specialized, experienced committees. Permanent committees also encouraged oversight of the executive branch. Members have called them "the eye, the ear, the hand, and very often the brain" of Congress.[14]

As committees acquired expertise and authority, they became increasingly self-reliant and resistant to chamber and party control. After the House revolt against domineering Speaker Joseph G. Cannon, R-Ill., in 1910, power flowed to the committee chairs. Along with a few strong party leaders, committee chairs held sway over House and Senate policy making during much of the twentieth century. In rare instances, committee members rebelled and diminished the chair's authority. But most members heeded the advice that Speaker John W. McCormack, D-Mass. (1962–1971), gave freshmen: "Whenever you pass a committee chairman in the House, you bow from the waist. I do."[15]

The chairs' authority was buttressed by the custom of seniority that flourished with the rise of congressional careerism. The majority party member with the most years of continuous service on a committee virtually always became its chair. As a result, committee chairs owed little or nothing to party leaders, much less to presidents. This automatic selection process produced experienced, independent chairs but concentrated authority in a few hands. The have-nots wanted a piece of the action and objected that seniority promoted the competent and incompetent alike. They objected, too, that the system promoted members from safe one-party areas—especially conservative southern Democrats and midwestern Republicans—who could ignore party policies or national sentiments.

The late 1960s and 1970s saw a rapid influx of new members, many from the cities and suburbs, who opposed the conservative status quo. (In the House, this surge was abetted by U.S. Supreme Court–mandated reapportionments, as discussed in Chapter 3.) Allying themselves with more senior members seeking a stronger voice in Congress, these reformers sponsored changes that diffused power and shattered seniority as an absolute criterion for leadership posts. Today, House and Senate committee chairs (and ranking minority members) are elected by their party colleagues. No longer free to wield arbitrary authority, they must abide by committee and party rules and be sensitive to majority sentiment within their party's caucus or conference.

TYPES OF COMMITTEES

Today, Congress boasts a shopper's bazaar of committees—standing, select, joint, and conference—and within each of these general types are variations. Standing committees, for example, can be classed as either authorizing or appropriating panels. Authorizing committees (such as Agriculture, Armed Services, and Judiciary) are the policy-making centers on Capitol Hill. As substantive committees, they propose solutions to public problems and advocate what they believe to be the necessary levels of spending for the programs under their jurisdictions. The House and Senate Appropriations Committees recommend how much money agencies and programs will receive. Not surprisingly, the two types of panels, authorizing and appropriations, tend to come into conflict. Typically, authorizers press for full funding for their recommendations, whereas appropriators usually recommend lower spending levels.

Standing Committees

A standing committee is a permanent entity created by public law or House or Senate rules. Standing committees continue from Congress to Congress, except in rare instances when they are eliminated or new ones are created. Table 7-1 identifies the standing committees in the 112th Congress.

Standing committees process the bulk of Congress's daily and annual agenda of business. Typically, measures are considered on the House or Senate floor after first being referred to, and approved by, the appropriate committees. At the same time, committees are the burial ground for most legislation—that is, committees select from the thousands of measures introduced in each Congress those that merit floor debate. Of the hundreds of bills that clear committees, fewer still are enacted into law.

Sizes and Ratios. The biennial election results frame the party negotiations over setting committee sizes and ratios (the number of majority and minority members on a panel). At the beginning of each new Congress, each chamber adopts separate resolutions, offered by Democrats and Republicans, that elect party members to the committees and thus set their sizes and ratios. In practice, committee sizes and ratios are established in the House by the majority leadership. Because the majority party has the votes, it is the final arbiter if the minority protests its allotment of seats.

At the opening of the 112th Congress, the ratio of Republicans to Democrats in the 435-member House was 56 percent (242 Republicans) to 44 percent (193 Democrats). In the main, this was the approximate ratio on most House committees. As a result, there was no public protest from minority members about being underrepresented on most committees, a common event in years past. To be sure, some committees, such as Rules (69 percent to 31 percent in the 112th) and Ways and Means (59 percent to 41 percent in the 112th), traditionally have disproportionate ratios to ensure firm majority party control. The Ethics Committee has an equal number of majority and minority members, and the Speaker names the committee chair.

| TABLE 7-1 **Standing Committees of the House and Senate, 112th Congress 2011–2013** ||

House	Senate
Agriculture	Agriculture, Nutrition, and Forestry
Appropriations	Appropriations
Armed Services	Armed Services
Budget	Banking, Housing, and Urban Affairs
Education and the Workforce	Budget
Energy and Commerce	Commerce, Science, and Transportation
Ethics	Energy and Natural Resources
Financial Services	Environment and Public Works
Foreign Affairs	Finance
Homeland Security	Foreign Relations
House Administration	Health, Education, Labor, and Pensions
Judiciary	Homeland Security and Governmental Affairs
Natural Resources	Judiciary
Oversight and Government Reform	Rules and Administration
Rules	Small Business and Entrepreneurship
Science, Space, and Technology	Veterans' Affairs
Small Business	
Transportation and Infrastructure	
Veterans' Affairs	
Ways and Means	

Sources: House and Senate committee web pages.

In the Senate, sizes and ratios are negotiated by the majority and minority leaders. (Senate rules, unlike those of the House, establish the sizes of the standing committees, but these can be adjusted up or down with the agreement of the majority and minority leaders.) Once it became clear after the 2010 elections by what margin the Democrats had retained Senate control (53D, 47R), the two party leaders—Democrat Harry Reid, Nev., and Republican Mitch McConnell, Ky.—were responsible for negotiating committee sizes and ratios. Determining ratios and making assignments for the sixteen new senators was put on hold for three weeks because of interparty negotiations over how to improve the operations of the Senate. Once this matter was resolved (see Chapter 8), the committees were impaneled: Democrats would hold a two-seat margin on most committees (such as Appropriations and Finance) —and a one-seat margin on others (such as Foreign Relations and Homeland Security). The Senate's Ethics Committee—which is chaired by a majority-party member—always has an equal number of majority and minority members.

Party leaders often enlarge panels to accommodate lawmakers competing for membership on the same committees. They recognize that intraparty harmony can be maintained by boosting the number of committee seats. In 2011, however, Speaker John Boehner, R-Ohio, downsized most House committees to boost productivity and to cut costs. For example, the Appropriations Committee went from sixty seats to fifty, Energy and Commerce from fifty-nine seats to fifty-four, Transportation and Infrastructure from seventy-five seats to fifty-nine, and Ways and Means from forty-one seats to thirty-seven. The Armed Services Committee maintained its size (sixty-two), becoming the largest House panel. Minority Leader Nancy Pelosi, D-Calif., faced some discontent from her Democratic flock once the size reductions became known. Many Democrats lost their seats on major committees with the GOP's reset of sizes and ratios. After bipartisan discussions, some committee sizes were adjusted. For example, Democrats were granted one more seat on the Energy and Commerce Committee to accommodate a returning Democrat who had taken a leave of absence. "Republicans also gave themselves an additional seat" on Energy and Commerce.[16]

Subcommittees. Subcommittees perform much of the day-to-day lawmaking and oversight work of Congress. Like standing committees, they vary widely in rules and procedures, staff arrangements, modes of operations, and relationships with the full committee as well as its other subcommittees. They are created for various reasons, such as lawmakers' need to subdivide a committee's wide-ranging policy domain into manageable pieces, their desire to chair these panels and to have a platform to shape the legislative agenda, and their desire to respond to the policy claims of specialized constituencies.

Under House rules, most standing committees are limited to no more than five subcommittees. Committees bound by the limit of five may create a sixth subcommittee if it is devoted to oversight. There are some exceptions to the limit of five, such as Appropriations (which has twelve subcommittees), Armed Services (seven), Foreign Affairs (seven), and Transportation and Infrastructure (six). Various reasons account for these deviations: long-standing custom, acquisition of additional jurisdiction, accommodations of lawmakers, and bicameral concerns. A committee authorized to establish additional subcommittees may choose not to do so. For example, a committee chair decided to reduce the number of subcommittees from seven to five. His new subcommittee structure was created "so that the jurisdiction of each subcommittee will have broad appeal and will engage the attention of the subcommittee members."[17]

Another House rule limits members to serving on no more than four subcommittees. Such limits—on the number of subcommittees for each standing committee and subcommittee assignment restrictions for each member—are designed to make Congress "more deliberative, participatory, and manageable by reducing scheduling conflicts and jurisdictional overlap."[18] Republicans are in control of the House of the 112th Congress, and their party conference rules state that the "method for the selection of Chairmen of the Committee's Subcommittees [and GOP subcommittee assignments] shall be at the discretion of the full Committee Chairman, unless a majority of the Republican Members of the full Committee disapprove the action of the Chairman." Furthermore, the chair "shall formalize in writing for the other Republican Members of the Committee the procedures to be followed in selecting Subcommittee Chairmen and individual subcommittee assignments and shall do so in advance of the Committee's organization." In the case of the Appropriations Committee, the chair submits nominees for subcommittee chairs to the Republican Steering Committee for approval.

The two Congresses are also evident in the composition of subcommittees. Judiciary chair Lamar Smith, R-Texas, passed over Steve King, R-Iowa, for chairmanship of the Immigration Subcommittee. King had been the ranking GOP member on the panel in the previous Congress. But, worried that King's inflammatory statements about immigrants would alienate Latino voters in the 2012 elections, Smith selected Elton Gallegly of California, "who has a lower profile and a less strident tone than King," to head the subcommittee.[19]

In dealing with House subcommittees, the minority Democrats in the 112th Congress followed the detailed procedures outlined in their party rules. Simply put, once the subcommittee structure and jurisdictions are established, committee Democrats bid for a subcommittee ranking slot (or assignment) in order of their seniority on the full committee (or seniority on the Appropriations subcommittee) with the most senior Democrat choosing first. The choices are then subject to approval by secret ballot of the Democratic committee members. The ranking positions on four of the most powerful committees— Appropriations, Energy and Commerce, Financial Services, and Ways and Means—require approval by the Democratic Steering and Policy Committee. If the Steering and Policy Committee rejects a member to serve as the ranking committee minority leader, the relevant committee is obliged to submit a new nominee to the party panel.

Assignment to the most important committees is generally "exclusive." Democrats who serve on exclusive committees may serve on no other standing committees unless they are granted an exemption, or waiver, from this requirement. (Waivers of the rule are quite common.) Waivers are granted to permit members to sit on an extra major committee that they deem important to their reelection prospects. This is another example of the two Congresses, the institution bending to suit the preferences and constituency needs of individual members. House Republicans refer to their generally exclusive panels as the "A" committees (Appropriations, Energy and Commerce, Rules, and Ways and Means).

Although silent on the number of subcommittees that standing committees may establish, Senate and party rules set subcommittee assignment limits for senators and prohibit them from chairing more than one subcommittee on any given committee. The number of subcommittees, not surprisingly, often equals the number of majority party members on a committee eligible to chair a subcommittee. Subcommittee chairs and assignments are determined in one of two ways: by the full chair in consultation with the ranking member or by senators' order of seniority on the full committee. It is traditional for committee members to defer to the chair on organizational matters, such as the number of subcommittees and their respective jurisdictions. These matters, however, are subject to majority approval of the panel.

Unlike in the House where every standing committee except Budget and Ethics has subcommittees, in the Senate four standing committees customarily function without subcommittees—Budget, Rules and Administration, Small Business, and Veterans' Affairs—as do four other permanent panels—Indian Affairs, Ethics, Intelligence, and Aging. These panels are able to process their legislative business without subcommittees because of their relatively small workloads compared with those of other Senate committees.

Select, or Special, Committees

Select, or special, committees are temporary panels that typically go out of business after the two-year life of the Congress in which they are created. But some select committees take on the attributes of permanent committees. The House, for example, has a Permanent Select Intelligence Committee. Select committees usually do not have legislative authority (the right to receive and report out measures) unless it is granted by their authorizing measure; they can only study, investigate, and make recommendations.

Select panels are created for several reasons. First, they can accommodate the concerns of individual members. Indeed, the chairs of these panels may attract publicity that enhances their political careers. For example, Democrat Harry S. Truman of Missouri came to the public's (and President Franklin D. Roosevelt's) attention as head of a special Senate committee investigating World War II military procurement practices. Second, special panels can be an access point for interest groups such as the elderly. Third, select committees supplement the standing committee system by overseeing and investigating issues that the permanent panels may lack adequate time for or prefer to ignore. A recent example of an issue-based select committee was the House's creation in the 110th and 111th Congresses of a select panel to pay full-time attention to, and act as a public focus for, global warming. When Republicans took charge of the House in the 112th Congress, they discontinued the global warming panel, contending that its demise would save money and that the panel duplicated the work of other standing committees. Republicans also wanted to "deny Democrats a key bully pulpit for advancing their environmental agenda."[20]

Finally, select committees can be set up to coordinate consideration of issues that overlap the jurisdictions of several standing committees. A good example occurred following the establishment in 2003 of the Department of

Homeland Security (DHS). It was formed by merging twenty-two federal agencies with a workforce at the time of 180,000 employees. Because numerous House committees exercised jurisdiction over parts of DHS, Speaker Dennis Hastert, R-Ill., created a select homeland security panel to determine whether a new, single-focused standing committee should be created to oversee DHS. As a result of the select panel's review, the House created a standing Committee on Homeland Security in the following Congress. (The formation of this panel is discussed in more detail later in this chapter.)

Joint Committees

Joint committees, which include members from both chambers, have been used since the First Congress for study, investigation, oversight, and routine activities. Unless the composition of a joint committee is prescribed in statute, House members of these committees are appointed by the Speaker; senators are appointed by that chamber's presiding officer. The chairmanship of joint committees rotates each Congress between House and Senate members. There are now four joint committees: Economic, Library, Printing, and Taxation. The Joint Library Committee and the Joint Printing Committee oversee, respectively, the Library of Congress and the Government Printing Office. The Joint Taxation Committee is essentially a holding company for staff who work closely with the tax-writing committees of each house. The Joint Economic Committee conducts studies and hearings on a wide range of domestic and international economic issues.

Conference Committees

Before legislation can be sent to the president to be signed, it must pass both the House and the Senate in identical form. One way this result is obtained is to create a conference committee (see Chapter 8 for more on conferences). Sometimes called the third house of Congress, these bicameral panels reconcile differences between similar measures passed by both chambers. They are composed of members of each house. A representative highlighted their importance:

> When I came to Congress I had no comprehension of the importance of the conference committees which actually write legislation. We all knew that important laws are drafted there, but I don't think one person in a million has any appreciation of their importance and the process by which they work. Part of the explanation, of course, is that there never is a printed record of what goes on in conference.[21]

Conference bargaining can be classified roughly in four ways: traditional, offer-counteroffer, subconference, and pro forma. Traditional conferences are those in which the participants meet face to face, haggle among themselves about the items in bicameral disagreement, and then reach an accord. The bulk of conferences are of this type. In offer-counteroffer conferences, often used by the tax-writing committees, one side suggests a compromise proposal; the other side recesses to discuss it in private and then returns to present a counteroffer. Conferences with numerous participants (on omnibus bills, for example) usually break into small units, or subconferences, to reconcile particular matters or to address special topics. Pro forma conferences are those in which issues are resolved informally—by preconference negotiations between conferee leaders or their staffs. The conference itself then ratifies the earlier decisions.[22]

Some scholars argue that congressional conference committees are powerful because they have unilateral authority to veto or negotiate alterations in legislation at a late stage in the process. Others dispute this contention and claim that the "ex post veto is not a significant institutional foundation of congressional committee power."[23] Another model suggests that conferees serve as agents of their respective chamber majorities, advocating their policy positions instead of conference committee viewpoints.[24] Whatever the claims, increasingly the top party leaders in each chamber are taking a direct and active role in determining those who should (or should not) be conferees. On occasion, the top leaders, such as the Senate majority leader or House majority leader, serve as conferees on priority measures to increase their leverage in the bicameral bargaining process.

THE ASSIGNMENT PROCESS

Every congressional election sets off a scramble for committee seats. Legislators understand the linkage between winning desirable assignments and winning elections. Newly elected representatives and senators quickly make their preferences known to party leaders, to members of the panels that make committee assignments, and to others—such as friendly lobbyists or generous contributors. They may be able to help the newcomers obtain their preferred committee seats. At the same time, incumbents may try to move to more prestigious panels.

The Pecking Order

The most powerful, and thus most desirable, standing committees are the House Ways and Means and Senate Finance, which pass on tax, trade, Social Security, and Medicare measures, and the House and Senate Appropriations Committees, which hold the federal purse strings. The Budget Committees, established in 1974, are sought-after assignments because of their important role in economic and fiscal matters and their guardianship of the congressional budgeting process. The House and Senate Commerce Committees, along with each chamber's banking and financial services committees, are also coveted panels: not only do they command broad jurisdictional mandates, but the many interest groups they affect can supply cash donations for the committee members' future election campaigns. To boost the reelection chances of some of the House Republican freshmen elected in 2010, the GOP leadership named twelve newcomers to Financial Services, five to Energy and Commerce, three to Appropriations, and two to Ways and Means. "The amount of money you can raise is almost entirely determined by committee membership," a GOP insider confided.[25]

Among those panels that seldom have waiting lists are the House and Senate Ethics Committees. These committees are not popular because legislators are reluctant to sit in judgment of their colleagues. "Members have never competed for the privilege of serving on the ethics committee, and I am no exception," remarked Rep. Howard L. Berman, D-Calif., after the Democratic leader prevailed on him to join the ethics panel. Or as one GOP member grumbled after serving as ethics chair, "I've paid my debt to society. It's time for me to be paroled."[26]

The attractiveness of committees can change. For example, the Senate Foreign Relations Committee was long a panel that elicited great interest among members, especially during the Vietnam War era. Once the Cold War ended, however, the panel often had trouble filling its vacancies. Throughout the 1990s, senators viewed it largely as a debating society without much influence either inside or outside the Senate. Today, because of heightened public concern about the global war on terrorism, an ongoing war in Afghanistan, instability in the Middle East, and a large array of other pressing global issues, the committee plays a major role in shaping the nation's policies in an uncertain world. "Yeah, they've got clout," one foreign policy expert explained. "You control money, you control nominations, you control treaties, and you control the microphone" to discuss an array of global issues. "That's a lot of power in Washington."[27]

Preferences and Politicking

In his analysis of six House committees, Richard F. Fenno Jr. found that three basic goals of lawmakers—reelection, influence within the House, and good public policy—affect the committee assignments that members sought. Reelection-oriented members were attracted to committees such as Natural Resources (then called the Interior Committee). Appropriations and Ways and Means attracted influence-oriented members. Policy-oriented members sought membership on the Education and Labor Committee (now Education and the Workforce) and the Foreign Affairs Committee. Members with similar goals found themselves on the same committees, Fenno concluded. Such homogeneity of perspectives may result in harmonious but biased committees (see Table 7-2).[28]

Since Fenno's study, scholars have elaborated on the link between members' goals and committee assignments. They have divided House committees into reelection (or constituency), policy, and power panels, and they concur that some mix of the three goals motivates most of the committees' activities. They agree, too, that members' goals "are less easily characterized in the Senate than in the House."[29] After all, most every senator has the opportunity to serve

TABLE 7-2 **House and Senate Committee Comparison**		
Category	House	Senate
Number of standing committees	20	16
Committee/subcommittee assignments per member	About 6	About 11
Power or prestige committees	Appropriations, Budget, Commerce, Financial Services, Rules, Ways and Means	Appropriations, Armed Services, Commerce, Finance, Foreign Relations[1]
Treaties and nominations submitted by the president	No authority	Committees review
Floor debate	Representatives' activity is somewhat confined to the bills reported from the panels on which they serve	Senators can choose to influence any policy area regardless of their committee assignments
Committee consideration of legislation	More difficult to bypass	Easier to bypass[2]
Committee chairs	Subject to party and speakership influence that can limit their discretionary authority over committee operations	Freer rein to manage committees
Committee staff	Often assertive in advocating ideas and proposals	More influential in shaping the legislative agenda
Subcommittee chairmanships	Representatives of the majority party usually must wait at least one term	Majority senators, regardless of their seniority, usually chair subcommittees

[1] Almost every senator is assigned to one of these committees.

[2] For example, by allowing riders—unrelated policy proposals—to measures pending on the floor.

on one of the top committees, such as Appropriations, Armed Services, Commerce, and Finance. Thus the power associated with a particular committee assignment is less important for senators than for representatives.

Members campaign vigorously for the committees they prefer. When Rep. Robert B. Aderholt, R-Ala., was a freshman, he set out to win a coveted spot on the Appropriations Committee. He solicited the help of the majority leader and lobbied each member who sat on the GOP's committee assignment panel. "It was almost like this was another congressional campaign," Aderholt explained. "While a lot of [new] members were driving around house hunting

---

BOX 7-1 How To Get the Committee Assignment You Want

The first step is to decide which committee assignments are right for you and your district. Soon after the organizational conference, you will receive a Dear Colleague letter from your leadership requesting that you submit your committee preferences. Expect this form by early December at the latest. Your personal policy interests, the needs of your district and state, and your future goals are important factors in deciding which committees to request.

Obtaining a seat on your preferred committee may be a multi-year process depending on vacancies and which committees you select. This applies especially to the "A" committees.

Second, be prepared to make your case as to why you should be selected to your committee of choice. The competition for committees such as Financial Services, Transportation and Infrastructure, and Armed Services can be intense.

Successful arguments may include highlighting your professional experience or policy expertise within the committee's jurisdiction, the critical needs of your district or state, the fact that your region of the country may be under-represented on the committee, or the fact that you may be a vulnerable freshman. Botton Line: This is about marketing yourself, your experience, you abilities, and your district.

Finally, you should engage the Steering Committee (the GOP's committee assignment panel). First, reach out its your class representative. They will be your primary voice on the Steering Committee and it is important that they be an advocate for your request. Keep in mind that your class representative must prioritize and balance the needs of your entire class.

You should also discuss your committee choices with the elected leaders. They hold a substantial block of votes on the Steering Committee. In addition, you may want to reach out to other members of the Steering Committee. Ideally, you want to have someone other than your class and regional representative speak in support of your request when the Steering Committee convenes.

---

and interviewing staff members, I was working" to win appointment to Appropriations.[30] In *Hit the Ground Running,* his guidebook for GOP newcomers to the 112th Congress, House majority leader Eric Cantor, R-Va., outlined the key steps for securing committee assignments (see Box 7-1).

Although both parties try to accommodate assignment preferences, some unlucky members still receive unwelcome assignments. A classic case was that of Democratic representative Shirley Chisholm of Brooklyn (1969–1983), the first African American woman elected to Congress. Initially, she was assigned to the House Agriculture Committee. "I think it would be hard to imagine an assignment that is less relevant to my background or to the needs of the predominantly black and Puerto Rican people who elected me," she said. Chisholm's protests won her a seat on the Veterans' Affairs Committee. "There are a lot more veterans in my district than there are trees," she later observed.[31] Yet some urban lawmakers welcome service on the Agriculture Committee, where they can fuse metropolitan issues with rural issues through food stamp, consumer, and other legislation.

How Assignments Are Made

Each party in each house has its own panel to review members' committee requests and dispense assignments to standing committees: the House Republican and Democratic Steering Committees, the Senate Republican Committee on Committees, and the Senate Democratic Steering and Outreach Committee. The decisions of these panels are the first and most important step in a three-step procedure. The second step involves approval of the assignment lists by each party's caucus. Finally, there is a pro forma election by the full House or Senate.

Formal Criteria. Both formal and informal criteria guide the assignment panels in choosing committee members. One formal rule is that each member be treated equitably. However, some lawmakers enjoy "grandfather" rights, meaning that newly adopted party rules governing committee service do not apply to them. For example, Senate GOP conference rules state that two Republicans from the same state should not serve on the same committee.

Since 1953 when Senate Democratic leader Lyndon B. Johnson of Texas announced his "Johnson rule," all Senate Democrats have been assigned one major committee before any party member receives a second major assignment. In 1965 Senate Republicans followed suit. Senate rules also classify committees into different categories, popularly called "A," "B," and "C." There is even a separate category of prestigious "Super A" committees. Senators may sit on only one of the four Super A panels: Appropriations, Armed Services, Finance, and Foreign Relations (unless they are granted a waiver of the rule). Senate Rule XXV states that members must serve on no more than two committees in the A category, which includes the four Super A panels; one in the B grouping (such as Budget, Rules and Administration, and Small Business); and any number of C committees (Ethics, Indian Affairs, Joint Library, Joint Printing, and Joint Taxation).

Informal Criteria. Many informal criteria affect committee assignments— including party loyalty, geography, substantive expertise, gender, or electoral vulnerability. In their party rules, House Democrats instruct the Steering Committee to consider "merit, length of service, degree of commitment to the Democratic agenda, and Caucus diversity" in granting committee assignments. Members' own wishes are another criterion. Lawmakers who represent districts or states with large military installations may seek assignment to the Armed Services Committee. Or lawmakers with a specific policy interest (education, health, and so on) may strive to win appointment to panels that deal with those topics. Finally, the committee assignment panels of each congressional party typically respect what is referred to as a "property norm." Returning lawmakers of each party are generally permitted to retain their committee seats (unless they are bumped because of committee ratio changes) before new members bid for vacant committee positions.

The two Congresses are always intertwined in committee assignment decisions. Each party seeks to boost the electoral resources of its members. House

Democratic and GOP leaders, for example, sometimes grant electorally vulnerable freshmen an extra committee assignment or two to broaden their appeal as they head toward their reelection contests. "All of these committees have constituents," said Democratic leader Steny Hoyer of Maryland. "And all of these [freshmen Democratic appointees] have people in their districts who are members of these constituencies."[32] More seasoned members who could face tough electoral competition may seek plum assignments as well to boost their influence and capacity for fund raising.

Party leaders also promise committee assignments to candidates to help them win election. In the 2010 elections, when Senate GOP leader Mitch McConnell, R-Ky., was campaigning in Arkansas for John Boozman, who was challenging incumbent senator Blanche Lincoln, D-La., he vowed he would appoint John Boozman to the Agriculture Committee. "John will be on the Agriculture Committee on Day One when we make the committee assignments," declared Senator McConnell. "I have the ability to put him on the Agriculture Committee, and I'm going to do that."[33] Senator Lincoln was the chair of the Agriculture Committee, and McConnell's promise helped to blunt Lincoln's claim that as the chair she could deliver for the farmers and consumers of Arkansas.

Seniority. Normally, the assignment panels observe seniority when preparing committee membership lists. The member of the majority party with the longest continuous committee service is usually listed first. Senate Republicans—unlike House Republicans and House and Senate Democrats—apply seniority rigidly when two or more GOP senators compete for either a committee vacancy or chairmanship. As a senator noted, "When I first came to the Senate, I was skeptical [of the seniority tradition]. But as I've become more senior, I've grown more fond of it."[34] (The Senate GOP leader fills half of all vacancies on the A committees; seniority determines the other half.)

By contrast, the two House parties do not observe seniority as strictly as Senate Republicans. House Democratic Caucus rules even state that the party's Steering and Policy Committee "need not necessarily follow seniority" in nominating members for committee posts (see Box 7-2 on party assignment committees). The following overview of how the four most recent Speakers—Newt Gingrich, R-Ga., Hastert, Pelosi, and Boehner—handled the selection of chairs reveals the changing character of the process.

Gingrich (1995–1999). Speaker Gingrich simply bypassed the seniority custom on several occasions to give chairmanships to lower-seniority colleagues whom he judged could move the party's agenda more vigorously than senior members. Gingrich also was instrumental in having the House adopt a rule imposing a six-year limit on committee and subcommittee chairs. This rule both promotes party direction of committees and triggers "musical chairs" whenever the chairs' six years have expired. (The Rules chair, appointed by the Speaker, is not subject by House rule to the six-year limit.) Republicans also adopted term limits as a party rule.

House Republicans. Before the 104th Congress began in 1995, incoming Speaker Newt Gingrich, R-Ga., revamped his party's committee on committees, which he would chair. Gingrich renamed it the Steering Committee; transformed it into a leadership-dominated panel; eliminated a weighted voting system wherein a GOP member of the assignment panel cast as many votes as there were Republicans in his state delegation; and granted the GOP leader the right to cast the most votes (five). These reforms continued in the subsequent Congresses. The Republican leader also appoints all GOP members of the Rules, House Administration, and Ethics Committees.

House Democrats. Democrats on the House Ways and Means Committee functioned as their party's committee on committees from 1911 until 1974, when the Democratic Caucus voted to transfer this duty to the Steering and Policy Committee. The Steering Committee, co-chaired by Rosa DeLauro of Connecticut and George Miller of California in the 112th Congress, recommends Democratic assignments to the caucus, one committee at a time.

Senate Republicans. The chair of the Republican Conference appoints the assignment panel of about eight members. In addition, the floor leader is an ex officio member. Idaho senator Michael D. Crapo chaired the panel during the 112th Congress.

Senate Democrats. The Steering and Outreach Committee makes assignments for Democrats. Its size (about twenty-five members) is set by the party conference and may fluctuate from Congress to Congress. The party's floor leader appoints the members of this panel and its chair (Sen. Mark Begich of Alaska, for the 112th Congress).

Hastert (1999–2007). When Dennis Hastert assumed the speakership, he decided to use an interview procedure to determine replacements for full committee chairs who had completed their six years. In a letter to GOP members, Speaker Hastert explained several features of the interview process: "The candidates [for each open chairmanship] will be given an opportunity to discuss their legislative agenda, oversight agenda, how they intend to organize the committees, and their communication strategy."[35] Party loyalty and fundraising prowess were also factors. "You can't tell me a Member who raises $1 million for the party and visits 50 districts is not going to have an advantage over someone who sits back and thinks he's entitled to a chairmanship. Those days are gone," said a top GOP leadership aide.[36] Even with term limits, there is no guarantee that chairs will be permitted to serve their full six years if they rouse the ire of party leaders. In an unprecedented event, GOP leaders ousted a colleague in 2004 (Christopher Smith of New Jersey) as chair of the Veterans' Affairs Committee, removed him from the panel, and named another member as chair. Smith's offense: his outspoken advocacy of more spending on veterans' benefits, which angered Speaker Hastert. The message of Smith's removal was plain to every Republican: toe the party line and be a team player or you will be benched.

Pelosi (2007–2011). Democratic Speaker Nancy Pelosi, unlike her GOP predecessors, chose to follow seniority in designating committee chairs. As a result, many of the Democratic chairs were liberal "old bulls" who either headed or were senior members of several of the most influential committees prior to the GOP takeover in 1995. The so-called old bulls included David Obey, Wis., of Appropriations; George Miller, Calif., of Education and Labor; Barney Frank, Mass., of Financial Services; John Conyers, Mich., of Judiciary; and Charles Rangel, N.Y., of Ways and Means. Few doubt that Pelosi exercised firm control of the Steering Committee's assignment process, however. The panel was chaired by two handpicked allies of the Speaker: California's Miller and Rosa DeLauro of Connecticut. Although Pelosi largely kept the chairs on a short leash, she did allow trusted allies, such as chairs Miller and Obey, greater independence. (Pelosi retained term limits for committee chairs in the 110th Congress, but dropped them from the House rulebook in the 111th.)

In the minority after the 2010 elections, a group of disgruntled Democrats wanted to reduce Pelosi's power by taking away her authority to name the Steering Committee co-chairs and transferring it to the Democratic Caucus. Pelosi, now minority leader, sidestepped that effort by offering an amendment to permit the members of the Steering Committee—stacked with Pelosi supporters—to select the co-chairs. Not surprisingly, committee members chose Miller and DeLauro.

What might have surprised the Steering Committee was the reversal (23–22) of their choice of Richard Neal, Mass., to replace Sander Levin, Mich.—who had chaired the Ways and Means Committee in the previous Congress—as the ranking member of that panel. The Democratic Caucus overturned the Steering Committee's recommendation by a 109–78 vote, confirming Levin as ranking member. A supporter of Levin explained that Neal was trying to leapfrog over four more senior Ways and Means Democrats to be the ranking member. "There is a certain amount of respect for not going against the seniority system, not going against an incumbent in that position," who was an effective chair, said Rep. Jan Schakowsky, Ill.[37]

Boehner (2011–). A former chair of the Education and the Workforce Committee and a principal author of the landmark "No Child Left Behind" law, Speaker Boehner announced that he would decentralize authority to the committees, empower them to do their job of recommending legislation for House consideration, and observe the "regular order" in lawmaking. "Regular order" meant that committees would hold hearings and markups and report their measures to the floor for an open and fair deliberative process. No longer would committees be bypassed and major bills written in secret by a select few in the Speaker's office. Speaker Boehner promised that the House would "operate in a manner that permits a free exchange of ideas and resolves our honest differences through a fair debate and vote."[38]

As chair of the GOP's Steering Committee with the right to cast more votes (five) than any other panel member, Speaker Boehner had to make several early chairmanship decisions because of the term limits on committee and subcommittee chairs. He wanted the term limit rule honored for the chairs of two influential committees, Appropriations and Energy and Commerce, and his position was upheld by the Steering Committee.

On Appropriations, Jerry Lewis, Calif., a former chair of the panel, wanted a waiver. He was challenged for the job by two other appropriators, Hal Rogers, Ky., and Jack Kingston, Ga. In individual appearances before the Steering Committee, all three promised to slash billions from the federal budget. Kingston was a favorite of Tea Party activists and conservative lobbyists, but much to their chagrin, in the three-way contest the Steering Committee chose Rogers as the new chair. Various conservative groups lamented that decision, because they viewed Rogers as insufficiently committed to cutting spending.

On Energy and Commerce, a former chair of the panel, Joe Barton of Texas, also sought a waiver. Speaker Boehner was not pleased that, as ranking member, Barton had publicly apologized to the head of BP for the federal government's heavy pressure on the company over the massive oil spill in the Gulf of Mexico. In the end, the Steering Committee named Fred Upton of Michigan to lead the panel, despite the opposition of many conservative and Tea Party activists. Upton's conservative critics argued that he had cooperated too much with Democrats and lacked sufficient zeal in cutting federal spending. (Upton, like every candidate for a committee chair, touted conservative credentials and promised to conduct vigorous oversight of the Obama administration.)

On the Senate side, Republicans adopted in 1997 a party rule restricting committee chairs (or ranking members) to six years of service. "The whole thrust behind this," said the Senate author of the term limit change, "is to try to get greater participation, so new members of the Senate don't have to wait until they've been here 18 years to play a role."[39] This goal is not easy to achieve, because long-serving Republicans are often senior on more than one committee. Thus when they hit the six-year limit, party rules permit them to seek the chairmanship (or ranking minority position) of another committee and leapfrog over a party member with less committee seniority. For example, after serving six years as either chair or ranking member of the Finance Committee, in the 112th Congress Sen. Charles Grassley, R-Iowa, became the ranking member on the Judiciary Committee. Grassley's predecessor on Judiciary was Sen. Orrin Hatch of Utah, who claimed the ranking post on Finance.

Senate Democrats have no term limit rule for their committee leaders. Their long-standing tradition is to allow seniority to determine who will be either the chair or ranking minority member of a standing committee. But Senate rules also limit members to one chairmanship. In 2011 Democratic senator Barbara Boxer, Calif., returned as head of the Environment and Public Works Committee, even though she was outranked by two of her colleagues, Max Baucus, Mont., and Joseph Lieberman, I-Conn. Baucus chose to continue to chair the Finance Committee, as did Lieberman to chair the Homeland Security and Governmental Affairs Committee.

Biases. The decisions made by the assignment panels inevitably determine the geographical and ideological composition of the standing committees. Committees can easily become biased toward one position or another. Farm areas are overrepresented on the Agriculture Committees and small business interests on the Small Business Committees. It is no wonder, then, that committees are policy advocates. They propose laws that serve the interests of their members and the outside groups and agencies that gravitate toward them.

Both who gets on a panel and who does not affect committee policy making. Committees that are carefully balanced between liberal and conservative interests can be tilted one way or the other by new members. Meanwhile, the number of women on a committee can sometimes change committee dynamics and outcomes. And new committee leaders can shift a panel's policy agenda and outlook. Senator Boxer's views on environmental policy diverged sharply from those of the previous chair, Sen. James Inhofe, R-Okla: "Inhofe calls global warming a hoax; Boxer ranks curbing global warming as one of her two top priorities."[40] A committee's political philosophy influences its success on the House or Senate floor. Committees ideologically out of step with the House or Senate majority are more likely than others to have legislation defeated or significantly revised by floor amendments.

Approval by Party Caucuses and the Chamber

For most of the last century, each chamber's party caucuses either simply ratified the assignment decisions of their committees on committees or took no action on them at all. Beginning in the 1970s, however, party caucuses became major participants in the assignment process. Chairs and ranking minority members were subjected to election by secret ballot of their party colleagues. Clearly, committee leadership is no longer an automatic right.

Although seniority still encourages continuity on committees, the seniority system has now become more flexible and is under party control. House Democratic rules for the 112th Congress state that upon "a demand supported by 10 or more Members, a separate vote, by secret ballot, shall be had on any member of a committee. . . . If the noes prevail on any such vote, the committee list . . . in question shall be returned to the [Steering Committee] for the sole purpose of implementing the direction of the Caucus." In the Senate, the parties can exercise control over committees but nearly always defer to the seniority rankings of lawmakers in determining who heads a committee or subcommittee.

Each chamber's rules require that all members of standing committees, including chairs, be elected by the entire House or Senate. The practice is for each party's leaders to offer the caucus-approved assignment lists to the full chamber. Normally, these are approved quickly by voice vote.

COMMITTEE LEADERSHIP

Committee chairs call meetings and establish agendas, hire and fire committee staff, arrange hearings, recommend conferees, act as floor managers, allocate committee funds and rooms, develop legislative strategies, chair hearings and markups, and regulate the internal affairs and organization of their committees.

A chair's procedural advantages are hard for even the most forceful minority members to overcome. The chair may be able to kill a bill simply by refusing to schedule it for a hearing. Or a chair may convene meetings when proponents or opponents of the legislation are unavoidably absent. The chair's authority derives from the support of a committee majority and a variety of formal and informal resources, such as substantive and parliamentary experience and control over the agenda, communications, and financial resources of the committee. When told by a committee colleague that he lacked the votes on an issue, House Energy and Commerce chair John Dingell, Mich., reminded him, "Yeah, but I've got the gavel."[41] Dingell banged his gavel, adjourned the meeting, and the majority had no chance to work its will before the legislative session ended.

The Dingell example highlights the formidable ability of chairs to stymie action on legislation they oppose. However, committee chairs also are among the most substantively and strategically knowledgeable members of their panel and of the chamber. They are advantageously positioned to advance ideas into law. When Bill Thomas, R-Calif., headed the Ways and Means Committee (2001–2007), he was acknowledged as hard-working, assertive, and shrewd. On many controversial issues (tax, trade, and health), he skillfully mobilized winning coalitions in committee, in the chamber, and in conference with the Senate. Thomas even sought out senatorial advice on how to move legislation in the House in a way that would maximize its chances in the Senate. "He will venture to the Senate floor to run options by key senators of both parties, or to stop in Senate leadership offices, before returning to the House to brief appropriate leaders on the latest state of play."[42]

The ranking minority party members on committees are also influential figures. Among their powers on various committees are nominating minority conferees, hiring and firing minority staff, sitting ex officio on all subcommittees, assisting in setting the committee's agenda, managing legislation on the floor, and acting as committee spokespersons for their party. Ranking members, as appropriate, present minority alternatives to majority proposals, challenge the chair on procedural and policy matters, develop tactics and strategies to foil the majority's plans, and highlight party goals and views to the attentive public.

Two examples from the 112th Congress involve ranking members who serve as party and policy advocates. Rep. Edward Markey, D-Mass., ranking member on the Natural Resources Committee, has been aggressive in confronting GOP members on the panel about their attempts to weaken federal environmental regulations. Elijah Cummings, D-Md., won the ranking position on the Oversight and Government Reform Committee over other competitors because he was viewed as more able than the others to counterattack the aggressive and media-savvy chair of the panel, Darrel Issa of California.[43]

POLICY MAKING IN COMMITTEE

Committees foster deliberate and collegial but often fragmented decisions. They encourage bargaining and accommodation among members. To move bills through Congress's multiple decision points from subcommittee to committee, authors of bills and resolutions typically make compromises in response to important committee members, among others. These gatekeepers may exact numerous alterations in a bill's substance. The proliferation of committees also multiplies the points of access for outside interests.

Overlapping Jurisdictions

The formal responsibilities of standing committees are defined by the rules of each house, various public laws, and precedents. Committees do not have watertight jurisdictional compartments. Any broad subject overlaps numerous committees. The Senate has an Environment and Public Works Committee, but other panels also consider environmental legislation. The same is true in the House. These House bodies, along with a brief sketch of some of their environmental responsibilities, are as follows:

Agriculture: pesticides; soil conservation; some water programs

Appropriations: funding for environmental programs and agencies

Energy and Commerce: health effects of the environment; environmental regulations; solid waste disposal; clean air; safe drinking water

Financial Services: open space acquisition in urban areas

Foreign Affairs: international environmental cooperation

Natural Resources: water resources; power resources; land management; wildlife conservation; national parks; nuclear waste; fisheries; endangered species

Oversight and Government Reform: federal executive branch agencies for the environment

Science, Space, and Technology: environmental research and development

Small Business: effects of environmental regulations on business

Transportation and Infrastructure: water pollution; sludge management

Ways and Means: environmental tax expenditures.

Jurisdictional overlaps can have positive results. They enable members to develop expertise in several policy fields, prevent any one group from dominating a topic, and promote healthy competition among committees. Committees with overlapping jurisdictions sometimes formulate a written memorandum of understanding that informally outlines how policy topics are to be referred among them.[44] But healthy competition can quickly turn into intercommittee warfare. Various House and Senate committees periodically clash over issues that do not fit neatly into any single panel's area of responsibility (energy and environmental issues, for example). Committees' formal jurisdictional mandates have not kept pace with change—nor can they given the constant emergence of new issues (such as global warming). Another trigger of turf battles is forum shopping by outside interests who want their carefully drafted bills referred to sympathetic committees.

The expansionist tendency of some committees also can create intercommittee tussles. The "bold jurisdictional power grab" by the House Energy and Commerce Committee for an intellectual copyright bill will not stand, declared the bipartisan leaders of the Judiciary Committee. "Rest assured, we will wholeheartedly oppose this move in a bipartisan fashion, as we would expect Energy and Commerce leaders to do if we attempted to write energy legislation."[45] At the start of the 112th Congress, the incoming chair of the Natural Resources Committee, Doc Hastings, R-Wash., urged GOP leaders to transfer energy jurisdiction from the Energy and Commerce Committee to his panel. "In terms of legislative power, it is a Goliath," Hastings declared. "[Energy and Commerce] is the committee that spawned Obamacare and the Democrats' cap-and-trade national energy tax."[46] Energy and Commerce chair Fred Upton, R-Mich., quickly defended his panel's jurisdiction. "To diminish the authority of the Energy and Commerce Committee," he wrote, "is to weaken the power of the House—the people's body-—and give an upper hand to the Democrat[ic] White House and Senate."[47] Another GOP Energy and Commerce panel member bluntly stated that Hastings's move "will not be successful. You don't spend four years getting back into the majority and immediately go into cannibal mode."[48] In the end, the GOP Steering Committee rejected Hastings's effort to capture part of the Energy and Commerce panel's jurisdiction.[49]

Multiple Referrals

When a bill is introduced in the House, it usually is referred to a single committee. House rules traditionally made no provision for multiple referrals, although informally at times more than one panel reviewed the same bill. In 1975, however, the rules were changed to permit several types of multiple referrals. This change augmented the Speaker's authority and granted him additional flexibility in referring measures to various committees.

When Republicans assumed control of the House in 1995, they streamlined multiple referrals and placed them firmly under the Speaker's control. The Speaker must "designate a committee of primary jurisdiction upon the initial referral of a measure to a committee." The primary committee concept increases accountability for legislation while retaining for the Speaker flexibility in determining whether, when, and for how long other panels can receive the measure.

At the time of initial referral, the Speaker identifies the primary committee. It has predominant responsibility for shepherding the legislation to final passage. The Speaker may also send the measure to secondary panels. The House parliamentarian calls this practice an additional initial referral. In the following example of referral language, the Energy and Commerce Committee is the primary committee and Judiciary is the additional initial panel:

> H.R. 650. A bill to establish reasonable legal reforms that will facilitate the manufacture of vital, life-saving vaccines, and for other purposes; to the Committee on Energy and Commerce, and in addition to the Committee on the Judiciary, for a period to be subsequently determined by the Speaker, in each case for consideration of such provisions as fall within the jurisdiction of the committee concerned.

Multiple referrals may promote integrated policy making, broader public discussion of issues, wider access to the legislative process, and consideration of alternative approaches. They also enhance the Speaker's scheduling prerogatives. The Speaker can use the referral power to intervene more directly in committee activities and even to set deadlines for committees to report multiply referred legislation. The reverse is also possible: the Speaker can delay action on measures by referring them to other committees. Thus multiple referrals can be employed to slow down legislative decision making.

The Senate usually sends measures to a single committee—the committee with jurisdiction over the subject matter that predominates in the legislation. Although multiple referrals have long been permitted by unanimous consent, they are used infrequently, mainly because senators have many opportunities to influence policy making on the floor. Senate procedures provide lawmakers with relatively easy ways either to bypass the referral of legislation to committees or to raise issues for chamber consideration.

Where Bills Go

Many bills referred to committee are sent by the chair to a subcommittee. Others are retained for review by the full committee. In the end, committees and subcommittees select the measures they want to consider and ignore the rest. Committee consideration usually consists of three standard steps: public hearings, markups, and reports.

Hearings. When committees or subcommittees conduct hearings on a bill, they listen to a wide variety of witnesses. These include the bill's sponsors, federal officials, pressure group representatives, business leaders, public officials, and private citizens—sometimes even celebrities. Celebrity witnesses can help give a bill national visibility. As Sen. Arlen Specter, D-Pa., put it, "Quite candidly, when Hollywood speaks, the world listens. Sometimes when Washington speaks, the world snoozes."[50]

Equally important are witnesses who add drama to hearings because of their first-hand experience with an issue or problem. The Senate Finance Committee, for example, attracted national headlines with its hearings on alleged wrongdoings by the Internal Revenue Service (IRS). Taxpayers recounted their horrendous experiences, and IRS agents donned black hoods to tell about the organization's mistreatment of taxpayers.[51] Testimony by employees who lost their jobs and retirement savings because of corporate scandals and mismanagement helped to galvanize congressional enactment of corporate accounting and accountability laws, such as the Dodd-Frank Wall Street Reform and Consumer Protection Act (P.L. 111–203).[52] Dueling hearings in the House and Senate during the 112th Congress featured as witnesses citizens who had experienced first-hand the effect of the health care overhaul. Witnesses in House hearings castigated and criticized what they called Obamacare. In response, Senate Democratic committee hearings in defense of the health care law heard "testimony from people who live outside the Beltway."[53] Hearings, then, are often orchestrated as political theater in which witnesses put a human face on a public problem and tell stories that may generate public momentum for or against legislation.[54]

Hearings also provide opportunities for committee members to be heard on issues. Frequently, lawmakers present their views on legislation in their opening statements and in the guise of questioning witnesses. By revealing the patterns and intensity of support or opposition and by airing substantive problems, hearings indicate to members whether a bill is worth taking to the full chamber. Most hearings follow a traditional format. Each witness reads a prepared statement. Then each committee member has a limited time (often five minutes) to ask questions before the next witness is called. To save time and promote give-and-take, committees occasionally use a panel format in which witnesses sit together and briefly summarize their statements.

Committees will sometimes convene joint hearings with other relevant House or Senate panels. They also may organize field hearings in cities around the country to generate and solicit public support for an issue, or, in a two Congresses theme, schedule hearings in the chair's state or district to win him or her favorable publicity and visibility prior to the November elections. Party committees, ad hoc legislative groups, or individual lawmakers also may conduct informal hearings of their own. Committees may even hold pre-hearings so committee members can be better informed about the issues likely to be raised during a scheduled hearing.

Committees are harnessing contemporary technology to conduct Capitol Hill hearings. Recent Speakers urged all committees to utilize technology to provide live broadcasts of their hearings online ("Webcasts") in order to make the legislative process "fully accessible and transparent" to the public.[55] House and Senate panels have used interactive video, teleconferencing, e-hearings, and other technology to collect testimony from witnesses who may be located in other parts of the nation or world. The Internet has been used to transmit testimony, and cable television viewers have e-mailed or faxed questions to witnesses.[56] And, in a first, an astronaut became the only person ever to deliver testimony from space to a committee hearing on Capitol Hill.[57]

Some of the overlapping purposes served by hearings are the following:

- To explore the need for legislation
- To build a public record in support of legislation
- To publicize the role of committee chairs
- To stake out committee jurisdictions
- To review executive implementation of public laws
- To provide a forum for citizens' grievances and frustrations
- To educate lawmakers and the attentive public on complex issues
- To raise the visibility of an issue

Hearings are shaped mainly by the chairs and staff, with varying degrees of input from party leaders, the ranking minority member, and others. Chairs who favor bills can expedite the hearings process; conversely, they can kill with kindness legislation they oppose by holding endless hearings. When a bill is not sent to the full chamber, the printed hearings are the end product of the committee's work. Committee chairs, mindful of the two Congresses, can also use hearings to try and win reelection by addressing issues that appeal to various voting groups in their state or district.

Markups. After hearings are held, committee members decide the bill's actual language—that is, they mark up or amend the bill (see Box 7-2 on committee decision making). Chairs may circulate their "mark" (the measure open for amendment) to committee colleagues and solicit their comments and suggestions.

To promote greater transparency and accountability, House Republicans adopted rules for the 112th Congress that require committees to make their markup vehicle available online to the public at least twenty-four hours prior to markup meetings. In addition, committees are obligated to make amendments adopted during markup publicly available online within twenty-four hours, and record votes during markups are to be publicly available in electronic form within forty-eight hours.

Some panels adhere closely to parliamentary rules during the committee amending phase; others operate by consensus with few or no votes taken on the issues; and still others have "conceptual markups." A senator explained that Finance Committee markups "are not about legislative language. There are concept documents that are then put into legislative language and brought to the floor."[58] Concepts may include, for example, whether going to school counts as work for welfare recipients or what kind of tax plan best fosters economic growth. Proponents try to craft a bill that will muster the backing of their colleagues, the other chamber, lobbyists, and the White House.

The markup process can be arduous because members often face the two Congresses dilemma: whether to support a bill that might be good for the nation or oppose it because of the opposition of their constituents. Not surprisingly, the bill that emerges from markup is usually the one that can attract the support of the most members. As a former chair of the House Ways and

Means Committee stated, "We have not written perfect law; perhaps a faculty of scholars could do a better job. A group of ideologues could have produced greater consistency. But politics is an imperfect process."[59] Or as Sen. Pat Roberts, R-Kan., said about a bill revamping the intelligence community: "While this is not the best possible bill, it is the best bill possible."[60]

Outside pressures often intensify during markup deliberations. Under House and Senate sunshine rules, markups must be conducted in public, except on national security or related issues. Compromises can be difficult to achieve in markup rooms filled with lobbyists watching how each member will vote. Thus committees sometimes conduct pre-markups in private to work out their positions on various issues.

After conducting hearings and markups, a subcommittee sends its recommendations to the full committee. The full committee may conduct hearings and markups on its own, ratify the subcommittee's decision, take no action, or return the matter to the subcommittee for further study.

Reports. If the full committee votes to send the bill to the House or Senate, the staff prepares a report, subject to committee approval, describing the purposes and provisions of the legislation. Reports emphasize arguments favorable to the bill, summarizing selectively the results of staff research and hearings. Reports are noteworthy documents. The bill itself may be long, highly technical, and confusing to most readers. "A good report, therefore, does more than explain—it also persuades," commented a congressional staff aide.[61] Furthermore, reports may guide executive agencies and federal courts in interpreting ambiguous or complex legislative language.

The Policy Environment

Executive agencies, pressure groups, party leaders and caucuses, and the entire House or Senate form the backdrop against which a committee makes policy. These environments may be consensual or conflictual. Some policy questions are settled fairly easily; others are bitterly controversial. Environments also may be monolithic or pluralistic. Some committees have a single dominant source of outside influence; others face numerous competing groups or agencies.

Environmental factors influence committees in at least four ways. First, they shape the content of public policies and thus the likelihood that these policies will be accepted by the full House or Senate. The Judiciary Committees are buffeted by diverse and competing pressure groups that feel passionately about volatile issues such as abortion, immigration, and gun control. The committees' chances for achieving agreement among their members or on the floor depend to a large extent on their abilities to deflect such issues altogether or to accommodate diverse groups through artful legislative drafting.

Second, policy environments foster mutual alliances among committees, federal departments, and pressure groups—the "iron triangles." The House and Senate Veterans' Affairs Committees, for example, regularly advocate legislation to benefit veterans groups, the second point in the triangle. This effort

BOX 7-3 Committee Decision Making: A Formal Model

Political scientists use a variety of sophisticated techniques to understand legislative decision making. Employing concepts from economics such as rational choice—the notion that individuals (or lawmakers) have preferences or desires and that they will act in their self-interest to achieve their goals—these scholars utilize a number of analytical tools to consider how lawmakers devise strategies to accomplish their policy objectives. One such analytical approach is called spatial theory. The term *spatial* refers to a mathematical idea that theorists rely on called a policy space. An easy-to-understand example is that certain policy preferences can all be arrayed along a straight line, or unidimensional continuum. So, for example, one end of the line might be labeled "more spending" and the other "less spending." Different spending preferences could be placed at different points, or spaces, along the line.

In employing spatial theory to model legislative decision making, scholars make a number of assumptions. Two are especially important: (1) lawmakers hold consistent preferences and (2) members have an ideal policy outcome that they prefer. Put differently, lawmakers will vote for policy alternatives that bring them closer to their policy ideal and oppose those that do the reverse. The work of these scholars highlights the importance of institutional rules and procedures in determining which of several policy alternatives will prevail. Analysts have also found that the median voter—the midpoint lawmaker with an equal number of other members to his left or right—is the ultimate determiner of outcomes in unidimensional cases. Another way to view the median voter is the 218th vote in the House, the Supreme Court justice who casts the fifth vote in a 5–4 decision, or the member who casts the sixth vote in a committee of eleven members.

To depict this graphically, assume that a House Appropriations subcommittee has sent to the floor a spending bill that reflects its committee median (CM). The subcommittee also must take into account a floor median (FM) if it wants its majority position to carry the day on the floor. The current policy status quo (Q) means that, if the bill does not pass, last year's funding level remains in force. If the subcommittee's bill is brought to the floor under a no-amendment rule, then the House membership can either accept or reject the panel's position. If the House rejects the subcommittee's policy recommendation, it has agreed to retain the status quo. Whether the subcommittee's position prevails on the floor can be depicted using these two examples.

If the subcommittee's position is to win on the House floor, it must devise a strategy that takes account of the majority preferences of the membership. Furthermore, the subcommittee

is backed by the Department of Veterans Affairs, the third point in the triangle. At the very least, issue networks emerge. These are fluid and amorphous groups of policy experts who try to influence any committee that deals with their subject area.[62]

Third, policy environments establish decision-making objectives and guidelines for committees. Clientele-oriented committees, such as the House and Senate Small Business Committees, try to promote the policy views of their clientele groups, small business enterprises. Alliances between committees and federal departments also shape decisions, such as the traditional support given the military by the House and Senate Armed Services Committees.

must have some way to acquire information about the policy options likely to be accepted by at least a majority of the House. These types of considerations are commonplace in the real world of Capitol Hill policy making.

Example 1

More spending   Less spending

      FM   CM   Q

In Example 1, the preferences of a majority of the House clearly are closer to the committee's position than the status quo. Thus, the committee's position prevails.

Example 2

More spending   Less spending

      FM   Q   CM

In Example 2, a majority of the House clearly favors the policy status quo instead of the committee's position, which loses in an up-or-down floor vote.

Most bills concern not a single dimension, such as more or less spending, but a multitude of dimensions. For example, a bill might be close to a member's ideal point on the spending dimension but be far away on another dimension, such as which governmental level (federal or state) should handle the issue. The introduction of additional dimensions (multidimensionality) produces greater difficulty in analyzing legislative decision making. By employing spatial theory and other analytical approaches, political scientists strive to better understand and explain congressional politics and decision making.[1]

[1] See, for example, Kenneth Shepsle and Mark Boncheck, *Analyzing Politics* (New York: Norton, 1977); Charles Stewart, *Analyzing Congress* (New York: Norton, 2001); and Gerald Strom, *The Logic of Lawmaking: A Spatial Theory Approach* (Baltimore: Johns Hopkins University Press, 1990).

Finally, environmental factors influence the level of partisanship on committees. Some committees are relatively free of party infighting, but other committees consider contentious social issues that often divide the two parties. The House Judiciary Committee is filled with conservative Republican and liberal Democratic firebrands. Their sharp ideological clashes sometimes receive wide publicity such as the panel's nationally televised impeachment of President Bill Clinton along party lines. To try to reduce the intense partisanship on the committee, Judiciary chair Lamar Smith, R-Texas, organized a bipartisan retreat early in the 112th Congress as a way for committee members "to find common ground despite the strong feelings on a lot of issues."[63]

COMMITTEE STAFF

Staff aides play a big role in the three principal stages of committee policy making—hearings, markup, and report. Representatives and senators (the latter to a greater degree because there are fewer of them) cannot handle their large workloads on their own, and so must rely heavily on their unelected employees. Indeed, Congress needs qualified professional staff to counter the expertise lodged in the executive branch and in the lobbying community. In the House and Senate, committee resources are roughly divided between the majority and minority parties on a two-thirds to one-third basis. Informally, both parties rely on a network of outside experts to help them evaluate proposals from the executive branch, forge policy proposals, or provide strategic advice. For example, some conservative think tanks, such as the Heritage Foundation, are developing for congressional Republicans health care ideas to serve as possible alternatives to what they call Obamacare.[64]

The discretionary agenda of Congress and its committees is powerfully shaped by the congressional staff. Their influence can be direct or indirect, substantive or procedural, visible or invisible. In the judgment of one former senator, "Most of the work and most of the ideas come from the staffers. They are predominantly young men and women, fresh out of college and professional schools. They are ambitious, idealistic, and abounding with ideas."[65] However, staff tenure is relatively short. According to a 2010 survey conducted by the House's Chief Administrative Office, the tenure of personal staff ranges from 6.7 years for chiefs of staff to 1.8 years for staff assistants. The average tenure for Senate aides is about 5.3 years. Many committee, personal, and leadership aides use their experience as a stepping-stone to other jobs, such as lobbying.

Policy proposals emanate from many sources—the White House, administrative agencies, interest groups, state and local officials, scholars, and citizens—but staff aides are strategically positioned to advance or hinder these proposals. As one Senate committee staff director recounted, "Usually, you draw up proposals for the year's agenda, lay out the alternatives. You can put in some stuff you like and leave out some you don't. I recommend ideas that the [chair is] interested in and also that I'm interested in."[66] Many committee staff members are active in outside communications and issue networks (health or environment, for example) that enhance lawmakers' abilities to make informed decisions.[67]

Staff aides negotiate with legislators, lobbyists, and executive officials on issues, legislative language, and political strategy. Staff members do the essential spadework that can lead to changes in policy or new laws. For example, a "team totaling 20 [Senate Governmental Affairs] aides, including detailees from the FBI and [Central Intelligence Agency]" drafted the 2004 bill that reorganized the nation's intelligence community.[68] Staff aides sometimes make policy decisions. Consider their crucial role on a defense appropriations bill:

The dollar figures in the huge piece of legislation [were] so immense that House-Senate conferees, negotiating their differences . . . , relegated almost every item less than $100 million to staff aides on grounds that the members themselves did not have time to deal with such items, which [a senator] called "small potatoes."[69]

During hearings, aides recruit witnesses, on their own or at the specific direction of the chair, and plan when and in what order they appear. In addition, staff aides commonly accompany committee members to the floor to give advice, draft amendments, and negotiate compromises. The number of aides who can be present on the floor is limited, however, by House and Senate regulations.

For information, analyses, policy options, and research projects, committee staff can turn to the three legislative support agencies: the Congressional Research Service, established in 1914; the Government Accountability Office, established in 1921 (as the General Accounting Office and renamed in 2004); and the Congressional Budget Office, established in 1974. Unlike committee or personal aides, the Congressional Research Service, the Government Accountability Office, and the Congressional Budget Office operate under strict rules of nonpartisanship and objectivity. Staffed with experts, they provide Congress with analytical talent matching that in executive agencies, universities, and specialized groups.

Staffing reflects members' dual roles in the two Congresses: national policy maker and constituency representative. It can be a controversial process. A New Jersey senator, for example, was criticized by African American clergy in his state for "failing to appoint blacks to important positions on his personal staff" as he had promised when running for office. The senator responded that he had hired professional black staffers and "defended his efforts to hire members of racial minorities."[70] During the electoral season, staffers frequently take unpaid leave to work as campaign volunteers for their boss or "to boost their party's prospects in pivotal races."[71]

COMMITTEE REFORM AND CHANGE

Since passage of the Legislative Reorganization Act of 1946, Congress has made numerous attempts to reform the committee system but has only rarely succeeded. Because of strong opposition from members who stood to surrender subcommittee chairmanships or favored jurisdictions, Congress has had only mixed success in reorganization efforts. Two changes to the committee system illustrate some of the difficulties associated with changing the committee structure. One revision created a homeland security panel in each chamber; another concerned the formation and then the demise of a select intelligence panel within the House Appropriations Committee. Needless to say, there were other committee changes during this period, such as the renaming of three House committees (from Education and Labor to Education and the Workforce, for example) at the start of the 112th Congress.

Homeland Security Committees

The National Commission on Terrorist Attacks upon the United States (the so-called 9/11 Commission) urged the House and Senate to each create a single authorizing committee for homeland security. Its report stated that at least eighty-eight committees and subcommittees in Congress had some jurisdiction over the Department of Homeland Security. Arguably, the formation of House and Senate homeland security panels would minimize turf conflicts, reduce the number of panels top DHS officials would have to appear before as witnesses, and strengthen congressional oversight of the new department. Eventually, both chambers responded to the commission's suggestion, but in different ways.

In the Senate, the GOP and Democratic leaders created in August 2004 a twenty-two-person working group (headed by Senators Mitch McConnell and Harry Reid) to review the commission's recommendations for improving oversight of intelligence and homeland security. Two months later, the Senate debated the McConnell-Reid plan (S. Res. 445), which called for renaming the Governmental Affairs Committee the Homeland Security and Governmental Affairs Committee and assigning it broad authority for overseeing domestic security and DHS. Achieving that objective, however, would require ten standing committees to give up some of their jurisdiction to the renamed Governmental Affairs panel.

During floor action on S. Res. 445, several amendments were successfully offered by committee chairs and ranking members that reclaimed the jurisdiction that would have been lost to the renamed Governmental Affairs Committee if the resolution was adopted unchanged. "We're creating a shell," lamented Joseph I. Lieberman of Connecticut, the ranking Democrat on the Governmental Affairs Committee. "We're calling a committee a homeland security committee. But if you pick up the shell, there's not much homeland security under it."[72] The chair of the Governmental Affairs Committee, Susan Collins, R-Maine, said the changes made to S. Res. 445 left her newly renamed panel with "less than 38 percent of the Department of Homeland Security's budget and 8 percent of its personnel."[73] Dismayed by these events, both Collins and Lieberman voted against S. Res. 445, which was approved on October 9, 2004, by a 79–6 vote. S. Res. 445 also called for the creation of a Senate Appropriations Subcommittee on Intelligence, but that proposal was not acted upon.

At the opening of the 109th Congress, the House replaced its temporary select panel on homeland security with a standing committee. The permanent panel was given, among other responsibilities, jurisdiction over overall homeland security policy and the organization and administration of the Department of Homeland Security. The new committee also was assigned broad oversight authority over all government "activities relating to homeland security, including the interaction of all departments and agencies with the Department of Homeland Security." Even with creation of the new panel, however, oversight of homeland security is still spread among nine other authorizing committees.

The turf-conscious committee chairs negotiated with their party leaders to preserve some portion of their panels' jurisdictions that had been given to the new standing committee. A detailed analysis of how homeland security legislation was to be referred among all the committees with homeland security jurisdiction was included in the *Congressional Record*.[74] To illustrate, the Homeland Security Committee is to receive bills dealing with "transportation security," and the Transportation and Infrastructure Committee retains its jurisdiction over measures dealing with "transportation safety." Plainly, this jurisdictional distinction is somewhat akin to the adage "two sides of the same coin."

At the start of the 112th Congress, House GOP leaders considered—and rejected—giving the Homeland Security Committee the predominance of jurisdiction over the Department of Homeland Security. Peter King, R-N.Y., the chair of the Homeland Security panel, urged party leaders to consolidate significant policy and oversight responsibility in his committee rather than maintain the status quo of having DHS subject to the marching orders of numerous committees and subcommittees. John Mica, R-Fla., the head of the Transportation Committee, along with other committee chairs, argued, however, that "their committees should get more homeland security turf, not less."[75] Plainly, GOP leaders did not want to open the new Congress with a bitter and divisive jurisdictional battle over committee turf and quietly quashed the matter.

Select Intelligence Oversight Panel

The 9/11 Commission declared congressional oversight of intelligence "dysfunctional." It recommended that the House and Senate create a single panel with the authority to both authorize and appropriate funds for the intelligence community. On the November 2006 campaign trail, the Pelosi-led Democrats vowed to implement all the outstanding recommendations of the commission, including the merger of the authorizing and appropriating processes for intelligence. In partial fulfillment of that promise, Speaker Pelosi successfully advocated a plan that achieved the goal of strengthening intelligence oversight without implementing the commission's exact recommendation.

Her proposal, which the House adopted on January 9, 2007, established a Select Intelligence Oversight Panel on Appropriations as a component of the Appropriations Committee. The panel is composed of thirteen members (eight majority members, five minority)—ten from the Appropriations Committee and three from the Permanent Select Intelligence Committee. The job of the select panel is to submit its recommendation for the intelligence community budget to the Appropriations Subcommittee on Defense, which would prepare, as stated in the select panel's authorizing resolution

(H. Res. 35), "the classified annex to the bill making appropriations for the Department of Defense." (Intelligence funding is largely hidden in the classified annex, or section, of the Pentagon's annual budget.)

During floor debate on H. Res. 35, Republicans said the arrangement neither merged the authorizing and appropriating functions in a single committee nor streamlined oversight of intelligence. As far as "I can tell," remarked one GOP lawmaker, "the only authority this [select panel] has is to write a report to the same people who serve on the [Appropriations Committee]. They could write a report and give it to themselves." In reply, Appropriations chair David Obey, who served on the select panel, argued that with the change the intelligence community could no longer ignore the House's intelligence authorizing committee because now it had a say in how much money would be allocated to intelligence (over $80 billion in 2010). "In this town," said Obey, "people follow the money." (The Senate Committees on Appropriations and Intelligence reached an agreement allowing selected staff with appropriate security clearances to "attend closed-door markups in both panels" and to have "access to both panels' budgets prior to markups."[76])

When Republicans reclaimed control of the House after the 2010 November elections, they abolished the Select Intelligence Oversight Panel. They argued that the panel was a redundant layer of committee bureaucracy. Other committees—Armed Services, Homeland Security, and Permanent Select Intelligence—could achieve the goal of intercommittee coordination between authorizers and appropriators that led to the select panel's formation in the first place. House Democrats urged Republicans to reestablish the panel, but they were not successful. Rush Holt, D-N.J., the outgoing chair of the select panel, said Republicans supported its elimination because the idea for it originated with their nemesis, Speaker Pelosi.[77] A House GOP leadership aide contended that the "sub-panel created by Democrats" did not establish one committee with both authorizing and appropriating authority over the intelligence community. Instead, the Democratic plan "diffused rather than consolidated oversight."[78] (See pp. 442–443 for more on this issue.)

Committees are remarkably durable, resilient, and stable institutions, despite the periodic forces for change that buffet them (such as public criticism of Congress and reformist sentiment among institutionally minded lawmakers). Major committee restructuring plans, as the several committee reform efforts in the post–World War II period attest, almost always fail or produce only marginal adjustments in committees' jurisdictional mandates, policy-making influence, or method of operation. Scholars and lawmakers posit various theories to explain why it is difficult to accomplish major jurisdictional realignment. For example, because the control of jurisdictional turf is viewed as power, Speaker Thomas P. "Tip" O'Neill Jr., D-Mass., explained the House's rejection of a major 1973–1974 committee realignment plan in this succinct manner: "The name of the game is power, and the boys don't want to give it up."[79] A political scientist offered an electoral explanation for the demise of committee reshuffling plans that embodies the two Congresses concept:

[A] primary and constant force hindering committee restructuring movements has been the electoral objectives of members of Congress. Under pressure to bolster their reelection prospects in order to achieve long-term legislative and personal goals, rational politicians with the ability to shape legislative structures utilize the arrangement of rules and procedures to secure targeted government benefits for needy constituents and voting blocs. Any widespread change in the established order of policy deliberation—particularly its center-piece—the committee system—would create far too much uncertainty in members' electoral strategies and therefore would be broadly opposed from the start.[80]

Whatever other factors (such as interest group, party leadership, or committee member and staff opposition) impede major committee overhaul, these workshops of Congress evolve in response to new events and circumstances. Several recent developments highlight the dynamic quality of the committee system. These include ebbs and flows in the authority of committee chairs, the use of task forces, and the circumvention of the committee process.

Constricting the Authority of Committee Chairs

When Republicans took control of both houses of Congress in the mid-1990s, many GOP committee chairs had to take more direction from their top leaders, especially in the House. Committee chairs "have been at the mercy of top House and Senate Republican leaders," wrote two congressional analysts, "who—given the high level of partisanship and the small size of their majorities—have resorted to dictating legislation from the top down in order to maintain some semblance of control."[81] Centralized control over committees was plainly evident during the speakership of Newt Gingrich (1995–1999), who sometimes circumvented committee consideration of legislation, dictated legislative changes to committees, used the Rules Committee to redraft committee-reported measures, and engaged in other actions that undermined the committee system, such as creating partisan task forces.

Speaker Hastert, too, was not reluctant to rein in committee chairs. The removal of the Veterans' chair, noted earlier, underscores that point. The Speaker also exercised tight control over the Appropriations Committee. After Hastert won adoption in 2003 of a party rules change requiring the Appropriations subcommittee chairs to be approved by the Steering Committee, one of the subcommittee leaders said, "Now the leadership gets to have the [subcommittee chairs] come in and grovel before them."[82] Two years later, the Steering Committee warned a subcommittee chair that he could lose the chairmanship of his Appropriations subcommittee if he "does not raise or donate more money to Republicans."[83]

Speaker Pelosi worked to keep the committee chairs under control and to shape the party message and agenda at the top leadership level. After all, a major focus of Pelosi was to retain Democratic control of the House in the

November 2008 and 2010 elections. She could not permit independent-minded committee chairs to do their own thing and jeopardize this fundamental party goal. At the same time, Speaker Pelosi recognized the need to have a productive relationship with her chairs, because much of the House's work is carried out by these "little legislatures." Achieving the right balance between "top-down" command and committee autonomy is no easy task. Henry Waxman, D-Calif., a committee chair and a Pelosi ally, put it this way: "I think there has to be a lot more direction from the leadership to the committees of jurisdiction. We don't want to return to the days of committee chairs that felt they didn't have to be accountable. There has to be a balance."[84] When asked, Waxman declined to say whether the correct balance had been achieved.

Boehner's speakership at this early stage is a work in progress. In sum, he has promised "no more bills written behind closed doors in the speaker's office. Bills should be written by legislators in committee in plain public view."[85] Nevertheless, some initial clues indicate that Boehner will, when necessary, provide guidance and direction to the committees. Four examples make the point. First, he is "looking to create a position in the Speaker's office for an oversight overseer to ride herd over numerous committees" investigating the executive branch. His objective is "to make sure that hearings are conducted in an orderly and politically manageable way (meaning, no inflated allegations, no duplicative topics, no from-here-to-eternity subpoenas)."[86] Second, Speaker Boehner opposed a gun-control measure introduced by the chair of the Homeland Security Committee. Mindful of the Speaker's action, and perhaps influenced by it, two weeks later the Judiciary chair turned down a request from all sixteen Democratic committee members to hold gun safety hearings in light of the Tucson shootings.[87] Third, Boehner has opposed earmarks over his entire legislative career, and he insists as leader that Republicans ban the practice. (Earmarks direct that federal agencies spend funds on particular projects or purposes in members' constituencies.) In the view of Rep. Patrick McHenry, R-N.C., "He stared the appropriators down, and he won."[88] Fourth, he named William "Mac" Thornberry, R-Texas, to coordinate the work of at least half a dozen committees and produce cybersecurity legislation.[89]

Senate committee chairs also are subject to direction from their party leadership, as these examples illustrate. Senate majority leader Harry Reid, instructed the Senate Finance and Budget Committee chairs "to take a look at what we can do with entitlements [mandatory spending programs]."[90] He also told Finance chair Max Baucus "to stop chasing Republican votes on [President Obama's] massive health care reform bill."[91] Earlier, when political momentum began to build for a patients' bill of rights measure, another majority leader took the issue away from the chair of the Health, Education, Labor, and Pensions Committee and "created a [party] task force . . . to write the . . . bill."[92] That majority leader also gave the Finance Committee a deadline to report a priority bill or else he would call up the proposal he favored.[93] The point is that, on measures of utmost party importance, congressional leaders will override the prerogatives of committee chairs to take control of crucial agenda items.

The ability of today's party leaders, particularly in the House, to exercise significant control over committee leaders represents a major change in how today's Congress works. Term limits, by design, have reduced the ability of chairs to create independent fiefdoms. The chairs are subject to centralized leadership direction on the party's top priorities and might face sanctions if their performance does not comport with party expectations. On the one hand, this development ensures that the chairs (and ranking minority members) are ultimately accountable for their actions to the Democratic Caucus or Republican Conference. On the other hand, tight leadership control, combined with term limits for House and Senate Republicans, could gradually diminish the traditional role of committees as the policy specialization system for the legislative branch. Why bother to devote years of effort to becoming substantive experts, some committee members might say, if policy on major issues is decided at the top and committee leaders are forced to relinquish their posts after six years (if not sooner)?

Party Task Forces

Speaker Gingrich was noted for creating numerous party task forces, in part because he could determine their mandate and timetable, appoint the chair and members, and assign a deadline for drafting a product. Many of these task forces did little, but some wrote legislation. Indeed, task forces can forge consensus, draft legislation, coordinate strategy, promote intraparty communication, and involve noncommittee members and junior members in issue areas.

Gingrich's use of task forces provides a practical look at the three theories of legislative organization: the distributional hypothesis, the informational hypothesis, and the party hypothesis. The Speaker's Task Force on California was established in large measure to ensure that the politically important state of California received its fair share of federal funds from the GOP-controlled House. This panel's formation buttressed the committee autonomy or distributive politics view of congressional organization: committees are designed to accommodate important constituencies. The Task Force on Immigration underscored the chamber-dominated, or informational, perspective. Its work enhanced the expertise of all members by providing them with specialized information on the complexities of immigration policy. Finally, the Task Force on the Environment was formed in part to promote the GOP's deregulatory agenda. A partisan perspective shaped much of its work.

Speaker Hastert de-emphasized the use of party task forces, but he still occasionally employed them to address issues of importance to the party. For example, Hastert created task forces to deal with health and terrorism issues. Speaker Pelosi established a bipartisan task force to consider whether the House should create an outside body to investigate ethical misconduct by lawmakers.[94] Her initiative led the House in March 2008 to create an independent Office of Congressional Ethics (OCE) with authority to initiate investigations of alleged misconduct by lawmakers.[95] Speaker Boehner, who retained the

OCE, relies on a GOP high-tech working group "to propose measures that would spur growth in the high-tech industry."[96]

Senate leaders also form party task forces, sometimes to showcase senators up for reelection and to promote party priorities. For example, a senator up for reelection was named by GOP leader McConnell to head the GOP's high-tech task force. The aims of the task force are "to advise the Republican Conference on technology issues and act as an advocate for the industry."[97] Party task forces are also created to develop legislative plans or ameliorate internal party conflict. For example, Senate GOP leader Bob Dole, Kan., established a task force to cool the passions of junior Republicans who wanted to oust the Appropriations chair (Mark Hatfield of Oregon) because he did not vote for a top GOP priority, a constitutional balanced budget amendment. The task force came up with term limits for committee chairs, which, as noted earlier, is still observed by Senate Republicans.

Bypassing Committees

It has not been unusual in recent years for House and Senate party leaders to bypass some or all of the stages of committee consideration of legislation. In general, the circumvention of committees reflects the dominance of party power over committee power. Specific reasons for bypassing committees are noteworthy. For example, heightened partisanship in certain committees encourages party leaders to take charge of priority measures to avoid negative media coverage of committee markups. Or factional disputes within committees may prevent them from reaching agreement on measures deemed important to party leaders. Time is a factor as well. Party leaders may believe there is not enough time for committees to hold hearings and markups on major bills they want to consider within a certain time period. Along these lines, Sen. Barbara Mikulski, D-Md., lamented that "legislative malpractice" occurred during the Senate debate on a medical liability bill. "First of all, the procedure for considering this bill is seriously flawed. The bill was brought to the full Senate without hearings, without consideration by the Judiciary Committee."[98] Senate GOP leader McConnell claimed that Democrats in the 111th Congress regularly bypassed Senate committees. Democrats set a record, declared McConnell, "bypassing committees 43 times or double the previous average."[99] The Democratic leader blamed dilatory procedural abuses by Republicans for the high number. Some analysts contend that "there are few consequences if [committees are bypassed] because nobody outside Congress cares whether a bill went through committee or not."[100] Today, committee review of major legislation can be problematic.

CONCLUSION

Several generalizations can be made about congressional committees today. First, they shape the House and Senate agendas. Not only do they have negative power—pigeonholing legislation referred to them—but they have positive power as well. The bills they report largely determine what each chamber will debate and in what form. As one House chair stated in his testimony before the Joint Committee on the Organization of Congress, committees

> provide Congress with the expertise, skill, and organizational structure necessary to cope with the increasingly complex and technical questions in both the domestic and international arenas. They also ensure a forum for the broadest possible participation of diverse interests and constituencies in the formative stages of the legislative process. They are, in short, the window through which much of the democratic participation in lawmaking is made possible.[101]

Second, committees differ in their policy-making environments, mix of members, decision-making objectives, and ability to fulfill individual members' goals. Recruitment methods reinforce committees' autonomy; they frequently are imbalanced ideologically or geographically. And they are likely to advocate policies espoused by agencies and outside groups interested in their work.

Third, committees often develop an *esprit de corps* that flows across party lines. Committee members usually will defend their panels against criticisms, jurisdictional trespassing, or any attempt to bypass them.

Fourth, committees typically operate independently of one another. This longtime custom fosters an attitude of mutual noninterference in the work of other committees. However, multiple referrals of bills spawn broader interrelationships among committees.

Fifth, the committee system contributes fundamentally to policy fragmentation, although a few committees—such as the House's Rules and Budget Committees—act as policy coordinators for Congress. "This is one of the anomalies here," remarked a House member. "In order to attain legislative efficiency, we say that we have to break down into committees with specialized jurisdictions. When you do that, you lose your ability to grapple with the big problems."[102] As a result, party leaders are more involved than ever in coordinating policy making and forging winning coalitions in committees and on the floor.

Finally, committee autonomy is under pressure from assertive party leaders who strive to move the party's agenda forward and enforce party discipline—with or without the committee leaders' cooperation. In theoretical terms, the pressure on autonomy may be seen as a shift in committee roles from distributional purposes to partisan-programmatic goals.

View from the House's "Back Benches." (Top): The Speaker's chair is in front of the flag and to the left of the Mace—a symbol of national unity that on rare occasions may be hoisted and displayed to quell disturbances in the chamber. The lower seats are occupied by clerks, and the box in the foreground is the "hopper," where members may place amendments for House consideration. (Bottom): The House chamber, seen from the rear, shows the Speaker's rostrum and the clerks' seats in front, but also the gallery and lawmakers' seats. Unlike senators, House members do not have assigned seats, but the majority and minority committee leaders' tables are seen to the right.

Congressional
Rules and Procedures

C ongress needs written rules to do its work. Compiling the Senate's first parliamentary manual, Thomas Jefferson stressed the importance of a known system of rules:

> It is much more material that there should be a rule to go by, than what the rule is; that there may be uniformity of proceeding in business not subject to the caprice of the Speaker or captiousness of the members. It is very material that order, decency, and regularity be preserved in a dignified public body.[1]

Jefferson understood that how Congress operates affects what it does. Thus Congress's rules protect majority and minority rights, divide the workload, help contain conflict, ensure fair play, and distribute power among members. Because formal rules cannot cover every contingency, precedents— accumulated decisions of House Speakers and Senate presiding officers—fill in the gaps. These precedents are codified by House and Senate parliamentarians, printed, and distributed. There are also informal, unwritten codes of conduct such as courtesy to other members. These folkways are commonly transmitted from incumbent members to newcomers.[2]

Before bills become laws, they typically pass successfully through several stages in each house (see Figure 8-1 for a simplified view of lawmaking). Bills that fail to attract majority support at any critical juncture may never be passed. Congress, in short, is a procedural obstacle course that favors opponents of legislation and hinders proponents. This defensive advantage promotes bargaining and compromise at each decision point.

Congressional rules are not independent of the policy and power struggles that lie behind them. There is very little the House and Senate cannot do under the rules so long as the action is backed by votes and inclination. And yet votes and inclination are not easily obtained, and the rules persistently challenge the proponents of legislation to demonstrate that they have both resources at their command. Little prevents obstruction at every turn except the tacit understanding that the business of the House and Senate must go on. Members recognize that the rules can be redefined and prerogatives taken away or

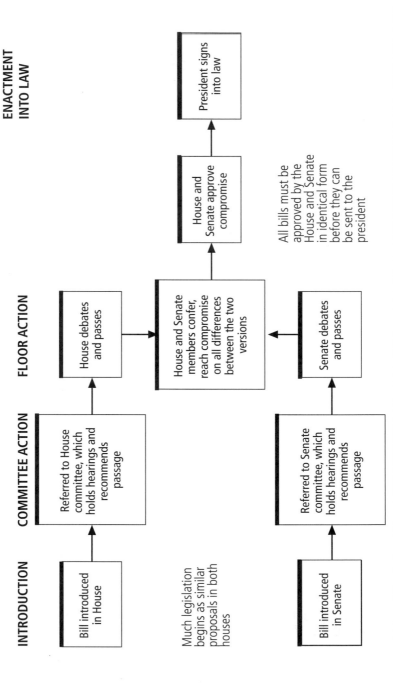

FIGURE 8-1 How a Bill Becomes Law

INTRODUCTION   COMMITTEE ACTION   FLOOR ACTION   ENACTMENT INTO LAW

Bill introduced in House

Referred to House committee, which holds hearings and recommends passage

House debates and passes

House and Senate members confer, reach compromise on all differences between the two versions

House and Senate approve compromise

President signs into law

Much legislation begins as similar proposals in both houses

Bill introduced in Senate

Referred to Senate committee, which holds hearings and recommends passage

Senate debates and passes

All bills must be approved by the House and Senate in identical form before they can be sent to the president modified. Rules also can be employed against those who use them abusively. In short, rules can be employed to block or advance actions in either chamber, and proponents or opponents of measures or matters do not look on them as neutral devices.

INTRODUCTION OF BILLS

Only members of Congress can introduce legislation. Often embedded in these measures are a number of assumptions—for example, that a problem exists; that it can best be resolved through enactment of a federal law instead of allowing administrative agencies or state and local governments to handle it; and that the proposed solution contained in the bill ameliorates rather than exacerbates the problem. When the 112th Congress convened in January 2011, the GOP-controlled House adopted a new rule requiring all lawmakers to provide with the bills (H.R.) and joint resolutions (H. J. Res.) they introduced a constitutional authority statement specifying "the power or powers granted to the Congress in the Constitution to enact the bill or resolution."

> The reasons that lawmakers introduce the measures they do are fascinating and numerous. They are led to their choice of legislation by many factors: parochial interest, party preference, crass calculation connected to campaign fund raising, and the two Congresses. For example, Sen. Robert Menendez, D-N.J., introduced comprehensive immigration reform legislation just weeks before the November 2010 elections to energize Latinos to turn out for Democratic congressional candidates.[3]

But there is also a motivator that is rarely discussed that can be just as potent: a personal brush with adversity. Congress is an intensely human place where personal experience sometimes has powerful repercussions.[4] As a senator stated, "Each of us, as United States senators, comes to . . . this public place with the sum of our beliefs, our personal experience and our values, and none of us checks them at the door."[5] For example, Sen. Pete V. Domenici, R-N.M., whose daughter suffers from mental illness, was Congress's acknowledged champion for the mentally ill. "In the field of mental health," said a Democratic House member, "I think it's possible that nothing at all would have been done by Congress if it weren't for legislators like Domenici who were galvanized by personal experience."[6] Rep. Carolyn McCarthy, D-N.Y., has long been a forceful advocate for gun control. Why? A deranged gunman on a commuter train killed her husband and seriously wounded her adult son. Personal experience, however, is not the only source of legislative proposals. Often members get ideas for bills from the executive branch, interest groups, scholars, state and local officials, constituents, the media, and their own staff.

A member who introduces a bill becomes its sponsor. He or she may seek cosponsors to demonstrate wide support for the legislation. Outside groups also may urge members to cosponsor measures. "We were not assured of a hearing," said a lobbyist of a bill that his group was pushing. "There was more hostility to the idea, so it was very important to line up a lot of cosponsors to show the over-all concern."[7] A two Congresses dimension is also evident in signing on (or not) to legislation. For example, a lawmaker may cosponsor a labor bill to win the support of union workers back home. Conversely, the lawmaker may decide against cosponsoring the labor bill because it would mobilize business groups to oppose his reelection. Vulnerable lawmakers up for reelection may cosponsor measures offered by opposition members to broaden their appeal to voters in both major parties.

Equally important as the number of cosponsors is their identity, especially their leadership status and ideological stance. Members often seek out cosponsors from the opposing party to signal that the bill transcends partisan politics. In an unusual cosponsorship pairing, the House chairs of their respective party campaign committees, Chris Van Hollen, D-Md., and Pete Sessions, R-Texas, joined to introduce bipartisan legislation.[8] When Sen. Ted Kennedy, D-Mass., an outspoken liberal, served in the Senate with Sen. Strom Thurmond, R-S.C., a southern conservative, he exclaimed, "Whenever Strom and I introduce a bill together, it is either an idea whose time has come, or one of us has not read the bill."[9]

Although identifying a bill's sponsors is easy, pinpointing its real initiators may be difficult. Legislation is "an aggregate, not a simple production," wrote Woodrow Wilson. "It is impossible to tell how many persons, opinions, and influences have entered into its composition."[10] President John F. Kennedy, for example, usually is given credit for initiating the Peace Corps. But Theodore Sorensen, Kennedy's special counsel, recalled that the Peace Corps was

> based on the Mormon and other voluntary religious service efforts, on an editorial Kennedy had read years earlier, on a speech by General [James] Gavin, on a luncheon I had with Philadelphia businessmen, on the suggestions of [Kennedy's] academic advisers, on legislation previously introduced and on the written response to a spontaneous late-night challenge he issued to Michigan students.[11]

In short, many bills have complex origins.

Required legislation, particularly funding measures, makes up much of Congress's annual agenda. Bills that authorize programs and specify how much money can be spent on them (authorization bills) and bills that provide the money (appropriation bills) appear on Congress's schedule at about the same time each year. Other matters recur at less frequent intervals, every five years perhaps. Emergency issues require Congress's immediate attention. Activist legislators also push proposals onto Congress's program. Bills not acted on die automatically at the end of each two-year Congress. "Anybody can drop a bill into the hopper [a mahogany box near the Speaker's podium where members place their proposed bills]," said a House GOP leader. "The question is, Can you make something happen with it?"[12]

Drafting

"As a sculptor works in stone or clay, the legislator works in words," observed one member.[13] Words are the building blocks of policy, and legislators frequently battle over adding, deleting, or modifying terms and phrases. Members increasingly give their bills eye-catching titles, such as the USA-PATRIOT Act (Uniting and Strengthening America by Providing Appropriate Tools Required to Intercept and Obstruct Terrorism) or the SOS Act (Stop Oil Spills). They may affix significant contemporary words ("jobs") or popular phrases to legislation, such as "bill of rights" (the patients' bill of rights, for example). As a Senate GOP leader pointed out, "If you ask [voters], 'Are you for the Bill of Rights?' Yeah, they're for the Bill of Rights. 'Bill of Rights' is a great term. It's the new term. It may even be supplanting reform."[14] And then there is the time that, instead of proposing to reduce or terminate estate taxes, Republicans called for an end to "the death tax."

Conversely, opponents of measures try to attach unattractive labels to them. Defenders of the estate tax refer to its abolition as the "Paris Hilton Benefit Act." Critics of an energy bill dubbed it the "Hooters and Polluters Bill" because the legislation contained a provision benefiting a Hooters restaurant in Louisiana. And "Obamacare" is how Republicans pejoratively characterized the president's landmark overhaul of the health care system. It was also referred to as "socialized medicine," a "government takeover," and a measure that contained "death panels." How measures are framed influences how the public will view them. "Whoever controls the language controls the debate," asserted one commentator.[15] And this is why in the current 24/7 media environment an effective "messaging" or public relations strategy is critical both to the fate of major legislation and to a party's electoral success.

Although bills are introduced only by members, anyone can draft them.[16] Expert drafters in the House and Senate offices of the legislative counsel assist members and committees in writing legislation. Executive agencies and lobbying groups also often prepare measures for introduction by friendly legislators. Many home-state industries, for example, draft narrowly tailored tariff or regulatory measures that enhance their business prospects. These proposals are then introduced by local lawmakers—another instance of the two Congresses linkage. As a senatorial aide explained, the senator "just introduces it as a courtesy to his constituents."[17] (See Box 8-1 outlining the four basic types of legislation: bills, joint resolutions, concurrent resolutions, and simple resolutions.)

Nowadays, Congress frequently acts on comprehensive (omnibus) bills or resolutions (sometimes called packages or megabills by the press). Packages contain an array of issues that were once handled as separate pieces of legislation. Their increasing use stems in part from members' reluctance to make hard political decisions without a package arrangement. A House Budget Committee chair once explained their attractiveness. To paraphrase:

BOX 8-1   **Types of Legislation**

Bill

◄ Most legislative proposals before Congress are in a bill form.

◄ Bills are designated H.R. (House of Representatives) or S. (Senate) according to where they originate, followed by a number assigned in the order in which they were introduced, from the beginning of each two-year congressional term.

◄ *Public bills* deal with general questions and become public laws if approved by Congress and signed by the president.

◄ *Private bills* deal with individual matters, such as claims against the government, immigration and naturalization cases, and land titles. They become private laws if approved and signed by the president.

Joint Resolution

◄ A joint resolution, designated H. J. Res. or S. J. Res., requires the approval of both houses and the president's signature, just as a bill does, and has the force of law.

◄ No significant difference exists between a bill and a joint resolution. The latter generally deals with limited matters, such as a single appropriation for a specific purpose.

◄ Joint resolutions are used to propose constitutional amendments, which do not require presidential signatures but become a part of the Constitution when three-fourths of the states have ratified them.

Concurrent Resolution

◄ A concurrent resolution, designated H. Con. Res. or S. Con. Res., must be passed by both houses but does not require the president's signature and does not have the force of law.

◄ Concurrent resolutions generally are used to make or amend rules applicable to both houses or to express their joint sentiment. A concurrent resolution, for example, is used to fix the time for adjournment of a Congress and to express Congress's annual budgeting plan. It might also be used to convey the congratulations of Congress to another country on the anniversary of its independence.

Resolution

◄ A simple resolution, designated H. Res. or S. Res., deals with matters entirely within the prerogatives of one house.

◄ It requires neither passage by the other chamber nor approval by the president and does not have the force of law.

◄ Most resolutions deal with the rules of one house. They also are used to express the sentiments of a single house, to extend condolences to the family of a deceased member, or to give advice on foreign policy or other executive business.

Large bills can be used to hide legislation that otherwise might be more controversial. By packaging difficult issues in measures that command broad support, they enable members to avoid hard votes that they would have to account for at election time and allow members to avoid angering special-interest groups that use votes [to decide] contributions to campaigns. Leaders can also use them to slam-dunk issues that otherwise might be torn apart or to pressure the President to accept provisions that he objects to.[18]

Sometimes, Congress has little choice but to use the omnibus approach. Difficulties in enacting twelve annual appropriations bills often mean that all or many ("omnibus") or two, three, or so ("minibus") are rolled into one comprehensive package. In this way, procedural action on the outstanding measures is expedited by majority party leaders, who, in doing so, minimize the opportunities for further delay. A goal of Speaker John Boehner, R-Ohio, is to "put an end to so-called comprehensive bills with thousands of pages of legislative text that make it easy to hide spending projects and [detrimental] policies."[19] (Interestingly, House Republicans used the size of the president's health overhaul measure—over 2,700 pages—as a symbol of big-government intervention in health care, a potent GOP electoral theme in the November 2010 elections and, perhaps, in the 2012 elections.) Some Democrats disagree with Speaker Boehner's view of big bills. "I don't think the issue's the length of the bills," said Rep. Diana DeGette, D-Colo. "I think the issue is the clarity of the explanation."[20]

Timing

"Everything in politics is timing," Speaker Thomas P. "Tip" O'Neill Jr., D-Mass., used to say. A bill's success or failure often hinges on when it is introduced or brought to the floor. A bill that might have succeeded early in a session could fail as adjournment nears. However, controversial legislation can sometimes be rushed through during the last hectic days of a Congress.

Elections greatly influence the timing of legislation. Policy issues can be taken off or kept on Congress's agenda because of electoral circumstances—a good illustration of how the two Congresses are inextricably connected. For example, coming off major electoral successes both House parties in recent years moved to capitalize on their momentum with quick action early in the new Congress. Examples are the House's action in 1995 on the ten-point, hundred-day Contract with America agenda heralded by Speaker Newt Gingrich, R-Ga., and the hundred-hour legislative agenda pushed in 2007 by Speaker Nancy Pelosi, D-Calif. And, as one of its first orders of business under Speaker Boehner, the House on January 26, 2011, voted to pass a bill entitled Repealing the Job-Killing Health Care Law Act.

REFERRAL OF BILLS

After bills are introduced, they are referred formally to the appropriate standing committees by the Senate presiding officer or the House Speaker. (In practice, however, measures are referred by the Senate or House parliamentarian, who is the official procedural adviser to each chamber's presiding officer.) A bill's phraseology can affect its referral and therefore its chances of passage.

This political fact of life means that members use words artfully when drafting legislation. The objective is to encourage the referral of their measures to sympathetic, not hostile, committees. If a bill mentions taxes, for example, it invariably is referred to the tax panels. In a classic case of circumventing the Finance Committee, Senator Domenici avoided the word *tax* in a bill proposing a charge on waterborne freight:

> If the waterway fee were considered a tax—which it was, basically, because it would raise revenues for the federal treasury—the rules would place it under the dominion of the Senate's tax-writing arm, the Finance Committee. But Finance was chaired by Russell B. Long, of Louisiana, whose state included two of the world's biggest barge ports and who was, accordingly, an implacable foe of waterway charges in any form. Domenici knew that Long could find several years' worth of bills to consider before he would voluntarily schedule a hearing on S. 790 [the Domenici bill]. For this reason, [Domenici staff aides] had been careful to avoid the word *tax* in writing the bill, employing such terms as *charge* and *fee* instead.[21]

Domenici's drafting strategy worked. His bill was jointly referred to the Commerce Committee and the Environment Committee, on which he served. Because committees' jurisdictional mandates are ambiguous and overlap, it is not unusual for legislation to be referred to two or more committees—the concept of "one bill, many committees." Indeed, multiple referrals are common in the House, less so in the Senate (see Chapter 7). In the Senate, they require unanimous consent to implement. Furthermore, all senators have many opportunities to influence committee-reported measures or matters, regardless of whether they serve on the panel of jurisdiction (see Box 8-2, which describes how parliamentary convention affects the reference of legislation).

Of the thousands of bills introduced each year, Congress takes up relatively few. During the 111th Congress (2009–2011), 10,770 public bills and joint resolutions were introduced, but only 342 (3.2 percent) became public laws. More public laws were enacted in earlier Congresses: for example, 640 in the 90th (1967–1969) and 590 in the 99th (1985–1987). Part of the general decline in the number of laws enacted can be explained by the use of omnibus or megabills. The decline may also stem from the widespread congressional sentiment that more laws may not be the answer to the nation's problems. But the decline also may reflect a political stalemate resulting from the complexity of issues, the intensity of partisanship, legislative-executive and bicameral conflicts, and the narrow party divisions in Congress. It is worth noting that lawmakers understand that most of the bills they introduce are unlikely, as stand-alone measures, to become law. However, the ideas encapsulated in their legislation can be "added as amendments to a larger bill or negotiated into a markup or conference report."[22]

Lawmaking is an arduous and intricate process. As a Senate GOP leader noted, "That's the way Congress works. You work for two years and finally you

BOX 8-2   **Rules and Referral Strategy**

Sometimes, the Senate's rules can be so arcane that it takes major strategy sessions to get even the most routine bills through the legislature.

That was the case when Sen. Bob Graham, D-Fla. (1987–2005), drafted a bill (targeted only at Florida) to permit the Forest Service to sell eighteen tracts of land and use the proceeds to buy up patches of private lands within the Apalachicola National Forest. To ensure that such a low-profile bill moved, Graham wanted it to go through the Energy and Natural Resources Committee, on which he sat.

Instead, Parliamentarian Alan S. Frumin told Graham's aides that the bill, which was soon to be introduced, would be referred to the Agriculture, Nutrition, and Forestry Committee. Because Graham was not a member, such a move could have guaranteed the bill a quiet death.

Why the Agriculture Committee? For at least four decades, the jurisdiction over land bills has been split between the two committees. Bills affecting land east of the 100th Meridian—which runs through North Dakota and South Dakota and the middle of Texas—are assigned to Agriculture, while bills that affect lands west of it go to Energy.

Graham's bill dealt with the wrong side of the country. To change Frumin's mind, Graham's aides needed to turn the rules to their advantage.

They found their opportunity by uncovering the roots behind the 100th Meridian rule. The idea was to divide jurisdiction between public lands and privately owned lands. Because most land on the East Coast is privately owned, that side of the country went to Agriculture, which had jurisdiction over private lands. Everything in the West fell to Energy, which had jurisdiction over public lands.

Graham's aides, however, found out that a majority of tracts in Florida were always public lands. That persuaded Frumin that the bill belonged to the Energy panel.

Source: Adapted from David Nather, "Graham Turns Rules to His Advantage," *CQ Weekly,* June 8, 2002, 1494.

get to the end and either it all collapses in a puddle or you get a break-through."[23] Or as John Dingell, D-Mich., the longest-serving House member ever, phrased it: "Legislation is hard, pick-and-shovel work," and it often "takes a long time to do it."[24] Perhaps this quote brings to mind the decades-long efforts by numerous lawmakers and presidents to overhaul the nation's health care system.

Once committees complete action on the bills referred to them, the House and Senate rules require a majority of the full committee to be physically present to report (vote) out any measure. If this rule is violated and neither waived nor ignored, a point of order can be made against the proposal on the floor. (A point of order is a parliamentary objection that halts the proceedings until the chamber's presiding officer decides whether the contention is valid.)

Bills reported from committee have passed a critical stage in the lawmaking process. The next major step is to reach the House or Senate floor for debate and amendment. The discussion that follows begins with the House because tax and appropriation bills originate there—the former under the Constitution, the latter by custom.

SCHEDULING IN THE HOUSE

All bills reported from committee in the House are listed in chronological order on one of several calendars—that is, the lists that enable the House to put measures into convenient categories. Bills that raise or spend money are assigned to the Union Calendar. The House Calendar contains all other major public measures, such as proposed constitutional amendments. Private bills, such as immigration requests or claims against the government, are assigned to the Private Calendar. There is no guarantee that the House will debate legislation placed on any of these calendars. The Speaker, in consultation with party and committee leaders, the president, and others, largely determines whether, when, how, and in what order bills come up. Outside events and influencers also shape agenda-setting. For example, the Speaker and other House GOP leaders solicited input for their 112th Congress agenda from citizens and bloggers around the country.[25] The power to set the House's agenda constitutes the essence of the Speaker's institutional authority. The Speaker's agenda-setting authority is bolstered by rules and precedents upholding the principle of majority rule. This means that in the House a united and determined voting majority—whether partisan or bipartisan—will prevail over resolute opposition.

Shortcuts for Minor Bills

Whether a bill is major or minor, controversial or noncontroversial, influences the procedure employed to bring it before the House. Most bills are relatively minor and are taken up and passed through various shortcut procedures.

One shortcut is the designation of special days for considering minor or relatively noncontroversial measures. An especially important routine and time-saving procedure is suspension of the rules. It is in order Monday, Tuesday, and Wednesday of each week. The procedure is controlled by the Speaker through the power of recognizing who may speak ("Mr. Speaker, I move to suspend the rules and pass H.R. 1234"). The vote simultaneously suspends House rules and enacts (or rejects) the measure. Most public laws enacted by the House are accomplished through this procedure. A study by Donald R. Wolfensberger, former staff director of the House Rules Committee, determined that since the early 2000s from 75 to over 80 percent of bills enacted into public law came to the House floor via this procedure, compared with about 33 percent two decades ago.

Legislation considered under suspension of the rules does not have to be reported from committee before the full House takes it up. Importantly, the suspension procedure permits only forty minutes of debate, allows no amendments, and requires a two-thirds vote for passage. The procedure is often favored by bill managers who want to avoid unfriendly amendments and points of order against their legislation. Bills that fail under suspension can return again to the floor by a rule issued by the Rules Committee (discussed later in this chapter). The heightened partisanship in the closely divided House raises the question of why the suspension procedure, which requires bipartisanship to attract the two-thirds vote, is being employed more and more in such a polarized institution. The answer seems to involve a trade-off. "As members are increasingly being denied opportunities in special rules to offer amendments to more substantive bills on the floor," explained Wolfensberger, "the leadership is providing alternative mechanisms to satisfy members' policy influence and reelection needs through the relatively non-controversial and bipartisan suspension process."[26] Thus greater use of suspensions serves two prime purposes: it provides an outlet for members to achieve their policy and political goals and keeps the lid on members' frustration with limited or closed amendment procedures.

The current rules of the House Republican Conference establish specific guidelines for using the suspension procedure. Under Conference Rule 28, bills and resolutions are not to be scheduled using the suspension procedure if, for example, they are opposed by more than one-third of the committee members reporting the bill; if they fail to include a cost estimate; or if they create new programs, unless they also eliminate or reduce a program of equal or greater size. The majority leadership "does not ordinarily schedule bills for suspension unless confident of a two-thirds vote."[27] In the House of the 112th Congress, however, the first two bills scheduled for suspension by the GOP leadership went down to defeat. The losses, they said, occurred because of their inexperience in managing the floor; the defection of GOP newcomers who believed the measures were taken up without adequate review; and the unexpected loss of support from Democratic lawmakers. In the view of Majority Leader Eric Cantor, R-Va., "It's very easy, when you bring things up under suspension, if the minority wants to take it down, they can. We used to do that . . . so that was kind of a learning day for us."[28]

At times, the minority party gets upset with the majority leadership for not scheduling enough of their bills via the suspension procedure. To protest, minority party members may vote against suspension bills until more of their routine measures are taken up on the floor. They also may castigate the majority leadership for using the suspension of the rules procedure on bills that in their estimation merit more debate than forty minutes and require the offering of amendments.

There are also occasions on which the minority will contend that noncontroversial bills that could easily pass by suspension are instead brought up with an open rule—which permits more than forty minutes of debate and allows amendments—granted by the Rules Committee. The aim, say minority members, is to boost the perception that the majority is running the House in a fair and deliberative manner. Or minority members will castigate the majority for taking up important measures under a procedure that restricts debate and prevents lawmakers from offering amendments. As one minority lawmaker exclaimed: "We have taken more legislation up under suspension of the rules, without any opportunity for people to be offering amendments. I think whatever side you're on, whatever party you're in, there really ought to be the opportunity for Members to offer amendments."[29]

Another expedited procedure is unanimous consent. The Speaker, however, will recognize a lawmaker to call up bills or resolutions by unanimous consent "only when assured that the majority and minority floor leadership and the relevant committee chairs and ranking minority members have no objection."[30] Without these clearances, unanimous consent is not a viable avenue to the floor.

Major measures reach the floor by different procedures. Budget, appropriation, and a limited number of other measures are considered "privileged"—meaning that the House rulebook grants them a "ticket," or privileged access, to the floor. Privileged measures may be called up from the appropriate calendar for debate at almost any time. (Remember, the Speaker sets the agenda, even for privileged business.) Most major bills, however, do not have an automatic green light to the floor. Before they reach the floor they are assigned a rule (a procedural resolution) by the Rules Committee.

The Strategic Role of the Rules Committee

The House Rules Committee has existed since the First Congress. During its early years, the committee prepared or ratified a biennial set of House rules and then dissolved. As House procedures became more complex because of the growing membership and workload, the committee became more important. In 1858 the Speaker became a member of the committee and the next year its chair. In 1880 Rules became a permanent standing committee. Three years later, the committee launched a procedural revolution. It began to issue rules (sometimes called special rules), which are privileged resolutions that grant priority for floor consideration to virtually all major bills.

Arm of the Majority Leadership. In 1910 the House rebelled against the arbitrary decisions of Speaker Joseph G. Cannon, R-Ill., and removed him from the Rules Committee. During the decades that followed, as the committee became an independent power it extracted substantive concessions in bills in exchange for rules, blocked measures it opposed, and advanced those it favored, often reflecting the wishes of the House's conservative coalition of Republicans and southern Democrats.

The chair of the Rules Committee from 1955 to 1967 was Howard W. "Judge" Smith, D-Va., a diehard conservative and a master at devising delaying tactics. He might abruptly adjourn meetings for lack of a quorum, allow requests for rules to languish, or refuse to schedule meetings. House consideration of the 1957 civil rights bill was temporarily delayed because Smith absented himself from the Capitol, and his committee could not meet without him. Smith claimed he was seeing about a barn that had burned on his Virginia farm. Retorted Speaker Sam Rayburn, D-Texas, "I knew Howard Smith would do most anything to block a civil rights bill, but I never knew he would resort to arson."[31]

Liberals' frustration with the bipartisan coalition of conservatives who dominated the committee finally boiled over. After John F. Kennedy was elected president in 1960, Speaker Rayburn recognized that he needed greater control over the Rules Committee if the House was to advance the president's activist New Frontier program. Rayburn proposed enlarging the committee from twelve members to fifteen. This proposal led to a titanic struggle between Rayburn and the archconservative Rules chair:

> Superficially, the Representatives seemed to be quarreling about next to nothing: the membership of the committee. In reality, however, the question raised had grave import for the House and for the United States. The House's answer to it affected the tenuous balance of power between the great conservative and liberal blocs within the House. And, doing so, the House's answer seriously affected the response of Congress to the sweeping legislative proposals of the newly elected President, John Kennedy.[32]

In a dramatic vote, the House agreed to expand the Rules Committee. Two new Democrats and one Republican were added, loosening the conservative coalition's grip on the panel.

During the 1970s, the Rules Committee came under even greater majority party control. In 1975 the Democratic Caucus authorized the Speaker to appoint, subject to party ratification, all Democratic members of the committee. (Thirteen years later, Republicans authorized their leader to name the GOP members of the Rules Committee.) The majority party maintains a disproportionate ratio on the panel (currently nine Republicans and four Democrats in the 112th Congress). The Rules Committee, in short, has once again become the Speaker's committee. As a GOP Rules member said about the panel's relationship with the Speaker, "How much is the Rules Committee the handmaiden of the Speaker? The answer is, totally."[33] Rep. David Dreier, R-Calif., heads the panel in the 112th Congress.

The Speaker's influence over the Rules Committee ensures that the Speaker can both bring measures to the floor and shape their procedural consideration. Because House rules require bills to be taken up in the chronological order listed on the calendars, many substantial bills would never reach the floor before Congress adjourned. The Rules Committee can put major bills first in line. Equally important, a rule from the committee sets the conditions for debate and amendment.

A request for a rule is usually made by the chair of the committee reporting the bill. The Rules Committee conducts hearings on the request in the same way that other committees consider legislation, except that only members testify. The House parliamentarian usually drafts the rule after consulting with majority committee leaders and staff. The rule is considered on the House floor and is voted on in the same manner as regular bills (see Box 8-3 for an example of a generally open rule from the Rules Committee).

Types of Rules. Traditionally, the Rules Committee has granted open, closed, or modified rules as well as waivers. An open rule means that any lawmaker may propose germane amendments. A closed rule prohibits the offering of amendments. A modified rule comes in two forms: modified open and modified closed (typically called a "structured" rule). The distinction hinges on the number of amendments made in order by the Rules Committee—few under modified closed, more under modified open. Waivers of points of order

BOX 8-3 **Example of a Rule from the Rules Committee**

*T*his is a modified open rule (H. Res. 92) that sets the terms for debating and amending the Full-Year Continuing Appropriations Act, 2011 (H.R. 1). It allows any member to offer a germane amendment as long as it is pre-printed in the Congressional Record. The House adopted the rule on February 15, 2011, by a 242–174 vote.

Resolved, That at any time after the adoption of this resolution the Speaker may, pursuant to clause 2(b) of rule XVIII, declare the House resolved into the Committee of the Whole House on the state of the Union for consideration of the bill (H.R. 1) making appropriations for the Department of Defense and the other departments and agencies of the Government for the fiscal year ending September 30, 2011, and for other purposes. The first reading of the bill shall be dispensed with. All points of order against consideration of the bill are waived. General debate shall be confined to the bill and shall not exceed one hour equally divided and controlled by the chair and ranking minority member of the Committee on Appropriations. After general debate the bill shall be considered for amendment under the five-minute rule. No amendment to the bill shall be in order except: (1) those received for printing in the portion of the Congressional Record designated for that purpose in clause 8 of rule XVIII dated at least one day before the day of consideration of the amendment (but no later than February 15, 2011); and (2) pro forma amendments for the purpose of debate. Each amendment so received may be offered only by the Member who submitted it for printing or a designee and shall be considered as read if printed. When the committee rises and reports the bill back to the House with a recommendation that the bill do pass, the previous question shall be considered as ordered on the bill and amendments thereto to final passage, without intervening motion except one motion to recommit with or without instructions.

Source: Congressional Record, 112th Cong., 1st sess., February 15, 2011, H815–H816.

set aside technical violations of House rules to allow bills or other matters to reach the floor. Waivers are commonly included in the different types of rules.

Whether Democrats or Republicans control the House, their majority on the Rules Committee displays procedural creativity and imagination:

> Instead of choosing from among a few patterns the Rules Committee has demonstrated a willingness to create unique designs by recombining an increasingly wide array of elements, or by creating new ones as the need arises, to help leaders, committees, and members manage the heightened uncertainties of decision making on the House floor.[34]

The trend toward creative use of complex rules reflects several developments. Among the most important are the wider use of multiple referrals, which requires Rules to play a larger coordinative role in arranging floor action on legislation; the rise of megabills hundreds of pages in length that contain priorities the Speaker does not want picked apart on the floor; the desire of majority party leaders to exert greater control over floor procedures; members'

BOX 8-4   **Examples of Creative Rules**

Queen-of-the-Hill Rule

◄ Under this special rule, a number of major alternative amendments—each the functional equivalent of a bill—are made to the underlying legislation, with the proviso that the substitute that receives the most votes is the winner.

◄ If two or more alternatives receive an identical number of votes, the last one voted upon is considered as finally adopted by the membership.

Self-Executing Rule

◄ This special rule provides that when the House adopts a rule it has also agreed simultaneously to pass another measure or matter.

◄ Adoption of a self-executing rule means that the House has passed one or more other proposals at the same time it agrees to the rule.

◄ Whether this rule is controversial or not usually depends on the nature of the policy being agreed to in the two-for-one vote.

Restrictive Rule

◄ The essential feature of the restrictive rule is that it limits the freedom of members to offer germane amendments to the bills made in order by those rules.

◄ The number of restrictive rules has increased since the 1980s.

◄ Rank-and-file members often rail against these rules because they restrict their opportunities to amend committee-reported measures or majority party initiatives.

Multiple-Step Rule

◄ This type of rule facilitates an orderly amendment process.

◄ One variation is for the Rules Committee to report a rule that regulates the debating and amending process for specific portions of a bill and then report another follow-on rule to govern the remainder of the measure and amendments to it.

◄ Another variation is for the Rules Committee to state publicly that, if a measure encounters difficulties on the floor, the panel will report a subsequent rule that limits time for further debate or further amendments.

Anticipatory Rule

◄ To expedite decision making on the floor, the Rules Committee may grant a rule even before the measure or matter to which it would apply has been reported by a House committee or conference committee.

impatience with dilatory floor challenges to committee-reported bills; members' demand for greater certainty and predictability in floor decision making; and efforts by committee leaders either to limit the number of amendments or to keep unfriendly amendments off the floor. The sharp rise in partisanship has also triggered an increase in creative, typically restrictive, rules (see Box 8-4 on examples of creative rules).

When Republicans took control of the House in 1995 after four consecutive decades in the minority, they remembered their bitter experience with rules that restricted their right to offer amendments. Speaker Gingrich promised more openness and greater opportunities for all lawmakers to offer floor amendments to pending legislation. Republicans did work to provide more open amendment procedures when they first took control of the House. However, as Republican majorities declined in subsequent Congresses, the number of open rules dropped markedly (see Table 8-1), the result of heightened partisan acrimony and the GOP's preference to enact its agenda priorities with few or no changes.

Like the Republicans in 1995 when Democrats reclaimed the House majority in the 110th Congress (2007–2009), Speaker Pelosi pledged to manage the chamber in an open, fair, and deliberative manner. But it was not long before the Democrats brought their legislative priorities to the floor under closed or structured rules. Meanwhile, regularly the Republicans took the floor to criticize the Democratic majority for reneging on its promises. The majority is "failing to live up to its commitment to run the House in an open and fair manner," exclaimed a Rules Republican.[35] In the next Congress, still under Democratic control, there were no open rules at all, even on the twelve appropriations measures, which traditionally are open to amendment, unless one counts as open a rule with a pre-printing requirement for amendments. The requirement that all amendments be printed in the *Congressional Record* prior to floor action (or be submitted in advance to the Rules Committee) aids the majority party in preparing its floor strategy. Overall, as one analyst wrote, the two Houses under Democratic control were "worse than Republicans were at their worst, producing restrictive amendment rules for 86 percent and 99 percent of legislation, respectively, versus 81 percent under Republicans in the 109th Congress."[36] In response to the GOP complaints, Democrats said the GOP's floor strategy was to offer "gotcha" amendments designed for campaign attack ads or to undermine the majority's policy priorities. Majority Leader Steny Hoyer, Md., added, "I said we were going to be fair, not stupid."[37]

Speaker Boehner has also promised to run an open, fair, and deliberative lawmaking process with ample opportunities for the minority Democrats to offer amendments. Let legislators legislate is his stated objective. "To my friends in the minority," he said, "I offer a commitment: Openness . . . will be the new standard. There were no open rules in the House in the last Congress. In this one, there will be many."[38] Note that Speaker Boehner did not say all rules would be open. Furthermore, he stated that the Democratic minority would not be allowed to disrupt floor proceedings. It is too soon to know whether and to what extent Speaker Boehner's good intentions will materialize. Early in the 112th Congress, Speaker Boehner brought a major spending reduction bill (H.R. 1) to the floor under an open amendment process (see Chapter 14). He has also used closed rules for various measures. Open rules generally clash with a fundamental objective of any majority party: passage of priority legislation.

TABLE 8-1 Open and Restrictive Rules, 95th–111th Congresses

Congress and years	Total rules granted	Open rules		Restrictive rules	
		Number	Percent	Number	Percent
95th (1977–1979)	211	179	85	32	15
96th (1979–1981)	214	161	75	53	25
97th (1981–1983)	120	90	75	30	25
98th (1983–1985)	155	105	68	50	32
99th (1985–1987)	115	65	57	50	43
100th (1987–1989)	123	66	54	57	46
101st (1989–1991)	104	47	45	57	55
102d (1991–1993)	109	37	34	72	66
103d (1993–1995)	104	31	30	73	70
104th (1995–1997)	151	86	57	65	43
105th (1997–1999)	142	72	51	70	49
106th (1999–2001)	184	93	51	91	49
107th (2001–2003)	112	41	37	71	63
108th (2003–2005)	128	33	26	95	74
109th (2005–2007)	138	24	17	114	83
110th (2007–2009)	159	23	15	136	85
111th (2009–2011)	95	0	0	95	100

Sources: Congressional Record, 103d Cong., 2d sess., October 7, 1994, H11278. For the 104th Congress, see House Rules Committee, press release, December 10, 1996. For the 105th Congress, the Rules Committee issued a total of 207 rules, but many did not directly involve bills and resolutions. As a result, the authors selected 142 as the number of rules granted for bills and resolutions. Minority Democrats have made their own calculation of the kinds of rules granted by the committee. They identify a total of 163 rules of which 38 are open (23 percent) and 115 (77 percent) are restrictive. See *Survey of Activities of the House Committee on Rules* (Washington, DC: Government Printing Office, 1999). For the 106th Congress, the Rules Committee issued 267 rules with 184 directly affecting the amending process on the floor. Thus, the authors employ the 184 figure instead of 267, which included rules, for example, that permitted the House to go to conference with the Senate. See *Survey of Activities of the House Committee on Rules* (Washington, DC: Government Printing Office, 2001). For the 107th Congress, the panel issued 191 rules with 112 directly related to the amendment process for the consideration of bills and resolutions. See *Survey of Activities of the House Committee on Rules* (Washington, DC: Government Printing Office, 2003). During the 108th Congress, the panel issued 192 rules with 128 either open (28), modified open (5), structured or modified closed (59), or closed (36). See *Survey of Activities of the House Committee on Rules* (Washington, DC: Government Printing Office, 2005). During the 109th Congress, the panel issued 193 rules with 138 directly related to the amending process. Of these, 22 were open, 2 modified open, 65 modified closed, and 49 closed. See *Survey of Activities of the House Committee on Rules* (Washington, DC: Government Printing Office, 2007), and *Survey of Activities of the House Committee on Rules* (Washington, D.C.: Government Printing Office, 2009). Data provided for the 110th and 111th Congresses provided by CRS congressional expert Christopher Davis. The count of special rules only includes those regulating the amending process on bills and joint resolutions.

In summary, rules establish the conditions under which most major bills are debated and amended. They determine the length of general debate, permit or prohibit amendments, and often waive points of order. Writing the rules is the majority party's way of ensuring that measures reach the floor under terms favorable to the party's preferred outcomes. Put differently, the majority party limits and structures the votes to get the legislative and political results it intends, keeping the two Congresses in mind. In this era of message politics and partisan polarization, innovative rules can both protect majority party members from casting electorally perilous votes or, alternatively, make amendments in order that appeal to diverse party constituencies.

For their part, minority lawmakers object strongly to the wider use of restrictive rules that block them from offering and getting votes on their policy alternatives. "We don't expect to win," said a minority member, "but we do expect to be able to at least offer amendments so the two parties can define their differences."[39] Special rules are often as important to a bill's fate as a favorable committee vote.

Dislodging a Bill from Committee

Committees do not necessarily reflect the point of view of the full chamber. What happens when a standing committee refuses to report a bill or when the Rules Committee does not grant a rule? To circumvent committees, members have three options: the discharge petition, the Calendar Wednesday rule, and the ability of the Rules Committee to extract a bill from committee. However, these tactics are rarely employed and seldom successful.

The discharge petition permits the House to relieve a committee of jurisdiction over a stalled measure. This procedure also provides a way for the rank and file to force a bill to the floor, even if the majority leadership, the committee chair, and the Rules Committee oppose it. If a committee does not report a bill within thirty legislative days after the bill was referred to it, any member may file a discharge motion (petition) requiring the signature of 218 members, a majority of the House. Once the signatures are obtained, the discharge motion is placed on the Discharge Calendar for seven days. It can then be called up on the second and fourth Mondays of the month by any member who signed the petition. If the discharge motion is agreed to, the bill is taken up right away. Since 1910, when the discharge rule was adopted, only three discharged measures have ever become law. Its threatened or actual use, particularly as the number of signatures closes in on 218, may stimulate a committee to act on a bill and the majority leadership to schedule it for floor action. The discharge procedure is rarely successful as a lawmaking device largely because members are reluctant to second-guess committees; to write legislation on the floor without the guidance of committee hearings and reports; and to use a procedure that may one day be used against committees on which they serve. Moreover, 218 signatures are not easy to obtain.

The minority party may employ discharge petitions to spotlight the two Congresses. For example, minority members may promote and publicize their high-priority issues and then circulate discharge petitions "in an attempt to force House votes—and provide a contrast with [the majority party] in an election year."[40] When Republicans were in the minority in the 111th Congress (2009–2011), they filed discharge petitions to try to force floor votes on repealing the health care law. Their objective was "to capitalize on the public's divided feelings on the health care law as the [2010] midterm elections approach."[41]

The discharge rule also applies to the Rules Committee. A motion to discharge a rule is in order after seven legislative days, instead of thirty days, as long as the bill made in order by the rule has been in committee for thirty days. Any member may enter a discharge motion, but majority members rarely break ranks with their party leaders to sign the petition. When Rep. Christopher Shays, R-Conn., signed a successful discharge petition to force House action on a landmark campaign finance reform bill (the Bipartisan Campaign Reform Act of 2002) opposed by the GOP leadership, there were charges of treason against Shays and rumblings that he might face a GOP challenger in the Republican primary. Signing discharge petitions, "along with other kinds of procedural betrayals, are being considered and discussed by members" of the GOP's committee on committees, remarked the Republican Conference chair.[42] Shays was subsequently passed over as chair of the Government Reform Committee, even though he had more seniority than the two other Republicans in contention.

Adopted in 1909, the Calendar Wednesday rule provides that on Wednesdays committees may bring up from the House Calendar or Union Calendar their measures that have not received a rule from the Rules Committee. However, the clerk will not call committees on Wednesdays unless the committee chair gives notice on Tuesday that he or she will seek recognition to call up a measure under the rule. Calendar Wednesday is cumbersome to employ, seldom used, and generally dispensed with by unanimous consent. Since 1943, fewer than fifteen measures have been enacted into law under this procedure.[43]

Finally, the Rules Committee has the power of extraction. The committee can propose rules that make bills in order for House debate even if the bills have been neither introduced nor reported by standing committees. Based on an 1895 precedent, this procedure is akin to discharging committees without the required 218 signatures. It stirs bitter controversy among members who think it usurps the rights of the other committees, and therefore it is seldom used.

HOUSE FLOOR PROCEDURES

The House meets Monday through Friday, often convening at noon. In practice, it conducts the bulk of its committee and floor business during the middle of the week (the so-called Tuesday to Thursday Club). To infuse greater predictability in the schedule, and to provide more time for members to spend in their districts, the GOP leaders of the 112th Congress crafted a legislative schedule for 2011 of 123 workdays over thirty-two weeks. "Under the new calendar, House members will have a cycle of being in session for two weeks in Washington [with five-day workweeks] and then spending the following week in their home districts."[44] Majority Leader Cantor also promised that there would be no votes each legislative day earlier than 1 p.m. (to permit committees to meet without interruption), no votes after 7 p.m., and on Fridays voting would conclude by 3 p.m.[45] However, this scheduling pattern may change in 2012 as the congressional and presidential election season heats up and lawmakers want to spend more time at home to campaign.

At the beginning of each day's session, bells ring throughout the Capitol and the House office buildings, summoning representatives to the floor. The bells also notify members of votes, quorum calls, recesses, and adjournments. Typically, the opening activities include a daily prayer; approval of the *Journal* (a constitutionally required record of the previous day's proceedings); recitation of the Pledge of Allegiance; receipt of messages from the president (such as a veto message) or the Senate; announcements, if any, by the Speaker; and one-minute speeches by members on any topic. On Mondays and Tuesdays, a period of morning hour debate takes place after the opening preliminaries but before the start of formal legislative business.

After these preliminaries, the House generally begins considering legislation. For a major bill, a set pattern is observed: adopting the rule, convening in Committee of the Whole, allotting time for general debate, amending, voting, and moving the bill to final passage.

Adoption of the Rule

The Speaker, after consulting other majority party leaders and affected committee chairs, generally decides when the House will debate a bill and under what kind of rule. When the scheduled day arrives, the Speaker recognizes a majority member of the Rules Committee for one hour to explain the rule's contents. By custom, the majority member yields half the time for debate to a minority member of the Rules Committee. At the end of the debate, which may take less than the allotted hour, the House votes on the previous question motion. Its approval brings the House to an immediate vote on the rule. Its rejection (a rare occurrence) allows the minority party to amend the rule—and then to vote on the rule.

Opponents of a bill can try to defeat the rule and avert House action on the bill itself. But rules are rarely defeated because majority party members generally vote with their leaders on procedural votes and the Rules Committee is sensitive to the wishes of the House. During the speakership of Dennis Hastert, R-Ill. (1999–2007), the House rejected only two rules offered by the Rules Committee. Splits within the majority party account for the defeats. Nancy Pelosi never lost a rule during her four years as Speaker (2007–2011). Once the rule is adopted, the House is governed by its provisions. Most rules state that "at any time after the adoption of [the rule] the Speaker may declare the House resolved into the Committee of the Whole."

Committee of the Whole

The Committee of the Whole House on the state of the Union is a parliamentary artifice designed to expedite consideration of legislation. It is simply the House in another form with different rules. For example, a quorum in the Committee of the Whole is only 100 members, compared with 218 for the full House. The Speaker appoints a majority party colleague to preside over the committee, which then begins general debate of a bill.

General Debate

A rule from the Rules Committee specifies the amount of time, usually one to two hours, for a general discussion of the bill under consideration. Controversial bills require more time, perhaps four to ten hours. Control of the time is divided equally between the majority and minority floor managers—usually the chair and ranking minority member of the committee that reported the legislation. (When bills are referred to more than one committee, a more complex division of debate time is allotted among the committees that had jurisdiction over the legislation.) The majority floor manager's job is to guide the bill to final passage; the minority floor manager may seek to amend or kill the bill.

After the floor managers have made their opening statements, they parcel out several minutes to colleagues on their side of the aisle who wish to speak. General debate rarely lives up to its name. Most legislators read prepared speeches. Give-and-take exchange occurs infrequently at this stage of the proceedings.

The Amending Phase

The amending process is the heart of decision making on the floor of the House. Amendments determine the final shape of bills and often dominate public discussion. Illinois Republican Henry J. Hyde, for example, repeatedly and successfully proposed amendments barring the use of federal funds for abortions.

An amendment in the Committee of the Whole is considered under the five-minute rule, which gives the sponsor five minutes to defend it and an opponent five minutes to speak against it. The amendment then may be brought to a vote. Amendments are routinely debated for more than ten minutes, however. Legislators gain the floor by saying, "I move to strike the last word" or "I move to strike the requisite number of words." These pro forma amendments, which make no alteration in the pending matter, simply serve to give members five minutes of debate time.

If there is an open rule, opponents may try to load a bill with so many objectionable amendments that it will sink under its own weight. The reverse strategy is to propose sweetener amendments that attract support from other members. Offering many amendments is an effective dilatory tactic because each amendment must be read in full, debated for at least five to ten minutes, and then voted on.

In this amending phase, the interconnection of the two Congresses is evident: amendments can have electoral as well as legislative consequences. Floor amendments enable lawmakers to take positions that enhance their reputations with the folks back home, put opponents on record, and shape national policy. For example, "put-them-on-the-spot amendments," as one representative dubbed them, can be artfully fashioned by minority lawmakers to force the majority to vote on issues such as gun control or stem cell research that can be used against them in the next campaign.[46] The majority party's control of the Rules Committee minimizes the use of this tactic because the panel may "script" the amendment process. For example, only the amendments made in order by Rules can be offered, often in a set order, and only by a specific member.

The minority guards the floor to demand explanations or votes on amendments brought up by the majority. As a minority floor guardian wrote, "So long as a floor watchdog exists all members of the House are afforded some additional protection from precipitous actions."[47] In the 112th Congress, various minority members assume this role for Democrats in the House.

Voting

Before passage of the 1970 Legislative Reorganization Act, the Committee of the Whole adopted or rejected amendments by voice votes or other votes with no public record of who voted and how. Today, any legislator supported by twenty-five colleagues can obtain a recorded vote. (The member who requested a recorded vote is counted as one of the twenty-five who rise to be counted by the chair.)

Since the installation of an electronic voting system in 1973, members can insert their personalized cards (about the size of a credit card) into one of more than forty voting stations on the floor and press the "Yea," "Nay," or "Present" button. A large electronic display board behind the press gallery provides a running tally of the total votes for or against a motion. The voting tally, said a representative, is watched carefully by many members:

> I find that a lot of times, people walk in, and the first thing they do is look at the board, and they have key people they check out, and if those people have voted "aye," they go to the machine and vote "aye" and walk off the floor.
>
> But I will look at the board and see how [members of the state delegation] vote, because they are in districts right next to me, and they have constituencies just like mine. I will vote the way I am going to vote except that if they are both different, I will go up and say "Why did you vote that way? Let me know if there is something I am missing."[48]

As noted earlier, both parties stage votes that can then be used against electorally vulnerable lawmakers or for other political purposes. For example, hours before President Obama delivered his 2011 State of the Union message, House Republicans required Democrats to vote on a resolution to cut nonsecurity discretionary spending, making them go "on the record" on spending cuts ahead of Obama's speech to Congress.[49]

After all pending amendments have been voted on, the Committee of the Whole rises. The chair hands the gavel back to the Speaker, and a quorum once again becomes 218 members.

Final Passage

As specified in the rule, the full House must review the actions of its agent, the Committee of the Whole. The Speaker announces that under the rule the previous question has been ordered, which means in this context that no further debate is permitted on the bill or its amendments. The Speaker then asks whether any representative wants a separate vote on any amendment. If not, all the amendments agreed to in the committee will be approved.

The next important step is the recommittal motion, which provides a way for the House to return, or recommit, the bill to the committee that reported it. The motion to recommit has two forms: (1) the rarely used "straight" motion to return the measure to committee (which effectively kills it), and (2) a motion to recommit with instructions that the committee report "forthwith," which means the bill never really leaves the House. If this form of the motion is adopted, the bill, as modified by the instructions, is automatically before the House again. By precedent, either form of the motion is always made by a minority party member who opposes the legislation. Each form of the motion is also subject to ten minutes of debate, five per side. Recommittal motions are usually not successful because they are so heavily identified as an opposition party prerogative, but they do serve to protect the rights of the minority. When Republicans won majority control in 1995, they amended the House rules to guarantee the minority leader or his or her designee the right to offer a recommittal motion with instructions (the instructions embody the minority's policy alternative and must be germane to the bill). This rule still remains in place.

The 110th and 111th Congresses, and even earlier ones, saw a change in the major purposes of the motion to recommit. Although still employed by the minority party to force the House to vote on its alternative policy proposal (the "instructions" in this motion), the motion to recommit is now frequently employed to achieve two political purposes: to defeat, delay, or eviscerate majority party policies and to force vulnerable majority lawmakers to vote on "gotcha amendments" certain to cause them electoral grief if they do not vote for the minority proposal. As Democratic leader Hoyer exclaimed, "The unfortunate fact is that the motion to recommit with instructions has for more than a decade become a hollow vehicle and farce."[50] For example, on a recent energy bill the Republican minority included in their motion to recommit with instructions the requirement that government contractors must "ensure that no employee had been convicted of child molestation and on a [science research reauthorization bill] that any federal employee who had viewed or downloaded pornography be fired."[51] Clearly, many lawmakers would be reluctant to vote against a motion to recommit with these kinds of instructions because they would likely face a barrage of campaign attack ads suggesting that they support child molestation and pornography. House Democrats, in the minority in the 112thCongress, have clearly taken notice. They plan to emulate the success the Republicans had in using the motion to recommit with instructions to require vulnerable Republicans to take electorally challenging votes. Minority Leader Pelosi and other party leaders are "trying to be more savvy about using the motions to put Republicans on the politically unpopular side of issues that Democrats want to champion ahead of the [2012] elections."[52] For example, Democrats have offered motions "barring a health care repeal bill from taking effect unless a majority of lawmakers forfeit their government-sponsored health insurance" and preventing "companies that outsource jobs from obtaining government contracts."[53]

If the motion to recommit with instructions is adopted, the minority proposal is incorporated into the bill. If it is rejected, the Speaker will declare, "The question is on passage of the bill." Passage of the measure, by the House in this case, marks about the halfway point in the lawmaking process. The Senate must also approve the bill, and its procedures are strikingly different from those of the House. It is an institution noted for protecting the rights of the minority, hence its reliance on the unanimous consent of all senators to accomplish much of the chamber's business.

SCHEDULING IN THE SENATE

Compared with the larger and more clamorous House, which needs and follows well-defined rules and precedents, the Senate operates more informally. And, unlike the House, where the rules permit a determined majority to make decisions, the Senate's rules emphasize individual prerogatives (unlimited freedom to debate and to offer amendments, including nonrelevant amendments) and minority rights (those of the minority party, a faction, or even a single senator). "The Senate," said one member, "is run for the convenience of one Senator to the inconvenience of 99."[54] No wonder some commentators say the Senate has only two rules (unanimous consent and exhaustion) and three speeds (slow, slower, and slowest). As Sen. Byron Dorgan, D-N.D., said, "The only thing it's easy to do in the Senate is slow things down. The Senate is 100 human brake pads."[55]

The scheduling system for the Senate appears relatively simple. The Calendar of Business is used for all public and private bills and the Executive Calendar for treaties and nominations. The Senate has nothing comparable to the scheduling duties of the House Rules Committee, and the majority and minority leadership actively consult about scheduling. The Senate majority leader is responsible for setting the agenda and is aided in controlling the scheduling by the priority given him when he seeks recognition on the floor. What this means is that if several senators are seeking recognition from the presiding officer and the majority leader is among them, the chair will always give preference to the majority leader.

Despite the Senate's smaller size, establishing a firm agenda of business is harder in the Senate than in the House. As a majority leader once said:

The ability of any Senator to speak without limitations makes it impossible to establish total certainty with respect to scheduling. When there is added to that the difficulty and very demanding schedules of 100 Senators, it is very hard to organize business in a way that meets the convenience of everybody.[56]

Legislation typically reaches the Senate floor in two ways: by unanimous consent or by motion. But senators, too, can also force Senate consideration of their proposals by offering them as nonrelevant amendments to pending business. Unanimous consent agreements are of utmost importance to the smooth functioning of the Senate.

Unanimous Consent Agreements

The Senate frequently dispenses with its formal rules and instead follows negotiated agreements submitted to the Senate for its unanimous approval (see Box 8-5 on unanimous consent agreements). The objectives are to expedite work in an institution known for extended debate, to impose some measure of predictability on floor action, and to minimize dilatory activities. As a party floor leader observed:

> We aren't bringing [measures] to the floor unless we have [a unanimous consent] agreement. We could bring child-care legislation to the floor right now, but that would mean two months of fighting. We want to maximize productive time by trying to work out as much as we can in advance [of floor action].[57]

It is not uncommon for party leaders to negotiate piecemeal unanimous consent agreements—limiting debate on a specific amendment, for example—and to hammer them out in public on the Senate floor.

Unanimous consent agreements (also called time-limitation agreements) limit debate on the bill, any amendments, and various motions. Occasionally, they specify the time for the vote on final passage and typically impose constraints on the amendment process. For example, to facilitate enactment of an omnibus crime package that contained provisions with widespread Senate support, senators agreed to a unanimous consent request barring floor amendments on controversial issues such as gun control or the death penalty.[58]

The Senate's unanimous consent agreements are functional equivalents of special rules from the House Rules Committee. Both waive the rules of their respective chambers and must be approved by the members—in one case by majority vote and in the other by unanimous consent. These accords are binding contracts and can be terminated or modified only by another unanimous consent agreement. Senators and aides often negotiate and draft unanimous consent agreements privately, whereas the Rules Committee hears requests for procedural rules in public sessions.

Ways to Extract Bills from Committee

If a bill is blocked in committee, the Senate has several ways to obtain floor action. It can add the bill as a nonrelevant floor amendment to another bill,

BOX 8-5 **Example of a Unanimous Consent Agreement**

*O*rdered, that at 10:00 a.m. on Tuesday, March 10, 2009, the Senate resume consideration of H.R. 1105, an act making omnibus appropriations for the fiscal year ending September 30, 2009, and for other purposes; provided, that the following be the only first degree amendments remaining in order to the bill; further, that no amendment be in order to the listed amendments prior to a vote in relation thereto; further, that the amendments must be offered and debated Friday, March 6, 2009, Monday, March 9, 2009, or Tuesday, March 10, 2009:

◄ Amdt. No. 615, offered by the Senator from Nevada (Mr. Ensign),

◄ Amdt. No. 621, offered by the Senator from Louisiana (Mr. Vitter),

◄ Amdt. No. 604, offered by the Senator from Alabama (Mr. Sessions),

◄ Amdt. No. 593, offered by the Senator from Arizona (Mr. McCain),

◄ Amdt. No. 662, offered by the Senator from South Dakota (Mr. Thune),

◄ Amdt. No. 637, offered by the Senator from Wyoming (Mr. Barrasso),

◄ Amdt. No. 668, offered by the Senator from Wyoming (Mr. Enzi),

◄ Amdt. Nos. 629, 630, 631, offered by the Senator from Arizona (Mr. Kyl),

◄ An amendment on dues notification offered by the Senator from Arizona (Mr. Kyl) or his designee, with a copy of the proposal at desk,

◄ Amdt. No. 673, offered by the Senator from Texas (Mr. Cornyn), and

◄ Amdt. No. 665, offered by the Senator from Kentucky (Mr. Bunning).

Ordered further, That on Tuesday, the remaining amendments be considered and debated and that after all debate has been concluded on the remaining amendments, the Senate proceed to vote in relation to the amendments in a sequence established under a subsequent order, with two minutes of debate, equally divided and controlled in the usual form prior to a vote in relation to each; provided, that after the first vote in the sequence, the remaining votes be limited to 10 minutes each.

Ordered further, That upon disposition of all remaining amendments, there then be 30 minutes of debate, equally divided and controlled between the Leaders or their designees, prior to a vote on the motion to invoke cloture on H.R. 1105.

Ordered further, That upon disposition of the amendments and the Senate having voted on the motion to invoke cloture on H.R. 1105 and cloture having been invoked, all post-cloture time be considered yielded back, the bill be read a third time, and the Senate proceed to vote on passage of the bill.

Ordered further, That with respect to the motion to invoke cloture on H.R. 1105, the mandatory quorum required under Rule XXII be waived.

Source: U.S. Senate, *Calendar of Business,* 111th Cong., 1st sess., March 10, 2009, 2.

bypass the committee stage by placing the bill directly on the calendar, suspend the rules, or discharge the bill from committee. Only the first two procedures are effective; the other two are somewhat difficult to employ and seldom succeed.[59] In recent years, however, various senators have employed motions to suspend the rules to force votes on amendments that would normally be out of order under Senate rules and precedents. The suspension rule requires one day's written notice (published in the *Congressional Record)* and a high voting threshold (two-thirds) to succeed.

Because the Senate has no general germaneness (or relevancy) rule, senators can take an agriculture bill that is stuck in committee and add it as a nonrelevant floor amendment to a pending health bill. "Amendments may be made," Thomas Jefferson noted long ago, "so as to totally alter the nature of the proposition." However, unanimous consent agreements can limit or prohibit nonrelevant amendments.

Senators can also bypass referral of measures to committee by invoking one of the chamber's formal rules (Rule XIV). Typically, when senators introduce bills or joint resolutions (or when bills or joint resolutions are passed by the House and sent to the Senate), they are referred to the appropriate committee of jurisdiction. Rule XIV specifies that those measures are to be read twice by title on different legislative days before they are referred. If a senator interposes an objection after the first reading and again the next day after the second reading, the bill or joint resolution is automatically placed on the Senate's Calendar of Business (see Box 8-6 for how Rule XIV works). Although not used for the vast majority of measures, Rule XIV is increasingly invoked on

---

BOX 8-6   Senate Rule XIV: Bypassing Committee Referral

MEASURE READ THE FIRST TIME—S. 192

Mr. BEGICH. Madam President, I understand that S. 192, introduced earlier today by Senator DEMINT, is at the desk and I ask for its first reading.

The PRESIDING OFFICER. The clerk will read the bill by title.

The bill clerk read as follows:

A bill (S. 192) to repeal the job-killing health care law and health care-related provisions in the Health Care and Education Reconciliation Act of 2010.

Mr. BEGICH. Madam President, I now ask for its second reading and object to my own request.

The PRESIDING OFFICER. Objection is heard.

The bill will be read the second time on the next legislative day.

Source: Congressional Record, January 26, 2011, S263.

MEASURE PLACED ON THE CALENDAR—S. 192

Mr. REID. Mr. President, I understand S. 192 is at the desk and is due for a second reading.

The ACTING PRESIDENT pro tempore. The clerk will read the title of the bill for the second time.

The legislative clerk read as follows:

A bill (S. 192) to repeal the job-killing health care law and health care-related provisions in the Health Care and Education Reconciliation Act of 2010.

Mr. REID. Mr. President, I object to further proceedings with respect to this legislation.

The ACTING PRESIDENT pro tempore. Objection having been heard, the bill will be placed on the calendar under rule XIV.

Source: Congressional Record, January 27, 2011, S295.

party issues of high priority. The majority leader, for example, may employ it to circumvent committees because no time is available for a lengthy committee review, or he wants an issue ready to be called up at his discretion. As Sen. Lamar Alexander, R Tenn., noted, "From the 103rd to the 109th Congress, Rule XIV to bypass [committees] was used on average 24 times per Congress. This was shattered in the 110th Congress when it was used 57 times."[60]

SENATE FLOOR PROCEDURES

The Senate, like the House, often convenes at noon, sometimes earlier, to keep pace with the workload. Typically, it opens with a prayer, followed by the Pledge of Allegiance and then leaders' time (usually ten minutes each to the majority leader and the minority leader to discuss various issues). If neither leader wants any time, the Senate typically either permits members who have requested time to make their statements, or it resumes consideration of old or new business under terms of a unanimous consent agreement. The Senate, too, must keep and approve the *Journal* of the previous day's activities. Commonly, the *Journal* is "deemed approved to date" by unanimous consent when the Senate adjourns or recesses at the end of each day.

Normal Routine

For most bills, the Senate follows four steps:

1. The majority leader secures the unanimous consent of the Senate to an arrangement that specifies when a bill will be brought to the floor and the conditions for debating it.
2. The presiding officer recognizes the majority and minority floor managers for opening statements.
3. Amendments are then in order, with debate on each amendment regulated by the terms of the unanimous consent agreement.
4. A roll call vote takes place on final passage.

As in the House, amendments in the Senate serve various purposes. For example, floor managers might accept "as many amendments as they can without undermining the purposes of the bill, in order to build the broadest possible consensus behind it."[61] Some amendments are designed with the two Congresses in mind. Such amendments may bestow benefits to the electorate or embarrass members who must vote against them. "My amendment can be characterized as a 'November amendment,'" remarked a Republican senator, "because the vote . . . will provide an opportunity for Senators to go home and say, 'I voted to reduce Federal taxes' and 'I voted to cut Federal spending.'"[62] Senate Democrats make "vigorous use of amendments to strike a contrast with Republican policies."[63] Unless constrained by some previous unanimous consent agreement, senators generally have the right to offer an unlimited number of floor amendments.

Significantly, recent majority leaders have increasingly used their right of first recognition on the floor to "fill the amendment tree." The right of first recognition brings up two points. First, the presiding officer always recognizes the majority leader first if other senators are trying to catch the eye of the chair. Second, despite Senate precedents stating that members lose the floor when they offer amendments, the first recognition principle trumps that determination, enabling the majority leader to offer amendment after amendment until the so-called amendment tree (a chart that depicts the number of permissible amendments to a measure) is filled. Majority Leader Harry Reid, D-Nev., used this procedural device forty-four times in the 111th Congress, "compared with the 40 times the previous majority leaders combined used the tactic."[64]

Senate precedents dictate how many amendments may be pending at any one time to a measure. Once the amendment tree is filled, no other senator may offer amendments—that is, the amending process is frozen. This practice is controversial and angers many lawmakers, especially those in the minority. It is done for various reasons, such as blocking unwanted, nonrelevant, amendments; protecting vulnerable colleagues from voting on amendments crafted to cause them electoral grief; or promoting negotiations with the opposition so an accord might be reached on the number of amendments each side is willing to vote on. If an accord is reached, the majority leader will drop some of his amendments so others may offer theirs.

A bill is brought to a final vote whenever senators stop talking. This can be a long process, particularly in the absence of a unanimous consent agreement. On some bills, unanimous consent agreements are foreclosed because of deliberate obstructive tactics, particularly the threat or use of the filibuster (extended debate). In these instances, bills cannot be voted upon until the filibuster has ended. Every measure might face at least two primary filibusters: the first on the motion to take up the legislation and the second on the consideration of the bill. "Double filibusters" underscore the expansive scope of minority rights that characterizes Senate procedure. (A number of laws, such as trade or reconciliation measures, restrict a senator's right to prolong debate. As a former Senate parliamentarian noted, "We have on the books probably a couple hundred laws that set up specific legislative vehicles that cannot be filibustered or only amended in a very restricted way.")[65]

Holds, Filibusters, and Cloture

The old-style filibuster has long been associated with the 1939 movie *Mr. Smith Goes to Washington,* which featured a haggard Jimmy Stewart conducting a dramatic solo talkathon on the floor of the Senate to inform the public about political wrongdoing. In its new incarnation, the filibuster is usually threatened more than invoked to gain bargaining power and negotiating leverage. Today, the threat to filibuster is sufficient to block action on many bills or nominations, in large measure because it is so hard to mobilize sixty votes to invoke cloture (closure of debate). Moreover, cloture is a time-consuming procedure (two days) that impedes the Senate's ability to process its extensive workload.

Filibusters involve many blocking tactics besides extended debate in which senators might hold the floor for hours of endless speeches. In today's polarized Senate, contemporary filibusters are commonly waged by those who skillfully exploit Senate rules. For example, senators might offer scores of amendments, raise many points of order, or demand numerous and consecutive roll call votes. Holds also function as a form of silent filibuster.

Holds. Long an informal custom, a hold permits one or more senators to block floor action on measures or matters by asking their party leaders not to schedule them. A hold, explained Sen. Charles E. Grassley, R-Iowa, is "a notice by a Senator to his or her party leader of an intention to object to bringing a bill or nomination to the floor for consideration."[66] The majority leader decides whether, or for how long, to honor a colleague's hold. The power of holds is grounded in the implicit threat of senators to conduct filibusters or to object to unanimous consent agreements.

Holds have come under criticism because they often lead to delays or even the death (choke holds) of measures or nominations. Originally intended as a way for senators to get information about when the majority leader planned action on a measure, holds have become devices to kill measures by delaying them indefinitely or to gain bargaining leverage by, for example, stalling action on presidential nominees. On one occasion, so many holds on nominations were pending before the Senate that a Democratic leader felt left out. As he explained, "I'm going to have to pick out a nominee to get to know him or her a lot better because it works that way. I mean, it's 'Hello, I'm your holder . . . come dance with me.'"[67]

For years, Senators Grassley and Ron Wyden, D-Ore., joined by Sen. Claire McCaskill, D-Mo., have tried to reform—not eliminate—the holds process. Specifically, they want to end secret holds where one anonymous senator can block bills or nominations. Some success for the trio came in 2007 when the Senate established a procedure for ending secret holds (formally called a "notice of intent to object"). Briefly, a senator would have a colleague object on his or her behalf to the consideration of a measure or matter. Then the senator had six session days to publicly claim the hold or drop it. However, there was no enforcement mechanism. Moreover, senators would relinquish their hold before the six-day period ended, but enlist another colleague to place the hold. A series of "revolving" holds undermined the attempt to end secret holds. When the 112th Congress opened, the Senate adopted a "standing order"—the functional equivalent of a formal rule—that requires every senator, after two session days, to make his or her hold public. If a senator does not come forward to be the claimant, then whoever objected on his or her behalf, including the two party leaders, would be identified in the *Congressional Record* as the "holder."

Filibusters and Cloture. The right of extended debate is unique to the Senate. Any senator or group of senators can talk continuously in the hope of delaying, modifying, or defeating legislation. In 1957 South Carolina senator

Strom Thurmond, then a Democrat, set the record for the Senate's longest solo performance—twenty-four hours and eighteen minutes; he was trying to kill a civil rights bill.

The success of a filibuster depends not only on how long it takes but also on when it is waged. A filibuster can be most effective late in a session because there is insufficient time to break it.[68] Even the threat of a filibuster can encourage accommodations or compromises between proponents and opponents of legislation.

Defenders of the filibuster say it protects minority rights, permits thorough consideration of bills, and dramatizes issues. "In many ways," noted Sen. Robert C. Byrd, D-W.Va., "the filibuster is the single most important device ever employed to ensure that the Senate remains truly the unique protector of the rights of our people."[69] Critics contend that talkathons enable minorities to extort unwanted concessions. During most of its history, the Senate had no way to terminate debate except by unanimous consent, exhaustion, or compromise. In 1917 the Senate adopted Rule XXII, its first cloture (debate-ending) rule. After several revisions, Rule XXII now permits three-fifths of the Senate (sixty members) to shut off debate on substantive issues or procedural motions. (A two-thirds vote is required to invoke cloture on a proposal to change the rules of the Senate.) Once cloture is invoked, thirty hours of debate time remain before the final vote occurs on the matter identified in the cloture motion.

Senators complain about the frequent use of filibusters, filibuster threats, and cloture attempts. In the past, filibusters generally occurred on issues of great national importance. Today, they occur on a wide range of less momentous topics. As one majority leader pointed out,

> Not long ago the filibuster or threat of a filibuster was rarely undertaken in the Senate, being reserved for matters of grave national importance. That is no longer the case. . . . The threat of a filibuster is now a regular event in the Senate, weekly at least, sometimes daily. It is invoked by minorities of as few as one or two Senators and for reasons as trivial as a Senator's travel schedule.[70]

Unsurprisingly, many commentators call it the "sixty-vote Senate." Or as a senator observed, "It isn't good enough to have the majority. You've got to have 60 votes."[71] Today, it is not uncommon for unanimous consent agreements to require bills or amendments to attract sixty votes for passage rather than a simple majority. The interests of both sides are served by this development. Majority advocates get a vote, and the supermajority threshold protects minority opponents. Moreover, this accord saves the Senate's time by avoiding use of the cloture procedure.

Attempts to invoke cloture also have increased, particularly in recent Congresses. For example, in the decade from 1961 to 1971 there were 5.2 cloture votes per Congress, but during the 109th Congress (2005–2007) there were fifty-two cloture votes.[72] The 110th Senate seemingly broke all records when the chamber voted on 112 cloture motions, "twice the number in the previous Congress and more than double the average number over the previous twenty years."[73] But then another new record was set in the 111th Congress 132 cloture votes.[74] Moreover, the norm of one cloture vote per measure has changed. The modern Senate reached a record of eight cloture votes (all unsuccessful) on a controversial campaign financing measure during the 100th Congress (1987–1989). Cloture is also sometimes employed for purposes unrelated to ending a filibuster. For example, if the sixty votes are obtained under Senate Rule XXII, there is the requirement that all amendments be germane to the clotured measure. Or the majority leader may schedule repeated cloture votes, knowing that they will fail, in order to tar the other party as "obstructionists" in the next election.

Contemporary senators' willingness to wield their procedural prerogatives for partisan advantage was plainly evident in the 111th Congress (2009–2011). It is not surprising, then, that the two parties provided different interpretations of the circumstances that provoked their dismay and frustration with Senate proceedings. Senate Democratic Policy Committee chair Byron Dorgan, who retired at the end of the 111th Congress, declared that there was "less cooperation and more determination to block almost anything than at any time I have seen in the 30 years I have served here." He added:

> We have a noncontroversial issue, a motion to proceed [to the consideration of] something on which there is no controversy, and it is subject to a filibuster, and then a cloture motion has to be filed. Then 2 days have to pass before it ripens. We have a cloture vote, and then following the cloture vote, the minority says: Well, we insist that the 30 hours postcloture be used. So 30 hours has to be burned off. Only then can you get a vote on a noncontroversial issue. Then you have a vote, and it is 98 to 1. That has happened throughout this [Congress]— continual efforts to block everything; deciding that the best strategy politically, apparently, for the minority here in the U.S. Senate is to block everything.[75]

Sen. Lamar Alexander, the chair of the Republican Conference, insists that the "real obstructionists have been the Democratic majority which, for an unprecedented number of times, have used their majority advantage to limit debate, not allow amendments and bypass the normal committee consideration of legislation." He continued:

> So the real "party of no" is the majority party that has been saying "no" to debate and "no" to voting on amendments that minority members believe improve legislation and express the voices of the people they represent. In fact, the reason the majority leader can claim there have been so many filibusters is because he actually is counting as filibusters the number of times he filed cloture—or moved to cut off debate.[76]

This clash of viewpoints on which party provoked the intense parliamentary warfare led a number of mainly junior senators to try—at the start of the 112th Congress—to change the Senate rules. One reform group favored use of the so-called constitutional or nuclear option.[77] Its advocates argue that a newly elected Senate should not be bound by preexisting rules. Instead, they argue, the Senate has the constitutional right "to determine the rules of its proceedings" by majority vote at the start of a new Congress, notwithstanding any inherited (or continuing) rules from the previous Congress. Under inherited Senate rules, however, ending a talkathon on any rules change requires a supermajority vote of two-thirds, a very high hurdle for reform proposals. Many senators on both sides of the aisle opposed the "constitutional" approach on the ground that it would change the fundamental character of the Senate by turning it into another House of Representatives where the governing principle is "majority rule." Reform-minded senators proposed other changes, such as lowering the number of senators required to invoke cloture and limiting debate on the motion to proceed to two hours.

In the end, the Senate adopted a series of modest changes, leaving Rule XXII (cloture/filibuster) untouched. The procedural modifications were negotiated for weeks among the key actors, including the majority and minority leaders and the chair and ranking member of the Committee on Rules and Administration. The revisions included an end to secret holds (noted earlier) on legislation and nominations; elimination of the reading requirement for amendments—employed as a dilatory tactic—if they have been available to lawmakers for at least seventy-two hours; and, as mentioned in Chapter 11, agreement that the number of federal positions subject to the advice and consent of the Senate should be reduced by one-third. In addition, the two party leaders announced a nonbinding "gentlemen's agreement." GOP leader Mitch McConnell, R-Ky., said that Republicans would restrict filibusters on the motion to proceed to consider legislation. For his part, Democratic leader Reid stated that he would exercise restraint in filling the tree to block Republican amendments. In addition, the two agreed that neither would pursue the constitutional option in the 112th Congress or in the next Congress.[78]

The threat of changing Senate rules by a simple majority, as well as other procedural "hardball" actions, reflects an erosion of the Senate's customary norms of collegiality, civility, and accommodation. The various explanations for this development include the election to the Senate of House members who bring with them the aggressive partisanship common to the House, heightened demands placed on senators by constituents and lobbyists, intense electoral competition, and the escalating costs of campaigns. "Daily priorities [are] shaped more by personal agendas—campaign needs, interest-group demands, personal staff, obligations to meet constituents, and off-the-Hill speeches—and less by the expectations of colleagues and the needs of

Senate colleagues," wrote Steven S. Smith. "Pressed by constituencies and lobbyists and more strongly motivated to grab a headline, senators now more routinely and more fully exploit their procedural prerogatives than at any other time in the Senate's history."[79] The upshot of these developments is a more individualistic and partisan Senate, which means that compromises and accommodations are harder to achieve on significant substantive and procedural issues.

RESOLVING HOUSE-SENATE DIFFERENCES

Before bills can be sent to the president, they must be passed by the House and the Senate in identical form. When the two chambers pass dissimilar versions of the same bill, another approach to resolving bicameral disagreements is to ping-pong House and Senate amendments between the chambers until each chamber is satisfied with the product. Recent Congresses have seen greater use of the ping-pong method because of the Senate's difficulty in getting to conference, largely because the procedural steps to convene a conference are subject to extended debate. If neither chamber will accept the other's changes via the exchange of amendment process, a House-Senate conference committee may be appointed to reconcile the differences. There are occasions, too, when ping-ponging is used in combination with conference committees. For example, the chambers may start out using the exchange of amendments and then convene a conference to resolve the outstanding matters in bicameral disagreement.

Most public laws are approved without conferences. Either they pass each chamber without any changes (roughly 70 percent), or the House and Senate amend a bill in turn until both chambers agree on the wording (about 20 percent of laws follow this shuttle route). Only about 10 percent of the measures passed by Congress—usually the most important and controversial—are subject to bicameral reconciliation by conference committees.

Under each chamber's rules and precedents, conference committees meet to resolve the matters in bicameral dispute; they are not to reconsider provisions already agreed to, and they are not to write new law by inserting matter that neither house may have considered. However, parliamentary rules are not self-enforcing, and either chamber can waive or ignore them. It is not unusual for conference reports to contain new matter that neither chamber debated nor amended in committee or on the floor. No wonder conference committees are called the third house of Congress. As Sen. Arlen Specter, D-Pa., stated, "[Conference committees] are when the work is concluded. Everything else which is done is really of much less significance than the conferences, where the final touches are put on legislation which constitutes the laws of the country."[80]

Selection of Conferees

Conferees usually are named from the committee or committees that reported the legislation. Congressional rules state that the Speaker and the Senate presiding officer select conferees. In fact, that decision typically is made by the relevant committee chairs and the ranking minority members. House and Senate party leaders commonly get involved in naming conferees on major legislation to ensure that the conferees will back leadership positions on the legislation.

House and Senate party leaders are sometimes named as conferees—a sign that they want to direct conference negotiations on high-stakes issues important to their party. The House majority leader, for example, often serves on important tax conferences. When the top majority party leaders of either chamber are named as conferees, this signals, as one senator declared, a "majority-party driven" conference.[81]

Each chamber may name as many conferees as it wants, and some conference delegations have become very large. The 1981 omnibus reconciliation conference set the record, with more than 250 House and Senate conferees working in fifty-eight subconferences to resolve more than three hundred matters in bicameral disagreement. The ratio of Republicans to Democrats on a conference committee generally reflects the proportion of the two parties in the House and Senate.

Today's conference committees represent a sharp departure in size and composition from the pre-1980 era, when conference delegations generally ranged from five to twelve conferees from each house. And before the mid-1970s, conferees nearly always were the most senior lawmakers from the committees that reported the legislation. Although seniority frequently determines who the conferees will be, it is not unusual for junior and even first-term members to be conferees. Furthermore, conferees today commonly are chosen from several standing committees and reflect intricate selection arrangements. For example, House conferees may be named to negotiate only certain items in disagreement instead of the entire bill. Multiple referrals and megabills are the driving forces behind these two developments.

In conference each chamber has a single vote determined by a majority of its conferees, who are generally expected to support the legislation as it passed their body. But, a senator confessed, as conference committees drag on, the "individual attitudes of the various members begin to show."[82] A standard objective of conferees is to fashion a compromise product (the conference report) that will be acceptable to a majority of the membership of both chambers and that the president will sign into law.

Openness and Bargaining

Secret conference meetings were the norm for most of Congress's history. In 1975 both houses adopted rules requiring open meetings unless the conferees from each chamber voted in public to close the sessions. Two years later, the

House went further, requiring open conference meetings unless the full House agreed to secret sessions. Sometimes, the Cable-Satellite Public Affairs Network (C-SPAN) televises conference proceedings.

The open conference is yet another instance of individual–institutional cleavage. Under the watchful eye of lobbyists, conferees fight harder for provisions they might have dropped quietly in the interest of bicameral agreement. And yet private bargaining sessions still permeate conference negotiations.

Senators and representatives expect certain bills to go to conference and plan their bargaining strategy accordingly. For example, whether to have a recorded vote on amendments can influence conference bargaining. In the absence of a recorded vote, amendments may be easier to drop in conference. Bargaining techniques in conference cover a range of techniques: from logrolling ("you accept my chamber's position on this provision and I'll accept yours on another provision") to threats to walk out of the negotiations unless the other side compromises. One side may fight hard for a position on which it plans to yield, so the conferees can tell their parent chamber that they put up a good battle but the other side would not relent. Conference committees are where the final version of the law is often written, sometimes making changes or additions to legislation that neither chamber ever reviewed or considered in committee or on the floor.

The Conference Report

A conference ends when its report (the compromise bill) is signed by a majority of the conferees from each chamber. House and Senate staff then prepare the conference report and the accompanying joint explanatory statement, which summarizes the conferees' recommendations. The House and Senate then vote on the conference report without further amendment. If either chamber rejects the conference report—an infrequent occurrence—a new conference may be called or another bill introduced. Once passed, the compromise bill is sent to the president for approval or disapproval.

CONCLUSION

The philosophical bias of House and Senate rules reflects the character of each institution. Individual rights are stressed in the Senate, majority rule in the House. In both chambers, however, members who know the rules and precedents have an advantage over procedural novices in affecting policy outcomes. The late senator Byrd—the longest-serving member ever in either chamber—was the acknowledged procedural expert in the Senate. Byrd understood that passing measures often involves unorthodox processes and procedures (for example, forgoing committee hearings or markups or even floor debate).[83]

In addition to congressional rules, persistence, strategy, timing, compromise, and pure chance are important elements in the lawmaking process. To make public policy requires building winning coalitions at successive stages where pressure groups and other parties can advance their claims. Political, procedural, personal, and policy considerations shape the final outcome. Passing laws, as one former representative said, is like the "weaving of a web, bringing a lot of strands together in a pattern of support which won't have the kind of weak spots which could cause the whole fabric to fall apart."[84]

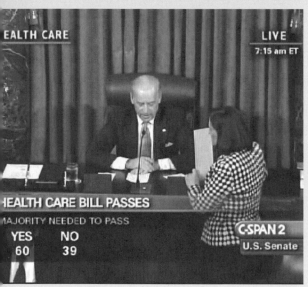

Congressional Decision Making. Covered by C-SPAN, the House votes along party lines to accept the Senate version of President Obama's health-care measure (top left). The House's electronic voting system records members' floor votes. (Middle), Members insert their plastic cards into voting boxes throughout the chamber and vote "yea," "nay," or "present." Vice President Joseph R. Biden Jr. (bottom left) announces the final Senate vote on the health-care bill as C-SPAN shows the tally. Members' votes are scrutinized and rated by hundreds of interest groups, including the Arab American Institute (bottom).

chapter 9

Decision Making in Congress

"I know that everyone is anxiously awaiting the 8:15 time," joked Senate majority leader Harry Reid to a group of unhappy senators waiting on the Senate floor at 8:40 p.m. on a Thursday evening. Only a few could even muster a smile in response.[1] Earlier that day, Reid had announced that senators could tentatively expect a roll call vote to take place at 8:15 p.m. Nearly half an hour after the vote was expected, it had become clear that Democrats lacked the support needed to advance a critical $410 billion omnibus spending measure. "It appears at this time that we are going to have to continue work on this bill," said Reid. "We would probably be a vote short."[2]

Democratic leaders were thrown off guard by dissent in their party's ranks. They had expected to pass the measure easily.[3] But passing the bill turned out to be a "tough slog."[4] Republicans denounced as wasteful the bill's increased spending—an average boost of 8 percent for domestic programs.[5] In the wake of the controversy, a few centrist Democrats signaled their concern and criticized the bill as "bloated" and "business as usual."[6] Even with these defections, however, Reid thought that he had won the needed support. Instead, he was blindsided by the opposition of Sen. Robert Menendez, D-N.J., who was "deeply offended" by a few provisions in the 1,132-page measure that would relax some travel and trade restrictions on Cuba.[7] Menendez's opposition was especially unexpected because senators serving in the party leadership— Menendez was chair of the Democratic Senate Campaign Committee (Sen. Patty Murray, D-Wash., heads the campaign panel in the 112th Congress)— rarely oppose their party on priority issues. "It's been surprising," Reid said of the failure to move the bill.[8]

Reid postponed the vote to buy time for building support. In the meantime, he was forced to allow Republicans to offer a series of amendments requiring Democrats to cast politically painful votes. Sen. David Vitter, R-La., for example, successfully demanded a vote on an amendment to eliminate automatic cost-of-living increases in congressional salaries.[9] Senators of both parties knew these votes would figure in future ads against Democratic candidates. "This is all about developing campaign commercials," said Sen. Mark Begich, D-Alaska.[10] "Democrats effectively used the pay raise issue against several Republican candidates in past cycles," noted a National Republican Senatorial Committee spokesman, "so I don't think they should be at all surprised if this emerges as an issue in some of their own campaigns."[11]

While the debate on amendments went forward, leaders began to round up new support for the bill. "We're working on it," said Majority Whip Richard J. Durbin, D-Ill. "I hope at the end of the day we don't lose [as many as four or five Democrats]."[12] Of the whip team's efforts, Sen. Claire McCaskill, D-Mo., commented, "I think it's fair to say that there's an extraordinary amount of pressure on this particular bill."[13] Treasury Department officials were dispatched to discuss the Cuba trade provisions with Menendez. Having received assurances about the way the administration would interpret the legislative language, Menendez finally announced his support of the bill at a Democratic Caucus meeting to a round of applause.[14] In the end, the Senate passed the legislation after an additional week of work, and President Barack Obama signed the measure into law.

This large-scale spending measure (and hundreds more that have a lower profile) required lawmakers to make tough policy choices collectively—after discussion, debate, bargaining, and problem solving. "The Senate requires consensus," remarked Senate leadership staffer Jim Manley. "Senator Reid is not a king. If he had the ability to snap his fingers and make things fall into place, he would."[15] The end product is almost always an imperfect compromise. Indeed, "imperfect" was precisely how President Obama described the omnibus spending bill when he signed it.[16] Legislative assemblies are deliberative bodies, and in the United States this deliberation always takes place in the context of the two Congresses. Individual members confront thousands of choices: how and when to participate, how to decide, how to find allies, and how to explain their actions to constituents back home.

THE POWER TO CHOOSE

All members of Congress have the ability to shape public policy, although some members are far more influential than others. At a minimum, every legislator has the right, indeed the obligation, to vote. Legislators must cast their own votes; no colleague or staff aide may do it for them. To exchange their votes or other official acts for money or for any other thing of value is a federal crime. But aside from bribery or corruption there are no legal grounds for challenging legislators' deliberations or decisions. As discussed in Chapter 2, the U.S. Constitution specifies that "for any speech or debate in either House, [members of Congress] shall not be questioned in any other place."

Policy making in Congress involves far more than casting roll call votes. Matters that come before Congress for a vote have already been shaped by the participation of members at many prior stages. Some of this work, like members' votes, is a matter of public record: formal meetings, markups, debates, and amending activities. Of equal importance are the less visible informal negotiations that surround nearly every enactment—away from the eyes of reporters and lobbyists. Separating formal and informal modes of participation in his study of members' committee activity, Richard L. Hall found that members' formal and informal activities do not always coincide.[17] Sometimes, members use formal actions to signal concern to constituents and other groups, but then do not follow through with the hard informal work needed to shape the legislation.

A full accounting of lawmakers' performance, then, would embrace not only how members participate in floor and committee deliberations but also how much effort they expend overall. How much attention do they pay to issues? How do they gain expertise? Whom do they consult for information on legislative decisions? How influential are party leaders? How do they hire, deploy, and supervise their staffs? Countless such decisions define what it means to be a member of Congress.

TYPES OF DECISIONS

One basic decision facing legislators is how to spend their time and energy while in the nation's capital. Some try to digest the mountains of studies and reports that cross their desks. They "do their homework," in Capitol Hill parlance. Others seem to know or care little about legislative matters. They pursue other duties—communication, outreach, visits with constituents or lobby groups, partisan politics, and fund raising. Such members may rarely contribute to committee or floor deliberations. Their votes usually follow cues from party colleagues, staff aides, the White House, or interest groups. Some are found in the ranks of the "Obscure Caucus," a list of unnoticed members compiled periodically by *Roll Call,* a Capitol Hill newspaper. "These Members pay strict attention to parochial issues and would much rather attend a hog-calling contest back home than appear on a cable news show. They deliver for their districts and shun any entreaties to become part of the Washington, D.C. culture."[18]

Specializing

Within the legislative realm, members may dig deeply in a particular area or range widely across issues and policies. Senators are more apt to be generalists, while representatives tend to cultivate a few specialties. Sen. Jim DeMint, R-S.C., once explained why members should specialize:

> If you've got twenty things you want to do, see where everything is. You'll find that maybe ten of those are already being worked on by people, and that while you may be supportive in that role, you don't need to carry the ball. But you can find those two or three things that are important to you that no one seems to be taking the lead on. But if you try to play the lead on everything, you'll be wasting your time.[19]

In both houses, key policy-making roles are played by those whom Rep. David E. Price, D-N.C., a political scientist, calls *policy entrepreneurs*—that is, those recognized for "stimulating more than . . . responding" to outside political forces on a given issue.[20] Often nearly invisible to the mass of citizens, these legislators are known to specialized publics for their contributions to specific policies—for example, Sen. John McCain, Ariz., on military readiness; Rep. Earl Blumenauer, D-Ore., on bike trails; Rep. Paul D. Ryan, R-Wis., on fiscal policy; and Sen. Tom Harkin, D-Iowa, on policies for the disabled.

Members' policy reaches can go beyond their committee assignments—through speeches, floor amendments, caucuses, and task forces, to name a few. When only in his second term, Rep. Dick Armey, R-Texas (1985–2003), who was not a member of the Armed Services Committee, devised an ingenious scheme to employ an outside commission—the Base Realignment and Closure Commission (BRAC)—to decide which unneeded military bases should be closed. His proposal smoothed political sensitivities and won bipartisan support for its enactment into law (P.L. 100–526). Such feats are not everyday occurrences, but the fluidity of today's procedures makes even the most junior member a potential policy entrepreneur.

A member's knowledge and perceived expertise on issues is a vital source of legislative influence. As Sen. Edmund S. Muskie, D-Maine (1959–1980), put it:

> People have all sorts of conspiratorial theories on what constitutes power in the Senate. It has little to do with the size of the state you come from. Or the source of your money. Or committee chairmanships, although that certainly gives you a kind of power. But real power up there comes from doing your work and knowing what you're talking about. Power is the ability to change someone's mind. . . . The most important thing in the Senate is credibility. Credibility! That is power.[21]

Timing of Decisions

Lawmakers do more than specialize in a particular policy field. They are constantly forced to make decisions on issues, many far from their areas of specialization. Timing is key. *When* members make decisions has important consequences for the deliberative process, a point that Richard F. Fenno Jr. elaborated in his work on the "politics of timing."[22]

From a study of a vote on selling AWACS (airborne warning and control system) reconnaissance planes to Saudi Arabia, Fenno identified three types of decision makers: early deciders, active players, and late deciders.

Early deciders are fervent supporters who want to get out front in the debate. "I'd rather come out early and be part of the fight," said Rep. Peter T. King, R-N.Y., of his ready support for fast-track trade authority.[23] These members are buoyed by friendly lobbyists but ignored by others because their commitments are known at the outset from declarations, bill sponsorship, or prior voting records.

Active players, by contrast, delay their commitments, inviting bids from various sides of the issue at hand and often gaining leverage over the final language of legislation.

Late deciders delay their decision (or reconsider an earlier commitment) until the very last moment. They forfeit influence over the basic framework of the measure. But late deciders are eagerly courted by all sides and may gain specific concessions. With every vote critical to Senate passage of President Obama's health care overhaul plan and pressure mounting to conclude action, Sen. Byron Dorgan, D-N.D., informed Majority Leader Reid that he would not vote for the Patient Protection and Affordable Care Act unless it included Indian health care. "That's not a threat, just a statement of fact," he said.[24] (Dorgan, now retired, was chair of the Committee on Indian Affairs.) Indian health care was included as part of the larger bill.

Taking the Lead

Senators and representatives differ widely in the rate at which they introduce and sponsor bills. Some lawmakers are inveterate initiators of bills and resolutions. Others shy away from sponsoring measures. Still others commonly take the lead in sponsoring legislation because of the position they occupy, such as the chair of the relevant committee of jurisdiction. A study by Wendy Schiller found that bills in the Senate are most likely to be introduced by senior senators, those who are chairs or ranking members of high-volume committees (such as Commerce), and those who represent large, diverse states.[25]

Senate and House rules do not limit the number of members who can cosponsor bills or resolutions. Thus cosponsorship has become common. Most bills are cosponsored; according to one study, over the study period the average Senate bill had 7.2 cosponsors and the average House bill had 22.2 cosponsors.[26] Authors of measures often circulate a "Dear Colleague" letter detailing the virtues of the bill and soliciting cosponsors to demonstrate broad support and urge committee action. One study found that more than 12,000 such letters were sent electronically by House members in 2007, an average of more than twenty-five letters per member.[27]

Occasionally, however, some members shun cosponsors. Introducing his waterway users' fee bill, Sen. Pete V. Domenici, R-N.M. (1973–2009), decided against seeking cosponsors for several reasons.[28] First, as ranking Republican on the subcommittee, he could arrange for hearings without the support of cosponsors. In addition, single sponsorship is easier. ("If you've got cosponsors you have to clear every little change with them.") And, finally, if the bill became law, he would get more credit on his own.

Do legislators favor the bills and resolutions they introduce? Normally they do, but as Sportin' Life, the *Porgy and Bess* character, said, "It ain't necessarily so." Members may introduce a measure to stake out jurisdiction for their committee or to pave the way for hearings and deliberations that will air a public problem. Or they may introduce measures they do not personally favor to oblige an executive agency or to placate an important interest group.

Taking Part

As members in any organization, some lawmakers take a passionate interest in what goes on; others pay selective attention to issues; a few seem just to be going through the motions. In his detailed study of three House committees, Richard L. Hall uncovered great variation in members' levels of participation.

Although members' attendance at committee and subcommittee sessions was respectable (about three-quarters of the members showed up for at least part of each session), active participation—taking part in markup debate, offering amendments, and the like—was far less common. Perhaps half a subcommittee's members could be considered players, by a generous counting. The rest were nonplayers. As a subcommittee staffer remarked, "On a good day half of [the members] know what's going on. Most of the time it's only five or six who actually mark a bill up."[29]

Constituency interests strongly propel members to participate in committee business. This is true even when the negotiations are informal and out of the public's sight. In formal subcommittee markup sessions, "the public forum has the benefit of allowing members at once to promote—through their votes, arguments, amendments, obstructionism—constituency interests and be seen doing so."[30]

Constituency-driven activity was especially common in the House Agriculture Committee, a panel historically buffeted by regional and commodity pressures. Because of the committee's composition, its membership is more favorable to agriculture programs than the House as a whole. Furthermore, only a subset of the committee's members participates in most matters, and those who choose to take part tend to be more biased in favor of the programs under consideration than even the rest of the Agriculture Committee. Hall found in his study that members representing constituencies with large numbers of dairy farmers and peanut growers, for example, were the most active in influencing policy affecting dairy and peanut interests. Neither the full committee nor floor deliberations counterbalanced the enthusiastic advocacy of the dozen or so lawmakers from districts that produced those commodities. Although participation on Agriculture was the most biased toward members with a constituency stake in the legislation being considered, Hall also found that in debates over job training legislation in another committee, participating members tended to represent areas with higher unemployment rates than those of nonparticipants. In cases in which concentrated district benefits were not at stake, Hall found no participatory biases.

Members in formal leadership positions are also more likely to take an active part in committee deliberations. Members often forgo participation because there are so many demands on their time that they must prioritize issues that are important to their constituents. Committee and subcommittee leaders, however, face fewer obstacles to participation because their seniority and authority "places them at the epicenter of the communications network in which most important legislative interactions take place."[31] In other words, holding leadership posts puts members "in the know" and enables them to be major players on legislation even when they do not personally have a significant constituency stake in the outcome.

Participation in House or Senate floor debates is equally varied: members who do not serve on the relevant committees, or who have only peripheral interests in the matter, are tempted to speak simply "for the record." "Congressional debate is typically no better than moderately informed," Gary Mucchiaroni and Paul J. Quirk concluded from their detailed analysis of three major congressional debates. "Legislators frequently assert claims that are inaccurate or misleading, and reassert them after they have been effectively refuted."[32] The good news about floor debates is that opposing members often—though not always—counter erroneous or distorted arguments.

Offering Amendments

Another important way of participating is to offer amendments to bills or resolutions. Amendments propose specific changes in legislative language: they delete or add words or substitute one provision for another. They are a chief means of shaping legislation during committee and floor deliberation. However, amendments are not always intended to enact policy changes. They can instead be used as a tool of obstruction. They also can serve political purposes by putting members on the record on specific issues.

House leaders, who control the floor agenda, regularly employ special rules to limit the amendments that members can offer to particular bills. By so doing, the leaders often can engineer favored policy outcomes, expedite floor action, and protect their vulnerable lawmakers from voting on politically difficult issues. During the 111th Congress, for example, minority Republicans were prohibited from offering amendments to appropriations bills, which typically are considered under an open amendment process. Why the clampdown on amendments? GOP members planned to force debates and votes on "abortion, school vouchers and medical marijuana, as well as gay marriage and gun control." The Democratic leadership said, "No way." Rep. David Dreier, Calif., the senior Republican on Rules, believed Democratic leaders wanted "to avoid tough votes on appropriations bills."[33] (Dreier chairs the Rules Committee in the 112th Congress.)

In the Senate, because of individual senators' prerogatives, germane and nonrelevant amendments are more freely offered and form a central part of floor debate. For example, in the 112th Congress when the Senate considered reauthorization of the Federal Aviation Administration (FAA), Minority Leader Mitch McConnell, R-Ky., forced a vote on an amendment modeled after the House-passed measure repealing the president's health care law. McConnell's amendment was rejected on a procedural vote, but Republicans remained determined to dismantle the law. McConnell warned: "We think this is just the beginning. This issue is still ahead of us, and we will be going back at it" again and again.[34]

Amendments can also derail legislation. For example, a 2009 effort to give the District of Columbia a voting seat in the House of Representatives ran into a serious legislative roadblock when the Senate adopted an amendment by Sen. John Ensign, R-Nev., that would have invalidated the District's restrictive gun control laws.[35]

Sometimes, amendments are offered simply to test the strength of support for a proposal rather than to immediately alter policy outcomes. During a debate on reauthorizing the National Aeronautics and Space Administration, a House member introduced an amendment to cancel the costly space station program. Instead of losing by a wide margin (as in previous years), the amendment failed by only a single vote. That narrow margin signaled plunging support for the space station and other "big science" projects.[36]

Some amendments are designed to force members to declare themselves on issues that command public attention. Sen. Vitter's amendment to the 2009 omnibus appropriations bill to end automatic cost-of-living increases in congressional salaries, noted earlier, is an example. Lawmakers who vote for salary increases, especially during hard economic times, risk having the voters turn them out of office.

Other amendments are poison pills. So-called killer amendments are intended to make a bill so unpalatable that, if adopted, they will kill the underlying measure. Senate and House sponsors of the landmark Bipartisan Campaign Reform Act of 2002 faced opponents who offered what are called nonseverability amendments, meaning that the entire act would fall if courts ruled against any portion of the measure. Advocates and opponents alike knew that one or more of the bill's provisions—the soft money ban, issue ad restrictions, or hard money limits—might well be struck down by the courts. (Recall from Chapter 4 that in 2010 the Supreme Court in *Citizens United v. FEC* did strike down the law's restrictions on issue ads.) The authors of the Senate bill, John McCain, R-Ariz., and Russ Feingold, D-Wis., beat back those amendments in close votes. Although killer amendments upset the sponsors and managers of bills, they rarely alter a measure's ultimate fate. Examining seventy-six killer amendments considered in the mid-1990s, John D. Wilkerson concluded that they "rarely, if ever, cause bills to fail. . . . Most were easily defeated."[37]

Casting Votes

Lawmakers' most visible choices are embodied in the votes they cast. Voting is a central ritual of any legislative body. Members know that their voting records communicate a great deal of information about their policy commitments to their constituents. Reflecting on his vote on a financial institutions bailout package, a House member said, "This is a legacy vote; these are the votes you have to live with for the rest of your life."[38] Several months after the 112th Congress convened, many Tea Party–supported congressional Republicans found themselves facing a legacy vote. These lawmakers, having promised in the 2010 elections to cut and curb government spending, now faced an unavoidable vote: the electorally painful decision to raise the national debt ceiling, allowing the government to spend hundreds of billions more. Raising the "must pass" debt ceiling is "beautiful politics—the brutal kind," declared former senator Alan Simpson, R-Wyo. (1979–1997), co-chair of President Obama's deficit reduction commission.[39]

Members anticipate that constituents will review their votes at reelection time. Outside groups closely follow members' votes on specific measures and publicize them during election campaigns. Groups may grade lawmakers as "heroes" or "zeros" based on their votes for environmental or business measures. Nevertheless, members' own personal judgments sometimes outweigh political expedience. "I'm willing to give up my seat over this," said Rep. Jim Marshall, D-Ga., a conservative in a Republican-leaning seat, explaining his vote on the 2008 bailout package.[40] Marshall was defeated in the next election.

Senators and representatives strive to be recorded on as many floor and committee votes as possible. Of the 660 House floor votes in 2010, members overall voted 94.2 percent of the time. During the same year, senators' average participation on 299 votes was 96.6 percent.[41] Members seek to compile a record of diligence to forestall charges of absenteeism by potential opponents. House and Senate leaders make it easier for members to fulfill high expectations by trying to schedule votes at predictable times, stacking votes back to back in midweek, or holding fewer votes on Mondays, when lawmakers are returning to Capitol Hill from their states or districts, and Fridays, when many members are anxious to depart for their constituencies.

If members cannot vote in person, they can still be recorded on an issue by announcing their views in floor statements or in press releases. Pairing is a voluntary arrangement that allows members to go on the record without voting or affecting the final tabulation. A member who wishes to be recorded on an issue but cannot be present for the roll call vote may also ask another member who plans to vote on the other side for a "pair" arrangement in which both announce their positions in the *Congressional Record* but neither casts a vote (they cancel each other out). Members often grant such requests as a courtesy to their colleagues.

What Do Votes Mean?

Like other elements of the legislative process, votes are open to multiple interpretations. House and Senate floor votes do not perfectly register members' views. Members sometimes vote against a bill that they prefer to the status quo because they hope that a better bill on the matter might emerge later. Members know that a weak reform can deplete political will for bolder action. Politicians will also refuse to accept a compromise when they can force a confrontation that will sharpen the differences between the parties. At times, members prefer to keep the issue alive rather than to pass a bill. As John B. Gilmour writes, "Advocates often anticipate that having the party differences clearly displayed will help them win in the next election, after which they will be able to enact an unadulterated form of the bill."[42] Killing a modest measure may lead to action on a more wide-ranging proposal later.

Members also may vote for a bill that they do not favor because they fear that if they fail to support it the end result will be something even worse. For example, some conservative Republicans voted for a federal program providing prescription drug coverage for elderly Americans because they believed it was the best bill they could get. "I don't think we'll write a better bill if we defeat this," explained a conservative senator.[43] Members will often go along with legislation because on the whole they deem the bill a step forward, even though they dislike specific portions.

In some cases, recorded votes are wholly misleading. Given the multiplicity of votes—procedural as well as substantive—on many measures, lawmakers can come out on more than one side of an issue, or at least appear to do so. For example, members may vote to authorize a program and later vote against funding it. Or they may vote against final passage of a bill but for a substitute version. This tactic assures the bill's backers that the lawmaker favors the concept, while pleasing voters who oppose the bill. Such voting patterns may reflect either a deliberate attempt to obscure one's position or a thoughtful response to complex questions. As in so many aspects of human behavior, lawmakers' motivations can be judged fully only in light of specific cases.

Members can also take advantage of "free votes" when their own individual vote will not affect the final outcome. Some members delay voting until the outcome of the vote is already assured. For example, during the debate on a constitutional amendment to prohibit flag burning, David C. King and Richard J. Zeckhauser observed "strategic waiting" on the part of members.[44] Democratic members were cross-pressured on the issue—Democratic leaders opposed the anti-flag burning amendment, but it was very popular with constituents. Before it was clear that the amendment was going to fail, only 28 percent of the voting Democrats supported the amendment. Once enough votes had been cast to defeat the amendment, 73 percent of the remaining Democrats voted in favor of it. After the amendment had failed, members could take the popular position without any legislative consequences. Opportunities for insincere votes proliferate in the U.S. system of the separation of powers. Members can deliberately vote for measures that they believe will fail in the other chamber of Congress or be vetoed by the president. And they can support popular measures that they expect the courts will strike down as unconstitutional.

Lawmakers' voting rationales are sometimes hard to explain to outsiders. In some cases, members face a dilemma: either vote their convictions and deal with the consequences, or swallow their misgivings and vote for appearance's sake. A GOP House member chose the former course when he joined fourteen other Republicans in voting against a popular bill authorizing U.S. sanctions against nations that persecute religious minorities—an appealing idea but fraught with problems. "This was an awfully awkward vote, and I know I'll hear from the folks back home," he explained. "But the devil was in the details."[45]

More often, lawmakers decide to go with the crowd. Regarding a highly appealing constitutional amendment requiring a balanced budget, Sen. Ernest

F. Hollings, D-S.C. (1967–2005), admitted that he planned to vote for it because he got "tired of explaining" its deficiencies. It was easier "just to say put it in."[46]

Scholars and journalists often mistakenly treat votes as if they are unambiguous indicators of legislators' views. Lobbyists, too, are prone to assess lawmakers on the basis of floor votes. Many groups construct voting indexes that label legislators as "friendly" or "unfriendly." Citizens should be cautioned to examine such indexes closely. How many votes does the index comprise? Are they a fair sample of the group's concerns? Does the index embody a partisan or ideological agenda, hidden or otherwise? The bottom line is: beware of an interest group's voting scorecards, even if you agree with its policy leanings.

DETERMINANTS OF VOTING

Votes, particularly on single issues, should be examined, interpreted, and categorized with care. Several factors shape congressional voting: party affiliation, ideological leanings, constituents' views, and presidential leadership.

Party and Voting

Party affiliation is the strongest single correlate of members' voting decisions. In a typical year, from half to two-thirds of all floor votes could be called party unity votes, defined as votes in which a majority of voting Republicans oppose a majority of voting Democrats. In the 111th Congress (2009–2011), 45 percent of all House votes and 75 percent of Senate votes fell into this category. House scores were low compared with Senate scores because the House passed numerous noncontroversial measures as it waited for the Senate to consider the big issues of 2010 (such as health care and financial regulation). When the House considered those measures, Speaker Nancy Pelosi, D-Calif. (2007–2011), "demanded, and got, unity from her party's caucus."[47] Figure 9-1 depicts House and Senate party unity votes from 1970 through 2010. Party voting is far more prevalent today than in the 1970s and early 1980s.[48] Indeed, contemporary levels of party voting recall the militant parties of the late nineteenth century.

Party unity scores can be calculated for individual members—the percentage of party unity votes in which the member voted in agreement with the majority of his or her party colleagues. According to these scores, the average legislator now toes the party line on nearly nine out of ten party unity votes. In 2010, for example, the average House Democrat voted with the caucus 89 percent of the time, with half "having party unity scores higher than 97 percent."[49] House Republicans, on average, voted with their party 88 percent of the time. In the Senate, Democrats voted together 91 percent of the time and Republicans 88 percent of the time. Aggregate party unity scores for Democrats and Republicans from 1970 through 2010 are displayed in Figure 9-2. Party voting levels in both houses have risen by about 20 percent since the 1970s.[50]

Party cohesion stems from a number of roots. Members of a political party vote similarly because they are elected by many of the same sorts of

FIGURE 9-1 **Party Unity Votes in Congress, 1970–2010**

Source: "Party Unity History," *CQ Weekly,* January 3, 2011, 36.

Note: Party unity votes are defined as the percentage of all House and Senate votes in which a majority of Democrats opposed a majority of Republicans.

constituencies and organized interests throughout the country. As one study noted, on a wide range of unrelated issues—"gun control, the economy, war, same-sex marriage, abortion, the environment, the financial bailout—the views of Republicans and Democrats have become increasingly monolithic."[51]

Party members also vote together because of their shared ideological commitments. Changes in the ideological composition and the constituency base of the two congressional parties have contributed to the increased levels of partisanship in the contemporary Congress. Each of these sources of party unity—constituency and ideology—is discussed here. However, it is important to note that congressional party unity also has a source in explicitly *partisan* motives, meaning party members' shared political interests in helping their party win elections and control Congress.[52] These interests bring fellow partisans together despite the diversity of their policy preferences. Indeed, even when interparty conflict in Congress was at a low ebb in the late 1960s and early 1970s, the parties still successfully organized the committees and leadership of Congress, and party affiliation remained the strongest single predictor of members' voting behavior.

Members of Congress cooperate with their fellow partisans in part because their personal fate as politicians is bound up with their party's

FIGURE 9-2   Levels of Party Voting in Congress, 1970–2010

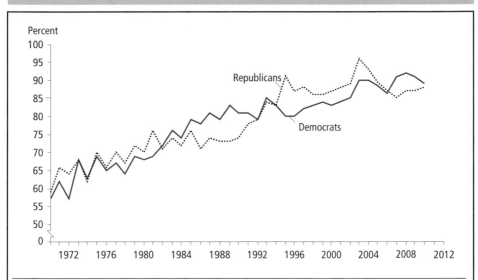

Source: Derived from annual CQ voting studies reported in *CQ Weekly,* January 3, 2011, 32.

Note: The graph shows the percentage of times the average Republican or Democrat in Congress voted with his party majority in partisan votes for the years listed. These composite party unity scores are based on votes that split the parties in the House and Senate—a majority of voting Republicans opposing a majority of voting Democrats. The scores have been recomputed to correct for absences.

public image. Members know that they do not win or lose elections solely as individual legislators. Voters' attitudes about the national parties affect their choices in particular congressional elections.[53] As a result, members take into account how their individual actions will affect public perceptions of their party as a whole. As one congressman explained to political scientist Randall Ripley, "We need a party record—and principles—as well as an individual record. The decline of the party image between 1962 and 1964 cost me 6 percent at the polls."[54]

Members also care about the collective image of their party because they want their party to command a congressional majority. Members gain power personally when their party is in the majority. Members of the majority party chair all committees and subcommittees, and majority leaders set the floor agenda. It is easier for members to advance their personal policy initiatives when they are in the majority.

Members concerned with winning elections and wielding influence will therefore pay attention to their party's collective image. To foster positive public impressions of their party, fellow partisans work to find common ground. They collaborate in efforts to construct an appealing policy agenda and then cooperate in promoting it. They also exploit opportunities to call into question the other party's competence and integrity.

Common political interests nurture bonds of trust and communication among fellow partisans. To deepen these bonds, the congressional parties hold regular lunches, conferences, and retreats for members. In addition, the socialization of new members largely takes place in partisan settings. Thus fewer friendships cross party lines these days. As one senator explained:

> If the only knowledge you have of "the other side of the aisle" is what you have read in an attack press release written by the party operatives, you wouldn't want to talk to them, and you certainly wouldn't want to be friends.[55]

Majority and minority party leaders regularly appeal to their members' common partisan interests in order to rally their troops behind the party agenda. The leaders of both parties strive to give the electorate a favorable view of the party's "brand." They hire consultants to devise messages and strategies crafted to generate broad public support for their policy goals and objectives. Contrasting his party's image with the clearer Republican brand, Senator Dorgan said, "I can tell you what the Republicans stand for in eight words: family values, strong defense, lower taxes and less government."[56] Reflecting on these partisan motives, political scientists Gary W. Cox and Mathew D. McCubbins write, "Modern political parties facing mass electorates, similar to corporations facing mass markets, have a strong incentive to fashion and maintain a brand name."[57]

The common political interests of Democrats and Republicans mean they are predisposed to support their party. Political scientists who have studied members' voting decisions have found that members decide mainly by consulting the views of their partisan colleagues.[58] The typical member of Congress feels "duty bound to ascertain the views of the party leaders and [to] go along in the absence of contrary inclinations."[59] In other words, members cooperate with their parties as a default position. They go along unless they have a reason to defect. Wavering members who have reservations about the party's position may be subject to heavy pressure from party leaders. A classic example involved House Speaker Newt Gingrich, R-Ga. (1995–1999), and his lieutenants. During the GOP's first year in power after forty consecutive years of Democratic control, a junior Republican described the leadership's approach at persuasion:

> They pull us into a room before almost every vote and yell at us. . . . They say, "This is a test of our ability to govern," or "This is a gut check," or "I got you here and you hired me as your coach to get you through, but if you want to change coaches, go ahead."[60]

Party leaders in both chambers can usually rely on a high level of reflexive support from fellow partisans, especially on procedural matters. Political scientists have repeatedly shown that members are more likely to vote with their parties on procedural motions than directly on the substance of legislation.[61] Indeed, members often support their party leaders on procedural matters related to a bill, even when they do not intend to support the bill on final passage. Procedural votes, in brief, are usually partisan votes. As a senator once observed, "This is a procedural vote, and in the Senate we traditionally stick with the leadership on such votes."[62]

Because leaders find it easier to muster support if a vote is defined in procedural terms, they use procedural tactics to engineer substantive policy outcomes. David W. Rohde calls this "process partisanship," which means "the degree to which each institution is structured or operates in a partisan fashion."[63]

House leaders have broad authority to exploit procedures to strengthen party unity. Through their control of key committees, scheduling powers, and use of special rules, majority party leaders arrange for votes they are likely to win and avoid those they are apt to lose.

Senate leaders have fewer procedural tools than House leaders, but they can use their right to be recognized first on the floor to regulate the timing, order, and content of debates to partisan advantage. For example, Senate majority leader Reid deliberately scheduled a series of votes he knew he would lose. Why? He wanted to portray Republicans as "obstructionists," to indicate to the bill's supporters that he tried, to demonstrate that Senate rules need revision (the measures were blocked by filibuster threats), and to direct the public's attention to these issues. Minority Leader McConnell viewed the entire exercise as political theater: "Are we here to perform, or are we here to legislate?"[64]

Ideology and Voting

Just as lawmakers are committed partisans, most of them also harbor broad ideological views on the proper role and purpose of government.[65] Indeed, many members of Congress entered politics through various ideological causes. The civil rights, environmental, and antiwar movements spurred political activism for many members on the left of the ideological spectrum. Many members on the right entered politics because of their small-government views or traditionalist social values. Long before they take their first oath of office, members bring ideological loyalties that inspire voting decisions throughout their political careers.

Both political parties encompass ideological diversity. The Republican Party, for example, embraces both economically conservative voters— educated, higher-income cohorts who are often associated with business— along with less-educated, lower- or middle-income people who are drawn to the party's traditional social values and its emphasis on limited government, national and border security, and a hard line on crime. How to balance the party's ideological wings is not an easy assignment for GOP congressional leaders. They work to accommodate both the party's social conservative and economically conservative business wings, not to mention the Tea Partiers.

One House GOP leader says that he seeks compromise positions that will be broadly acceptable to Republicans: "The journey to the middle starts from both ends of the spectrum."[66]

The journey to an acceptable compromise seems much longer and more difficult in the 112th Congress, however. Many first-term Republicans are in no mood to contain their zeal to cut spending, repeal health care, and overturn unwanted federal regulations. During a House GOP Conference meeting, freshman representative Steve Southerland, Fla., said he understood the party leadership's plea for party unity. "I want you to know there is a limit to how far I will follow. I may lose in 2012, but I will not lose me."[67]

The Democratic Party also embraces ideological variety. It includes across-the-board liberals who are committed to a vigorous government redressing economic grievances, to tolerant stances on social and lifestyle issues, and to international treaties and institutions guiding foreign policy. The party's diversity reflects its voters, who range from union members—who are concerned with economic issues but unsupportive of liberalism on social causes—to the "creative class" professionals in university towns and urban enclaves who are far more libertarian on social issues.[68] Free trade pacts also tend to split these groups: union members fear losing jobs to low-wage foreign labor, while educated professionals tend to be more open toward globalization. Democratic leaders have to navigate these ideological divisions, often by avoiding issues that fracture the party.

When political scientists began seriously to analyze congressional roll call voting in the 1950s, ideological diversity within each of the two parties was far greater than it is today. Conservatives and liberals had a meaningful presence in both legislative parties. Although members often voted along party lines, at other times they would unite across parties in recognizable ideological coalitions. Frequently, Republicans and southern Democrats would cooperate in a voting pattern known as the conservative coalition.[69] Historically, this coalition was stronger in the Senate than in the House, but its success rate was impressive in both chambers during the 1939–1965 period—no matter which party controlled the White House or Capitol Hill.

Since the 1960s, the two legislative parties have sorted themselves out along ideological lines, with conservatives largely in the Republican Party and liberals exclusively in the Democratic Party. Of the polarized 111th Congress (2009–2011), a scholar noted that "the most conservative Democrat is more liberal than is the most liberal Republican."[70] As a consequence, the cross-party conservative coalition surfaces so rarely these days that the respected *CQ Weekly* has stopped scoring it.[71] Bipartisan conservatism fell victim to the increasing ideological consistency of both political parties. "Democrats are perched on the left, Republicans on the right, in both the House and the Senate as the ideological centers of the two parties have moved markedly apart," writes Sarah A. Binder.[72]

The polarization of the contemporary Congress—in which partisanship and ideology are closely intertwined—can be shown spatially on a left–right (liberal–conservative) continuum. Using the congressional roll call voting record, political scientists Keith T. Poole and Howard Rosenthal have devised a scaling methodology to generate ideological scores for all members of Congress.[73] Their data show marked divergence between the parties in recent years.

Figure 9-3 displays the distribution of ideological preferences for Republicans and Democrats among activists and the general public and within Congress. When voters are asked to locate themselves on the ideological spectrum, the result roughly follows a normal bell-shaped curve. As shown in panel A, citizens are bunched together around the middle of the ideological spectrum, with relatively few respondents identifying themselves as very liberal or very conservative.[74] The same centrist pattern appears when voters are asked to position themselves on specific policy issues, even on hot-button topics such as taxes and abortion. By contrast, political activists are more likely to identify as either liberal or conservative. The surveys of delegates to the national presidential nominating conventions displayed in panel A of Figure 9-3 reveal Republican and Democratic activists clustering to the left or right of the median, with far less overlap between the two parties at the elite level than exists in the mass public.

In 1968 the ideological divisions in the House of Representatives (displayed in panel B in Figure 9-3) looked similar to those of the party elites. Democrats appeared in almost every ideological niche, from far left to far right. Although Republicans were more tightly clustered on the right, a number spilled over to the liberal side of the scale.[75] Political moderates— members at or near the midpoint between the parties—constituted a substantial bloc.

The contemporary Congress (represented by panel C) is almost completely polarized along party lines. Only a handful of members fall at the midpoint—not a single Republican falls on the liberal side of the scale, and only a few Democrats stray into the conservative category. (Panels B and C were compiled from the Poole-Rosenthal data by scholar Sean M. Theriault.)

In today's Congress, members' party affiliation and ideological views overlap almost perfectly. (These figures are for the House; patterns in the Senate are similar though somewhat less dramatic.) This polarization and the resulting collapse of the middle (the "shrinking center") have produced clear ideological battle lines between the parties. Although partisan rigidity gets a bad rap from commentators, one must consider how closely political convictions are linked to partisanship in the minds of lawmakers and their activist supporters. "If you can't find common ground, that doesn't mean you're partisan," explained Speaker Nancy Pelosi. "It just means you believe different things." Of her Republican foes—often blamed for obstructing her party's proposals—she noted, "They vote the way they believe. . . . I think that they vote with more integrity than they get credit for."[76]

The proportion of political moderates—conservative Democrats or liberal Republicans—hovered at about 30 percent in the 1960s and 1970s. Today,

FIGURE 9-3 Ideological Divisions in Congress and the Public

Percent   A. Ideological distribution of general public and party activists

- 50
- 40
- 30
- 20
- 10
- 0

Democratic activists

General public

Republican activists

Very liberal — Liberal — Moderate — Conservative — Very conservative

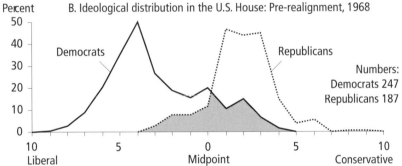

Percent   B. Ideological distribution in the U.S. House: Pre-realignment, 1968

- 50
- 40
- 30
- 20
- 10
- 0

Democrats

Republicans

Numbers:
Democrats 247
Republicans 187

10 Liberal — 5 — 0 Midpoint — 5 — 10 Conservative

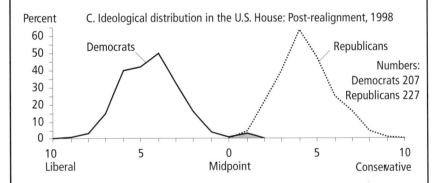

Percent   C. Ideological distribution in the U.S. House: Post-realignment, 1998

- 60
- 50
- 40
- 30
- 20
- 10
- 0

Democrats

Republicans

Numbers:
Democrats 207
Republicans 227

10 Liberal — 5 — 0 Midpoint — 5 — 10 Conservative

Sources: Panel A: *Washington Post*/ABC News survey, *Washington Post,* August 11, 1996, M8, and August 25, 1996, M4. Panels B and C: Adapted from Sean M. Theriault, "The Case of the Vanishing Moderates: Party Polarization in the Modern Congress" (paper presented at the Western Political Science Association, Denver, Colorado), March 2003, fig. 1. These data are derived from Keith T. Poole and Howard Rosenthal's DW-NOMINATE ideology scores. See Keith T. Poole and Howard Rosenthal, *Congress: A Political-Economic History of Roll-Call Voting* (New York: Oxford University Press, 1997). Scores for adjacent years (1969–1970 and 1999–2000) yield virtually identical results. See Morris P. Fiorina et al., *Culture War? The Myth of a Polarized America,* 2d ed. (New York: Pearson Longman, 2006), fig. 2.2.

however, fewer than one in ten lawmakers fall into this centrist category.[77] Conservative Democrats, the larger of the two centrist groupings, once represented a third of their party's members; today they could caucus in a small cloakroom. The fiscally conservative "Blue Dog" Democrats, as they called themselves, saw their ranks cut in half (from a little over fifty to twenty-six) in the November 2010 elections. Even rarer are moderate Republicans, who account for no more than 2 percent of all House GOP members and no more than 3 to 6 percent of senators.[78]

Constituency and Voting

Constituency context is another powerful influence on members' vote choices. Constituencies control lawmakers' choices in two ways. First, people usually elect representatives whose views mirror their own. In this sense, representatives vote their constituency because they are simply transplanted locals. Second, members listen to constituents because it is politically imperative to do so. Representatives feel great electoral pressure to respond to the dominant political interests and opinions in their constituencies.

Constituency concerns can either reinforce or undermine party unity in Congress. For much of the twentieth century, it was not unusual for conservative-leaning states to elect Democrats and for liberal-leaning states to elect Republicans. During that period, constituency influence often led members to buck their party. But since the 1960s, constituencies have gradually sorted themselves out according to ideological and policy preferences. In the current era, constituency pressure tends to bolster party unity.

Relatively few Democrats in the 112th Congress represent conservative districts or states. In 1960 all senators from the South were Democrats, and they constituted a large conservative bloc who often resisted Democratic Party leaders and cooperated across party lines with Republicans. But in the current Congress, only six southern Democrats are in the Senate.[79] By the same token, many areas once represented by GOP liberals have been captured by Democrats. New England, an area of the country that was once a moderate Republican stronghold, now elects Democrats almost exclusively. The decline of conservative Democrats and moderate Republicans underlies much of the ideological cohesion within, and the chasm between, today's Capitol Hill parties.[80]

Partisans in the contemporary Congress vote together in great part because they reflect the same kinds of states and districts. Republicans tend to represent rural areas and outer suburbs. Democrats tend to represent urban areas, inner-ring suburbs, and majority-minority districts.[81]

The few remaining party mavericks in today's Congress tend to come from parts of the country where their party generally does not do well electorally. Democratic mavericks tend to be from nonminority southern or midwestern areas. The Senate Democrat most likely to defect from the Democratic Party's position in 2010 was Nebraska's senator Ben Nelson, who opposed his party on 46.4 percent of party unity votes.[82] Similarly, the most independent

Republicans are those representing northeastern and mid-Atlantic states. In 2010, for example, Maine's two Republican senators, Susan Collins and Olympia Snowe, opposed their party on 31.5 and 27.2 percent of party unity votes, respectively.[83] (Retiring senator George Voinovich, R-Ohio, was actually the GOP lawmaker who voted most often against his party.)

Constituency affects congressional decision making as politicians take both attentive and inattentive publics into account. Political scientist R. Douglas Arnold has tracked how both groups can influence members' electoral calculations.[84] Attentive publics are those citizens who are aware of issues facing Congress and hold decided opinions about what Congress should do. It is thus relatively easy for politicians to consider their views. A politician's natural instinct is to yield to the strongly voiced preferences of an attentive public, unless the issue in question mobilizes two equally vociferous but opposing interests. Especially feared are single-interest groups that threaten to withhold electoral support if their preferences—for example, on abortion or gun control—are ignored.

Inattentive publics are those who lack extensive knowledge or firm preferences about a specific issue. Frankly, this definition describes most people most of the time. People pay attention to only a small fraction of the issues before Congress. Yet a reelection-minded legislator dare not ignore those who seem indifferent to an issue. "Latent or unfocused opinions," Arnold cautions, "can quickly be transformed into intense and very real opinions with enormous political repercussions. Inattentiveness and lack of information today should not be confused with indifference tomorrow."[85] Legislators are well advised to approach even the most minor choices with this question in mind: will my decision be defensible if it were to appear on the front pages of major newspapers in my state or district?

Calculating the electoral consequences of a lawmaker's multitude of daily decisions is no easy task. Arnold summarizes the components of such calculations:

> To reach a decision, then, a legislator needs to (1) identify all the attentive and inattentive publics who might care about a policy issue, (2) estimate the direction and intensity of their preferences and potential preferences, (3) estimate the probability that the potential preferences will be transformed into real preferences, (4) weigh all these preferences according to the size of the various attentive and inattentive publics, and (5) give special weight to the preferences of the legislator's consistent supporters.[86]

Fortunately, lawmakers need not repeat these calculations every time they face a choice. Most issues have been around for some time. The preferences of attentive and even inattentive publics are fairly well known. Moreover, Congress is well structured to amass and assess information about individual and group preferences. And prominent officials—party leaders and acknowledged policy experts, for example—can often legitimize members' choices and give them cover in explaining those choices to voters.

The Presidency and Voting

Although Congress often pursues an independent course and members differ in their feelings toward the occupant of the White House, presidents can persuade members to support their agendas. Figure 9-4 depicts the percentage of the time presidents—from Dwight D. Eisenhower to Barack Obama—have prevailed in congressional roll call votes on which they announced a position. Presidents take positions on a wide range of issues, from the momentous (health care and financial reforms, in Obama's case) to large numbers of routine and noncontroversial matters (most Senate confirmations of executive nominations, for example).[87]

During President Barack Obama's first two years in office, he enjoyed large success in winning congressional support on those issues where he took a clearly stated position. In fact, in 2009 he had a 96.7 percent success rate, the best score since *CQ Weekly* (a well-known and respected Washington journal published by Congressional Quarterly Inc.) began its voting pattern studies in 1953. A year later, his success rate dropped to 85.8 percent, "the tenth highest on record and the fourth highest for a president in his second year." Moreover, his 2010 score "does not capture the sheer size of the legislation enacted during his second year: the tax deal [extending President Bush's 2001 and 2003 tax cuts to 2012], in addition to overhauls of [the] health care system and financial regulations, not to mention student loans, food safety, a strategic weapons treaty with Russia and a repeal of the ban on gays serving openly in the military."[88]

Figure 9-4 reveals several important points. First, presidents do far better with their own partisans than with those of the opposition party. Members of the president's party feel obliged to lend their support whenever they can. The party ratio that presidents confront in Congress is the single most important determinant of success or failure.

By the same token, party control of Congress dramatically affects presidential success rates. As long as their party controls Congress, presidents win at least three of every four votes on which they take a position; when the government is divided, presidents fall well below that level. In his first two years in office, with Democrats controlling both chambers, President Bill Clinton prevailed on 86.4 percent of all roll call votes. After the GOP took over Congress in 1995, Clinton's success rates on Capitol Hill plummeted to its modern-day low of 36 percent.[89]

Another important pattern that emerges from Figure 9-4 is that presidents tend to lose congressional support as their administrations age. Presidents' best years in dealing with Congress are usually their first. A downward trend is evident for almost all modern presidents, though it was less pronounced for Clinton, whose congressional support settled at a relatively

FIGURE 9-4 **Presidential Success History, 1953–2010**

Source: *CQ Weekly*, January 3, 2011, 20.

Note: Presidential success is defined as the percentage of the times the president won his way on roll call votes on which he had taken a clear position.

steady low level after the Republican takeover of Congress. The pattern of declining support over time was also evident over George W. Bush's first six years in office, even though Republicans maintained control of Congress throughout that period.

LEGISLATIVE BARGAINING

Whatever their sources of influence, in the end individual legislators have only a single vote on any given bill or, more typically, on an amendment. At that moment, the vote is reduced to a "yea" or "nay" question, with no hedging or nuance allowed. Legislators have to decide how to cast these binary votes on a bewildering array of issues. They rarely have adequate—or even much—information on any particular bill or amendment. Legislators must weigh their goals—which often may conflict—and process their limited information in a relatively short period of time to arrive at a decision.[90]

Such a state of affairs—disparate goals and widely scattered influence—is hazardous. Stalemate is a constant threat. The "collective action problem" is how political scientists refer to the challenge of merging individual goals into group achievements. To overcome this predicament, members have to resort to politicking—that is, they must trade off goals and resources to get results. It is no wonder, then, that Congress is "an influence system in which bargain and exchange predominate."[91]

Implicit and Explicit Bargaining

Bargaining is a general term that refers to several related types of behavior. It describes in an overall sense, the process by which two or more parties arrive at a mutually beneficial exchange. Such processes may be implicit or explicit.

Implicit Bargaining. Implicit bargaining occurs when legislators take actions designed to elicit certain reactions from others, even though no negotiation has taken place. For example, legislators often introduce bills or sponsor hearings not because they expect the measure to pass but to prod someone else—an executive branch official, or a committee chair with broader jurisdiction on the question—to take action. Or a bill's managers may accept a controversial amendment knowing full well that the objectionable provision will be dropped in the other chamber or in conference. These are examples of the so-called law of anticipated reactions.[92]

Another type of implicit bargaining occurs when legislators seek out or accept the judgments of colleagues with expertise on a given matter, expecting that the situation will be reversed in the future. Exchanges of voting cues are endemic in both chambers. What is being traded is information. The exchange not only saves the recipient the time and trouble of mastering the subject matter, but it also can provide credible cover in defending the vote. Exchanging cues is a key element in John W. Kingdon's model of representatives' decisions, derived from interviews with members immediately after their votes on specific issues.[93]

Legislators have little difficulty making up their minds when they receive no conflicting cues from party leaders, respected fellow members, constituents, or key interest groups. If all the cue-givers in their field of vision concur, members operate in a consensus mode of decision making. If the actors are in conflict, the lawmaker will have to weigh the alternatives. For example, a liberal senator who finds himself alone in voting on the same side as most conservative senators may reevaluate his position.

Fellow members emerge in Kingdon's study as the most influential cue-givers, with constituencies ranking second. As one lawmaker observed:

> I think that the other members are very influential, and we recognize it. And why are they influential? I think because they have exercised good judgment, have expertise in the area, and know what they are talking about.[94]

When members deviate from a consensus stance among their cue-givers, it is usually to follow their own conscience or their constituencies. Adding up these short-term forces, Kingdon's model successfully predicted about 90 percent of the decisions.

Explicit Bargaining. Explicit bargains also take several forms. In making compromises, legislators may agree to split their differences. Compromises are straightforward on issues dealing with quantitative elements that can easily be adjusted upward or downward—for example, funding levels or eligibility criteria. Compromise on substance is also possible. For example, members who favor a major new program and members who oppose any program at all may agree to a two-year pilot project to test the idea.

"You cannot legislate without the ability to compromise," declared Sen. Alan Simpson, R-Wyo., who often found fault with militant junior members of his own party. He recounted the following tale:

> On a recent bill, I went to [conservative House members] and said: "Here's what I'm doing. I've got six senators who will vote this far, and then the next time if you go any further, they will not be there." So [my GOP colleague] and I delivered on this singular bill, and they said, "We want you to get more." And we said, "There is no more to get." Next vote on this bill, we lost six votes. Then they came in and said, "We are going to probably kill the whole thing. . . ." [A]nd they got nothing.[95]

The lesson is that compromise is inevitable in crafting laws; those who are unwilling to give ground are bound to be disappointed. On occasion, both parties avoid compromise and engage in brinksmanship, with each expecting the other to "blink" first before the interparty deadlock produces bad political and policy repercussions. Winning concessions from the opposing side is a key aim of this form of bargaining.[96]

Logrolling

Logrolling is bargaining in which members exchange support so that all parties to the deal can attain their individual goals. The term originated in the nineteenth century when neighbors helped each other roll logs into a pile for burning. Its most visible form is a something-for-everyone enactment, sometimes called a "Christmas tree" bill. Such bills are prevalent in legislative areas such as public works, omnibus taxation, or tariffs and trade. Describing a classic logroll, former representative Edward J. Derwinski, R-Ill. (1959–1983), explained how the country's two million farmers put together a majority coalition every five years to pass the omnibus farm bill's basket of price supports, acreage allowances, and marketing agreements:

> What [the farmers] do is very interesting. The agriculture people from North Carolina, where agriculture means tobacco, discuss their problems with the man representing the rice growers in Arkansas or California. The sugar beet growers in Minnesota and sugar cane interests in Louisiana and Hawaii and the wheat and corn and soybean and other producers just gather together in one great big happy family to be sure there is a subsidy for every commodity. They put

those numbers together again so that they have at least 218 support-ers in the House and 51 in the Senate. A supporter of the tobacco subsidy automatically becomes a supporter of the wheat subsidy, or the sugar quota, or the soybean subsidy, or whatever else follows.[97]

Logrolling draws lawmakers into the finished legislative product by embracing their special interests, proposals, or amendments. Henry M. "Scoop" Jackson, D-Wash. (House, 1941–1953; Senate, 1953–1983), when asked how he had assembled a majority for a new proposal, responded something like this: "Maggie said he talked to Russell, and Tom promised this if I would back him on Ed's amendment, and Mike owes me one for last year's help on Pete's bill."[98] Such reciprocity especially pervades the Senate, dominated as it is by individu-als. Sponsors of a Senate bill often must placate most or all interested legislators to gain clearance to bring a bill to the floor.

Lawmakers who enter into, and stand to profit from, a logroll are expected to support the final package, regardless of what that package looks like. A broad-based logroll is thus hard to stop. "It's not a system of punishment. It's a system of rewards," explained Rep. Bill Frenzel, R-Minn. (1971–1991).[99]

In a hostile fiscal environment, logrolling is often aimed at equalizing sac-rifices instead of distributing rewards. Broad-spectrum bills—authorizations, omnibus tax measures, continuing resolutions, and budget resolutions—may include numerous less than optimal provisions, many of which would fail if voted on separately. Such a negative logroll enables lawmakers to support the measure as "the best deal we can get."

Logrolling often turns narrowly targeted programs into broad-scale ones as many lawmakers want a piece of the policy pie. This development can dilute a program's impact by spreading funds throughout the nation rather than in targeted areas. Similarly, if resources are spread too thinly among too many sites, the program may not make a noticeable difference in any single area.

In a time logroll, members agree to support one measure in exchange for later support for another measure. A time logroll was crucial to the initial House passage of the new prescription drug benefit for seniors in 2003. Rep. Jo-Ann Emerson, R-Mo., had been fighting for years to allow U.S. consumers to purchase generic drugs from Canada and other countries where prices were lower, but she could not convince her Republican leadership to permit a vote. "I felt like a darned broken record," Emerson said.[100] When Emerson realized that Republican leaders would need her vote to pass the new prescription drug benefit, she took advantage of the opportunity. She demanded that they prom-ise to bring her reimportation bill up for a vote, and eventually she was able to get a good-faith pledge from the leadership to greenlight her bill. "I'm extremely pleased with the outcome," she said.[101] Republican leaders fulfilled their promise to Emerson the following month by permitting the House to take a vote on the matter.[102]

Sometimes, logrolls can be constructed on the basis of side payments, in which support is exchanged for benefits on an unrelated issue—for example, a federal project for the state or district, a better committee assignment, inclusion in an important conference, help with fund raising, or access to the White House. Although such side payoffs may seem trivial or parochial, they can enable members to achieve valued goals.

Bargaining Strategy

For bargaining to take place, participants in the House and Senate must be able to rely on one another's future actions. Rep. John P. Murtha, D-Pa. (1974–2010), a master dealmaker, cited two elements of power on Capitol Hill: "Develop expertise on an issue that makes you vital to colleagues, and keep your word."[103] Relying on his expertise and contacts within the defense community, he often cut deals quietly in the back corner of the Democratic side of the House. His orbit embraced liberal legislators and even ultraconservative former Republican floor leader Tom DeLay of Texas, whom Murtha regarded as an honest broker. When DeLay needed something, he would sometimes approach Murtha for assistance. On the Senate side of the Capitol, the same kind of deal-making occurs. Majority Leader Reid, for example, was not reluctant to provide Senators Ben Nelson and Mary Landrieu, D-La., with what each wanted in order to win their votes for the president's controversial health overhaul plan. The press soon called the special health benefits each received for their states, respectively, the "Cornhusker Kickback" and the "Louisiana Purchase."[104]

For bargaining to succeed, the participants must agree on the need for a legislative product—that is, the benefits of reaching a decision must exceed the costs of failing to do so. In many cases, politicians may prefer a course of strategic disagreement, which John B. Gilmour describes as "efforts of politicians to avoid reaching an agreement when compromise might alienate supporters, damage their prospects in an upcoming election, or preclude getting a better deal in the future."[105]

According to bargaining theory, a measure's sponsors will yield only what they absolutely must to gain a majority of supporters. "Parties wish to use their votes efficiently, winning victories at the cheapest possible price."[106] By this logic, if bargainers act rationally and have perfect information about one another, minimum winning coalitions should predominate.[107] Recounting Senate majority leader Lyndon B. Johnson's meticulous vote counting before a floor fight, political scientist John G. Stewart concluded, "And once a sufficient majority had been counted, Johnson would seldom attempt to enlarge it: Why expend limited bargaining resources which might be needed to win future battles?"[108]

Most legislative strategists, however, lack Johnson's extraordinary skills. Uncertainty about outcomes leads them to line up more than a simple majority of supporters. Moreover, at many points in the legislative process supermajorities are required—for example, in voting under suspension of the rules, in overriding vetoes, or in ending Senate filibusters. Not surprisingly, therefore, minimum winning coalitions are not typical of Congress, even in the majoritarian House of Representatives.[109]

Yet coalition size is the crux of legislative strategy. Bargainers repeatedly face the dilemma of how broadly or how narrowly to frame their issues and how many concessions to yield in an effort to secure passage.

CONCLUSION

Congressional deliberation is at risk today. With both parties unified and seemingly uninterested in debate or compromise, life on Capitol Hill has become, in Hobbes's words, "nasty" and "brutish" (though hardly "short"). Take-no-prisoners strategies are encouraged by today's highly competitive, polarized party system. As a senator observed,

> The pressure on congressional leaders both from interests in the party and from outside groups is severe. Many would rather fight and lose, rather than reach out and find common ground. Congress should not be like the Super Bowl, in which one team always has to win and the other team inevitably loses. There's nothing wrong with reaching legitimate compromise and getting something done for the American people.[110]

Sarah Binder's findings echo this sentiment. "The decline of the political center," she writes, "has produced a political environment that more often than not gives legislators every incentive not to reach agreement."[111] The result is often legislative inaction, which may be criticized as stalemate or gridlock.

Yet the enterprise of lawmaking rests on the premise that, at least where urgent matters are concerned, bargainers will normally prefer some sort of agreement to none at all. As Everett M. Dirksen, R-Ill., the legendary Senate Republican leader (1959–1969), once remarked, "I am a man of fixed and unbending principle, and one of my principles is flexibility."[112] Flexibility is especially crucial with "must-pass" legislation that, if not approved, can imperil government functions. When dealing with some reauthorizations, appropriations, and debt ceiling adjustments, the alternative to action can be shutdown of the federal government. Indeed, budget impasses have resulted in government shutdowns seventeen times in the last twenty-five years.[113] An eighteenth shutdown was averted in mid-April 2011 when Congress passed a continuing resolution covering government spending for the rest of fiscal year 2011.

Bargaining is a necessary part of legislative life. It shapes the character of bills, resolutions, and other forms of congressional policy making. It also underlies many attributes of the legislative process—delay, obfuscation, compromise, and norms such as specialization and reciprocity.

Deliberation is the hallmark of legislative decision making. Coalitions are constructed as diverse views are voiced and a variety of members and interest groups participate. It is yet another point of contact and conflict between the two Congresses—the Congress of individual wills and the Congress of collective decisions.

***M**ultiple Presidential Roles.* President Bara
Obama meets with bipartisan Senate leade
to discuss his Supreme Court nomination of Sor
Sotomayor (top). From left to right, Sen. Jeff Sessio
R-Ala., ranking minority member of the Judicia
Committee; Minority Leader Mitch McConnell, R-K
Vice President Joseph R. Biden Jr.; President Oban
Majority Leader Harry Reid, D-Nev.; and Judicia
Committee chair Patrick Leahy, D-Vt. Preside
Obama (middle left) signs the Caregivers a
Veterans Omnibus Health Services Act. The preside
is mobbed by lawmakers seeking a handsha
before he delivers the annual State of the Uni
address in January 2011 (middle right). (Bottom le
The president meets with House majority lead
John R. Boehner, R-Ohio, and minority leader Nar
Pelosi, D-Calif.

Congress and the President

Barack Obama, the nation's forty-first president, took office in 2009 with the hopes and goodwill of the majority of Americans. Most people recognized that he had inherited huge economic problems: a financial system in tatters, major automobile companies nearing bankruptcy, growing joblessness, home foreclosures, bank failures—not to mention the unfinished wars in Iraq and Afghanistan. The president addressed these issues, and many more, with varying degrees of legislative success, public support, and personal frustration.

During his first two years in office, the president enjoyed huge—even transformative—legislative achievements, comparable to President Lyndon B. Johnson's "Great Society" accomplishments such as Medicare in 1965. A few examples make the point. With a Democratic-controlled Congress, the president won enactment of a massive overhaul of the health care system, something many of his predecessors had wanted but had failed to do. He revamped the financial regulatory system, championed a $787 billion stimulus package to revive the economy and prevent another Great Depression, and, during one of the most productive "lame-duck" sessions in decades, succeeded in winning Senate approval of a major nuclear arms treaty with Russia, terminating the "don't ask, don't tell" law that prevented gays from serving openly in the military, and—in a bipartisan deal he made with congressional Republicans that angered many liberal Democrats—gaining approval of an $858 billion tax reduction package that extended President George W. Bush's 2001 and 2003 tax cuts to 2012. Among other things, the tax package also continued unemployment benefits for the jobless at a time when the unemployment rate was hovering just below 10 percent.

Major legislative successes were hard to come by in the 112th Congress, with the House in GOP hands and more Republicans in the Senate. Moreover, House and Senate Republicans acted quickly but unsuccessfully to fulfill their campaign pledge to "repeal and replace" the Obama-championed Patient Protection and Affordable Care Act (which they derisively called Obamacare). In doing so, they proposed legislation to eviscerate the act, held numerous hearings and offered floor amendments to castigate the health law, and enlisted outside groups and media outlets to continue their drumbeat of criticism against the act.

The GOP-controlled House also launched scores of hearings to review critically the administration's issuance of rules and regulations viewed as economically harmful to business. The House even passed a resolution directing its standing committees to highlight regulatory overreach by federal agencies. For example, Spencer Bachus, R-Ala., chair of the House Financial Services Committee, exclaimed that the "more than 300 new rules and regulations being written per the new [Dodd-Frank Wall Street Reform and Consumer Protection Act, P.L. 111–203] are proving detrimental to businesses and the economy."[1]

Tensions between the executive and legislative branches are inevitable. The two policy-making branches have divergent responsibilities and different constituencies and terms of office, and typically they are jealous of each other's prerogatives. Executive officials see the decentralized Congress as inefficient and meddlesome. Legislators perceive the hierarchical and highly centralized executive branch as arrogant and arbitrary. At times, these differences lead to conflicts that the news media dramatize as the "battles on the Potomac."

And yet day in and day out Congress and the president work together. Even when their relationship is guarded or hostile, bills are passed and signed into law. Presidential appointments win Senate approval. Budgets are eventually enacted and the government is kept afloat. This cooperation continues even when control of the White House and the Congress is divided between the two major parties.

Early in 2011, for example, a government shutdown was averted when the GOP-controlled House and Democratic-controlled Senate—in the face of profound differences over the $61 billion in spending reductions proposed by the cost-cutting House—managed to reach a compromise to keep the government funded temporarily until the two sides could reach a permanent settlement of their bicameral spending differences. The essence of the compromise was to use the president's budget proposals. Federal agencies would continue to operate "at current funding levels, except for eight programs that were marked for deep cuts or termination in the budget request Obama delivered to Capitol Hill" in February.[2]

Divided government often complicates relationships between Congress and the executive branch, as is evident in the 112th Congress (2011–2013). But unified partisan control of both branches is no guarantee of harmony, as Presidents Jimmy Carter and Bill Clinton (in his first two years in office) learned. Political scientist Ross K. Baker has summarized President Clinton's rocky start with Congress:

> Clinton's problems started with his proposal to enable gays to serve openly in the armed forces. His principal antagonist in this fight was not a Republican, but the Democratic chairman of the Senate Armed Services Committee, Sam Nunn of Georgia. After backing down on

that issue, Clinton proposed an emergency stimulus package that quickly passed the House but was scuttled by the outnumbered Republicans in the Senate through a filibuster—Democrats didn't have the 60 votes to end it. Clinton's early missteps, combined with collapse of the national health insurance initiative, captained by Hillary Clinton, contributed to the Republican capture of both houses of Congress in the 1994 elections.[3]

President Obama also experienced push back from various congressional Democrats to his major initiatives. Some pointed out that the president was overloading the legislative circuits by proposing so many major initiatives all at once—a massive stimulus package and major proposals to reform health care, energy, and education. "There's only so much that we can absorb and do at one time," explained Sen. Daniel Inouye, D-Hawaii, chair of the Senate Appropriations Committee.[4] The president responded that Congress is capable of dealing with more than one major problem at a time.

THE PRESIDENT AS LEGISLATOR

The president is sometimes called the chief legislator because of his close involvement in congressional decision making. Article II, section 3, of the Constitution directs the president from time to time to "give to the Congress Information of the State of the Union and recommend to their Consideration such Measures as he shall judge necessary and expedient." (Today, this means annually and during television's prime time.) Soon after delivering the annual State of the Union address, the president sends to Congress draft administration bills for introduction on his behalf. By enlarging the list of messages required from the president—the annual budget and economic reports, for example—Congress has further involved the chief executive in designing legis lation. Indeed, Congress often delegates authority to the president because it appreciates the strengths of the White House—such as its capacity for coordination—and recognizes its own shortcomings, such as its decentralized committee structure, which inhibit swift and comprehensive policy making. Crises, partisan considerations, and public expectations all make the president an important participant in congressional decision making. And the president's constitutional veto power ensures that White House views will be listened to, if not always heeded, on Capitol Hill.

The legislative presidency emerged after World War II. By then, it was conceded that this new presidential role was institutionalized, performed not because of some unique combination of personality and circumstance but because everyone expected it—including Congress, the press, and the public.[5] This deeply entrenched expectation will not change anytime soon.

Understanding the chief executive's relations with Congress is no easy task. The founders did not clearly define the legislative-executive relationship, and so it has always been a work in progress. Presidents bring their own style to the relationship, which political scientist Charles O. Jones characterizes as either the "partnership model" or the "independent model." The partnership model means that presidents consult regularly with lawmakers and involve them directly in the policy and political affairs of the White House. The independent model holds that presidents should minimize their involvement with Congress and strive on their own to accomplish their top priorities.[6]

Scholars and others have long analyzed America's complex system of separate institutions sharing, and competing for, power. Different theories, such as Jones's, have been formulated to define effective presidential leadership. In recent decades, scholars have produced an array of studies, "a bewildering succession of new models of the presidency, each the product of an admixture of empirical and normative assessments."[7] Some studies focus on the person in the White House; others examine the bureaucracy and the institutional functions and structures of the presidency; and still others analyze discrete aspects of the relationship between Congress and the president, such as presidential spending power versus the legislative branch's power of the purse.[8] Here we discuss four prominent presidential theories—persuasion, rhetoric, administrative, and the "two presidencies"—as a way to illuminate important aspects of the chief executive's relations with Congress. To varying degrees, these analytical perspectives overlap and capture the activities of all presidents.

The Power to Persuade

"Presidential power is the power to persuade," wrote Richard E. Neustadt, a former staff aide in the Truman White House and adviser to President-elect John F. Kennedy.[9] Power, Neustadt asserted, meant more than the executive's ability to persuade Congress to enact a bill. "Strategically, the question is not how he masters Congress in a peculiar instance, but what he does to boost his chances for mastery in any instance."[10] Presidents striving to be successful are urged to employ all their powers—constitutional, political, bureaucratic, personal, and more—to persuade Congress and others to follow their lead. Setting Congress's agenda—that is, determining the policies that the legislature heeds by taking them up in committee and on the floor—epitomizes the president's power to persuade.

Presidents have shaped Congress's agenda since the earliest days of the Republic. The First Congress of "its own volition immediately turned to the executive branch for guidance and discovered in [Treasury Secretary Alexander] Hamilton a personality to whom such leadership was congenial."[11] Two decades later (by 1825), the "initiative in public affairs remained with [Speaker Henry] Clay and his associates in the House of Representatives" and not with the president.[12] Thus dominance in national policy making may pass from one branch to the other. Strong presidents sometimes provoked efforts by Congress to reassert its own authority and to restrict that of the executive. Periods of presidential ascendancy are often followed by eras of congressional assertiveness. Still, Congress has usually expected the White House to outline its legislative program in the annual State of the Union message and in other formal and informal presidential messages.

Presidents follow different patterns in setting agendas. They also study the decisions of their predecessors to learn from their mistakes and successes. For example, President Ronald Reagan (1981–1989) analyzed why his predecessor, Jimmy Carter (1977–1981), had difficulties in dealing with Congress so that he could follow a different tack when he became president. Reagan found that Carter quickly overloaded Congress's agenda and never made clear what his priorities were. Three major consequences resulted:

> First . . . there was little clarity in the communication of priorities to the American public. Instead of galvanizing support for two or three major national needs, the Carter administration proceeded on a number of fronts. . . . Second, and perhaps more important, the lack of priorities meant unnecessary waste of the President's own time and energy. . . . Third, the lack of priorities needlessly compounded Carter's congressional problems. . . . Carter's limited political capital was squandered on a variety of agenda requests when it might have been concentrated on the top of the list.[13]

Carter lacked the temperament for personal lobbying. Although he met in formal sessions with a large number of members, he shunned informal, personal contacts. He did not view informal discussions or negotiating meetings with members as a productive use of his time.

By contrast, agenda control was the hallmark of Reagan's leadership during his first year in office. By limiting his legislative priorities, Reagan focused Congress's and the public's attention on one priority issue at a time. Most were encapsulated as "Reaganomics"—tax and spending cuts. He exploited the usual honeymoon period for new presidents by moving his agenda quickly, during a moment of widespread anticipation of a new era of GOP national political dominance.

Reagan also dealt skillfully with Congress, meeting, negotiating, and socializing with lawmakers, including a private dinner with Democratic Speaker Thomas P. "Tip" O'Neill Jr. of Massachusetts and his wife. Enjoying a Republican majority in the Senate, the Reagan White House focused primarily on lobbying the Democratic-controlled House to pass the president's economic program—the "greatest selling job I've ever seen," said Speaker O'Neill. Reagan personally called or telegraphed all of the "Boll Weevils," the forty-seven southern Democrats in the Conservative Democratic Forum.[14] And he persuaded several governors to meet with members from their states who were opposing the program. Top executive officials were dispatched to targeted Democratic districts to drum up public support. On the key House vote, all 191 GOP members and sixty-three Democrats backed the president's budget plan.

Overall, after only eight months in office Reagan scored some of the biggest victories of his entire eight years in office. Later, when his control over the agenda slackened, Congress was still confined to a playing field he had largely set out. Lawmakers were forced to respond to, though not always accept, the positions the president had staked out on taxes, spending, defense, and social issues.

President Obama—the first sitting senator since John Kennedy (1960) to move directly to the White House—promised the voters "change" if elected. He delivered. His "big bang" domestic agenda is as strikingly ambitious as that of any president since Johnson's Great Society program. Taking office during one of the worst economic recessions in decades and benefitting from a Congress controlled by Democrats by wide margins, Obama won enactment of landmark comprehensive laws, such as the economic stimulus package (American Recovery and Reinvestment Act), financial regulatory reform, and health care reform. In 2009 his success score—"the share of votes on which Congress acceded to his clearly stated position"—was a historically high 96.7 percent.[15] The next year, as noted in Chapter 9, it dropped to 85.8 percent, still the tenth "highest on record and the fourth highest for a president in his second year."[16] Obama might also be dubbed the "transparency" president; he has placed more government data and information online than any of his predecessors.

And yet despite the president's high success rate with Congress and his signal policy achievements, many people across the ideological spectrum disapproved or were skeptical of his policies. In a September 2010 Gallup Poll, respondents approved of only one of Obama's five major achievements during his first two years in office—reform of the financial regulatory process, 61 percent approving to 37 percent disapproving. The other four achievements were supported by only a minority of respondents: rescue of the financial system, 37 percent to 61 percent; the stimulus package, 43 percent to 52 percent; the bailout of the automotive companies, 43 percent to 56 percent; and health reform, 39 percent to 56 percent.

Many Americans do not give the president much credit for his initiatives because, says Andrew Kohut, president of the Pew Research Center, his "achievements are seen through the prism of, 'He hasn't fixed the economy.'" And President Obama concurs in that assessment: "It's perfectly sensible that they are holding out an overall assessment [of my presidency] until they see changes in their lives."[17]

Several other factors also account for the disconnect between major policy success and public discontent, even giving rise to an influential Tea Party movement. Four merit some mention.

First, the president seemingly misinterpreted the meaning of his historic 2008 victory. His resounding 53 percent victory margin reflected many things—public disapproval of George W. Bush and the Iraq war, the woeful state of the economy, and so on—but it is doubtful that the electorate endorsed a "new New Deal" that would dramatically expand the role, reach, and cost of government.

Obama campaigned on "change you can believe in," but to many people it was change they did not want or support, especially when confidence in government was low and federal expenditures were a Niagara Falls of red ink. A Gallup pollster remarked that it was paradoxical that in 2008, when trust in government was at an historic low of about 25 percent, Obama was offering "government as the primary solution to most of the nation's woes."[18] What people wanted most from the government and the private sector were three things: jobs, jobs, jobs.

Second, the president's governing agenda was summed up by many as too much spending (trillions), too much debt ($14.3 trillion and rising), too much government (scores of new federal programs, entities, and regulations), and too little success in creating economic growth. "Where's my bailout?" was the refrain heard on Main Street. By contrast, on Wall Street many business executives awarded themselves large bonuses from the bailout funds provided by taxpayers. The president could claim that his policies prevented another 1930s depression, but it is hard to gain much public credit for preventing something that did not happen.

Third, public expectations for the president were simply too high, as they often are for presidents. He and his supporters wanted many things to happen fairly quickly (recall White House Chief of Staff Rahm Emanuel's comment that great crises should not be wasted because they beget great opportunities): revival of the economy, enactment of climate change legislation, closure of the Guantánamo Bay detention camp, labor law reform, an overhaul of the health care system (including a public option), immigration reform, and more. The founders, however, had devised a complex three-way bargaining process among the House, Senate, and White House that is inherently slow-moving. And added to that reality are the difficulties of moving legislation through the Senate, where sixty votes have become the new norm to advance legislation.

Senate Republicans employed a confrontational "party of no" strategy in the 111th Congress (2009–2011), blocking numerous measures and nominations. As Senate GOP leader Mitch McConnell, Ky., said of Obama's program, "I wish I could have blocked more"; it was anathema to many Republicans. Absent GOP votes on many administration priorities, the public watched a messy sausage-making process as Democratic leaders attracted ("bought" from the public's perspective) votes by including in the legislation special-interest provisions sought by their party colleagues. It was of little surprise, then, that Obama's goal of being a postpartisan president who could change the way Washington works was never reached.

Fourth, as scholar William Galston put it, there was a clash between the president's "agenda of choice"—his campaign promises—and his "agenda of necessity"—the economic crisis.[19] His agenda of choice prevented a laser-like focus on what seemed to interest the public most: restoration of a healthy economy that would put many unemployed people back to work. Health care, climate change, education reform, and other important issues absorbed the president's time and energy, reinforcing the view among many people that Obama was a "big government" liberal who was taking the country in a direction they did not want to go.

In short, President Obama was unable to convince an angst-ridden public going through tough times that his agenda would produce a strong foundation for twenty-first-century growth. Meanwhile, he tried out a slogan for his agenda—the "New Foundation"—to rally public support. But historian Doris Kearns Goodwin told him it sounded "like a woman's girdle."[20] Thus in 2011 he changed his slogan to "Win the Future." As for the future, it is worth noting that many policy provisions in laws such as health care and financial reform will not take effect until after Obama's first term—"and in some cases well past a second."[21] Front-loading benefits and back-loading costs are a strategy often employed by elected officials to win passage of significant measures.

President Obama's record of accomplishment during his first two years in office is something that most chief executives would not be able to achieve over their full four-year terms. Big legislative achievements may still emerge over the next two years, but the political odds suggest a more modest, incremental approach to policy making with an emphasis on cost-cutting and implementing laws already on the books. No doubt, much of the president's time dealing with the 112th Congress will be spent defending and protecting from GOP assaults the policy successes of his first two years.[22]

For the most part, presidents recognize the importance of maintaining informal contacts with Congress because they understand it is not easy to persuade Congress to act in a certain way. As Lyndon Johnson—who had served as Senate minority leader (1953–1955) and majority leader (1955–1960)—once declared, "Merely placing a program before Congress is not enough. Without constant attention from the administration, most legislation moves through the congressional process at the speed of a glacier."[23] Johnson regularly (and sometimes crudely) admonished his aides and departmental officers to work closely with Congress. "[Get off] your ass and see how fast you can respond to a congressional request," he told his staff. "Challenge yourself to see how quickly you can get back to him or her with an answer, any kind of an answer, but goddamn it, an answer."[24]

At least since Harry S. Truman, presidents have maintained a formal White House legislative liaison office. It promotes the administration's program in Congress; lobbies outside groups, state officials, and others to do the same; targets members who could be coaxed for votes on certain issues, and, more generally, fosters a cooperative legislative-executive atmosphere.

To persuade members to support their programs, presidents often grant or withhold their patronage resources. Broadly conceived, patronage involves not only federal and judicial positions but also federal construction projects, location of government installations, campaign support, access to strategic information, plane rides on *Air Force One*, White House entree for important constituents, and countless other favors, large and small. Some presidents even keep records of the political favors they grant to lawmakers, IOUs that they can cash in later for needed support in Congress. There are limits, however, to the persuasive power of patronage. As one White House congressional relations chief said, "The problem with congressional relations is that with every good intention, at the end of the day you can't accommodate all the requests that you get."[25] More important, many factors influence how members vote on issues important to the White House. Although a president's persuasive skills can sometimes tip the balance, other considerations—lawmakers' constituency interests, policy preferences, and ideological dispositions, as well as public opinion and the number of partisan seats in each chamber—usually are more important in shaping congressional outcomes.

Going Public: The Rhetorical President

"With public sentiment, nothing can fail; without it nothing can succeed," Abraham Lincoln once observed.[26] Lincoln's idea is the essence of the rhetorical presidency: how and when a chief executive strategically employs contemporary campaign techniques and the technology of the mass media to promote "himself and his policies in Washington by appealing to the American public."[27] The rhetorical president's ultimate objective is to produce an outpouring of public support that encourages lawmakers to push his ideas through the congressional obstacle course. Indeed, "if he had the votes he would pass the measure first and go to the public only for the bill-signing ceremonies."[28]

Going public on an issue, however, is not without its risks. The strategy may alienate legislators who feel that the president is going over their heads, cutting them out of the process, and disregarding their constitutional role. The president can also raise expectations that cannot be met, make inept appeals, or stiffen the opposition. Furthermore, many legislators are more popular than the president in their districts or states.

President Reagan was an acknowledged master at using the electronic media to orchestrate public support. The Hollywood actor-turned-president was at home in front of cameras and microphones, and he had a keen sense of public ritual and symbolism as means of rallying support. After the March 30, 1981, assassination attempt, Reagan returned a month later and made a dramatic appeal for his economic program. "The White House shrewdly tied Reagan's return to action to the budget and tax debate, scheduling an April 28 comeback speech before a joint meeting of Congress. It was a triumph, and people began to call him the 'Great Communicator.'"[29] Reagan's adroitness with the media, primarily during his first year in office, is a legacy that looms large for subsequent presidents and Congresses. He showed that "one man using the White House's immense powers of communication can lift the mood of the nation and alter the way it does business."[30]

President Clinton used various media technologies to reach voters and employed campaign-style practices to generate public support for his programs. His empathetic response to the April 1995 bombing of a federal office building in Oklahoma City reminded people of the human face of the federal government, the very entity House Republican "revolutionaries" were warring against. When Republicans added provisions that Clinton opposed to a flood relief bill, the president used the bully pulpit to paint the GOP position as "extreme" and generated a flurry of favorable publicity for his position. As one reporter noted,

> News accounts portrayed Republicans as, well, crazy extremists bent on playing games with flood victims. Rank-and-file Republicans writhed in political agony. Michigan Republican Fred Upton's mother watched the news accounts with alarm and warned her son, "You're getting killed." "When your mom tells you that, you know you're in trouble," said Upton.[31]

The White House also used "nightly tracking polls and weekly focus groups to help determine its daily message and the approach President Clinton should take to important national issues."[32]

George W. Bush was initially dubbed "the reticent president" by some analysts on several grounds: his preference for not seizing the public spotlight and addressing every major event or issue that might arise; his determination to stay "on message" by sticking to prepared talking points; his predilection for carefully staged and scripted appearances; and his propensity for committing verbal gaffes. Nevertheless, Bush worked diligently to win public and political support for his policy and political objectives.[33] Bush also became the first president to deliver his weekly radio address in Spanish—political recognition of the electoral potential of the growing Hispanic population.

Bush came into his own as both communicator in chief and commander in chief in the aftermath of the terrorist attacks on the World Trade Center in New York City and the Pentagon. He gave powerful and eloquent speeches in a variety of forums, such as before Congress and at the United Nations (UN), on the need to go after terrorists who threatened the United States and to disarm Saddam Hussein's regime in Iraq. His direct and confident manner resonated with most Americans and boosted domestic and congressional support for his antiterrorism and war plans.

In addition, the Bush White House went to great lengths to use television to promote the president, employing former network television aides with expertise in lighting, camera angles, and backdrops. The most elaborately staged event was Bush's flight to and speech on the aircraft carrier *Abraham Lincoln,* during which he prematurely announced the end of major military combat in Iraq. White House aides "choreographed every aspect of the event, even down to the members of the *Lincoln* crew arrayed in coordinated shirt colors over Mr. Bush's right shoulder and the 'Mission Accomplished' banner placed to perfectly capture the president and the celebratory two words in a single shot."[34] As the war continued for years without producing stability and security in Iraq, those same images were used to ironic effect by war critics, Democratic candidates, and late-night comedians.

After the Democrats won control of Congress in 2006, President Bush continued to go public against Congress in pursuit of his war policies. However, that strategy became increasingly untenable as the violence in Iraq escalated, antiwar sentiment grew in the United States, and Bush's job approval ratings plummeted to less than 30 percent.[35] In the end, Bush left office in January 2009 "with some of the lowest [popular approval] marks of any president in recent history."[36]

President Obama, like Reagan, is an exceptionally skilled and eloquent speaker who enjoys addressing citizens in a variety of locales and settings. Winston Churchill once said that of "all the gifts bestowed upon [modern leaders], none is so precious as the gift of oratory."[37] Obama has that gift.[38] In a modern version of Franklin Roosevelt's "fireside" chats, Obama became the first president to appear on *The Tonight Show,* a late-night television program that draws about five million viewers. The president's purpose was "to broaden his audience beyond cable news junkies and political elites, appealing to those who don't already know the intricacies of his budget blueprint and health care overhaul plan."[39]

President Obama recognizes that "in a fragmented media universe, presidents must communicate nearly constantly across an array of platforms, both traditional and new."[40] One of those new platforms was a live Internet "town hall" meeting in which Obama fielded questions in the White House from citizens across the nation as well as from a live audience in the East Room. That video chat was the first of its kind for any modern presidency.[41] In the Internet age with its 24/7 media cycle, presidents must exploit an array of traditional and nontraditional communication methods if they are to influence and shape the public conversation.

Despite his communication innovations and gifts as a speaker, which helped him win the presidential nomination, Obama—by many accounts, including his own—has not employed the "bully pulpit" in an effective manner as chief executive. He delivered many major and thoughtful speeches and interviews during his first two years in office, but they appeared to do rather little in moving public opinion toward supporting his ambitious agenda. As Democratic governor Ed Rendell of Pennsylvania put it, "Ironically, the best communicator I ever saw in a campaign has turned out to be not so good at getting out the message as president."[42] A liberal House Democrat bluntly stated, "The messaging has been terrible almost since day one. One of the best communicated campaigns I've ever seen and the worst messaging presidency."[43]

The president agreed with some of this criticism. As Obama said during an interview:

> What I have not done as well as I would have liked to is to consistently communicate to the general public why we're making some of these decisions. Because we've been so rushed over the course of the last [two years], just issue after issue and crisis after crisis, we haven't been as effective.[44]

By not employing the huge megaphone of the White House, the president enabled congressional Republicans, hostile media outlets, and others who opposed his agenda to dominate the public relations battle. Health care is a prime example. Republicans constantly and successfully framed the national debate on health care reform as a "government takeover," "socialized medicine," or a bill with "death panels." President Richard Nixon made a keen observation on how administrations can win favorable congressional action on their policies: "In the final analysis, [legislative successes] are not won or lost by programs. They are won or lost on how these programs are presented to the country, and how all the political and public relations considerations are handled."[45] His comment underscores the importance of presidential communication strategies, especially in this fast-paced, competitive media environment.

The Administrative President

Presidents understand that getting Congress to pass legislation is an arduous process, and that even when laws are enacted bureaucratic indifference may hamper implementation of presidential initiatives. Thus a president's core administrative strategy is to win policy goals by statute whenever feasible, but, when such an effort falls short, to accomplish those aims through organizational or managerial techniques. Administrative presidents employ a variety of methods, such as naming loyal political appointees to supervise and monitor agency activities, reorganizing executive departments to advance presidential goals, using the budget process to reduce unwanted programs or increase favorite activities, and employing executive orders and rule-making authority to achieve outcomes blocked by Congress.[46]

Using executive orders and reorganization plans, presidents can act on their own to create entirely new administrative entities. In doing so, presidents are able to institutionalize policies that Congress would never have created. Based on a study of all the administrative agencies established between the end of World War II and 1995, William G. Howell and David E. Lewis report that "presidents have unilaterally created over half of all administrative agencies in the United States."[47] Among them are such important agencies as the Peace Corps. Facing significant opposition in Congress to the Peace Corps idea, President Kennedy opted to create the agency by executive order. By the time Congress got around to reviewing the president's actions, the Peace Corps already had 362 employees and 600 volunteers at work in eight countries.[48] By establishing this "fact on the ground," the president pressured Congress into accepting the new organization. Another example stems from the September 11, 2001, terrorist attacks. In the immediate aftermath of the attacks, President Bush unilaterally created an Office for Homeland Security in the White House, constructed a prison for suspected terrorist noncitizens at Guantánamo Bay, Cuba, and established a new court system for handling cases involving "unlawful enemy combatants."[49] Despite candidate Obama's campaign promises and two years of unified Democratic control, the Guantánamo prison remains open, with military tribunals there set to resume in 2011 after a two-year hiatus.

For his part, President Obama created by executive order several executive entities. Examples are the Export Coordination Enforcement Center, the

President's Council on Jobs and Competitiveness, and the National Commission on Fiscal Responsibility and Reform, co-chaired by Erskine Bowles, former White House chief of staff to President Clinton, and former senator Alan Simpson, R-Wyo.

Presidents have long employed executive orders—a form of administrative lawmaking using (or expanding) authority that the legislative branch has delegated—to achieve objectives not explicitly authorized by Congress.[50] President Truman, for example, issued an executive order racially integrating the armed services. Stymied by the GOP-controlled Congress on issues such as antismoking legislation, a patients' bill of rights, and subsidies for school construction, President Clinton made extensive use of executive orders. "His formula include[d] pressing the limits of his regulatory authority, signing executive orders and using other unilateral means to obtain his policy priorities when Congress fail[ed] to embrace them."[51] Congressional Republicans railed against Clinton's "go-it-alone" governing.

George W. Bush similarly exploited administrative tools to advance his policy goals. First, he used the appointment power to staff the White House and executive branch with people who shared his goals and to place conservatives in prominent posts. Many of his allies claimed that Bush surpassed even Ronald Reagan in the ideological commitment of his appointments.[52] Bush also placed high value on loyalty in naming people to important governmental positions. For example, Condoleezza Rice, the president's national security adviser, confidante, and a frequent visitor to Camp David, replaced Colin Powell as secretary of state in Bush's second term.

Second, Bush quickly exercised executive authority to roll back, suspend, or challenge many Clinton-era regulations. He also was not reluctant to implement by executive fiat administration programs stalled in Congress. For example, when the Senate blocked action on Bush's faith-based initiative (assisting religious groups in winning government grants for charitable and social service work), the president ordered his administration to implement the program through executive orders and changes in agency regulations.[53]

Third, like presidents before him, Bush encouraged his departments and agencies to move rapidly to enact a wide array of so-called "midnight regulations." Rushing them through in the administration's waning months, executive officials could burnish the president's legacy and—as a senior think tank analyst observed—"extend its influence into the future."[54] Speaker Nancy Pelosi, familiar with the last-minute issuance of regulations by an outgoing administration, issued on Halloween a list of eleven Bush administration rules that she dubbed the "Ghoulish Midnight Regulations."[55]

Upon entering office, the Obama administration moved quickly to block or reverse many of Bush's rules and regulations. Even before he was sworn into office, Obama's transition team "compiled a list of about 200 Bush administration actions and executive orders that could be swiftly undone to reverse White House policies on climate change, stem cell research, reproductive rights and other issues."[56] True to form, in his first seven days in office President Obama blocked action on Bush's last-minute rules, banned the use of torture, ordered a review of detention policies for suspected terrorists, overturned the ban on funding international health groups that provide counseling on terminating pregnancies, directed the Transportation Department to develop new fuel efficiency standards, and ordered the Environmental Protection Agency (EPA) to consider granting California and other states the ability to impose tailpipe emission standards tougher than the federal standards.

In addition, President Obama imposed new ethics standards on administration officials, issued a Freedom of Information Act memorandum instructing "all members of his administration to operate under principles of openness, transparency and of engaging citizens,"[57] and issued two other memoranda (an Open Government Initiative and an Open Government Directive) instructing departments and agencies on how they are, among other actions, to implement "the principles of transparency, participation, and collaboration."[58]

The "Two Presidencies"

"The United States has one president, but it has two presidencies; one presidency is for domestic affairs, and the other is concerned with defense and foreign policy."[59] According to this formulation by political scientist Aaron Wildavsky, presidential proposals are likely to achieve more success in the international arena than in the domestic arena, in part because Congress asserts itself more in domestic policy making than in foreign policy. Since its emergence, Wildavsky's thesis has sparked considerable controversy on, for example, how to measure success rates in the two arenas and whether the concept is relevant today in a world in which the international and domestic constantly overlap.[60] Whatever the strengths or weaknesses of the two-presidencies idea as Wildavsky laid it out, the concept seems relevant to the presidency of George W. Bush before and after the September 11, 2001, terrorist attacks. The pre-9/11 period constituted George W. Bush's first presidency with its focus on domestic issues, then the post-9/11 era constituted his second presidency, with its strong focus on defense and national security issues.

The Pre-9/11 Phase. Despite Vice President Al Gore's plurality in the 2000 popular vote tally, the absence of any mandate from the voters, and the lack of any presidential coattails (the GOP lost seats in both chambers, though it held onto the majority in each), President Bush quickly advanced an ambitious agenda as though he had won a huge victory. This approach surprised the many pundits who had predicted that Bush would move slowly to implement his "compassionate conservative" campaign promises. "This is the farthest thing from a caretaker administration you could get," declared a Brookings Institution analyst. "It's the farthest thing from a president saying I lost the popular vote, I'm here because of a 5 to 4 vote on the Supreme Court [*Bush v. Gore*]. I'd better [advance] some centrist positions."[61]

Bush scored major policy successes early in his first term, largely by staking out an assertive policy-making approach that combined bipartisan and partisan governing strategies. Three days after being sworn into office, for example, Bush proposed the No Child Left Behind Act, which was later signed into law. The measure established standards of learning and accountability for elementary and junior high schools across the nation. A bipartisan and bicameral group of lawmakers—Rep. John Boehner, R-Ohio, and Rep. George Miller, D-Calif., and Sen. Edward Kennedy, D-Mass., and Sen. Judd Gregg, R-N.H., worked cooperatively with the administration to win passage of the legislation. Bush took a more partisan approach in pushing Congress to enact the largest across-the-board tax cut ($1.35 trillion) since Ronald Reagan's presidency. Although there were partisan complaints that the tax cut was too large, lawmakers on both sides of the aisle were reluctant to vote against tax reductions for their constituents.

A different legislative dynamic emerged after May 2001, when Vermont GOP senator Jim Jeffords switched parties, and Senate Democrats suddenly found themselves the majority party (Jeffords became an independent but caucused with the Democrats). Democratic control of the Senate produced significant problems for the Bush administration. Now the Democrats could initiate and force votes on their priorities, hold hearings to spotlight their agenda and critique Bush's, modify or block administration bills coming from the GOP House, reject the president's nominations, and require the White House to develop "a defensive strategy for responding to Democratic ideas."[62] Bush responded by renouncing bipartisanship and adopting a partisan model of governance.

But the president soon encountered vocal opposition to many of his ideas in Congress and the country. Polls indicated public concern about the country's direction and revealed that the public preferred the Democrats' positions over GOP ones. By June 2001, Bush's public standing had fallen "to a tepid 50 percent approval rating, the lowest presidential approval rating in more than five years."[63] As a result, congressional Democrats became increasingly optimistic that they could reclaim control of Congress in the midterm elections of November 2002. It was not to be, however.

The Post-9/11 Phase. The George W. Bush presidency was transformed by the terrorist attacks. After an uncertain response during the first days, Bush became a confident, resolute, decisive, and strong commander in chief. Images of the president consoling firemen and others at the site of the World Trade Center, his calm and confident demeanor, and his eloquent statements to the public—including the September 20, 2001, national address before a joint meeting of Congress—rallied the nation to fight a global war against terrorists and the states that provided them safe haven. He called this global struggle "the first war of the twenty-first century," a war that could go on for years or even decades.

Meanwhile, Bush's public approval ratings soared to a record-level 91 percent, breaking his father's record of 89 percent during the 1991 Persian Gulf War.[64] The levels of bipartisanship on Capitol Hill were also remarkable in the first weeks after the terrorist attacks. Congress moved quickly to enact some significant measures, including passage of legislation authorizing the president to employ "all necessary and appropriate force" against those groups or nations involved in the terrorist attacks. Subsequently, as directed by the president, the military ousted the Taliban regime in Afghanistan, which had provided safe haven for Osama bin Laden, the al Qaeda leader behind the September 11 attacks. (On May 2, 2011, the world's most wanted terrorist, Osama bin Laden, was killed at his compound in Pakistan in a daring Navy commando operation authorized by President Obama.)

President Bush's focus then turned to Iraq, a nation he declared to be part of the "axis of evil" that threatened the world. In October 2002, the administration persuaded Congress to enact a joint resolution granting the president unilateral authority to launch a preemptive military strike against Iraq. On March 19, 2003, President Bush went on national television and informed the nation of the start of the war in Iraq. Three weeks later, on April 9, U.S. forces entered Baghdad, ending the regime of longtime dictator Saddam Hussein.

President Bush justified the invasion of Iraq on several grounds: al Qaeda operated in Iraq, and Saddam Hussein was somehow involved in the 9/11 attacks; Saddam had weapons of mass destruction (chemical and biological) and posed a threat to American and world safety; and, as the president stated in his 2003 State of the Union address, Saddam was obtaining uranium from Niger for his nuclear weapons program. However, the rationales for invading Iraq proved to be false. A few weeks before he left office, in a valedictory interview with ABC News, President Bush came close to suggesting that the invasion of Iraq had been a mistake. "The biggest regret of all the presidency has to have been the intelligence failure in Iraq," the president said.[65]

The Iraq war eventually dominated national politics and policy making. It consumed the time and energy of the administration and Congress and divided the country. Reflecting their unhappiness about the Iraq war, President Bush, and political scandals on Capitol Hill, voters put the Democrats in charge of the House and Senate in the November 2006 elections. The return of divided government was a major power shift in national governance in at least two respects: first, the Democratic-controlled Congress launched hard-hitting investigations of executive branch actions—such as contracting abuses in Iraq and in the aftermath of Hurricane Katrina—that had received little attention from Republican Congresses fearful of embarrassing the White House.

Second, Democratic leaders of the 110th Congress worked to restore Congress's role as a "check and balance" by confronting and challenging the president on a range of issues, such as trying to impose a timetable for the withdrawal of U.S. troops from Iraq. During his presidency, Bush and Vice President Richard B. "Dick" Cheney expanded executive power through a combination of unilateral decision making; minimizing, even ignoring, the role of Congress; and interpreting broadly the commander in chief's wartime role. The Democratic Congress devised its legislative strategies and battled the White House in the court of public opinion, but lawmaking on many significant issues proved difficult because of the combined potency of the president's veto and the difficulty in obtaining the sixty votes needed to overcome GOP filibusters in the Senate.

Divided government, a common occurrence since World War II, does not necessarily mean a legislative stalemate. Major policy achievements have occurred during periods of divided government, largely because it prompts the search for bipartisan solutions to difficult problems. Even with heightened partisan tensions between Bush and congressional Democrats, the 110th Congress won enactment of several major laws, such as a $700 billion bailout of banks and financial institutions, a major tightening of ethics rules for lawmakers and lobbyists, higher fuel efficiency standards for automobiles, a new G.I. Bill of Rights for veterans, and a $300 billion reauthorization of a farm bill (overriding Bush's veto).

President Obama confronts an array of overlapping issues that involve the two presidencies because so many of today's problems are transnational in character. They range from global warming to international criminal organizations to global economic crises. No single nation is capable of effectively addressing these global issues alone, nor is any nation insulated from the effects of these issues. If global economic markets are declining, the United States is directly affected—that is, thousands of workers are likely to be laid off because foreign purchasers are not able to buy U.S. exports in the quantities they once did. The president understands that America's prosperity and security are inextricably linked to the well-being of the global economy.

THE VETO POWER

Article I, section 7, of the Constitution requires the president to approve or disapprove bills passed by Congress. When the president disapproves (vetoes) a measure, it dies unless it "shall be repassed by two thirds of the Senate and House of Representatives." Because vetoes are so difficult to override, the veto power transforms the president into, in Woodrow Wilson's words, a "third branch of the legislature."[66] Presidents can usually attract enough of their supporters in Congress to sustain a veto, who may also publicly pledge to sustain vetoes of certain bills to show solidarity with the chief executive. From 1789 through the end of the George W. Bush administration, thirty-six of forty-four presidents exercised their veto authority on 2,562 occasions. Congress overrode these vetoes on 110 occasions (4.3 percent).[67] During his first two years in office, President Obama vetoed just two bills, which is the average (one veto per year) during periods of unified government[68] (see the section "Pocket Vetoes" for more discussion of Obama's two vetoes).

When contemplating a veto, presidents seek advice from numerous administration sources such as agency officials, the Office of Management and Budget, and White House aides. Presidents commonly give various reasons for vetoing a bill: the bill is unconstitutional, it encroaches on the president's independence, it is unwise public policy, it cannot be administered, or it costs too much. Political calculations may underlie any or all of these reasons. The veto is more than a negative power, however. Presidents use the threat of a veto to advance their policy objectives by, for example, inducing legislators to accommodate executive preferences and objections. "We try to use the veto threat wisely, to change votes or to change the language of the underlying document," explained a top White House legislative aide. "And we succeed."[69]

Presidents also practice the politics of differentiation through the veto: a veto fight with Congress may suit presidents who want to underscore how their views differ from the other party's. For its part, Congress can discourage vetoes by adding items to must-pass legislation or to measures the president strongly favors. Congress may also deliberately send the president of the opposite party a measure that lawmakers want him to veto, so that they can use the issue on the campaign trail—a "winning by losing" strategy. Bills may also be signed in a public ceremony closer to the November elections as a way to energize the electoral base of the president's party—another example of the two Congresses.

Veto Options

Once the president receives a bill from Congress, he has ten days (excluding Sundays) in which to exercise one of four options:

1. He can sign the bill. Most public and private bills presented to the president are signed into law. The president also may issue a signing statement that expresses his interpretation of the provisions of the new law.

2. He can return the bill with his veto message to the originating house of Congress.

3. He can take no action, and the bill will become law without his signature. This option, which is seldom employed, is reserved for bills the president dislikes but not enough to veto.

4. He can pocket veto the bill. Under the Constitution, if a congressional adjournment prevents the return of a bill, the bill cannot become law without the president's signature.

Veto Strategies

George H. W. Bush (1989–1993) was among the most successful chief executives in employing the veto against an opposition Congress. He used it to block unwanted legislation and as a potent bargaining weapon to wring concessions from the Democratic-controlled Congress. Not until his term was nearly over, and after thirty-five consecutive veto victories, did Congress manage to override a Bush veto—on a 1992 measure to reregulate the cable television industry. Part of the explanation for Bush's veto successes was that he announced his intentions early and stuck by them unless the compromises he wanted were agreed to. Furthermore, he convinced congressional Republicans that their strength depended on sustaining his vetoes. (Of his forty-six vetoes, only the cable bill veto was overridden by Congress.)

By contrast, President Clinton did not veto a single measure during his first two years in office—something that had not happened since the days of Millard Fillmore in the 1850s. Part of the explanation is that Clinton was dealing with a Democratic Congress. Not until 1995 did Clinton use his veto pen, rejecting an appropriations bill sent to him by the Republican Congress. Subsequently, the president either exercised or threatened to exercise the veto against numerous GOP-sponsored bills.

President George W. Bush claimed that he would not hesitate to use his veto power to enforce his budgetary goals if Congress passed legislation he considered excessive or objectionable. But he did not veto a single bill, spending or otherwise, during his entire first term, although he did issue 145 veto threats during that time. One has to reach back all the way to James Garfield (1881) to find a veto-less president, and Garfield did not even serve a full year before being assassinated. Partial-term presidents William Henry Harrison, Zachary Taylor, and Millard Fillmore never issued a veto, nor did one-termers John Adams and John Quincy Adams. Only Jefferson survived two terms without one.[70]

Several factors account for Bush's no-veto first term: unified Republican control of the House and Senate during much of the period and the resulting consensus on many issues; the refusal of top party leaders, such as Speaker Dennis J. Hastert, R-Ill., to send to the White House bills that Bush might veto; the desire of Republicans to demonstrate their capacity to govern with narrow majorities; the ability of the White House and GOP congressional leaders to work out their disagreements; and the president's pragmatism in redefining his positions "to accommodate the direction in which lawmakers were leaning."[71]

Bush issued his first veto in July 2006 on a stem cell research bill that violated his antiabortion beliefs.[72] With the Democratic takeover of the 110th Congress (2007–2009), the number of vetoes and veto threats increased. Bush vetoed seven measures in 2007 and four more the next year. In 2003, with the GOP in charge of Congress, Bush issued ninety-one statements of administration policy (which often included veto threats); 141 were sent to the Democratic Congress in 2007.[73] Congress overturned four of Bush's twelve vetoes.

The Bush White House sometimes choreographed bill-signing ceremonies to reward supporters and send messages. For example, "Bush signed [a bill dealing with corporate corruption] on a table adorned with a sign saying 'Corporate Responsibility,' a technique used by the White House image-makers to associate the president's picture with the gist of his message."[74] In a first, President Bush invited bloggers as a group to a signing ceremony for a measure creating a database of federal spending—"a recognition of their role in forcing the bill through Congress over the objections of senior senators."[75] For their part, the Democratic leaders of the 110th Congress, Speaker Nancy Pelosi and Senate majority leader Harry Reid, D-Nev., sometimes held their own media-covered signing ceremonies, affixing their signatures to bills before they were sent to the White House.[76]

Like other presidents, Barack Obama has threatened several times to veto measures because of objections to provisions in the legislation. During

President Obama's 2011 State of the Union address, he declared, "If a bill comes to my desk with earmarks in it, I will veto it" (as discussed in Chapter 14, earmarks are special-interest provisions in measures that benefit members' districts or states). The president's threat had a direct effect on the lawmakers. As Senate majority whip Richard Durbin, D-Ill., exclaimed, "We're out of the earmark business."[77]

Once Congress has enacted a bill, it is printed on special paper called "parchment" and delivered by hand to the White House. A copy is also sent to the Government Printing Office for online public distribution.

Post-Veto Action

Just as the president may feel strong pressure to veto or to sign a bill, Congress may feel intense political heat after it receives a veto message. A week after President Nixon's televised veto of a 1970 bill funding welfare programs, House members received more than 55,000 telegrams, most of them urging support for the veto. And Congress did uphold the veto, in part because of Nixon's televised appeal. However, despite a massive telephone campaign to congressional offices (as many as eighty thousand calls an hour) urging members to sustain President Reagan's veto of a 1988 civil rights bill, the House and Senate easily overrode the veto.[78]

Actually, Congress need not act at all on a vetoed bill. If party leaders lack the votes to override, the chamber that receives a vetoed measure may refer it to committee or table it. Even if one house musters the votes to override, the other body may do nothing. A vetoed bill cannot be amended—it is all or nothing at this stage—and the Constitution requires that votes on vetoed bills be recorded.

Signing Statements

At times, presidents issue proclamations called "signing statements" to accompany bills they have signed into law. Even though they are not mentioned in the Constitution, signing statements have been used since James Monroe's presidency (1817–1825). George W. Bush, however, employed them more often than any other president to reassert and strengthen the so-called unitary theory of executive power.[79] As interpreted by Bush, this theory allowed the president to override laws that he claimed would impinge upon his constitutional prerogatives as commander in chief. When Congress banned torture of war prisoners, for example, the president held that the law trespassed on his powers as commander in chief. Ronald Reagan was the first president to use signing statements as a way to challenge congressional enactments on constitutional grounds. Of his 276 signing statements, 71 (or 26 percent) raised constitutional objections. By comparison, 127 (or 85 percent) of President Bush's 149 signing statements contained "multiple constitutional and statutory objections . . . to over 700 distinct provisions of law"[80] (see Box 10-1 for three examples of Bush's signing statements).

Even though the Constitution requires the president to "take care that the laws be faithfully executed," Bush's signing statements asserted that he had "the

BOX 10-1 **Examples of Signing Statements**

	Congressional directive	Signing statement
Intelligence Reform and Terrorism Prevention Act of 2004 (P.L. 108-458) Signed December 17, 2004	Created a position for a national intelligence director in response to past intelligence failures, and required the president to consult with Congress on the person's responsibilities.	"To the extent that provisions of the Act ... purport to require consultation with the Congress as a condition to execution of the law, the executive branch shall construe such provisions as calling for, but not mandating, such consultation."
Fiscal 2006 Defense Appropriations (P.L. 109-148) Signed December 30, 2005	Outlawed "cruel, inhumane or degrading treatment" of suspected terrorists in U.S. custody.	"The executive branch shall construe Title X in Division A of the Act, relating to detainees, in a manner consistent with the constitutional authority of the President to supervise the unitary executive branch and as Commander in Chief."
Department of Defense Appropriations Act, 2007 (P.L. 109-289) Signed September 29, 2006	Blocked money from being spent to process foreign intelligence if it was gathered unlawfully. Stipulated that information gathered on U.S. citizens must comply with constitutional limits on searches and seizures.	"The executive branch shall construe [the provision] in a manner consistent with the President's constitutional authority as Commander in Chief, including for the conduct of intelligence operations, and to supervise the unitary executive branch."

Source: Adapted from Chris Wilson, "Memo to Congress: Bush Asserts Final Say," *CQ Weekly,* October 30, 2006, 2863.

power to set aside the laws when they conflict with his legal interpretation."[81] Signing statements have raised concerns in Congress because they seem to provide the president with an unofficial line-item veto, allowing him to decide which parts of bills to implement or ignore. However, some observers believe that signing statements have little effect on the administration of laws. Studies have shown that "federal agencies seem to have generally complied with thousands of legislative provisions that [Bush] had questioned."[82]

When campaigning for president, Obama criticized President Bush's use of signing statements. As president, Obama vowed he would use such statements with restraint and "only when it is appropriate to do so as a means of discharging my constitutional responsibilities."[83] On March 11, 2009, President Obama issued his first signing statement, "reserving a right to bypass dozens of provisions in a $410 billion government spending bill even as he signed it into law."[84] Sen. Charles E. Grassley, R-Iowa, blasted the signing statement for setting back "whistleblower protections and [violating] two promises with one stroke of the pen."[85] The two promises, according to Grassley, were protecting whistleblowers and avoiding Bush's sentiment that some parts of laws are optional. In a White House memorandum to all departments and agencies, President Obama made clear that signing statements are appropriate in limited circumstances, and that "they promote a healthy dialogue between the executive branch and Congress."[86]

Healthy dialogue or not, Obama's signing statement on a supplemental war funding bill raised the ire of four key Democratic lawmakers, including David Obey, Wis., the Appropriations chair, and Barney Frank, Mass., chair of the Financial Services panel. They warned Obama against overusing signing statements as a way to circumvent congressional intent. The four lawmakers wrote in a letter to the president:

> We were surprised to read your signing statement in which you expressed the view that you are constitutionally free to ignore the conditions duly adopted in the legislative process regarding funding for [the International Monetary Fund and the World Bank]. The policy of using signing statements . . . may result not in the invalidation of those various provisions, but rather in insufficient congressional support for further funding of these institutions.[87]

Pocket Vetoes

The pocket veto has been a source of some controversy and confusion over the years. Article I, section 7, of the Constitution states:

> If any bill shall not be returned by the President within ten days (Sundays excepted) after it shall have been presented to him, the same shall be a law, in like manner as if he had signed it, unless Congress by the adjournment prevents its return, in which case it shall not be a law.

The framers wanted to ensure that presidents would not be forced into signing last-minute legislation and that Congress would have time to consider, and perhaps override, the president's objections. The issue, however, is exactly when a congressional adjournment prevents the return of the president's veto. Several court decisions, such as *Kennedy v. Sampson* (1974), established the principle that pocket vetoes are not to be used during congressional sessions but only after Congress's final adjournment at the end of its second session.

The Ford and Carter administrations adhered to this understanding, but not other administrations. For example, President Reagan twice used intersession (between the first and second sessions) pocket vetoes, and President Clinton employed intrasession (in the middle of a session) pocket vetoes. Clinton even returned the pocket vetoes to Congress, which tried unsuccessfully to override them. In December 2007, President Bush invoked the pocket veto and returned it to the House (which originated the measure) "to leave no doubt the bill is being vetoed." The House majority voiced strong objection, with Speaker Pelosi declaring, "Your successful return of H.R. 1585 establishes that you were not prevented from returning it."[88]

President Obama's two vetoes were what some refer to as "hybrid vetoes" or "protective return" pocket vetoes (see Box 10-2). Obama returned the two unsigned bills to the originating chamber as if he were exercising a regular (or traditional) veto. In both cases, Congress objected to his pocket veto approach, treated it as a regular veto, and sustained the veto.

BOX 10-2   **Deep Presidential Pockets**

When he quietly vetoed his first piece of legislation last week—a stopgap military appropriation that turned out not to have been needed—**Barack Obama** renewed a rather obscure constitutional debate about the way recent administrations have employed the "pocket veto," in which a president fails to either sign or veto a bill after Congress has already adjourned.

In his Dec. 30 "memorandum of disapproval," the term usually applied when announcing a pocket veto, Obama indicated that he was withholding his signature from the short-term continuing resolution that Congress sent him to ensure military spending until the fiscal 2010 Defense spending bill could be signed into law—which Obama had done Dec. 19. But the president also returned the short-term bill to the House.

There is no question that, as Obama asserts in his memorandum, his signing the Defense bill made the short-term continuing resolution unnecessary. But constitutional law experts question whether Obama and other recent presidents who have done the same thing actually have the authority to issue hybrid veto messages that combine both a traditional and pocket veto.

"This never made any sense," says **Louis Fisher**, a specialist on constitutional law at the Library of Congress. "It seems you have either a returned veto or a pocket veto, but not both".

President **Gerald R. Ford** was the first to use one of these "protective return" vetoes, though he agreed to limit its use after a court challenge by Democratic Sen. **Edward M. Kennedy** of Massachusetts, who prevailed in federal District Court, according to Robert Spitzer, a political science professor at the State University of New York at Cortland, who wrote a 2005 book on the presidency and the Constitution.

Nevertheless, presidents of both parties subsequently issued several hybrid vetoes. The most recent example was **George W. Bush's** rejection of the fiscal 2008 defense authorization bill in Dec. 2007. Bush objected to a provision that could have allowed lawsuits against Iraq in U.S. courts for acts committed under **Saddam Hussein's** regime.

Although it may seem like just "constitutional trivia," Spitzer says he views it as a way that presidents of both parties have quietly tried to expand executive power.

Presidents view the pocket veto, originally envisioned as protection against Congress passing laws and then skipping town before a president had a chance to veto them, as particularly attractive because there's no way legislators can override them.

"This whole protective return pocket veto is a back-door way to expand the pocket veto so that the president can use it any time Congress is literally not in session," Spitzer says.

Source: The following is reprinted from Seth Stern, "Deep Presidential Pockets," *CQ Weekly,* January 4, 2010, 10.

Thus it appears that neither an intra- nor an intersession pocket veto prevents its return to Congress. Until the Supreme Court makes a definitive ruling involving the use of the pocket veto both during and between legislative sessions, it is likely that legislative-executive conflicts over the pocket veto will occur periodically. In summary, the scope of the pocket veto power, as public law scholar Louis Fisher has written, "has been left largely to practice and to political understandings developed by the executive and legislative branches."[89]

The Line-Item Veto

Congress's habit of combining numerous items into a single measure obliges the president to accept or reject the entire package. Presidents and supporters of executive power have long advocated allowing the president to veto items selectively. They argue that it would give the president an effective way to eliminate wasteful spending and reduce the federal deficit. Opponents counter that the item veto is about interbranch power and not fiscal restraint. Granting the item veto to the president, they argue, would undermine Congress's power of the purse and give chief executives added bargaining leverage over lawmakers. "The president could say, 'I'm going to zap your dam, but I've got another piece of legislation coming around, and I won't be so inclined to do that [if you support me],'" said Rep. Jack Kingston, R-Ga.[90] Critics also say that presidents already have the only tool they need to control spending: the veto.

After much debate, Congress in 1996 expanded the president's rescission (cancellation of spending) authority. It eventually passed the line-item veto, as part of the "Contract with America," despite concern among congressional Republicans that President Clinton would use it against GOP-passed riders (extraneous policy provisos) in appropriations bills. The Line-Item Veto Act gave the president a fifth veto option. After a president signed a bill into law, he could exercise the line-item veto prerogative to cancel dollar amounts specified in any appropriations law, or even in the accompanying House or Senate committee reports; strike new entitlement programs or expansions of existing programs; and delete tax breaks limited to one hundred or fewer beneficiaries. The measure required the president, after using the line-item veto, to send a special message to Congress identifying what he had rescinded. To overturn his decisions, Congress would have to pass another bill that the president could then veto, requiring Congress to override it by a two-thirds vote of each chamber. Under the law, then, the president could block something if he had the support of only one-third plus one of the members of each chamber. The act became effective on January 1, 1997, and was originally set to expire at the end of 2004.

Contrary to the expectations of pundits, President Clinton exercised caution in his use of the line-item veto. The president apparently chose not to anger lawmakers whose support he might need later to enact administration priorities. As one account noted, the president "has deferred to Congress on the overwhelming majority of projects that members added to budget bills, even when the Administration could find no compelling public interest to justify them."[91]

On June 25, 1998, in the case *Clinton v. New York City,* the Supreme Court by a 6–3 vote held the Line-Item Veto Act to be unconstitutional because it gave the president "unilateral authority to change the text of duly enacted statutes," as Justice John Paul Stevens wrote for the majority.[92] The Clinton administration soon announced that it would release funds for the projects that had been subjected to line-item vetoes.

Since the Court's decision, and in view of today's record expenditures during the economic crisis and heightened concern about wasteful spending, there has been renewed interest in enacting a constitutionally valid line-item veto. For example, Sen. Thomas Carper, D-Del., and Sen. John McCain, R-Ariz., introduced the Unnecessary Spending Act (S. 102) early in the 112th Congress. If enacted, it would grant the president the ability to cancel, or rescind, provisions in appropriations bills. The president would then return his recommendations for cancellation to Congress for expedited consideration in the House and Senate. Ostensibly, the bill would be constitutional because both houses would be required to pass a rescission measure before it might become law. President Obama also supports enactment of enhanced rescission legislation that would guarantee within a specified number of days an up or down vote on a package of spending cuts. Many lawmakers oppose the Carper-McCain bill; they believe it would cede too much power to the president.

SOURCES OF LEGISLATIVE-EXECUTIVE COOPERATION

Unlike the legislative assemblies of many nations where executive authority is lodged in the leader of parliament—called the prime minister or premier—Congress truly is separate from the executive branch. And yet the executive and legislative branches are mutually dependent in policy making. The 124 volumes (as of 2011) of the *United States Statutes at Large* underscore the cooperative impulses of the two branches. Each volume contains the joint product of Congresses and presidents over the years, from the 108 public laws enacted by the First Congress (1789–1791) to the 342 enacted by the 111th Congress (2009–2011). These accomplishments are the result of party loyalties and public expectations, bargaining and compromise, and informal links between the president and lawmakers.

Party Loyalties and Public Expectations

Presidents and congressional leaders have met informally to discuss issues ever since the First Congress, when George Washington frequently sought the advice of Virginia representative James Madison. But meetings between the chief executive and House and Senate leaders were not common until Theodore Roosevelt's administration (1901–1909). Today, congressional party leaders are two-way conduits who communicate legislative views to the president and inform other members of executive preferences and intentions.

A president and the members of his party are linked psychologically and ideologically. This means that "bargaining 'within the family' has a rather different quality than bargaining with members of the rival clan."[93] Congressional Democrats want President Obama to succeed in moving his agenda, even though they do not always share his priorities. As Rep. Chris Van Hollen, Md., said, "Our political fortunes are tied to Barack Obama's" and that the 2010 midterm elections would be "a report card not only on Congress but the White House, too."[94] The voters did in fact send the report card home, and congressional Democrats suffered, as Obama said, a "shellacking."

Bargaining and Compromise

The interdependence of the two branches provides each with the incentive to bargain. Legislators and presidents have in common at least three interests: shaping public policy, winning elections, and attaining influence within the legislature. In achieving these goals, members of Congress may be helped or hindered by executive officials. Agency personnel, for example, can heed legislators' advice in formulating policies, help them gain favorable publicity back home, and give them advance notice of executive actions. Meanwhile, executive officials rely on legislators for help in pushing administrative proposals through the legislative process.

President Obama and his cabinet heads and top aides have courted the legislative branch to gain favorable action on his agenda priorities. During the 111th Congress, Obama spent considerable time with House and Senate Democrats, visiting, for example, with all Senate Democrats at their weekly luncheon session. Sen. Ron Wyden, D-Ore., described how, during a White House meeting with Senate Democrats, the president indicated he was open to a range of budgetary compromises: "If you don't care for ideas that I have, I'm going to be open to alternatives."[95]

Before the Democrats suffered big losses in the November 2010 elections, Obama had had little contact with congressional Republicans, including their House and Senate leaders. However, much to the chagrin of House and Senate Democratic leaders, President Obama met with Senate GOP leader McConnell during the lame-duck session of the 111th Congress. As noted earlier, they reached a deal to extend the Bush-era tax cuts for two years for everyone, including the wealthy (the tax cuts were set to expire December 31, 2010). In return, the president received Republican support for an extension of jobless benefits and a Social Security payroll tax cut.

Many congressional Democrats were furious with Obama for reversing his position. After all, during the 2008 campaign Obama had pledged he would let the Bush tax cuts expire for the wealthy but not for the middle class. In the end, though, many Democrats voted for the bipartisan agreement. As Sen. Sherrod Brown, D-Ohio, explained, "I think that we know that he's our ally, that his success is our success, [and that] we fight for, overwhelmingly, the same things.

We've had differing views on how to go about the [tax extension] negotiations, but I have differences with my wife too."[96]

Informal Links

Some presidents deal with Congress more adeptly than others. Lyndon Johnson assiduously courted members. He summoned legislators to the White House for private meetings, danced with their wives at parties, telephoned greetings on their birthdays, and hosted them at his Texas ranch. He also knew how to twist arms to win support for his programs. Johnson's understanding of what moved members and energized Congress was awe-inspiring. "There is only one way for a President to deal with the Congress," he said, "and that is continuously, incessantly, and without interruption."[97]

President Obama meets periodically with the bicameral leadership—the Speaker, House minority leader, Senate majority leader, and Senate minority leader—to discuss issues of common concern. His top legislative aides are present at every key stage of a bill's development, suggesting ways to resolve contentious issues. As a former senator, the president also has informal and friendly relationships with many lawmakers, such as Sen. Tom Coburn, R-Okla. Meanwhile, Vice President Joe Biden is serving as a lead liaison to the House and Senate, working with lawmakers to, for example, craft agreements on tax and budget issues.[98]

Since the 2010 midterm elections, in an effort to establish a personal relationship with Speaker Boehner and Senate GOP leader McConnell, President Obama has had them to the White House for lunch and has telephoned them—that is, he has reached out to them more frequently. His goal is to build rapport, mutual understanding, and a common bond. McConnell—who stated after the 2010 elections that his number-one priority was to make Obama a one-term president—joked that he is "talking so much to the president that he's on Obama's speed dial."[99] Speaker Boehner said he talks with the president "every couple of weeks" and that their relationship is open, honest, and fair.[100]

Whether the informal personal discussions between or among these three national leaders lead to more productive problem-solving remain's to be seen. "These kinds of relationships just don't pop up out of the air or out of necessity," observed a former aide to Speaker Boehner. "They require trust, and they take time. You just don't grow that necessary trust and relationship overnight."[101] Presidential scholars suggest, however, that the chief executive's style and skills affect legislative success only "at the margins."[102] Far more important are contextual factors: the mood of the country, the state of the economy, the popularity of the president, and, most especially, the president's partisan strength in Congress.

SOURCES OF LEGISLATIVE-EXECUTIVE CONFLICT

Legislative-executive conflicts were evident in 1789, they are present today, and they can be expected in the future for at least three reasons. First, the Constitution specifies neither the precise policy-making roles of Congress and the president nor the manner in which they are to deal with one another. Second, presidents and Congresses serve different constituencies. Third, important variations exist in the timetables under which the two branches operate.

Constitutional Ambiguities

Article I invests Congress with "all legislative powers," but it also authorizes the president to recommend and to veto legislation. In several specific areas the Constitution splits authority between the president and Congress. The Senate, for example, is the president's partner in treaty making and nominations under "advice and consent" clauses. And before treaties can take effect, they require the concurrence of two-thirds of the Senate. The Constitution is silent, however, on how or when the Senate is to render its advice to the president.[103]

In 1919 and 1920, a historic confrontation occurred when the Senate vehemently opposed the Treaty of Versailles negotiated by President Woodrow Wilson. The treaty contained an agreement binding the United States to the proposed League of Nations. Many senators had warned the president against including the League provision in the treaty, and during floor deliberations the Senate added several reservations that the president strongly opposed. Spurning compromise, Wilson launched a nationwide speaking tour to mobilize popular support for the treaty. Not to be outdone, senators opposed to the pact organized a "truth squad" that trailed the president and rebutted his arguments. During his tour, Wilson suffered a stroke from which he never fully recovered. And in the end, the treaty was rejected. This historical example illustrates that, under the Constitution's separation of powers, presidents' abilities to achieve even their most urgent foreign policy goals are limited by Congress's institutional prerogatives.

Different Constituencies

Presidents and their vice presidents are the only public officials elected nationally. To win, they must create vastly broader electoral coalitions than are necessary for legislators, who represent either states or districts. Only presidents, then, can claim to speak for the nation at large. It is important to note, however, that

> there is no structural or institutional or theoretical reason why the representation of a "single" broader constituency by the President is necessarily better or worse than the representation of many "separate" constituencies by several hundred legislators. Some distortion is inevitable in either arrangement, and the question of the good or evil of either form of distortion simply leads one back to varying value judgments.[104]

Presidents and legislators tend to view policies and problems from different perspectives. Members of Congress often subscribe to the view that "what's good for Portland is good for the nation." Presidents are apt to say that "what's good for the nation is good for Portland."

In other words, public officials may view common issues differently when they represent diverging interests. For example, a president might wish to reduce international trade barriers. A representative from a district where a manufacturer is threatened by imported products is likely to oppose the president's policy, whereas retailers of imported products are likely to support the president. The challenge to national policy making is to forge consensus within an electorate that simultaneously holds membership in two or more competing constituencies.

Disparities in constituencies are underscored by differences in the ways voters judge presidents and members of Congress. Studies of presidential popularity ratings suggest that presidents are judged on the basis of general factors—economic boom or bust, the presence or absence of wars or other crises, the impact of policies on given groups.[105] The news media, too, can affect the assessment of presidents. Legislators, by contrast, tend to be assessed on the basis of their personalities, their communication with constituents, and their service in material ways to the state or district. Not only do presidents and legislators serve different constituencies, but they also labor under divergent incentives.

Different Time Perspectives

Finally, Congress and the president operate on different timetables. Presidents have four years, at most eight, to win adoption of their programs. They are usually in a hurry to achieve all they can before they leave office. In practice, they have even less time because of the typical falloff in presidential support after the initial "honeymoon." Indeed, presidents and their advisers actually often have a year, perhaps less, to sell their basic programs to Congress and the public. "A president's most effective year is his first," explained Sen. Richard Durbin, D-Ill., President Obama's close friend and confidant. "He is brand new to the office, has a national mandate of varying degrees, and Congress is usually more open to working with him. After the first year, an election year is under way and people look at him differently."[106] Presidents think in terms of four years; most lawmakers think in terms of two.

On major, long-standing issues, however, Congress typically moves slowly. Seldom does it pass presidential initiatives quickly unless an emergency or crisis of some sort is looming. Moreover, many legislators are careerists. Once elected, House members are likely to be reelected, and senators serve six-year terms. Most members hold office a good deal longer than the presidents they deal with. Skeptical legislators, reluctant to follow the president, realize that if they resist long enough someone else will occupy the White House.

THE BALANCE OF POWER

"The relationship between the Congress and the presidency," wrote Arthur M. Schlesinger Jr., "has been one of the abiding mysteries of the American system of government."[107] Part of the mystery inheres in the Constitution, which enumerates many powers for Congress as well as those "necessary and proper" to carry them out, while leaving the president's powers largely unstated. Where does the balance of power lie? There is no easy answer, but at certain times the scale has tipped toward Congress and at other times toward the president. Scholars have even identified periods of "congressional government" or "presidential government."[108]

Four points need to be remembered about the ups and downs of Congress and the presidency. First, even during periods in which one branch appears to dominate, the actual balance of power in specific policy areas is complex. The stature of either branch is influenced by issues, events, partisan circumstances, personalities, or public opinion.

The mid-1960s and early 1970s, for example, are cited as a time of "imperial presidents" and compliant Congresses.[109] Although Congress enacted much of President Johnson's Great Society program, it also initiated scores of laws, including consumer, environmental, health, and civil rights legislation. Nor did executive actions go unchallenged. Nationally televised hearings conducted in 1966 by the Senate Foreign Relations Committee helped to mobilize congressional and public opposition to the Vietnam War. The refrain "imperial presidents" and compliant Congresses was heard again when Republicans were in charge of Congress from 2001 to 2007 and George W. Bush was in the White House. But Congress was by no means passive during that period.

Second, power also shifts within each branch. In Congress, aggressive leaders may be followed by less assertive leaders. In the executive branch, the forces for White House leadership regularly battle the forces for agency decentralization. These internal power fluctuations clearly affect policy making. During the Eisenhower presidency in the 1950s, powerful committee and party leaders could normally deliver blocs of votes to pass legislation. Today, even with the resurgence of partisanship on Capitol Hill, the president can never be sure which of the 535 members will form a winning coalition.

Third, legislative-executive relationships are not zero-sum games. If one branch gains power, the other does not necessarily lose it. If one branch is up, the other need not be down. The expansion of the federal government since World War II has augmented the authority of both branches. Their growth rates were different, but each expanded its ability to address complex issues, initiate legislation, and frustrate the proposals of the other. According to the conventional wisdom, wars, crises, nuclear weapons, military expansion, and public demands fostered the imperial presidency. Such factors certainly enlarge the likelihood of executive dominance, but in the wars of 1812 and 1898, for example, military action was encouraged in part by aggressive Congresses. Economic panics and depressions under Presidents James Monroe, James Buchanan, and Ulysses S. Grant did not lead to losses of congressional power.

Political scientist David Mayhew has asserted that, with respect to productivity of laws and investigations, it "does not seem to make all that much difference whether party control of the American government happens to be unified or divided."[110] Mayhew examined the period from 1946 to 1990, when the mobilization of cross-party majorities on Capitol Hill was commonplace. President Ronald Reagan, for example, enjoyed large successes on his policy priorities (tax cuts, defense hikes, and program reductions) in 1981 when he won the support of conservative "Reagan Democrats" in the Democratic-controlled House. Today, in an era of strong, largely cohesive, and ideologically distinct congressional parties—reflecting the conditional party government model discussed in Chapter 6—presidents confront a heightened potential for partisan impasses, especially in the Senate, regardless of whether the government is unified or divided.

Conflict between Congress and the president is embedded in the system of separation of powers and checks and balances. But the founders also expected their governmental arrangement to promote accommodation between the branches. Historical patterns have veered between these two extremes. The two branches worked together in the early days of Woodrow Wilson's progressive New Freedom (1913–1916), during the New Deal (1933–1937) and World War II (1941–1945), during the brief Great Society years (1964–1966) following John F. Kennedy's assassination in 1963, for the even briefer "Reaganomics" juggernaut during Ronald Reagan's first year in office (1981), during most of George W. Bush's first six years in office (2001–2007), and during Barack Obama's first two years (2009–2010). At other times, the two branches fought fiercely—during Wilson's second term (1919–1921); after 1937 during the Franklin Roosevelt administration; after 1966 during the Lyndon Johnson administration; and for much of the Nixon, Reagan, George H. W. Bush, and Clinton administrations, and the final two years of George W. Bush's presidency.

Finally, a wide gap often separates what presidents want from what they can achieve. Congress can influence what, when, how, or even whether executive recommendations are sent to Capitol Hill. Expectations of what will pass Congress frequently shape White House agendas. This indirect priority-setting power of the House and Senate can affect whether the president even transmits certain proposals to Congress. It also works in the other direction. Recommendations may be forwarded or endorsed because the White House knows they have broad legislative support. "The president proposes, Congress disposes" is an oversimplified adage.

Congress and the president are institutions shaped by diverging imperatives. Executive officials want flexibility, discretion, and long-range commitments from Congress. They prefer few controls and consultations with a limited number of legislators. The executive tends to be hierarchical, or vertical, in decision making, whereas Congress tends to be collegial and horizontal—with power spread among 535 independent-minded lawmakers. One of the legislative branch's strengths is that it is able to give voice and visibility to diverse viewpoints that the executive branch may have overlooked or ignored. The dispersion of power can slow down decision making, but it also can promote public acceptance of the nation's policies. Thus what are often viewed as Congress's vices are also genuine virtues.

CONCLUSION

Conflict would seem to be the inevitable result of a system that intentionally divides lawmaking and other powers between the executive and legislative branches. Much of the relationship between Congress and the executive, however, is better characterized as accommodation than as conflict. Neither branch is monolithic. Presidents find supporters in both chambers even when presidents are opposed by congressional majorities. Both branches seek support for their policy preferences from each other and from outside allies. Congress and the president must find ways to work together to achieve common goals.

Nevertheless, confrontation is a recurring element in dealings between Capitol Hill and the White House. The framers of the Constitution consciously distributed and mixed power among the three branches. They left it unclear how Congress or the president would assert control over the bureaucracy and over policy making. Even when both houses of Congress are controlled by the same party as the White House, the two branches have different constituencies and often become adversaries.

Finally, legislative-executive relations are constantly evolving. Either branch may be active on an issue at one time and passive at another time. So many circumstances affect how, when, what, or why shifts occur in the relationship that it is impossible to predict the outlook.

Over the past generation, Congress clearly has equipped itself with a formidable arsenal of resources. As a result, it can play a more active role, initiating policies of its own and overseeing executive branch actions. This development need not be a formula for stalemate. "Our proper objective," counseled Sen. J. William Fulbright, D-Ark. (1945–1974), "is neither a dominant presidency nor an aggressive Congress but, within the strict limits of what the Constitution mandates, a shifting of the emphasis according to the needs of the time and the requirements of public policy."[111]

Government Regulators— *A Far-flung Bureaucracy.* Securities and Exchange Commission chair Mary Schapiro and Commodity Futures Trading Commission CFTC chair Gary Gensler (top left) examine their records while testifying before House Financial Services Committee. (Top right), Rep. Darrell Issa, R-Calif. (center), now chair of the House Oversight and Government Reform Committee, leads his party's oversight of the Obama administration, with former chair Edolphus Towns, D-N.Y., looking on. A Transportation Safety Administration (TSA) officer (middle left) shows a passenger how to go through a full-body scanner at Washington's Dulles International Airport. Another passenger (middle right) finds a unique way to protest TSA's intrusion of privacy at Phoenix Sky Harbor Airport. President Obama (bottom) makes his fourth trip to examine the Gulf oil spill damage—this time in southern Alabama with local officials and Coast Guard Admiral Thad Allen, his on-the-scene coordinator.

Congress and the Bureaucracy

I n 1996 President Bill Clinton proclaimed, "The era of big government is over." Today, the era of big government is back, if it ever went away. The national government has grown under presidents of both parties throughout the modern era. The administration of Republican president George W. Bush oversaw substantial governmental growth, only in part triggered by new domestic security, law enforcement, and military requirements after the terrorist attacks of September 11, 2001. As journalist David S. Broder wrote, President Bush presided over one of the largest expansions of government in history: "He has created a mammoth Cabinet department [Department of Homeland Security], increased federal spending, imposed new federal rules on local and state governments, and injected federal requirements into every public school in America."[1]

In January 2009, Democratic president Barack Obama took office in the midst of the most serious national economic crisis since the Great Depression. Even though the National Bureau of Economic Research declared that the recession technically ended in June 2009, unemployment in early 2011 still exceeded 9 percent, with home foreclosures continuing to spread and one in seven Americans (44 million) living below the poverty line, the highest level in half a century.[2] The government intervened dramatically in the marketplace, spending trillions of taxpayer dollars to try and revive the ailing economy. The effort undoubtedly helped halt the recession's downward spiral, perhaps preventing another depression. "Not since Lyndon B. Johnson and Franklin D. Roosevelt," wrote a congressional journalist, has a president like Obama "moved to expand the role of government so much on so many fronts—and with such a demanding sense of urgency."[3] As one scholar said about this government-directed model of capitalism:

> We've gone from debates over privatizing the public sector to big steps toward governmentalizing the private sector. We're writing this new social contract with three guides: more public money in the private economy, more rules to shape how the private sector behaves, and more citizen expectations that government will manage the risks we face.[4]

Public reaction against "governmentalizing" the economy and escalating spending contributed to, as President Obama put it, the "shellacking" congressional Democrats received in the November 2010 elections. The landslide GOP victory occurred for many reasons. One factor was the emergence of a resurgent conservative movement led by the so-called Tea Party, for whom a smaller and fiscally responsible government is a top priority. Fully 86 percent of Tea Party supporters, according to exit polls of voters in the 2010 congressional elections, "want less government intrusion on people and businesses."[5] Whether this cutback sentiment leads to less expansive and expensive government remains unclear at this juncture. Five weeks after the November 2010 elections, a reporter asked President Obama if the era of big government was over. The president answered: "It's not an issue of big government versus small government. It's an issue of smart government," where "we can probably do more and do it smarter with less money, if we are actually making some tough choices."[6]

Why is it difficult for presidents or Congress to shrink the size, role, or reach of the federal government? Setting aside war and other national crises, one basic reason is the ambivalence of the public. Although they profess to wanting to get the government off their backs, Americans of virtually all ideological persuasions often turn to the government to help fulfill their goals and to provide assistance during times of need. As William S. Cohen, former GOP senator from Maine (1979–1997) and defense secretary during the Clinton administration, put it: "The government is the enemy until one needs a friend."[7]

The paradox, then, is that citizens and groups such as the Tea Party oppose the general idea of big government, but they support many of the government's specific roles—and may even welcome selective expansion of those roles—in ensuring clean air and water, a strong national defense, access to quality health care, the safety of food and prescription drugs, crime prevention, and protection from terrorist attacks. Understandably, lawmakers typically defend government programs supported by their constituents. To implement any government program, an organized bureaucracy is required—often federal *and* state bureaucracies.

The recent expansion of the federal government has spawned a wave of interest in "states' rights." Governors, state legislatures, and attorneys general have shown no reluctance to challenge federal authority. Legislative leaders in twelve states, for example, back a "repeal amendment" to the U.S. Constitution that would permit any federal law or regulation to be overturned "if the legislatures of two-thirds of the states voted to do so."[8] Many states, too, have adopted "sovereignty resolutions," which allow state legislatures, referendums, or special conventions to declare federal laws, such as the recent health care reforms, "null and void within their state borders."[9]

Tension is common in the U.S. system of federalism, in part because of conflicts over which level of government can best perform what types of functions. The federal government can preempt state laws or impose federal mandates on the states. When the national government fails to address important issues (such as immigration, energy conservation, or climate change), states step in to deal with them. Meanwhile, the national government looks to the states for ideas and innovations. For example, President Obama's landmark health care overhaul plan was patterned after various state initiatives. The reality is that today's federal-state relationship is usually more symbiotic than confrontational. Each level of government needs the other. Washington relies on the states to administer various national programs, and states rely on federal resources to fund many of their health care, transportation, and education priorities.

The two Congresses contribute to an expanding bureaucracy. In today's complex and interdependent world, constituents typically look to the national government rather than the private sector to secure collective goods such as security, justice, and protection. Members of Congress respond to their constituents' demands. Regardless of which party is in control, the national government is not reluctant to supersede state authority to regulate electricity, define what constitutes drunk driving, or combat child abductions. Similarly, nationwide corporations often lobby for federal regulation so they do not have to contend with the different rules of the fifty states. Indeed, businesses often prefer federal regulations because these are sometimes "considerably weaker than those being imposed these days by many of the tougher states."[10] As former senator Ernest F. Hollings, D-S.C. (1966–2005), said, "We have armies who protect us from enemies from without and the [Federal Bureau of Investigation] protects us from enemies within. We have Social Security to protect us from the ravages of old age. We have Medicare to protect us from ill health. We have clean air and clean water [laws] to protect our environment. We have [laws that mandate] safe working places and safe machinery. Our fundamental duties here are to protect."[11]

CONGRESS ORGANIZES THE EXECUTIVE BRANCH

Just as the president and Congress share influence over lawmaking, they share responsibility for the executive branch of government—the bureaucracy. The Constitution requires the president to implement the laws, and by implication it empowers him to manage the executive branch. But Congress "has at least as much to do with executive administration as does an incumbent of the White House."[12] Congress is constitutionally authorized to organize and fund the executive branch. The Framers, of course, did not foresee the huge federal bureaucracy that has arisen from their sparse references to "executive departments." George Washington supervised only three departments (State, War, and Treasury); Barack Obama heads fifteen. Beyond the cabinet departments, the federal bureaucracy also includes independent agencies (such as the Central Intelligence Agency), independent regulatory commissions, and government corporations (see Figure 11-1).

Congress has extensive influence over the structure and composition of the federal bureaucracy.[13] Among other things, it can enact statutes that

FIGURE 11-1 The Government of the United States

The Constitution

Legislative Branch

Congress

Senate **House**

Architect of the Capitol
U.S. Botanic Garden
Government Accountability Office
Government Printing Office
Library of Congress
Congressional Budget Office

Executive Branch

The President
The Vice President

Executive Office of the President

White House Office
Office of the Vice President
Council of Economic Advisers
Council on Environmental Quality
National Security Council
Office of Administration
Office of Management and Budget
Office of National Drug Control Policy
Office of Policy Development
Office of Science and Technology Policy
Office of the U.S. Trade Representative

Judicial Branch

The Supreme Court of the United States

Article III Courts:
U.S. Circuit Courts of Appeals
U.S. District Courts
Territorial Courts
U.S. Court of International Trade
Administrative Office of the U.S. Courts
Federal Judicial Center
U.S. Sentencing Commission

Article I Courts:
U.S. Court of Federal Claims
U.S. Court of Appeals for the Armed Forces
U.S. Tax Court
U.S. Court of Veterans Appeals

Agriculture Department	Commerce Department	Defense Department	Education Department	Energy Department
Health and Human Services Department	Homeland Security Department	Housing and Urban Development Department	Interior Department	Justice Department
Labor Department	State Department	Transportation Department	Treasury Department	Veterans Affairs Department

Independent Establishments and Government Corporations

African Development Foundation
Broadcasting Board of Governors
Central Intelligence Agency
Commodity Futures Trading Commission
Consumer Product Safety Commission
Corporation for National and Community Service
Defense Nuclear Facilities Safety Board
Environmental Protection Agency
Equal Employment Opportunity Commission
Export-Import Bank of the U.S.
Farm Credit Administration
Federal Communications Commission
Federal Deposit Insurance Corporation
Federal Election Commission
Federal Housing Finance Board
Federal Labor Relations Authority
Federal Maritime Commission
Federal Mediation and Conciliation Service
Federal Mine Safety and Health Review Commission
Federal Reserve System

Federal Retirement Thrift Investment Board
Federal Trade Commission
General Services Administration
Inter-American Foundation
Merit Systems Protection Board
National Aeronautics and Space Administration
National Archives and Records Administration
National Capital Planning Commission
National Credit Union Administration
National Foundation on the Arts and the Humanities
National Labor Relations Board
National Mediation Board
National Railroad Passenger Corporation (Amtrak)
National Science Foundation
National Transportation Safety Board
Nuclear Regulatory Commission
Occupational Safety and Health Review Commission
Office of the Director of National Intelligence
Office of Government Ethics

Office of Personnel Management
Office of Special Counsel
Overseas Private Investment Corporation
Peace Corps
Pension Benefit Guaranty Corporation
Postal Rate Commission
Railroad Retirement Board
Securities and Exchange Commission
Selective Service System
Small Business Administration
Social Security Administration
Tennessee Valley Authority
Trade and Development Agency
U.S. Arms Control and Disarmament Agency
U.S. Commission on Civil Rights
U.S. Information Agency
U.S. International Development Cooperation Agency
U.S. International Trade Commission
U.S. Postal Service

Source: The United States Government Manual, 2009–2010 (Washington, DC: Office of the Federal Register, Government Printing Office), 21.

TABLE 11-1 **Growth of the Cabinet**	
Department	Year created
State	1789
Treasury	1789
War (reorganized and renamed Defense in 1947)	1789
Interior	1849
Justice (position of attorney general created in 1789)	1870
Agriculture	1889
Commerce (created as Commerce and Labor)	1903
Labor (split from Commerce and Labor)	1913
Health, Education, and Welfare (reorganized and renamed Health and Human Services in 1979)	1953
Housing and Urban Development	1965
Transportation	1966
Energy	1977
Education	1980
Veterans Affairs	1989
Homeland Security	2002

Source: CQ Daily Monitor, January 10, 2003, 3.

establish or abolish executive agencies and departments (see Table 11-1). The newest cabinet creation is the Department of Homeland Security (DHS). Congress can also instruct departments and agencies to reorganize themselves or establish an outside commission to recommend how departments or agencies might be merged or abolished. Or it can authorize the president to reorganize on his own initiative or to propose reorganization plans that will then be subject to some form of congressional review. In addition to establishing federal entities such as DHS, Congress extends its long arm into the bureaucracy in many different ways. The Senate confirms (or not, as the case may be) presidential appointments of high-level officials. Congress authorizes the basic personnel systems of federal entities. It also grants rule-making authority to administrative agencies.

Senate Confirmation of Presidential Appointees

High-level federal appointments—executive, diplomatic, and judicial—are subject to the Senate's "advice and consent" under Article II, section 2, of the Constitution. After the president has decided whom to nominate, the Senate decides whether to confirm (see Figure 11-2).

FIGURE 11-2   **The Appointments Process**

Source: Reprinted with permission of The Free Press, a Division of Simon & Schuster, Inc., from *The Politics of Presidential Appointments* by G. Calvin MacKenzie. Copyright © 1981 by the Free Press. All rights reserved.

Senators use their confirmation power to wield influence over executive branch priorities. Senate committees usually elicit the following promise from departmental and agency nominees they have confirmed: "The above nomination [a cabinet secretary, for example] was approved subject to the nominee's commitment to respond to requests to appear and testify before any duly constituted committee of the Senate."[14] Or as Sen. Charles Grassley, R-Iowa, declared, "I'm going to hit every [Obama] nominee with the question, 'Are you open to congressional oversight?'"[15] The confirmation process also reflects the two Congresses principle. As a top Senate official once remarked, "It looks very, very good in California or some place to put out a press release that says, 'Today, I questioned the new Secretary of Transportation about the problems of our area.'"[16]

Presidents can bypass the Senate's advice and consent role in three broad ways. Constitutionally, presidents can make recess appointments during Senate breaks, either within or between sessions.[17] The Constitution (Article II, section 2) provides that "[t]he President shall have Power to fill up all Vacancies that may happen during a Recess of the Senate, by granting Commissions which shall expire at the End of their next Session." Recess appointees then serve until the end of the next Senate session—for example, a person named in 2011 could serve until late 2012. Presidential recess appointments are not unusual. During his two terms in office, President George W. Bush made 171 recess appointments, "surpassing Bill Clinton's 139 recess appointments."[18] President Obama, after two years, made twenty-eight recess appointments, compared with Bush's twenty-three for the same time period.[19]

Senators often resent presidential use of this option. Upset with President Obama's recess appointment of a physician to head the Centers for Medicare and Medicaid Services, GOP leader Mitch McConnell of Kentucky retaliated by blocking floor debate on two of Obama's judicial nominees.[20] Moreover, when senators left town for six weeks for the November 2, 2010, midterm elections, Senator McConnell won a key concession from Democratic majority leader Harry Reid of Nevada. In exchange for not blocking fifty-four of Obama's nominations and not invoking a Senate rule that returns nominations to the White House if they have not been acted on for more than thirty days,[21] (McConnell won Reid's promise that he would keep the Senate in *pro forma* session during the six-week period.) In a *pro forma* session, the Senate convenes for only a few seconds each day during a recess and thus would technically be able to act on nominations received from the White House.[22] Use of these sessions prevented President Obama from using recess appointments for people opposed by Senate Republicans.

The president can also name individuals, on a temporary acting basis, to fill vacant positions that require confirmation by the Senate. Senate dissatisfaction with this procedure led to enactment of the Federal Vacancies Reform Act of 1998 (P.L. 105-277), which imposed time restrictions on how long officials can serve in an acting capacity, typically 210 days. In some cases, Congress has enacted laws that permit the president, an agency head, or an automatic mechanism to fill temporary vacancies. For example, if the director of the Office and Management and Budget (OMB) is absent or unable to serve, the deputy director then acts as the OMB director.[23]

Many prominent officials, such as White House advisers, are not subject to the advice and consent of the Senate. President Obama may be a record-breaker in naming so many individuals, informally called "czars," to head up important policy initiatives—the "environmental czar," the "economic czar," the "information czar."[24] Czars oversee and coordinate the forming of coherent policies that cut across the jurisdictions of several departments and agencies. For example, Harvard professor Elizabeth Warren was asked to set up the new Bureau of Consumer Financial Protection in the Treasury Department. The bureau was created as part of the landmark financial regulatory reform bill (P.L. 111-203), and she was largely the intellectual force behind its creation. Because of significant Senate opposition to Warren, President Obama bypassed the nominations process and named Warren an assistant to the president and special adviser to the Treasury secretary. GOP senator Bob Corker of Tennessee dubbed Warren "the czar of all czars."[25]

The appointment of numerous czars reflects the amassing of further power in the White House. Sen. Robert C. Byrd, D-W.Va., objected to Obama naming multiple czars because they are not answerable to Congress, they confuse the lines of administrative authority, and they "obscure the decisionmaking process."[26] Yale law professor Bruce Ackerman added, "We need to seriously consider requiring Senate approval of senior White House staff positions."[27] And yet the slow pace of confirmations no doubt provides incentives for presidents to name policy czars as a way to avoid lengthy Senate approval.

Indeed, today nominations to high-level executive posts are subject to standards of judgment and evaluation that go far beyond reasonable questions of competence or conflict of interest; nominees' personal lives and backgrounds are scrutinized as well. As one commentator explained:

> These days, if you want to run for office or accept a position of public trust, everything is relevant. Your moral, medical, legal and financial background, even your college records, become the subject of public scrutiny. In the old days, the scrutiny was done in private, and certain transgressions could be considered irrelevant.[28]

This shift in standards stems in part from a change in attitudes by the press, the public, the White House, and the Senate. The press, for example, now more aggressively reports on the private activities of public officials.[29] In the 1980s, use of marijuana could derail nominees. In the 1990s, it was hiring an illegal immigrant as a nanny or domestic helper. In 2009 tax issues caused problems for several of Obama's top nominees, such as Thomas Daschle, the former Senate Democratic leader. He was forced to withdraw as the president's choice to head the Department of Health and Human Services because of his failure to pay $146,000 in taxes.[30] This trend is also driven in large measure by a hyperpartisan environment in which the president's opponents seek to embarrass or obstruct the administration at every turn.

These developments have produced a rigorous vetting process for nominees. Each nominee must fill out several lengthy questionnaires and undergo security checks. According to Norman Ornstein, "Each security check is a massive operation, involving up to 40 face-to-face interviews, and is basically the same for the assistant secretary of Education for public affairs as it is for the Secretary of State."[31] The Senate Finance Committee "borrowed" staff from the Internal Revenue Service (IRS) to examine the tax returns of Obama's nominees. Investigators from the White House, Federal Bureau of Investigation (FBI), the IRS, and Senate ask nominees difficult and uncomfortable questions about their personal and professional lives. "I have never been subjected to such personally insulting and expensive scrutiny in my life," said one Obama nominee, who was asked for receipts for furniture he donated to charity more than a decade ago. Another nominee was asked about "his wife's sexual activity when she was at university."[32] The importance of a thorough vetting process was emphasized by an Obama adviser: "The real purpose of vetting is to understand the person's ability to perform the job and be confirmed for the position. We also want to avoid surprises."[33] "Avoiding surprises" is a goal not always achieved. For example, Treasury secretary Timothy Geithner encountered unexpected tax problems that delayed his eventual confirmation.

A study by the Brookings Institution, a Washington, D.C.–based think tank, found that one result of the rigorous vetting process is a drop-off in "the number of talented Americans willing to accept the call to presidential [service]. Presidential recruiters report that it takes more calls to find candidates willing to subject themselves to the process and more work to keep the candidates from bolting once the process begins."[34]

Today, there is substantial frustration with the confirmation process. "The nomination system is a national disgrace," wrote a scholar of the presidential appointment process.[35] The problems are many, afflicting the administrations of both parties—even when the same party controls the White House and the Senate. Although the Senate eventually confirms most nominees, three concerns with the process merit mention.

First, it takes longer and longer to fill the full-time cabinet and agency positions requiring Senate confirmation. Whereas President John F. Kennedy had his administrative appointees in place by April 1961, only 2.4 months after his inauguration, "the first Bush administration was not fully confirmed until early October [1989], and the Clinton administration not until mid-October [1993], more than eight months after the start of their respective presidencies."[36] Four months into George W. Bush's first-term administration, "only 11 percent of its most senior government positions" had been filled.[37] For Bush's second term, however, all of his new cabinet secretaries were in place by mid-February 2005, with most confirmed during January. Public administration expert Paul C. Light studied five hundred of Obama's nominees for full-time jobs in his administration "and found they've waited an average of more than nine months to be confirmed, longer than at any time since the 1960s."[38] About two hundred of Obama's nominations remained pending before the Senate nearly two years into his term. As White House press secretary Robert Gibbs noted, "There is certainly an advise and consent, a very important [constitutional] provision. It is not advise, delay and consent. It should not be that way."[39]

To try and resolve this problem as well as related issues, the bipartisan Senate leadership created on the opening day of the 112th Congress a "working group," headed by Senators Charles Schumer, D-N.Y., and Lamar Alexander, R-Tenn., to suggest reforms to the confirmation process.[40] The working group, with the support of the bipartisan leadership, recommended that a statute be developed to reduce the number of executive positions from fourteen hundred to about a thousand that require Senate confirmation. Schumer and Alexander "singled out assistant secretary posts for legislative affairs and communications, as well as part-time members of commissions, for exemption."[41] This proposal aims "to ease the Senate workload while speeding the ability of the White House to fill jobs."[42]

Second, the expanding bureaucracy contributes to the slowness of the confirmation process. Congress and the president have created more executive positions requiring Senate confirmation. President Kennedy nominated fifteen undersecretaries and eighty-seven assistant secretaries in 1961; President George W. Bush appointed almost fifty undersecretaries and more than 220 assistant secretaries.[43] For his fifteen cabinet departments, President Obama must fill more than seven hundred positions, all confirmable by the Senate. Overall, when other agencies are included in the count 1,141 positions must be confirmed by the Senate.[44] Senators sometimes complain that confirmation delays are the result of presidents' dilatoriness in nominating individuals to fill executive positions.

In the 1970s, writes Paul Light, "Congress discovered executive structure . . . and began to mine it."[45] Since then, Congress and the president have made many changes in the top four layers of officials in cabinet departments (secretary, deputy secretary, undersecretary, and assistant secretary), all while creating more new job titles in the top echelons of government than ever before. The result is additional layers of bureaucracy—in some federal agencies as many as fifty layers are between the president and frontline executive employees—"a bureaucratic fog in which Congress and the president are hopelessly isolated from the people they most need to guide."[46] Among the numerous new titles are deputy associate deputy secretary, principal assistant deputy undersecretary, principal senior deputy assistant secretary, deputy associate assistant secretary, and deputy executive associate administrator.[47]

As a result of "title creep," Light explains that it is difficult to know whom to hold accountable for what goes wrong in the executive branch, and "impossible for the bottom to hear the top when messages go through dozens of interpretations on their journey down."[48] The Pentagon is a glaring example of the burgeoning bureaucracy. In 1960 there were seventy-eight deputy assistant secretaries of defense, and today there are 530.[49] Light brands title creep as the "thickening of government" and attributes much of it to "an indelible belief that more leaders equals more leadership."[50] Several other reasons accounting for the invention of new titles include the "use of promotions rather than pay raises to reward senior employees [and] the creation of new positions by Congress and attempts by presidents to tighten their hold on the bureaucracy with a greater number of political appointees."[51] New political posts are created by redefining civil service jobs as political or simply by creating new positions. Whatever the reason for their creation, the addition of nominees subject to advice and consent slows the confirmation process.

The third concern is that the Senate's confirmation process can be mean and nasty, especially in this period of polarized politics. "With law so hard to make and so hard to change, influencing the choice of the implementers and adjudicators of the law becomes an essential strategic option."[52] Many nominees are therefore subjected to rough treatment. Ideological groups, for example, may organize attack campaigns to defeat nominees who appear unsupportive of their agendas. Sometimes, the purpose of Senate confirmation hearings "seems less to ensure that nominees are fit than to cripple the chief executive's political leadership. A defeated nomination can embarrass a president, demoralize his supporters, and reduce public confidence in his judgment."[53] Others argue that although the confirmation process may be tough, so are the positions for which nominees seek assignment. "If you can't fight your way through the process," says a former head of the Central Intelligence Agency (CIA), "you might not just do a hot job as director."[54]

Individual senators, too, are not reluctant to threaten filibusters or to place holds on nominations—that is, senators notify party leaders that they oppose floor consideration of certain nominees. In 2010 President Obama missed the statutory deadline by a week for submitting his fiscal 2012 budget proposal to Congress in part because Sen. Mary Landrieu, D-La., had placed a six-week hold on Jacob J. Lew's nomination to be director of the Office of Management and Budget (OMB). The hold thus slowed development of the president's spending blueprint (see Box 11-1). The Senate may also refuse to consider a nominee if members invoke senatorial courtesy. This tradition, dating from the nation's earliest years, means that the Senate will usually delay or not act on nominees for offices in a state if opposed by a senator of the president's party from that state.

The Personnel System

Congress wields constitutional, legal, and informal authority over the federal personnel system. The civil service itself was created after a disgruntled job seeker assassinated President James A. Garfield in 1881. That event prompted Congress to curb the abuses of the spoils system, the practice of handing out federal jobs to supporters of the party that had won the presidency. In 1883 Congress passed the first civil service law that substituted merit for patronage. But those patronage practices have a modern equivalent: the political appointee system. The latest figures show that the fifteen cabinet departments are home to more than 2,500 political appointees (see Table 11-2).[55] The number of political appointees, however, is small compared with the number of federal employees: 2.7 million civil servants and 1.4 million uniformed personnel.

Not all political appointees have the requisite experience to meet the challenges of their office. When Hurricane Katrina devastated the Gulf Coast in late August 2005, the chief of the Federal Emergency Management Agency (FEMA) was Michael Brown. A former commissioner of the International Arabian Horse Association, Brown had little experience in emergency management. Despite President Bush's praise—"Brownie, you're doing a heck of a job"—FEMA's response to this crisis was inept and inadequate. One response by Congress was to pass the Post-Katrina Emergency Management Reform Act of 2006 (P.L. 109-295), which requires that any nominee named to head FEMA must meet certain qualifications.[56]

Periodically, various lawmakers recommend a reduction in the number of political appointees. They contend that there are simply far more appointees than the president can manage effectively. Far from enhancing responsiveness, said one senator, the large number of political appointees undermines "presidential control of the executive branch."[57] Not everyone agrees. Amid

BOX 11-1 **Lew Confirmed to Head OMB after Landrieu Lifts Hold in Senate**

After lengthy delays in the Senate unrelated to his nomination, Jacob J. Lew won confirmation last week for a return engagement to direct the federal budget office.

By voice vote, the Senate on Nov. 18 confirmed Lew's nomination to lead President Obama's Office of Management and Budget (OMB). Lew's confirmation was assured after Mary L. Landrieu, D-La., lifted a hold she had placed on the nomination over issues with the Obama administration's implementation of an offshore oil-drilling moratorium.

As recently as Nov. 16, Landrieu had said she saw no "light at the end of the tunnel" in her standoff with the administration. But several subsequent meetings with administration officials apparently set her mind at ease.

Lew, 55, is widely respected among both Republicans and Democrats and received strong support from both the Homeland Security and Budget committees, which sent his nomination to the full Senate in September. His confirmation had been stalled since then, after Landrieu's hold.

Lew held the same job during the Clinton administration and won praise for his role in bringing about the Balanced Budget Act of 1997 (P.L. 105-33), a bipartisan effort that resulted in a short series of federal surpluses. He will succeed Peter R. Orszag, who left in July.

The confirmation is welcome news for OMB, which is in a critical stage of putting together the president's budget request for fiscal 2012, due in early February.

In comments on the floor Nov. 18, Landrieu called Lew "a terrific nominee," noting several times that her concerns were not personally connected to him.

"It was a horrible accident," Landrieu said of the April oil spill in the Gulf of Mexico that led to the drilling ban, "but to place a moratorium on an entire industry because one company and their contractors made some serious and terrible mistakes, I think, is really unprecedented. It was unwise, and it was extremely harmful to the Gulf Coast."

Earlier in the week, White House spokesman Robert Gibbs had said it was important to fill the OMB post quickly.

"There are deadlines that—that have to be met in this year to get a budget worked through and ultimately get one that can be sent up to Capitol Hill," Gibbs said. "That's work that needs to be going on as soon as possible."

Lew has been serving as deputy secretary of State for management and resources, a post described by the White House as chief operating officer for the department. He was confirmed by voice vote for his State Department post in January 2009.

Source: Niels Lesniewski and Paul M. Krawzak, "Lew Confirmed to Head OMB After Landrieu Lifts Hold in Senate," *CQ Weekly,* November 22, 2010, 2718.

rising partisanship one scholar argued, "presidents need to stock departments with people who understand politics and the importance of interaction with Congress, lobbyists and the media."[58]

Pay and Other Legal Standards. By law, Congress has wide control over federal employees. It can establish retirement programs; special requirements for holding office; personnel ceilings; employee performance standards; wages,

TABLE 11-2	**Political Appointees by Department and Appointment Type, 2010**				
Department	Pres. Appt. Requiring Senate Approval	Pres. Appt. Not Requiring Senate Approval	Non-Career Senior Executive Service	Schedule C	Total
Agriculture	16	0	43	168	227
Commerce	23	2	33	103	161
Defense	53	0	94	134	281
Education	17	1	14	112	144
Energy	22	0	30	66	118
Health and Human Services	20	1	48	66	135
Homeland Security	20	1	61	102	184
Housing and Urban Development	15	0	18	49	82
Interior	17	0	30	36	83
Justice	223	0	45	68	336
Labor	19	0	29	105	153
State	222	3	36	125	386
Transportation	23	0	31	41	95
Treasury	33	0	23	45	101
Veterans Affairs	15	0	8	9	32
Total	738	8	543	1,229	2,518

Source: Henry B. Hogue, Maureen Bearden, and Betsy Palmer, "Filling Advice and Consent Position at the Outset of a New Administration," Congressional Research Report RLWP19, April 1, 2010, 2.

benefits, and cost-of-living adjustments (COLAs); and protections from reprisals for whistleblowers (employees who expose waste and corruption). The 1939 Hatch Act, named for Sen. Carl Hatch, D-N.M. (1933–1949), restricts federal employees' partisan activity. The act was passed during the New Deal after reports that civil servants were being coerced to back President Franklin D. Roosevelt in his reelection efforts. Today, civil servants can engage in political activity in accord with regulations prescribed by the U.S. Office of Special Counsel. For example, most career civil servants can run for nonpartisan office, contribute to political organizations, or distribute campaign literature. They may not run for partisan office, use their authority to exert influence over an election, or wear political buttons while on duty.[59] As a sign of the times, the special counsel's office has also issued guidelines for federal employees on the use of social media such as Facebook and Twitter in election campaigns.[60]

Other limits are placed on bureaucrats as well. After leaving public office, many executive officers, top legislative staffers, and legislators themselves pass through the "revolving door" to jobs with private firms that deal with the government. However, various laws impose a "cooling-off" period before these officials and employees may lobby their former agencies, departments, or branches of government. For example, under the Honest Leadership and Open Government Act, which President Bush signed into law on September 14, 2007, high government officials and senators are subject to a two-year cooling-off period after leaving office; House members must comply with a one-year cooling-off period.[61] Nevertheless, government officials regularly move to the private sector and vice versa. Enactment of the landmark Dodd-Frank Wall Street Reform and Consumer Protection Act (P.L. 111-203) in 2010 saw many government regulators walk through the revolving door to join various Wall Street firms.[62] Similarly, top White House officials have also left the administration to take high-paying jobs in business, law, and public relations firms, despite signing Obama-required pledges barring them for two years from trying to influence executive officials on behalf of their clients. However, the pledge does not prevent "outgoing Obama aides from lobbying Congress or from helping employers or clients influence the administration by charting strategy or even supervising lobbyists."[63]

The revolving door issue became a major issue for the Department of Interior after the massive oil spill in 2010 in the Gulf of Mexico (British Petroleum's Deepwater Horizon oil rig disaster). It was not uncommon, for example, for Interior officials—whose job it is to oversee the safety of deepwater oil drilling—to adopt regulations promulgated by the American Petroleum Institute and then take high-paying jobs in the oil and gas industry. Interior secretary Ken Salazar even told Congress that in certain cases he could support a lifetime revolving door ban for federal oil regulators.[64]

Size of Government. Americans have debated the size and reach of the federal government since the nation's founding. At least since the twentieth century—from the Progressive Era to World War I, from the New Deal to the Great Society to today's governmental interventions in the private sector—the national government has expanded dramatically. Growth has been driven by overlapping factors. Wars and crises, of course, expand federal obligations. The intelligence community mushroomed during the Cold War as the United States faced a major threat from the other nuclear-armed superpower, the Soviet Union, and expanded dramatically after the September 11, 2001, terrorist attacks. As a result, some 854,000 people with supersecret clearances are now in place at ten thousand sites across the United States.[65]

Complexity is another factor triggering governmental growth. New problems and issues repeatedly demand national action. Today, the federal government must address issues with global dimensions, from trade to currency exchange rates to climate change. As the nation's population grew to over 300 million and government expanded its responsibilities and capacities, it was only natural that individuals and groups would look to their national office-holders to solve problems in health care, transportation, law enforcement, energy, and so on.

People often complain about the overly large federal establishment, but what does "too big" really mean? Much of the disagreement centers on how government size should be measured: the share of the gross domestic product (GDP) devoted to federal expenditures, the magnitude of the federal budget, or the number of federal employees. As to the first standard, federal spending relative to the size of the U.S. economy is a mixed picture, from 21.8 percent of GDP in 1990 to 18.4 percent in 2000, 19.8 percent in 2004, 20.2 percent in 2008, and 23.8 percent in 2010. Another measure is the federal budget, which keeps growing (reaching $3.7 trillion in 2011), but so, too, have the nation's population and obligations.

Contrary to what many people believe, the federal workforce has remained relatively constant in size. How can the government continue to perform services while generally keeping its size down? One answer is that much of what the federal government does is to transfer money to eligible recipients, such as the elderly who receive Social Security. This function does not require large numbers of federal workers. Another answer is that federal work has been outsourced to contract firms, or privatized. The Pentagon, for example, reached a milestone in 2001 when the number of its private sector employees (734,000) exceeded its civilian workforce (700,000). Nine years later, the Defense Department said it employed 766,000 contractors compared with 745,000 civilian employees; however, another study calculated that Pentagon-employed contractors numbered 1.2 million.[66] These contract employees "perform service jobs from mowing lawns to testing weapons systems."[67] As one analyst explained, "Everybody wants the federal government to look smaller than it really is. By contracting out jobs rather than having civilian workers in those jobs, you can say, 'Look, the government's smaller.'"[68] Another scholar has put the true personnel size of the government at about 15 million employees: the 4.1 million civilian, military, and postal workers plus the 10.5 million "shadow" employees who work "under federal contracts and grants or mandates imposed on state and local governments."[69]

However this debate about government size is reconciled, privatizing (or outsourcing) the federal government's work has certain benefits and costs. Outsourcing has distinct advantages in many instances: contractors can be faster, more flexible, and cheaper than the career bureaucracy. They can provide security services, technological skills, intelligence capabilities, and other benefits that government agencies are unable to fulfill. However, many analysts believe that certain functions are inherently governmental, which means they are "so intimately related to the public interest as to require performance by a federal government employee."[70] There is concern that the government loses vital expertise when it outsources critical functions to the private sector.[71] As a result, there is renewed debate on Capitol Hill on questions such as: What is appropriate to outsource? Should certain functions be insourced? Is there a right balance between the federal and contractor workforce? Moreover, because contractors are not directly responsible to Congress, the so called third-party (or shadow) government raises serious questions of accountability, resulting in fraud, waste, and cost overruns, as shown by the contracting abuses associated with post–Hurricane Katrina and Iraq reconstruction.[72]

The Rulemaking Process

Congress creates and funds executive agencies and defines their legal mandates, but rarely can it specify the details needed to implement policies and programs. By statute, Congress delegates to federal entities its inherent legislative authority to craft the implementing rules and regulations (the terms are interchangeable) for carrying out the mandates contained in laws. As Senator Grassley explained, "All regulations are based ultimately on the authority granted by this Congress. When an agency promulgates a rule, it is engaging in a legislative task—in effect, filling in the gaps on the implementation that we in Congress have established through statute."[73] Executive agencies through their rule-writing authority (their final regulations have the full force and effect of statutes) enact more "laws" annually than the legislative branch. In other words, executive branch officials who write regulations are lawmakers operating in a bureaucratic context.

A Controversial Example: Health. In March 2010, President Obama signed the landmark 2,700-page health overhaul bill into law (Patient Protection and Affordable Care Act). Its over forty separate provisions permit or require various federal entities, such as the Department of Health and Human Services (HHS), to issue scores of regulations implementing the health care law.[74] Moreover, all fifty states have major responsibilities for issuing regulations to carry out various provisions of the law. Because many Republican governors, legislatures, and attorneys general dislike the law, some have chosen to "slow walk" its implementation and join efforts to invalidate its key parts.

On January 19, 2011, every House Republican, plus three Democrats, voted 245–189 to pass a bill (H.R. 2) repealing what they pejoratively call "Obamacare." The next day, the House adopted a resolution directing four House committees to draft replacement health care legislation. With Democrats in control of the White House and Senate, it is unlikely that Republicans can muster the sixty votes in the Senate to break a filibuster blocking a repeal vote, or a two-thirds vote in either chamber to override a presidential veto. Still, as Senate GOP conference chair Lamar Alexander exclaimed, "We're committed to trying to repeal it, and, if that doesn't work, to go step by step" to minimize its effect.[75] In the House, Speaker John Boehner, R-Ohio, declared, "I am committed to doing everything I can do . . . to prevent 'Obamacare' from being implemented. Now, when I say everything, I mean everything."[76]

The notion of two Congresses pervades all these developments. Congressional Republicans plan to persist in casting the law and accompanying regulations in a negative light in the hope of boosting their chances of winning both legislative chambers and the White House in the November 2012 elections. As a GOP senator put it, "We won the 2010 elections by bashing what the Democrats did on healthcare. Maybe we can win the 2012 election by the same strategy."[77] However, the health care law has many popular features, such as prohibiting insurers from dropping their coverage of sick people and allowing adult children to remain on their parents' health policies until the age of twenty-six. Democrats believe—and are working to drive home their view— that as more people realize and reap the benefits of the health overhaul, the harder it will be to repeal the law, particularly its popular parts.[78] Republicans view matters differently. "It is telling that the more Americans learn about [the health law], the more discouraged they are by its harmful effects," exclaimed House majority leader Eric Cantor, R-Va.[79]

In their multifrontal assault on the law (in the judiciary, the states, the court of public opinion, and Congress), Republicans can employ an array of legislative techniques against the health care law such as:

- Using the appropriations process to eliminate or reduce funding for regulation-writing by the health agencies;[80]
- Holding aggressive oversight hearings to require executive officials to defend their health rules;
- Scheduling regular floor debates to showcase the weaknesses of the health care law and the virtues of the GOP's alternative health care ideas;
- Acting repeatedly on measures to undermine the law; and
- Attaching targeted amendments to "must pass" bills that dilute or dismantle key health care provisions before they can take effect.

In addition, congressional Republicans can employ the Congressional Review Act (CRA) to try to nullify, one at a time, unwanted health or other regulations promulgated by executive agencies. The CRA is a section of the 1996 small business regulatory fairness law requiring regulators to submit all proposed major rules and regulations—those with an economic impact over $100 million in any one year—to the House and Senate. Lawmakers then have sixty legislative days from the time a regulation is published in the *Federal Register*—the government's publication of regulatory activities—to reject it under expedited procedures by enacting a joint resolution of disapproval (see Box 11-2).[81]

House and Senate Republicans are likely to use the CRA with increasing frequency in the 112th Congress to try to suspend, delay, or kill unnecessary regulations. However, President Obama can veto joint resolutions of disapproval, and neither chamber is likely to muster the two-thirds vote needed to override the chief executive. Nevertheless, as an aide to a former Senate GOP majority leader noted, the CRA "provides an important public relations tool to highlight real concerns and perhaps force the administration to make some changes [to the challenged regulation] that they would otherwise not be willing to make."[82]

BOX 11-2   **Resolution of Disapproval**

Republicans may be in the minority in the Senate, but they have a number of tools that will allow them to bring up votes on the health care law that Democrats may want to avoid. One little-discussed method allows opponents of the law to bring up a resolution that could kill health policy regulations that the administration issues. Such a resolution would not have to overcome amendments, filibusters or motions to move to other business.

The technique, authorized in the 1996 Congressional Review Act (CRA), gives Congress 60 days to overturn a major regulation after an agency publishes a rule or informs Congress of its release (whichever is later).

If Congress succeeds in shepherding through a disapproval resolution that the president will sign, federal regulators cannot publish a new rule that is "substantially" similar to the one that was rejected.

Earlier this year, Sen. Michael B. Enzi was the first to target a regulation resulting from the health care overhaul. The Wyoming Republican sought to overturn a rule setting guidelines for grandfathering health plans that were in existence when the health care law passed in March.

Enzi's proposal (SJ Res 39) was rejected, 40–59, on a party-line vote. Even if Congress had passed the measure, President Obama probably would have vetoed it.

Opponents of rules have succeeded only once in overturning a policy. In March 2001, the House and Senate Republicans who controlled Congress, joined by moderate Democrats, over-turned an Occupational Safety and Health Administration ergonomics rule that was issued during the waning days of the Clinton administration. President George W. Bush signed the resolution into law.

Even though the prospects for killing a regulation are slim under the CRA, Republicans still see it as a valuable tool that can keep the issue in the public's sights and force Democrats to defend the law.

Source: Rebecca Adams, "The Anti-Regulation Route," *CQ Weekly*, November 29, 2010, 2757.

Disapproval resolutions also signal regulatory agencies that Congress is keeping a close eye on their work. According to Texas Republican John Carter, the GOP Conference secretary, the CRA will be a major weapon, able "to block the implementation of these bad laws, and to educate the public with laser clarity on the specifics of what these regulations will do to our freedoms."[83]

Statutory Standards for Rulemaking. In the Administrative Procedure Act (APA) of 1946 and later amendments to it, Congress established standards for rulemaking by government agencies. Under the APA, regulatory agencies are required to publish a notice in the *Federal Register* of their proposed rulemaking. The notice includes such information as where and when "interested parties" can comment on the proposed rule. Typically, the public comment period runs for at least thirty days. Interested parties can take part in the process by testifying in public about the merits or demerits of proposed regulations. Citizens can comment on federal rulemaking through the government's official websites—www.federalregister.gov or www.reginfo.gov—as well as through comparable sites. The Obama administration has been considering a nontraditional change in how rulemaking would work: agencies would first draft a rule, then solicit public comments, make revisions based on the comments, and then publish the final rule. The new approach would use blogs, electronic town hall meetings, and social media sites to involve the citizenry in determining whether a rule is needed, and, if so, what should be in it. As the White House's deputy chief technology officer said, "Instead of starting with a finished product, we're co-creating from the get-go and asking people what should be in such a rule before we write it."[84]

The federal courts also ensure that executive officials do not repeal rules by fiat. A federal appeals court has held that once a rule is published in the *Federal Register,* "it cannot be reversed without a lengthy administrative process, even if [the rule] has not yet taken effect."[85] Although presidents can overturn executive orders with the stroke of a pen, they cannot treat regulations the same way. "It is not easy for a president to stop a final rule that has been published in the *Federal Register* short of putting the whole process [as prescribed in the Administrative Procedures Act of 1946] in reverse and beginning the process of rule making anew—with public notices, comment periods and agency reviews that could take years."[86]

Legislative-Executive Clashes. Congress and the White House frequently skirmish over rulemaking. GOP administrations tend to have a pro-business regulatory bias, favoring voluntary compliance and giving key regulatory jobs to corporate and industry officials who are keen on easing or reducing regulation. Democratic presidents appoint individuals to head agencies who support worker safety, consumer, and environmental protections. As incoming administrations frequently do, just hours after being sworn into office President Obama ordered "work halted on all federal regulations left unfinished at the end of the [George W.] Bush era until they can be reviewed by the new president's team."[87] Regulations surged during the first two years of the Obama administration, more than doubling the number issued during the Bush administration.[88]

A regulatory counterattack followed the Republican takeover of the House in the November 2010 elections. Recognizing that Republicans were seeking to challenge and limit new administrative rule-writing, President Obama issued an executive order requiring federal agencies "to review health and safety [and environmental] regulations to determine if they are burdensome on businesses, in which case they may be changed or repealed."[89]

A recent ongoing controversy between Congress and the executive agencies has centered on the authority of the Environmental Protection Agency (EPA) to regulate carbon emissions. When the Democratic-controlled 111th Congress (2009–2011) failed to enact legislation to curb greenhouse gas emissions found to promote climate change and to endanger public health and welfare, the EPA used its authority under the Clean Air Act (P.L. 101–549) to require power plants, electric utilities, and oil refineries to employ the best available technologies to reduce their carbon emissions. (On April 2, 2007, the U.S. Supreme Court, in *Massachusetts v. EPA*, agreed that greenhouse gases were air pollutants and subject to regulations imposed by the EPA.) In response to the EPA's actions, House and Senate members from energy-producing states immediately went on the offensive to limit or strip the EPA's climate change authority. "We are not going to let this administration regulate what they've been unable to legislate," declared House Energy and Commerce chairman Fred Upton, R-Mich.[90] Upton also promised that EPA administrator Lisa Jackson would be testifying so frequently before his committee "that he'll guarantee her a permanent parking space on Capitol Hill."[91] In the Senate, Jay Rockefeller, D-W.Va., and Lisa Murkowski, I-Alaska—both of whom represent energy-producing states—either want to delay the regulations for two years or "to strip EPA entirely of its regulatory power over carbon emissions."[92]

Some six hundred major rules and regulations issued each year by executive agencies must be reviewed by the White House regulatory "czar." This czar is the chief of the Office of Information and Regulatory Affairs (OIRA) within the Office of Management and Budget. OIRA analyzes regulations that would impose more than $100 million in costs on affected industries. It can then reject them, require their revision, or approve them in line with the president's priorities. Proposed rules and regulations are typically subject to cost-benefit review.

Measuring costs and benefits is at best a tricky undertaking. Risk analysis experts hold that this traditional tool should be used "to sort through a complex world of threats to human and environmental health so we can identify the choices that will do the most people the most good at the least cost."[93] Critics of this approach, however, point out that measuring costs is usually easier than estimating benefits; costs are more easily quantified, whereas benefits are often intangible and long-term. In a 2011 review of regulations, the Office of Management and Budget stated that major "federal rules and regulations . . . cost between $6.5 billion and $12.5 billion but resulted in between $23.3 billion and $82.3 billion in benefits."[94] How valuable are regulations? Lawmakers, like their constituents, are of two minds. Some, such as Sen. Barbara Boxer, D-Calif., emphasize their positive achievements:

> The purpose of the Federal regulatory process is to improve and protect the high quality of life that we enjoy in our country. Every day, the people of our Nation enjoy the benefits of almost a century of progress in Federal laws and regulations that reduce the threat of illness, injury, and death from consumer products, workplace hazards, and environmental toxins.[95]

Others call for "more rational regulations," with "better analysis of costs, benefits, and risks, so that regulators will issue smarter, more cost-effective regulations."[96] A difficult challenge is to distinguish between inflexible, pointless, or overly burdensome and costly regulations and the beneficial regulations that are necessary to promote and protect the public's health and safety.

Whatever their view of the regulatory process, legislators must act as intermediaries between their constituents and federal agencies. Constituents' problems are handled within members' offices by personal staff aides called caseworkers. In addition to courting the electoral payoff of effective casework—evidence of the two Congresses once again—some members appreciate its value as oversight. "The very knowledge by executive officials that some Congressman is sure to look into a matter affecting his constituents acts as a healthy check against bureaucratic indifference or arrogance," wrote a former senator.[97]

CONGRESSIONAL CONTROL OF THE BUREAUCRACY

"Congressional power, like chastity," explained a scholar, "is never lost, rarely taken by force, and almost always given away."[98] Because no law can be sufficiently detailed to cover every conceivable circumstance, Congress allows executive officials wide discretion in implementing the laws it passes. This delegation of authority occurs because legislators lack the time, knowledge, or expertise to address the complexities of contemporary administration.

Congress is often sharply criticized for drafting vague or sloppy legislation that gives executive officials and judges too much leeway in interpretation and administration. "Administration of a statute is, properly speaking, an extension of the legislative process," pointed out political scientist David B. Truman, and therefore Congress must watch over its programs lest they undergo unintended change.[99] Because of the size and reach of the executive establishment, Congress's oversight role is even more important today than when Woodrow Wilson wrote in 1885, "Quite as important as lawmaking is vigilant oversight of administration."[100]

The Constitution does not refer explicitly to the oversight role, but it does implicitly flow from Congress's right, among other things, to make laws, raise and appropriate money, give advice and consent to executive nominations, and impeach federal officials. Congress has, however, formalized its oversight duties. The Legislative Reorganization Act of 1946 directed all House and Senate committees to exercise "continuous watchfulness" over the programs and agencies under their jurisdiction. Subsequent statutes and House and Senate rules have extended Congress's authority and resources for oversight. The Government Accountability Office (GAO), the chief investigative arm of the legislative branch, provides the House and Senate at the start of each new Congress with "high risk" reports on the management and accounting practices of federal agencies and departments. The high risk reports also identify "areas in need of broad-based transformation."[101] Overall, GAO issues annually more than a thousand audits and reports on administrative management.

Members understand their review responsibilities. "Congress's duty didn't end in passing this law," remarked a senator. "We have to make sure the law works." Another senator said, "I have always felt that one-third of the role of Congress should be in oversight."[102] The purposes of oversight are many, but three are especially important: (1) to check the power of the executive branch; (2) to determine how laws are being implemented and whether they need adjustments and refinements; and (3) to shine the spotlight of public attention on significant executive actions and activities. As Woodrow Wilson wrote in 1885, "The informing function of Congress should be preferred even to its legislative [lawmaking] function." He went on to say:

> Unless Congress [has] and use[s] every means of acquainting itself with the acts and dispositions of the administrative agencies of government, the country must be helpless to learn how it is being served; and unless Congress both scrutinize[s] these things and sift[s] them by every form of discussion, the country must remain in embarrassing, crippling ignorance of the very affairs which it is most important it should understand and direct.[103]

Political purposes are served by oversight as well, such as generating favorable publicity for programs; urging the elimination or reduction of agencies; responding to requests from special interests to influence agency decisions; or winning electoral support from constituents or groups. Oversight thus occurs in a political context, within which Congress's relationship with administrative agencies can range from cooperation to conflict.

To ensure that laws are working, Congress relies on a varied array of formal and informal processes and techniques. Each has its strengths and weaknesses, and it is often necessary to use several in combination if the House and Senate are to challenge or assess executive branch performance. Many oversight activities are indirect, ad hoc, and not subject to easy measurement or even recognition. "Oversight isn't necessarily a hearing," said John D. Dingell, D-Mich., a noted House overseer when he chaired the Energy and Commerce Committee. "Sometimes it's a letter. We find our letters have a special effect on a lot of people."[104]

Hearings and Investigations

Many of Congress's most dramatic historical moments have occurred during legislative probes into administrative or business misconduct or manmade or natural disasters. Examples are the Teapot Dome inquiry (1923), the Senate's Watergate hearings (1973–1974), the Iran-contra investigation (1987), the joint hearings into the disintegration of the space shuttle *Columbia* (2003), the hearings on the Iraq war (2007), the hearings into taxpayer-funded bonuses for Wall Street executives (2009), or, more generally, the scores of 2011 hearings by the GOP-controlled House committees searching for ways to slash federal spending. The mere threat of a congressional hearing is often enough to keep agencies in line. But Congress's investigative authority is not without limits.

Earl Warren, when he was chief justice of the U.S. Supreme Court, wrote in *Watkins v. United States* (1957):

> There is no general authority to expose private affairs of individuals without justification in terms of the functions of Congress. . . . Nor is the Congress a law enforcement or trial agency. These are functions of the executive and judicial departments of government. No inquiry is an end in itself; it must be related to, and in furtherance of, a legitimate task of the Congress.[105]

By collecting and analyzing information, House and Senate inquiries can clarify whether new laws are needed to address public problems. They also sharpen Congress's ability to scrutinize executive branch activities, such as the expenditure of funds, the implementation of laws, and the discharge of duties by administrative officials. Investigations also inform the public by disseminating and revealing information. "Congress provides a forum for disclosing the hidden aspects of governmental conduct," wrote two Senate members of the Iran-contra investigating committee. It allows a "free people to drag realities out into the sunlight and demand a full accounting from those who are permitted to hold and exercise power."[106] Hearings and investigations are, in short, valuable devices for making government accountable to the people. They can spawn new laws or their functional equivalent: change in bureaucratic operations.

Congressional Vetoes

Congress has little choice but to delegate sweeping authority to administrative agencies. The question is then how Congress can control those agencies. One answer historically has been the legislative veto (or congressional veto), a statutory enactment that permits presidents or agencies to take certain actions subject to later approval or disapproval by one or both houses of Congress (or in some cases by committees of one or both houses). Legislative vetoes are arrangements of convenience for both branches. Executives gain decision-making authority they might not have otherwise, and Congress retains a second chance to examine decisions.

In 1983 many forms of the legislative veto were declared unconstitutional by the Supreme Court (*Immigration and Naturalization Service v. Chadha*). The Court's majority held that the device violated the separation of powers, the principle of bicameralism, and the presentation clause of the Constitution (legislation passed by both chambers must be presented to the president for his signature or veto). The decision, wrote Justice Byron R. White in a vigorous dissent, "strikes down in one fell swoop provisions in more laws enacted by Congress than the court has cumulatively invalidated in its entire history."[107]

Congress has repealed some veto provisions since *Chadha* and amended others, while continuing to employ a wide range of oversight techniques to monitor executive actions. Yet despite the *Chadha* ruling, legislative vetoes of the committee variety continue to be enacted into law. Public law scholar Louis Fisher has summed up the status of legislative vetoes:

> Are they constitutional? Not by the Court's definition. Will that fact change the behavior between committees and agencies? Probably not. An agency might advise the committee: "As you know, the requirement in this statute for committee prior-approval is unconstitutional under the Court's test." Perhaps agency and committee staff will nod their heads in agreement. After which the agency will seek prior approval of the committee.[108]

Self-interest impels agencies to pay close attention to the wishes of members of Congress, especially those who sit on their authorizing or appropriating panels.

Mandatory Reports

Congress can require the president, federal agencies, or departments to assess programs and report their findings.[109] Reports can act "as a mechanism to check that laws are having the intended effect." Moreover, they can "drive a reluctant bureaucracy to comply with laws it would otherwise ignore."[110] Each year, executive agencies prepare several thousand reports for submission to Congress. Because of the massive size and important role of the Defense Department, it is not surprising that the Pentagon is tasked with preparing numerous reports for Congress. During an August 2010 departmental briefing, Defense Secretary Robert Gates noted, "In 1970, the Pentagon produced a total of 37 reports for the Congress, a number that topped off at more than 700 reports in last year's cycle."[111] Trying to reduce the number of outdated or duplicative reports—which Congress does periodically—often comes with the requirement that agencies be more responsive to committees' requests for information. A spokesperson for Howard "Buck" McKeon, R-Calif., the chair of the House Armed Services Committee, said his boss would be happy to work with Secretary Gates to eliminate various reporting requirements if the Pentagon would do "a better job of providing specific programmatic and policy information in a timely manner" to the committee.[112]

Nonstatutory Controls

Congressional committees also use informal means to review and influence administrative decisions. These range from telephone calls, letters, personal contacts, and informal understandings to statements in conference reports, hearings, and floor debates.[113] Committee reports frequently contain phrases such as "the committee clearly intends that the matter be reconsidered" or "the committee clearly intends for the Secretary to promote" or "the committee clearly expects."

On occasion, OMB directors tell federal agencies to ignore report language because it is not legally binding. Lawmakers of both parties and chambers (and even executive officials), however, may seek to thwart such directives. Sometimes, members threaten to make all report language legally binding on agencies, thereby limiting the agencies' flexibility and discretion in resolving issues.[114] Although their usage is not measured, nonstatutory controls may be the most common form of congressional oversight.

Inspectors General

In 1978 Congress created a dozen independent offices for inspectors general (IGs). Since then, Congress has established inspectors general offices in nearly every federal department and agency. IGs conduct audits and investigations of agency programs and operations; prevent and detect fraud and abuse in such programs and operations; and keep Congress and agency heads fully informed on a timely basis about problems and the need for corrective actions. Granted wide latitude and independence, IGs are "the government's first line of defense against fraud."[115]

Inspectors general testify frequently before congressional committees and submit directly to Congress reports on their efforts to root out waste, fraud, and abuse. For example, the Labor Department IG determined that a departmental initiative to improve worker safety in hazardous industries "rarely fulfilled its promise" because of uneven inspections and enforcement. The result was fifty-eight fatalities that might have been prevented.[116] The Pentagon's IG detailed billions of dollars in waste and fraud by military contractors.[117]

The Appropriations Process

Congress probably exercises its most potent oversight of agencies and programs through the appropriations process. By cutting off or reducing funds (or threatening to do so), Congress can abolish agencies, curtail programs, or obtain requested information. Upset that the secretary of the Department of Housing and Urban Development (HUD) was flying off to various conferences rather than dealing with the housing foreclosure crisis, appropriators eliminated the secretary's travel budget. "Frankly, I want to cause [HUD] officials a little personal pain," declared one legislator. I want them to "just plant their butts at their desks and do the job that they were appointed to do."[118] In another case, a House Appropriations subcommittee chair, angry because the Homeland Security Department had not provided reports on its spending priorities, declared, "They've just been ignoring us. They'll pay for that."[119] By the same token, Congress can build up program areas by increasing their appropriations—sometimes beyond the levels that the administration has requested.

The appropriations power is exercised mainly through the House and Senate Appropriations Committees, especially through each panel's standing subcommittees. These panels annually recommend funding levels for federal agencies and departments so that they have the funds to carry out their program responsibilities. The budgetary recommendations of the Appropriations subcommittees are generally accepted by their parent committee and by the House or Senate.

The Appropriations Committees and their subcommittees, or members from the House or Senate floor, may offer amendments that limit the purposes for which money may be spent ("limitation riders") or that impose other spending limits on federal agencies. Funding bills also may contain various policy directives to federal agencies—for example, prohibiting agencies from using funds to promulgate or issue certain regulations. Such directives are often in the form of floor amendments. "These amendments," wrote two GOP senators, "are an important way for Congress to save taxpayers from wasteful agency spending, and they enjoy a long-standing precedent because of their use by Republican and Democratic Congresses alike to rein in the excesses of Republican and Democratic administrations."[120] Political scientist Jason A. McDonald has also underscored the legislative importance of limitation amendments in influencing agency actions. They provide "Congress with much more influence than scholars have appreciated over not only everyday policy decisions within agencies (which in and of itself would be significant), but also over the substance of regulations about which members of Congress, and their constituencies, care for political and policy reasons."[121]

Impeachment

Article II, section 4, of the Constitution states: "The President, Vice President, and all Civil Officers of the United States, shall be removed from office on Impeachment for, and Conviction of, Treason, Bribery, or other high Crimes and misdemeanors." This removal power is the ultimate governmental check vested in Congress.[122] The House has the authority to impeach an official by majority vote. It then tries the case before the Senate, where a two-thirds vote is required for conviction.

Only impeached federal judges have been convicted by the Senate. The most recent case occurred on December 8, 2010, when the Senate voted for only the eighth time to convict and remove from office a federal district judge in Louisiana.[123] As for presidents, the House impeached President Andrew Johnson in 1868, after Radical Republicans in the House charged that he had violated the Tenure of Office Act by dismissing the secretary of war. The Senate acquitted Johnson by a single vote. Facing probable impeachment and conviction, President Richard M. Nixon resigned in 1974 after the House Judiciary Committee voted articles of impeachment. In December 1998, President Clinton became the first elected president to be impeached by the House. (Johnson was not elected; he became president when Abraham Lincoln was assassinated.) The charges against Clinton were perjury and obstruction of justice. Two months later, the Senate voted acquittal on both articles of impeachment.[124]

Oversight: An Evaluation

Congress's willingness to conduct regular and meaningful oversight stems from several factors: public dissatisfaction with government; revelations of executive agency abuses; the influx of new legislators skeptical of government's ability to perform effectively; concern about the growth of a regulatory state; the availability of seasoned congressional staff; and recognition by Congress that it must make every dollar count.[125] Of these several factors, two stand out as especially important motivators of oversight since Republicans' capture of the House in November 2010. First, top GOP leaders have made cutting agencies and programs a major priority, and, second, many in the populace want to rein in the reach of the federal government. In response, House GOP leaders have developed a strategic plan to make oversight of the Obama administration a top priority:

> [Speaker] Boehner will coordinate all long-term committee oversight planning and strategy, deciding which issues to investigate, which committees to put in charge, and how to package oversight findings to build momentum for bills that Republicans want to pass. [Majority leader] Eric Cantor will handle day-to-day management of all committees conducting oversight. . . . Boehner and Cantor have ordered up a 24/7 war-room model where attacks on administration policy are developed by chosen committees, relayed to rank-and-file members (with high visibility roles envisaged for members of the hard-charging freshmen class), and, eventually, coordinated with GOP governors.[126]

The perspective of the two Congresses highlights the electoral, political, and policy incentives that encourage members to oversee the bureaucracy. One of these incentives is the opportunity to claim credit for assisting constituents and to receive favorable publicity back home. Another is the prodding by interest groups and the media. Committee and subcommittee chairs "seek a high pay off—in attention from both the press and other agencies—when selecting federal programs to be their oversight targets."[127] Members on the relevant committees of jurisdiction are also motivated to induce favorable agency and departmental action on pet policies or programs.

Divided government—the president of one party, Congress (or one chamber) controlled by the other—encourages vigorous congressional oversight. Oversight simultaneously enables opposition lawmakers to supervise agency activities and look for ways to undermine the administration's policy goals or public reputation. Simply responding to scores of subpoenas issued by committees controlled by the opposition party can sap the time and energy of the White House and agency officials. By comparison, under unified government, the majority party in Congress tends to engage in less oversight. As one senior GOP lawmaker said of the unified period (2003–2007) when Republicans were in charge, "Our party controls the levers of government. We're not about to go out and look beneath a bunch of rocks to cause heartburn."[128] Party loyalty, in short, overcame institutional responsibility.

Whether within unified or divided government, congressional oversight may not probe as deeply as some might wish. "We have not done our job in terms of oversight," declared Sen. Tom Coburn, R-Okla. in 2010.[129] Friendly alliances can develop among the committees that authorize programs, the agencies that administer them, and the interest groups that benefit from governmental services. Many committees are biased toward the programs or agencies they oversee. They want to protect and nurture their progeny and make program administration look good. Without concrete allegations of fraud or mismanagement, committees may lack the incentive to scrutinize and reevaluate their programs. This kind of cooperative oversight can dissuade committees from conducting meaningful inquiries that require agencies to justify their existence and contribution to the public's well-being

A standard rationale for oversight is that it ensures that laws are carried out according to congressional intent. But because many laws are vague and replete with multiple objectives, they are difficult to assess. Moreover, proof that programs are working as intended may not emerge for years. Congressional patience may wane as critics conclude that there are no demonstrable payoffs for the taxpayer. Alternatively, oversight may identify program flaws but not reveal what would work or even whether there is any ready solution.

In the 112th Congress, the need to establish oversight priorities was underscored by Darrell Issa, R-Calif., the House's leading investigator as chair of the Oversight and Government Reform Committee. "I don't need to be looking at every failure of government," he said. "I need to be looking at where failure of government needs reform. You bring it back to Congress and we fix it."[130] Chairman Issa solicited the input of 150 companies, trade associations, think tanks, and scholars, "asking them to come up with a list of the most onerous existing and proposed regulations that are hurting job creation and economic growth."[131] Democrats complained that this initiative catered too much to moneyed interests rather than the broad middle-class.

Each oversight technique has limitations. Hearings may provide dramatic episodes, but they often result in minimal follow-up. The appropriations process is usually hemmed in by programmatic needs for financial stability. And statutes are often blunt instruments of control. Other obstacles to effective oversight include inadequate coordination among committees sharing jurisdiction over a program; sporadic review by committees of departmental activities; and frequent turnover among committee staff aides, a situation that limits their understanding of the programs created by Congress.

Critics who fault Congress's oversight may be erecting unattainable standards. Many analysts are looking for what scholars have come to call "police-patrol" oversight—active, direct, systematic, planned surveillance of executive activities. Instead, Congress often waits until the "fire alarms" sound—set off by interest groups, the press, staff aides, and others concerned about administrative violations—before it begins to review in detail agencies' activities.[132]

Congress may be benefitting from some extra police patrol assistance offered by a combination of civic-minded individuals and technology. A new trend is the "public as watchdog." A good example is the enactment in 2006 of the Federal Funding Accountability and Transparency Act, informally called the "Google your government" law, because it required OMB "to provide a user-friendly, searchable database" of nearly $1 trillion in federal grants and contracts.[133] Websites such as recovery.gov or stimuluswatch.org allow citizens to monitor the projects that receive taxpayer dollars. The GAO has a website and hotline to enable citizens to report allegations of waste, fraud, or misman-agement of federal funds. And Chairman Issa has established a whistleblower website where agency employees can alert committee staff of fraud and abuse in their agency. Majority Leader Cantor's website, dubbed YouCut, permits the public to vote on "which government programs should be cut."[134]

There are even informal "citizen regulators" who test children's toys and clothing to protect them from harmful chemicals. "I'm not going to rely on an agency that changes personnel based on administrations and takes years to make any kind of change," remarked the mother of a three-year-old.[135] The promise of these actions is that they enable any interested person or watchdog group to monitor federal spending or products available in stores across the nation and make their evaluations known to congressional law-makers. The blogosphere, in short, adds millions of extra eyes to congres-sional oversight.

Micromanagement

Because oversight often means legislative intrusion into administrative details, executive branch officials sometimes complain about congressional micromanagement. Even though the executive bureaucracy may react with dismay, Congress's focus on administrative details is as old as the institution itself. The structural fragmentation of the House and Senate encourages examination of manageable chunks of executive actions. Members realize that power inheres in details, such as prescribing personnel ceilings for agen-cies. Presidents who oppose certain programs can starve them to death by shifting employees to favored activities. Thus Congress may specify personnel ceilings for some agencies. "It is one of the anomalies of constitutional law and separated powers," writes Louis Fisher, "that executive involvement in legislative affairs is considered acceptable (indeed highly desirable) while legislative involvement in executive affairs screams of encroachment and usurpation."[136]

CONCLUSION

Because of continual shifts in the balance of legislative and executive preroga-tives, the age-old issue of executive independence versus congressional scrutiny will not be settled. Yet the recent interest in oversight has had almost no dis-cernible effect on the size and scale of the executive branch or on the main roles and responsibilities of the legislative branch. After all, committees are not dis-interested overseers, but rather guardians of the agencies and programs under their purview. Together with their satellite interest groups, committees and agencies form subgovernments or issue networks that dominate many policy-making areas.

Court Politics. Solicitor General Elena Kagan (top) begins the third day of Judiciary Committee hearings on her nomination to the Supreme Court. President Obama hugs Justice Ruth Bader Ginsburg (whose husband had recently passed away) as he arrives in the House chamber for his 2011 State of the Union message (middle), as Justices Anthony Kennedy (left) and Stephen Breyer look on. Members of the Westboro Baptist Church of Topeka, Kan. (bottom), picket in front of the Supreme Court building in October 2010. The father of a slain soldier brought suit against the church—whose members had appeared with similar placards at the son's funeral. The Court ultimately ruled in the church's favor: no matter how hateful or offensive the language, it is nonetheless protected under the First Amendment.

12

Congress and the Courts

"Scarcely any political question arises in the United States that is not resolved, sooner or later, into a judicial one," wrote the famous French chronicler Alexis de Tocqueville in *Democracy in America*, his classic 1835 study of early American life.[1] From the beginnings of the Republic, when federal courts handed down decisions that strengthened the national government, to many of today's most hotly debated issues—health care, immigration, gun rights—federal judges have been at the storm center of numerous controversies. The U.S. Supreme Court first asserted the prerogative of judicial review in the landmark case of *Marbury v. Madison* (1803).[2] Over time, the American public has come to view the highest court as the primary interpreter of the Constitution.[3] Bolstered by both public legitimacy and legal precedent, federal judges regularly pass judgment on the compelling issues that confront the nation.[4] At the same time, Congress and the White House also interpret the Constitution. As the Supreme Court stated in *United States v. Nixon* (1974), "In the performance of assigned constitutional duties each branch of the Government must initially interpret the Constitution, and the interpretation of its powers by any branch is due great respect from the others."[5]

Conflicts between Congress and the federal courts are inevitable. A famous instance occurred during the New Deal when the Supreme Court invalidated thirteen acts of Congress in one term (1935–1936). So frustrated was President Franklin D. Roosevelt that he proposed legislation expanding the size of the Court so he could nominate judges more sympathetic to his program. However, widespread legislative and public opposition defeated Roosevelt's Court-packing scheme. Nevertheless, the Court, perhaps sensitive to the changes under way in the country, became more accommodating in interpreting key constitutional provisions. In 1937 the Court handed down a decision that upheld a state minimum wage law similar to one that it had previously ruled unconstitutional.[6] In that same year, the Court also upheld a federal law regulating management-labor relations, recognizing a far greater congressional power to regulate commerce than the Court's precedents had permitted. This abrupt turnaround by the Court was, as a wit of the period put it, "the switch in time that saved nine."

THE FEDERAL COURTS

Although the framers outlined the structure and authority of Congress in some detail in Article I of the Constitution, Article III, which deals with the courts, is much less detailed. Indeed, Article III leaves the creation of the federal courts other than the Supreme Court wholly to the discretion of Congress. Thus the judicial branch owes less to constitutional mandates and more to the legislation establishing its structure and the rulings of the early justices such as Chief Justice John Marshall (1801–1835). As a noted legal scholar explained:

> Congress was created nearly full blown by the Constitution itself. The vast possibilities of the presidency were relatively easy to perceive and soon, inevitably materialized. But the institution of the judiciary needed to be summoned up out of the constitutional vapors, shaped and maintained. And the Great Chief Justice, John Marshall—not single-handed, but first and foremost—was there to do it and did.[7]

The most important constitutional provision related to the courts is the guarantee of lifetime tenure for Article III judges. The framers of the Constitution wanted an independent judiciary—that is, a judiciary insulated from political pressure. This independence is an important part of the American system of separation of powers, and yet it is a source of friction between Congress and the courts. Although, as discussed later in this chapter, Congress is not without influence, the federal courts, including the Supreme Court, have the institutional ability to frustrate congressional policy.

The federal court system today comprises district courts, courts of appeals, and the Supreme Court. The district courts are the federal trial courts, which deal with a range of civil matters and federal criminal cases. In addition to Article III district judges, the district courts are staffed by magistrate judges, who serve a fixed term and assist the district judges in handling the civil and criminal caseloads. The district courts also house the federal bankruptcy courts, which are staffed by specialized judges serving a fixed term.

District courts are similar to congressional committees in the sense that most of the work of the federal courts is done at that level. Like congressional districts, district courts are organized by state. Each state, and the District of Columbia, has at least one, with larger states (such as Texas and California) having as many as four. The primary function of the district courts is "norm enforcement"—that is, applying relatively settled law to disputes.

Above the district courts are the courts of appeals, which are organized in eleven regional circuits. There is also a circuit for the District of Columbia, and one additional circuit, the Federal Circuit, with a nationwide but specialized jurisdiction centering mainly on appeals of administrative agency rulings. Parties unhappy with the outcome of a case at the district court level typically have an automatic right of appeal to the appellate level. These courts are staffed by judges typically called circuit judges. The courts of appeals hear oral arguments and decide cases in three-judge panels. In rare circumstances, a three-judge panel's decision will be reviewed by a larger number of circuit judges, sitting "en banc." The primary function of the courts of appeals is "error correction"—that is, reviewing the work of lower courts, and some executive branch agencies, for mistakes of law or fact.

Parties unhappy with the outcome of an appeal can seek Supreme Court review of their cases, but unlike at the court of appeals level, Supreme Court review is almost never automatic. Instead, the Court decides which cases from the courts of appeals and the state courts of last resort it will hear. Typically, the Supreme Court will hear and decide about 1 percent of the cases in which one or both parties have requested review. As a result, the Court's docket is dominated by cases raising important questions of constitutional and statutory interpretation. Unlike the lower federal courts, the Supreme Court does not engage in norm enforcement, and it rarely takes a case for the sole purpose of correcting an error committed by a lower court. Instead, its policy-making role is paramount.

The Supreme Court's policy making is carried out in three main ways. First, its interpretive decisions can uphold or broaden the legislative powers of Congress. "Congress acted within its authority," said Supreme Court justice Ruth Bader Ginsburg, when the Court upheld a law further extending copyright privileges for authors, inventors, and artists such as commercial artist Walt Disney.[8] Second, it can check overreaching by Congress through its implied power of judicial review. Third, and equally significant, the Supreme Court can act as a policy-making catalyst, especially when the House or Senate is stymied in making decisions. The landmark civil rights case of *Brown v. Board of Education* (1954) is a classic example. The decision struck down the separate-but-equal doctrine that had upheld state laws mandating racially segregated public schools. Until this decision, filibusters by southern senators had thwarted enactment of meaningful civil rights bills. The *Brown* ruling galvanized Congress to enact the Civil Rights Act of 1957, the first civil rights law enacted by Congress since 1875. "The genius of a system of divided powers," wrote one law professor, "is that when one branch is closed to the desires of the populace or the demands of justice, another may open up."[9] The *Brown* decision alone had little impact on the actual desegregation of public schools until Congress began to pass landmark legislation such as the Civil Rights Act of 1964 and the Elementary and Secondary Education Act of 1965.

THE COURT AS REFEREE AND UMPIRE

The Supreme Court serves as both referee between the two nationally elective branches and the umpire in federal-state relations. Ever since the Court claimed the power of judicial review in 1803, it has considered a large number of separation-of-powers and federalism issues, most notably during the New Deal and over the last few decades. Whether acting as referee or umpire, the

Supreme Court is often subjected to criticism for usurping the prerogatives of the other national branches, or of the state and local governments. Members of Congress "often reserve their most vituperative criticism of federal courts for decisions that, in their view, unduly limit the prerogatives of state and local governments to regulate such matters as abortion, school prayer, prison overcrowding, school busing, local elections, and so on."[10]

A common refrain in criticism of the courts is that judges are acting as a "super legislature" in their rulings—that is, they are legislating from the bench. The charge of "judicial activism" is premised on the view that, at least in some cases, judges are making decisions based on their personal values and not the dictates of law, or that they are making decisions that their critics believe should be settled by the elective branches of government.

Judicial activism, however, is frequently in the eye of the beholder. When, for example, the Supreme Court ruled 5–4 in *District of Columbia v. Heller*[11] that the Second Amendment protects an individual's right to own a gun— thereby overturning long-standing law to the contrary in the District and, by implication, elsewhere—relatively few conservative commentators charged the Court with judicial activism. Many liberals, by contrast, saw the *Heller* case as a clear example of conservative judicial activism.[12] On the other hand, when the Supreme Court ruled, also 5–4, in *Kelo v. City of New London* that a city had the power of eminent domain to condemn a private residence to promote local economic development, liberals praised the case as exhibiting judicial restraint, permitting democratically accountable local governments to make such decisions free from judicial second-guessing.[13] Meanwhile, conservatives denounced the case as "liberal activism."[14]

The charge of judicial activism often serves as a way of denouncing judicial decisions that politicians and opinion leaders oppose on other grounds. In the broader context of partisan and ideological polarization, the judiciary has come in for harsh attacks from many quarters. Retired Supreme Court justice Sandra Day O'Connor commented that "the breadth and intensity of rage currently being leveled at the judiciary may be unmatched in American history. The ubiquitous 'activist judges' who 'legislate from the bench' have become central villains on today's domestic political landscape."[15]

The Referee

Like the federal courts, Congress interprets the Constitution. When it makes national policy through its lawmaking processes, it is also asserting that it has the constitutional power to do so. As a result, it is not uncommon for the two branches to view issues differently. To be sure, the Supreme Court often exercises restraint when it addresses the powers of Congress or the president for two key reasons: to avoid charges of judicial overreaching and to acknowledge that only the elective institutions can implement judicial judgments. The following case reveals how a decision restricting Congress's authority under the commerce clause (Article I, section 8) of the Constitution can trigger a fast reassertion of legislative power.

In *United States v. Lopez* (1995), the Supreme Court overturned a federal law banning guns near school grounds. For the "first time since the New Deal . . . the Court found Congress to have exceeded the bounds of its constitutional authority to regulate interstate commerce"—in this case the presence of guns that had undoubtedly moved across state lines before ending up on school playgrounds.[16] In response, Congress moved quickly to pass legislation reasserting its authority under the commerce clause to restrict the presence of guns in school zones. The measure, which the president signed, stated: "It shall be unlawful for any individual knowingly to possess a firearm that has moved in or that otherwise affects interstate or foreign commerce at a place that the individual knows, or has reasonable cause to believe, is a school zone."[17] When the revised statute was challenged in the lower federal courts, it was upheld as a constitutional exercise of Congress's power to regulate interstate commerce. The Supreme Court has not yet reviewed these lower-court decisions.

Lopez takes on added importance in the contemporary context because of the ongoing litigation over the constitutionality of the individual mandate, a key provision of the 2010 health care reform legislation. When it goes into effect, the individual mandate will require most Americans to have health insurance, either through an employer, a government program, or self-purchased. Defenders of the law argue that the individual mandate is a necessary part of a comprehensive reform of the national health insurance market, and is thus justified, according to one of several legal theories, as an exercise of Congress's power over interstate commerce. Whether Congress can regulate individuals in this way turns, at least in part, on the Court's interpretation of the breadth of the commerce power. *Lopez* and a few other cases suggest the limits of that power.

Mindful of the courts' referee role, lawmakers have sought to employ it for their own goals. Thus on a number of occasions members of Congress have asked the courts to defend congressional prerogatives against usurpation by the president. War making is the principal example. Not since World War II has Congress declared war, although it has enacted legislation that is functionally equivalent. Recent presidents of both parties have committed American troops to combat on their own initiative. As for war power suits brought by lawmakers, scholar Louis Fisher takes a cautionary view:

> From the Vietnam War to the present day, members of Congress have gone to court to contest presidential wars and defend legislative prerogatives. In most of these cases, the courts held that the lawmakers lacked standing to bring the case. Even when legislators were granted standing, the courts refused relief on numerous grounds. Judges pointed out that the legislators represented only a fraction of the congressional membership and that often another group of legislators had filed a brief defending the president's action. Courts regularly note that Congress as a whole has failed to invoke its institutional powers to confront the president.[18]

Usually courts dismiss these suits and offer two rationales: first, the lawsuits raise political questions best left to the elective branches to resolve; and second, they represent conflicts between groups of lawmakers, not constitutional clashes between Congress and the president.

The fundamental question is how deferential the courts should be to laws enacted by the popularly elected Congress or to executive use of its war powers. Lawmakers and presidents are accountable to their constituents every time they face reelection. Although judges are not immune to the tides of public opinion, they do not face accountability through elections. On the other hand, a key virtue of an independent judiciary is that it can, in theory, protect unpopular or politically weak minority groups against unconstitutional deprivations of liberty. The tension between policy making by elected officials versus judge-made decisions is perennial.

The Umpire

As the federalism umpire, the Supreme Court is the arbiter of federal and state powers. The claims of the federal government are anchored in the supremacy clause (Article VI) of the Constitution, which posits that the federal Constitution, as well as federal laws and treaties, prevail over conflicting state constitutions or laws. The states' claims are grounded in the Tenth Amendment, which reserves certain powers to the states or to the people, and the Eleventh Amendment, which protects states from being sued in federal court. The Eleventh Amendment comes into play when Congress seeks to make state governments subject to federal regulation.

Legal controversies arising out of the 1990 Americans with Disabilities Act (ADA) illustrate the Supreme Court's role as federalism umpire. In *Alabama v. Garrett* (2001), the Court held that states are immune from suits brought by handicapped state employees under the ADA. The Court held that states were not required "to make special accommodations for the disabled, so long as their actions toward such individuals had a rational basis." The reason lay in an expanded notion of states' "sovereign immunity" from suits by private citizens—a theory disputed by many legal scholars.[19] In a dissenting opinion, Justice Stephen G. Breyer countered: "In fact, Congress compiled a vast legislative record documenting 'massive, society-wide discrimination' against persons with disabilities." Breyer, a one-time Capitol Hill staff member, went on to remind his colleagues of the constitutional primacy of legislative judgments.

Unlike the courts, Congress can readily gather facts from across the nation, assess the magnitude of a problem, and more easily find an appropriate remedy. And unlike the courts, Congress directly reflects public attitudes and beliefs, enabling it to better understand where and to what extent refusals to accommodate disability amount to behavior that is callous or unreasonable to the point of lacking constitutional justification. Unlike judges, members of Congress can directly obtain information from constituents who have first-hand experience with discrimination and related issues.

Three years later, in *Tennessee v. Lane,* the Court took a different view from *Garrett* regarding state sovereignty under the ADA. Briefly, George Lane, a paraplegic who had been charged with a crime, had to crawl up two floors to reach a county courtroom in Tennessee because there was no elevator. At a subsequent hearing, he refused to crawl up the stairs and was arrested for failure to appear at the hearing on his case. He sued Tennessee under the ADA and won a financial settlement, which the court upheld. Why the different outcomes in *Lane* and *Garrett*? Part of the explanation is that the Court considered a wider range of evidence. In *Garrett,* the Court considered only state employers such as the University of Alabama; in *Lane,* it also examined the treatment of the disabled by Tennessee's county and city employees. Significantly, *Lane* involved access to the courts, one of the country's key political institutions. Although the Court is concerned about disabled persons' access to employment, it has traditionally shown greater sympathy for access to political institutions by disadvantaged groups. Such disputes highlight the many dimensions and complexities associated with federalism decisions.

Statutory Interpretation

The distinction between statutory and constitutional interpretation is very important. In statutory interpretation, federal judges construe the meaning, or intent, of the often vague language embedded in laws. Constitutional interpretation occurs when federal or state laws are challenged as violating the U.S. Constitution.

The Lily Ledbetter case decided in May 2007 is an example of the Supreme Court engaging in statutory interpretation. Despite doing the same job as her male counterparts at Goodyear Tire and Rubber Co., Ledbetter received less pay. When after twenty years on the job she learned of Goodyear's discriminatory treatment, she sued on the grounds of gender-based pay and employment discrimination. To decide this case, the Supreme Court had to determine whether the statute of limitations in the relevant federal law, Title VIII of the Civil Rights Act, had expired and precluded Ledbetter's suit. The Court ruled, in a 5–4 decision, that Ledbetter's lawsuit was not timely because she did not file the suit within 180 days of the date on which the lower pay had been agreed on by the parties. The Court majority rejected the argument that the statute of limitations restarted with every discriminatory paycheck. A vigorous dissent by Justice Ruth Bader Ginsburg chided the Court's majority for their ignorance of workplace realities and noted that Congress could clarify the law.

Many lawmakers strongly disagreed with the *Ledbetter* decision and its interpretation of legislative intent. In one of its first actions, the 111th Congress (2009–2011) passed legislation, which President Obama signed into law, overturning *Ledbetter* and resetting the statute of limitations with every discriminatory paycheck, thereby making it easier for workers to challenge gender-based employment discrimination.[20]

In determining whether national or state actions violate the Constitution, federal judges examine the text of the Constitution, the intentions of the drafters, and judicial precedents relevant to the controversy. In the death penalty area, the Court also considers society's evolving standards regarding such punishment because the Eighth Amendment forbids "cruel *and unusual* punishments" (emphasis added).

The major difference between statutory and constitutional interpretation is the ease with which Congress can reassert its understanding of the law against the Supreme Court. When the Court misinterprets a statute, Congress can simply amend or clarify the law, as it did in the *Ledbetter* case. By contrast, a constitutional decision of the Court is binding on Congress and can be undone only by a subsequent constitutional amendment—which is very rare—or by the Court itself when it overrules one of its precedents.

Judicial interpretation of federal statutes is fraught with difficulty because communications between Congress and the federal courts are highly imperfect. Neither branch understands the workings of the other very well.[21] Ambiguity, imprecision, or inconsistency can often be the price of winning enactment of legislative measures. The more legislators try to define precisely the language of a bill, the more they may divide or dissipate congressional support for it. Abner J. Mikva, a four-term House Democrat from Chicago who went on to become a federal judge and later counsel to President Bill Clinton, recounted an example from his Capitol Hill days. The issue involved a controversial strip-mining bill being managed by Arizona Democrat Morris K. Udall, then chair of the House Interior (now called Natural Resources) Committee:

> They'd put together a very delicate coalition of support. One problem was whether the states or the feds would run the program. One member got up and asked, "Isn't it a fact that under this bill the states would continue to exercise sovereignty over strip mining?" And Mo replied, "You're absolutely right." A little later someone else got up and asked, "Now is it clear that the Federal Government will have the final say on strip mining?" And Mo replied, "You're absolutely right." Later, in the cloakroom, I said, "Mo, they can't both be right." And Mo said, "You're absolutely right."[22]

Called upon to interpret statutes, judges may not appreciate the efforts required to get legislation passed on Capitol Hill or understand how to examine legislative history, as manifested in hearings, reports, and floor debate. Within the courts and among legal scholars, there is a lively debate over the proper way to approach statutory interpretation. Should judges focus only on the plain meaning of the statutory language, or should they delve into legislative history to ascertain what Congress intended when it employed certain statutory phrases? A group of federal judges, led by Supreme Court justice Antonin Scalia, argues that legislative history is unreliable as an indicator of legislative intent because it is open to manipulation by lawmakers, executive officials, and congressional staffers.

One remarkable example of the manipulation of legislative history occurred in the context of the Senate passage of the Detainee Treatment Act

(DTA) in late 2005. An important issue before the federal courts at the time was whether the DTA would retroactively nullify all the pending legal challenges of the Guantánamo detainees. Two sponsors of the legislation, Sen. Lindsey O. Graham, R-S.C., and Sen. Jon Kyl, R-Ariz., sought to quash all such challenges, while another sponsor, Sen. Carl Levin, D-Mich., wanted to allow cases filed before the passage of the DTA to go forward.[23] But just before passage of the legislation, Graham and Kyl inserted into the *Congressional Record* a colloquy designed to show that in passing the DTA the Senate intended to invalidate all pending legal challenges brought by Guantánamo detainees. Written in informal style, the colloquy contained controversial banter suggesting that the exchange occurred live on the Senate floor. Such a colloquy would have alerted all senators that Graham and Kyl believed the legislation would foreclose all pending cases, and the absence of subsequent objections would imply that senators agreed with this interpretation. However, a C-SPAN recording showed that the discussion never actually occurred on the Senate floor. Justice Department lawyers nevertheless cited the colloquy in their legal brief arguing that Congress intended to remove all the pending cases from federal jurisdiction.[24] In response, a lawyer for one of the detainees objected. "This colloquy is critical to the government's legislative history argument, and it's entirely manufactured and misrepresented to the court as having occurred live on the Senate floor before a crucial vote."[25]

Rather than relying on legislative history, Scalia contends that justices should follow a textualist approach, examining the wording of laws or constitutional clauses and interpreting them according to what they meant at the time of enactment.[26] Other federal judges, including Supreme Court Justice Stephen Breyer, defend the value of legislative history, finding it useful in statutory interpretation. "It is dangerous," Breyer asserted, "to rely exclusively upon the literal meaning of a statute's words."[27]

The dispute over legislative history is well illustrated by Congress's passage of the Civil Rights Act of 1991. The law overturned, in whole or in part, seven civil rights cases decided by a conservative-leaning Supreme Court.[28] And yet because the 1991 legislation was filled with ambiguities, interested lawmakers created their own legislative history during floor debate. A memorandum was even put in the *Congressional Record* stating that the written statement was the exclusive legislative history for certain contested provisions. During debate on the legislation, a Republican senator pointed out the pitfalls of relying on legislative history. His position essentially endorsed Scalia's view that Congress should state clearly what it means or wants in the law itself rather than in floor debates or other explanatory statements.[29]

Supreme Court Justice John Paul Stevens expressed a contrary opinion, saying that a "stubborn insistence on 'clear statements' [in the law] burdens the Congress with unnecessary reenactment of provisions that were already plain enough." Rep. Barney Frank, D-Mass., once remarked that if Scalia's view on legislative history became dominant, Congress would be required to develop a new category of legislation: "the 'No, we really meant it' statute."[30] The chief counsel of the Senate Judiciary Committee observed that difficulty in textual interpretation "encourages us to write clearer legislation. But unclear bills are still written. If they were not, we would not have this fight over [the confirmation of] judges."[31]

Legislative Checks on the Judiciary

Many factors are likely to generate conflict between Congress and the courts. With federal judges serving life tenure, turnover on the courts is often far slower than in Congress. Meanwhile, the ideological and partisan composition of Congress can diverge widely from that of the federal courts. In addition, some Supreme Court rulings have direct and profound effects on Congress and its members. Cases involving the redistricting of House seats and campaign finance are recent examples. Scores of interest groups also monitor court decisions, and, when they disagree with them, these groups are not reluctant to lobby Congress to seek their statutory reversal.

Congress has a variety of tools by which it can influence the Supreme Court and lower federal courts. In addition to the Senate's constitutional advice and consent role regarding judicial nominations, four legislative powers merit some mention: (1) to withdraw jurisdiction, (2) to impeach judges, (3) to influence the size, procedures, and pay scales of the courts, and (4) to pass constitutional amendments.

Withdrawal of Jurisdiction. The jurisdiction of the federal courts, including the Supreme Court, is based in both Article III, which sets the outer limits of federal jurisdiction, and in statute. Because it is based in statute, Congress can alter the jurisdiction of the federal courts to achieve policy goals.

In some circumstances, Congress may seek to expand federal court jurisdiction—usually at the expense of state courts—to achieve particular policy goals. In the post–Civil War period, for example, Congress expanded federal court jurisdiction in an effort to protect the civil rights of African Americans.[32] Republican Congresses in the latter half of the nineteenth century expanded federal court jurisdiction in order to protect commercial interests against state controls.[33] Similarly, the Class Action Fairness Act of 2005 expanded federal jurisdiction over many large class-action lawsuits, a key goal of business groups who had been frustrated by plaintiff lawyers' "forum shopping" to find the most friendly state courts.

But Congress's power over the jurisdiction of the federal courts, including the Supreme Court, serves as a potential check on judicial overreach. Under its constitutional authority to determine the Supreme Court's appellate jurisdiction, for example, Congress may threaten to withdraw the Court's authority to review certain categories of cases. Recent years offer several examples of such threats. One issue concerned a Ninth Circuit Court of Appeals decision that a 1954 federal law adding the phrase "one Nation under God" to the Pledge of Allegiance was unconstitutional on First Amendment grounds. In response, House majority leader Tom DeLay, R-Texas, remarked, "I think that [legislation limiting the court's jurisdiction] would be a very good idea to send a message to the judiciary [that] they ought to keep their hands off the Pledge of Allegiance."[34] Other topics—such as same-sex marriage and the public display of the Ten Commandments—evoked similar responses. Some scholars have argued that such threats of court-curbing legislation affect judicial decision making. One recent study found that the Supreme Court responds to the introduction of court-curbing legislation by striking down fewer laws in subsequent years.[35]

Despite the ongoing conflicts between Congress and the courts, on only one occasion in U.S. history did Congress prevent the Supreme Court from deciding a case by removing its appellate jurisdiction:

> This extraordinary action was taken by a Congress dominated by Radical Republicans who wanted to prohibit the Supreme Court from reviewing the constitutionality of the Reconstruction Acts of 1867. The acts substituted military rule for civilian government in the ten southern states that initially refused to rejoin the Union and established procedures for those states to follow to gain readmittance and representation in the federal government.[36]

Congress simply passed legislation repealing the Supreme Court's right to hear appeals involving these matters, thereby preventing "a possibly hostile Court from using the power of judicial review to invalidate a piece of legislation."[37] Various scholars have identified a variety of reasons why court-curbing legislation is so rarely adopted: "the historically broad consensus in Congress to protect, or at least tolerate, an independent judiciary; judicial opponents' reluctance to emasculate an institution that they may someday need as an ally; . . . and resistance by the organized bar."[38]

Impeachment of Judges. Federal judges, like other national civil officers, are subject to impeachment under Article II of the Constitution. They are appointed "during good behavior," effectively for life. Only one Supreme Court justice, Samuel Chase, has ever been impeached by the House. It occurred in 1804, during bitter partisan battles between Federalists and Jeffersonian Republicans. The judiciary was the last bastion of Federalist influence after Thomas Jefferson won the presidency in the 1800 election. Chase's intemperate and arrogant behavior—he even campaigned for John Adams's reelection in 1800—raised the ire of Jefferson and his allies in Congress. On March 12, 1804, the House voted 73–32 along party lines to impeach Chase. The Senate, however, failed to convict (and thus remove) him. The importance of Chase's acquittal by the Senate was underscored in a book by Chief Justice William Rehnquist:

> The acquittal of Samuel Chase by the Senate had a profound effect on the American judiciary. First, it assured the independence of federal judges from congressional oversight of the decisions they made in the cases that come before them. Second, by assuring that impeachment would not be used in the future as a method to remove members of the Supreme Court for their judicial opinions, it helped to safeguard the independence of that body.[39]

Other Supreme Court justices have been either threatened with impeachment or subjected to impeachment investigations. One example is William O. Douglas in 1953 and in 1970.

Fifteen federal judges have been impeached, and eight have been removed by a two-thirds vote in the Senate.[40] The 111th Congress (2009–2011) actually saw active impeachment proceedings against two district judges. In May 2009, Judge Samuel B. Kent of the Southern District of Texas was convicted of obstruction of justice, resulting from an investigation of claims that he had sexually abused two female court staffers. He was sentenced to thirty-three months in prison. He did not, however, resign from the bench, meaning that he continued to collect his judicial salary. His refusal to step down drew protests from Capitol Hill, which prompted Kent to announce that he would resign in one year. Press reports suggested that Kent and his attorney believed that it would take at least that long for the House and Senate to act. This frankness led to immediate initiation of impeachment proceedings in the House, and the House soon voted unanimously to impeach Kent. He then resigned, before the Senate could try him, effective June 30, 2009.

On December 8, 2010, the Senate voted unanimously to remove Judge Thomas Porteous Jr. of the Eastern District of Louisiana from the bench. Porteous was impeached on four articles, based on corruption and making false statements on his financial disclosure reports.

These recent examples of judicial impeachments are representative of such cases throughout U.S. history. Judges have been impeached for unethical and illegal acts, but not because of the legal and policy judgments rendered during the course of their judicial duties. The "Impeach Earl Warren" billboards and bumper stickers that appeared all across the South in the 1960s in the wake of *Brown v. Board of Education* were outside the norm. Congress has not used impeachment as a mechanism to exert political influence over the judiciary.

Size, Procedure, and Pay. Historically, the size of the Supreme Court has varied anywhere from six to ten members. "Generally, laws decreasing the number of justices have been motivated by a desire to punish the president; increases have been aimed at influencing the philosophical balance of the Court itself" (such as Roosevelt's Court-packing plan).[41] But since 1869 Congress has not changed the Court's size from its current nine justices, so this power is unlikely to be invoked in the foreseeable future.

Procedurally, lawmakers have occasionally proposed that court decisions overturning federal laws be accomplished by a supermajority vote of the justices. Some of the "more extreme proposals have urged that such decisions be unanimous."[42] None of these proposals has been adopted. Instead, they serve as signals to the judiciary of lawmakers' disapproval of certain court decisions. Lawmakers have communicated their complaints to the unelected members of the judicial branch by calling for stronger ethical guidelines for judges to ensure their impartiality.[43] Legislative proposals for the creation of an inspector general post to oversee judicial branch ethics have met with judicial branch

claims that such oversight would violate the separation of powers and undermine judicial independence.

Another legislative proposal that has generated interbranch controversy is
opening federal courtrooms to television cameras. Several justices have
opposed televising Supreme Court proceedings, in part because the cameras
might alter decision making, intrude on the privacy of the justices by making
them public celebrities, and threaten their personal security. During an appearance before the Senate Judiciary Committee, Justice Anthony Kennedy
implored senators to not pass legislation mandating the televising of their open
proceedings.[44] His concern was that televised Court sessions would eventually
undermine the collegial character of the Court and encourage the justices to
speak in sound bites. Attitudes toward cameras in the courtroom may be
changing, however. In her confirmation hearings, the Court's newest member,
Elena Kagan, said that she thought "it would be a great thing for the institution
and for the American people" to be able to watch Supreme Court arguments
on television.[45] Justice Sotomayor has expressed similar views. In the fall of
2010, the Judicial Conference of the United States, the policy-making body for
the lower federal courts, approved a proposal to study implementing digital
video recording of civil proceedings in district courts. [46]

A current concern is that fewer aspirants are seeking federal judgeships.
Part of the reason is pay. "Salaries are far lower [for federal judges] than what
fresh-faced law-school grads can make at big corporate firms."[47] Chief Justice
John Roberts devoted much of his 2008 annual year-end report on the federal
judiciary to the inadequacy of judicial salaries. The judicial branch as a whole
made a major push in the 110th Congress for a judicial pay increase. The effort
at what the judges term "salary restoration"—because judicial salaries had not
kept pace with inflation—won the support of House and Senate leaders and
President Bush. But opposition from a few powerful members of Congress
axed the bill.

Congressional opposition to increased judicial pay stems from so-called
linkage. Under current law, the salaries of federal judges and members of
Congress are linked.[48] Lawmakers' reluctance to raise their own salaries—for
obvious political reasons—is a large part of the reason federal judges' salaries
have not kept pace with inflation. To raise judicial salaries substantially, members of Congress would have to agree to "de-link" their salaries from those of
judges, thereby depriving members of some political cover on the occasions
when they decide to raise their own salaries. The chief justice currently receives
an annual salary of $223,500, associate justices $213,900, appeals court judges
$184,500, and federal district judges $174,000.[49] By comparison, law school
deans can earn over $400,000 a year and top law firm partners $1 million or
more a year.[50] Some analysts, however, question whether there are benefits to
paying judges more.[51] The present state of the federal budget makes any substantial increase in judges' salaries unlikely in the near future.

Constitutional Amendments. On four occasions, Congress successfully
used the arduous process of amending the Constitution to overturn decisions

of the Supreme Court. In *Chisholm v. Georgia* (1793), the Court held that citizens of one state could sue another state in federal court.[52] To prevent a rash of citizen suits against the states, Congress oversaw passage of the Eleventh Amendment to reverse this decision. It protects states' sovereign immunity from lawsuits brought by citizens of other states and foreign countries. The *Dred Scott v. Sandford* (1857) decision[53]—denying African Americans citizenship under the Constitution—was nullified by the Thirteenth Amendment (abolishing slavery) and Fourteenth Amendment (granting African Americans citizenship). The Sixteenth Amendment overturned *Pollock v. Farmer's Loan and Trust Co.* (1895), which struck down a federal income tax. The Twenty-sixth Amendment invalidated *Oregon v. Mitchell* (1970), which held that Congress had exceeded its authority by lowering the minimum voting age to eighteen for state elections.[54]

Generally, lawmakers are reluctant to amend the Constitution. The view of Rep. Melvin Watt, D-N.C., reflects that of many members: "I just think the Constitution has served us very well over a long, long period of time, and one needs to make a compelling case before we start amending the Constitution to do anything."[55] However, certain constitutional amendments have appeared regularly on the legislative agenda. One would ban desecration of the American flag. The proposal is a response to a 1989 Supreme Court ruling in *Texas v. Johnson* that state laws banning flag burning violate the First Amendment right of free speech. Justice William Brennan, who wrote the majority opinion in *Johnson,* declared, "We do not consecrate the flag by punishing its desecration, for in doing so we dilute the freedom that this cherished emblem represents."[56] The House has passed the legislation several times, but the Senate has never approved the measure.

Eliminating life tenure for federal judges is another proposal that sometimes surfaces on Capitol Hill. Bitter judicial nomination battles have prompted some observers to suggest term limits (such as fifteen years) for federal judges. "If the Senate can't figure out how to reach a [partisan] truce in its battles over these all-important jobs," wrote one analyst, "maybe the best solution is to make the jobs not quite so important."[57] Others simply contend that Supreme Court justices serve too long (18.7 years was the average length of service on the Rehnquist Court). Aging justices, it is argued, may become overly arrogant, out of touch with contemporary values, or too impaired to serve. To avoid the difficulties of winning approval of a constitutional amendment, they propose a complex legislative approach that would move "justices into senior status after roughly eighteen years on the high court."[58]

ADVICE AND CONSENT FOR JUDICIAL NOMINEES

Article II, section 2, of the Constitution states that the president "shall nominate, and by and with the Advice and Consent of the Senate, shall appoint . . . Judges of the Supreme Court." The founders rejected giving the power to appoint solely to the executive, or solely to Congress as a whole or to the Senate in particular. But they compromised and required for judicial selections joint action by the president and the Senate. The president has the sole prerogative to nominate, but the power to confirm (or not) belongs to the Senate. Alexander Hamilton, in *Federalist* No. 66, viewed this division of responsibility in stark terms: "There will, of course, be no exertion of CHOICE on the part of the Senate. They may defeat one choice of the Executive and oblige him to make another; but they cannot themselves CHOOSE—they can only ratify or reject the choice he may have made."

Hamilton's perspective, however, requires some refinement. Giving two elective institutions a voice in the appointments process necessarily means that the Senate is able to influence the president's choice of nominees. Indeed, individual senators, House members, interest groups, the American Bar Association (which since 1952 has rated judicial candidates), the Federalist Society, the press and media, and even sitting judges can all sometimes influence both the choice of judicial nominees and Senate action, if any, on those nominees.[59] The fact that federal district and appellate court jurisdictions are geographically based means that senators from those states (especially if they are of the president's party) commonly have a big say in recommending judicial candidates to the White House (see Table 12-1 for judgeship appointments by presidents).

Any discussion of the various norms, practices, and controversies associated with the confirmation process for federal judges must be prefaced by a description of the half-dozen principal stages in filling a vacancy on the Supreme Court.

First, the president puts together a short list of nominees. Considerable thought and research go into the list. Presidents want to nominate individuals who reflect their political and policy views and who are generally perceived as highly competent and knowledgeable. Many political considerations also enter the selection process. The gender, race, geographic, and religious make-up of the Court may be relevant to the choice. Presidents consider the nominee's age, seeking a qualified candidate who will be able to serve a lengthy tenure on the Court. And they look to the composition of the Senate and assess the prospects of an easy or difficult confirmation battle.

The contemporary selection process also includes careful vetting of potential nominees' personal and professional lives. Typical of recent presidents, the research process conducted for the nominees on Obama's short list when Justice David Souter announced his retirement was highly intensive. Researchers scoured "the real estate transactions, taxes, ethics, the backgrounds of spouses and adult children, as well as a particularly close look at the early jobs held right after law school—often at the Justice Department—when early views could have been formed and when a paper trail of thousands of documents was probably created."[60]

Second, once the president has made his choice, he sends a written nomination to the Senate, which is then referred to the Judiciary Committee. The nominee is escorted to various Hill offices to meet and talk with key senators. Meanwhile, the nominee begins extensive preparation for the hearings before

TABLE 12-1   **Judgeship Appointments by President, 1933–2011**

President	Supreme Court	Regional Court of Appeals	USCAFC[1]	District Courts	Total
F. Roosevelt (1933–1945)	9	52	—	136	197
Truman (1945–1953)	4	27	—	102	133
Eisenhower (1953–1961)	5	45	—	127	177
Kennedy (1961–1963)	2	20	—	102	124
L. Johnson (1963–1969)	2	41	—	125	168
Nixon (1969–1975)	4	48	—	182	231
Ford (1974–1977)	1	12	—	52	65
Carter (1977–1981)	0	56	—	206	262
Reagan (1981–1989)	3	78	5	292	378
G. H. W. Bush (1989–1993)	2	37	5	149	193
Clinton (1993–2001)	2	62	4	306	374
G. W. Bush (2001–2009)	2	61	2	261	326
Obama[2] (2009–2011)	2	16	1	50	69

Source: Adapted from "Judgeship Appointments by President," *The Third Branch,* newsletter of the Federal Courts, February 2009. Data for the Obama administration are from the Federal Judicial Center, www.fjc.gov/history/home.nsf/page/research_categories.html.

[1] The U.S. Court of Appeals for the Federal Circuit (USCAFC) was established in 1982.

[2] Data are through March 3, 2011.

the Judiciary Committee. Part of the preparation commonly involves participation in mock confirmation hearings called "murder boards."

Third, the Judiciary Committee launches its own investigation of the nominee's background and qualifications. After that stage is completed, the Judiciary chair schedules public hearings on the nomination. The members of the committee have the opportunity to ask the nominee questions and also to receive testimony from other witnesses. Although it is unthinkable today that the committee would not proceed in this way, it is notable that for most of the nation's history confirmation hearings were unheard of. In 1925 Attorney General Harlan Fiske Stone was the first Supreme Court nominee to testify in public before the Judiciary Committee. Stone had made political enemies cleaning up the Justice Department in the midst of the Teapot Dome Scandal—and in vigorously enforcing the nation's antitrust laws. Certain senators signaled that they might block Stone's appointment in light of the Justice Department's handling of a related indictment against Sen. Burton K. Wheeler, D-Mont. To answer questions about his handling of the Wheeler case, Stone apparently offered to appear before the committee in a public hearing.[61] Still, confirmation hearings did not become customary until the mid-1950s.

Fourth, after the hearings are concluded, the Judiciary Committee meets in open session to report the nomination to the Senate either with a favorable or negative recommendation, or with no recommendation at all. Dating back to at least the 1880s, the "Judiciary Committee's traditional practice has been to report even those Supreme Court nominations that were opposed by a committee majority, thus allowing the full Senate to make the final decision on whether the nominee should be confirmed."[62] (This practice does not apply to nominees for district or appellate court judgeships.) Once reported by the committee, the nomination is assigned to the Senate's executive calendar.

Fifth, the Senate majority leader decides when to call up the nomination for chamber consideration after consultation with various lawmakers, including the minority leader, and other pertinent individuals. Once the nomination reaches the floor, all senators have an opportunity to discuss the nominee's credentials, philosophy, or anything else they believe is relevant for the public record. Extended debate, or a filibuster, is unusual on Supreme Court nominations. Cloture is available to curb talkathons but has been moved only four times: in 1968, on Abe Fortas's nomination to chief justice; in 1971, on William Rehnquist's nomination to be an associate justice; in 1986, on Rehnquist's nomination to be chief justice;[63] and in 2006, on Samuel A. Alito's nomination to replace Justice O'Connor. After debate ends, in a practice begun in 1967, the Senate decides whether to confirm the Supreme Court nominee by a roll call vote.[64]

Sixth, if a majority of the Senate votes to confirm, the secretary of the Senate transmits the resolution of confirmation to the president. The president then signs a document called a commission that officially appoints the nominee to the Supreme Court. The attorney general signs the engraved commission and delivers it to the nominee, who then takes the constitutional oath of office making him or her a justice of the U.S. Supreme Court.

Norms and Practices

Extraconstitutional norms and practices shape the confirmation process. President George Washington quickly learned the importance of the newly emerging norm of senatorial courtesy—an informal practice in which presidents consult home-state senators before submitting nominees for federal positions in their state. When he "failed to seek the advice from the Georgia senate delegation regarding a nomination for a federal position in Savannah, Washington was forced to withdraw the nomination in favor of the person recommended by the senators."[65]

Related to senatorial courtesy is the blue-slip policy of the Judiciary Committee, which applies only to district and court of appeals nominees. It refers to "blue approval papers that senators are asked to submit on nominees for federal judgeships in their states. For the past few years, both home-state senators have to submit a positive blue slip for a nominee to be considered by the Judiciary Committee."[66] Although exceptions have been made to this policy, Judiciary chair Patrick J. Leahy, D-Vt., announced that for the 111th Congress he would follow the traditional practice of not advancing judicial nominees unless both home-state senators agreed, but senators would not "be able to withhold blue slips anonymously."[67] Senate Republicans underscored that they expected to be consulted on nominations when they sent a letter to Senator Leahy and President Obama stating that "if we are not consulted on, and approve of, a nominee from our states, the Republican Conference will be unable to support moving forward on the nominee," implicitly threatening to employ dilatory tactics such as the filibuster.[68]

An array of other Senate practices also influence whether any action occurs on judicial nominations, such as the hold, the committee chair's prerogative of determining whether hearings will be held, and the majority leader's willingness to schedule floor consideration of the nominations. As for holds, the 112th Congress adopted Res. 28, the Wyden/Grassley/McCaskill Secret Holds Resolution, with the intention of eliminating the practice of secret holds.[69] Sen. Wyden said of the resolution, "If you want to exercise that extraordinary power, you ought to do it in the sunlight."[70] Whether eliminating secret holds—which can be used to block judicial nominees—will actually reduce delays in confirming judges remains to be seen.

An unresolved issue is the balance between advice and consent. Presidents usually favor consent over advice. The Senate tilts in the other direction. "It's advice and consent, not nominate and rubber stamp," declared Senator Leahy.[71] The qualifications appropriate for service as a federal jurist are not self-evident. The Constitution makes no reference to what presidents or senators should consider when exercising their respective roles (being a lawyer is not even a prerequisite). Setting aside the standard qualifications that everyone expects in prospective judges—legal experience, ethical behavior, recognized competence, and so on—an age-old question is whether people should be subject to litmus tests to be either nominated or confirmed for a judicial position. Should judicial nominees disclose their views on hot-button issues likely to come before the Court? Most recent nominees have studiously refused to reveal much about their views on such issues when questioned by senators.

Nomination Battles

Over the last two centuries, the Senate has "rejected about 20 percent of all Supreme Court nominees."[72] Most of the rejections occurred in the nineteenth century, with President John Tyler holding the record: five of his six nominees were rejected by the Senate (see Table 12-2).

The bitter confirmation battles of the present day date from President Ronald Reagan's nomination of conservative Robert H. Bork to the Supreme Court in 1987. A Democratic-controlled Senate rejected Bork, who was perceived as too conservative, by a 58–42 margin. The political campaign mobilized against the nomination gave rise to a new verb, to bork. Four years later, a Democratic-controlled Senate narrowly approved Clarence Thomas by a vote of 52–48, despite claims by law professor Anita Hill that Thomas had sexually harassed her while she served in his employ in a federal workplace. Conservative groups were outraged by the ways in which Bork and Thomas were treated by the Democratic-controlled Senate.

Since the failed Bork nomination, senators have become increasingly unwilling to support Supreme Court nominees selected by presidents of the opposing party.[73] In 1986 Antonin Scalia was confirmed by the Senate 98–0, even though it was entirely clear that he was a staunch judicial conservative. President Clinton's two nominees in the early 1990s—Ruth Bader Ginsburg in 1993 and Stephen Breyer in 1994—each garnered opposition from a handful of conservative senators. President George W. Bush's nominees—John Roberts and Samuel Alito—were met with even more widespread Democratic opposition, with only half of Senate Democrats voting in favor of Roberts and only four Democrats in favor of Alito. Senate votes on President Obama's Supreme Court nominations—Elena Kagan and Sonia Sotomayor—broke down along party lines, with only nine Republicans voting for Sotomayor and only five Republicans voting for Kagan. "We have shifted from a basic expectation that absent a reason to vote against a nominee members of the opposing party will support a president's nominee," said Benjamin Wittes, senior fellow at the Brookings Institution. "In a very short period of time, that has reversed to a presumption that members of the opposition party will oppose the president's nominee, absent a reason to support him or her. That is a very profound change."[74]

The Kagan nomination in many ways illustrates the underlying partisan logic of opposition to Supreme Court nominees in the contemporary era. One criticism raised of Kagan's nomination was her lack of judicial experience. Other than Kagan, every current justice is a former federal appeals court judge. It is, of course, an open question whether membership on the highest court should reflect a broader diversity of backgrounds. From Chief Justice John Marshall's day through Earl Warren's, for example, the Court typically included members steeped in legislative or executive experience. In the Court's recent history, only Supreme Court justice Sandra Day O'Connor ever held an elective office; she was an Arizona state senator. Some legal scholars suggest that a wider range of occupational experiences on the Court would serve an important representational function and enhance decision making "with a variety of issues in the electoral and legislative spheres."[75] Opponents of her nomination, nevertheless, cast Kagan's lack of judicial experience as a "qualifications" issue.

TABLE 12-2 **Supreme Court Nominations Not Confirmed by the Senate**

Nominee	President	Date of nomination	Senate action	Date of Senate action
William Paterson	George Washington	February 27, 1793	Withdrawn[1]	December 15, 1795
John Rutledge[2]	Washington	July 1, 1795	Rejected (10–14)	February 3, 1811
Alexander Wolcott	James Madison	February 4, 1811	Rejected (9–24)	February 2, 1829
John J. Crittenden	John Quincy Adams	December 17, 1828	Postponed	March 3, 1835
Roger Brooke Taney	Andrew Jackson	January 15, 1835	Postponed (24–21)[3]	January 31, 1844
John C. Spencer	John Tyler	January 9, 1844	Rejected (21–26)	
Reuben H. Walworth	Tyler	March 13, 1844	Withdrawn	
Edward King	Tyler	June 5, 1844	Postponed	June 15, 1844
Edward King	Tyler	December 4, 1844	Withdrawn	
John M. Read	Tyler	February 7, 1845	Not acted upon	
George W. Woodward	James K. Polk	December 23, 1845	Rejected (20–29)	January 22, 1846
Edward A. Bradford	Millard Fillmore	August 16, 1852	Not acted upon	
George E. Badger	Fillmore	January 10, 1853	Postponed	February 11, 1853
William C. Micou	Fillmore	February 24, 1853	Not acted upon	
Jeremiah S. Black	James Buchanan	February 5, 1861	Rejected (25–26)	February 21, 1861
Henry Stanbery	Andrew Johnson	April 16, 1866	Not acted upon	
Ebenezer R. Hoar	Ulysses S. Grant	December 15, 1869	Rejected (24–33)	February 3, 1870

Nominee	President	Date	Action	Date
George H. Williams[2]	Grant	December 1, 1873	Withdrawn	
Caleb Cushing[2]	Grant	January 9, 1874	Withdrawn	
Stanley Matthews	Rutherford B. Hayes	January 26, 1881	Not acted upon[1]	
William B. Hornblower	Grover Cleveland	September 19, 1893	Rejected (24–30)	January 15, 1894
Wheeler H. Peckham	Cleveland	January 22, 1894	Rejected (32–41)	February 16, 1894
John J. Parker	Herbert Hoover	March 21, 1930	Rejected (39–41)	May 7, 1930
Abe Fortas[2]	Lyndon B. Johnson	June 26, 1968	Withdrawn	
Homer Thornberry	Johnson	June 26, 1968	Not acted upon	
Clement F. Haynsworth Jr.	Richard M. Nixon	August 18, 1969	Rejected (45–55)	November 21, 1969
G. Harrold Carswell	Nixon	January 19, 1970	Rejected (45–51)	April 8, 1970
Robert H. Bork	Ronald Reagan	July 1, 1987	Rejected (42–58)	October 23, 1987
Douglas H. Ginsburg	Ronald Reagan	October 29, 1987	Withdrawn	
Harriet Miers[3]	George W. Bush	October 3, 2005	Withdrawn	

Source: Joan Biskupic and Elder Witt, Guide to the U.S. Supreme Court, 3d ed., vol. 2 (Washington, DC: Congressional Quarterly, 1997), 707: authors' notes.

[1] Later nominated and confirmed.

[2] Nominated for chief justice.

[3] Later nominated for chief justice and confirmed.

Rather than oppose a nominee based on ideology, there is every reason to think that a president's partisan opponents prefer to fight Supreme Court nominations on the qualifications issue. Sen. Charles E. Schumer, D-N.Y., has argued that senators should forthrightly take ideology into account in voting on Supreme Court nominations rather than look for other pretexts for opposing judges with whom they disagree. "For one reason or another, examining the ideologies of judicial nominees has become something of a Senate taboo," writes Schumer. "Unfortunately, the taboo has led senators who oppose a nominee for ideological reasons to justify their opposition by finding non-ideological factors, like small financial improprieties from long ago. This 'gotcha' politics has warped the confirmation process."[76]

Recent research suggests that the relationship between qualifications and the ideology of nominees has shifted since the Bork nomination fight. Political scientist Lee Epstein and her coauthors found that before Bork, senators were willing to vote for moderately qualified nominees, even if there was some ideological distance between them and the nominee. Post-Bork, however, they found that senators were less willing to vote for ideologically distant nominees, regardless of qualifications. Epstein and her coauthors summed up the situation as "the president's discretion over whom to nominate to the Supreme Court has grown far more circumscribed over the last two decades."[77] Perhaps this observation helps to explain recent presidents' preferences for nominees with court of appeals experience.

Consent and Dissent

Until recently, little controversy was associated with scrutinizing judges named to serve on the lower federal courts. Today, fierce political, strategic, and tactical conflicts between the parties and branches overlay the confirmation process for many judicial nominees, especially for the appellate courts. "The politicization of the judiciary has recently been the most focused, and most virulent, at the appellate, or circuit level," said federal judge James Robertson.[78]

The George W. Bush presidency saw intense clashes over federal appeals court nominees, with minority-party Democrats using numerous obstructionist techniques to delay Senate consideration of the president's nominees.[79] In the spring of 2005, Republican frustration over judicial filibusters became so great that Senate majority leader Bill Frist, R-Tenn., threatened to use a parliamentary maneuver called the "nuclear option" to end the talkathons. Under the maneuver, the majority leader would raise a point of order that further debate on a controversial nominee was dilatory. The Republican presiding officer would rule in his favor, and if the Democrats appealed the ruling, Frist would move to table (or kill) the appeal. The result: judicial nominations would be subject to an up-or-down majority vote rather than the Senate's cloture process (which requires sixty votes). The maneuver was never executed, however, because a bipartisan group of fourteen senators opposed Frist's plan while also simultaneously providing sufficient votes to secure Senate approval of some of the disputed nominees.

The level of conflict over judicial nominations has not abated under President Obama. In fact, during the first two years of the Obama administration even district court nominations became more controversial. Several factors explain these developments.

First, interest groups are aware that federal judges make critical decisions across a broad spectrum of policy issues. Both parties understand that although the Supreme Court is viewed as the court of last resort, it decides only about seventy to eighty cases each year (a decade ago the number was 107).[80] By contrast, the twelve regional appeals courts and the federal circuit courts decide more than 63,000 cases annually.[81] The courts of appeals are "playing a more important role in setting law for vast areas of the country. A decision by the Ninth Circuit, for example, is binding on nine states, where 19 percent of the nation's population lives."[82] According to one law professor, the courts of appeals are "the Supreme Courts for their region."[83] Interest groups may also be growing more sensitive to the discretion of district judges, especially in complex commercial litigation and employment discrimination cases. Many of the procedural rulings of district judges in such cases are not generally reviewed by appellate courts, but can seriously affect the value of cases involving corporate defendants.

Second, some confirmation fights are clearly warm-ups for potential Supreme Court vacancies down the line. Because of the preferences of recent presidents for court of appeals judges, blocking a (potentially) controversial nominee from the appellate bench likely eliminates that person from future consideration for the high court.

Third, the contemporary Senate is a highly partisan institution for the reasons recounted in Chapter 6. The ideological chasm between the two parties—also evident on the Judiciary Committee—is wider than it has been in decades. It is, then, simply far more difficult for the Senate to provide advice and consent for lifetime judicial appointments in such a polarized environment. Unlike legislation, once the Senate confirms a judicial nominee there is no opportunity for subsequent Senates to reverse the decision except through the impeachment process. As a scholar explained:

Because presidents overwhelmingly seek to appoint judges who hail from the president's party, Senate scrutiny of judicial nominees should be particularly intense when different parties control the White House and Senate. Not a surprise then that nominees considered during a period of divided control take significantly longer to be confirmed than those nominated during a period of unified control. Judicial nominees are also less likely to be confirmed during divided government: Over the past six decades, the Senate has confirmed on average 87 percent of appellate court nominees considered during a period of unified control, while confirming 70 percent of nominees during divided government.[84]

Moreover, in presidential election years there is often a drop-off in the number of judges confirmed by the Senate. Majority Leader Harry Reid, D-Nev., has even called this informal slowing down the "Thurmond rule," after former senator Strom Thurmond, R-S.C. "After June," noted Senator Reid, "we will have to take a real close look at judges in a presidential election year."[85] Although some senators dispute that there is a so-called Thurmond rule, the political reality is indeed a marked decline in the number of appellate judges confirmed during presidential election years. One study concluded that for "all judicial nominations submitted between 1947 and 2008, appointees for the Courts of Appeal pending in the Senate in a presidential election year were nearly 40 percent less likely to be confirmed than nominees pending in other years."[86] A law professor explained why this pattern occurs: "The priority for the party not in control of the White House is not so much in stopping candidates based on their ideology, but keeping as many vacancies open as possible on the theory that the next president may be someone of your party and will be able to fill those slots."[87]

Fourth, the confirmation battles represent a clash between the president and the opposition party in the Senate over who will control the ideological balance of power on the courts. President George W. Bush, for example, was "more consistent and insistent than, say, [Gerald R.] Ford or Reagan" in nominating conservatives to the bench.[88] "If Democrats just rolled over on Bush's nominations," said one political analyst, "they would be guilty of oppositional malpractice."[89] There is no doubt that President Bush was successful in recasting federal courts in a more conservative direction.

President Obama has not been equally aggressive. Many of the president's supporters have expressed dismay at the administration's relatively slow rate of making lower-court nominations. In February 2011, there were 101 vacancies on the lower courts, but only forty-eight Obama nominees were awaiting Senate consideration.[90] In other words, the Obama administration had not yet put forward names for more half the vacancies. However, a recent study by political scientists Sarah Binder and Forrest Maltzman found that presidents in the postwar period have been taking progressively longer in making lower-court nominations, even after taking into account other factors.[91] It remains to be seen whether the Obama administration's slow rate of nominations is in keeping with these broader historical trends.

It is likely that much of the growing delay in making nominations is resulting from enhanced vetting of potential nominees. Binder and Maltzman suggest that, because of the increased incentives of the opposition party to obstruct lower-court nominations, presidents may react by scouring nominees' backgrounds in search of possible grounds for Senate opposition. In other words, to avoid a stalled nomination, presidents may be stalling before making the nominations. Whatever the reason, the sixty lower-court judges confirmed during Obama's first two years in office is the lowest number in thirty-five years.[92]

CONCLUSION

Federal courts, like Congress and the president, are central forums for resolving the political, social, and economic conflicts that characterize American society. All three branches of government interact constantly to shape and influence the laws under which Americans live. Sometimes, as presidents say, "the buck stops here." In Congress, the buck may stop nowhere, and either elective branch may pass the buck to the courts when it is unable to resolve certain issues. "Through this process of interaction among the branches," writes scholar Louis Fisher, "all three institutions are able to expose weaknesses, hold excesses in check, and gradually forge a consensus on constitutional values."[93]

Interest Group Influence. A staff member for AARP (American Association of Retired Persons)—the nation's largest membership lobby—weighs members' responses to the controversial Medicare prescription drug bill, which the organization backed (top). A poster from the physicians' trade group, the American Medical Association (AMA), urges citizens to oppose cuts for Medicare providers (bottom left). Mass demonstrations (bottom right) seek to impress lawmakers through sheer numbers: Hundreds of dissidents march to the Capitol to protest the Obama Adminstration's health-care bill.

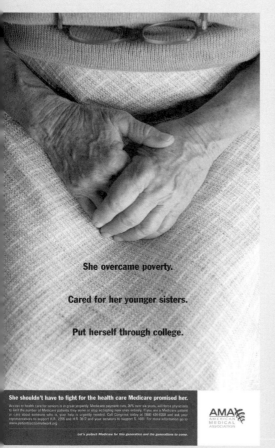

She overcame poverty.

Cared for her younger sisters.

Put herself through college.

She shouldn't have to fight for the health care Medicare promised her.

Access to health care for seniors is in great jeopardy. Medicare payment cuts, 26% over six years, will force physicians to limit the number of Medicare patients they serve or stop accepting new ones entirely. If you are a Medicare patient or care about someone who is, your help is urgently needed. Call Congress today at (888) 434-6200 and ask your representatives to support H.R. 2396 and H.R. 3617 and your senators to support S. 1081. For more information go to www.patientsactionnetwork.org

AMA AMERICAN MEDICAL ASSOCIATION

Let's protect Medicare for this generation and the generations to come.

Congress and
Organized Interests

Three weeks before the landmark health care overhaul plan—the Patient Protection and Affordable Care Act—was signed into law by President Barak Obama on March 23, 2010, five thousand protestors picketed the Ritz Carlton Hotel in Washington, D.C. Inside, American's Health Insurance Plans (AHIP), the trade association of the health insurance industry, was holding its annual lobbying conference. Among the goals of the conference was to lay out a strategy to oppose passage of health reform unless it protected the interests of the industry. The protestors outside the conference, members of a broad coalition of over a thousand organizations (such as labor, consumer, and civil rights), had were seeking to confront the insurance industry and win media attention, gain public support for health care reform, and secure legislative backing for President Obama's health care plan. "The message we have is simple," exclaimed the director of Health Care for Americans Now (HCAN), the group that organized the protest at the Ritz Carlton, "Congress should listen to us, not the insurance industry."[1]

Meanwhile, lawmakers could not help but hear the cacophony of messages and voices advocating for and against health care reform. Record numbers of pressure group lobbyists and citizen activists were swarming Washington, seeking influence over virtually every facet of the health plan. Health companies and trade associations hired "more than 4,500 lobbyists to influence health reform—amounting to about eight lobbyists for each member of Congress."[2] MoveOn.org sponsored a "virtual march" on Capitol Hill, sending more than one million pro-reform e-mails to lawmakers' offices. Conservative groups such as the National Right to Life Committee purchased television ads and organized grassroots campaigns to pressure wavering congressional Democrats to vote against "Obamacare." Marches, rallies, demonstrations, conferences, radio and television advertising, the print media, YouTube, blogs, and more were all used to influence congressional decision makers. The U.S. Chamber of Commerce even commissioned an economic study to portray the health bill as a job killer and harmful to the nation's economy, and budgeted $50,000 to hire a prominent economist to do the study. The next step called for the economist to circulate "a sign-on letter to hundreds of other economists saying that the bill will kill jobs and hurt the economy." The open letter would be used "to produce advertisements, and as a powerful lobbying and grass-roots document."[3]

Groups on all sides of the health care issue spent huge sums to mold the final product. The medical interests alone (doctors, hospitals, drug companies, and various health businesses), which were not monolithic in their preferences, spent a record $876 million (for a business sector) over fifteen months (January 2009 to March 2010) to influence the debate and shape the measure to their liking. Unlike during the introduction of the Clinton administration's 1993–1994 health reform plan, when the health industry was united in its opposition, much of the $876 million was spent in support of President Obama's plan. Even after enactment of the plan into law, lobbying expenditures on health care continued. According to Tony Podesta—whose firm, the Podesta Group, ranked second in fees received during the debate on Obama's plan—his clients are keen on influencing "how the measure is implemented and in any corrections Congress might make."[4] (In 2010 spending on lobbying was estimated at $3.5 billion.[5])

AMERICAN PLURALISM

The fifteen-month battle to enact comprehensive health care reform—an idea advocated since at least the administration of President Teddy Roosevelt— illustrates the dual nature of American pluralism. On the one hand, a vast array of organized interests, most of them headquartered in the nation's capital, seek to influence government policy. This is the "Washington system" of lobbyists and insider access that inspires so much populist rhetoric and public distaste.[6] Narrow profit motives were hardly absent from the health reform debate, as manifold lobbyists sought legislative concessions to line their clients' pockets.

On the other hand, also weighing in on the issue were membership organizations, some of them huge. By means of such organizations, Americans assemble "to petition the government for redress of grievances," in the words of the Constitution's First Amendment. Groups of Americans legitimately concerned about how health care reform might affect the quality, affordability, and accessibility of medical treatments made their concerns known.

The controversy surrounding health care reform illustrates the ambivalence that characterizes both scholarly and journalistic considerations of American pluralism. The world of interest groups prompts fears of a government corrupted by narrow special interests. And yet organized interests are not only constitutionally protected, but also a foundation of civil society and a natural by-product of democratic freedom. President Harry S. Truman, in a wry response to a reporter's question—"Mr. President, would you be against lobbyists who are working for your program?"—remarked: "Well, that's a different matter. We probably wouldn't call these people lobbyists. We would call them citizens appearing in the public interest."[7]

A Capital of Interests

Capitol Hill lobbyists regularly fill committee hearings and markups, jam into conference committee rooms, and pack House and Senate galleries. These emissaries of organized interests do more than observe congressional events. They wield their vast resources—money, connections, personnel, information, and organization—to win passage of legislation they favor and reward the politicians who help them. Practically every major corporation, trade association, and professional group has Washington lobbyists. Lobbyists even have their own association: the American League of Lobbyists. Mindful that lobbyists have long been criticized and demonized by scores of public officials, pundits, and others, the league's president organized a public relations offensive to "help people understand that the 'L' word is not a bad word." He added:

> We're going to be demonstrating that everybody has a lobbyist out there. The second you get up in the morning and you have your toast and eggs, the wheat and poultry lobbyists are involved. Then you get into your car, and you have the Toyota lobbyists. When you log on to your computer and surf the Web, don't forget about the Google lobbyists. Most people have no idea that they have so many lobbyists in their day.[8]

A look inside the Washington telephone directory under "associations" reveals as much as the Constitution about what moves Congress. Washington is home to more national associations (and the 260,000 people they employ) than any other city.[9] Numerous law, financial, technology, and public relations firms have opened offices in the District of Columbia, and the growing cadres of consultants and lawyers represent diverse clients, including foreign governments. As the head of a financial trade group noted, "A financial institution—whether it's a bank or a nonbank of any size—needs to have a Washington office. It puts you at a competitive advantage to have a Washington presence [because you] can have input into the [lawmaking] process."[10]

The lobbying community probably constitutes the third largest industry employer in the nation's capital, behind government and tourism. Indeed, President Obama's successful initiative to overhaul the financial regulatory system prompted banks, securities firms, and Wall Street firms to hire "more than 3,000 lobbyists to shape the bill," or roughly five lobbyists per Capitol Hill lawmaker.[11] "The more the government gets involved in an industry's affairs," declaimed an experienced lobbyist, "the more industry hires people to figure that out."[12] When control of one or both houses of Congress moves from one party to another, the changeover often sparks a boost in lobbying hiring and expenditures as organized interests seek out better access to new congressional leaders. "It's standard operating procedure in Washington that whenever there is a shift in power, there is a scramble by companies to make sure they have adequate representation with the new power brokers," explained the head of the Center for Responsive Politics, a D.C.-based think tank.[13]

Spending on lobbying has continued to grow, despite broader economic downturns. Lobbying expenditures by companies, associations, and their clients totaled $3.5 billion in 2010, as noted earlier, over twice as much as in 2000.[14] "Lobbying appears recession-proof," remarked the director of a D.C. think tank. "Even [though] companies are scaling back other operations, many view lobbying as a critical tool in protecting their future interests, particularly when Congress is preparing to take action on issues that could seriously affect their bottom lines."[15] Lobbyists of all sorts converged on Congress as it considered and passed in 2009 a $787 billion economic stimulus package, the American Recovery and Reinvestment Act (AARA).[16] High-tech and pharmaceutical companies wanted tax breaks for offshore income. Labor unions pressed for guarantees that green technology spending would produce jobs with good pay and benefits. Florida citrus growers and California wine producers, along with other agricultural interests, urged more generous tax treatment for cultivating new fields. The industries in the sectors hardest hit by the recession, real estate and financial services, hired multitudes of lobbyists from across Washington to seek various kinds of assistance for these industries.[17]

A Nation of Joiners

Americans' zest for joining groups was noted long ago by the French political observer Alexis de Tocqueville. Americans of all "conditions, minds, and ages daily acquire a general taste for association and grow accustomed to the use of it," he wrote in 1835.[18] Throughout American history, groups speaking for different subsets of "the people" have swayed public policies and politics. The nineteenth-century abolitionists fought to end slavery. The Anti-Saloon League crusaded for the prohibition of alcohol in the 1900s. Liberal movements in the 1960s and 1970s protested the Vietnam War, racial discrimination, and abuse of the environment. In the 1970s and 1980s, interest groups galvanized support for or against equal rights for women. In the 1990s, conservative groups pushed term limits for lawmakers, a balanced budget amendment, and tax cuts. More recently, antiabortion groups, immigration reform advocates, and both liberal and conservative membership organizations, from Moveon.org to the Tea Party Patriots, have played a prominent role in the political debate.

A free society nurtures politically active groups. "Liberty is to faction what air is to fire," wrote James Madison in *The Federalist* No. 10. In recent years, interest groups have grown in number and diversity. For example, the American Medical Association dominated health lobbying for decades, but today hundreds of health advocacy groups woo lawmakers and orchestrate grassroots activity, up from about ninety in 1975 to at least 750 today. "You name a disease, there's probably a Washington lobby for it," said an official of the American Heart Association.[19] Overall, there are more narrowly based groups that focus on a single issue such as abortion or gun control. Many factors account for the proliferation of interest groups: social and economic complexity; scientific and technological developments; the government's regulatory role; the competition for federal dollars; and the diffusion of power in Congress and throughout the government, which enhances access for outside interests (see Box 13-1 on theories of interest group formation).

BOX 13-1   **Some Theories on Interest Group Formation**

Scholars have suggested a number of theories to explain the development of interest groups. Special interests have long been a source of fascination, in part because of their ability to influence policy making even though they may not reflect majority sentiment within the country. The case of intense minorities prevailing over apathetic or disengaged majorities often rivets scholarly attention. Among the various theories of group formation are the following.

▶ *The proliferation hypothesis* suggests that as society becomes more complex and interdependent, groups naturally form to reflect the country's intricate array of issues and entities. As new conditions, issues, or forces emerge, new groups are formed to reflect or respond to these developments. "The reasoning behind the proliferation hypothesis is straightforward: groups need a clientele from which to draw members."[1]

▶ *The disturbance hypothesis* posits the notion of an unstable equilibrium among groups. If something disturbs the equilibrium, such as war, technological innovations, the emergence of new concerns (acquired immune deficiency syndrome [AIDS], homeland security, and so on), and the like, then new groups emerge. As two scholars wrote, "Groups organize politically when the existing order is disturbed and certain interests are, in turn, helped or hurt." As an example, they noted: "Mobilization of business interests since the 1960s often has resulted from threats posed by consumer advocates and environmentalists, as well as requirements imposed by the steadily growing role of the federal government."[2]

▶ *The exchange hypothesis* states that groups form because of the efforts of "entrepreneurs." The argument asserts that "group organizers invest in a set of benefits which they offer to potential members at a price—joining the group. Benefits may be material [private gains], solidarity [camaraderie], or expressive [the reward of belonging to a group with shared values and causes]."[3] The implication is that organized interests are "deemed more powerful than unorganized interests."[4]

---

[1] Scott H. Ainsworth, *Analyzing Interest Groups* (New York: W. W. Norton and Co., 2002), 40.

[2] Alan J. Cigler and Burdett A. Loomis, eds., *Interest Group Politics,* 6th ed. (Washington, D.C.: CQ Press, 2002), 8. See also David B. Truman, *The Governmental Process,* 2d ed. (New York: Knopf, 1971).

[3] Robert Salisbury, "An Exchange Theory of Interest Groups," *Midwest Journal of Political Science* (February 1969): 1. Mancur Olson, in *The Logic of Collective Action* (Cambridge: Harvard University Press, 1965), suggests that many individuals are unlikely to join organizations that may benefit them personally because they will still receive the gains without the costs (fees, attending meetings, and so on) of participating in the group. This is called the free-rider problem. "For Olson, a key to group formation—and especially group survival—was 'selective' benefits. These rewards—for example, travel discounts, informative publications, and cheap insurance—go only to members." See Cigler and Loomis, *Interest Group Politics,* 9.

[4] Ainsworth, *Analyzing Interest Groups,* 39.

Some scholars contend that Americans' civic engagement has declined. Harvard University professor Robert Putnam has argued that citizen participation in associations is on the wane, drawing his most famous example from the nation's bowling alleys. Putnam's data show that more people are bowling, but are doing so outside of traditional bowling leagues, resulting in a drop in the number of bowling leagues.[20] They are, in short, "bowling alone." As for people generally, they "would rather be alone in front of a television set than out with a group," Putnam wrote.[21] Several years later, Putnam presented a more optimistic assessment of America's civic life, spotlighting citizens' engagement in a dozen community-building activities around the country.[22] Other scholars note that although membership in older groups such as Lions Clubs, Elks, or Moose is down, membership is rising in newer organizations such as environmental groups and youth soccer leagues.[23] The social media (such as blogs, Facebook, and Twitter) also enable the formation of new social and political communities. Other important indicators of civic engagement—especially volunteering—have registered increases in participation.[24] Meanwhile, scholars have generally found that during times of economic crisis there is a falloff in civic participation (the Tea Party is certainly an exception). The unemployed feel depressed and pessimistic and tend to withdraw from community organizations. According to a study conducted by UCLA professor Jennie Brand, "People who lose their jobs, even once, were roughly 30% less likely to participate in community activities, and that lasted through their lives."[25]

Biases of Interest Representation

Not all societal interests are organized and represented in the pressure group system. Organizations do not necessarily emerge just because people share a common policy goal or political interest. Economist Mancur Olson Jr. famously analyzed the difficulties of organizing to bring about policy change.[26] Organizing requires time, energy, and money, and individuals know that the small contributions they can make usually will not be decisive or even important. If a group exists and successfully presses for policy changes, the benefits will spread beyond those who worked to bring about the results. If, for example, an environmental group successfully calls for clean air regulations, urban residents will benefit from the reduced smog, regardless of whether they personally made any contribution to the group's efforts. As a consequence, individuals will prefer to free-ride on the work of others.

The problem of free-rider is especially problematic for large groups, where failure to help with the collective effort is totally anonymous. According to Olson's analysis, organizing is easier for small groups with a strong material stake in policy outcomes. In small groups, social pressure can be effectively applied to discourage free-riding. In some cases, a single individual or firm will bankroll the cost of organizing, because it can benefit even after bearing the costs alone. Under this logic, the pressure group system should be tilted toward narrow economic interests that are easier to organize, and it should underrepresent broad public interests.

According to Olson's theory of collective action, Congress will receive more input from narrow groups with a financial stake in policy issues than from groups representing broader societal interests. Consistent with this theory, there are indeed biases in the composition of the interest group universe. One survey found that business interests make up 72 percent of all interests having Washington representation.[27]

The composition of the interest group world also reflects economic inequality. Put simply, it takes money to create and sustain organized interests, and so groups representing the well-off are more likely to emerge and survive. As political scientist E. E. Schattschneider famously put it, "the flaw in the pluralist heaven is that the heavenly chorus sings with a strong upper-class accent."[28] Frank Baumgartner, a political scientist who was part of a group that studied the lobbying community over a ten-year period, underscored how the poor and less-well-off are disadvantaged in having their issues advocated on Capitol Hill. "The biggest indictment of the lobbying community is that it amplifies the voice of those who already have the most resources in society and leaves the people with the greatest needs completely voiceless."[29]

The well-off and the well educated in U.S. society participate more in politics than the less fortunate, and lawmakers hear disproportionately from them. In her analysis of legislator-constituent interactions in health care policy, Kristina C. Miler discovered that legislators' perceptions of their constituencies were systematically distorted by the fact that they and their offices interacted so much more frequently with resource-rich groups.[30] The rich and poor are interested in different things. The advantaged talk about taxes, government spending, and social issues, whereas the disadvantaged are primarily concerned about "basic human needs . . . [food], jobs, housing, and health."[31] Elected officials are inundated with messages from groups that represent the politically active (such as the elderly, veterans, and small business owners). But lawmakers receive comparatively little information about the policy preferences of the needy, who are often only marginally engaged in civic life.

PRESSURE GROUP METHODS

Since the birth of the Republic, groups have influenced Congress's decisions. During the nation's early technological and industrial expansion, railroad interests lobbied for federal funds and land grants to build their routes. Some of these early lobbyists' methods—such as offering bribes—fueled public suspicion of pressure tactics. In 1874 Sen. Simon Cameron, R-Pa., described an honest politician as one who "when he is bought, stays bought."[32] Samuel Ward, the "king of the lobby" for fifteen years after the Civil War, once wrote to his friend Henry Wadsworth Longfellow:

> When I see you again I will tell you how a client, eager to prevent the arrival at a committee of a certain member before it should adjourn, offered me $5,000 to accomplish this purpose, which I did, by having

[the member's] boots mislaid while I smoked a cigar and condoled with him until they could be found at 11:45. I had the satisfaction of a good laugh [and] a good fee in my pocket.[33]

Lobbying methods have evolved in variety, sophistication, and subtlety. As government has expanded in size and scope, the mutual dependence of legislators and lobbyists has deepened. The legislator-lobbyist connection is a two-way street:

> Groups turn to Congress as an institution where they can be heard, establish their positions, and achieve their policy goals. Members of Congress in turn rely on groups to provide valuable constituency, technical, or political information, to give reelection support, and to assist strategically in passing or blocking legislation that the members support or oppose. Groups need Congress, and Congress needs groups.[34]

Modern-day methods vary according to the nature and visibility of the issue and groups' resources. Among the most important practices are direct and social lobbying, group alliances, grassroots support, and electronic advocacy.

These diverse techniques are typically employed in tandem. For example, House and Senate Democratic leaders and aides meet regularly with their lobbying allies, such as labor unions.[35] Sen. Debbie Stabenow, D-Mich., who heads the Democratic Steering and Outreach Committee, works "hand in hand with outside advocacy groups to raise public support for bills on the Democratic agenda."[36] Similarly, business lobbyists regularly consult with congressional GOP leaders and their top aides to formulate strategy on the party's issues and goals. For example, in the summer of 2010 House Republican leader John Boehner of Ohio even streamed live on the Internet a Capitol Hill meeting with twenty GOP lobbyists. The session was directed at gathering "suggestions for a new [GOP] policy agenda" for the November 2010 elections and the 112th Congress (2011–2013).[37] The lobbyists then mobilize grassroots support for these initiatives through petition drives, rallies, radio and television advertising blitzes, national door-to-door campaigns, and other techniques.[38] In 2009 Sen. John Thune, R-S.D., the chair of the Republican Policy Committee, was tapped to meet regularly with business groups and key GOP-leaning grassroots organizations to discuss ways to move the party's policy initiatives.[39]

Direct Lobbying

In the traditional method of direct lobbying, lobbyists present their clients' cases directly to members and congressional staff. When a group hires a prominent lawyer or lobbyist, such as Ken Duberstein, Heather Podesta, or Gerald Cassidy, the direct approach involves personal contact with senators or representatives. An aide to Speaker Thomas P. "Tip" O'Neill Jr., D-Mass. (1977–1987), explained the importance of the personal touch:

[Lobbyists] know members of Congress are here three nights a week, alone, without their families. So they . . . [s]chmooze with them. Make friends. And they don't lean on it all the time. Every once in a while, they call up—maybe once or twice a year [to] ask a few questions. . . . Anne Wexler [a former official in the Carter White House, and later a lobbyist] will call up and spend half an hour talking about . . . politics, and suddenly she'll pop a question, pick up something. They want that little bit of access. That's what does it. You can hear it. It clicks home. They'll call their chief executive officer, and they've delivered. That's how it works. It's not illegal. They work on a personal basis.[40]

A variation on direct lobbying is when private citizens who have the resources hire lobbyists to present their issue or case to lawmakers. The private citizens range from "victims of Bernard Madoff's infamous Ponzi scheme to William Weld, a former two-term governor of Massachusetts" to individuals who "want presidential pardons or congressional help with immigration troubles."[41]

Former members of Congress are particularly effective at direct lobbying. Recognizing their value, lobbying firms and clients eagerly enlist the services of former lawmakers. "Each member is part of a network of reciprocity," observed scholar James A. Thurber, "You help me, and I'll help you. That's what a lobbying client is buying."[42] A retired twenty-year House member wrote to prospective clients that he could "unravel red tape, open doors, make appointments, work with the Administration or government agencies, influence legislation, and assist in any other service required."[43] Drawing on recent disclosure filings, the nonpartisan Center for Responsive Politics reported that "315 former members are registered or are involved with lobbying entities."[44] Nearly a quarter of the members who retired or were defeated in the 2008 elections have registered as lobbyists.[45] (A website—www.opensecrets.org—allows citizens to track public officials who move between the government and the private sector: the so-called revolving door.) Former top Capitol Hill staff aides are similarly sought after because of their personal knowledge and understanding of key members and congressional processes.[46] Many former lobbyists also take high-ranking staff jobs on Capitol Hill.[47] Advantaged in direct lobbying are Hollywood movie stars, famous sports figures, prominent business executives (such as Microsoft's Bill Gates), and the children and spouses of powerful members.[48]

Member-to-member lobbying can be uniquely effective. No outsider has the same access to lawmakers (and to certain precincts of Capitol Hill) that former colleagues have. For example, ex-GOP senators who may be lobbyists can attend the regularly scheduled Tuesday Republican Policy Committee lunch, "where legislative tactics are plotted on issues ranging from tax cuts to foreign policy"—information "that gives them a decided edge over other lobbyists."[49] Some are offended by the access that lobbyists who are former legislators have to the floor and to other Capitol Hill locations that are not generally open to the public. Ethics rules do impose restrictions on the former lawmakers (for example, they may not lobby their colleagues while in the chamber), but former members still retain privileges denied to others. As former House Speaker J. Dennis Hastert, R-Ill., explained, "It's hard to take away benefits from former members. We're all going to be former members one day."[50] (Hastert is now a lobbyist with the D.C.-based firm Dickstein and Shapiro.) Turnover in Congress hampers direct lobbying by former members. The longer former members have been out of Congress, the fewer personal contacts they have with current members.

Direct lobbying takes many forms. For one thing, lobbyists may organize focus groups of Hill staff aides to determine which arguments will most appeal to lawmakers.[51] The president of a telephone trade association underscored the importance of keeping congressional staffers informed. He even organized a retreat for congressional aides, in part to glean political intelligence about how best to frame his association's issues on Capitol Hill.[52] Lobbyists monitor committees; testify (or have their clients appear as witnesses) at hearings; interpret Hill decisions for clients; articulate clients' interests to legislators; draft legislation, speeches, and "Dear Colleague" letters for members; and give campaign assistance. The House offers more occasions for contacting members directly than does the Senate, where lobbyists are more likely to target staff aides.

Taken together, lobbyists are major players in congressional policy making. "Lobbyists contribute a lot to democracy," observed Rep. James P. Moran, D-Va. "They provide continuity and institutional memory. Most of them have been around longer than members."[53] Or as a GOP senator put it, "I would have to say the best information I get in the legislative process comes from people directly involved in the industry that is going to be affected—and from people who represent them: the 'nefarious' lobbyists."[54] A financial services lobbyist skilled in policy development bluntly emphasized the important role that he and his colleagues play in the lawmaking process. "Most members may know one or two issues well, if that. Then you have a 26-year-old kid, maybe he's even 30 and went to a good law school, who's on the staff working 10 hours a day and is supposed to tell his boss how to do derivatives regulation or credit-card reform. Are you kidding?"[55]

Social Lobbying

Lobbying also occurs in social settings outside the legislative context, such as at dinner parties, receptions, sporting and entertainment events, or on the golf course or tennis court. Successful direct lobbying is grounded in trust.[56] Legislators must believe that lobbyists are credible and knowledgeable before they will accept advice from or even devote time listening to them. Social interactions are extremely useful for fostering and developing the personal relationships that lobbyists need to be effective. Lobbyists thus seek out opportunities to interact casually with lawmakers, even when no client business will be discussed. On some occasions, of course, a conversation in a social setting can produce results for a lobbyist's client. As one experienced power dealer explained, "When you want to make an end run, meet someone at a party."[57]

Travel with members of Congress has long afforded many opportunities for lobbyists to engage in social lobbying, but recent ethics laws have placed new restrictions on the practice. Until the 2007 ethics rules were in place it was not unusual, for example, for legislators to accept flights on corporate jets, reimbursing their sponsors only for the cost of commercial airfare. Such settings afforded many possibilities for relationship-building and casual interaction among lobbyists, legislators, and lobbyists' clients. The 2007 ethics reforms, however, "effectively ban travel with registered lobbyists."[58] Lobbyists "may not accompany lawmakers or aides 'on any segment' of a trip."[59] And lawmakers must receive prior approval for all such travel from the Committee on Ethics of their chamber.

Lobbyists are not permitted to pay for meals for legislators, banning the lobbyist-funded lavish dinners that were the source of so much public distaste. There is, however, the "reception exception" or the "toothpick rule," which permits "members and aides to [eat] food [on toothpicks] at receptions, but bans them from attending sit-down meals with lobbyists."[60] As one lobbyist hosting a reception for legislators ruefully put it, "I'm sitting here as vice president of corporate affairs for the National Association of Manufacturers, and I'm making sure that there's nothing you need a fork for."[61] Members and aides may also attend lobbyist-paid events when carrying out "official duties" and when more than twenty-five people not connected with Congress are in attendance.

A large loophole in all these ethics rules involves political fund raising. Social and direct lobbying is unrestricted at campaign events. Many fund-raising events such as golf outings, fishing trips, and sit-down dinners offer wide-open opportunities for casual interactions with lawmakers. For example, Heather Podesta hosted a dinner at her home for five Democratic female senators. The fee for attendees, who in return were given a chance to discuss issues with the senators in a private setting, was $30,400 for a "co-chair" of the event, $10,000 for a "vice chair," $5,000 for a "co-host," and $1,000 for an "individual sponsor." Checks, said Podesta, were to be made payable to the Democratic Senatorial Campaign Committee (DSCC).[62] Lawmakers can continue to invite lobbyists to attend "lavish birthday parties in a lawmaker's honor ($1,000 a lobbyist), weekend golf tournaments ($2,500 and up), a Presidents Day weekend at Disney World ($5,000), or parties in South Beach in Miami ($5,000)."[63] Lobbyists end up paying for such events because "they pay a political fund-raising committee set up by the lawmaker. In turn, the committee pays the legislator's way."[64] In short, what is illegal if done directly—such as paying for legislators' meals, travel, or gifts—is legal if done indirectly through campaign contributions. "I can get a $2 million earmark" setting aside money for a particular interest, remarked Sen. Tom Coburn, R-Okla., "and then they can give money through their friends to my campaign, but they can't buy me a $20 dinner."[65]

A variation on social lobbying is worth noting. Although members are banned by law from receiving honoraria, they can ask corporations or groups to make a donation on the lawmakers' behalf to charities or other tax-exempt groups. Critics suggest that this arrangement enables members to "obtain political benefits by directing contributions to favored organizations, and some tax exempt groups are affiliated with politicians."[66] An analysis by the *New York Times* found "at least two dozen charities that lawmakers or their families helped create or run that routinely accept donations from businesses seeking to influence them."[67] There are no financial limits on these donations, and they "typically far exceed what companies are permitted to give to candidates in campaign contributions."[68] Meanwhile, tax-exempt organizations are under increasing scrutiny by the Internal Revenue Service and other entities to determine whether lawmakers and lobbyists "are using charities as a political-money subterfuge."[69] The year 2009 saw a drop in charitable contributions (from $40 million to $25 million) to members' favorite causes, perhaps because of the sluggish economy or new regulations requiring more public reporting of the donations made by corporate, labor, and other groups.[70]

Still, ethics experts remain concerned that companies, banks, and other groups with business before Congress are providing thousands and even millions of dollars to fund endowed university chairs or institutes named after influential lawmakers. Examples are the McConnell Center for Political Leadership at Louisville University (named after GOP senator Mitch McConnell) and the Dan and Maggie Inouye Distinguished Chair in Democratic Ideals at the University of Hawaii (named after Democratic senator Dan Inouye). "The simple fact is these things should not be named after people when they are in office," declared a congressional analyst. "We all know what is going on here: the donors are trying to influence the lawmakers."[71] The donors contend that their contributions are for good causes, and various lawmakers state that they have received prior approval of congressional ethics officials to participate in these donations, or they "avoid requesting the donations themselves, instead leaving such pleas up to staff from the universities or charities involved."[72]

Coalition Lobbying

To enhance their chances of success, lobbyists often construct coalitions in support of their legislative initiatives. Coalitions bring more resources, contacts, and money to lobbying efforts. With the diffusion of power on Capitol Hill, coalitions are better able than single groups to touch all the legislative bases. When individuals and organizations "band together and support one another," noted former senator John B. Breaux, D-La. (1987–2005), now a partner in a major Washington lobbying firm, it makes for "a smoother and more effective [legislative] operation than if fifty or more voices [are] all arguing for the same principle without any coordination."[73]

Examples of such coalitions abound. In 2011 environmental and public health groups came together to work against legislative efforts to strip the Environmental Protection Agency of its authority to regulate greenhouse gas emissions. Some years earlier, the Pharmaceutical Research and Manufacturers of America (PhRMA) worked with a variety of technology and financial interests to push for more favorable tax treatment of corporate income earned overseas, and a provision was inserted in the American Jobs Creation Act of 2004. A study by researchers at the University of Kansas determined that this single tax break earned companies $220 for every dollar they spent lobbying on the issue, "a 22,000 percent rate of return on their investment."[74] With the January 1, 2011, expiration of the President George W. Bush–era tax cuts approaching, the Tax Relief Coalition—which includes trade associations representing large and small businesses—launched a public relations blitz to win legislative support for keeping the revenue rates in place.[75] Elsewhere, those with a different view of the tax cuts formed a countercoalition to keep the Bush-era tax rates for middle- and lower-income families but not for wealthy earners.[76]

"We have no permanent friends or permanent enemies—only permanent interests." That oft-repeated line helps to explain why "coalitions, like politics, make strange bed fellows."[77] Rival lobbying interests sometimes forge temporary coalitions to promote or defend shared goals. For example, a group of trade unions and liberal-leaning consumer groups joined with PhRMA and the health insurers' main trade association, America's Health Insurance Plans, in a coalition known as the "Healthcare Reform Dialogue" to seek points of agreement when the Obama administration began its successful effort to revamp the national health care system.[78] During the 110th Congress (2007–2009), an unusual coalition formed on a major farm bill to reduce subsidies for the traditional commodity crops—corn, wheat, cotton, rice, and soybeans—and provide more assistance for specialty crops, land conservation, environmental issues (such as biofuels research), and nutrition programs. Meanwhile, upset that customary farm bills mainly subsidize rich farmers while hurting poor farmers in developing countries and in rural areas of the United States, sixteen faith-based groups formed the Religious Working Group on the Farm Bill. They were joined in the effort by the liberal Environmental Defense Fund and Oxfam and the conservative Club for Growth and Citizens against Government Waste.[79] In opposition were the large commodity trade associations such as the American Farm Bureau Federation, American Soybean Association, and National Corn Growers Association.

A drawback of coalitions is that they are marriages of convenience—the coalition between the American Petroleum Institute and the Environmental Working Group is but one example. As the head of the environmental group observed, "This is not a sign of any great, broad alliance with the oil industry."[80] Multiple organizations are unlikely to cooperate on more than one issue, or for extended time periods. Lawmakers may also be wary of a coalition whose organizers, membership, or funding sources are murky. An attractive name (such as the Coalition for Asbestos Reform or the Climate Policy Group) may simply be a way for a single interest to bankroll an initiative while masking its identity. To combat such efforts, Congress adopted reforms in 2007 that require more disclosure of the groups that fund and lead coalition efforts.

Grassroots Lobbying

From the abolitionist crusade to women's suffrage to the civil rights struggle to today's Tea Party movement, grassroots lobbying is perhaps the most effective pressure technique. Instead of contacting members directly, many organizations mobilize citizens in districts and states across the country to pressure their senators and representatives. For example, when eBay, the online auction website, wanted to influence federal telecommunications policy so that phone and cable companies could not favor certain types of Web traffic at the expense of others, it sent an e-mail to more than a million eBay users urging them to contact their members of Congress in support of "network neutrality."[81] Similarly, the Service Employees International Union (SEIU) announced a plan to enlist its members to make ten million telephone calls to pressure members of Congress to support universal health insurance coverage.[82]

Interest groups often send mass mailings to targeted congressional districts with letters or postcards enclosed for constituents to sign and mail to their legislators. Although lawmakers recognize that lobbying groups orchestrate such mail campaigns, they also realize they may serve as a rough measure of sentiment and organizational strength behind an issue:

> Members have to care about this mail, even if it's mail that is almost identically worded. Labor unions do this sort of thing a lot. The congressman has to care that somebody out there in his district has enough power to get hundreds of people to sit down and write a postcard or a letter—because if the guy can get them to do that, he might be able to influence them in other ways. So, a member has no choice but to pay attention. It's suicide if he doesn't.[83]

Washington lobbying and public relations firms market grassroots lobbying services to clients. Masters of grassroots lobbying know how to guide citizens in their communications with members of Congress. For example, here is what one lobbyist said when he called a sportsman about a proposal that would have made hunting no longer tax-deductible as a business expense: "Hello, Johnny Bob? This is J. D. in Washington. Got a pencil handy? Now, this is who your congressman is. This is how you write him."[84] Although the lack of disclosure requirements makes it difficult to track expenditures on grassroots lobbying, it has become a vital part of the Washington influence industry. "We are talking about lobbying firms that are providing paid advertising to influence specific legislation," observed campaign finance expert Thomas E. Mann. "These are massively funded lobbying campaigns using paid media."[85]

Lawmakers seek to distinguish between genuine grassroots and fake grassroots (often called "Astroturf"). Many so-called grassroots groups function as front organizations for their financial backers. One group with an environmentally friendly name, the Save Our Species Alliance, was actually pushing "a rewrite of the Endangered Species Act to ease paper and logging business's access to federal lands where those species live."[86] And when the House debated a major telecommunications bill, lawmakers were flooded with bogus mail from children, dead people, and constituents who said they had not sent any mailgrams. The uproar from members led to an investigation of the affair by the Capitol Police.[87]

Proponents contend that groups or individuals who can hire lobbying firms to concoct sham grassroots activity should be required to disclose publicly who they are and how much they are spending. "The point is to identify the messengers behind these communications," said a public interest advocate, "because that helps [people] evaluate the information."[88] Opponents argue that disclosure requirements run counter to the Constitution's guarantee of free speech and the right to petition the government. As noted in one federal court decision, "In a representative government such as this, these branches of government act on behalf of the people and, to a very large extent, the whole concept of representation depends upon the ability of the people to make their wishes known to their representatives."[89]

Mass mobilizations have become so common that some firms now specialize in "grass tops" lobbying. Whereas the goal of grassroots lobbying is to mobilize the masses, the goal of grass tops lobbying "is to figure out to whom a member of Congress cannot say no: his chief donor, his campaign manager, a political mentor. The lobbyist then tries to persuade that person to take his client's side" during talks with the lawmaker.[90] Big corporations may also hire "stealth" lobbyists—public relations specialists who work quietly to "influence the news media, sponsor grassroots activities and generate favorable scientific reports."[91]

Electronic Lobbying

As in most other areas of life, advances in communication technology have transformed lobbyists' work. The mobile telephone, the Blackberry, the iPad, and many other digital tools allow lobbyists sitting in a congressional markup to send out alerts on legislative developments to clients, coalition partners, and their home offices. Text messaging, e-mail, and the array of social networking sites available such as Twitter, YouTube, and Facebook have all greatly increased the speed with which lobbyists can influence the legislative process and galvanize their supporters. Much grassroots lobbying now occurs over the Internet. During the Senate Judiciary Committee's confirmation hearings on Supreme Court nominee Elena Kagan, a prominent advocate for Kagan sent "live Twitter updates from the confirmation deliberations" to her followers.[92] The conservative Family Research Council, which opposed Kagan, hosted webcasts with legal experts who explained why Kagan should not serve on the Supreme Court. The council also provided people visiting their website with a letter they could send to their senators objecting to Kagan's confirmation. Individuals only had to put in their ZIP code and hit "Enter."[93] Messages can now be conveyed immediately to sympathizers anywhere in the country to bring pressure to bear when and where it is most needed. The potent combination of technology and politics makes "it easier to organize and send a political message across the country at warp speed."[94]

Groups use computer databases to identify supporters, target specific constituencies, recruit people, and generate personalized mass mailings.[95] With the emergence of interactive websites, lobbyists can communicate directly with prospective supporters, assign tasks, and get immediate feedback on any issue. "[Lobbying] groups get to more of my voters, more often, and with more information than any elected official can do," complained one House member. "I'm competing to represent my district against the lobbyists and the special interests."[96]

Bloggers can activate an electronic network of political activists and organizations to lobby Congress on behalf of policies or issues they support or oppose. Talk radio hosts such as Rush Limbaugh (who is heard weekly on more than six hundred stations by perhaps fourteen million listeners a week), can trigger an outpouring of letters, telegrams, e-mails, YouTube videos, and Tweets to lawmakers. In 2010 Fox News host Glenn Beck mobilized tens of thousands of antitax, pro–limited government, and anti–excessive spending Tea Party members to attend a rally at the Lincoln Memorial in Washington, D.C., on the forty-sixth anniversary of Martin Luther King's momentous "I Have a Dream" speech.[97]

A subtle form of electronic lobbying occurs when advocacy groups purchase or establish websites or newspapers and buy radio and television stations to disseminate their views, blurring the "distinction between legitimate media and propaganda to promote their causes."[98] The National Rifle Association (NRA), for example, believes that, like the NRA, more advocacy groups will emulate traditional media formats or buy radio stations to present their views to the general public without identifying them as group-owned. "We have as much right to be at the table delivering news and information to the American public as anyone else does," NRA's executive director explained.[99] Perhaps with that in mind, heeding federal court decisions upholding the Second Amendment right to bear arms, the NRA has expanded its portfolio beyond guns, such as opposing Elena Kagan's nomination to the Supreme Court and campaign finance reform. One of the most influential of all lobbying groups, the NRA has been able to increase its leverage on Capitol Hill because congressional battles are "so closely fought now that powerful interest groups hold more sway even if they can deliver a handful of votes."[100]

GROUPS AND THE ELECTORAL CONNECTION

Today it is often hard to differentiate the roles of interest groups and political parties in electoral politics. "The standard distinction between interest groups and parties used to be that parties were committed to winning elections and that pressure groups let elections happen and then tried to influence the people who got elected," remarked a political scientist. "Now interest groups through

---

BOX 13-2 **Union Workers Trained as Lobbyists**

T he United Steel Workers brings a group of legislative interns to the capital several times a year. It pays them what they make in their normal jobs plus expense allowances, lodges them in hotels, and gives them desks in the Steel Workers' offices near Dupont Circle. The visitors are technically on sabbaticals authorized by the union's collective bargaining agreements.

The program combines schooling and work. Interns often are sent to Capitol Hill to track down lawmakers or congressional aides to make the union's case on legislative issues. During a typical week, they also study congressional procedures and history, attend hearings, and observe union policy meetings. The purpose is to give rank-and-file workers a deeper knowledge of Congress and to inspire activism at the local level. The union hopes its interns will go home more politically savvy and better prepared to rally coworkers on union issues and at election time.

The steel union's program is unusual in intensity, length, and agenda. The union wants to bolster its grassroots efforts and deepen its pool of potential candidates for elected offices. A spokesman for the Steel Workers said the union hopes the six-year-old program will "get more plumbers and steamfitters and electricians into public office."

Source: Adapted from Matthew Tully, "Union Program Fields Blue-Collar Washington Lobbyists," *CQ Daily Monitor,* March 29, 1999, 7.

---

their PACs [political action committees] and a variety of other methods are very much involved in the pre-policy arena."[101] As one example, the grassroots operation of the U.S. Chamber of Commerce "has begun to rival those of the major political parties."[102] Box 13-2 provides an interesting example of a group that is blending issue advocacy and electoral politics. Union workers are being trained as lobbyists in order to make them more effective advocates, organizers, and potential candidates for elective office.

Some groups are so extensively involved in partisan electoral politics that they are effectively "party allies," a vital part of their party's "enduring multi-layered coalition," in the words of Paul S. Herrnson.[103] Increasingly, the electoral coalitions of the two parties exhibit greater ideological homogeneity. For Democrats, group allies include labor unions, environmental and women's rights organizations, and liberal membership groups such as People for the American Way and Moveon.org. For Republicans, allied groups include the U.S. Chamber of Commerce, pro-life and pro-gun organizations, and conservative ideological groups such as the Club for Growth and Freedom Works. Between elections, congressional party leaders and their allied interest groups cooperate to promote their party's message, enhance its public image, and advance its agenda.

Interest groups help elect members to Congress in three principal ways: They raise funds and make financial contributions through political action committees, they conduct their own independent campaigns for or against issues and candidates, and they rate the voting records of legislators.

Groups and Campaign Fund Raising

Legislators who dislike raising money—seemingly a majority of them—turn to lobbyists or professional fund-raisers to arrange parties, luncheons, dinners, or other social events to which admission is charged. Lobbyists buy tickets or supply lists of people who should be invited. They even serve as treasurers of members' reelection campaigns or political action committees.[104]

Fund-raising events consume more and more of legislators' limited time and create new scheduling conflicts—further evidence of the imperatives of the two Congresses, the representative assembly versus the lawmaking institution. Members cannot chase money and do legislative work at the same time. To minimize these conflicts, "windows" are opened in the Senate's schedule:

> A window is a period of time in which it is understood that there will be no roll-call votes. Senators are assured that they won't be embarrassed by being absent for a recorded vote. Windows usually occur between six and eight in the evening, which is the normal time for holding fund-raising cocktail parties.[105]

Sen. Robert C. Byrd, D-W.Va., the longest-serving lawmaker ever in either chamber, complained that members must spend more time raising money than legislating.[106] A former senator said he "had to become an expert [at fund-raising] to survive in California politics." He described three principles of raising money based on his experiences: First, "people who give once are likely to give again." If you stop asking, they will stop giving or give to someone else. Second, "it's a compliment . . . to ask someone for a large sum." Third, "people who have given to other causes may give to yours." For this reason, "keep track of all who give what to whom."[107] Congressional critics, and even legislators and lobbyists themselves, question the propriety of fund-raising practices. Members are concerned about implied obligations when they accept help or money from groups. For their part, lobbyists resent pressure from members to give repeatedly.

"Bundling" is a widely used fund-raising technique that allows lobbyists and fund-raising entities to raise more money for candidates than they can contribute individually under campaign finance laws. Political action committees (PACs), for example, are limited to giving a candidate $5,000 for use in the primary and general election. There are no limits, however, on "how much a PAC can forward to candidates from other donors."[108] To bundle, a lobbyist or another type of fund-raiser will solicit checks from various sources and then give them all at once to a candidate's campaign committee or to the House and Senate party campaign committees. The candidate knows the bundler's identity because the checks are submitted to the campaign together or, in some cases, because the checks contain identifying information. Lobbyists are not "bundling this cash for altruistic reasons," said the president of a nonpartisan election watchdog group": They want to get the [lawmakers'] attention and interest."[109] Until the 2007 ethics reforms, the public was entirely in the dark about the identities of bundlers and the amounts they raised. Under the current rules, limited disclosure requirements are imposed. Campaign committees must identify persons "reasonably known" to be registered lobbyists if they have provided two or more "bundled" contributions totaling more than $16,000 during any semiannual reporting period.[110]

Groups and Advocacy Campaigns

Elections are contested today on interest group turf, with incumbents fighting opposing interests as well as other candidates. Interest group allies develop and fund advertising campaigns that are designed to influence electoral outcomes. Two major labor unions—the AFL-CIO and the Service Employees International Union—coordinated spending of $88 million or more in twenty-six targeted states to try to help Democrats retain control of Congress in the November 2010 elections. The unions also put more campaign workers in the field than in previous elections, "knocking on doors of union households and handing out leaflets at work sites."[111] Not to be outdone, the U.S. Chamber of Commerce set aside $75 million to help Republicans win back control of Congress. Moreover, fifteen conservative groups budgeted $300 million to wrest control of Congress from the Democrats, with the bulk of the money concentrated in swing states and districts.[112]

Reverse lobbying also occurs. Lawmakers lobby the lobbyists to achieve their policy priorities. They aggressively solicit legislative input, as well as campaign funds, from their interest group allies. For example, members will try to persuade key groups that are on the fence to back their proposals or not publicly oppose them. The passage in 2003 of a major prescription drug benefit for Medicare enrollees was facilitated by Speaker Hastert's wooing of the AARP—the multimillion-member seniors' lobby. Seven years later, congressional Democrats and President Obama lobbied the AARP and won its backing for enactment of the most significant health care overhaul in two generations.

Rating Legislators

About a hundred groups keep pressure on members of Congress by issuing "report cards" on their voting records. Groups select a number of major issues and then publicize members' scores (on a scale of zero to one hundred) based on their "right" or "wrong" votes on them. Members are often warned by colleagues that certain votes will be scored. "You'll hear this as you walk into the chamber: 'This is going to be a scored vote. The environmentalists are going to score this vote, or the AFL-CIO is going to score this vote,'" explained a House member.[113] Congressional aides sometimes check with lobbying groups to determine whether certain votes will be scored.

Interest groups use scorecards to influence members' decisions on selected issues. The liberal Americans for Democratic Action and the conservative American Conservative Union issue score-based ratings that are well known and widely used. The ratings game, however, is suspect; it is always simplistic. The selected votes are often inadequate to judge a member's full record, because they are selected with an agenda in mind. Group strategists defend ratings as "a shorthand way for voters to tell something about their congressman."[114] In targeting members in upcoming elections, many interest groups assign attention-getting names based on their scorecards, such as "heroes and zeroes" (from consumer advocates) or the "dirty dozen" (environmental polluters).

Groups use legislative scorecards to determine which candidates will win endorsement and receive campaign contributions. Vulnerable incumbents who hold closely contested seats and are mindful of the two Congresses are usually careful when casting their votes to avoid antagonizing powerful interest groups back home. As a lawmaker who represents a marginal district once said, "If I cast a vote, I might have to answer for it. It may be an issue in the next campaign. Over and over I have to have a response to the question: Why did you do that?"[115] Some of the groups that rate lawmakers maintain websites that allow visitors to compare how they personally would vote on issues with the actual voting record of their senators or representatives.[116] Interest groups may also canvass door to door in certain areas, "to talk to voters about the results" of their scorecards.[117] Worth mention is that various Tea Party groups are monitoring the votes and promises of the lawmakers they helped to elect to the 112th Congress.[118]

GROUPS, LOBBYING, AND LEGISLATIVE POLITICS

How much influence do organized interests wield over congressional legislation? The American public is convinced that their sway is excessive. Overwhelming majorities of survey respondents agree with the statement "Congress is too heavily influenced by interest groups."[119] Political science research, by contrast, offers no such clarity on this question. According to a thorough review of the literature, the subject of interest group influence has "generated more smoke than fire, more debate than progress, more confusion than advance."[120] Moreover, the results of empirical research do not support sweeping populist characterizations of Congress as bought and paid for by moneyed interests. A ten-year study by a group of political scientists who examined ninety-eight issues found that the side with the most PAC donations, lobbyists, money, and members won only half of the time. They concluded, "A better predictor than money in winning or killing legislation was the support of government agency heads, congressmen-turned-lobbyists, high-level congressional and government officials—and best of all—party leaders and the president."[121] The study also pointed out that it is difficult for lobbyists to change the policy status quo, because there are "people benefiting from the status quo" and entrenched interests on both sides of the issue.[122]

The Role of Money

Journalists and campaign reform groups often posit a direct linear correlation between members' votes and the amounts they have received from various groups. Scholarly researchers reject such simple cause-and-effect inferences. Simply correlating the campaign contributions legislators receive with their voting behavior ignores the possibility that members might just as well have voted as they did without any group influence or campaign contributions. Instead, it is necessary to determine whether lawmakers *change* their behavior after having received campaign assistance. The more careful research designs used by scholars frequently fail to find any causal connection between PAC contributions and members' votes.[123] As the manager of a corporate PAC pointed out, money is "only one tool. We use it to defeat people who do not agree with us and elect those who do. I wish we could just 'buy' votes, but we can't. That's not the way it works in the real world."[124]

Rather than altering members' behavior, the principal finding of empirical research on interest group behavior is that lobbyists tend to donate to members who are already friendly to their objectives. Labor unions, for example, donate the bulk of their funds to Democrats.[125] Similarly, oil and gas interests contribute primarily to Republicans.[126] Generally speaking, groups do not regard it as a good investment of their campaign money to donate to legislative opponents. Citing [E. E.] Schattschneider who said, "moneyed interests sing with an upper-class accent," write political scientists Richard L. Hall and Frank W. Wayman "they also spend a good deal of effort singing to the choir."[127] Furthermore, as discussed in Chapter 3, the amount that interest groups can contribute to legislators' campaigns is limited. With the proliferation of interest groups and PACs, candidates have many different groups to which they can turn for fund-raising help. No single group is likely to exert overwhelming financial leverage over any given member of Congress.

In short, the patterns in campaign contributing simply do not conform to crude vote-buying theories. The relationship between lobbyists and legislators rarely resembles a simple economic exchange of money for support. Contributions signal and reinforce a relationship more often than they create one. The influence of money must be weighed along with other considerations influencing members' votes, including constituency pressures, party ties, friendships with fellow legislators or lobbyists, and personal conscience, idiosyncrasies, and prejudices. As Rep. Barney Frank, D-Mass., put it: "Votes will beat money any day. Any politician forced to choose between his campaign contributions and strong public sentiment is going to vote public sentiment. Campaign contributions are fungible, you can get new ones. You can't get new voters."[128]

This is hardly to claim that the enormous sums that interest groups spend on political campaigns have no effect on legislative politics and policy making.

Contributions almost certainly buy access to legislators. "There is no question—if you give a lot of money, you will get a lot of access. All you have to do is send in the check," explained one corporate executive.[129] Nevertheless, the linkages between money and policy making are not simple or easy to trace. Under the right circumstances, organized interests can reframe issues, sway members, mobilize support, or demobilize opposition, but there is very little evidence that organized interests are able to convert outright opponents.[130]

Lobbying and Legislation

An open, decentralized institution, Congress presents lobbyists with multiple opportunities to shape the fate of legislation. Groups play a direct or indirect part throughout the congressional environment in individual members' work, committee activities, legislative agenda setting, and floor decision making. Nevertheless, tracing the nature and extent of lobbyists' influence on legislation is no less difficult than untangling the relationship between campaign contributions and lawmaking.

Just as organized interests contribute primarily to their legislative allies, lobbyists also spend most of their time with friendly legislators. Lobbyists rarely target their opponents in Congress, nor do they generally devote significant effort trying to influence fence-sitters.[131] Instead, they work with lawmakers who share their policy views—providing them with appropriate information, data, and political intelligence that they can perhaps use to persuade wavering colleagues.

Along these lines, many organized interests have ties to sympathetic informal congressional groups. For example, the steel industry maintains links with the Steel Caucus and textile manufacturers with the Textile Caucus. Interest groups can be instrumental in forming these informal legislative entities. The idea for the Mushroom Caucus (to protect mushroom producers from foreign imports) originated at a May 1977 luncheon for House members sponsored by the American Mushroom Institute.[132] The Institute of Scrap Recycling Industries lobbied for two years (successfully) to encourage formation of the Senate Recycling Caucus and the House Recycling Caucus. These two recycling groups focus "on ways Congress can help improve recycling and develop new markets for recycled products."[133] Several of the informal legislative caucuses are closely affiliated with nonprofit entities such as the Congressional Black Caucus Foundation, which can collect unlimited donations from corporations, unions, and others. The nonprofits often sponsor policy forums, meetings, conventions, and other events where lobbyists can mingle with lawmakers and discuss the issues of the day.[134]

The relationship between lobbyists and legislators is better understood as a "legislative subsidy" than as a simple exchange in which legislators trade policy for political support.[135] Legislators benefit from the help of lobbyists because successful legislating requires so much work and expertise. Lobbyists' primary role is to assist and underwrite the efforts of their legislative allies. Lobbyists provide their congressional supporters with information, legislative language, policy analysis, useful arguments, and political advice. Working with friendly legislators, lobbyists steer policy toward their clients' goals, exerting influence that in practice is hard to distinguish from legislators' own policy preferences.

The value of lobbyists to legislators thus extends far beyond campaign contributions. "Essentially, we operate as an extension of congressmen's staff," explained one lobbyist. "Occasionally we come up with the legislation, or speeches—and questions [for lawmakers to ask at hearings] all the time. We look at it as providing staff work for allies."[136] Or, as one of Washington's premier lobbyists, Thomas Hale Boggs Jr. (son of former House majority leader Thomas Hale Boggs Sr., D-La. [1941–1943, 1947–1973], and former representative Lindy Boggs, D-La. [1973–1991]), explained, "Congressional staffs are overworked and underpaid. Lobbyists help fill the information vacuum."[137]

Lobbyists' information and expertise are thus one of their most valuable assets. An annual survey conducted by the American League of Lobbyists revealed that lobbyists rated "good information/analysis" given directly to the member as the most effective way to influence a lawmaker.[138] Reflecting on the changing styles of modern lobbying, a lawyer-lobbyist said, "Because of the increasing sophistication of staff, you have to be armed with facts, precedents and legal points. Sure it's a political environment, but it's much more substantive. The old-style, pat-'em-on-the-back lobbyist is gone, or at least going."[139] Lobbying is substantive because Washington is a town filled with experts and saturated with data, analyses, and reports on all sides of an issue. The result: "Facts compete in Washington, just like Democrats and Republicans."[140]

Subgovernments

Many congressional committees deal with policies of concern to specific groups such as farmers, teachers, or veterans. Lawmakers whose constituencies contain many members of these groups tend to seek seats on the relevant committees. Members from farming areas seek assignment to the agriculture committees; members from states with many users of federal lands (such as ranchers and miners) seek assignment to the natural resources committees. Such committees often form alliances with the bureaucrats and lobbyists who regularly testify before them and with whom members and staff aides frequently meet. At hearings before the House or Senate veterans' affairs committees, for example, the triple alliance is on public view. In attendance are the committee members, along with witnesses from various veterans' organizations (such as the American Legion) and executive officials from the Department of Veterans Affairs. Scholars and journalists use the term *subgovernment* for the three-way policy-making alliances of committees, executive agencies, and interest groups.

These triangular relationships dominate policy making less today than in the past. Other contending forces (citizens' groups, aggressive journalists, assertive presidents) have ended their policy monopoly. Fluid issue networks, in which diverse participants and groups influence decision making, better characterize current relationships within and among policy domains.

REGULATION OF LOBBYING

For more than a hundred years, Congress intermittently considered ways to regulate lobbying—a right protected by the First Amendment's free speech principle and "the right of the people . . . to petition the Government for a redress of grievances." Not until 1946 did Congress enact its first comprehensive lobbying law, the Federal Regulation of Lobbying Act (Title III of the Legislative Reorganization Act). The ineffectiveness of this law finally led to passage of the Lobby Disclosure Act of 1995.[141] In 2007 Congress enacted another major lobbying reform measure, the Honest Leadership and Open Government Act (P.L. 110-181). In general, there have been three main statutory approaches to the regulation of lobbying: defining and prohibiting abusive lobbying practices, requiring registration for lobbyists, and providing for disclosure of lobbyists' activities.[142]

The 1946 Lobbying Law

The main objective of the 1946 act was public disclosure of lobbying activities. Persons trying to influence Congress were required to register with the clerk of the House or the secretary of the Senate and to report quarterly the amounts of money they received and spent for lobbying. The law's drafters, although reluctant to propose direct control of lobbying, believed that "professionally inspired efforts to put pressure upon Congress cannot be conducive to well-considered legislation." Thus the law stressed registration and reporting:

> The availability of information regarding organized groups and full knowledge of their expenditures for influencing legislation, their membership and the source of contributions to them of large amounts of money, would prove helpful to Congress in evaluating their representations without impairing the rights of any individual or group freely to express its opinion to the Congress.[143]

The lobby law soon proved ineffective. In 1954 the Supreme Court upheld its constitutionality, but the decision (*United States v. Harriss*) significantly weakened the law.[144] First, the Court said that only lobbyists paid to represent someone else must register—exempting lobbyists who spent their own money. Second, the Court held that registration applied only to persons whose "principal purpose" was to influence legislation. As a result, many trade associations, labor unions, professional organizations, consumer groups, and law firms avoided registering because lobbying was not their principal activity. Some lobbyists claimed immunity from the law on the pretext that their job was to inform, not influence, legislators. Finally, the Court held that the act applied only to lobbyists who contacted members directly. This interpretation excluded indirect lobbying activities that, for example, generated grassroots pressure on Congress.

Lawmakers tried repeatedly to plug the 1946 law's loopholes. The attempts foundered largely because it was difficult to regulate lobbying without trespassing on citizens' rights to contact their elected representatives. After repeated efforts to "change the way Washington does business"—a campaign theme that many members advocated—the two parties finally came together to enact the first major overhaul of the 1946 act.

The Lobby Disclosure Act of 1995

The Lobby Disclosure Act of 1995 applied new rules to individuals and firms that lobby Congress and senior executive branch officials. The law broadened the definition of those who must register as lobbyists to include all those who spend at least one-fifth of their time trying to influence lawmakers, congressional aides, or high-level executive officials, and who are paid $5,000 or more over a six-month period. Registrations of lobbyists quickly soared. A study by the Government Accountability Office determined that when the law took effect "only 6,078 individuals and organizations had registered" under the outdated 1946 act. "After the new law took effect, a total of 14,912 lobbyists registered," 10,612 of them first-time registrants.[145] In 2009 there were about 15,000 registered lobbyists, although many more people who lobby do not register, in part because the statutory requirements do not apply to them. The law is administered by the public records offices of the House and Senate.

Lobbyists are required to "provide semi-annual disclosures showing who their clients are, what policies they are trying to influence, and roughly how much money they are spending for lobbying."[146] Civil fines of up to $50,000 can be imposed on those who fail to comply. Grassroots lobbying is exempt from the law, as are lobbyists paid $5,000 or less semiannually and organizations that use their own employees to lobby.

Although the 1995 lobby law was an improvement over the old one, it was minimally enforced. A 2005 report by the Center for Public Integrity said that the disclosure system was in disarray.[147] Lee H. Hamilton, former Indiana representative, vice chair of the 9/11 Commission, and cochair of the 2006 Iraq Study Group, described the situation:

> Roughly one in five of the companies registered to lobby failed to file the required forms, and overall, 14,000 documents that should have been filed are missing, while another fifth of the required lobbying forms were filed late. The Center [for Public Integrity] found that "countless forms are filed with portions that are blank or improperly filled out. An unknown number of lobbyists neglect or refuse to file any disclosure forms whatsoever." In essence, we have a lobby disclosure system in name only.[148]

Some firms and organizations also underreport their lobbying expenditures. "Companies, trade associations, and lobby firms often misreport—intentionally or inadvertently—how much money they shell out or take in."[149]

The Honest Leadership and Open Government Act of 2007

A confluence of events beyond the perception that the 1995 law was weakly enforced compelled the 110th Congress (2007–2009) to take up another major lobbying reform bill. Those events included, among other examples of transgressions by lawmakers, the Jack Abramoff bribery scandal (2005–2006), which led to the imprisonment of Abramoff and several lawmakers. Lobbyist Abramoff had developed close ties to influential lawmakers and staff aides, in part by providing them with lavish travel, meals, and gifts. As one staff aide said, "I was given tickets to sporting events, concerts, free food, free meals. In return, I gave preferential treatment to my lobbying buddies."[150] Democrats made the "culture of corruption" on Capitol Hill a major theme of the November 2006 elections, which won them majority control of both chambers. Highlighting the two Congresses theme, Democratic leaders realized that they had to make ethics and lobbying reform a top priority or they could face electoral defeat in the next election. Turning the tables, Republicans used the corruption issue in the November 2010 elections because several prominent congressional Democrats were confronting allegations of ethical and legal misconduct.[151]

Some of the most notable provisions of the 2007 ethics reforms are highlighted in Box 13-3. Allegations of ethical violations are handled by each chamber's ethics committee; lobbying violations are under the purview of the Department of Justice. In March 2008, the House created an Office of Congressional Ethics (OCE) composed of eight private citizens. The OCE may investigate any alleged rules violations by members and report their findings to the House Ethics Committee for further review. OCE reports are eventually made public even if the ethics panel chooses to dismiss the cases submitted to them.[152] Whether statutory or rule-based, enforcement of the requirements is essential to gain public trust.

Public trust and enforcement remain significant issues. To promote public trust, President Obama took office promising to change the way Washington did business. He targeted "the outsized influence of lobbyists" on both ends of Pennsylvania Avenue.[153] During his administration, guidelines, memoranda, and executive orders have been issued restricting and limiting communications between federally registered lobbyists and executive branch officials and banning lobbyists from political appointments. (On occasion, however, executive nominees have received waivers from the president's ethics rules so they could serve in his administration.)[154] Restrictions have been placed on the number of lobbyists who may serve on federal advisory panels and commissions. According to the General Services Administration, "52 government agencies use 915 advisory committees organized under the law, with a total membership of more than 60,000."[155] In his January 27, 2010, State of the Union message, President Obama urged Congress to pass new lobbying restrictions: "It's time to require lobbyists to disclose each contact they make on behalf of a client with my administration or with Congress."

BOX 13-3   The Honest Leadership and Open Government Act of 2007

LOBBY REGISTRATION

The clerk of the House and the secretary of the Senate are required to make registration and disclosure forms available, in a searchable and suitable format, on the Internet for public inspection.

LOBBYING DISCLOSURE

Lobbyists must file quarterly reports for an electronic database, with a maximum fine of $200,000 for not complying.

GIFTS, MEALS, AND TRAVEL

Lobbyists may not give lawmakers or staff gifts, even those less than $50 in value, and they cannot pay for lawmakers' or staffers' meals or travel expenses.

Members and staff must receive advance approval from the appropriate ethics committee before accepting any travel with any private organization.

REVOLVING DOOR

Senators and very senior executive officials are prohibited from lobbying for two years after they leave government; House members, for one.

Senior staff members who left Capitol Hill would be prohibited from lobbying for one year.

All Senate staff members are prohibited from lobbying the member or committee for whom they worked for one year after leaving.

CAMPAIGN CONTRIBUTIONS

Registered lobbyists would have to reveal all their political contributions, including bundling of contributions from friends and colleagues.

LOBBYING THE EXECUTIVE BRANCH

Lobbyists who contact executive branch officials, called "covered officials," must register with the clerk of the House and secretary of the Senate and disclose their contacts and activities. (The 1946 act did not address lobbying the executive branch.)

Source: Adapted from Jack Maskell, Legislative Attorney, "Lobbying Law and Ethics Rules Changes in the 110th Congress," Congressional Research Service Report RL34377, September 17, 2007.

Enforcement of the registration and disclosure requirements under the 1995 and 2007 laws remains problematic. A 2010 report by the Government Accountability Office stated that the "Justice Department has now received referrals regarding 2,680 lobbyists or organizations that have not filed required reports on their campaign contributions or their political spending," but the Department of Justice has taken "little or no follow-up action."[156]

Moreover, there appears to be a trend of registered lobbyists "de-registering," perhaps because of Obama's restrictions, the paperwork burdens, or their assertion that they do not engage in lobbying.[157] Some Washington insiders say, "I don't lobby," because they do not meet with lawmakers directly. For example, a former Senate party leader does not register as a lobbyist even though he provides clients with lawmaking and other relevant advice. "I provide my clients with analysis, not access," he said. "I offer them strategic advice on public policy matters, including analysis of the substance, procedure and politics associated with different policy initiatives, whether they be legislative, regulatory or otherwise."[158]

Foreign Lobbying

The 1995 Lobby Disclosure Act also amended the Foreign Agents Registration Act of 1938, which required those who lobby on behalf of foreign governments or political parties to register with the Justice Department. The 1995 law broadened the definition of foreign lobbyists to include individuals who lobby on behalf of foreign-owned commercial enterprises. About five hundred lobbyists have registered with the Justice Department as agents representing foreign governments or parties (see www.usdoj.gov/criminal/fara).

Because of the role of the United States in the global economy and in military security, many foreign governments and lobbyists who work for foreign clients spend considerable time and money promoting their interests on Capitol Hill and with the broader citizenry. For example, to hasten passage of a trade agreement with the United States, the South Korea's embassy "signed four different lobbying and public relations firms to advocate for the trade deal."[159] Concerned that Congress might pass resolutions condemning its human rights record, Egypt's President Mubarak (now deposed) "accelerated his lobbying spending in Washington from $214,000 in 2006 to $1.5 million" three years later.[160] Many other nations also hire lobbyists to forge closer ties with Congress, the executive branch, and various U.S. industries, such as oil.[161]

Local lobbyists also operate globally. Many U.S.-based corporations hire lobbyists who can protect their interests in Europe or other parts of the world when disputes arise about trade, agriculture, antitrust laws, the environment, and other issues.[162] The National Rifle Association formed a transnational organization of gun groups and firearm manufacturers from eleven other countries (the World Forum) to fight international restrictions and regulations that might adversely affect the gun trade.[163]

Globalization of the world's economy also influences congressional lobbying. Toyota is the world's largest auto manufacturer, with plants located in eleven states. By locating plants around the country, the company enhances its political clout on Capitol Hill, gaining supporters in the House, Senate, and state houses. Toyota can now "call on 151 House members, 22 senators, and 11 governors from the states where it operates."[164]

CONCLUSION

Since the nation's beginning, lobbying and lawmaking have been closely intertwined. Lobbying "has been so deeply woven into the American political fabric that one could, with considerable justice, assert that the history of lobbying comes close to being the history of American legislation."[165]

Recent years have witnessed an explosion in the number and types of groups organized to pursue their ends on Capitol Hill. Compared with decades past, many more industry associations, public affairs lobbies (such as Common Cause), single-issue groups, political action committees, and foreign agents are engaging in the influence trade. Some of these groups employ new grassroots and technological lobbying techniques. Many victories today are won in Washington because of sophisticated lobbying campaigns waged in home states or districts.

No one questions that groups and lobbyists have a rightful public role, but some aspects of lobbying warrant concern. Groups often push Congress to pass laws that benefit the few and not the many. They inflate disagreements and hinder compromise. They often misrepresent the voting records of legislators in their rating schemes and pour money into the campaigns of their allies (mainly incumbents). Lawmakers who defy single-issue groups find at election time that those organizations are bent on defeating them.

Built-in checks constrain group pressures, however. The immense number of organized interests enables legislators to play one competing group off against another. Knowledgeable staff aides also provide members with information to counter lobbyists' arguments. Lawmakers' own expertise is another informal check on lobbyists. Finally, there are self-imposed constraints. Lobbyists who misrepresent issues or mislead members soon find their access permanently closed off. As Rep. Barney Frank, explained: "I feel better about a position when I can hear from both sides. . . . You can use [lobbyists] to inform you, as long as they know that if they lie, they lose. They will never be allowed to come back to this office."[166]

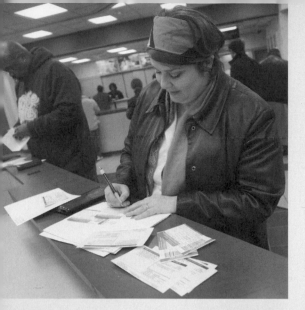

Budgets, Taxes, and Policies during Hard Times. Two citizens (top) fill out last-minute tax returns at a post office in northwest Washington, D.C. Copies of the U.S. budget for Fiscal 2012 (middle left) are stacked up at the Government Printing Office, February, 2011. GOP Budget chair Rep. Paul Ryan, Wis., and ranking minority member Sen. Jeff Sessions, Ala. (middle right), deliver their party's response to the president's proposed 2012 budget. Policy makers face the worst economic downturn since the Great Depression of the 1930s. Expecting a bear market in their search for jobs and careers (bottom), students and others line up to attend a job fair at Miami Dade College.

Congress, Budgets, and Domestic Policy Making

Barack Obama campaigned on the theme of change. After he took the oath of office in January 2009, his most pressing task was to change the downward trajectory of an economy already in a deep recession. During Obama's first two years in the White House, billions, even trillions, of dollars were spent or committed by the federal government to revive the ailing economy. Indeed, bailing out the sinking financial sector cost taxpayers over $3 trillion. "It's like having a second US budget dedicated solely to saving the US financial system, and that is truly surreal," proclaimed Sen. Max Baucus, D-Mont., the chair of the Finance Committee.[1] It was also unreal to the mass of voters who went to the polls in November 2010—many outraged by the tidal wave of red ink. They elected numerous cost-cutting, Tea Party–endorsed GOP deficit hawks to take control of the House. Republicans also upped their numbers in the Senate from forty-one to forty-seven.

Not surprisingly, the major priority for House Republicans in the 112th Congress (2011–2013) was to slash domestic discretionary spending. Their opportunity came quickly because the 111th Congress had failed to pass any of the twelve annual appropriations bills to fund the government. Instead, on December 21, 2010, the Democratic Congress passed a continuing resolution (CR), which the president signed into law, temporarily extending government funding until March 4, 2011. Funding the government beyond March 4 to avert a shutdown thus became the responsibility of the incoming 112th Congress.

In mid-February 2011, the House took up a GOP-crafted CR (H. J. Res. 144) that would reduce nonsecurity federal expenditures (only 12 percent of a $3.7 trillion annual budget) by over $61 billion from 2010 levels. It also funded the government until the end of the fiscal year (September 30, 2011). "Never before has a CR been used to reduce spending so dramatically," exclaimed a senior House staffer, "and never before has one been considered under anything approaching an open [amendment] process."[2] House members filed 583 amendments to the measure, voted on over 100, and passed about 70 during a lengthy and freewheeling debate.[3]

The two Congresses were evident in some of the amendments. For example, GOP representative Denny Rehberg, Mont., who is challenging incumbent Democratic senator Jon Tester in the 2012 elections, won approval of an amendment defunding implementation of the health care law—Tester voted for the health law. The Senate GOP campaign committee quickly put out a statement that said in part, "Today's vote to defund ObamaCare highlights the stark contrasts between Montana Republicans and Senator Tester," who repeatedly has "put his love of ObamaCare ahead of the wishes and interests of his state."[4] At 4:30 a.m. on Saturday, February 19, 2011, an exhausted House concluded its debate on the continuing resolution, approved the measure, and adjourned to reconvene nine days later.

The House's CR, carrying an "H.R. 1" bill number to signify it as the GOP's top priority, now went to the Democratic Senate, which had already been in recess for two weeks. Like the House, it returned for business on February 28, only four days before funding for the government was set to expire. Because of the huge political and policy disagreements between the chambers—for example, House Republicans eliminated or reduced funding for favorite Democratic priorities such as the Environmental Protection Agency, Planned Parenthood, public radio, and Pell Grants for higher education—it was unrealistic to expect that the two chambers could in a few days resolve their vast differences.

To avoid a government shutdown, both houses passed a two-week CR (to March 18) to allow three-way negotiations to continue among the House, Senate, and White House (the president named Vice President Joe Biden to lead the White House's negotiating team). But two weeks proved insufficient to produce a breakthrough. In an attempt to move the negotiations along, Senate leaders agreed to hold test votes on the two competing plans, with each requiring sixty votes for approval. The GOP's plan ($57.5 billion in cuts) won the support of forty-four senators, with fifty-six opposed. The Democratic proposal ($4.7 billion in cuts) attracted the support of forty-two senators, with fifty-eight opposed.[5] The votes, held on March 9, aimed "to demonstrate that neither proposal would pass the Senate and that Republicans would be forced to negotiate down from the amount of cuts they want."[6] Or as Sen. Charles Schumer, D-N.Y., said, "We're looking for some give on the Republican side. Those two votes failing might actually be progress."[7] Speaker John Boehner, R-Ohio, called for the Democrats to get serious about the budget negotiations.

Because under the two-week CR little progress was being made in negotiations to end the budget standoff, the House and Senate agreed to continue government funding for another three weeks (to April 8). As one account noted, the two sides appeared in agreement on only two things: "Congress should avoid a government shutdown, and spending bills should include some measure of funding reduction."[8]

A little more than an hour before the midnight expiration of the CR and the start of a government shutdown, the three principal negotiators—President Obama, Speaker Boehner, and Senate majority leader Harry Reid, D-Nev.—reached an agreement after days of tense and arduous negotiations. Unwanted concessions were made by the negotiators, but those compromises permitted both parties to claim victory. The president and Senator Reid agreed to $38.5 billion in spending cuts—tens of billions more than they initially proposed—that represented, according to the president, "the biggest annual spending cuts in history."[9] Speaker Boehner dropped his party's insistence on including controversial policy riders in the CR, such as defunding the health care law and Planned Parenthood. With the deal in hand, President Obama quickly signed a one-week CR to keep the government open and to provide time for legislation to be drafted reflecting the specifics of the eleventh-hour accord. Subsequently, both chambers passed the measure funding the government for the rest of the 2011 fiscal year.

Plainly, conflicts about policies and the money to pay for them lie at the vortex of today's lawmaking process. Whether the 112th Congress's zeal for budget-cutting represents a "culture change" on Capitol Hill is unclear at this juncture. One thing does appear clear, however: tough budget battles are ahead for Congress and the White House as they move beyond cuts in the 12 percent discretionary domestic portion of the budget and address the truly large areas of fiscal expenditures, such as the mandatory spending programs (entitlements) and defense. Big policy-making challenges and conflicts loom as national officeholders strive to reach consensus on how to drive down the nation's escalating deficit and debt. Some lawmakers argue for a "grand compromise" to bring down the deficit and debt. In this compromise, Democrats would accept revisions to the major entitlement programs, including Social Security, as well as further domestic spending reductions. Republicans would agree to tax hikes and defense cuts.

DEFINITIONS OF POLICY

Defining the term *public policy* with any precision is difficult because the concept is inextricably entwined with the purposes of government. Nevertheless, several definitions exist. David Easton famously defined public policy as society's "authoritative allocation" of values or resources. To put it another way, policies can be regarded as determining "who gets what, when, and how" in a society. Randall B. Ripley and Grace A. Franklin offer a more serviceable definition of policy: policy is what the government says and does about perceived problems.[10]

How can one recognize policies? The answer is not as simple as it may seem. Many policies are explicitly labeled and recognized as authoritative statements of what the government is doing, or intends to do, about a particular matter. The measures may be far-reaching (financing the Social Security system, for example), or they may be trivial (naming federal buildings after deceased public officials). Nevertheless, these are obvious statements of policy. They are usually written down, often in precise legal language, and they boast documented legislative histories in committee hearings, reports, and floor deliberations that indicate what lawmakers had in mind as they hammered out the policy's final provisions.

Not all policies, however, are so formal. Some are articulated by officials but, for one reason or another, are never set down in laws or rules. The Monroe

Doctrine, which declared U.S. resistance to European intervention in the Western Hemisphere, was inserted into President James Monroe's 1823 State of the Union message, and it was written by Secretary of State John Quincy Adams. Successive generations of policy makers have adhered to it ever since. Other policies, especially of a symbolic or hortatory nature, gain currency in the eyes of elites or the public without formal or legal elaboration.

Some policies stress substance—programs designed to build the nation's defense, for example. Others stress procedure, such as those imposing personnel ceilings on federal agencies, mandating program management standards, or requiring contractors' insurance for military weapons. Still others are amalgams of substance and procedure, such as the fast-track provisions (renamed "trade promotion authority") written into trade laws and other laws that expedite committee and floor action in each house. Fast-track statutory provisions include time limits on committee consideration of a bill and on floor debate of a measure, prohibitions against floor amendments, and a requirement that each chamber pass identical legislation, thereby dispensing with conference committees to iron out bicameral differences.

Finally, sometimes public policy is defined by the government's inaction. The United States had no general immigration law before 1924 and no overall national medical care program before 1965, but its policy of unregulated private activity and self-help on these issues was unmistakable.

The process of arriving at these policies is policy making. The process may be simple or complex, highly publicized or nearly invisible, concentrated or diffuse. The policy may happen suddenly, such as military air strikes ordered by the president. Or it may require years or even decades to formulate, such as civil rights or Medicare for the elderly.[11]

STAGES OF POLICY MAKING

Whatever the time frame, policy making normally has four distinct stages: (1) setting the agenda, (2) formulating policy, (3) adopting policy, and (4) implementing policy.

Setting the Agenda

At the initial stage, public problems are spotted and moved onto the national agenda, which can be defined as "the list of subjects to which government officials and those around them are paying serious attention."[12] In a large, pluralistic country such as the United States, the national agenda at any given moment is extensive and vigorously debated.

How do problems move onto the agenda? Some emerge as a result of a crisis or an attention-grabbing event—an economic depression, a terrorist attack, a school shooting, a devastating hurricane or earthquake, or a high-visibility corruption scandal. Others are occasioned by the gradual accumulation of knowledge—for example, rising awareness of an environmental hazard such as global warming. Still other agenda items represent the accumulation of past problems that no longer can be avoided or ignored such as the safety of the nation's food supply and the crumbling infrastructure.

Agendas are also set in motion by political processes—election results (1964, 1980, 1994, 2006, 2008, and 2010 are good examples), turnover in Congress, or shifts in public opinion.[13] The 1994 election results gave the GOP control of the House for the first time in forty years and a chance to pursue its "revolution" in downsizing government. The next eight elections produced different outcomes. For example, the election of 2006 resulted in a Democratic Congress, and with it came a new set of priorities, including opposition to the president's handling of the Iraq war and aggressive congressional oversight of the executive branch. The 2008 elections ended with the Democrats in charge of Congress and the White House and an agenda driven in large measure by a major economic crisis. In the 2010 elections, Democrats took a "shellacking." The eighty-seven House GOP freshmen, backed by an assertive Tea Party movement, made cost-cutting and downsizing government their top priorities. Scores of members in both parties and both chambers shared their concerns and mobilized to address the nation's mounting deficit and debt.

Agenda items are pushed by policy entrepreneurs—that is, people who are willing to invest their time and energy in promoting a particular issue. Especially at the beginning of a new president's term, many of Washington's think tanks and interest groups issue reports that seek to influence the economic, social, or foreign policy agenda of the nation. For example, various think tanks have long advocated Social Security reforms. Elected officials and their staffs or appointees are more likely to shape agendas than are career bureaucrats.[14] Notable policy entrepreneurs on Capitol Hill are party and committee leaders.

Lawmakers frequently are policy entrepreneurs because they are expected to voice the concerns of their constituents and organized groups and to seek legislative solutions. Politicians generally gravitate toward issues that are visible, salient, and solvable. Tough, arcane, or controversial problems such as entitlements may be shunned or postponed because they arouse significant public controversy.

The nation's recent experience with record gasoline prices placed pressure on lawmakers to address difficult questions of energy policy. Energy independence has been a decades-long goal of the United States, particularly since the 1970s when the Organization of Petroleum Exporting Countries (OPEC), a cartel, began to deliberately slow down oil production. The result was long gas lines in cities across America as citizens waited for hours to fill their tanks before the stations ran out of fuel. Some energy-saving and conservation innovations were introduced, but these largely lapsed with the return of a global oil glut. Forecasters continue to predict more short- and long-term energy woes unless steps are taken to develop clean alternative fuels, change consumption habits, encourage conservation, and reduce the spiraling demand for oil, especially oil from the volatile Middle East. The reality is that there are no quick fixes to the demand for energy. As one analyst suggested,

We need an energy policy that understands that the world is going to require much more energy in the future. The math is pretty simple. Today, there are about 6.7 billion people on earth. By 2050 there will be 9 billion. To sustain these extra 2.3 billion people while still raising standards of living everywhere, we will need to consume about twice as much energy as we do today. So the debate about oil vs. natural gas vs. biofuels vs. alternative energy is wholly unrealistic. If we are going to sustain and support this kind of population and economic growth, we'll need everything.[15]

This kind of creeping crisis is often difficult for members of Congress to grapple with, in part because of the two-Congresses dilemma. As conscientious lawmakers, members might want to forge long-term solutions. But as representatives of their constituents, they must respond to more immediate constituent concerns about, as Obama's energy secretary phrased it, being "at the mercy of [energy] price spikes" because of the country's oil dependency.[16]

Formulating Policy

In the second stage of policy making, lawmakers and others discuss items on the political agenda and explore potential solutions. Members of Congress and their staffs play crucial roles by conducting hearings and writing committee reports. They are aided by the policy experts in executive agencies, interest groups, legislative support agencies, think tanks, universities, and private sector organizations.

Another term for this stage is *policy incubation*, which entails "keeping a proposal alive while it picks up support, or waits for a better climate, or while a consensus begins to form that the problem to which it is addressed exists."[17] Sometimes, this process takes only a few months; more often it requires years. During Dwight D. Eisenhower's administration (1953–1961), for example, congressional Democrats explored and refined domestic policy options that, while not immediately accepted, were ripe for adoption by the time their party's nominee, John F. Kennedy, was elected president in 1960.[18]

The incubation process not only brings policies to maturity but also refines the solutions to problems. The process may break down if workable solutions are not available. The seeming intractability of many modern issues complicates problem solving. Thomas S. Foley, D-Wash. (Speaker, 1989–1995), held that in the years after he entered Congress in 1965 issues became far more perplexing. At that time "the civil rights issue facing the legislators was whether the right to vote should be federally guaranteed for blacks and Hispanics. Now members are called on to deal with more ambiguous policies like affirmative action and racial quotas."[19] Complex topics such as stem cell research, genetic discrimination, unconventional warfare, and global climate change are contemporary examples of the difficult issues facing lawmakers. Solutions to problems normally involve "some fairly simple routines emphasizing the tried and true (or at least not discredited)."[20] A repertoire of proposals—for example, blue-ribbon commissions, trust funds, or pilot projects—can be applied to a variety of unsolved problems. Problem solvers also must guard against recommending solutions that will be viewed as worse than the problem.

Adopting Policy

Laws often embody ideas whose time has come. The right time for a policy is what scholar John W. Kingdon calls the "policy window": the opportunity presented by circumstances and attitudes to enact a policy into law. Policy entrepreneurs must seize the opportunity before the policy window closes and the idea's time has passed.

Once policies are ripe for adoption, they must gain popular acceptance. This is the function of legitimation, the process through which policies come to be viewed by the public as right or proper. Inasmuch as citizens are expected to comply with laws or regulations—pay taxes, observe rules, and make sacrifices of one sort or another—the policies themselves must appear to have been properly considered and enacted. One of the lingering liabilities of the landmark Patient Protection and Affordable Care Act of 2010 is the impression among some Americans that it was rammed through without bipartisan support.

Symbolic acts, such as members voting on the House or Senate floor or the president signing a bill, signal to everyone that a policy was adopted within the traditional practices. Hearings and debates serve to fine-tune policies as well as to cultivate support from affected interests. As for the pace of the overall process, responding to critics of Congress's glacial progress in adopting energy legislation, a senator posed these questions:

> Would you want an energy bill to flow through the Senate and not have anyone consider the impacts on housing or on the automotive industry or on the energy industries that provide our light and power? Should we ignore the problems of the miner or the producer or the distributor? Our legislative process must reflect all of the problems if the public is to have confidence in the government.[21]

Legitimating policies, in other words, often requires a measured pace and attention to procedural details. But a measured pace and painstaking attention to procedural niceties often provide opponents of change with an opportunity to mobilize. In many circumstances, policy makers may be forced to enact bold changes quickly in response to public outcry or demand, knowing that the details will have to be refined and adjusted later. The legislative passage in three weeks of President Obama's economic stimulus package is an example.

Implementing Policy

In the final stage, policies shaped by the legislature and at the highest executive levels are put into effect, often by a federal agency. Most policies are not self-executing; they must be promulgated and enforced. A law or executive order rarely spells out exactly how a particular policy should be implemented.

Congress and the president usually delegate most decisions about implementation to the responsible agencies under broadly worded guidelines. Implementation determines the ultimate effect of policies. Officials of the executive branch can thwart a policy by foot-dragging or sheer inefficiency. By the same token, overzealous administrators can push a policy far beyond its creators' intent.

Congress, therefore, must exercise its oversight role. It may require executive agencies to report to or consult with congressional committees or to follow other formal procedures. Members of Congress receive feedback on the operation of federal programs through a variety of channels: media coverage, interest group protests, and even casework for constituents. With such information Congress can adjust funding, introduce amendments, or recast the legislation on which the policy is based.

TYPES OF DOMESTIC POLICIES

One way to understand public policies is to analyze the nature of the policies themselves. Scholars have classified policies in many different ways.[22] Our typology identifies three types of domestic policies: distributive, regulatory, and redistributive.

Distributive Policies

Distributive policies or programs are government actions that convey tangible benefits—subsidies, tax breaks, or advantageous regulatory provisions—to private individuals, groups, or firms. These benefits are often called "pork," a derogatory term for program benefits or spending specifically designated for members' states or districts. But pork is often difficult to define objectively. After all, "one person's pork is another person's steak." The projects come in several varieties, including "old-fashioned pork" (bridges and roads), "green pork" (wind, solar, and other alternative energy projects), "academic pork" (research grants to colleges and universities), or "high-tech pork" (cybersecurity).

Distributive policy making, which makes many interests better off and few, if any, visibly worse off—comes easy to Congress, a collegial and nonhierarchical institution that must build coalitions to function. A textbook example was the $1 billion-plus National Parks and Recreation Act of 1978. Dubbed the "Park Barrel Bill," it created so many parks, historic sites, seashores, wilderness areas, wild and scenic rivers, and national trails that it sailed through the Interior (now Resources) Committee and passed the House 341–61. "Notice how quiet we are. We all got something in there," said one House member after the Rules Committee cleared the bill in five minutes flat. Another member quipped, "If it had a blade of grass and a squirrel, it got in the bill."[23] Distributive politics of this kind throws the two Congresses into sharp relief: national policy as a mosaic of local interests.

The politics of distribution works best when tax revenues are expanding, fueled by high productivity and economic growth. When productivity declines or tax cuts squeeze revenues, it can become difficult to add new benefits or expand old ones. Yet distributive impulses remain strong even in these circumstances as lawmakers in both parties work to ensure that money is spent for specific purposes in their districts or states. This type of particularistic spending is known by a variety of different names—"pork," "spending with a Zip code," "member projects," "congressional initiatives," "congressional directed spending," or, more common today, "earmarks." By whatever name, the fundamental purpose of this spending is to "bring home the bacon." Recently, earmarks have fallen into some disfavor, in part because of their cost, political use ("greasing" the legislative wheels), and the circumvention of competitive procedures for funding such constituency-based projects.

The Controversy over Earmarks. During the last two decades, the number of earmarks in spending bills increased in number and dollar value. In 1993 there were 892 earmarks worth $2.6 billion; in 1998 nearly 2,000 earmarks worth $10.6 billion; and by 2005 "nearly 14,000 earmarks, costing $27.3 billion."[24] The cost of over 9,000 earmarks peaked at $29 billion in 2006, with a falloff to $15.9 billion (9,500 earmarks) in 2010.[25] (The 2010 expenditures for earmarks represented less than half of 1 percent of the $3.7 trillion federal budget.)

Various factors accounted for the explosion in earmarks and then their rapid drop-off. As for the increase, with narrow partisan divisions in the House and Senate, party and committee leaders used earmarks to attract the votes they needed to pass priority legislation and, in a two-Congresses tactic, helped electorally vulnerable lawmakers facing tough challenges at home. A longtime GOP appropriator also stated that in 1995, when Republicans took control of the House, they "democratized the earmark process," by making earmarks "available to everyone, Republican or Democrat, leader and rank-and-file alike."[26]

The decline in earmarks occurred for three principal reasons. First, there was significant criticism of wasteful and unnecessary earmarks, especially in an era of rising fiscal deficits. The classic example highlighted by opponents of earmarks was "the bridge to nowhere"—a $230 million bridge connecting a small Alaskan town of eight thousand to an island with fifty residents.[27]

Second, there was an unseemly and sometimes corrupt connection between earmarks and campaign contributions. One lawmaker (who ended up in jail) took $2.4 million in bribes from lobbyists to insert earmarks for defense contractors, who would then contribute to his reelection campaign.

Third, aggressive watchdog groups, bloggers, and several lawmakers, such as Rep. Jeff Flake, R-Ariz., or Sen. John McCain, R-Ariz., exposed and challenged on the floor what they viewed as bad earmarks.

Earmark Reform. The 110th and 111th Congresses, as well as President Obama, instituted reforms intended to bring transparency and accountability to the earmark process. For example, the procedures required public disclosure of the lawmaker requesting an earmark; the name and location of the intended recipient; the purpose of the earmark; and certification that neither the requesting lawmaker nor his or her spouse has a financial interest in the earmark.

The 112th Congress went even further. The GOP-controlled House imposed a complete ban on earmarks for all House members. Their party regulation stated that "no Member shall request a congressional earmark, limited tax benefit, or limited tariff benefit, as such terms have been described in the Rules of the House." Some House committees also established their own guidelines for excluding earmarks from their measures.[28]

The Senate resisted for a time but then moved to ban earmarks. After President Obama declared in his 2011 State of the Union message that he would veto any legislation containing earmarks and the House indicated that it would not pass any bills that contained them, Senate Appropriations chair Daniel Inouye, D-Hawaii, said in a statement: "Given the reality before us, it makes no sense to accept earmark requests that have no chance of being enacted into law."[29] But Senator Inouye, a strong proponent of earmarks, promised that he would revisit the issue and "explore ways to improve the earmarking process."[30]

The debate over earmarks did not end in either chamber for a fundamental two-Congresses reason. As one lawmaker explained, earmarking is "part of the genetic makeup of a legislator," who must try to find a way to help out his or her community.[31] Earmark advocates in both chambers argued that a blanket ban impeded the lawmaking process; granted too much authority to unelected bureaucrats to make spending decisions that reside constitutionally with House and Senate members; and urged a rethinking of how to define an earmark. Writing to their Appropriations Committee's leaders, several senators stressed the need "to operationalize a clear definition" of earmarks. Authorized earmarks that benefit the entire nation, they argued, "are quite different from congressionally directed spending items, which only benefit a separate state, congressional district or region, and change year-to-year."[32]

Members also employed other, less transparent means to finance projects back home: earmarks by another name. They include "lettermarking"—lawmakers writing to administrators to urge that home-based projects be funded; "phonemarking"—calling executive officials to request money for projects in their states or districts; and "soft earmarks"—simply "suggesting" to agency officials that money should be spent on the lawmaker's project. Members also might hike the dollar amounts in certain budgetary accounts and "then forcefully request that the agency spend the money on the member's pet project."[33] Some lawmakers continue to solicit funding for earmarked local projects. They ask constituents to send in letters identifying community projects in need of federal money. As Rep. Mike Thompson, D-Calif., wrote in a letter to constituents:

I disagree with this decision [banning earmarks] because it prevents full and open congressional consideration of many worthwhile project proposals critical to the health, safety and economic well-being of the people of our district. As your representative in Congress, I am committed to working with you to pursue alternative strategies to support critical infrastructure improvements in our communities.[34]

To sum up, many lawmakers and analysts contend that eliminating earmarks saves a trivial amount of money, and that the lengthy debates over earmarks only detract from the big-budget items that dominate spending such as entitlements and defense, which need members' attention. Moreover, many earmarks are not wasteful and serve worthwhile national purposes, such as repairing decrepit bridges, establishing the Human Genome Project, and requiring the Pentagon "to procure Predator drone aircraft as well as to buy more body armor for troops and provide more armor protection for vehicles used in Iraq."[35]

Regulatory Policies

Regulatory policies are designed to protect the public from the harm or abuse that might result from unbridled private activity. For example, the Food and Drug Administration monitors standards for foodstuffs and tests drugs for purity, safety, and effectiveness, and the Federal Trade Commission guards against illegal business practices, such as deceptive advertising.

Federal regulation against certain abuses dates from the late nineteenth century, when the Interstate Commerce Act and the Sherman Antitrust Act were enacted to protect against abuses in transportation and monopolistic practices. As the twentieth century dawned, scandalous conditions in slaughterhouses and food-processing plants led to meatpacking, food, and drug regulations. The stock market collapse in 1929 and the Great Depression of the 1930s paved the way for the New Deal's regulation of the banking and securities industries and of labor-management relations. Consumer rights and environmental protection policies came of age in the 1960s and 1970s. The reversal of some of the protections of the 1930 enactments, plus lax oversight by federal agencies, contributed to the banking crisis of 2008–2009, which in turn fueled the Great Recession. Predictably, the fresh wave of Wall Street scandals led to a new round of regulatory fervor. Among its legacies is the Consumer Financial Protection Bureau (P.L. 111-203). Its job is to act as a watchdog for consumers in their purchase of various financial products, such as credit cards or mortgages.

Regulation inevitably arouses controversy. Much of the clean air debate, for example, involves the basic issue of costs versus benefits: do the public health benefits of cleaner air outweigh the financial costs of obtaining it?[36] Environmentalists and health advocates argue that tougher standards for regulating air pollution would prevent suffering and save the lives of thousands who are afflicted with asthma and other lung diseases. Industries and conservative groups attack these claims, contending that the "regulations are unnecessary, would be too costly and would yield only marginal health benefits."[37] A by product of new regulations such as the sweeping health care and financial reform laws enacted by the 111th Congress—has been the skyrocketing revenues for "Washington lobbyists positioned to help companies influence and comply with the new regulations."[38]

Reviewing federal agencies' regulating-writing process is a priority of the 112th Congress and of President Obama. Like presidents before him, President Obama took steps to further centralize overall control over regulation writing in the Office of Management and Budget (OMB), specifically OMB's Office of Information and Regulatory Affairs (OIRA). For example, the president issued an executive order on January 18, 2011 (E.O. 13563) requiring agencies to produce affordable and less intrusive regulations. "We're looking at the [regulatory] system as a whole to make sure we avoid excessive, inconsistent and redundant regulation."[39] To achieve these regulatory goals, the president relies on OMB, which uses cost-benefit analysis to curb excessive and burdensome regulations. Darrell Issa, R-Calif., the chair of the House Oversight and Government Reform Committee also cites regulatory reform as a top priority.

Redistributive Policies

The most difficult of all political feats is redistributive policy—that is, one in which the government purposefully shifts resources from one group to another. Typically controversial, redistributive policies engage a broad spectrum of political actors, not only in the House and Senate but also in the executive branch and among interest groups and the public at large. Redistributive issues tend to be ideological, dividing liberals and conservatives on fundamental questions of equality, opportunity, and property rights. Tax cuts for the wealthy at a time of rising income inequality is an example of a redistributive controversy. (Despite the controversy, when the tax cuts are brought up for a vote, they are usually approved by a solid margin.) Redistribution can even be future-oriented: excessive amounts of deficit spending today mean larger financial burdens for the next generation.

Most of the divisive socioeconomic issues of the past generation—civil rights, affirmative action, school busing, welfare, immigration, tax reform—were redistributive problems. A redistributive issue for the twenty-first century is the growing share of the federal budget that goes to the elderly compared with everyone else in society. Spending on entitlement programs, principally Social Security and Medicare, absorbs an ever-increasing proportion of federal dollars, which then are unavailable for other important social, domestic, or security needs.

When redistributive issues are at stake, federal budgeting is almost always marked by conflict. In recent years, the conflicts have tended to be over how to cut entitlements. Various techniques have been employed to disguise cuts and to make them more palatable. Omnibus budget packages permit legislators to approve cuts en bloc instead of one by one, and across-the-board formulas (such as freezes) give the appearance of spreading the misery equally to affected groups. In all such vehicles, provisions of this sort are added to placate the more vocal opponents of change.

CHARACTERISTICS OF CONGRESSIONAL POLICY MAKING

As a policy-making body, Congress displays the traits and biases of its membership and structure, as well as those of the larger political system. As for the first, the two houses of Congress have divergent electoral and procedural traditions. As for the second, Congress is representative, especially where geographic interests are concerned, and it is decentralized, having few mechanisms for integrating or coordinating its policy decisions. As for policy itself, Congress is often inclined toward enacting symbolic measures instead of substantive ones. Finally, Congress is rarely ahead of the curve—or the public—tending to reflect conventional perceptions of problems.

Bicameralism

Differences between the House and Senate—their relative sizes, members' terms of office, the character of their constituencies—shape the policies they make. Six-year terms, it is argued, allow senators to play statesmen for at least part of each term before the approaching elections force them to concentrate on fence-mending. Although this distinction may be more apparent than real, empirical studies of senators' behavior lend some support to the claim.[40]

Various constituencies tend to pull in divergent directions. Homogeneous House districts often promote clear, unambiguous positions on a narrower range of questions than those embraced by an entire state. A senator, then, as a representative of an entire state, must weigh the claims of many competing interests on a broad range of matters.

The sizes of the two chambers dictate procedural biases. House rules are designed to allow majorities to have their way. By contrast, Senate rules give individual senators great latitude to influence action. As a GOP senator once said, "The Senate has the strongest minority of any minority on Earth, and the weakest majority of any on Earth."[41]

In short, the two chambers differ in outlook, constituency, and strategy. Bicameralism is less important in promoting or discouraging particular kinds of policies, writes Benjamin I. Page, than in "the furtherance of deliberation, the production of evidence, and the revealing of error."[42]

Localism

Congressional policies respond to constituents' needs, particularly those that can be mapped geographically. Sometimes, these needs are pinpointed with startling directness. For example, an aviation noise control bill required construction of a control tower "at latitude 40 degrees, 43 minutes, 45 seconds north and at longitude 73 degrees, 24 minutes, 50 seconds west"—the very location of a Farmingdale, New York, airport in the district of the Democratic representative who requested the provision.[43]

Usually, however, programs are directed toward states, municipalities, counties, or geographic regions. Funds are often transferred directly to local government agencies, which in turn deliver the aid or services to citizens. But sometimes Congress will require states and localities to fund some national priorities without federal assistance. These "unfunded mandates" strain state budgets and rouse the ire of state and local officials. In 1995 President Bill Clinton signed into law the Unfunded Mandates Reform Act, which requires Congress either to make provision to pay for any mandate that the CBO estimates will cost state and local governments $50 million or more, or to "take a separate recorded vote to waive the requirement, thus holding members of Congress accountable for their decision."[44]

Lawmakers are therefore now supposed to consider the costs of any federal requirements they impose on state and local governments. For example, the No Child Left Behind (NCLB) education law (P.L. 107-110), which President Obama is urging the 112th Congress to revise and reauthorize before 2014 (the statute's expiration date), prescribes mandatory standardized testing in all public schools in today's cash-strapped states. School systems in many states complain that the federal government has failed to provide enough money to cover the expense of meeting the law's requirement. The law's fundamental goal is to ensure that by 2014 every student in grades 3–8 is proficient in reading and math. If not, schools might close and teachers could be fired.

National and local policies are necessarily intertwined. National policies can be advanced by state and local governments; in turn, states or localities can develop innovations that spur national action. The threat of terrorist attacks in the United States demands that any such calamity be confronted by first responders—police officers, firefighters, public health officials, and others—at the state and local levels. On other issues as well, the states are the testing grounds, or laboratories, for social, economic, and political experiments.

Many policy debates revolve around not only which government level can most effectively carry out a responsibility, but also which level best promotes particular values. Liberals tend to prefer that the national government lead in enforcing civil rights and environmental protection. Conservatives support an activist national government on defense and security matters. When it suits their purposes, both liberals and conservatives are capable of advocating either national mandates or local autonomy, depending on which level of government would best serve their objectives.

Piecemeal Policy Making

Policies all too often mirror Congress's scattered and decentralized structure. Typically, they are considered piecemeal, reflecting the patchwork of committee and subcommittee jurisdictions. Congress's segmented decision making is typified by authorizing and appropriating processes in which separate committees consider the same programs, often without consulting each other.

The structure of a policy frequently depends on which committees have reported it. Working from varying jurisdictions, committees can take different approaches to the same problem. The taxing committees gravitate toward tax provisions to address problems; the appropriations committees will prefer a fiscal approach to issues; the commerce panels typically adopt a regulatory perspective; and so forth. Each approach may be well or ill suited to the policy objective. The approach adopted will depend on which committee is best positioned to promote the bill.

Symbolic Policy Making

Congressional policy making can be more about appearance than substance. Bills are often passed to give the impression that action is being taken, even when the measure adopted is unlikely to have any real impact on the problem. The general public and interest groups continually demand, "Don't just stand there, do something." Doing something is often the only politically feasible choice, even when no one knows exactly what to do or whether inaction might be just as effective.[45]

Still, symbolic actions are important to all politicians. This is not the same thing as saying that politicians are merely cynical manipulators of symbols. Words and concepts—*equal opportunity, income inequality, cost of living, parity, affirmative action*—are contested earnestly in committee rooms and on the House and Senate floor. The result, however, is that federal goals are often stated in vague, optimistic language and not spelled out in terms of specific measures of success or failure.

Reactive Policy Making

It would be naive to expect a deliberative body to routinely adopt bold or radical solutions to problems. Elected officials are seldom far ahead of or far behind the collective views of their constituencies. Members know that out-of-the-mainstream views are unlikely to attract widespread public support. Indeed, Congress is essentially a reactive institution. As one House member explained,

> When decision rests on the consent of the governed, it comes slowly, only after consensus has built or crisis has focused public opinion in some unusual way, the representatives in the meantime hanging back until the signs are unmistakable. Government decision, then, is not generally the cutting edge of change but a belated reaction to change.[46]

Ending the statutory "don't ask, don't tell" policy toward gays in the military, for example, came late in 2010—only after public attitudes on the matter had shifted and the Joint Chiefs of Staff had assured lawmakers that the change would not adversely affect military performance.

The reactive character of Congress's policy making is evident in its budget process. Under pressures to reform, Congress reacted in 1974, 1985, and again in the 1990s with formal and informal changes in the way it makes budget decisions. The current budget process, dating from the mid-1970s, was intended to bring coherence to the way standing committees handle the president's budget. It has decisively shaped both Congress's internal decision making and its relations with the executive.

CONGRESSIONAL BUDGETING

Congressional budgeting is a complex process that involves two types of federal spending: discretionary and mandatory (entitlements). Discretionary spending is under the jurisdiction of the House and Senate Appropriations Committees; mandatory or entitlement spending embedded in statutes is the purview of the authorizing (or policy-recommending) committees of each chamber. Virtually all House and Senate members and committees, the president and executive branch officials, and scores of other participants actively seek to influence Congress's power of the purse. That congressional budgeting is usually contentious should come as no surprise considering the high political and policy stakes associated with fiscal decision making (see Box 14-1 for some of the terminology used in budgeting).

Authorizations and Appropriations

Congress's budget procedures are shaped by two customary and longtime processes: authorizations and appropriations. Generally, legislative rules stipulate that before agencies or programs receive any money, Congress should first pass authorization laws that do three fundamental things: (1) establish or continue (reauthorize) federal agencies and programs; (2) define the purposes, functions, and operations of programs or agencies; and (3) recommend (that is, authorize) the appropriation of funds for programs and agencies. As Senate Democratic leader Harry Reid explained, "Authorizations allow programs to be created and funded. When we pass an authorizing bill, we hope the authorized level will be looked at in [the] appropriations committee—as I did as a longtime member. But we realize there are competing priorities, and full funding doesn't come very often."[47]

As an example, the defense authorization bill might authorize the construction of three new submarines and recommend $15 billion for this purpose. Does that mean the Pentagon has the money to build the submarines? No. Congress must enact the defense appropriations bill that would grant the Pentagon legal authority to spend a specific amount of money for the submarines. In short, an authorization can be viewed as a "hunting license" for an appropriation, a law that actually supplies programs and agencies with public funds (budget authority).

By custom, the House initiates appropriations bills. The House Appropriations Committee (usually one of its twelve subcommittees) would recommend how much money the Pentagon should receive for the submarines. The amount is called "budget authority" (BA), and it is equivalent to depositing money in a checking account. The budget outlay (BO) is the check

BOX 14-1 **A Budget Glossary**

Appropriations. The process by which Congress provides budget authority, usually through the enactment of twelve separate appropriations bills.

Budget authority. The authority for federal agencies to spend or otherwise obligate money, accomplished through enactment into law of appropriations bills.

Budget outlays. Money that is spent in a given fiscal year, as opposed to money that is appropriated for that year. One year's budget authority can result in outlays over several years, and the outlays in any given year result from a mix of budget authority from that year and prior years. Budget authority is similar to putting money into a checking account. Outlays occur when checks are written and cashed.

Discretionary spending. Programs that Congress can finance as it chooses through appropriations. With the exception of paying entitlement benefits to individuals (see mandatory spending below), almost everything the government does is financed by discretionary spending. Examples include all federal agencies, Congress, the White House, the courts, the military, and programs such as space exploration and child nutrition. About a third of all federal spending falls into this category.

Fiscal year. The federal government's budget year. For example, fiscal year 2012 runs from October 1, 2011, through September 30, 2012.

Mandatory spending. Made up mostly of entitlements, which are programs whose eligibility requirements are written into law. Anyone who meets those requirements is entitled to the money until Congress changes the law. Examples are Social Security, Medicare, Medicaid, unemployment benefits, food stamps, and federal pensions. Another major category of mandatory spending is the interest paid to holders of federal government bonds. Social Security and interest payments are permanently appropriated. And although budget authority for some entitlements is provided through the appropriations process, appropriators have little or no control over the money. Mandatory spending accounts for about two-thirds of all federal spending.

Pay-as-you-go (PAYGO) rule. This Senate rule requires that all tax cuts, new entitlement programs, and expansions of existing entitlement programs be budget-neutral—that is, offset either by additional taxes or by cuts in existing entitlement programs.

Cut-as-you-go (CUTGO) rule. This House rule requires new mandatory spending to be offset with cuts to existing entitlement programs. Tax increases cannot be used to offset new spending.

Reconciliation. The process by which tax laws and spending programs are changed, or reconciled, to reach outlay and revenue targets set in the congressional budget resolution. Established by the 1974 Congressional Budget Act (P.L. 93-344), it was first used in 1980.

Rescission. The cancellation of previously appropriated budget authority. This is a common way to save money that already has been appropriated. A rescissions bill must be passed by Congress and signed by the president (or enacted over his veto), just as an appropriations bill is.

Revenues. Taxes, customs duties, some user fees, and most other receipts paid to the federal government.

Sequester. The cancellation of spending authority as a disciplinary measure to cut off spending above preset limits. Appropriations that exceed annual spending caps can trigger a sequester that will cut all appropriations by the amount of the excess. Similarly, tax cuts and new or expanded entitlement spending programs that are not offset under the pay-as-you-go law could trigger a sequester of nonexempt entitlement programs.

Source: Adapted from Andrew Taylor, "Clinton's Strength Portends a Tough Season for GOP," *CQ Weekly,* February 6, 1999, 293.

written by the Pentagon to the contractors hired to construct the submarines. The House Appropriations Committee can provide up to the authorized $15 billion (but not more), propose less funding, or refuse to fund the submarine purchases at all. Assume that the House votes to approve $10 billion. The Senate Appropriations Committee, acting somewhat like a court of appeals, then hears Navy officials asking the Senate to approve the full $15 billion. If the Senate accedes, a House-Senate compromise is worked out, either in a conference committee or by the bicameral exchange of amendments.

The authorization-appropriation sequence, which is often observed in the breach, is not required by the U.S. Constitution. The dual procedure dates from the nineteenth century and stems from inordinate delays caused by adding riders—extraneous policy amendments—to appropriation bills. "By 1835," wrote a legislator, "delays caused by injecting legislation [policy] into these [appropriations] bills had become serious and [Massachusetts representative] John Quincy Adams suggested that they be stripped of everything save appropriations."[48] Two years later, the House required authorizations to precede appropriations. The Senate followed suit. Both chambers have rules and precedents designed "to segregate decisions about what the government should do [authorizations] from those about how much it can afford [appropriations]."[49] However, as discussed shortly, policy riders are often added to appropriations bills despite the dual procedure.

The Constitution provides that "No Money shall be drawn from the Treasury, but in Consequence of Appropriations made by Law" (Article I, section 9). As a result, appropriations have priority over authorizations. An appropriations measure may be approved even if the authorization bill has not been enacted. Some programs have not been authorized for years, but they still continue to operate. Why? If money is sprinkled on programs or agencies, they continue to exist and function even if their authorization has lapsed. As one House Appropriations subcommittee chair said about the "must-pass" appropriations bills, "It's not the end of the world if we postpone the Clean Air Act or a tax measure. But the entire government will shut down if . . . appropriations [are not enacted annually]."[50]

Authorizations can be annual, multiyear, or permanent. Through the end of World War II, most federal agencies and programs were permanently authorized. They were reviewed annually by the House and Senate Appropriations Committees, but not by the authorizing committees (such as Agriculture or Commerce). Since the 1970s, the trend has been toward short-term authorizations, giving the authorizing committees more chances to control agency operations.[51] Generally, authorizing committees are eager to enact their bills on a timely basis, because otherwise they cede their lawmaking power to the appropriating panels. As Sen. Dianne Feinstein, D-Calif., the chair of the Intelligence Committee, exclaimed, "If this committee can't pass authorization bills . . . which give scope and force of law to what we do, we are in fact a paper tiger."[52] But authorizers also try from time to time to hitch a ride on an appropriations bill heading to the White House. "Ideally, it's not great to use [appropriations] bills," remarked Rep. Barney Frank, D-Mass. "But they may be the only vehicles we can use [for] some [authorization measures] where we're facing a veto or we have problems in the Senate."[53]

In practice, it is hard to keep the two stages distinct, in large measure because the availability of money affects whether policies can be carried out. Authorization bills sometimes carry appropriations, and appropriations bills sometimes contain legislation (or policy provisions). Chamber rules that forbid these maneuvers can be waived. In the House, so-called limitation riders make policy under the guise of restricting agency use of funds. Phrased negatively ("None of the funds may be used for a specified purpose . . ."), limitations on the use of federal funds bolster congressional control of the bureaucracy. A well-known limitation amendment—barring the use of federal funds for abortions except under limited circumstances—was first adopted in 1976 and has been readopted ever since in appropriations bills. The Senate, too, is not reluctant to add extraneous policy proposals to appropriations bills. Angered that a major immigration proposal was added to a supplemental appropriations bill, Democratic leader Harry Reid exclaimed, "This is the mother of all authorizing legislation on an appropriations bill."[54] Policy riders can provoke, as noted by Rep. Frank, bicameral, party, and legislative-executive disputes.

Committee Roles and Continuing Resolutions. Among the authorizing committees, House Ways and Means and Senate Finance have especially powerful roles in the budget process. These tax panels have access to the staff experts of the Joint Taxation Committee. Because the House under the Constitution initiates revenue measures, it usually determines whether Congress will act on legislation to raise, lower, or redistribute the tax burden. Occasionally, however, the Senate takes the lead. The Senate technically complies with the Constitution by appending a major tax measure to a minor House-passed revenue bill. In 1981 the Republican-controlled Senate used this tactic to act on President Ronald Reagan's sweeping tax cut plan. It used the same ploy the next year on the president's tax increase package. The House jealously guards its constitutional authority to originate tax measures and typically will return to the Senate any bill that violates the origination clause.[55]

Whenever Congress cannot complete action on one or more of the twelve regular appropriations bills (generally one for each subcommittee) by the beginning of the fiscal year (October 1), it provides temporary, stopgap funding for the affected federal agencies through a joint resolution known as a continuing resolution, as noted earlier in this chapter. In the past, continuing resolutions were usually employed to keep a few government agencies in operation for short periods (usually one to three months). In some years, Congress has packaged all the regular appropriations bills into one massive continuing resolution. (A record twenty-one continuing resolutions were needed in 2000 before the GOP Congress and President Clinton compromised their differences on several appropriations bills that had not been enacted by the start of the fiscal year.[56]) Each year, Congress also passes one or more supplemental appropriations bills to meet unforeseen contingencies. To sum up, there are three basic types of appropriations: *regular* (made annually), *supplemental* (furnishing funds for unexpected contingencies), or *continuing* (providing funds when one or more annual appropriations bills have not been enacted by the start of the fiscal year).

A Shift in Thinking. Significantly, the 112th Congress may be witnessing a shift in the role and culture of the two Appropriations Committees. Once known as guardians of the federal Treasury, the two panels gradually developed an affinity for spending as they evaluated and compared the budgetary requests of federal agencies and departments. Some lobbyists even referred to the committees as "favor factories" where taxpayer dollars could be won for their clients. Several committee members won the appellation the "King of Pork" or the "Prince of Pork" for the hundreds of millions of dollars they earmarked for projects in their states or districts.

Recently, a House appropriator called the panel "the Dis-Appropriations Committee."[57] Subtraction, not addition, characterizes budgeting by the two panels. As Harold Rogers, R-Ky., the chair of House Appropriations, said, "The atmosphere in the country is that government has to get serious about cutting spending. We've finally come to the realization, and now we understand how deep the [deficit] problem is. And the place where the spending is controlled is the Appropriations Committee."[58]

To what extent and for how long the "atmosphere in the country" will support program funding reductions are unclear. Government programs have constituencies—which is often why they were created in the first place—likely to oppose severe funding cuts or outright program terminations. As scholars and others have long known, people favor spending cuts in the abstract but not for programs they support and benefit from. For example, senior citizens often tell lawmakers, "Keep your hands off my Social Security!" A key question, then, is, are Americans finally ready and willing to shrink the size and scope of government and roll back federal spending?[59]

Backdoor Spending Techniques

To sidestep appropriators' abilities to slash their recommended funding levels, authorizing committees evolved backdoor funding provisions to bypass the front door of the two-step authorization-appropriation sequence. Backdoors are authorization laws that mandate, rather than simply recommend, the expenditure of federal funds. This type of spending legislation, which is reported solely by the authorizing committees, is called direct (or mandatory) spending, as opposed to the discretionary spending under the House and Senate Appropriations Committees. There are three types of backdoor or direct spending provisions: (1) contract authority permits agencies to enter into contracts that subsequently must be covered by appropriations; (2) borrowing authority allows agencies to spend money they have borrowed from the public or the Treasury; and (3) entitlement programs grant eligible individuals and governments the right to receive payments from the national government.

The fastest-growing of the three types is entitlements, which establish legally enforceable rights for eligible beneficiaries. Spending for entitlement programs (such as Medicare and Social Security) is determined by the number of citizens who qualify and the benefit levels established by law. No fixed dollar amount is established for these programs. Budget wonks sometimes call entitlements "uncontrollable under existing law." Statutory changes, however, are difficult to make because entitlements benefit millions of people. Tellingly, the GOP-controlled House of the 112th Congress has considered defunding President Obama's health care law by changing into discretionary spending the mandatory spending features embedded in the health law. If such a law were enacted, it would be easier for House appropriators to defund the statute's implementation.[60]

The Challenge of Entitlements

Entitlements are the real force behind the escalation of federal spending (see Figure 14-1). More than half of all federal spending consists of entitlements that avoid the annual appropriations review process. This ratio of discretionary (determined through yearly appropriations) to mandatory spending represents a dramatic reversal from that of a half-century ago. Unlike defense or domestic discretionary programs—for which the Appropriations panels recommend annual amounts and on which all lawmakers may vote—entitlement spending occurs automatically under the terms outlined in the statute.

Congress has done a reasonable job of containing discretionary spending. But reining in costly entitlements has proved to be a much more difficult task. In 1996 Congress passed legislation ending a decades-old national welfare entitlement program, Aid to Families with Dependent Children.[61] However, the recipients of the largest share of entitlement spending—senior citizens—are highly protective of these programs and also very likely to vote. A classic example of how hard it is to revamp entitlements occurred in the second term of President George W. Bush. He launched an intense lobbying drive to win public and congressional support for replacing Social Security with individual retirement accounts, but his reform effort failed to gain any traction. Even many Republicans opposed the plan's reliance on private accounts. "Social Security [is] the bedrock of support for seniors," said Sen. Olympia J. Snowe, R-Maine, "precisely because it's defined and guaranteed. What cost and what risk is it worth to erode the guaranteed benefit [through variable stock or bond investments]?"[62]

President Obama also faces the challenge posed by the escalating costs of the big three entitlement programs—Medicare, Medicaid, and Social Security. But this is hardly news. Public officials and analysts have been warning for years—without too much effect—that the projected expenditures of entitlement programs are unsustainable. For example, Medicare faces a prospective funding gap of at least $36 trillion. Moreover, because of the current recession, during which fewer payroll taxes are collected, the Medicare fund is expected to run out of money in 2017.[63] Social Security is slated to pay full benefits to

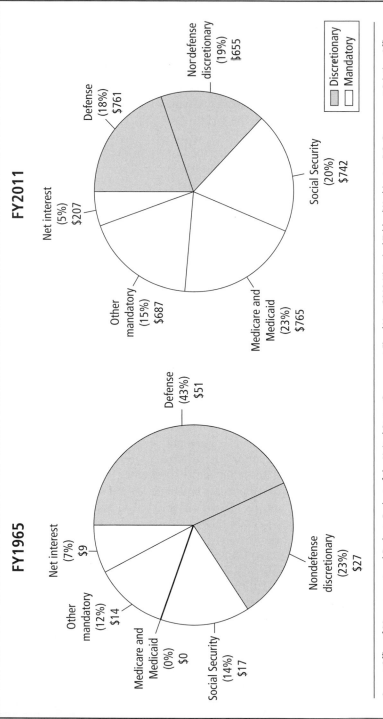

FY2011

Defense
(18%)
$761

Nondefense
discretionary
(19%)
$655

Net interest
(5%)
$207

Social Security
(20%)
$742

Other
mandatory
(15%)
$687

Medicare and
Medicaid
(23%)
$765

Discretionary
Mandatory

FY1965

Defense
(43%)
$51

Net interest
(7%)
$9

Nondefense
discretionary
(23%)
$27

Other
mandatory
(12%)
$14

Medicare and
Medicaid
(0%)
$0

Social Security
(14%)
$17

Source: Office of Management and Budget, *Budget of the United States Government Fiscal Year 2012 Historical Tables* (Washington DC: Government Printing Office, 2011, 145, 159. Charts prepared by Robert Keith and Bill Heniff Jr., Government and Finance Division, Congressional Research Service.

the elderly until 2037, after which seniors would receive 75–80 percent of their promised benefits unless changes are made to the existing laws.[64]

The long-term demographic challenge confronting Social Security and Medicare is that the United States is an aging society with a population that is living longer, thanks in part to advances in often-expensive medical technology. The nation is already witnessing the gradual retirement of the seventy-six million members of the "baby boom" generation (those born between 1946 and 1964), creating a pool of the largest number of retirees in the history of the country. This development will lead to huge retirement and medical expenditures for those who are eligible to receive Social Security and Medicare benefits. But, according to the projections, fewer workers (a "birth dearth") will be paying taxes to support the retirement and medical expenditures that will make up retirees' expected benefits. As a chair of the Senate Budget Committee pointed out,

> In 1950 there were about 16 Americans working for every 1 American retired. That meant programs such as Social Security . . . not only generated money to support those who were retired, they actually generated more money than needed to support the people who retired. That is happening today even. But the number of people retiring compared to the number of people working has been changing. It has gone from 16 in 1950 down to about 3 and a half today. And further into this century, as the baby boom generation retires, it will drop to 2 people working for every 1 person retired. . . . It becomes pretty obvious, if you have only two people working to pay for one person retired, those two people are going to have to pay a lot more in taxes to support that one person. . . . So this creates a huge . . . unfunded liability [in future years as more money is taken out of Social Security than is paid in]. We do not know how we are going to pay for [Social Security and Medicare] in the outyears.[65]

Many proposals have been advanced to deal with the long-term funding challenge, but each is controversial. For Social Security, the proposed changes include raising the retirement age, reducing benefits for future retirees, increasing the payroll tax rate, requiring affluent retirees to pay taxes on their benefits, and raising the amount of income subject to Social Security payroll taxes.[66]

Politically, there are risks for any lawmaker or political party that advocates such recommendations. In the 112th Congress, Rep. Paul Ryan, R-Wis., the chair of the Budget Committee, is one of many members of the fiscally conservative GOP-controlled House who is willing to take that risk. Representative Ryan has suggested overhauling Medicare and partially privatizing Social Security and cutting benefits. Many Democrats strongly oppose such proposals, arguing in Social Security's case that it will have no effect on escalating deficits ($1.5 trillion in 2012) until 2037. "Blaming Social Security for our deficit is nothing but an ideological attempt to slash benefits and privatize the program," declared Sen. Charles Schumer, D-N.Y.[67]

Why would congressional Republicans hand Democrats a political weapon that could erode GOP support among elderly voters in the next election? A Republican pollster suggested an answer. "It may be hard to understand why someone would try to jump off a cliff" to resolve a long-term entitlement spending issue, he said, "unless you understand that they are being chased by a tiger, and that tiger is the tea party."[68] Other GOP strategists disagree. They underscore that because of crushing budget realities the time is right politically for entitlement reform, provided the party does not move so fast as to "outstrip public opinion."[69]

Many analysts and public officials contend that the real entitlement budget buster of the future is not Social Security but the soaring costs of Medicare and health care in general: "The long-term fiscal problem truly is fundamentally one involving the rate at which healthcare costs grow. Social Security and aging are important, but it is not where the money is, explained President Obama's former budget director."[70] Representative Ryan's 2012 budget plan proposes a major overhaul of Medicare—federally subsidized vouchers for seniors so they can purchase health insurance in the private sector—and Medicaid—block grants to the states to care for low-income individuals and families. Public wariness of Ryan's plan makes its enactment unlikely.

With health care costs rising faster than inflation, with the graying of society, and with the advent of costly new medical technologies, Medicare is already paying out more in benefits than it is receiving in taxes. President Obama's landmark health care law, the Patient Protection and Affordable Care Act, aims to slow rising health care costs, but the outcome is unclear, in part because key features of the law do not take effect until 2014. Medicare's actuaries wonder whether the savings expected from the law's provisions will be enough "to reduce the perverse economic incentives [such as defensive medicine] and costs built into the health care system."[71] In short, citizens want Lexus health services on a Chevrolet budget.

Elected officials often focus first on Social Security because there is a rough consensus on the solutions to constrain its soaring cost. Not so with Medicare. Setting aside the president's health care law and Representative Ryan's health proposals, the other steps "Congress could take now to restrain Medicare's growth are politically perilous. Deny end-of-life care? Restrict eligibility? Reduce treatments? Raise costs?"[72] Even more frightening from a budget perspective is the prospect of providing long-term nursing home or other care for the elderly. Long-term care, said Rep. Earl Pomeroy, D-N.D., is "the elephant in the living room that no one's talking about."[73] And Medicaid, a federal entitlement program for indigent and low-income persons that is jointly funded by the national and state governments has "now surged past Medicare to become the nation's largest health care program."[74]

In short, an entitlement revolution is under way as the government today transfers more than half of federal monies to eligible families and individuals. "Call it government by ATM," remarked an analyst. "You walk up, hit the buttons, and the cash to which you're entitled pops out."[75] This transformation in the federal budget—away from discretionary to direct (or mandatory) spending—raises the question of whether this funding ratio is sustainable. Congress and the president face at least a dual fiscal challenge: the battle for scarce resources between entitlements and discretionary spending, and the struggle within the discretionary category between domestic versus defense and homeland security spending.

Two other forms of mandatory spending merit separate mention as well: tax expenditures and raising the debt ceiling, including interest on the national debt.

Tax Expenditures. An estimated $1 trillion is consumed by indirect spending, also called tax expenditures or tax preferences. This is the revenue that is forgone through various tax credits, subsidies, or deductions such as the home mortgage interest deduction. Rep. Jim Cooper, D-Tenn., declared that if "there is anything more out of control than entitlement spending," it is tax expenditures.[76] Compared with mandatory or discretionary spending, these expenditures receive scant public attention. One study noted that "much like entitlement programs, [tax expenditures] are on automatic pilot and do not receive sufficient scrutiny as part of the budget process."[77] Significantly, the total value of all tax preferences is virtually equal to the total value of all discretionary spending.

In the 112th Congress, a so-called bipartisan "gang of six" senators considered a combination of savings from entitlements and tax expenditures, as well as various spending cuts, to trim $4 trillion from the deficit over ten years.[78] Like other government programs, tax expenditures have their own political constituencies that will fight attempts to eliminate or reduce this conglomeration of tax breaks and subsidies. Of the some 250 tax expenditures, most "disproportionately benefit those at the top of the economic ladder."[79] Scholars who study tax expenditures sometimes refer to this form of federal largess as "the submerged state" or the "hidden welfare state."[80]

Raising the Debt Ceiling—Interest on the Debt. The national debt—the accumulation of annual deficits—is slated to rise from over $14 trillion to over $15 trillion by the summer of 2011, if not earlier. Under the Constitution, Congress has the authority—statutorily assigned to the Treasury Department— to borrow money to cover the shortfall between federal spending and tax receipts. By law, Congress caps the amount of outstanding debt as a way, in theory, to better control legislative spending. However, Congress has raised the debt ceiling more than forty times since 1980 (twice in 2008 and twice in 2009) to stay ahead of the escalating debt—triggered by factors such as borrowing to pay the cost of three conflicts (Iraq, Afghanistan, and Libya).[81]

If the debt ceiling is not raised, the "federal government would have to eliminate all spending on discretionary programs, cut nearly 70 percent of outlays for mandatory programs, increase revenue collection by nearly two-thirds or take some combination of these actions."[82] Failure to raise the ceiling would constitute the nation's first default on paying its debt obligations. Austan Goolsbee, the chair of the President Obama's Council of Economic

Advisers, bluntly warned, "If we get to the point where we damage the full faith and credit of the United States, that would be the first default in history caused by pure insanity."[83]

Goolsbee made that comment because of widespread speculation that congressional Republicans in both chambers plan to play "political chicken." Backed by the Tea Party movement and others, GOP lawmakers have indicated they would vote for the politically unpopular debt ceiling hike—adding additional indebtness to already record-setting deficits and debt—only if the Obama administration accepted deep reductions in discretionary spending and agreed to add to the debt ceiling legislation a process to curb entitlement spending.[84] The outcome is unclear, but it seems likely that experienced party leaders in both chambers will mobilize the votes to pass a stand-alone measure increasing the debt ceiling to over $15 trillion. (In 2011 House Republicans amended the rules of their chamber to require a direct vote on raising the debt ceiling. Previously, House rules provided that passage of the annual budget resolution, discussed shortly, would automatically result in adoption of a measure raising the debt ceiling.)

"There is a cancer eating away at the budget from within," wrote a journalist, and it is the ever-increasing interest that must be paid to service the national debt.[85] Interest payments in 2011 on the national debt exceed $200 billion, and in 2021 they are projected to be over $925 billion. This development further compounds the difficulty of resolving the long-term deficit. In 2014 interest payments are projected to "surpass the amount spent on education, transportation, energy, and all other discretionary programs outside of defense." In 2018 interest payments will surpass Medicare spending.[86] The options for Congress to slow the growth of interest payments on the debt appear straightforward, but they are politically controversial and substantively complex: tax more, spend less, combine those two, and foster economic growth.

To focus greater attention on issues such as tax expenditures, the debt ceiling, interest on the debt, entitlements, and much more, Congress passed almost forty years ago a landmark budgetary measure, the Congressional Budget and Impoundment Control Act of 1974. The goals of that act included bringing greater coordination and coherence to legislative budgeting and strengthening Congress's power of the purse. However, the results have been mixed, because it is no easy task to control and monitor federal budgeting.

THE 1974 BUDGET ACT

Congress refocused its budgetary attention in the 1970s after its loose control of the purse strings gave rise to charges of financial irresponsibility. President Richard Nixon blamed Congress for annual deficits, consumer price hikes, high unemployment, and inflation. He also refused to spend monies duly appropriated by Congress, a practice called impoundment. Even though his administration lost every court challenge to the impoundments, Nixon held the political high ground. These diverse pressures prompted Congress to tighten its budget procedures.

The Budget and Impoundment Control Act of 1974 was landmark legislation. Among its principal features was the creation of House and Senate Budget Committees, as well as the Congressional Budget Office (CBO). The nonpartisan CBO prepares economic forecasts for Congress, estimates the costs of proposed legislation, and issues fiscal, monetary, and policy reports. The 1974 act also limited presidential use of impoundments and established a timetable for action on authorization, appropriation, and tax measures. The timetable has been changed periodically, and Congress commonly misses some of the target dates (see Box 14-2 for the timetable).

Of the many complex features of the 1974 act, two are central components of Congress's current budget process: the concurrent budget resolution and reconciliation. These two elements compel much of the time-consuming work of each annual legislative session, attract the attention of many interests and participants clamoring for fiscal resources, and influence policy decisions and outcomes.

BOX 14-2   **The Congressional Budget Timetable**

Deadline	Action to be completed
First Monday in February	President submits budget to Congress
February 15	Congressional Budget Office submits economic and budget outlook report to Budget Committees
Six weeks after president submits budget	Committees submit views and estimates to Budget Committees
April 1	Senate Budget Committee reports budget resolution
April 15	Congress completes action on budget resolution
May 15	Annual appropriations bills may be considered in the House, even if action on budget resolution has not been completed
June 10	House Appropriations Committee reports last annual appropriations bill
June 15	House completes action on reconciliation legislation (if required by budget resolution)
June 30	House completes action on annual appropriations bills
July 15	President submits mid-session review of his budget to Congress
October 1	Fiscal year begins

Source: Bill Heniff Jr., *The Congressional Budget Process Timetable,* Congressional Research Service Report 98–472 GOV, March 20, 2008.

Concurrent Budget Resolution

The core of Congress's annual budget process is adoption of a concurrent budget resolution. This measure is formulated by the House and Senate Budget Committees, which consider the views and estimates of numerous committees and witnesses.

The resolution consists of five basic parts. First, the budget resolution estimates what the federal government will spend in a fiscal year and for at least the four following fiscal years. For each fiscal year, the spending is expressed in terms of both budget authority and budget outlays. Second, the total aggregate spending is then subdivided among twenty functional categories such as defense, agriculture, or energy. For each category, the spending indicates what Congress expects to expend in those substantive areas. Third, the budget resolution stipulates the recommended levels of federal revenues needed to pay for the projected spending during each of the fiscal years. Fourth, because the federal government consistently runs deficits, the budget resolution identifies the estimated deficits (or surpluses should they occur, which is infrequent). Fifth, the total outstanding public debt (savings bonds, Treasury securities, and other government obligations) permitted by law is also specified for at least the five-year period. In effect, the budget resolution sets the overall level of discretionary spending for each fiscal year. For 2012 the concurrent budget resolution set a spending ceiling of just over $1 trillion for appropriations bills in an overall budget of $3.7 trillion.[87]

The budget resolution is Congress's fiscal blueprint. It establishes the context of congressional budgeting; guides the budgetary actions of the authorizing, appropriating, and taxing committees; and reflects Congress's spending priorities. A senator described the purposes of the budget resolution: "[The budget] resolution would be analogous to an architect's set of plans for constructing a building. It gives the general direction, framework, and prioritization of Federal fiscal policy each year. Those priorities then drive the individual appropriations and tax measures which will support that architectural plan."[88]

In a period of polarized politics, partisan issues dominate debate on these resolutions as Democrats and Republicans battle over spending levels for their competing priorities. In a bold and politically risky move, House Budget Committee chair Paul Ryan unveiled a budget resolution for 2012 that would slash nearly $6 trillion in federal spending over ten years, including, as noted earlier, the two health care entitlement programs (Medicare and Medicaid). Ryan called his budget blueprint the "path to prosperity." House Democratic leader Nancy Pelosi dubbed it a "path to poverty."[89] It is not unusual for minority party members in both chambers to vote as a bloc against the majority party's budget resolution.

The House and Senate each consider a budget resolution. In the House, budget resolutions are typically considered under special rules from the Rules Committee, which limit debate and impose restrictions on the number and types of amendments. In the Senate, the 1974 budget act sets a fifty-hour limitation for consideration of the budget resolution, unless members accept a unanimous consent agreement imposing other time restrictions. Amendments can be taken up and voted on after the fifty hours, but without debate. This circumstance often leads to "vote-a-ramas" over several days, when senators may "cast back-to-back votes on a dizzying array of dozens of amendments," often with the two Congresses in mind. As national policy makers, members of Congress may have to cast tough, but responsible, votes, which will "serve as valuable campaign fodder" for opponents in the next election.[90]

When the chambers pass budget resolutions with different aggregate and functional spending levels, as is normal practice, House and Senate members usually meet in conference to resolve their disagreements. The conference report is then submitted to both chambers for final action. Because Congress's budget resolution is not submitted to the president, it has no binding legal effect. Instead, it outlines a fiscal framework that enables Congress, through its Budget Committees, CBO, and other entities, to monitor all budget-related actions taken during the course of a year. When the House and Senate are late or unable to adopt a concurrent budget resolution—as has occurred several times because of bicameral disagreements over priorities and expenditures— each chamber usually adopts a resolution (H. Res. or S. Res.) reflecting the budget levels and enforcement procedures contained in the resolution adopted by one chamber but not the other.

Reconciliation

The 1974 budget act established a special procedure called reconciliation, which is an optional process authorized when Congress adopts the budget resolution. Its basic purpose is to bring revenue and direct spending (entitlement) legislation into conformity (or reconciliation) with the fiscal targets established in the concurrent budget resolution. As Sen. Robert C. Byrd, D-W. Va., explained, "A budget reconciliation process was established as an optional procedure to enhance Congress's ability to change current law in order to bring revenue and [direct] spending levels into conformity with the targets of the budget resolution."[91] Its basic objective is to make changes in federal policies that result in budgetary savings. First used in 1980, reconciliation has been employed over twenty times since. It is a controversial process that "forces committees that might not want to reduce spending for entitlements under their jurisdiction to act and report legislation."[92]

Reconciliation is a two-step process. In the first step, Congress adopts a budget resolution containing a provision that usually instructs two or more House and Senate committees to report legislation that changes existing law. The instructions name the committees required to report legislation; they give each committee a dollar figure for mandated savings but do not specify the policies to achieve those goals; and they establish a deadline for reporting legislation to achieve the savings. In the second step, the House and Senate Budget Committees compile into an omnibus reconciliation bill the legislative changes in revenue or direct (entitlement) spending programs recommended by the named committees. If the instructions involve only one committee in each chamber, then those panels would bypass the Budget Committee and report their recommendations to the full House or Senate. On several occasions, reconciliation directives have provided for the maximum of three reconciliation bills during each fiscal year: one involving taxes, another on spending, and a third on raising the statutory debt limit.

Reconciliation in the House is considered under the terms of a rule from the Rules Committee. Procedurally, however, reconciliation is focused on the Senate, because measures governed by that optional process are treated differently from other bills or amendments. Reconciliation bills cannot be filibustered (a statutory time limit of twenty hours is placed on debate); passage requires a simple majority instead of the supermajority (sixty votes) needed to stop a talkathon; and amendments must be germane (the Senate has no general germaneness rule) and deficit-neutral (tax cuts or spending increases must be offset by equivalent revenue increases or spending reductions). Little surprise that measures likely to arouse controversy in the Senate, such as tax bills, are attached to filibuster-proof reconciliation measures that could pass by majority votes. Democratic senator Robert Byrd lamented that reconciliation "can be used by a determined majority to circumvent the regular rules of the Senate in order to advance partisan legislation. We have seen one party, and then the other, use this process to limit debate and amendments on non-budgetary provisions that otherwise may not have passed under the regular rules."[93]

To prevent just such a usage of reconciliation bills, senators adopted the so-called Byrd Rule (named after Senator Byrd) in the mid-1980s. Under this complex rule, measures cannot be included in the Senate reconciliation package, including conference reports, if they are viewed as extraneous provisions that do not reduce the deficit. Sixty votes are needed in the Senate to waive the Byrd Rule.[94] As a result, many senators can challenge inserted provisions as "Byrd droppings." As the former staff director of the Senate Budget Committee explained, "On something as massive as President Obama's health care reform, there will be a number of provisions that don't have direct budgetary consequences."[95] In the end, reconciliation was employed on the health care overhaul. However, because the pertinent bill was given a careful "Byrd bath" by each chamber's Democratic leaders, the Senate parliamentarian ruled only one minor provision in violation of the Byrd rule.

The Democratic-controlled Senate decided to use reconciliation on health care, knowing full well it angered Republicans. In a stunning January 2010 special election upset in Massachusetts, Republican Scott Brown won the Senate seat long held by Democrat Edward Kennedy, with the result that Senate Democrats could no longer muster the sixty votes required to end filibusters solely from within their own ranks. Therefore, Democrats, to the displeasure of Republicans, used reconciliation in which fifty-one votes could win Senate approval of the president's health overhaul plan.

In summary, reconciliation offers a powerful procedure for fiscal policy. In a classic case, President Ronald Reagan and GOP congressional leaders used it for the first time on a grand scale in 1981. A reconciliation bill dictated deep, multiyear reductions (about $130 billion over three years) in domestic spending. Not long afterward, Congress also agreed to Reagan's tax legislation, the Economic Recovery Tax Act of 1981, which sharply cut tax rates for individuals and businesses. The revenue losses caused by the tax cut, combined with increased defense and entitlement expenditures and insufficient spending reductions in other areas, soon pushed annual budget deficits to levels unprecedented in peacetime, from double- to triple-digit shortfalls. Since the 1980s, Congress has been grappling with large deficits, with only a brief interlude of surpluses during the Clinton presidency.

A Revised Budget Process

The growth of budgetary deficits after 1981 became the prime congressional issue, as lawmakers and presidents adapted to a new world: the politics of deficit reduction. Numerous proposals were put forth to deal with the problem. A notable example in the mid-1980s was the *Gramm-Rudman-Hollings* plan, named after Senators Phil Gramm, R-Texas; Warren B. Rudman, R-N.H.; and Ernest F. Hollings, D-S.C.

The plan's core feature was annual deficit-reduction targets. If Congress did not meet the targets, the president would have to confiscate funds—that is, impose automatic, across-the-board spending cuts (called sequestration) evenly divided between defense and domestic programs. This dire prospect was supposed to give Congress and the president the incentive to decide how best to achieve deficit reduction. However, the plan did not work, and deficits continued to climb because the yearly targets were met through budgetary gimmicks.

As a result of the dissatisfaction with this law, Congress enacted another major budgetary reform, the *Budget Enforcement Act (BEA)* of 1990. The BEA once again changed Congress's fiscal procedures. Three basic features undergirded the new legislation. First, it shifted Congress's attention from deficit reduction to spending control. Thus the law removed the threat of sequestration if conditions beyond Congress's control (inflation, a worsening economy, or emergency funding for crises or disasters) pushed the deficit upward.

Second, the BEA established caps, or limits, for discretionary spending. The spending caps could be changed, but Congress and the president would have to agree to the modification. A loophole in the law enabled Congress and the president to escape tight spending caps if they designated expenditures above the cap as emergency spending.

Third, the BEA subjected tax and entitlement programs to a new pay-as-you-go (PAYGO) procedure, which required that any tax reductions or any increases in mandatory (entitlement) spending be offset by tax hikes or reductions in other entitlement programs. As the chief counsel of the Senate Budget Committee explained, "The 'pay-as-you-go' label implies that Congress and the President may cut taxes or create [new entitlement spending] programs—that is 'go'—if they also agree to provide offsetting increased revenues or spending reductions—that is 'pay.'"[96]

Throughout much of the 1990s, the GOP-controlled Congress and President Clinton waged fierce battles over deficit reduction. As part of their political game plan, Republicans sent Clinton appropriations and reconciliation bills making deep cuts in federal programs. The president vetoed the measures, forcing two partial shutdowns of the government—the longest in congressional history. A fiscal breakthrough soon emerged, however.

THE ARRIVAL OF UNEXPECTED SURPLUSES

To the surprise of many lawmakers and pundits—especially those who were constantly lamenting the pain and sacrifice (tax hikes and spending cuts) that balancing the budget would require—balanced budgets appeared sooner than anyone expected. By the end of September 1998, the national budget was $70 billion in the black, something that had last occurred in 1969. David A. Stockman, President Reagan's director of the Office of Management and Budget (OMB), once predicted deficits as far as the eye could see. Now economic forecasters were predicting surpluses as far as the eye could see.

Why the surge of black ink? Several factors contributed to the fiscal turnaround. First, the robust economy, combined with a booming stock market, flooded the federal Treasury with revenue from the capital gains taxes paid mainly by the richest one percent of the populace. Second, the Federal Reserve kept inflation and interest rates under control through an effective monetary policy that promoted economic expansion. Third, presidential and congressional budgetary decisions during the first George Bush administration, such as passage of the BEA of 1990, as well as President Clinton's 1993 economic package encouraged fiscal restraint and led to budgetary savings. Fourth, the end of the Cold War led to reductions in defense expenditures. Finally, luck and timing contributed to the fiscal mix. "Just about everything broke right that could have broken right," said Robert Reischauer, a former CBO director.[97]

Not everyone believed that the politics of plenty had arrived or, if it had, that it would last indefinitely. Some lawmakers suggested to their colleagues that budget surpluses stood for "BS." Another economic recession, they said, could be around the corner. "The truth is there is no surplus," exclaimed a senator, citing a national debt at the time of $5.7 trillion.[98] Nevertheless, on January 30, 2001, the CBO revised its surplus projections over the next decade upward to $5.6 trillion.

THE RETURN OF DEFICITS

Shortly after President George W. Bush entered office, he and congressional Democrats began to argue about what to do with the huge projected surplus. Although many lawmakers and pundits recognized that the ten-year projection might never materialize—a slowing economy, international crises, or other reasons could intervene—politicians of both parties had their own ideas on how the surplus should be spent. It was a case of fiscal projections driving policy making, even though the money was not yet in the bank.

President Bush's top priority when he took office was a sizable tax cut. And on June 7, 2001, he signed into law the largest tax cut ($1.35 trillion) since Reagan's twenty years earlier. A little more than three months later, terrorists attacked the United States, and new demands and challenges confronted the country. The brief era (1998–2002) of surpluses had come to a quick end.

What happened to the surplus? It disappeared because the factors that produced it reversed themselves. Instead of defense and intelligence cutbacks, the nation was paying for military conflicts in Afghanistan and Iraq, reconstruction of those countries, and enhanced homeland security. A record ten years of uninterrupted economic growth ended and the stock market performed poorly, shrinking federal revenues. The large tax cuts pushed by the Bush administration, year after year, also contributed to the growing revenue shortfalls. Moreover, Congress's statutory fiscal constraints—spending caps and PAYGO—expired on September 30, 2002. Thus policy makers were now free to let the deficit increase without worrying about how to pay for tax cuts or spending hikes.

Subsequently, both chambers restored nonstatutory spending caps and PAYGO provisions. Spending caps are set in the concurrent budget resolution. Similarly, in 1993 the Senate included for itself a pay-as-you-go provision in the budget resolution. Modified and extended several times, the provision has a current expiration date of September 30, 2017. The House also adopted PAYGO rules. These rules obligated lawmakers to search for "payfors" or "offsets" to fund their policy objectives, such as using unspent money in various federal programs. In 2009 both chambers also enacted a new PAYGO law.

When the Republicans took control of the House in the 112th Congress, they rescinded their PAYGO rule. Instead, they put in place a "cut-as-you-go rule" (CUTGO), which focuses on spending cuts to mandatory (entitlement) programs. Thus increases in entitlement spending must be offset only by spending reductions in other mandatory programs. However, tax initiatives are exempt from the CUTGO rule. As one account noted, House Republicans "could extend Bush [era] tax cuts for the wealthy past their 2012 expiration or create a significant new tax break for businesses without regard for the holes those policies would blow in the nation's finances."[99] CUTGO also might foster House-Senate budgetary conflicts because the Senate follows PAYGO. This means that tax hikes—off the table in the House—can be used in the Senate to offset new entitlement spending.[100]

Today, President Obama and Congress confront projected yearly deficits of more than a trillion dollars. How much is a trillion dollars? President Reagan explained it this way: "If you had a stack of thousand-dollar bills in your hand only 4 inches high, you'd be a millionaire. A trillion dollars would be a stack of thousand-dollar bills 67 miles high."[101]

If deficits continue to rise significantly in the years ahead, the federal government faces a serious dilemma: how to fund competing priorities and commitments. As one budget analyst put it, "What we have done in the last several years is decide we can cut taxes, fight two wars, increase homeland security, expand government entitlement benefits, and leave the bill to future generations."[102] The air war over Libya can be added to this list.

The problem for Congress and the White House is determining what set of policies aimed at improving the nation's fiscal prospects can attract the necessary votes. As one analyst observed, on one side are people who stress the "national neglect" theory. Being competitive globally and flourishing at home require major government investments in areas such as education and transportation. On the other side are those who emphasize the "national gluttony" model, which holds that excessive federal spending must be curbed first, based on the theory that a nation cannot spend its way to prosperity.[103] Any attempt to reconcile these competing worldviews underscores the fact that federal budgeting is about more than numbers. It reflects the divergent views of the two political parties about what policies best serve the country's short- and long-term interests.

CONCLUSION

Today, lawmakers are preoccupied with scores of important policy issues: an ailing economy, defense and homeland security, joblessness, energy sources and usage, and the health of various domestic social programs. Rep. Barney Frank, D-Mass., has posed a question that crystallizes the debate over these various concerns: "What is the appropriate level of public activity in our society?"[104] Democrats and Republicans tend to answer that question differently. Governing, however, means making choices. Future decisions about budgeting and national priorities will surely reflect the values, goals, and interests that result from the confrontations and accommodations inherent in America's pluralist policy-making system.

"Hard" versus "Soft" Power for National Security. U.S. Army soldiers board a helicopter in south-central Afghanistan (top), as part of a surge against Taliban militants. The survivor from a pirate crew captured by Navy SEALS—accused of hijacking a U.S. merchant ship and taking its captain hostage—is led to a New York courtroom (center). Another use of power is diplomacy with foreign nations, in which Congress plays a necessary though subordinate role. (Bottom left), Senate Foreign Relations chair John Kerry, D-Mass., greets visiting Australian Prime Minister Julia Gillard before she addresses a joint session of Congress. Likewise, the Agriculture Department's P.L. 480 program (bottom right) distributes surplus farm products abroad.

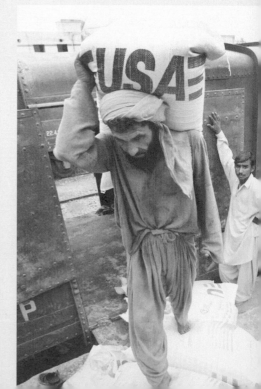

chapter

15

Congress and
National Security Policies

On March 19, 2011, the United States and its NATO allies launched an air campaign against the Libyan regime headed by the brutal dictator Muammar Gaddafi. The immediate goals were to eliminate Libya's air defense systems, establish a "no-fly" zone (preventing Libya's air force from bombing Gaddafi's opponents), and degrade the regime's military capabilities. The popular uprisings across the Middle East in countries such as Egypt and Tunisia had succeeded in ending their oppressive regimes, and so encouraged thousands of Libyans to take to the streets to end Gaddafi's tyrannical rule. Unlike the relatively nonviolent responses to the earlier uprisings in Egypt and Tunisia, Gaddafi ordered his military leaders to use their guns and bombs to slaughter the protestors, who had taken control of large portions of Libya. The protestors were a badly armed, untrained ragtag rebel army of civilians who were no match for Gaddafi's army and air force.

To prevent a huge massacre, the United Nations Security Council adopted a resolution on March 17 authorizing "all necessary measures" to protect Libyan civilians. The Arab League also urged an international force to impose a no-fly zone over Libya. In response, the United States initially led a multilateral force in imposing the no-fly zone to help protect the rebel force from being crushed. Clandestine operatives of the Central Intelligence Agency (CIA) were also on the ground in Libya, gathering "intelligence for military airstrikes and to contact and vet the beleaguered rebels battling" Gaddafi's military.[1]

President Barack Obama emphasized that the nation's role was limited in time, scale, and scope, and that direction of the Libyan campaign would soon be handed over to NATO commanders. The hand-off took place in less than two weeks. Despite the humanitarian impulse behind the air campaign—preventing a dictator from killing his own people—the president realized that U.S. forces were already stretched thin by the wars in Iraq and Afghanistan and that the public was nearing "intervention fatigue."

The sudden nature of the air attack sparked the bipartisan ire of many in Congress. Lawmakers complained that they were not consulted and had not authorized the air strikes. They also raised tough questions for the administration such as: What is the nation's goal or long-term strategy? What if Gaddafi remains in power even though the president had declared several times that the dictator must go? Who are the rebel dissidents? Would the United States provide the rebel forces with military weapons? What would constitute success? What would be the U.S. exit strategy?

When President Obama addressed the nation on March 28 to explain his decision on Libya, he emphasized the mission's humanitarian imperative and the U.S. partnership with its allies. The president also dispatched his top cabinet officers to brief the House and Senate on the military campaign. One commentator noted the uniqueness of the Libyan situation: "using American military power to [participate in] a war, then dialing back to become more of an equal partner with international allies."[2]

International cooperation has not always marked U.S. foreign policy. Earlier generations of Americans tended to view themselves as special people set apart from the world's conflicts. Having forsaken old world "wars and alarms," U.S. citizens—protected by two oceans—historically resolved to remain aloof from other nations' struggles. The most famous passage of President George Washington's 1796 Farewell Address counsels:

> The great rule of conduct for us, in regard to foreign nations is in extending our commercial relations to have with them as little political connection as possible. . . . 'Tis our true policy to steer clear of permanent alliances, with any portion of the foreign world. . . . Taking care to keep ourselves, by suitable establishments, on a respectable defensive posture, we may safely trust to temporary alliances for extraordinary emergencies.[3]

Although Washington's Farewell Address is dutifully read in the chambers of Congress every year on the first president's birthday, Washington's vision bears little resemblance to twenty-first century conditions. As a world power today with lasting alliances spanning the globe, the United States and its foreign policies would scarcely be recognized by the nation's founders.

Formulating and implementing U.S. foreign and national security policies are not episodic activities but continual obligations. Congress and the president share in these duties—just as in domestic and budgetary matters. Congress has broad constitutional authority to take part in foreign and domestic security decisions. Even the most decisive chief executives can find themselves constrained by active, informed, and determined policy makers on Capitol Hill.

CONSTITUTIONAL POWERS

The U.S. Constitution is, in Edward S. Corwin's classic words, "an invitation to struggle for the privilege of directing American foreign policy."[4] In other words, foreign and military powers are divided between the branches. "While the president is usually in a position to *propose*, the Senate and Congress are often in a technical position at least to *dispose*."[5] The struggle over the proper role of each branch in shaping foreign policy involves conflict over policy as well as over process.

The President Proposes

The chief executive enjoys certain innate advantages in dealing with foreign affairs. As John Jay wrote in the *Federalist* No. 64, the office's unity, its superior information sources, and its capacity for secrecy and dispatch give the president daily charge of foreign intercourse.[6] In Jay's time, Congress was not in session the whole year, whereas the president was always on hand to make decisions.

The president's explicit international powers are to negotiate treaties and appoint ambassadors (powers shared with the Senate), to receive ambassadors and other emissaries, and to serve as commander in chief of the armed forces. The latter power looms large over the interbranch politics of the modern period, during which presidents have at their disposal huge military, security, and intelligence capabilities. Presidents have claimed not only their explicit prerogatives but also others not spelled out in the Constitution. Whether they are called "implied," "inherent," or "emergency" powers, presidents increasingly invoke them in conducting foreign policy. President George W. Bush, according to GOP senator Lindsay Graham, S.C., "came up with a pretty aggressive, bordering on bizarre, theory of inherent authority that had no boundaries. As [the Bush administration] saw it, the other two branches were basically neutered in the time of war."[7] President Obama's leadership style differs from Bush's—generally more deliberative, cautious, and pragmatic. But he was not reluctant to bypass Congress and claim that his Libyan actions were "consistent with his powers as the country's commander in chief."[8]

The executive branch tends to be favored by foreign policy specialists, who often denigrate legislative involvement in foreign policy. Speaking to his fellow Republicans just after they ascended to power on Capitol Hill in 1995, former secretary of state James Baker cautioned the new majority "not to meddle too much" in the (then Democratic) administration's foreign policy. U.S. leadership in the world, he declared, could be sustained only "if we understand that the president has primary responsibility for the conduct of the nation's foreign policy."[9] Many lawmakers and scholars take a perspective different from Baker's. Edward Corwin, the noted presidential and constitutional scholar mentioned earlier, provided this balanced assessment of the legislative-executive relationship in foreign policy:

> What the Constitution does, *and all that it does,* is to confer on the President certain powers capable of affecting our foreign relations, and certain other powers of the same general kind on the Senate, and still other powers upon the Congress; but which of these organs shall have the decisive and final voice in determining the course of the American nation is left for events to resolve.[10]

The president's advantages are magnified in times of warfare or crisis. It was Congress's clumsy management of affairs during the Revolutionary War that, among other things, led the founders to champion an independent, energetic executive and to designate the president as commander in chief. Authority tends to become more centralized during wars and crises, so presidential powers reach their zenith at such times. This held true during the Cold War between the United States and the Soviet Union (1947–1989) and the hot wars in Korea (1950–1953) and Vietnam (1965–1974). The same pattern was evident in the period following the terrorist attacks of September 11, 2001, on the United States. Heightened security fears and the wars in Afghanistan and Iraq brought new and sometimes unprecedented assertions of executive authority. Initially at least, Congress's voice was muted.

A number of lawmakers were nevertheless quick to criticize President Obama for his unilateral decision to commit U.S. military forces to Libya. Sen. Richard Lugar, R-Ind., the ranking member on the Senate Foreign Relations Committee, declared that Congress "should have a debate on this war, even if a belated one," to bring "the clarity that our fighting men and women deserve." He went on to say that Americans had waded into a conflict supporting one side without really knowing who they were supporting or what they believed. He added: "A clear assessment of America's true national interests in the region is essential so that we don't back into the next war, as we did this one."[11]

Presidential powers usually contract and are subjected to sharper scrutiny from Capitol Hill when tensions ease or when the public tires of a prolonged conflict. Public opinion eventually came to oppose the Korean and Vietnam conflicts, a pattern that has repeated itself in the Iraq and Afghanistan wars. A 2011 poll found that nearly two-thirds of Americans agreed that "the war in Afghanistan is no longer worth fighting."[12] Divided control of the two policy-making branches spurs Congress to cast a more critical eye upon executive actions.

Perhaps the most sensible statement of the separation of powers came from Justice Robert Jackson in *Youngstown Sheet and Tube Co. v. Sawyer* (1952). He wrote that "the president might act in external affairs without congressional authority, but not that he might act contrary to an act of Congress."[13]

Congress Reacts

Congress has an impressive arsenal of explicit constitutional duties, such as the power to declare war, to regulate foreign commerce, to raise and support military forces, and to make rules governing military forces, including for "captures on land and water" (Article I, section 8). Paramount is the power of the purse. According to Crabb, Antizzo, and Sariedinne, "It is within the power of Congress to determine the course of American diplomacy, by virtue of its control over expenditures by the federal government."[14]

From examining the historical record, Crabb and his colleagues identify three conditions for congressional activism in foreign and defense affairs:

(1) periods of weak presidential leadership in foreign policy, (2) public groundswells of concern over America's international role, and (3) pressing domestic issues that impinge on foreign affairs. Their assessment of legislative activism in foreign affairs is pessimistic. They contend that legislative activism has been associated with "the least successful and impressive chapters in the annals of American diplomacy."[15]

Our own review of the historical record, however, yields a more positive assessment of legislative influence on foreign policy. Congress asserted itself following the Revolutionary War and at the outset of the other nineteenth-century wars. At the same time, it moved to rein in excessive presidential assertions of authority both before, during, and after those wars—an impulse that extends to the more recent wars: Korea, Vietnam, Afghanistan, and Iraq, as well as the later phases of the Cold War.

WHO SPEAKS FOR CONGRESS?

The wide-ranging subjects of foreign policy and military affairs fall within the purviews of some twenty-three congressional committees. Other House panels and Senate panels consider matters with a tangential bearing on foreign and military policy.

The foreign affairs and national security panels are among the most visible on Capitol Hill. The Senate Foreign Relations Committee considers treaties and the nominations of key foreign policy officials. It normally regards itself as a working partner and adviser to the president. In the late 1960s and early 1970s, during the height of dispute over the Vietnam War, the committee became a forum for antiwar debate under the leadership of its chair, J. William Fulbright, D-Ark. (1959–1974). A later chair, Jesse Helms, R-N.C. (1995–2001), attacked international agencies and thwarted many of the Clinton administration's diplomatic objectives. When Sen. (now Vice President) Joseph R. Biden Jr. chaired the panel, he and his Senate committee colleagues laid out alternatives to President George W. Bush's international policies.

Sen. John Kerry, D-Mass, chairs the panel today. At the age of twenty-seven, Kerry was the first Vietnam veteran to appear before the panel. On April 22, 1971, Kerry posed a now-famous question: "How do you ask a man to be the last man to die for a mistake?"[16] A senator steeped in international issues, Kerry has an agenda for the 112th Congress that includes, among other issues, global terrorism; the conflicts in Afghanistan, Iraq, and Libya; the spread of nuclear weapons; and climate change. With Obama in the White House, Senator Kerry will tend to be "a facilitator for the president," said a foreign policy scholar. "That is his style."[17]

For most of its history, the House Foreign Affairs Committee worked in the shadow of its Senate counterpart. This situation changed after World War II, when foreign aid programs thrust the House—with its special powers of the purse—into virtual parity with the Senate.[18] Today, the House committee addresses nearly as wide a range of issues as the Senate committee. For example, Rep. Ileana Ros-Lehtinen, R-Fla., the chair of the panel in the 112th Congress, plans to restore fiscal discipline to foreign affairs, impose stronger sanctions on the nation's enemies (for example, North Korea), reform the United Nations, and champion human rights. Foreign Affairs tends to attract members with a more global outlook than the House as a whole.

The Senate and House Armed Services Committees, which traditionally have a culture of bipartisanship, oversee the nation's military establishment. Annually, they authorize Pentagon spending for research, development, and procurement of weapons systems; construction of military facilities; and rules for civilian and uniformed personnel. The latter jurisdiction includes the Uniform Code of Military Conduct, which governs the lives of men and women in uniform and which has attracted congressional scrutiny of diverse matters such as sexual orientation, sexual harassment, treatment of enemy prisoners, overseas voting rights, and even the right of Jewish officers to wear yarmulkes while in uniform. Although global strategy and military readiness are important matters for the committees' members, what rivets their attention are issues closer to home such as force levels, military installations, and defense contracts. Thus constituency politics often drives military policy.

Because of their funding jurisdictions, House and Senate Appropriations subcommittees exert detailed control over foreign and defense policies. Tariffs and other trade regulations are the domains of the taxing committees (House Ways and Means, Senate Finance). Committees involved in banking handle international financial and monetary policies. And the commerce committees have jurisdiction over foreign commerce generally. With the creation of the Homeland Security Department, and despite the formation of homeland security committees in the House and Senate, scores of other panels assert jurisdiction linked in some way to local and national security.

The House and Senate Select Intelligence Committees were created in the late 1970s, following revelations of widespread abuses, illegalities, and misconduct on the part of intelligence agencies, particularly the Central Intelligence Agency (CIA) and the Federal Bureau of Investigation (FBI). After forty years, however, the two oversight panels are still hampered in conducting vigorous scrutiny of the intelligence community because, according to a scholar, they have "limited expertise and weak budgetary authority."[19]

The 2004 report of the National Commission on Terrorist Attacks upon the United States (9/11 Commission) called for revitalized oversight of the intelligence community through either a joint committee or separate House and Senate panels with authorizing and appropriating jurisdiction.[20] But neither chamber followed this advice. The House did create a select oversight panel in 2007 that combined membership from the authorizing and appropriating committees, as noted in Chapter 7, but it was disbanded four years later. However, Mike Rogers, R-Mich., the chair of the House Intelligence panel in the 112th Congress devised a new arrangement between his panel and the House Appropriations Committee. Three appropriators now participate in

Intelligence Committee hearings and meetings. For its part, the relevant Senate committees (Appropriations and Select Intelligence) signed a memorandum of agreement "pledging greater cooperation."[21]

Congress's organization for policy making is far from tidy. But it would be a mistake to draw any sharp contrast with the executive branch in this regard. Executive branch agencies are equally scattered: consider the long-standing coordination problems among the four military services or sixteen intelligence agencies.[22] In December 2004, the intelligence community received a major overhaul after enactment of the Intelligence Reform and Terrorism Prevention Act. The act created a director of national intelligence (DNI) who could look at the intelligence community as a whole and work to coordinate its work. However, an inspector general's report sharply criticized the DNI for "a failure to end the turf battles among America's spy agencies."[23] To bolster the DNI's role, the Intelligence Authorization Act (P.L. 111-259) granted the DNI several new authorities over budget and personnel matters. Whether these changes are sufficient for the DNI to coordinate the work of the intelligence community remains an open question. (Here it is important to note the successful U.S. commando operation in May 2011 that led to the demise of al Qaeda leader Osama bin Laden. The success of the operation demonstrates the progress that has been made since 9/11 in information sharing and cooperation among the nation's intelligence and national security agencies.)

Faced with a profusion of congressional power centers, executive branch policy makers complain that they do not know whom to consult when crises arise, that they have to testify before too many committees, and that leaks of sensitive information are inevitable with so many players. But the executive branch or their emissaries are often free to consult with as few or as many lawmakers as they choose—in some cases with only the joint party leaders, in others with chairs and ranking members of the relevant committees. And when Congress tries to step in to influence administration policies, executive officers predictably complain about "micromanagement."

TYPES OF FOREIGN AND NATIONAL SECURITY POLICIES

Foreign policy is the total of decisions and actions governing a nation's relations with other nations and consists of national goals to be achieved and resources for achieving them. Statecraft is the art of selecting preferred outcomes and marshaling the appropriate resources to attain them. As former secretary of state Henry A. Kissinger, a foreign policy pragmatist, put it, "Values are essential for defining objectives; strategy is what implements them by establishing priorities and defining timing."[24]

Defining a nation's goals is no simple matter. The subject has sparked intense conflict both between Congress and the president and within Congress itself. Momentous congressional debates have displayed widely diverging views on subjects such as ties to England and France during the nation's early decades, American expansion abroad, tariff rates, involvement in foreign wars, approaches to combating terrorists, and U.S. involvement in nation building or forcible regime change.

In 1998 Lee H. Hamilton, D Ind., chair of the House Foreign Affairs Committee and an acknowledged authority on international relations, summarized what he viewed as the major components of the national interest: (1) to preserve the territorial integrity of the United States and the safety and security of its people; (2) to sustain U.S. economic prosperity; (3) to promote democratic values; (4) to promote basic human rights; and (5) to protect the health and welfare of the American people.[25]

As for resources for meeting such goals, military strength and preparedness immediately come to mind. However, other assets such as wealth, productivity, creativity, political ideals, cultural values, and global credibility are even more potent in the long run. Hamilton observes that it is essential to determine "what resources—both human and capital—we are prepared to risk or expend to protect the American national interest." How to allocate resources among competing priorities means making difficult decisions because, said Hamilton, "we simply cannot do it all."[26] Recently, former House member Jane Harman, D-Calif.—an expert in national security policy making and Hamilton's successor as president of the Woodrow Wilson Center for International Scholars— emphasized the importance of assessing the nation's strategic interests: "It should be obvious that both our resources and our power are less than they have been in prior decades, and that requires a new assessment of how to deploy our scarce assets against the biggest threats to the U.S. homeland."[27]

In balancing national goals and national resources, policy makers confront several different and sometimes overlapping types of foreign and national security policies. Structural policies involve procuring and deploying resources or personnel; strategic policies advance the nation's objectives militarily or diplomatically; and crisis policies protect the nation's safety against specific foreign or domestic threats.

STRUCTURAL POLICIES

National security programs involve millions of workers and the expenditure of billions of dollars annually. Decisions about deploying such vast resources are called structural policy decisions. Examples include choices of specific weapons systems, contracts with private suppliers, the location of military installations, sales of weapons and surplus goods to foreign countries, and trade policies that affect domestic industries and workers. Structural policy making on foreign and defense issues is virtually the same as distributive policy making in the domestic realm.

The last sixty years have seen a growing imbalance in the military versus nonmilitary elements of foreign policies. In fiscal year 2012, the U.S. military budget will be larger than those of the next nineteen nations of the world combined.[28] But the singular military machine of the United States is, historically speaking, a fairly recent phenomenon. After earlier wars, the United States quickly "sent the boys home" and, under congressional pressure, shrank its armed forces—though each time to somewhat higher plateaus.[29] After World War II, however, the Cold War threat led to unprecedented levels of peacetime preparedness. By 1960, when retiring president Dwight D. Eisenhower, a career military officer, warned against the "military-industrial complex" (his speech draft said "military-industrial-congressional complex"), the new militarism was already deeply embedded in the nation's political and economic system.

Department of Defense (DOD) spending—more than $675 billion in fiscal 2012—is the biggest discretionary portion of the federal budget. Worth noting is that from 2003 to 2010 the cost of the Iraq conflict was put at $784 billion, surpassing in inflation-adjusted dollars the Vietnam War (1965–1975) at $738 billion. The war costs for Afghanistan (2001–2010) were $321 billion. Together, the two wars have cost over $1 trillion.[30] After its first two weeks, the Libyan conflict had already cost $550 million and, according to Defense Secretary Robert Gates, the price tag going forward is expected to be $40 million a month.[31] As the nation's largest employer, its largest customer, and its largest procurer of equipment and services, DOD controls a huge number of structural outlays, which attract a wide swath of political interests. As a venture capitalist put it, "The military is like a Fortune No. 1 company."[32]

The State Department, by contrast, makes relatively few such decisions. For every twenty-one federal dollars spent on the military, only about one dollar goes to international affairs—including not only diplomatic representation but also military assistance, foreign development, and humanitarian aid.[33] The State Department's services and achievements are largely intangible, and in any event it spends much of its energy and money overseas. It is little surprise, then, that it has few strong domestic clients and, compared with DOD, fewer champions on Capitol Hill. A surprising advocate for the State Department was Defense Secretary Robert Gates—after all, State and Defense are typically rivals for resources and influence. Gates urged Congress to provide more money for State, and he stressed the importance of strengthening national security by better integrating diplomacy (soft power) with military action (hard power). "We must focus our energies beyond the guns and steel of the military, beyond just our brave soldiers, sailors, marines, and airmen," said Gates. His vision was of global conflicts fundamentally political in nature: "Success will be less a matter of imposing one's will and more a function of shaping [the] behavior of friends, adversaries and, most importantly, the people in between."[34]

The Congressional-Military-Industrial Complex

Defense dollars for projects, contracts, and bases, among other things, are sought by business firms, labor unions, and local communities. The Pentagon's ties to the business community are so cozy that an estimated 40 percent of its contracts are awarded without competitive bidding, according to an independent study of some 2.2 million contracts.[35] As champions of local interests, members of Congress are naturally drawn into the process. The impulse is wholly bipartisan.

(Some observers have even suggested that a "surveillance-industrial complex" has emerged in the post-9/11 era in which the government's interception of communications is contracted to private companies.[36])

Weapons Systems. Pentagon procurement officers anticipate congressional needs in planning and designing projects. The perfect weapons system, it is said, is one with a component manufactured in every congressional district in the nation. The Air Force's F-22 Raptor jet fighter, which has a price tag of nearly $300 million each, is assembled at Georgia and Texas factories from parts made by a thousand suppliers in forty-three states. "What it means to the company is the technology and the jobs," explained a factory manager.[37]

In a dramatic break with previous defense budgets, Defense Secretary Gates proposed major changes for the military budget. Spending priorities would shift from big weapons programs to more funds for fighting unconventional wars such as the battles against al Qaeda and Taliban insurgents. Under his plan, which eliminated several big weapons programs, 50 percent of the Pentagon's budget would go to countering conventional threats, 10 percent to unconventional ("irregular") warfare, and 40 percent to weapons that can be used in both conventional and unconventional conflicts.[38] As one account noted,

> Defense spending traditionally reflects conventional threats such as China or perhaps Iran. But Secretary Gates's . . . budget [plan] recommends billions of dollars for the counterinsurgency needs of unconventional conflicts such as Iraq and Afghanistan, while making broad and controversial cuts to weapons programs such as the F-22 stealth fighter that Gates sees as part of an outdated, Cold-War mind-set.[39]

Lawmakers responded quickly to Gates's budget plan. "I will work to overturn the secretary's recommendation" regarding the F-22, declared Republican senator Saxby Chambliss of Georgia (the F-22 was assembled in Marietta, Georgia). The entire Connecticut congressional delegation wrote to Gates to say that stopping the F-22 program would "end jobs for 2,000 Connecticut engineers, machinists, and aerospace workers."[40] The House Armed Services Committee chair said he appreciated Gates's hard work on the defense budget, but made it clear that "the buck stops with Congress, which has the critical Constitutional responsibility to decide whether to support these proposals."[41] Eliminating or reducing weapons systems is especially problematic during a recession when thousands of people are losing their jobs. In 2009 a strong veto threat by President Obama, along with the backing of the Pentagon, the air force, and key lawmakers on Capitol Hill, prompted Congress to agree to limit the further procurement of F-22s to 187 aircraft, effectively ending their production.

The 112th Congress is in the midst of another multiyear battle over an aircraft: the development of an alternate engine for the F-35 (the Joint Strike Fighter), which is the Pentagon's largest weapons program. President Obama and the Pentagon do not want another engine developed for the fighter jet;

they view it as a waste of money. Manufacturer Pratt & Whitney won the primary contract to produce the engine that will power the F-35, but General Electric (GE) and Rolls Royce, along with various lawmakers, are vigorous advocates of developing a backup engine for the fighter jet and are lobbying strenuously to win funding for the engine. The corporate competitors of Pratt & Whitney want a share of the multibillion-dollar market for the F-35, and their supporters in Congress want jobs for their states and districts. A spokesperson for Republican senator Rob Portman of Ohio, where hundreds of people work for GE, has argued that the second engine "encourages competition, which forces companies to develop a better product at a lower cost, saving taxpayer money in the long run."[42] However, in this period of enormous fiscal deficit and debt, the odds appear to favor the elimination of funding for the development of a second engine for the F-35.

Indeed, it is possible that the larger debate over fiscal policy may impose some constraint on the congressional politics of defense spending. In January 2011, during the House debate on H.R. 1, the stopgap funding measure discussed in Chapter 14, Tea Party Republicans and many Democrats voted to eliminate $450 million in funding for development of the alternative F-35 engine. Nevertheless, Speaker Boehner backed the second engine, in part because of the jobs it provided for hundreds of his constituents. The fate of the backup engine remains unclear.

Even when military planners decide to phase out a weapon, lawmakers may compel them to keep the item in production. One example is the marines' V-22 Osprey, a tilt-rotor aircraft that flies like a conventional plane but takes off and lands like a helicopter. Conceived during the Cold War, the planes— now over $100 million apiece—were intended to change the way the marines fight wars. But there were design problems; several planes crashed, claiming the lives of two dozen soldiers. Defense Secretary Richard B. "Dick" Cheney canceled the program in 1989, judging that it was too costly, but he was overruled by Congress and its fierce lobbying. The Tilt-Rotor Caucus, a group of representatives from regions in which the plane is manufactured, worked with contractors to keep the project alive.[43] In 2005, twenty years after the program was conceived, DOD's Defense Acquisition Board approved full-scale production of the Osprey. "It is the only major weapons system program that was canceled and then resurrected," claimed a member of the House Armed Services Committee.[44]

In March 2008, DOD signed a multiyear procurement contract through 2012 with the Boeing Company and Bell-Textron for the manufacture and delivery of V-22s.[45] Through 2009, 181 V-22s have been procured. So the Ospreys fly on. "It is the hardest thing to do, to take a weapon out of the budget," a Defense undersecretary noted. "It is just so easy to put one in."[46]

Lawmakers and lobbyists exploit the differing priorities of the four services (army, air force, navy, marines), which persist in the face of determined efforts at coordination by civilian managers over several presidencies, Republican and Democratic alike. The air force's projects include new jets, refueling tankers, and space weapons. The marines want the Osprey. The navy covets new aircraft carriers, and the army needs new artillery and combat vehicles.

On April 28, 2011, President Obama, made two major changes in his national security team. The president named CIA director Leon Panetta to replace the soon-to-retire (June 30) Robert Gates as defense secretary. Panetta, an acknowledged authority on federal budgeting, is a former director of the Office of Management and Budget, and he served as chair of the Budget Committee during his service in the U.S. House. Because of escalating budget-cutting pressures, Panetta will have the critical strategic job of determining which defense programs should be trimmed or terminated and which will require additional resources. Gen. David Petraeus, the commander of allied forces in Afghanistan, was named by the president as Panetta's replacement at the CIA. Petraeus's appointment underscores that today's fight against non-state terrorists requires intelligence, information, and technology, combined with a sophisticated understanding of when and how to apply military force. (The Panetta and Petraeus nominations require Senate confirmation.)

Military Base Closures. The proliferation and geographic dispersion of military installations are another example of distributive military policy making. L. Mendel Rivers, D-S.C., chair of the House Armed Services Committee from 1965 to 1971, kept defense money flowing to bases in Charleston, South Carolina, campaigning on the slogan "Rivers delivers!" More recently, Sen. Trent Lott, R-Miss. (1989–2007), hailed a Pascagoula, Mississippi, firm that builds ships for the navy: "It's one of the most impor-tant shipyards in the country, and if I were not supportive of my hometown, that shipyard and the workers in that shipyard, I wouldn't deserve to be in Congress, now would I?"[47]

In the post–Cold War era, Congress tried to surmount the politically unpalatable problem of closing unneeded military installations. In 1988 it passed a law intended to insulate such decisions from congressional pressure by delegating them to bipartisan Base Realignment and Closing Commissions (BRACs). The BRACs were also intended to eliminate pressure on lawmakers to vote for an administration's programs in exchange for keeping open military bases in their districts. As Rep. Richard Armey, R-Texas, the champion of the BRAC legislation, stated: "The fact is, unfortunate as it is, that historically base closings have been used as a point of leverage by administrations, Democratic and Republican administrations, as political leverage over and above Members of Congress to encourage them to vote in a manner that the administration would like."[48]

Using the defense secretary's recommendations, a BRAC would draw up a list of installations targeted for closure. To make the decisions hard to overturn, the list had to be accepted or rejected as a whole by the president and Congress. Base closings were also part of Congress's wider effort to balance the budget.

Five rounds of BRACs (1988, 1991, 1993, 1995, and 2005) reduced or eliminated hundreds of defense installations. The political pressures were intense. One commission chair was greeted at base entrances by parents holding children who, they said, would starve if the base closed.[49] Lawmakers from affected areas fought the closure lists and nearly succeeded in overturning them. From the Pentagon's perspective, the closures of excess infrastructure meant that the savings could be spent on higher military priorities. Communities where bases were shuttered looked for new uses for the military facilities, such as the land and buildings, and in some cases requested federal assistance for the cleanup of environmental contamination at these installations.

Trade Politics

Another arena for distributive politics is foreign trade. Since the First Congress (1789–1791), the legislative branch's constitutional power to "regulate commerce with foreign nations" and to "lay and collect taxes, duties, imposts, and excises" has been used to protect and enhance the competitive position of U.S. goods and industries, whether cotton or wheat or textiles or computer software. Until the 1930s, tariff legislation—long the primary source of federal revenue—was contested on Capitol Hill by political parties and economic regions. Northern manufacturers, for example, wanted protectionist tariffs, and southern exporting states wanted low tariffs to avoid other nations' retaliatory tariffs against their agricultural products.

Starting with the Reciprocal Trade Agreements Act of 1934 (P.L. 73-316), however, Congress began to delegate the details of tariff negotiations to the executive branch. The 1974 Trade Act is a key statute that transfers trade negotiating authority to the president, subject to Congress's ability to approve or disapprove the agreements under expedited procedures (for example, limited floor debate and no amendments in either chamber). Expedited procedures provide assurances to trading partners that Congress will act on any negotiated agreements within a certain time period. Important to note is that the 1974 trade law specifically recognized the constitutional authority of either chamber to make or change their own rules regardless of any statutory provisions addressing the procedural operations of the House or Senate.

Divergent Views on Trade. Protectionist impulses have not waned, however; myriad trade interests are represented on Capitol Hill. One trade expert suggests that three groups largely shape the trade debate in Congress.[50] To varying degrees, the perspectives of all three groups are represented in both parties. Republicans are generally "trade liberalizers," which reflects the views of many in the business community, among others. They tend to favor lowering trade barriers at home and combating them abroad in order to open world markets for U.S. goods. After all, "95 percent of the world's consumers now live somewhere other than the United States."[51] Trade advocate David Dreier, R-Calif., chair of the House Rules Committee in the 112th Congress, wrote: "Opening up new markets for U.S. producers, farmers, service providers and investors is essential for spurring growth and creating new job opportunities for both union and nonunion workers."[52]

Republicans' long-term commitments to free trade may be undergoing some change, however. As one account noted:

> While the modern GOP has traditionally been a bastion of support for free markets, times have changed. The public's embrace of trade has loosened considerably as American jobs have disappeared. That appears particularly true among grass-roots Tea Party activists, who often echo Democratic complaints about corporate outsourcing as well as popular concerns about the influence of global economic organizations that facilitate trade, such as the World Trade Organization (WTO) and the International Monetary Fund (IMF).[53]

Many Democrats are in the "fair trade" camp. They represent areas of union strength and favor barriers to curb the loss of jobs to low-wage countries. Fair traders argue that the poor labor, human rights, and environmental conditions in many countries enable them to undercut U.S. businesses through lower production costs. Fair traders want trade agreements—before they are entered into—to stipulate that nations must meet specific labor, environmental, and human rights standards.

The third group could be called "trade skeptics." They contend that trade agreements undermine U.S. sovereignty and largely benefit multinational corporations over small businesses, small farmers, and workers. Lawmakers who support labor unions and the Tea Party movement generally believe that trade has hurt the American economy by lowering wages and outsourcing jobs overseas.

The three different perspectives underscore the complexities and crosscurrents that suffuse trade policy and politics. Because both parties contain lawmakers in all three groups, it is too simple to identify one party (Republicans) as free trade and the other (Democratic) as protectionist.

A two-Congresses example illustrates the point. Republican senator Jeff Sessions of Alabama blocked a bipartisan trade bill supported by numerous business associations. His purpose was to prevent the duty-free import of sleeping bags from Bangladesh. Alabama is home to the only domestic manufacturer of inexpensive sleeping bags. As Senator Sessions explained:

> I do believe in trade. I think it's best for the world. But I would say to my colleagues we have got to have fair trade. And nations around the world . . . have taken advantage of the United States and . . . [think] that they can cheat on agreements and manipulate agreements and close down businesses . . . and somehow we're just going to pass on by.[54]

From a bicameral perspective, the Senate generally leans toward free trade because export-minded agricultural interests are overrepresented. The House, with its constituency-attentive focus, has stronger protectionist leanings.

Two Case Examples. Most battles over trade bills call forth variations of the lineups and perspectives just described. In the thirteen months of negotiations leading up to the landmark 1993 North American Free Trade Agreement (NAFTA)—a trading bloc consisting of the United States, Canada, and Mexico—the U.S. trade representative, Carla A. Hills, logged forty consultations with individual lawmakers and no fewer than 199 meetings with congressional groups, from the House Ways and Means and Senate Finance Committees to the Northeast-Midwest Congressional Coalition and the Senate Textile Group.[55]

When the bill implementing NAFTA reached Capitol Hill, a bipartisan effort was needed to approve it. President Clinton launched a high-profile public relations campaign, trumpeted the bill's job creation benefits, welcomed support from Republican leaders, and cut deals to meet individual legislators' objections. Opposing the bill were many Democrats, including the House majority leader and chief whip. In the end, only 40 percent of House Democrats supported the president, but their 102 votes along with those of 132 Republicans were enough to gain House passage. NAFTA then easily passed the Senate. The final enactment was a huge patchwork of provisions aimed at placating disparate interests.[56]

More than a decade later, the modest Central American Free Trade Agreement (CAFTA), a centerpiece of President George W. Bush's trade agenda, encountered similar resistance, with many members complaining that previous administrations had failed to implement promised retraining programs for workers whose jobs went overseas.[57] The agreement was narrowly approved (the Senate vote was 54–45, the House vote 217–215) with scant Democratic support. Republican leaders pulled off the victory with a combination of arm-twisting and concessions to sugar growers, textile mills, and hosiery makers.

Other Pertinent Issues. In the debate over U.S.-China trade status, representatives splintered across the political spectrum. Christian conservatives allied with liberal, pro-labor Democrats in opposing a trade deal with China because of their concerns about Beijing's persecution of Christian and other religious leaders.[58] The lure of China's vast potential market for U.S. goods vied with doubts over China's unpredictable government and its poor human rights, worker safety, and environmental records. Trade policy and negotiations, asserts Rep. Sander M. Levin, D-Mich., "now involve virtually every area of what used to be considered U.S. domestic law—from antitrust and food safety to telecommunications."[59] Separating local from global issues is difficult. As President Obama has said, "We have learned that the success of the American economy is inextricably linked to the global economy."[60]

Having delegated most decisions to the executive, lawmakers who want to review specific trade deals must struggle to get back in the game. The Trade Act of 1974, as noted earlier, addressed this dilemma. The president, it said, must actively consult, notify, and involve Congress as he negotiates trade agreements. These agreements would take effect only after an implementing law is enacted, and such legislation would be handled under a fast-track procedure.

Most presidents since 1974 have been awarded fast-track (or trade promotion) authority to negotiate trade pacts subject to up-or-down votes in both houses of Congress within ninety days. However, that authority lapsed during the Clinton presidency and was not renewed by the Republican-led Congress. In 2002, after a vigorous lobbying effort, President Bush won a five-year renewal of the fast-track procedure. Even so, the House vote was close— 215–212 (the Senate margin was 64–34). To gain the needed House votes, numerous concessions were made to placate textile workers and citrus growers, among others. The measure also featured a Democratic-sponsored hike in aid for workers who had lost jobs to foreign competition.[61] The fast-track authority lapsed again in 2007 because of heightened national concern about the loss of U.S. jobs overseas, a trend toward economic nationalism, and sharper partisanship in Congress over trade deals.

Several lawmakers in the 112th Congress are urging that President Obama be granted trade promotion authority. They are worried that many nations such as China are busily negotiating these pacts and gaining a global economic advantage. Furthermore, they realize that "countries are much less likely to negotiate trade deals with the U.S. when the president lacks fast-track [trade promotion] authority, for fear that trade deals will be changed when they are brought to Congress."[62]

Distributive politics underlies many other foreign and defense programs as well. For example, P.L. 480 (Food for Peace) dispenses agricultural surpluses to needy nations. This law is intended to serve humanitarian purposes, but it has at times inhibited local agricultural development in Third World countries because its subsidized products undermine the ability of local farm workers to compete and sell their commodities.

The United States is also the world's largest seller of arms to developing nations. The value of all arms transfer agreements with developing nations in 2009 was over $45 billion. The Pentagon also trains military forces in numerous nations to use its weapons. Arm sales are a profitable enterprise for the government that—for good or ill—affects civil and military affairs in every corner of the globe.[63]

STRATEGIC POLICIES

To protect the nation's interests, decision makers design strategic policies on spending levels for international and defense programs; total military force levels; the basic mix of military forces and weapons systems; arms sales to foreign powers; foreign trade inducements or restrictions; allocation of economic, military, and technical aid to developing nations; treaty obligations to other nations; U.S. responses to human rights abuses abroad; and its stance toward international bodies such as the United Nations (UN), the North Atlantic Treaty Organization (NATO), and world financial agencies.

Strategic policies overlap and embrace most important foreign policy questions. They engage top-level executive decision makers as well as congressional committees and mid-level executive officers. Such debates can express citizens' ideological, ethnic, racial, or economic interests.[64] Strategic issues typically involve broad themes and invoke policy makers' long-term attitudes and beliefs. The key agencies for strategic decision making include the State Department, the Office of the Secretary of Defense, the intelligence agencies, and the National Security Council—all advising the president.

The Power of the Purse

Congress uses its spending power to establish overall appropriation levels for foreign and defense purposes. Under those ceilings, priorities must be assigned among military services; among weapons systems; between uniformed personnel and military hardware; and to economic, cultural, or military aid—to name just a few of the choices. The president leads by presenting the annual budget, lobbying for the administration's priorities, and threatening to veto options deemed unacceptable. Yet if it chooses, Congress also can write its own budget down to the smallest detail. And the omnibus character of appropriations measures places pressure on the president to accede to the outcome of legislative bargaining on expenditures. To get the 95 percent of the budget the administration wants, the president may have to swallow the 5 percent he opposes.

Post–Cold War Spending: Down and Up. Congress responds both to perceived levels of international tension and to shifting public views on the salience of global engagement. After the collapse of the Soviet Union, a bipartisan consensus in the Pentagon and in Congress agreed that defense funding and force levels could be cut gradually. That consensus arose either from the belief that a sizable "peace dividend" could be realized or from the hope that savings could be gained from smarter planning and trimming waste, fraud, and abuse. Downsizing the military establishment, however, is politically and economically disruptive. Defense Secretary Gates cautioned against cutting military expenditures significantly in the aftermath of the conflicts in Iraq and Afghanistan. In an address at the Naval War College in 2009, he argued:

> Every time we have come to an end of a conflict, somehow we have persuaded ourselves that the nature of mankind and the nature of the world have changed on an enduring basis and so we have dismantled our military and intelligence capabilities. My hope is that as we wind down in Iraq and whatever the level of our commitment in Afghanistan, that we not forget the basic nature of human kind has not changed.[65]

Footing the bill for combat operations poses dilemmas for Congress. How much money is needed, and how much freedom should the president have in spending it? President Lyndon B. Johnson gradually deepened U.S. involvement in Vietnam, but he hesitated to ask Congress to appropriate the needed funds. Thus the first supplemental funding bill was passed in February 1966, even though Congress had signed on to the war as early as August 1964 (with the Gulf of Tonkin Resolution). Johnson's effort to hide the escalating war costs while maintaining domestic programs elevated both inflation and the federal debt.

After the September 11, 2001, attacks on the United States, Congress acted swiftly to pass a $40 billion supplemental appropriations package, one-fourth of which was under the president's near-total control. After the U.S. invasion of Afghanistan in October 2001, Congress approved another $30 billion, again featuring flexibility. However, some lawmakers, especially on the funding committees, expressed their doubts. "All presidents want unlimited authority. In any time of conflict, there's a tendency to allow a little more leeway," said an Appropriations subcommittee chair. "We have a responsibility to maintain a balance . . . and we're struggling with that."[66]

In the years following the terrorist attacks, however, Congress approved hundreds of billions of dollars in supplemental expenditures that reflected only marginal congressional adjustments. These bills were intended to exempt wartime spending from compliance with the annual spending caps. The Obama administration took a different tack; it reduced reliance on supplemental appropriations to fund war operations and included those costs in the Pentagon's normal budget.

The power of the purse is a blunt instrument in time of war. In the final analysis, no major foreign or military enterprise can be sustained unless Congress provides money and support. A president can conduct an operation for a time using existing funds and supplies, just as Johnson did at first in Vietnam and Obama is doing in Libya, but sooner or later Congress must be asked for funding. The U.S. role in South Vietnam finally ended in 1974, when Congress simply refused to provide emergency aid funds.

Today because of the ballooning deficit, the size of the military budget makes it a prime target for spending reductions (after 9/11, the defense budget doubled in size). Defense Secretary Gates recognized the need for fiscal discipline in defense spending and recommended, among other cost-saving actions, that the military services find $100 billion in savings over five years to invest in military forces in the field and still another $78 billion in planned spending.[67] His cost-cutting objectives seem at least four-fold: (1) preempt even deeper cuts at a time when, after three wars, the equipment and personnel needs of the military require restorative expenditures; (2) direct the cost-cutting toward unwanted and lower-priority programs, projects, and missions; (3) shift the culture of the Pentagon from one of "endless money" to one of "savings and restraint";[68] (4) and underscore that the strength of the economy is a paramount national security issue. In the view of a defense specialist, we can't afford to keep policing a world in which many of our trading partners are growing faster and our military [missions] are contributing to national bankruptcy. The last thing America needs is a concept of its role in the world that is beyond the capacity of our economy and our political system to sustain, purchased with borrowed dollars that will make the emergence of new "peer competitors" more likely.[69]

Spending on Diplomacy. Unlike national defense, international affairs funding represents a relatively small expenditure (see Figure 15-1). For 2012, President Obama requested $47 billion for the State Department and the U.S. Agency for International Development (AID), but the 112th Congress seemed certain to reduce this figure. Sen. Rand Paul, R-Ky., proposed cutting foreign aid entirely, and other lawmakers suggested reducing the State Department's

FIGURE 15-1 **Defense and Foreign Policy Spending as Percentage of Total Budget Outlays, 1940–2010**

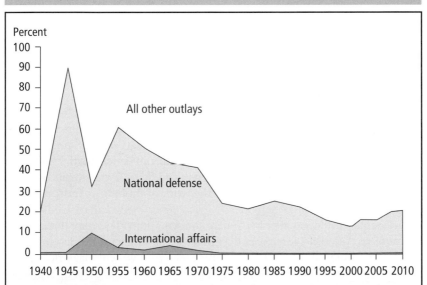

Sources: Historical figures from *Budget of the United States Government, Fiscal Year 2010,* Historical Tables (Washington, DC: Government Printing Office, 2009), table 3-2. Projections for 2010 are from *Budget of the United States Government, Fiscal Year 2010,* Current Services Budget Authority and Outlays by Function, Category, and Programs (Washington, DC: Government Printing Office, 2009), table 24-14.

Note: Figures are fiscal year outlays, according to current statistical conventions for treating off-budget items. The total budget in billions of dollars was $9.5 in 1940, $42.6 in 1950, $92.2 in 1960, $195.6 in 1970, $590.9 in 1980, $1,253.2 in 1990, $1,825.0 in 2000, and (projected) $3,644.4 in 2010.

budget to 2008 levels.[70] Historically, the nation's foreign operations required relatively small outlays. In the immediate post–World War II years of 1947–1951, however, programs to rebuild devastated Europe and Japan consumed as much as 16 percent of U.S. annual spending. Throughout the Cold War, the United States was a major provider of economic, military, and technical aid throughout the world.

In recent years, Department of State operations have accounted for about one percent of all expenditures. U.S. economic assistance to promote democracy, address poverty, and improve health and education is a fraction of that, and most of this aid goes to a handful of frontline states (Israel, Egypt, Afghanistan, and Iraq, most prominently). In a pork-barrel approach to foreign aid, Congress appropriated more than $30 billion—through DOD rather than State—to rebuild Iraq. "What appeared to be a remarkably generous foreign aid package," writes T. Christian Miller, "was in fact a remarkable program of domestic handouts and corporate welfare."[71] Most of the money enriched well-placed U.S. businesses; very little reached average Iraqis.

In opinion surveys, citizens indicate only lukewarm support for foreign aid spending, and they grossly overestimate how much is actually spent. In a 2010 University of Maryland poll, respondents said that 25 percent of the federal budget goes to foreign aid; a year earlier a Kaiser Foundation poll found that 45 percent believed that foreign aid is one of the largest categories of federal spending.[72] Perhaps that is the reason U.S. foreign aid, although high in pure dollar terms, ranks low among the world's wealthiest nations as a proportion of the gross domestic product.[73]

Some observers point to this imbalance between military and other aid as a weakness in the nation's ability to use diplomacy to prevent armed conflicts. As Adm. Michael Mullins, chairman of the Joint Chiefs of Staff, pointed out, "Preventing wars is as important as winning them and far less costly."[74] Despite the funding imbalance between the Defense and State Departments, and the multitude of foreign policy challenges, the work of diplomacy fundamentally involves three categories of activities. As Secretary of State Hillary Clinton told departmental employees after her Senate confirmation, "There are three legs to the stool of American foreign policy: defense, diplomacy, and development. And we are responsible for two of the three legs. And we will make clear, as we go forward, that diplomacy and development are essential tools in achieving the long-term objectives of the United States."

One of Secretary Clinton's rather new tools in promoting democratic development is the social media such as Facebook, Twitter, and YouTube. In 2011 social media websites were instrumental in mobilizing thousands of protestors to oust the dictators of Tunisia and Egypt. And yet the Internet also can be used by authoritarian regimes to track down dissidents and put them in jail, or worse. The clash between Internet censorship and freedom, secrecy and openness, highlights the challenge of maintaining, as Clinton said, "an Internet that delivers the greatest possible good to the world."[75]

Treaties and Executive Agreements

The Constitution calls for Congress and the president to be partners in a key element of strategic policy: treaties with foreign powers. Under Article VI of the Constitution, all treaties "shall be the supreme Law of the Land" unless the treaty itself requires implementing legislation.

Although the president initiates them, treaties are made "by and with the advice and consent of the Senate." The Senate's consent is signified by the concurrence of two-thirds of the senators present and voting. Treaty approval by the Senate entails more than a simple up-or-down vote; it is conducted in two steps. First, the Senate takes up the treaty. If it must be amended, an infrequent occurrence, it must be renegotiated with the nations that were parties to it.

Second, the Senate considers a resolution of ratification. To this document can be added reservations, declarations, or understandings; their adoption by majority vote does not require renegotiation of the treaty. According to one scholar, the "three qualifiers demarcate future U.S. behavior, intent, or policy positions as a result of the treaty. . . . They can also specify U.S. policy on unrelated issues."[76] The Senate, of course, can simply refuse to consider a treaty. (Technically, ratification is a prerogative of the president and involves the exchange of pertinent documents between or among the nations who signed the treaty.)

Congress may or may not be taken into the president's confidence when treaties and executive agreements are negotiated. To avoid humiliation like that experienced by President Woodrow Wilson when the Senate rejected the Treaty of Versailles after World War I, modern chief executives typically inform key senators during the negotiation process. Rarely does the Senate reject a treaty outright. In fact, it has turned down only twenty treaties since 1789. One study found that the Senate had approved without change 69 percent of those treaties submitted to it.[77] Such was the case in March 2003, when the Senate unanimously approved a U.S.-Russia treaty requiring cuts in the two nations' arsenals of long-range missiles. Despite critics' charges that the deal was "flimsy," senators opted to send a positive signal to Russia during the run-up to the Iraq war.

A different fate befell a major multilateral pact, the Comprehensive Test Ban Treaty (CTBT), in the fall of 1999. From the moment it reached the Senate two years earlier, the pact met fierce resistance from conservatives, who argued that it would jeopardize the nation's nuclear superiority and weaken deterrence against would-be nuclear powers. Senate Republicans realized from private consultations that they had the votes to kill the treaty. Normally, the Senate would have simply declined to act. But when pressed by President Clinton and Democratic leaders to bring the treaty to the floor, Republican leaders suddenly scheduled a flurry of hearings, quickly followed by floor debate. No bargaining was evident at either stage.[78] The treaty's foes seemed bent on humiliating the president and signaling their unilateralist approach to future arms control efforts. By the time the treaty's advocates realized they had fallen into a trap (partially of their own making), it was too late to turn back. After debate described as "nasty, brutish and short," the treaty failed by a 48–51 vote short of a majority, much less the required two-thirds.[79] "While there was nothing improper or illegal in their parliamentary tactics," one commentator wrote, "it was nonetheless a nasty and contemptuous way of doing business quite out of character with the [Senate's] stately, sometimes ponderous way of doing business."[80]

A major success for President Obama was winning Senate approval of a major arms control treaty with Russia during the December 2010 lame-duck session of the 111th Congress (the legislative branch was convening after the November elections). Dubbed "New START" (Strategic Arms Reduction Treaty)—the original START treaty was negotiated in the late 1980s during the closing stages of the Cold War—the treaty received the Senate's consent on December 22, 2010, by a 71–26 vote. The president won the treaty approval battle after an intensive lobbying campaign:

> He mounted a five-week campaign that married public pressure and private suasion. He enlisted the likes of Henry Kissinger, asked Chancellor Angela Merkel of Germany to help and sent a team of officials to set up a war room of sorts on Capitol Hill. Vice President Joseph R. Biden, Jr. had at least 50 meetings or phone calls with Senators.[81]

Because of the hurdle of obtaining a two-thirds Senate vote, since World War II presidents have relied increasingly on executive agreements—international accords that are not submitted to the Senate for its advice and consent. As explained by two legal scholars:

> As a matter of historical practice, the president may also make international agreements if authorized to do so by a law passed by Congress. (These are called "congressional–executive" agreements; the North American Free Trade Agreement is a prominent example.) And in some narrow cases, the president may create an international agreement all by himself through his own constitutional powers. [All are] legally binding on the United States and future presidents.[82]

Executive agreements may also be made pursuant to an earlier treaty. "Narrow cases" often involve military matters.

According to a legal expert, between 1939 and 2009 the United States concluded about 16,500 executive agreements compared with some 1,100 treaties.[83] Kiki Caruson describes the subject matter of the agreements:

> The vast majority of executive agreements concern routine procedural matters such as postal agreements, mutual legal assistance, cooperation in the fields of science and technology, conservation, civil aviation agreements, and other relatively non-controversial issues. But the executive agreement has also been used to address important foreign policy issues, such as security and defense matters.[84]

Although the conventional wisdom typically attributes the rise of executive agreements to presidential evasion of the Senate's treaty confirmation role, political scientists Glen S. Krutz and Jeffrey S. Peake argue that executive agreements constitute "a rational response by the president and Congress to the challenges faced by the United States during the daunting complexity brought on by the emergence of its international leadership in the twentieth century."[85] Executive agreements go into force more quickly than treaties and offer a much less cumbersome process for management of international affairs—efficiency gains that can benefit Congress as well as the president.

In federal court cases challenging whether such agreements should have been treaties, the justices have invoked the political questions doctrine and declined to rule on the merits. This doctrine holds that the issue is best left "to the discretion and expertise of the legislative and executive branches."[86]

According to the Case-Zablocki Act of 1972, copies of all executive agreements must be transmitted to Congress within sixty days of their going into effect. From time to time, a constitutional amendment to require Senate ratification of executive agreements has been proposed, but none has ever received the two-thirds vote in both chambers of Congress that would send the proposal to the states for ratification.

Other Policy Making Powers of Congress

In addition to its control of the purse strings, Congress employs an array of other techniques to shape or influence strategic policies. The most common tools of congressional policy leadership are informal advice, legislative prodding through nonbinding resolutions or policy statements, policy oversight, legislative directives or restrictions, and structural or procedural changes.[87]

Advising, Prodding. Congressional leaders and key members routinely provide the president and other executive officials with informal advice. Sometimes, this advice proves decisive. In 1954 President Eisenhower dispatched Secretary of State John Foster Dulles to meet with a small bipartisan group of congressional leaders to determine whether the United States should intervene militarily in Indochina (Vietnam). The leaders unanimously declined to sponsor a resolution favoring involvement until other nations indicated their support of military action. Lacking assurances from either Congress or foreign allies, Eisenhower decided against intervening.[88]

Congress engages in legislative prodding by proposing legislation or suggesting ideas to the administration. During the 111th Congress, for example, congressional Democrats urged President Obama to develop an exit strategy for Afghanistan and to devise benchmarks to measure the progress of the mission. As Sen. Carl Levin, D-Mich., the chair of the Armed Services Committee, explained, "We need metrics to measure progress to report to the American people and, importantly, to hold people accountable."[89] And prodding of the White House by various lawmakers no doubt contributed to President Obama's release of four secret Department of Justice legal opinions written during the George W. Bush administration detailing the harsh interrogation techniques that could be used to extract information from terrorist suspects.

More frequently, Congress passes resolutions that are not legally binding or enforceable. Every recent Congress has approved numerous simple or concurrent resolutions. These measures may lend support to the executive branch, advance certain policies, or signal assurances or warnings to other nations. Occasionally, nonbinding resolutions put forward fresh policy ideas; at other times they are little more than posturing.

Congressional speeches are also important in framing media and public opinion. These speeches, two scholars note, can "shape media coverage of prospective uses of force, which in turn impacts public opinion about the war." They add: "All sorts of trouble, political or otherwise, await the president who loses public support for an ongoing military venture."[90]

Oversight. Congress shapes foreign policy through oversight of the executive branch's performance. Hearings and investigations often focus on foreign policy issues. Recurrent hearings on authorizing and funding State Department and Defense Department programs offer many opportunities for lawmakers to voice their concerns, large and small. Another device is to require that certain decisions or agreements be submitted to Congress before they go into effect. Congress and its committees may also require reports from the executive that "provide not only information for oversight but also a handle for action."[91] Hundreds of foreign and defense policy reporting requirements are embedded in current statutes.

Oversight in time of war or crisis is especially hazardous. The president resists intrusions, and lawmakers are reluctant to impede the action. "The trick is to rein in the White House but not seem unpatriotic," writes historian Bruce J. Schulman.[92] The boldest legislative foray into wartime oversight occurred during the Civil War. While Confederate guns were threatening Washington, D.C., the Joint Committee on the Conduct of the War (1861–1865), controlled by Radical Republicans, held hearings on Capitol Hill and published reports that questioned President Abraham Lincoln's war policies, criticized military operations, berated generals who failed to pursue the enemy, and exposed waste and fraud in military procurements.

During World War II, Missouri senator Harry S. Truman headed the Special Committee to Investigate the National Defense Program (1941–1948), which uncovered profiteering, contract abuses, and shoddy workmanship in wartime projects. The committee saved taxpayers billions of dollars and, not incidentally, boosted the career of its chair (it was the "Truman Committee," proclaimed its letterhead). The Senate Foreign Relations Committee hearings launched in 1966 raised doubts in the public's mind about the Vietnam War.

After the Vietnam War, Congress uncovered long-standing abuses by law enforcement and intelligence agencies. A Senate committee headed by Sen. Frank Church, D-Idaho (1957–1981), found that the FBI, CIA, and National Security Agency (NSA) had spied on politicians, protest groups, and civil rights activities; opened mail illegally; and sponsored scores of covert operations abroad. Oversight during the Cold War period had neglected these matters. As a result of the findings, Congress set up new permanent intelligence committees, required presidents to report covert operations, and in 1978 passed the Foreign Intelligence Surveillance Act (FISA, P.L. 95-511), which "squarely repudiated the idea of inherent executive power to spy on Americans without obtaining [judicial] warrants." "The United States must not adopt the tactics of the enemy," the Church committee declared, "for each time we do, each time the means we use are wrong, our inner strength, the strength that makes us free, is lessened."[93]

After the burst of 1970s reforms, however, Congress reverted to a Cold War mode of complacency. Abuses reminiscent of the Vietnam era were again alleged. Presidents of both parties exercised secret and unchecked powers and evaded or resisted legislative scrutiny. For example, intelligence agencies during the George W. Bush years were found to have wiretapped U.S. citizens without warrants from the FISA-created courts. "The White House became a keen user of unilateral executive orders that bypassed Congress."[94]

Most observers of Congress agree that Republican Congresses (1995–2007) actively probed the Clinton administration's scandals, but "when George Bush became president, oversight [of issues that could embarrass the administration] largely disappeared. From homeland security to the conduct of the war in Iraq, from the torture issue uncovered by the Abu Ghraib revelations to the performance of the IRS, Congress has mostly ignored its responsibilities."[95] When Democrats took charge of the 110th Congress, as noted in Chapter 11, they aggressively investigated the Bush administration. They continued to exercise vigorous oversight in the 111th Congress, even though their party was in charge of the executive establishment.

When the GOP took charge of the 112th House, Speaker Boehner adopted intensive oversight of the Obama administration as a major theme. The topics include a host of national security issues such as cybersecurity, the withdrawal of troops from Iraq and Afghanistan, and the administration's 2011 handling of the "Arab Spring" in the Middle East. Of particular importance to the leadership is achieving fiscal savings in national security without jeopardizing the capacity of the military, intelligence, and homeland security agencies to deal with future terrorist threats.

Legislative Mandates. Congress sometimes makes foreign policy by legislative directives—to launch new programs, to authorize certain actions, or to set guidelines. A landmark enactment of the Cold War era was the Jackson-Vanik amendment to the Trade Act of 1974 (named for Sen. Henry M. "Scoop" Jackson, D-Wash., and Rep. Charles Vanik, D-Ohio). Prompted by concern over the Soviet Union's treatment of its Jewish minority, the amendment denied government credits and most-favored-nation trade status (now called "normal trade relations") to any communist country that restricted the free emigration of its citizens.

Foreign policy statutes may include explicit legislative restrictions, which perhaps are Congress's most effective weapon. Often they are embedded in authorization or appropriations bills that the president is unlikely to veto. Throughout the Reagan presidency, for example, Congress passed many limits on military aid to Central American countries. Most notable were the Boland amendments (named for House Intelligence Committee chair Edward P. Boland, D-Mass.) attached to various bills after 1982 to forbid nonhumanitarian aid to the contra rebels in Nicaragua. The 1987 Iran-contra scandal brought to light how President Reagan and his National Security Council had circumvented this prohibition.[96]

Even the threat of passing legislation may bring about the desired result. Dissatisfied with the Reagan administration's weak "constructive engagement" policy toward South Africa's apartheid policy (a brutal form of racial segregation practiced by that nation's former government), a pro–civil rights coalition on Capitol Hill threatened to pass legislation imposing economic and other sanctions. But just before a sanctions bill was to be approved in 1985, President Reagan issued an executive order imposing limited sanctions. (The next year, over Reagan's veto, Congress enacted tougher restrictions.)

Legislation also shapes the structures and procedures through which policies are carried out. "Congress changes the structure and procedures of decision making in the executive branch in order to influence the content of policy," writes James M. Lindsay.[97] When lawmakers wanted to reform military procurement, they restructured the Defense Department to clarify and streamline the process; when they wanted more say in trade negotiations, they wrote themselves into the process by enacting various trade laws.

CRISIS POLICIES: THE WAR POWERS

An international crisis endangering the nation's safety, security, or vital interests pushes aside other foreign policy goals. Examples range from Japan's attack on the U.S. naval fleet in Pearl Harbor in 1941 to the al Qaeda attacks of September 11, 2001.

Crisis policies engage decision makers at the highest levels: the president, the secretaries of state and defense, the National Security Council, and the Joint Chiefs of Staff. Congressional leaders are sometimes brought into the picture. More rarely, congressional advice is sought out and heeded—as in President Eisenhower's 1954 decision against military intervention in Indochina. Often when executive decision makers fear congressional opposition, they simply neglect to inform Capitol Hill until the planned action is under way. A failed attempt in 1980 to rescue American hostages in Iran, for example, was planned in strictest secrecy, and no consultations were undertaken.

As long as a crisis lingers, policy makers keep a tight rein on information flowing upward from line officers. The attention of the media and the public is riveted on crisis events. Patriotism runs high. Citizens hasten to "rally round the flag" and support, at least initially, whatever course their leaders choose.[98]

Constitutional Powers

War powers are shared by the president and Congress. The president is the commander in chief of the military and naval forces of the United States (Article II, section 2), but Congress has the power to declare (authorize) war (Article I, section 8). The framers vested the power to declare war in Congress because they understood that monarchs and presidents often took their nations to war for diverse motives, such as ambition or military glory. As John Jay wrote in *Federalist* No. 4, "These and a variety of other motives, which affect only the mind of the sovereign, often lead him to engage in wars not sanctified by justice or the voices and interests of his people." The framers expected the commander in chief to defend the nation against sudden attacks, implying a limited military role for the president. Lawmakers and scholars have argued for decades about this division of the war powers.

Congress has declared war only five times: the War of 1812 (1812–1814), the Mexican War (1846–1848), the Spanish-American War (1898), World War I (1917–1918), and World War II (1941–1945). In four instances, Congress readily assented to the president's call for war, acknowledging in the declaration that a state of war already existed. Only once did Congress delve into the merits of waging war, and that was in 1812, when the vote was close. In two cases—the Mexican and Spanish-American conflicts—lawmakers later had reason to regret their haste.

In an age of undeclared wars, more problematic than formal declarations are the more than three hundred other instances in which U.S. military forces have been deployed abroad. (The number is uncertain because of quasi engagements involving military or intelligence advisers.)[99] The examples range from an undeclared naval war with France (1798–1800) to the invasion of Iraq (2003). Since the end of the last declared war—World War II—in 1945, numerous military interventions have taken place abroad. Some were massive and prolonged wars: Korea (1950–1953), Vietnam (1964–1975), Afghanistan (2001–), and Iraq (1991, 2003–). Still others were short-lived actions (for example, military coordination of medical and disaster relief after the U.S. embassies in Kenya and Tanzania were bombed in 1998) and rescue or peacekeeping missions, some of which involved casualties (Lebanon, 1983; Somalia, 1992–1993).

Most of these interventions were authorized by the president as commander in chief on the stated grounds of protecting American lives, property, or interests abroad. Some were justified on the grounds of treaty obligations or "inherent powers" derived from a broad reading of executive prerogatives. Others were peacekeeping efforts under UN or NATO sponsorship.

A fundamental change has occurred in the division of war powers between Congress and the president. The change occurred in 1950 when President Harry Truman took the nation to war against North Korea without seeking a declaration of war or any formal congressional authorization. Instead, he received war-making authority from the Security Council of the United

Nations. Since that time, explained scholar Andrew J. Bacevich, the "perceived imperative of waging the Cold War all but nullified [Congress's power to declare war]. When it comes to using force, presidents exercised wide discretion, ordering American troops into action and [often] notifying Congress after the fact."[100] Congress has an arsenal of tools to challenge the president (such as the purse strings, advice and consent, lawmaking, investigations, and debate), but it often defers to the chief executive rather than asserting its formidable constitutional prerogatives.

Members of Congress, though wary of armed interventions, are reluctant to halt them: "No one actually wants to cut off funds when American troops are in harm's way," a House leadership aide explained. "The preferred stand is to let the president make the decisions and, if it goes well, praise him, and if it doesn't, criticize him," observed former representative Lee Hamilton, who co-chaired the 9/11 Commission and the Iraq Study Group after he retired from Congress.[101] Interventions go well if they come to a swift, successful conclusion with few American lives lost. Actions that drag on without a satisfactory resolution or that cost many lives will eventually tax both lawmakers' and citizens' patience. As the sense of urgency subsides, competing information appears that may challenge the president's version of the event. Congressional critics thus are emboldened to voice their reservations. This reaction occurred as the undeclared wars in Korea and Vietnam dragged on and after U.S. troops suffered casualties in Lebanon and Somalia.

Although Congress has rarely used its power of the purse to withhold funds for executive war-making, it has many other indirect mechanisms to influence military policy. Tough congressional oversight, public criticism of the president in the news media, and resolutions of disapproval can all raise the political costs to presidents of continuing a military action. In a recent study, political scientist Douglas L. Kriner finds that the level of congressional opposition that presidents encounter to their military policies depends heavily on the share of Congress held by the opposition party.[102] Based on his analysis of all major U.S. military actions between 1877 and 2004, Kriner finds that presidents who encounter significant congressional opposition are more likely to limit the scope and duration of military engagements.

The War Powers Resolution

The Johnson and Nixon administrations' conduct of the war in Vietnam left many lawmakers skeptical of presidential war-making initiatives. In 1973 Congress passed the War Powers Resolution (WPR, P.L. 93-148) over President Richard Nixon's veto. This law requires the president to consult with Congress before introducing U.S. troops into hostilities; report to Congress any commitment of forces within forty-eight hours; and terminate the use of forces within sixty days if Congress does not declare war, does not extend the period by law, or is unable to meet. (The president may extend the period to ninety days, if necessary.)

By the end of 2010, presidents had submitted over 130 reports to Congress that troops had been deployed abroad. President Obama reported on March

21, 2011, "consistent with the War Powers Resolution" that he had deployed U.S. military forces "with the support of European allies and Arab partners, to prevent a humanitarian catastrophe and address the threat posed to international peace and security by the crisis in Libya."[103] In still other cases, the executive branch claimed that reports were not required because U.S. personnel were not confronting actual or imminent hostilities.

The WPR is an awkward compromise of executive and legislative authority, and presidents still intervene as they see fit. Members of Congress tend to sit on the sidelines, only later questioning presidential initiatives; but sometimes deployments are debated heatedly. President Reagan dispatched two thousand marines to Lebanon in 1982, but it was not until the troops came under hostile fire in 1983 that Congress seriously debated invoking the War Powers Resolution. Later, a compromise was reached in which the president signed congressional legislation invoking the WPR, and Congress authorized U.S. troops to remain in Lebanon for eighteen months (P.L. 98-119). Shortly afterward, 241 marines were killed by a suicide truck bombing, raising new complaints from Congress and the public. The president subsequently withdrew the troops.

Afghanistan, Iraq, and Libya

Post–September 11, 2001, authorizations under the WPR found Congress in a reactive posture. Three days after the terrorist attacks, with smoke still lingering above the damaged Pentagon building, both chambers passed S. J. Res. 23, authorizing the president "to use all necessary and appropriate force against those nations, organizations, or persons he determines planned, authorized, committed, or aided the terrorist attacks." The debate was scant, and all but one member in the two chambers voted for it. The measure included the assertion that "[n]othing in this resolution supersedes any requirement of the War Powers Resolution." But as Ivo H. Daalder and James M. Lindsay contend, "In effect, Congress declared war and left it up to the White House to decide who the enemy was."[104]

Some three weeks later, President George W. Bush notified Congress that he had launched an assault "designed to disrupt the use of Afghanistan as a terrorist base of operations." Once the operation had toppled Afghanistan's Taliban regime, however, the White House resumed its drumbeat of war threats against its preferred Mideast target: Saddam Hussein's Iraq regime. That regime had already survived the 1991 Gulf War, in which an international force led by the United States evicted the Iraqi military from Kuwait after they had invaded that country.

To sell the Iraq war to the American media and people, the White House framed the debate in three ways: (1) Saddam's weapons of mass destruction (WMD) posed an imminent threat (the WMD frame); (2) the Iraqi people should be freed from a cruel dictator (the liberation frame); and (3) Saddam sponsored terrorist activities (the terrorism frame).[105] The WMD argument prevailed until after the fighting began and no WMDs were found. Thereafter, the liberation rationale dominated the administration's rhetoric. Elite and public opinion agreed that regime change in Iraq was desirable, but it was sharply divided over whether the United States should act unilaterally or work through the UN and a broad coalition of allies, as in 1991. These battles were waged more on news media talk shows and editorial pages than in the halls of Congress.

The president's advisers initially asserted that the president could launch a preemptory attack without further approval. But surveys showed that a large majority of the public—including a majority of Republicans—wanted the president to gain Congress's approval.[106] So as his father had done before the Gulf War in 1991, George W. Bush sought congressional consent.

By the 1991 Gulf War standards—extended deliberation in both houses— debate on invading Iraq was muted and desultory. Sen. Robert C. Byrd, D-W. Va., railed against what he termed the president's demand for "power to launch this nation into war without provocation and without clear evidence of an imminent attack on the United States. And we are going to be foolish enough to give it to him."[107] Lopsided majorities backed the resolution: 296–133 in the House, 77–23 in the Senate. Along with almost all Republicans, many skeptical Democrats went along with the president—more than had backed his father's Gulf War resolution.

In March 2003, the president launched the war. Even lawmakers with misgivings signed onto resolutions of "support for the troops." After no weapons of mass destruction were found in Iraq, the Bush administration found itself with a big problem. Moreover, soon public opinion began to turn against the war as the years of sectarian conflicts and suicide bombings in that nation were highlighted by the news media. By 2008, however, President Bush's "surge" strategy of sending more troops to Iraq (correcting the initial error of not deploying enough troops) was improving the security environment.

The election in 2008 of Barack Obama brought policy shifts in the nation's security policies. On Iraq, the president announced that U.S. troops would end all combat operations by August 2010, with all American troops departing that country by the end of 2011. The fundamental question, then, is what will happen when American military forces leave Iraq? Will terrorist attacks increase in various parts of Iraq? Will private contractors be able to protect adequately the U.S. diplomatic community? Are the Iraqi forces suffi- ciently trained to maintain stability? As one account noted, "After the thou- sands of American lives lost and billions spent, it would be tragic if Iraq collapsed again into war or fell prey to Iran or other neighbors because of a security vacuum created by the U.S. withdrawal."[108] Iraq's future, in short, will be in the hands of the Iraqi people.

Obama's strategic focus shifted to shoring up a deteriorating situation in Afghanistan as a renewed Taliban insurgency threatened the security and stability of the country. In 2009, emulating Bush's military "surge" in Iraq,

President Obama dispatched thirty thousand more troops to Afghanistan to salvage a deteriorating war. His fundamental goals for Afghanistan are to secure a stable nation that can defend itself and that cannot, as under the Taliban, serve as a base of terrorist operations against the United States. However, after a decade of military battles in Afghanistan polls show that nearly two-thirds of Americans believe the war is not worth fighting. Lawmakers and voters are also skeptical about the cost of nation-building in a feudal country, not to mention the cost of military operations (estimated to be $120 billion in 2011) during a period of U.S. economic stress.[109]

Press accounts indicate that the president's goal of pulling troops from Afghanistan starting in July 2011 does not sit well with some military commanders.[110] The clash appears to be between administration officials who want a faster drawdown of military forces and military officers who want a slower drawdown of forces, say sometime in 2012. The decision, of course, will be made by the commander in chief.

The uprising in Libya in the spring of 2011 raised the underlying question: what is the purpose of war? Philosophers and scholars have debated this question for centuries. To put the matter simply, there are "wars of necessity," where the safety and survival of the country are at stake, and "wars of choice."[111] Libya falls in the latter category. Its stated objective, as noted earlier, was to prevent an imminent humanitarian catastrophe in that country.

Congress's constitutional war-declaring role was again ignored, although various lawmakers pondered legislative action "on a resolution that would retroactively bless the president's military actions."[112] The president and his aides contended that he had authority under the WPR "to send U.S. troops into combat without congressional authorization for up to 90 days in the case of an emergency," and the Libyan situation was an emergency[113] (see Box 15-1). The Libyan intervention had its supporters and critics, but it elevated anew a principle officially adopted by the United Nations in 2006: the "international community has the responsibility to protect populations from atrocities."[114]

Just as the doctrines of war change so too does the nature of warfare. The "spectrum of conflict," said Defense Secretary Gates, "ranging from unsophisticated insurgents or terrorists at the low end to sophisticated national armies at the high end, is becoming blurred." He further explained that

> the black-and-white distinction between irregular war and conventional war is an outdated model. We must understand that we face a more complex future than that, a future where all conflict will range along a broad spectrum of operations and lethality. Where near-peers will use irregular or asymmetric tactics and non-state actors may have weapons of mass destruction or sophisticated missiles. . . . This kind of warfare will require capabilities with the maximum possible flexibility to deal with the widest possible range of threats.[115]

BOX 15-1 **A Question of Authority**

Once again, lawmakers are up in arms over the president's failure to consult Congress before sending U.S. troops into action overseas. And yet another president is claiming that his actions are consistent with his powers as the country's commander in chief.

President Obama's decision to order the U.S. military to join in attacks on Libyan air defenses and government forces has reopened the much-argued question of who—the president or Congress—has the authority to commit American troops to combat.

"We need to have a debate in the Congress on a declaration of war against the Libyan state," Indiana Republican Richard G. Lugar, the ranking Republican on the Senate Foreign Relations Committee, said in remarks that capture the sentiments of lawmakers from both parties. "A no-fly zone is a military action. That requires the advice and consent of Congress."

To be sure, the Constitution gives Congress the sole power to declare war. But that prerogative has not been exercised since December 1941, when the United States declared war against Japan, Germany, and Italy. Since then, presidents of both parties have cited either congressional resolutions or UN Security Council resolutions to send U.S. forces into combat.

These actions have created what some legal scholars describe as common-law principles that have made such practical alternatives to an official declaration of war the order of the day.

Obama did discuss his plans for the military mission in Libya with a handful of congressional leaders just before it was launched. But many lawmakers still feel slighted, particularly because Obama, who once taught constitutional law, took a limited view of presidential war powers during his campaign. . . .

[I]n his formal notification to Congress that he was joining U.N.-sanctioned operations against Libya, Obama asserted that his actions were consistent with the 1973 War Powers Resolution, which requires presidents to get congressional authorization to send U.S. troops into combat. The law makes an exception for emergencies, in which case the president must withdraw troops after 60 or 90 days without retroactive approval from Congress.

White House officials argued the Libya mission qualifies as an emergency, given the imminent threat . . . of humanitarian catastrophe as Muammar el-Qaddafi's forces stood poised to retake the rebel-held city of Benghazi. The officials also insist that U.S. forces will hand the mission in Libya to coalition allies well before the law's deadlines.

Still, for new members of Congress, especially those supported by the Constitution-wielding tea party, the manner in which Obama launched the first U.S. military campaign under their watch has come as a shock. "The biggest issue here, whether you are for it or against it, there's a process to follow and it wasn't followed," said Republican freshman Ann Marie Buerkle of New York, a member of the House Foreign Affairs Committee. The president "needs congressional approval."

But senior lawmakers such as Lugar have been around long enough to know that, historically, Congress is unlikely to insist, and once again, the president will have his way.

Source: Jonathan Broder and Emily Cadei, "A Question of Authority," *CQ Weekly*, March 28, 2011, 670.

A think tank analyst identifies other complexities of today's defense and foreign policy environments by adding, among others, multinational corporations, religious radicals, humanitarians, and mercenaries to the mix.[116] Moreover, unlike wars of the past, it appears improbable that today's conflicts will end with formally signed peace treaties. Today's nonstate, and perhaps unknown, enemies could be located anywhere in the world.

Congress's War Powers in Today's World

With each new crisis, the War Powers Resolution is attacked or defended, depending on the view held of the proposed intervention. Although presidents are encouraged to pause and consult before acting, experience since 1973 reveals that the WPR has not prevented them from boldly exercising military powers, including military responses to sudden threats.

For the record, every post-1973 president has denied the WPR's legality, but few at either end of Pennsylvania Avenue are willing to risk having the Supreme Court resolve the question. Lawmakers strive vainly to be consulted, but they support the action as long as it is politically feasible. However, if the crisis persists and the president's actions backfire, Congress moves in and sometimes threatens or curtails the action by refusing funds. Congress unquestionably has the constitutional authority to end wars. As Brad Berenson, who served as an attorney in the Bush White House, has stated, "I am not aware of a serious dispute over whether it is constitutional for Congress to defund or otherwise terminate the war in Iraq. The big debate is over whether it is wise."[117] An outstanding issue, according to Andrew Bacevich, is whether a Congress that is often too compliant will recognize that its first responsibility "is not to support the commander in chief. It is to exercise independent judgment [about committing the nation to war], an obligation that transcends party."[118]

The WPR has few outright defenders, but lawmakers are not ready to repeal or replace it. Although it diminishes Congress's constitutional power of declaring war, the WPR has some practical virtues. It accommodates the rapid use of armed force without the traditional step of formally declaring war. In the current context, declaring war may not be a viable option. "You can't just go off and declare war when you don't know who you are declaring war against," remarked Sen. John B. Breaux, D-La., after the September 11, 2001, attacks.

The WPR gives at least a nodding respect to the framers' belief that Congress, the branch most representative of the people, is the sole source of legal and moral authority for major military enterprises. Presidents may succeed at short-lived actions without a legislative mandate and public support, but longer and more costly engagements will surely falter, as the Korean and Vietnam Wars did. For the time being, then, the enactment stands as a reminder of the ultimate need to gain congressional approval for major military deployments.

CONCLUSION

Some politicians still claim that citizens are preoccupied with domestic concerns and thus are uninterested in world affairs, but that is apparently a misreading of public sentiment. Researchers have found that a strong majority of citizens endorse an active role for the United States in world affairs. The Iraq war was a prime policy concern of voters in the 2004, 2006, and 2008 elections. And although people are reluctant to use U.S. troops overseas, they support fights against international terrorism, nuclear proliferation, and drug trafficking.[119]

Several developments enhance Congress's obligations in foreign policy. First, the United States continues to exert influence in every corner of the globe: militarily, diplomatically, and culturally. Second, global interdependence blurs the line that once demarked domestic policy from foreign policy. Insofar as the resulting issues trespass upon traditional domestic matters, they are bound to encourage congressional intervention and influence. Finally, the question of whether the nation is willing or able to underwrite its costly international projects is forcing Congress and the White House to reassess the nation's global commitments, relying more on multilateral rather than unilateral actions and policies.[120]

Members of Congress cannot avoid foreign and national security policies. As the world grows ever more interdependent, those policies impinge upon every citizen and every local community. An internationally minded electorate, sensitive to famines and plagues in Africa, deforestation in the Amazon, foreign competition for jobs and trade, earthquakes and tsunamis in Japan, and anti-Americanism and terrorism in various regions, draws fewer distinctions between domestic and global matters than in the past.

Today's legislators know that global developments touch their local constituencies, and they believe (rightly or wrongly) that they will be judged to some degree on their understanding of those subjects. It especially behooves lawmakers to debate, challenge, and question presidential war-making policies that could involve the blood and treasure of the nation. As West Virginia senator Byrd stated, "Two constitutional power centers—set up by the framers to check and balance one another—and do battle over politics, policies, and priorities—occupy their distinct ends of Pennsylvania Avenue. What makes it all work for the good of the nation is the character of the individuals who serve."[121]

Citizens and Congress. *Tourists in the 1930s* gawk at the Capitol's elaborately decorated rooms (left). Today's tourists (top right) can take a Segway tour of Capitol Hill, stopping at the Capitol's east front plaza (Bottom), the $621-million Capitol Visitors Center, opened in 2008, informs people about Congress's duties and achievements, guides them toward tours of the building and its chambers, offers food and restrooms, and treats citizens to an unusual underground view of the Capitol dome.

The Two Congresses and the American People

"That meeting was one of the most astounding experiences I've had in my 34 years in politics," remarked Sen. Charles E. Schumer, D-N.Y.[1] Schumer had just emerged from a summit with Treasury Secretary Henry M. Paulson Jr. and Federal Reserve chairman Ben Bernanke. House and Senate leaders, along with a group of lawmakers responsible for oversight of financial markets, had assembled at 7:00 p.m. on September 18, 2008. Seated under a portrait of Abraham Lincoln, Bernanke somberly detailed the unfolding financial crisis and warned that the entire economy "was on the brink of a heart attack."[2]

Over the preceding ten days, the government had seized Fannie Mae and Freddie Mac, the investment bank Lehman Brothers had filed for bankruptcy, Merrill Lynch had been sold at a fire-sale price, and the giant insurance firm American International Group (AIG) had been pulled back from collapse by the federal government's $85 billion emergency loan. Credit markets were frozen, denying credit access to consumers and small businesses throughout the country. "I gulped," said Schumer. "We all realized we're not in normal times."[3]

To contain the crisis, George W. Bush and his administration sought immediate congressional support for a plan that would allow the Treasury Department to buy up to $700 billion of the distressed assets weighing down the balance sheets of major financial institutions. To put this request in context, $700 billion is more than the Pentagon's annual budget.[4] The three-page proposal asked for unfettered authority to spend these vast sums, with nothing more than semiannual reports to Congress.

"Do you know what you are asking me to do?" said Senate majority leader Harry Reid, D-Nev. "It takes me 48 hours to get the Republicans to agree to flush the toilets around here."[5] The administration wanted Congress to act in a matter of days. "This is the United States Senate," said Reid. "We can't do it in that time frame."[6]

The 2008 financial crisis was so urgent that "the Capital almost had the feel of wartime."[7] Still, lawmakers understandably balked at authorizing so much taxpayer money with so little deliberation. "Just because God created the world in seven days doesn't mean we have to pass this bill in seven days," quipped Rep. Joe Barton, R-Texas.[8] Not all members were willing to trust the administration's claims of impending financial disaster. "Where have I heard this before? The Iraqis have weapons of mass destruction, and they're ready to use them," complained Rep. Gene Taylor, D-Miss. "I'm in no rush to do this."

The bailout proposal was extremely unpopular with constituents, who flooded members' offices with calls that ran as much as 30–1 against.[9] The first effort to pass the bill, on September 30, went down to defeat 228–205 in the House of Representatives.[10] The House's action caused a large-scale sell-off on Wall Street, with the Dow Jones stock index plunging 7 percent in one day.

As days unfolded without a congressional consensus, opinion leaders began to speak of "financial Armageddon" and a "credibility test for Congress."[11] Congress eventually acceded to the administration's $700 billion request, but first lawmakers imposed some limits on the administration of the program. They amended the administration's proposal in order to restrict executive compensation, mandate program oversight, and require aid to Americans in danger of losing homes to foreclosure. The amended proposal was approved by Congress and signed into law on October 3, 2008.

In the end, however, Congress's efforts to assert more control over the implementation of the bailout failed. In carrying out the program, the administration made a quick reversal, using the funds not to buy toxic assets but to recapitalize banks. It quickly became clear that the banks could not be held accountable for their use of these funds. Treasury also refused to act on mortgage relief. A Brookings Institution report concludes:

> Congress designed a financial package that allowed the Treasury to spend nearly $350 billion with no accountability for how the money was used, little transparency in how institutions were selected for infusions, no metrics for determining program effectiveness, and no mechanism for forcing the Treasury to comply with the terms of the law that required action to mitigate foreclosures.[12]

Congressional handling of the financial crisis was flawed in many respects. And long afterward, the bailout remained highly unpopular with voters.[13] Nevertheless, the program proved not nearly so expensive for taxpayers as had been expected: most of the funds disbursed to financial firms had been paid back by March 2011, and the U.S. Treasury estimates that the program will turn a profit.[14] Many economists judged that the program helped to stabilize the financial system and forestall further damage.[15]

A crisis poses a severe challenge for legislative assemblies. The demand for immediate action runs counter to the deliberative processes that legislatures follow. The congressional process is inherently ponderous as different perspectives and interests are consulted and majorities are constructed. The United States is not, as some people have claimed, a "presidential nation"; it is a "separated system" marked by the ebb and flow of power among the policy-making branches of government.[16] As former Speaker Newt Gingrich, R-Ga. (1995–1999), said of the nation's complex and frustrating governing arrangements,

> We have to get the country to understand that at the heart of the process of freedom is not the presidential press conference. It is the legislative process; it is the give and take of independently elected, free people coming together to try to create a better product by the friction of their passions and the friction of their ideas.[17]

The legislative "give and take" Gingrich describes inevitably takes time. As a result, fast-moving crises—all too common in an interconnected world of complex financial and security relationships—often demand that Congress act quickly, frequently without due deliberation.

Anxious or fearful citizens need to keep in mind that the American system of government is one of deliberate and fragile interplay among institutions. Citizens' ambivalence toward the popular branch of government is yet another reminder of the dual character of Congress—the theme that has pervaded our explanations of how Congress and its members work. The two Congresses are manifest in public perceptions and assessments. Citizens evaluate Congress using standards and expectations that differ from the ones they use to assess their own senators and representatives.[18] This same duality appears in media coverage: the two Congresses are covered by different sets of reporters working for different kinds of media organizations.

CONGRESS-AS-POLITICIANS

Lawmakers' working conditions and schedules are far from ideal and beg for periodic examination.[19] The hours are killing, the pay comparatively modest, the toll on family life heavy, and the psychic rewards fleeting. A 2007 *Washington Post Magazine* profile of freshman representative Joe Courtney, D-Conn., sketched his life as follows:

> Rising, going to hearings, meeting with lobbyists, fundraising, speaking on the House floor, taking more meetings, walking to the apartment, crashing, rising. . . . The [DCCC] continues to send him reminders about his fundraising goals: *Get off the Capitol grounds; get to the phone bank; make the call.* . . . Another knock. An aide pops in with a reminder: The fundraiser back home is that weekend. . . . 'It just never stops. Never.'"[20]

"Your schedule is not your own," remarked Sen. Fred Thompson, R-Tenn. (1994–2003), on announcing his retirement.[21] Rep. Joe Scarborough, R-Fla. (1995–2001), complained that "the conflict between being a good congressman and full-time father has grown even greater in recent years."[22] "I'm basically single-parenting," said Courtney's wife.[23]

Members' Bonds with Constituents

Despite their job pressures, elected representatives are by no means an endangered species. Diligence and attentive home styles yield dividends at the polls. If voters regard elected officials as a class as rascals, they tend to exempt their own elected representative. For example, just before the 2010 midterm elections public approval of Congress stood at a mere 21 percent.[24] At the same time, only 31 percent of likely voters said their own member of Congress should not be reelected.[25] In the end, despite staggeringly low approval ratings for Congress as a whole—its average approval rating throughout 2010 was only 19 percent[26]—about 85 percent of members seeking reelection were returned to office (see Table 4-4). The 2011 reelection rate was the lowest since 1948, and yet it still reflected the sharp distinction voters draw between their own representatives and Congress overall.

Such large discrepancies between citizens' assessments of their own representatives and of Congress as an institution derive, in part, from divergent expectations. The public places different demands on individual members compared with Congress as a whole. From the institutional Congress, the public expects answers to the nation's problems developed in an open and fair policy process. By contrast, in assessing their own representatives voters take into account far more than lawmakers' positions on national policy issues. They also weigh members' service to the state or district, their communication with constituents, and their home style. Put differently, Congress is viewed as a national policy-making institution, but individual members of Congress are only partly assessed in terms of their stances on national issues. Local representatives are also evaluated in light of the personal bonds they forge with constituents.

Members' high visibility in their states or districts reinforces their local ties. Constituents receive mail from their local representatives, read about them in newspapers and magazines, and see them on television. Large numbers of citizens report having contacts with them. Incumbents miss few opportunities to do favors for constituents, gestures that are usually appreciated and remembered. It is no wonder, then, that constituents view their local representatives in more sympathetic, personal terms than they view the institution of Congress as a whole.

Senators and representatives present themselves to constituents largely on their own terms through advertising, self-promotion, and uncritical coverage by local or regional news media. Members devote countless hours to fund raising to ensure that they have the money to purchase all the paid media they need. Reflecting on the hundreds of fund-raising calls he makes daily, Representative Courtney said, "You could be Abraham Lincoln, but if you don't have the heart of a telemarketer, you're not going to make it to Congress."[27]

Members and their staffs devote constant attention to generating publicity and local press. "I am never too busy to talk to local TV," said a prominent House member. "Period. Exclamation point."[28] A survey of House press secretaries showed virtually unanimous agreement: "We'd rather get in [the hometown paper] than on the front page of the *New York Times* any day."[29] Individual lawmakers tend to bask in the flattering light cast by their local media. Hometown reporters, especially for broadcast media, usually work on general assignment and are ill prepared to question the lawmaker in detail about issues or events. Often their primary goal is simply to get the legislator on video or audio. For politicians, this is an ideal situation. They can express their views in their own words with a minimum of editing and few challenges from reporters.

The importance of personal connections and public relations does not mean that constituents are uninterested in their representatives' issue stances. Lawmakers also forge bonds with voters out of mutual agreement on important national issues. The recruitment process typically yields representatives who faithfully reflect local views and prejudices. As Donald Manzullo, R-Ill., chair of the House Small Business Committee, put it, "Members of Congress see the world through people they represent."[30] At the same time, members' personal ties with voters can help insulate them from disapproval on the occasions when their issue positions diverge from local preferences.

Questions of Ethics

Congressional ethics, however, are perennially in doubt. In a 2010 survey, a mere 9 percent of respondents rated the honesty and ethical standards of Congress members as high or very high.[31] Voters, however, do view their own representatives as more ethical than the rest of Congress. In a 2006 poll, for example, although 69 percent of respondents assessed the honesty of members of Congress generally as either "not so good" or "poor," only 30 percent took such a negative view of their own representative.[32]

Public assessments of congressional ethics stand at odds with the views of most political scientists and close observers of the institution. The conventional wisdom among experts is that the vast majority of lawmakers are dedicated and ethical in their behavior. "Members of Congress behave better than people think," declared former representative Lee H. Hamilton, D-Ind. (1965–1999).[33]

Despite public distrust, lawmakers' behavior today is more transparent and less corrupt than in the past. Members' rising qualifications, more intense media scrutiny, and reforms in campaign finance and ethics procedures have all helped to curtail corruption.[34] Money used to flow freely under the table. "Back in the old days, it was a common occurrence that you walked around with envelopes of cash in your pocket" to hand out to powerful lawmakers, recalled a Washington lobbyist.[35] Today, campaign contributions and direct lobbying expenses are subject to considerably more scrutiny by reporters and civic groups. Although large loopholes remain, financial abuses today are rare by pre-1970s standards.

Why, then, do citizens and commentators remain so contemptuous of lawmakers' ethics? A variety of factors, some of which are beyond members' control, drive public skepticism.

Unethical Behavior. One reason the public distrusts members' ethics is that, unfortunately, unethical behavior persists despite the network of laws and rules intended to restrain it. In 2010, for example, the House summoned veteran lawmaker Charlie Rangel, D-N.Y., to stand in the well of the House to receive formal censure for ethics violations.[36] The House of Representatives took this action after an internal House investigation concluded that Rangel had failed to pay taxes he owed, neglected to disclose several sources of income, and improperly solicited funds from corporations and lobbyists for a Charles B. Rangel Center for Public Service at City College of New York. During the 111th Congress, ethics investigations forced five other members to reimburse expenses for a Caribbean trip that received corporate funding in violation of House rules. More troubling, four members of Congress resigned under ethical clouds in 2006, including two sentenced to jail terms for bribery.[37]

Scandals, even when they are uncovered and punished, weaken public confidence. Most notable was the recent mega-scandal centered on lobbyist Jack Abramoff, who advanced the interests of the gambling industry by means of donations, luxury trips, and favors for some half-dozen lawmakers. "I don't think we have had something of this scope, arrogance, and sheer venality in our lifetimes," observed Norman J. Ornstein, longtime analyst of the Hill scene.[38] Abramoff pleaded guilty in 2006 to fraud, tax evasion, and conspiracy to bribe public officials.[39] Association with the Abramoff case ended the political careers of at least six members of Congress, along with those of many congressional staffers and lobbyists.[40]

Ethics Rules and Processes. Congress's internal processes to police members' ethical violations fail to inspire public confidence. Members typically cringe at passing judgment on their peers. The result of this reluctance is often "a moribund ethics process."[41] But even energetic ethics enforcement does not improve public perceptions. The House Ethics Committee was far more active in the 111th Congress (2009–2011) than it had been in recent years, conducting 111 inquiries into members' activities. Despite all this enforcement activity, a poll of likely voters in twelve competitive congressional districts in November 2010 revealed that only 7 percent believed that congressional ethics had improved; 57 percent said that congressional ethics had deteriorated.[42]

Paradoxically, the intensified regulation of public life actually fuels public distrust. So many rules govern the public activities of lawmakers that they can run afoul of them unintentionally. "High-level public officials are particularly good targets for investigation," explains law professor Cass R. Sunstein, "if only because of the complex network of statutes that regulate their behavior."[43] Elected officials are scrutinized by the Federal Election Commission, the House and Senate ethics committees, the Office of Congressional Ethics, and occasionally by the Justice Department and federal prosecutors (see Box 16-1 on congressional ethics). A number of "watchdog" groups such as Citizens for Responsibility and Ethics in Washington and Judicial Watch also closely monitor ethics issues and publicize the results of their investigations.

Changing Standards of Personal Behavior. Politicians today are held to higher standards of personal habits and conduct than were politicians in the past. The contemporary news media exert great enterprise and energy investigating personal indiscretions and ethical violations, a shift from the journalistic

---

BOX 16-1   Congressional Ethics

Members of Congress are bound by the U.S. Constitution, federal laws, party provisions, and House and Senate rules and conduct codes. Although many observers criticize loopholes, the panoply of regulations is extensive.

- ▶ **Constitution.** Each chamber has the power to punish its members for "disorderly behavior" and, by a two-thirds vote, to expel a member. Members are immune from arrest during attendance at congressional sessions (except for treason, felony, or breach of peace) and "for any speech or debate in either house, they shall not be questioned in any other place" (Article I, section 6). This latter provision protects lawmakers from any reprisals for expressing their legislative views.
- ▶ **Criminal Laws.** Federal laws make it a crime to solicit or accept a bribe; to solicit or receive "anything of value" for performing any official act or service, or for using influence in any proceeding involving the federal government; to enter into or benefit from any contracts with the government; or to commit any fraud against the United States. Lawmakers involved in the so-called Abscam affair were convicted in 1981 for violating these statutes.
- ▶ **Ethics Codes.** Adopted in 1968 and substantially tightened in 1977, 1989, 1995, 1997, and 2007, the House and Senate ethics codes apply to members and key staff aides. The codes require extensive financial disclosure; restrict members' outside earned income (to 15 percent of salaries); prohibit unofficial office accounts that many members used to supplement official allowances; impose stricter standards for using the frank for mailings; and ban lawmakers from accepting most meals and gifts from lobbyists. The House Committee on Standards of Official Conduct and the Senate Select Ethics Committee implement the codes, hear charges against members, issue advisory opinions, and recommend disciplinary actions.
- ▶ **Party Rules.** Congressional parties can discipline members who run afoul of ethics requirements. House Democratic and Republican rules require a committee leader who is indicted to step aside temporarily; a leader who is censured or convicted is automatically replaced.
- ▶ **Federal Election Campaign Act Amendments of 1974.** As amended again in 1976 and 1979, the Federal Election Campaign Act imposes extensive requirements on congressional incumbents as well as challengers. Additional rules and penalties are set in the Bipartisan Campaign Reform Act of 2002.
- ▶ **Office of Congressional Ethics.** Established by the House of Representatives in 2008, the Office of Congressional Ethics is an independent, nonpartisan board of eight private citizens charged with reviewing allegations of misconduct against House members and staff and, when appropriate, referring matters to the Committee on Standards of Official Conduct.

---

norms of earlier eras. The effect on public perceptions is to heighten awareness of congressional shortcomings, regardless of how atypical such failings might be. The diligent work of law-abiding members attracts little attention, while an ethical lapse—or even rumors of one—makes headlines.

In particular, sexual misconduct and substance abuse are far less tolerated today than they were a generation ago. In March 2011, Sen. John Ensign, R-Nev., declined to run for reelection, citing "consequences to sin," after admitting an affair with the wife of a top campaign staffer.[44] Just the previous month, Rep. Chris Lee, R-N.Y., resigned from office after a gossip website revealed that he, a married man, had been seeking dates from women on the website Craigslist and had sent a shirtless photo of himself to a woman online.[45] Indeed, reports of adulterous affairs have ended the careers of several other members in recent years.[46]

Opposition Research. Many scandals are merely driven by political opponents of the accused. Members of Congress, challengers, and party operatives all opportunistically seize on any ethical miscue, real or manufactured, for political advantage. In the early weeks of the 110th Congress (2007–2009), some media outlets ran stories criticizing the new Speaker, Nancy Pelosi, for apparently demanding a larger jet for trips home than the one used by her predecessor. It later surfaced that the request for a larger jet came not from the Speaker herself but from the House sergeant at arms because of security concerns and the added distance (Pelosi lived in California, her predecessor in Illinois).[47] That did not, however, prevent Speaker Pelosi's detractors from using the story to push a media narrative that she was abusing the privileges of her office.

In his study of the impact of what he calls the "ethics culture" on federal appointments, G. Calvin Mackenzie writes:

> Instead of getting out of the way so the winners can govern, the losers begin guerrilla operations that never cease, using every weapon and every opportunity to attack, harass, embarrass, and otherwise weaken those who hold office. If you cannot beat them in an election, current practice now suggests, then do everything in your power to keep the winners from governing and implementing their policy priorities.[48]

In other words, ethics charges and countercharges are often nothing more than "politics by other means."[49] Nevertheless, the political uses of ethics charges ensure that they are continually in the public eye, undercutting perceptions of lawmakers generally.

"A Small Class of People." Do these hazards of public life deter "the best and the brightest" from seeking elective office? It is hard to answer that question. Young people, for example, show lamentably scant interest in government careers, and yet their idealism often leads them to pursue other paths of public service.[50] The difficulties of balancing a parental or care-giving role with the round-the-clock demands of the lawmaker's life do appear to fall especially hard on women. Research suggests that the relentless schedule is an important reason why so few women run for political office.[51] The poor esteem in which the public holds Congress may also be another deterrent for potential candidates.[52]

American democracy requires that ambitious people put themselves forward as candidates. But many of the ablest individuals—especially in one-party areas—decide to sit on the sidelines. Although open seats seem to have little shortage of claimants, the unwillingness of talented, experienced politicians to challenge sitting incumbents raises the specter of unaccountability. The fact is, parties frequently have great difficulty recruiting good challengers to run against officeholders. Indeed, the absence of strong challengers, especially for House seats, is a major factor in the persistently high incumbent reelection rates. Meanwhile, the outcomes of congressional elections almost always reveal at least a few underperforming incumbents who would have been vulnerable to defeat, had they only drawn a credible opponent.[53] Congressional elections would be more competitive and voters would have better choices if greater numbers of talented individuals were willing to enter the fray.

The rising demands and costs of congressional life probably lie beyond the reach or interest of average men and women. Reflecting on the multiplicity of presidential duties, Woodrow Wilson once remarked that Americans might be forced to pick their leaders from among "wise and prudent athletes—a small class of people."[54] The same might now be said of senators and representatives.

CONGRESS-AS-INSTITUTION

Americans expect Congress to be active and productive. Opinion surveys have consistently found that people prefer that Congress play a strong, independent policy-making role. They want Congress to check the president's initiatives and to examine the president's proposals carefully.[55] Related to that desire, they often endorse the notion of divided government—that is, the White House controlled by one party and Capitol Hill controlled by the other.

Policy Success and Stalemate

Americans are often unaware of the ways in which Congress affects their daily lives. Lee Hamilton tells the following story:

> [A] group of [young people] visiting my Indiana office told me that Congress was irrelevant. So I asked them a few questions. How had they gotten to my office? On the interstate highway, they said. Had any of them gone to the local university? Yes, they said, admitting they'd got some help from federal student loans. Did any of them have grandparents on Social Security and Medicare? Well sure, they replied, picking up on where I was headed. Their lives had been profoundly affected by Congress. They just hadn't focused on all of the connections before.[56]

Indeed, most citizens do believe that Congress is an important institution that should share power equally with the president. When Indiana University's

Center for Congress asked in the fall of 2010 how much of an impact Congress had on citizens' lives, 52 percent of respondents said "a great deal" and another 36 percent said "some." Majorities also found it easy to "find out what's happening in Congress" (56 percent agreed strongly or somewhat) and easy to express their views to their senators and representatives (58 percent).[57]

Its poor public reputation notwithstanding, Congress has produced many innovative and effective policies. In an intriguing experiment, Paul C. Light of the Brookings Institution set out to identify the federal government's most influential actions over a fifty-year period.[58] A survey of historians and political scientists served to winnow a preliminary roster of 588 items to a list of fifty "greatest achievements." For the record, the top three successes were judged to be rebuilding Europe after World War II (the Marshall Plan, 1947), expanding the right to vote (Voting Rights Act of 1965), and promoting equal access to public accommodations (Civil Rights Act of 1964).

In every case Light uncovered, Congress played a vital role in the policy's inception, ratification, or implementation. Although Congress was not always the initiator, many programs associated with given presidents—for example, the Marshall Plan (Harry S. Truman) and Medicare (Lyndon B. Johnson)—began as proposals on Capitol Hill. "No one party, Congress, or president can be credited with any single achievement. . . . Rather, achievement appears to be the direct product of endurance, consensus, and patience."[59]

Despite its past achievements, most people could compile a must-do legislative agenda that would include many items left unattended by recent Congresses. According to a recent survey, the American public is concerned that Congress fails to debate and take leadership on important matters. Citizens are worried that Congress pays too little attention to long-term problems such as the cost of entitlements, the mushrooming public debt, energy issues, and infrastructure maintenance. The survey's analyst, Paul Light, concluded: "What we found is there is tremendous demand for answers. [The citizens] may not know exactly what to do, but they're very, very worried."[60]

The 111th Congress, with unified Democratic control in President Obama's first two years in office, achieved some remarkable legislative breakthroughs, including comprehensive reforms of the national health insurance marketplace, federal student loan policies, and regulations of financial institutions. But it also left much work undone. No progress was made on immigration policy, despite widespread agreement that the current system is profoundly deficient. No energy legislation was passed, even though it was a top administration priority. Congress failed entirely to write a budget for fiscal year 2011. And, most remarkably, Congress did not pass any of the twelve annual appropriations bills needed to keep the federal government operating through 2011.

The early months of the 112th Congress (2011–2013) point to renewed stalemate. Bogged down over last year's appropriations, more than two months into the session Congress still had not arrived at an agreement to prevent a shutdown of the federal government. Stacks of executive appointments and judicial nominations languished unprocessed in the Senate. Meanwhile, because of the wide differences between the Republican-controlled House of Representatives and the Democratic-controlled Senate, few issues offer any realistic prospect of bicameral agreement or potential for significant action. These difficulties suggest that the successes of the 111th Congress were fleeting. Now back to the pattern of recent years, Congress has difficulty just processing the institution's routine workload, much less addressing longer-term issues.

Assessing the Congressional Process

Congress's institutional shortcomings are numerous and obvious. Beyond its structural and procedural complexities, the quality of its deliberations often falls short of democratic ideals. Lack of comity and bipartisanship, the growth of Senate roadblocks, and questions surrounding transparency contribute as well to Congress's muddied reputation. Are reforms possible?

Deliberation. Legislative assemblies are primarily designed to foster deliberation. "The assembly makes possible a deliberation in which conflicting judgments about the public good . . . can be examined, debated, and resolved," writes Richard Hall. "And through such a process the actions of government achieve legitimacy."[61] Recent developments have significantly undermined the quality and quantity of congressional deliberation. In order to cope with the pressures of lawmaking in a highly polarized and partisan environment, leaders of both parties tend to "short-circuit regular deliberative procedures in committee, on the floor, and in conference."[62]

The legislative process has morphed into a wide variety of highly centralized improvisations—what Barbara Sinclair has termed "unorthodox lawmaking."[63] Leaders package together disparate policies into omnibus vehicles so bulky that only a small number of staff aides and members know what provisions have been inserted or left out. Outcomes are normally predetermined, especially in the House, where majority party leaders oversee the pre-floor negotiations and craft the rules for debate. Most important House measures are considered under restrictive or closed rules permitting few or no amendments.[64] Floor deliberations are just a series of desultory recitations—public speaking in this country has become something of a lost art. Under such circumstances, lawmakers are often embarrassed by provisions they have voted into law.

Committee deliberation has been similarly weakened. Committee meetings are frequently poorly attended, with the outcomes laid out by the chair and the chair's majority-party colleagues. Leaders routinely bypass committee consideration altogether, bringing unreported bills directly to the floor. Staff resources for House and Senate committees were cut by more than a third between 1979 and 2005.[65] In 2011 the House cut all committee budgets by 5 percent, except for Appropriations, which received a 9 percent cut. The Senate effectively froze committee budgets for the 112th Congress. According to two analysts, "Committees have been marginalized in myriad ways, from central party direction to ad hoc groups to omnibus bills."[66] As committees become less consequential policy-making arenas, members have less incentive to develop policy expertise in the matters before their committees.

Even House-Senate interactions are less deliberative in character. Today's congressional leaders frequently avoid the conference process altogether, convening "pro forma" conferences to ratify deals worked out in leadership offices or exchanging bills back and forth between the chambers. On occasion, House-Senate negotiations have even excluded minority-party conferees. Such tactics streamline the legislative process but forfeit the benefits of deliberation.

Another factor weakening congressional deliberation is Congress's frantic stop-and-go work schedule. Although earlier members did not live in the nation's capital, most of them stayed in town for weeks at a stretch, their days dominated by extended hearings or deliberations. By the mid-twentieth century, a minority of members—mostly from the eastern corridor—constituted a "Tuesday–Thursday club," spending long weekends at home. Nowadays, nearly all members follow such a schedule, which often shrinks to Tuesday night to Thursday afternoon. And extended nonlegislative or "district work periods" surround all the major holidays.

Thirty-four-year House veteran Hamilton has offered a blunt assessment of the situation:

> Congress doesn't work enough at its true job. Members of Congress spend too much of their week campaigning, and not enough of it doing the hard work of governing. Building a consensus behind an approach to a national problem is tough; it takes negotiation, extended discussion, and hard study. This is impossible when you spend three days on Capitol Hill and then rush home for an extended weekend of appearances.[67]

One remedy would seem simple: longer sessions (two weeks at least), alternating with periods for constituency work or official travel. Because of the pressures of campaigning in today's highly competitive environment, it is unlikely that the congressional calendar will become any more favorable to extended deliberation. Indeed, according to plans for the first session of the 112th Congress (2011), members of Congress would be in Washington even less than in recent years. Majority Leader Eric Cantor, R-Va., announced a calendar in which the House would be in session only 123 days during 2011, "the lightest House schedule in a non-election year since 2005 and, before that, 1983."[68] Workweeks were to be no longer than four consecutive days, and votes were to be scheduled before 7:00 p.m. The goal, stated Cantor, was to stress "quality over quantity."[69]

Comity and Bipartisanship. Another institutional malady is the decline of interpersonal comity. This decline is the product of several converging factors, most notably the escalating cohesion within, and polarization between, the two parties. Nelson W. Polsby has termed the contemporary period an "era of ill feeling" in Congress.[70]

Critics have persuasively faulted the contemporary Congress for engaging in a "destructive form of partisanship" that prevents bipartisan give-and-take.[71] As leaders centralize power, minority-party members are less likely to be heard. "Oh, those were frustrating years," recalled former Republican leader Robert Michel of Illinois, who served in the minority for all of his thirty-eight years in the House (1957–1995):

> But . . . I never really felt I was out of the game or that I had no part to play. Under the rules of the House, the traditions of the House . . . there is a role to play for the minority. . . . We struck a deal, we made a bargain [and worked at] bringing dissident factions together . . . to craft good legislation for the country. That was the joy of it![72]

Michel's successor and former staff aide representative Ray LaHood, R-Ill. (now President Obama's secretary of transportation), explained that Michel "taught us by example that the House floor should be a forum for reasoned debate among colleagues equal in dignity. He came to the House every day to do the work of the people, and not to engage in ideological melodramas or political vendettas."[73]

Observing the unpredictable and not always coherent policies produced by bipartisan deal-making in the mid-twentieth-century Congress, many political scientists lamented the absence of "party government." They preferred a democratic politics in which parties would run on coherent platforms and command the leadership and unity to enact their programs into law. Key elements of the party government model have now come to pass. The parties are far more internally homogeneous; the caucuses meet regularly to decide policy; members' party-line voting presents clear alternatives to voters. But no analyst has contended that these changes have lifted the quality of policy making. Instead, partisanship has been blamed for escalating the level of rancor and stalemate. Former representative and deputy GOP whip Mickey Edwards of Oklahoma (1977–1993) decries "partisanship in the extreme," which extends beyond policy or ideological differences:

> Instead of morphing from candidates to members of Congress on the day they are sworn in, today's legislators engage in permanent campaigning. Neither party is willing to allow the other to gain credit for an achievement that might help it in the next election, so the center aisle that divides Democrats from Republicans in the House has become a wall.[74]

Intense and pervasive partisan conflict has also become a barrier to public trust in government. A recent political science study demonstrates that changes in the level of congressional partisanship have a direct, lasting, and negative effect on Americans' assessment of the institution.[75] According to the study's author, Mark D. Ramirez,

Citizens appear to equate partisan conflict with partisan biases and the notion that members of Congress are avoiding the facts—whatever they may be—when formulating policy. . . . [T]he public perceives partisan conflict as a waste of time and resources that could be spent trying to solve the nation's problems rather than trying to put the other party down for personal or partisan electoral gains.[76]

Senate Roadblocks. Nowhere has the rise of partisanship created more obstacles for policy making than in the Senate. For much of the Senate's history, filibusters were rare, employed for matters of great constituency or regional importance. Today, they have become "a partisan tool."[77] The partisan filibuster—in which most or all of the Senate majority party's agenda is systematically blocked by an organized minority-party filibuster—is a recent innovation. Barbara Sinclair's research dates the organized partisan filibuster to the first two years of the Clinton presidency (the 103d Congress, 1993–1995), in which Republican-led filibusters obstructed half of all major measures.[78]

Because of the partisan filibuster, the Senate has evolved into an institution that is encountering exceptional difficulty in governing. "The reality is that because of Senate rules, it takes 60 votes to order pizza, let alone to consider and vote on important pieces of legislation," quipped Rep. Jim McGovern, D-Mass.[79] "Requiring a supermajority to pass legislation that is at all controversial makes the coalition-building process much more difficult and increases a status quo–oriented system's tendency toward gridlock," writes Barbara Sinclair. "The costs of gridlock can be severe: a government that cannot act, that cannot respond satisfactorily to its citizens' demands, loses its legitimacy."[80]

The widespread use of delaying tactics in the Senate has effects that extend far beyond the highly controversial issues. It is not merely that the Senate's majority party faces great obstacles to passing its partisan agenda. The delays also impede the Senate's ability to manage the rest of its workload. As Scott Lilly, senior fellow at the Center for American Progress, explains, "The legislative calendar is so consumed by extended debate" that there is not enough time for the Senate to reauthorize expiring programs; nearly half of the funds appropriated for nondefense discretionary spending in fiscal year 2010 "had to be appropriated without legal authority."[81] In addition, appropriations bills almost never pass on time, denying federal agencies the information they need to plan budgets, evaluate competing contract proposals, and maximize value for taxpayers. Many uncontroversial matters that pass the House never receive Senate consideration simply because of the lack of floor time.

Transparency. Another important issue in evaluating Congress is transparency, the ability of the public to monitor and understand congressional proceedings. Questions of transparency present difficult trade-offs for legislative assemblies. On the one hand, a lack of transparency is a major source of public mistrust. People fear that a lack of public access will allow special interests to dominate the legislative process in secret. The Sunlight Foundation, a nonprofit group founded to champion congressional transparency, has pushed popular initiatives such as the online availability of members' financial statements, lobbying expenses, "earmarks" (members' requests for constituency spending projects); senators' "holds" (halting floor debate on bills); and reports of Hill support agencies such as the Congressional Research Service (CRS). Generally speaking, the public does not trust legislators to act in the public interest in the absence of public scrutiny and accountability.

On the other hand, transparency can hamper internal legislative bargaining and compromise. It is more difficult for members to accept trade-offs that impose costs on their constituencies when those decisions are made in full public view.[82] Instead, lawmakers have a greater incentive to play to their external constituencies and refuse to engage in meaningful negotiations. One of the most significant transparency reforms ever adopted was to permit C-SPAN to telecast congressional proceedings.[83] This reform gave Americans much more access to the lawmaking process. But, just as opponents of televising Congress feared, it may have hindered congressional work. Television "has probably done more to make the Senate a more partisan place," points out veteran senator Orrin G. Hatch, R-Utah. "There's a lot of posturing before the camera."[84]

The Perils of Reform.   Reforming Congress is often touted as a solution to its organizational or procedural faults. The House and Senate themselves periodically engage in self-examination (the last broad-scale inquiry took place in 1993). But such efforts are often impeded by the two-Congresses dilemma— that is, structural reforms can threaten members' electoral interests. E. Scott Adler warns, for example, that "any widespread change in the established order of policy deliberation—particularly in its centerpiece, the committee system— would create far too much uncertainty in members' electoral strategies."[85]

Congress's history nevertheless includes some major planned innovations affecting deliberation as well as electoral arrangements. Reformers with different and often conflicting goals—enhancing legislative power and efficiency, gaining partisan or policy advantage, or augmenting individual lawmakers' perquisites— have coalesced around significant reforms. Because of the variety of goals involved, however, the results achieved are often different from those anticipated.

In his survey of forty-two major institutional innovations over the last century, Eric Schickler finds that "preexisting institutions create constituencies for their preservation that typically force reformers with new goals to build upon, rather than dismantle, these structures."[86] An example was the series of new budget procedures piled like so many building blocks on top of the existing authorization-appropriations process. Little wonder that such reforms typically fall short of their sponsors' objectives. Instead of achieving stable, effective arrangements, the reforms result in "a set of institutions that often work at cross-purposes."[87]

Media Coverage

The most open and accessible of the three branches of government, Congress is covered by a large press corps populated by some of the nation's most skilled journalists. CBS News reporter Bob Schieffer claims that Capitol Hill is the best news beat in Washington.[88] Paradoxically, however, neither reporters nor their editors are able to convey the internal subtleties or the external pressures that shape lawmaking. Moreover, the very media best suited to reporting on Congress—serious daily newspapers and magazines—are suffering long-term declines in circulation.[89] In response, newspapers have curtailed their coverage of Congress and national and global politics in general. Pressrooms have been downsized; most foreign bureaus have been closed. Bottom-line pressures on the media threaten the nation's democratic processes by leaving people less informed.

Even prestigious news magazines have curtailed public affairs coverage in favor of stories about celebrities, entertainment, and lifestyle issues. The first cover of *Time* magazine in 1926 portrayed former House Speaker Joseph G. Cannon, R-Ill. (1903–1911). Today, political figures—other than presidents— are rarely seen on the covers of *Time* and its competitors.

The decline has been equally drastic in television (including the so-called all-news channels). "Apart from technology," says journalist Bill Moyers, "the biggest change in my thirty years in broadcasting has been the shift of content from news about government to consumer-driven information and celebrity features."[90]

Political news has changed in content as well as coverage. Fewer stories appear on policy issues and more on scandal, wrongdoing, or corruption. Following the canons of investigative journalism, reporters play the role of suspicious adversaries on the lookout for good guys and bad guys, winners and losers. Ethical problems, congressional pay and perquisites, campaign war chests, and foreign junkets are frequent targets. Generally speaking, political radio and TV talk shows are ill-informed, combative, and contemptuous of politicians and their work.[91]

As mentioned earlier, divergent press coverage—local versus national media—widens the gap between the two Congresses' distinct images: it is more positive for individual members than for the institution. Congress as an institution is covered by the national press with lots of skepticism and cynicism, while individual lawmakers are covered respectfully by the local media.

Citizens' Attitudes toward Congress

Individual members of Congress may receive respectable marks, but people often seem ready to flunk Congress as a whole (see Table 16-1). The institutional Congress usually ranks well below respondents' own representatives in public esteem. Citizens' ratings of the job Congress is doing fluctuate with economic conditions, wars and crises, scandals, trust in government overall, and levels of partisan conflict (see Figure 16-1). Approval of Congress surged briefly after it handled the Watergate affair in 1974, after the Republican takeover twenty years later, and after the terrorist attacks of September 11. The overall trend has been markedly downward since 2002, however, with Congress plumbing historic depths of public dissatisfaction in 2010.

TABLE 16-1   **High Approval for Members, Low Approval for Congress**

Individual members	Congress as an institution
Serve constituents	Resolves national issues only with difficulty or not at all
Run against Congress	Has few defenders
Emphasize personal style and outreach to constituents	Operates as collegial body that is difficult for citizens to understand
Are covered by local media in generally positive terms	Is covered by national media, often negatively (with focus on scandals and conflicts)
Respond quickly to most constituent needs and inquiries	Moves slowly with cumbersome processes that inhibit rapid responses
Are able to highlight personal goals and accomplishments	Has many voices, but none can speak clearly for Congress as a whole

Sources: Timothy E. Cook, "Legislature vs. Legislator: A Note on the Paradox of Congressional Support," *Legislative Studies Quarterly* 4 (February 1979): 43–52; Glenn R. Parker and Roger H. Davidson, "Why Do Americans Love Their Congressmen So Much More Than Their Congress?" *Legislative Studies Quarterly* 4 (February 1979): 53–61; Richard Born, "The Shared Fortunes of Congress and Congressmen: Members May Run from Congress but They Can't Hide," *Journal of Politics 52* (November 1990): 1223–1241.

Congress is not well understood by the average citizen. Partly to blame are the institution's size and complexity, not to mention the arcane twists and turns of the legislative process. But many citizens simply find the whole legislative process distasteful.

Dissention is on display on Capitol Hill to a greater extent than in other branches of government. Although this same messiness is found in the other branches of government, it is more visible and continuous in Congress. The president speaks with one voice: even though there is fierce competition for the president's ear, a statement from the president defines the administration's position. As for the judiciary, opinions are frequently divided or unclear as judges and justices disagree about law and policy, but their decisions are usually accepted as law. By contrast, no single member, not even the institution's top leaders, speaks for Congress.

The public's ambivalence toward Congress goes far deeper than unhappiness with specific policies or disgust with scandals, if the sobering conclusions of John R. Hibbing and Elizabeth Theiss-Morse are to be believed:

> People do not wish to see uncertainty, conflicting opinions, long debate, competing interests, confusion, bargaining, and compromised, imperfect solutions. They want government to do its job quietly and efficiently, sans conflict and sans fuss. In short . . . they often seek a patently unrealistic form of democracy.[92]

FIGURE 16-1   Public Assessments of the Two Congresses, 1974–2010

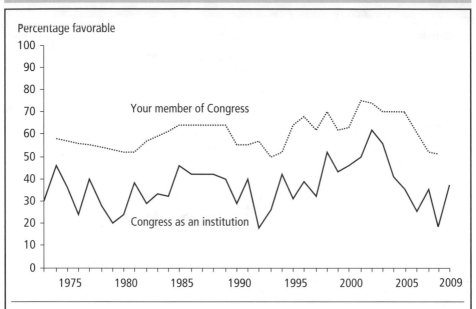

Source: Authors' interpolations of survey results, primarily drawn from the Gallup Organization and the Harris Survey.

Note: The Gallup Organization's questions are "Do you approve of the way the U.S. Congress is handling its job? Do you approve or disapprove of the way the representative from your own congressional district is handling his/her job?" The Harris Survey's question is "How would you rate the job done this past year by [Congress] [your member of Congress]—excellent, pretty good, only fair, or poor?" Responses are dichotomized as favorable ("excellent," "pretty good") or unfavorable ("only fair," "poor"). The plotted points in the figures indicate respondents having opinions who approve of or are favorable toward congressional performance. Polling data for 2010 are from an ABC News/*Washington Post* poll using the Gallup Organization's traditional questions.

In other words, people seem to abhor the very attributes that are the hallmarks of robust representative assemblies. As Hibbing and Theiss-Morse observe, Congress "is structured to embody what we dislike about modern democratic government, which is almost everything."[93]

TWENTY-FIRST-CENTURY CHALLENGES

The U.S. Congress is now in its third century. Survival for more than two centuries is no mean feat. Perhaps it resembles Dr. Johnson's dog (noted not for its proficiency at walking on its hind legs but for being able to do so at all). Congress has withstood repeated stress and turbulence, including a civil war, political assassinations, terrorist attacks, domestic scandals, and contentious foreign involvement. The U.S. constitutional system is far older than most of the world's existing governments.

Global Threats and Alarms

The physical setting of the U.S. Capitol now exhibits the stepped-up security arrangements prevalent elsewhere since the September 11, 2001, terrorist attacks. Just a decade ago, visitors and Hill personnel moved freely in and out of the Capitol and surrounding office buildings. Members of the public may still visit most Capitol Hill facilities, but they now encounter uniformed officers, metal detectors, and concrete barriers. In the wake of the attempted assassination of Rep. Gabrielle Giffords in Tucson in January 2011, congressional leaders and members are contemplating additional security precautions.[94] One welcome development, however, is the long-needed U.S. Capitol Visitor Center—constructed under the East Front—that enhances the building's safety while introducing visitors to Congress and its work.

Congressional Continuity. The 9/11 terrorist attacks prompted people to think the unthinkable about the physical continuity of Congress. If the Capitol were attacked, how could the House members killed be quickly replaced? Nearly every state empowers governors to fill Senate seats temporarily, but under the Constitution those who fill House seats must be elected, which would entail time-consuming special elections. What could be done about incapacitated members? What would happen if the nation's capital were destroyed or uninhabitable?

Various constitutional amendments have been suggested to allow for the temporary appointment of House members in the event a catastrophe caused mass vacancies. A bipartisan Continuity of Government Commission recommended an amendment empowering Congress to enact legislation addressing a range of continuity questions.[95] But House majorities have opposed the idea of appointing temporary members, even to fill vacancies caused by some calamity. Reformers have been greatly frustrated by the lack of progress on this issue. "Our leaders' failure to establish a plan to ensure that our Constitution survives is irresponsible," writes Norman Ornstein. "Do we really have to wait until the nightmare scenario becomes a reality to do something?"[96]

Policy Challenges. Mere survival, though, may be the least of Congress's problems. In a world of uncertain global challenges, Congress continues to face difficult and controversial domestic issues such as high unemployment, large and growing budget deficits, energy sustainability, climate change, immigration, infrastructure renewal, and widening economic inequality. On top of these continuing domestic issues are global challenges such as unrest across the Middle East, the European debt crises, plus war and reconstruction in Afghanistan and Iraq.

Checks and Imbalances?

The constitutional system of divided powers and competing branches does not yield a stable equilibrium. Powers ebb and flow among the branches. Crises tend to empower the executive branch, whereas more peaceful times are friendlier to congressional power. An activist bench can drive the judiciary into political thickets; at other times the bench defers to the other branches.

Executive Hubris. Executive branch encroachments upon legislative prerogatives are neither new nor confined to crisis periods. Most modern presidents have fought for broader leeway in spending appropriated funds and freedom to reorganize agencies and redeploy their personnel. Presidents and their appointees naturally seek to control information about what they are doing. Despite the ebb and flow of institutional power over time, however, there is no question that recent presidents have pushed the boundaries of presidential authority in ways that threaten to eclipse Congress.

Executive dominance is most apparent in military affairs. Throughout the post–World War II era, presidents have regularly embroiled the United States in military conflicts without seeking congressional support. In fact, since President Truman single-handedly intervened in the Korean War in 1950 without asking for congressional support, none of the U.S.'s military actions has been accompanied by a congressional declaration of war.[97] Truman asserted the power to act without Congress under the United Nations Charter, UN Security Council resolutions, and NATO treaties; Congress did not contest those claims. Although Presidents George H. W. Bush and George W. Bush both asked for congressional authorizations of the use of force in Iraq, they—along with all other contemporary presidents—contended that they did not need congressional approval to act. President Bill Clinton did not ask for any kind of congressional support before launching cruise missiles against the Iraqi intelligence services in 1993, nor did he seek congressional authority before launching air strikes against the Serbs in 1994 and 1995.

The pattern continues in the Obama administration. When President Obama decided at a contentious White House meeting in March 2011 to support military action against the Qaddafi regime in Libya, he did so without either broadly consulting with Congress or seeking any kind of congressional authorization.[98]

Presidents have also become more assertive in denying information to Congress. The George W. Bush administration made secrecy a watchword. The White House refused to share documents with Congress, permit certain executive officials to testify before congressional committees, or otherwise cooperate with investigative hearings.[99] Staunch GOP committee chairs Charles E. Grassley of Iowa (Senate Finance), Henry J. Hyde of Illinois (House International Relations), and F. James Sensenbrenner Jr. of Wisconsin (House Judiciary) repeatedly protested the executive's failure to provide information.[100]

Despite such complaints, it is also clear that Congress has been complicit in its loss of power. In its haste to respond to terrorist attacks of 9/11, for example, Congress gave scant attention to details of the vast grants of power it ceded to the president and the executive branch by approving open-ended military action, the problematic USA Patriot Act, and the 180,000-employee Homeland Security Department. Sen. Robert C. Byrd, D-W.Va. (1959–2010), rebuked congressional inaction on the eve of the Iraq war in an eloquent speech to an almost empty chamber:

We stand passively mute in the Senate today, paralyzed by our own uncertainty, seemingly stunned by the sheer turmoil of events. . . . But today we hear nothing, almost nothing, by way of debate. . . .

The rafters should ring. The press galleries should be filled. Senators should be at their seats listening to questions being asked about this war, questions to which the American people out there have a right to expect answers. The American people are longing for information and they are not getting it. This chamber is silent. . . . We are truly sleepwalking through history.[101]

"Congress has ceded its war power to the president," concludes former representative Hamilton.[102]

Party polarization in recent years may also have contributed to Congress's refusal to assert its prerogatives more vigorously. During conditions of unified government, it is in the partisan interest of the congressional leadership to avoid vigorous executive oversight and any other actions that might weaken the president. Reflecting on the relationship between Congress and President George W. Bush during the years of unified party control, Rep. Ray LaHood conceded the point: "Our party controls the levers of government. We're not about to go out and look beneath a bunch of rocks and try and cause heartburn."[103]

Loyalty to a president from the majority party should be no excuse for congressional timidity. Partisan loyalties did not immunize past presidents of both parties, from Franklin D. Roosevelt to Ronald Reagan to Bill Clinton, against probing oversight and sometimes fierce opposition led by their party's leaders on Capitol Hill—even in wartime. If lawmakers do not fiercely defend their prerogatives, they have only themselves to blame when executives ignore them.

Judicial Lawmaking. Congress also faces attacks upon its powers from an activist federal judiciary, which has invalidated federal enactments in more than thirty cases since 1995. Since the 1990s, the courts have challenged federal laws in areas such as interstate commerce and civil rights, raising questions that were last litigated in the 1930s. By narrow majorities, for example, the U.S. Supreme Court curbed the 1990 Americans with Disabilities Act on the grounds it had not dared to apply to earlier civil rights statutes. Other recent court rulings have progressively restricted Congress's ability to impose any meaningful regulations on campaign finance.

Members of Congress regularly criticize the courts for "judicial activism," by which they typically mean a handful of ideological issues, principally involving abortion and religious establishment clause jurisprudence. These hoary complaints, however, seem to speak to an earlier era rather than the judicial branch of today, overwhelmingly staffed by Republican nominees.[104] Meanwhile, relatively few seem troubled by rulings regarding fundamental state and federal authority. Senior federal circuit court judge John T. Noonan

Jr., a Reagan appointee, argues that the Supreme Court has "invented criteria for Congress that invaded the legislative domain."[105] The judiciary retains the capacity to constrict legislative powers in much the same way that late nineteenth-century courts gutted the Civil War constitutional amendments. As Noonan explains, "If five members of the Supreme Court are in agreement on an agenda, they are mightier than five hundred members of Congress with unmobilized or warring constituencies."[106]

Is Congress Permanently Damaged? Following the Vietnam War and the Watergate scandal, Congress tried valiantly to reclaim prerogatives that had slipped away during the Cold War period. A new equilibrium seemed to have been established, but the reform fervor was short-lived. In his detailed account of congressional initiatives, James L. Sundquist sums up that era:

> The 1970s were a period of upheaval, of change so rapid and so radical as to transform the pattern of relationships that had evolved and settled into place over the span of half a century or more. But by the end of the decade the spirit of resurgence . . . had waned.[107]

Although a brief period of balance between the branches ensued, Sundquist accurately predicted the coming of "a new cycle of slow decline of the Congress in favor of the president."[108]

Reflecting on that new cycle of events, Andrew Rudalevige of Dickinson College revisits the 1970s question: is there a new imperial presidency? His short answer is yes: "Presidents have regained freedom of unilateral action in a variety of areas, from executive privilege to war powers to covert operations to campaign spending. . . . The default position between presidents and Congress has moved toward the presidential end of the inter-branch spectrum—and irreversibly so."[109]

Is this trend irreversible? As defenders of the constitutional system, we remain cautiously hopeful of the future. After all, partisans of all stripes have a long-term stake in an active, robust legislative branch. Executive initiatives, as popular as they may seem, demand critical review; executive programs must be overseen and evaluated.

What does the future hold? Much depends on a series of unanswered questions: Will members of Congress fulfill their constitutional duties and mount credible critiques of executive power-seeking? Will citizens reignite their interest in politics—to learn, speak, and vote in order to counteract excesses of power, whatever their source? Former representative Hamilton's assessment is on the mark. Citizens, he says, "must understand that they need to get involved if they want our system to improve. They need to know that the nature of this relationship between the representative and the represented—and the honesty of the exchanges between the two—shapes the strength of our representative democracy."[110]

Unfortunately, no advocate of the framers' constitutional design can offer confident solutions to these dilemmas. So we conclude with a question for the twenty-first century. Are the two Congresses ultimately compatible, or are they diverging, each detrimental to the other? The burdens placed on both Congresses become increasingly heavy from an ever-growing and diverse nation in an increasingly complex world. Congress-as-institution is expected to resolve all kinds of problems, not only by processing legislation but also by monitoring programs and serving as an all-purpose watchdog. Legislators struggle to keep abreast of these demands.

Recent events are not encouraging, but the question remains whether representative democracy will in the end be a winning or losing effort. History is only mildly reassuring, and the future poses new and difficult challenges for which the margin of error may be narrower than ever before. And yet representative democracy itself is a gamble. The proposition that representation can yield wise policy making remains a daring one. As always, it is an article of faith whose proof lies inevitably in the future.

Reference Materials

APPENDIX A   Party Control: Presidency, Senate, House, 1901–2013

Congress	Years	President	Senate			House		
			D	R	Other	D	R	Other
57th	1901–1903	William McKinley/ Theodore Roosevelt	31	55	4	151	197	9
58th	1903–1905	T. Roosevelt	33	57	—	178	208	—
59th	1905–1907	T. Roosevelt	33	57	—	136	250	—
60th	1907–1909	T. Roosevelt	31	61	—	164	222	—
61st	1909–1911	William Howard Taft	32	61	—	172	219	—
62d	1911–1913	Taft	41	51	—	228	161	1
63d	1913–1915	Woodrow Wilson	51	44	1	291	127	17
64th	1915–1917	Wilson	56	40	—	230	196	9
65th	1917–1919	Wilson	53	42	—	216	210	6
66th	1919–1921	Wilson	47	49	—	190	240	3
67th	1921–1923	Warren G. Harding	37	59	—	131	301	1
68th	1923–1925	Calvin Coolidge	43	51	2	205	225	5
69th	1925–1927	Coolidge	39	56	1	183	247	4
70th	1927–1929	Coolidge	46	49	1	195	237	3
71st	1929–1931	Herbert Hoover	39	56	1	167	267	1
72d	1931–1933	Hoover	47	48	1	220	214	1
73d	1933–1935	Franklin D. Roosevelt	60	35	1	313	117	5
74th	1935–1937	F. D. Roosevelt	69	25	2	319	103	10
75th	1937–1939	F. D. Roosevelt	76	16	4	331	89	13
76th	1939–1941	F. D. Roosevelt	69	23	4	261	164	4
77th	1941–1943	F. D. Roosevelt	66	28	2	268	162	5
78th	1943–1945	F. D. Roosevelt	58	37	1	218	208	4
79th	1945–1947	Harry S. Truman	56	38	1	242	190	2
80th	1947–1949	Truman	45	51	—	188	245	1
81st	1949–1951	Truman	54	42	—	263	171	1
82d	1951–1953	Truman	49	47	—	234	199	1
83d	1953–1955	Dwight D. Eisenhower	47	48	1	211	221	1
84th	1955–1957	Eisenhower	48	47	1	232	203	—
85th	1957–1959	Eisenhower	49	47	—	233	200	—
86th[a]	1959–1961	Eisenhower	65	35	—	284	153	—
87th[a]	1961–1963	John F. Kennedy	65	35	—	263	174	—
88th	1963–1965	Kennedy/ Lyndon B. Johnson	67	33	—	258	177	—

Congress	Years	President	Senate			House		
			D	R	Other	D	R	Other
89th	1965–1967	Johnson	68	32	—	295	140	—
90th	1967–1969	Johnson	64	36	—	247	187	—
91st	1969–1971	Richard M. Nixon	57	43	—	243	192	—
92d	1971–1973	Nixon	54	44	2	254	180	—
93d	1973–1975	Nixon/ Gerald R. Ford	56	42	2	239	192	1
94th	1975–1977	Ford	60	37	2	291	144	—
95th	1977–1979	Jimmy Carter	61	38	1	292	143	—
96th	1979–1981	Carter	58	41	1	276	157	—
97th	1981–1983	Ronald Reagan	46	53	1	243	192	—
98th	1983–1985	Reagan	45	55	—	267	168	—
99th	1985–1987	Reagan	47	53	—	252	183	—
100th	1987–1989	Reagan	55	45	—	258	177	—
101st	1989–1991	George H. W. Bush	55	45	—	260	175	—
102d	1991–1993	Bush	57	43	—	268	166	1
103d	1993–1995	Bill Clinton	56	44	—	258	176	1
104th	1995–1997	Clinton	47	53	—	204	230	1
105th	1997–1999	Clinton	45	55	—	207	227	1
106th	1999–2001	Clinton	45	55	—	211	223	1
107th	2001–2003	George W. Bush	50	49	1	210	222	3
108th	2003–2005	Bush	48	51	1	205	229	1
109th	2005–2007	Bush	44	55	1	202	232	1
110th[b]	2007–2009	Bush	49	49	2	233	202	—
111th[c]	2009–2011	Barack Obama	58	40	2	257	178	—
112th	2011-2013	Obama	51	47	2	193	242	—

☐ Republican control   ☐ Democratic control

Sources: Encyclopedia of the United States Congress, ed. Donald C. Bacon, Roger H. Davidson, and Morton Keller (New York: Simon and Schuster, 1995), 1556–1558; data compiled by authors for 103d through 112th Congresses.

Note: Figures are for the beginning of the first session of each Congress and do not include vacancies, subsequent shifts, or changes in party affiliation.

[a] The House in the 86th and 87th Congresses had 437 members because of an at-large representative given to both Alaska (January 3, 1959) and Hawaii (August 21, 1959) prior to redistricting in 1962.

[b] The two Senate independents caucused with the Democrats, giving them a 51–49 majority for the purpose of organizing the chamber.

[c] For the Senate, we have counted as Democrats Arlen Specter, who shifted parties in April 2009, and Al Franken of Minnesota, who was sworn in on July 7, 2009.

Capitol Hill is an excellent place to obtain first-hand experience with the U.S. government. With 541 lawmakers (representatives, senators, delegates, and resident commissioners); hundreds of committees and subcommittees; scores of informal caucuses; and three congressional support agencies (the Congressional Research Service, Government Accountability Office, and Congressional Budget Office), intern opportunities abound for students interested in experiencing Congress and its members up close and personal.

Undergraduates will find useful information about landing an internship on Capitol Hill in several sources. One of the best is published under the auspices of the American Political Science Association and is titled *Studying in Washington: Academic Internships in the Nation's Capital.* Political scientist Stephen E. Frantzich discusses how to get a good internship, make the most of the experience, and find a place to live in Washington, D.C.

From our own years of "soaking and poking" around Capitol Hill, we offer five observations about getting congressional experience. First, no central clearinghouse exists for internships. Every congressional office, committee, caucus, and support agency manages its own internship program. Contact information and intern applications may be found on member and committee websites (www.house.gov and www.senate.gov). Many intern opportunities are available for minority students, such as through the Congressional Hispanic Caucus Institute (www.chci.org) or the minority access internship program (www.minorityaccess.org). You must be persistent, patient, and determined to find a position that will be a rewarding learning experience. Not only should you find out what duties and functions will be assigned to you as a volunteer intern (it is sometimes possible to secure paid internships), but you also need to remember that you have something useful to offer. Most congressional offices and committees are understaffed and subject to high staff turnover. Although the market for interns is competitive, congressional lawmakers, committees, and staffers want and need your talent.

Second, develop some notion as to where you would like to intern. Do research on the committee, lawmaker, support agency, or caucus that interests you. Remember that every office has its own personality. Senate offices, for example, are often large enterprises with many staff aides, while House offices are generally smaller. Interns thus will have more opportunities for personal, day-to-day contact with House members than with senators. The best way to determine the office environment is by interviewing people who have worked in a particular office, talking with the internship coordinators at your college or university, or visiting the office yourself.

Third, target your own representative and senators. Many congressional members prefer interns from their own state or district who are likely to be familiar with the geography and concerns of that area. In addition, potential interns probably will have family and friends who are constituents of the lawmaker. Do not hesitate to use your contacts. You might also volunteer to work in a state or district office of the lawmaker. Before accepting an internship, consider your own views and ideals. If your views are conservative, working for a lawmaker who espouses liberal causes may be difficult. However, if you are tactful and open-minded, working for someone whose views differ from yours may be instructive. Because you are a student, an internship with someone who holds divergent ideological views probably will not be held against you later in landing a position.

Fourth, intern placement opportunities are plentiful. Many colleges and universities sponsor semester programs in Washington, D.C. Several schools, including American University, Boston University, Hamilton College, State University of New York, University of Southern California, and University of California run programs in Washington, D.C. Some accept students from other accredited colleges and universities. The Washington Center for Internships and Academic Seminars, in existence since 1975, has placed thousands of students from hundreds of colleges.

Finally, Congress needs and welcomes the influx of new ideas and experiences that interns bring with them. The work at times may be drudgery—answering mail and telephones, entering information into computers, and running errands—but the opportunity to learn about Congress and to pick up political smarts not easily available from textbooks is nearly without equal. You may even want to keep a private journal of your experiences: what you have done and what you have learned. In sum, a volunteer job on Capitol Hill is likely to be rewarding intellectually and in other ways that are impossible to predict.

RESOURCES

The Congressional Intern Handbook. Washington, DC: Congressional Management Foundation, 2006.

Fleishman, Sandra. "The Annual Scramble: Washington Interns Line Up for Their First Lesson—in Housing Supply and Demand." *Washington Post,* May 29, 2004, F1.

Frantzich, Stephen E. *Studying in Washington: Academic Internships in the Nation's Capital.* 5th ed. Washington, DC: American Political Science Association, 2002.

Joyce, Amy. "Interns Seek Their Place in the Sun." *Washington Post,* July 11, 2004, F4.

Lee, Jennifer. "Crucial Unpaid Internships Increasingly Separate the Haves from the Have-Nots." *New York Times,* August 10, 2004, 16.

Manning, Jennifer E., and Elli K. Ludwigson, "Internships, Fellowships, and Other Work Experience in the Federal Government," CRS Report 98-654, July 27, 2010. Provides useful listings and bibliographies of internships.

Maxwell, Bruce. *Insider's Guide to Finding a Job in Washington: Contacts and Strategies to Build Your Career in Public Policy.* Washington, DC: CQ Press, 1999.

Peterson's Internships. Princeton, NJ: Peterson's Guides. Annual.

Reeher, Grant, and Mack Mariani, eds. *The Insider's Guide to Political Internships: What to Do Once You're in the Door.* Boulder, CO: Westview Press, 2002.

Strand, Mark, Michael S. Johnson, and Jerome F. Climer. *Surviving Inside Congress.* Washington, DC: Congressional Institute, 2009.

Washington Center for Internships and Academic Seminars. Address: 2301 M Street N.W., Washington, DC 20037. Telephone: (202) 336-7600 or (800) 486-8921. Website: www.twc .edu/internships/index.htm.

Washington Information Directory. Washington, DC: Congressional Quarterly. Annual publication that provides information about governmental and nongovernmental groups as well as addresses and phone numbers for congressional offices and committees.

CHAPTER 1

Bianco, William, ed. *Congress on Display, Congress at Work.* Ann Arbor: University of Michigan Press, 2000.

Hamilton, Lee H. *How Congress Works, and Why You Should Care.* Bloomington: Indiana University Press, 2004.

Hibbing, John R., and Elizabeth Theiss-Morse. *Congress as Public Enemy.* Cambridge: Cambridge University Press, 1995.

———. *Stealth Democracy: Americans' Beliefs about How Government Should Work.* Cambridge: Cambridge University Press, 2002.

Mayhew, David R. *Congress: The Electoral Connection.* 2d ed. New Haven, CT: Yale University Press, 2004.

CHAPTER 2

Binder, Sarah A. *Minority Rights, Majority Rule: Partisanship and the Development of Congress.* Cambridge: Cambridge University Press, 1997.

Polsby, Nelson W. *How Congress Evolves: Social Bases of Institutional Change.* New York: Oxford University Press, 2004.

Rakove, Jack N. *Original Meanings: Politics and Ideas in the Making of the Constitution.* New York: Vintage, 1997.

Remini, Robert V. *The House: The History of the House of Representatives.* Washington, D.C./New York: Smithsonian Books/Harper Collins Publishers, 2006.

Schickler, Eric. *Disjointed Pluralism: Institutional Innovation and the Development of the U.S. Congress.* Princeton, N.J.: Princeton University Press, 2001.

Swift, Elaine K. *The Making of an American Senate: Reconstitutive Change in Congress, 1787–1841.* Ann Arbor: University of Michigan Press, 1996.

Wirls, Daniel, and Stephen Wirls. *The Invention of the United States Senate.* Baltimore: Johns Hopkins University Press, 2004.

CHAPTER 3

Brunell, Thomas L. *Redistricting and Representation: Why Competitive Elections Are Bad for America.* New York and London: Routledge, 2008.

Canon, David T. *Race, Redistricting, and Representation.* Chicago: University of Chicago Press, 1999.

Ehrenhalt, Alan. *The United States of Ambition.* New York: Random House, 1991.

Fowler, Linda L., and Robert D. McClure. *Political Ambition: Who Decides to Run for Congress.* New Haven, CT: Yale University Press, 1989.

Jacobson, Gary C. *The Politics of Congressional Elections.* 7th ed. New York: Pearson Longman, 2009.

Jacobson, Gary C., and Samuel Kernell. *Strategy and Choice in Congressional Elections.* New Haven, CT: Yale University Press, 1981.

CHAPTER 4

Abramowitz, Alan I. *The Disappearing Center: Engaged Citizens, Polarization, and American Democracy.* New Haven, CT: Yale University Press, 2010.

Dolan, Kathleen A. *Voting for Women: How the Public Evaluates Women Candidates.* Boulder, CO: Westview Press, 2003.

Fiorina, Morris P., Samuel J. Abrams, and Jeremy C. Pope. *Culture War? The Myth of Polarized America.* 2d ed. New York: Pearson Longman, 2005.

Herrnson, Paul S. *Congressional Elections: Campaigning at Home and in Washington.* 5th ed. Washington, DC: CQ Press, 2008.

Jacobson, Gary C. *The Politics of Congressional Elections.* 7th ed. New York: Pearson Longman, 2009.

Thurber, James A., ed. *The Battle for Congress: Consultants, Candidates, and Voters.* Washington, DC: Brookings, 2001.

Wattenburg, Martin. *Is Voting for Young People?* New York: Pearson Longman, 2007.

CHAPTER 5

Arnold, R. Douglas. *Congress, the Press, and Political Accountability.* Princeton, N.J.: Princeton University Press, 2004.

Baker, Ross K. *House and Senate.* 3d ed. New York: Norton, 2001.

Burden, Barry C. *Personal Roots of Representation.* Princeton, N.J.: Princeton University Press, 2007.

Davidson, Roger H. *The Role of the Congressman.* Indianapolis: Bobbs-Merrill, 1969.

Fenno, Richard F., Jr. *Home Style: House Members in Their Districts.* Boston: Little, Brown, 1978.

Fiorina, Morris P. *Congress: Keystone of the Washington Establishment.* 2d ed. New Haven, CT: Yale University Press, 1989.

Price, David E. *The Congressional Experience: A View from the Hill.* 3d ed. Boulder, CO: Westview Press, 2004.

Sellers, Patrick. *Cycles of Spin: Strategic Communication in the U.S. Congress.* New York: Cambridge University Press, 2010.

Swers, Michele L. *The Difference Women Make: The Policy Impact of Women in Congress.* Chicago: University of Chicago Press, 2002.

CHAPTER 6

Aldrich, John H. *Why Parties? The Origins and Transformation of Party Politics in America.* Chicago: University of Chicago Press, 1995.

Baker, Richard A., and Roger H. Davidson, eds. *First among Equals: Outstanding Senate Leaders of the Twentieth Century.* Washington, DC: Congressional Quarterly, 1991.

Cox, Gary W., and Mathew D. McCubbins. *Setting the Agenda: Responsible Party Government in the U.S. House of Representatives.* New York: Cambridge University Press, 2005.

Davidson, Roger H., Susan Webb Hammond, and Raymond W. Smock, eds. *Masters of the House: Congressional Leaders over Two Centuries.* Boulder, CO: Westview Press, 1998.

Green, Matthew N. *The Speaker of the House: A Study of Leadership.* New Haven, CT: Yale University Press, 2010.

Lee, Frances E. *Beyond Ideology: Politics, Principles, and Partisanship in the U.S. Senate.* Chicago: University of Chicago Press, 2009.

Rohde, David W. *Parties and Leaders in the Postreform House.* Chicago: University of Chicago Press, 1991.

Sinclair, Barbara. *Legislators, Leaders, and Lawmaking: The U.S. House of Representatives in the Postreform Era.* Baltimore: Johns Hopkins University Press, 1995.

——— *The Transformation of the U.S. Senate.* Baltimore: Johns Hopkins University Press, 1989.

Strahan, Randall. *Leading Representatives: The Agency of Leaders in the Politics of the U.S. House.* Baltimore: Johns Hopkins University Press, 2007.

CHAPTER 7

Deering, Christopher J., and Steven S. Smith. *Committees in Congress.* 3d ed. Washington, DC: CQ Press, 1997.

Evans, C. Lawrence. *Leadership in Committee: A Comparative Analysis of Leadership Behavior in the U.S. Senate.* Ann Arbor: University of Michigan Press, 1991.

Fenno, Richard F., Jr. *Congressmen in Committees.* Boston: Little, Brown, 1973.

Hall, Richard L. *Participation in Congress.* New Haven, CT: Yale University Press, 1998.

King, David C. *Turf Wars: How Congressional Committees Claim Jurisdiction.* Chicago: University of Chicago Press, 1997.

Krehbiel, Keith. *Information and Legislative Organization.* Ann Arbor: University of Michigan Press, 1991.

Maltzman, Forrest. *Competing Principals: Committees, Parties, and the Organization of Congress.* Ann Arbor: University of Michigan Press, 1997.

Wilson, Woodrow. *Congressional Government.* Reprint of 1885 ed. Baltimore: Johns Hopkins University Press, 1981.

CHAPTER 8

Binder, Sarah A. *Stalemate: Causes and Consequences of Legislative Gridlock.* Washington, DC: Brookings, 2003.

———. Sarah A., and Steven S. Smith. *Politics or Principle? Filibustering in the United States Senate.* Washington, DC: Brookings, 1996.

Cox, Gary W., and Matthew D. McCubbins. *Setting the Agenda: Responsible Party Government in the U.S. House of Representatives.* New York: Cambridge University Press, 2005.

Evans, Diana. *Greasing the Wheels: Using Pork Barrel Projects to Build Majority Coalitions in Congress.* New York: Cambridge University Press, 2004.

Krehbiel, Keith. *Pivotal Politics: A Theory of U.S. Lawmaking.* Chicago: University of Chicago Press, 1998.

Krutz, Glen. *Omnibus Legislating in the U.S. Congress.* Columbus: Ohio State University Press, 2001.

Longley, Lawrence D., and Walter J. Oleszek. *Bicameral Politics: Conference Committees in Congress.* New Haven, CT: Yale University Press, 1989.

Loomis, Burdett, ed. *Esteemed Colleagues: Civility and Deliberation in the U.S. Senate.* Washington, DC: Brookings, 2000.

Oleszek, Walter J. *Congressional Procedures and the Policy Process.* 8th ed. Washington, DC: CQ Press, 2011.

Sinclair, Barbara. *Unorthodox Lawmaking: New Legislative Processes in the U.S. Congress.* 3d ed. Washington, DC: CQ Press, 2007.

Smith, Steven S. *Call to Order: Floor Politics in the House and Senate.* Washington, DC: Brookings, 1989.

CHAPTER 9

Arnold, R. Douglas. *The Logic of Congressional Action.* New Haven, CT: Yale University Press, 1990.

Binder, Sarah A. *Stalemate: Causes and Consequences of Legislative Gridlock.* Washington, DC: Brookings, 2003.

Brownstein, Ronald. *The Second Civil War: How Extreme Partisanship Has Paralyzed Washington and Polarized America.* New York: Penguin Press, 2007.

Edwards, George C. *At the Margins: Presidential Leadership of Congress.* New Haven, CT: Yale University Press, 1989.

Kingdon, John W. *Congressmen's Voting Decisions.* 3d ed. Ann Arbor: University of Michigan Press, 1989.

Mucchiaroni, Gary, and Paul J. Quirk. *Deliberative Choices: Debating Public Policy in Congress.* Chicago: University of Chicago Press, 2006.

Sulkin, Tracy. *Issue Politics in Congress.* New York: Cambridge University Press, 2005.

Theriault, Sean M. *Party Polarization in Congress.* New York: Cambridge University Press, 2008.

CHAPTER 10

Binkley, Wilfred. *President and Congress.* New York: Knopf, 1947.

Bond, Jon R., and Richard Fleisher, eds. *Polarized Politics: Congress and the President in a Partisan Era.* Washington, DC: CQ Press, 2000.

Canes-Wrone, Brandice, *Who Leads Whom? Presidents, Policy, and the Public.* Chicago: University of Chicago Press, 2006.

Edwards, George C., III. *On Deaf Ears: The Limits of the Bully Pulpit.* New Haven, CT: Yale University Press, 2006.

Fisher, Louis. *Constitutional Conflicts between Congress and the President.* 4th ed. Lawrence: University Press of Kansas, 1997.

Gilmour, John B. *Strategic Disagreement: Stalemate in American Politics.* Pittsburgh: University of Pittsburgh Press, 1995.

Howell, William G. *Power without Persuasion: The Politics of Direct Presidential Action.* Princeton, NJ: Princeton University Press, 2003.

Mayhew, David R. *Divided We Govern: Party Control, Lawmaking, and Investigations, 1946–1990.* New Haven, CT: Yale University Press, 1991.

Rudalevige, Andrew. *The New Imperial Presidency.* Ann Arbor: University of Michigan Press, 2005.

CHAPTER 11

Aberbach, Joel D. *Keeping a Watchful Eye: The Politics of Congressional Oversight.* Washington, DC: Brookings, 1990.

Arnold, R. Douglas. *Congress and the Bureaucracy: A Theory of Influence.* New Haven, CT: Yale University Press, 1979.

Foreman, Christopher J., Jr. *Signals from the Hill: Congressional Oversight and the Challenge of Social Regulation.* New Haven, CT: Yale University Press, 1988.

Light, Paul C. *A Government Ill Executed: The Decline of the Federal Service and How to Reverse It.* Cambridge, MA: Harvard University Press, 2008.

———. *The New Public Service.* Washington, DC: Brookings, 1999.

———. *The True Size of Government.* Washington, DC: Brookings, 1999.

Mackenzie, G. Calvin, with Michael Hafken. *Scandal Proof: Do Ethics Laws Make Government Ethical?* Washington, DC: Brookings, 2002.

Rosenbloom, David. *Building a Legislative-Centered Public Administration: Congress and the Administrative State, 1946–1999.* Tuscaloosa: University of Alabama Press, 2000.

CHAPTER 12

Berger, Raoul. *Congress v. The Supreme Court.* Cambridge, MA: Harvard University Press, 1969.

Binder, Sarah A., and Forrest Maltzman. *Advice and Dissent: The Struggle to Shape the Federal Judiciary.* Washington, DC: Brookings, 2009.

Fisher, Louis. *Constitutional Dialogues.* Princeton, NJ: Princeton University Press, 1988.

Geyh, Charles Gardner. *When Congress and Courts Collide.* Ann Arbor: University of Michigan Press, 2006.

Katzmann, Robert A. *Courts and Congress.* Washington, DC: Brookings, 1997.

Noonan, John T., Jr. *Narrowing the Nation's Power: The Supreme Court Sides with the States.* Berkeley: University of California Press, 2002.

Wittes, Benjamin. *Confirmation Wars: Preserving Independent Courts in Angry Times.* Lanham, MD: Rowman and Littlefield, 2006.

CHAPTER 13

Baumgartner, Frank R., et al., *Lobbying and Policy Change: Who Wins, Who Loses and Why.* Chicago: University of Chicago Press, 2009.

Birnbaum, Jeffrey H., and Alan S. Murray. *Showdown at Gucci Gulch: Lawmakers, Lobbyists, and the Unlikely Triumph of Tax Reform.* New York: Random House, 1987.

Cigler, Allan J., and Burdett A. Loomis, eds. *Interest Group Politics.* 7th ed. Washington, DC: CQ Press, 2007.

Hall, Richard L., and Alan V. Deardorff. "Lobbying as Legislative Subsidy." *American Political Science Review* 100 (February 2006): 69–84.

Hojnacki, Marie, and David Kimball. "Organized Interests and the Decision of Whom to Lobby in Congress." *American Political Science Review* 92 (December 1998): 775–790.

Rozell, Mark, Clyde Wilcox, and David Madland. *Interest Groups in American Campaigns: The New Face of Electioneering.* 2d ed. Washington, DC: CQ Press, 2005.

Truman, David B. *The Governmental Process, Political Interests, and Public Opinion.* 2d ed. New York: Knopf, 1971.

CHAPTER 14

Elving, Ronald D. *Conflict and Compromise: How Congress Makes the Law.* New York: Simon and Schuster, 1995.

Hilley, John L. *The Challenge of Legislation.* Washington, DC: Brookings, 2008.

Kelman, Steven. *Making Public Policy.* New York: Basic Books, 1987.

Kingdon, John W. *Agendas, Alternatives, and Public Policies.* Boston: Little, Brown, 1984.

Mettler, Suzanne, *The Submerged State: How Invisible Government Policies Undermine Democracy.* Chicago: University of Chicago Press, 2011.

Schick, Allen. *Congress and Money: Budgeting, Spending, and Taxing.* Washington, DC: Urban Institute, 1980.

———. *The Federal Budget: Politics, Policy, Process.* Rev. ed. Washington, DC: Brookings, 2007.

CHAPTER 15

Crabb, Cecil V., Jr., Glenn J. Antizzo, and Leila E. Sarieddine. *Congress and the Foreign Policy Process.* Baton Rouge: Louisiana State University Press, 2000.

Daalder, Ivo H., and James M. Lindsay. *America Unbound: The Bush Revolution in Foreign Policy.* New York: Wiley, 2005.

Fisher, Louis. *Constitutional Conflicts between Congress and the President.* Lawrence: University Press of Kansas, 2007.

———. *The Constitution and 9/11.* Lawrence: University Press of Kansas, 2008.

Goldsmith, Jack. *The Terror Presidency: Law and Judgment inside the Bush Administration.* New York: Norton, 2007.

Hinckley, Barbara. *Less Than Meets the Eye: Foreign Policy Making and the Myth of the Assertive Congress.* Chicago: University of Chicago Press, 1994.

Howell, William G., and Jon C. Pevehouse. *While Dangers Gather: Congressional Checks on Presidential War Powers.* Chicago: University of Chicago Press, 2007.

Kriner, Douglas L. *After the Rubicon: Congress, Presidents, and the Politics of Waging War.* Chicago: University of Chicago Press, 2010.

Lindsay, James M. *Congress and the Politics of U.S. Foreign Policy.* Baltimore: Johns Hopkins University Press, 1994.

Rundquist, Barry S., and Thomas M. Carsey. *Congress and Defense Spending: The Distributive Politics of Military Procurements.* Norman: University of Oklahoma Press, 2002.

CHAPTER 16

Adler, E. Scott. *Why Congressional Reforms Fail: Reelection and the House Committee System.* Chicago: University of Chicago Press, 2002.

Binder, Sarah A., Thomas E. Mann, Norman J. Ornstein, and Molly Reynolds. *Mending the Broken Branch: Assessing the 110th Congress, Anticipating the 111th.* Brookings Institution Report, January 2009, www.brookings.edu/papers/2009/0108_broken_branch_binder_mann.aspx.

Bok, Derek. *The Trouble with Government.* Cambridge, MA: Harvard University Press, 2001.

Cook, Timothy E. *Making Laws and Making News: Media Strategies in the U.S. House of Representatives.* Washington, DC: Brookings, 1989.

Davidson, Roger H., ed. *Workways of Governance: Monitoring Our Government's Health.* Washington, DC: Governance Institute/Brookings, 2003.

Hamilton, Lee H. *How Congress Works, and Why You Should Care.* Bloomington: Indiana University Press, 2004.

Hibbing, John R., and Elizabeth Theiss-Morse. *Stealth Democracy: Americans' Beliefs about How Government Should Work.* Cambridge: Cambridge University Press, 2002.

Mackenzie, G. Calvin, with Michael Hafken. *Scandal Proof: Do Ethics Laws Make Government Ethical?* Washington, DC: Brookings, 2002.

Mann, Thomas E., and Norman J. Ornstein, *The Broken Branch: How Congress Is Failing America and How to Get It Back on Track.* New York: Oxford University Press, 2006.

Rudalevige, Andrew. *The New Imperial Presidency: Renewing Presidential Power after Watergate.* Ann Arbor: University of Michigan Press, 2005.

Wolfensberger, Donald. *Congress and the People: Deliberative Democracy on Trial.* Washington, DC: Woodrow Wilson Center Press, 2000.

CHAPTER 1

1. Ron Barber's vivid account was related in "Tucson Victim Barber: 'Almost Right Away, He Shot Me,'" *Washington Post,* January 21, 2011.
2. Staff of Congressional Quarterly, *CQ's Politics in America 2010: The 111th Congress,* ed. Chuck McCutcheon and Christina L. Lyons (Washington, DC: CQ Press, 2009), 48.
3. Sheryl Gay Stolberg and William Yardley, "For Giffords, Tucson Roots Shaped Views," *New York Times,* January 15, 2011, A1, A15.
4. Jeremy Duda, "Up Close with U.S. Rep. Gabrielle Giffords," *Arizona Capitol Times,* July 10, 2009; San Pedro Valley News-Sun staff, "Some Seek to Recall U.S. Rep. Giffords . . . Will Congress and the Constitution Let Them?" *San Pedro Valley News-Sun,* August 19, 2009.
5. Quoted in Duda, "Up Close with U.S. Rep. Gabrielle Giffords."
6. Philip Elliott, "They Saved Obama's Bill; Can He Save Their Seats?" Associated Press, March 25, 2010.
7. Randal C. Archibold, "Ranchers Alarmed by Killing near Border," *New York Times,* April 4, 2010, A9.
8. Quoted in Editors, "Send Rep. Giffords Back to Congress; It's a No Brainer," *Arizona Republic,* September 27, 2010.
9. Archibold, "Ranchers Alarmed."
10. Ted Robbins, "Arizonans, Border Patrol Clash over Checkpoints," National Public Radio, August 24, 2007; "U.S. Rep. Gabrielle Giffords Statement on Border Patrol Checkpoint," press release, Office of Gabrielle Giffords, September 21, 2007.
11. Michael Barone, Richard E. Cohen, and Jackie Koszczuk, *Almanac of American Politics, 2010* (Washington, DC: National Journal Group, 2009).
12. Bob Christie, "Rep. Giffords Wins Re-Election in AZ 8th District," Associated Press, November 5, 2010.
13. Quoted in Reid Wilson, "Arizona Dems Have, at Times, Bucked Leadership," *Arizona Capitol Times,* September 23, 2009.
14. Like Representative Giffords, in late 2006 Sen. Tim Johnson, D-S.D., required emergency brain surgery and months of therapy—he had a stroke. Two years later (in 2008, a Democratic year), he handily defeated his GOP opponent.
15. Barone, Cohen, and Koszczuk, *Almanac of American Politics.*
16. Paul S. Herrnson, *Congressional Elections: Campaigning at Home and in Washington,* 5th ed. (Washington, DC: CQ Press, 2008), 272.
17. Sam Rayburn, *Speak, Mr. Speaker,* ed. H. G. Dulaney and Edward Hake Phillips (Bonham, TX: Sam Rayburn Foundation, 1978), 263–264. Rayburn was Speaker from 1940 to 1947, 1949 to 1953, and 1955 to 1961.
18. Quoted in Marin Cogan, "Allen West Gets Brushback from Veteran Bishop," *Politico's On Congress: Congressional News and Analysis Blog,* December 21, 2010, www.politico.com/blogs/glenthrush.
19. U.S. Congress, House Committee on Administrative Review, *Administrative Management and Legislative Management,* 2 vols., H. Doc. 95–232, 95th Cong., 1st sess., September 28, 1977, 2:18–19.
20. Frank E. Smith, *Congressman from Mississippi* (New York: Random House, 1964), 127.
21. David R. Mayhew, *Congress: The Electoral Connection* (New Haven, CT: Yale University Press, 1974), 16.

22. Alan Abramowitz, "A Comparison of Voting for U.S. Senator and Representative in 1978," *American Political Science Review* 74 (September 1980): 633–640; Richard F. Fenno Jr., *The United States Senate: A Bicameral Perspective* (Washington, DC: American Enterprise Institute, 1982), 29ff; Frances E. Lee and Bruce I. Oppenheimer, *Sizing Up the Senate: The Unequal Consequences of Equal Representation* (Chicago: University of Chicago Press, 1999), 111–113.

23. U.S. Congress, Joint Committee on the Organization of Congress, *Organization of the Congress, Final Report*, 2 vols., H. Rep. 103–14, 103d Cong., 1st sess., December 1993, 2: 275–287. Also see Table 5–1 in this book.

24. Glenn R. Parker and Roger H. Davidson, "Why Do Americans Love Their Congressmen So Much More Than Their Congress?" *Legislative Studies Quarterly* 4 (February 1979): 53–61; Kelly D. Patterson and David B. Magleby, "Public Support for Congress," *Public Opinion Quarterly* 56 (Winter 1992): 539–540; and Randall B. Ripley, Samuel C. Patterson, Lynn M. Mauer, and Stephen V. Quinlan, "Constituents' Evaluations of U.S. House Members," *American Politics Quarterly* 20 (October 1992): 442–456.

25. On how the public's perceptions of the policy process affect Congress's institutional image, see John R. Hibbing and Elizabeth Theiss-Morse, *Congress as Public Enemy: Public Attitudes toward American Political Institutions* (New York: Cambridge University Press, 1995).

26. Alexander Hamilton, James Madison, and John Jay, *The Federalist Papers*, No. 51, ed. Clinton Rossiter (New York: Mentor, 1961), 322.

27. *Federalist Papers*, No. 52, 327.

28. Edmund Burke, "Speech to Electors at Bristol," in *Burke's Politics*, ed. Ross J. S. Hoffman and Paul Levack (New York: Knopf, 1949), 116.

29. Ibid.

30. Quoted in *Roll Call*, September 9, 1993, 16.

31. *U.S. Term Limits v. Thornton*, 115 S.Ct. 1842 (1995).

32. Quoted in Mark Carl Rom, "Why Not Assume That Public Officials Seek to Promote the Public Interest?" *Public Affairs Report* 37 (July 1996): 12.

33. For an accessible discussion of different voting systems, see Douglas J. Amy, *Behind the Ballot Box: A Citizen's Guide to Voting Systems* (Westport, CT: Praeger, 2000), 65.

34. For an analysis of members facing this representational difficulty, see Richard F. Fenno Jr., *Home Style: House Members in Their Districts* (Boston: Little, Brown, 1978), especially pages 91–99 and 102–114.

35. Alan I. Abramowitz, *The Disappearing Center: Engaged Citizens, Polarization, and American Democracy* (New Haven, CT: Yale University Press, 2010), 37.

36. Morris P. Fiorina, with Samuel J. Abrams, *Disconnect: The Breakdown of Representation in American Politics* (Norman: University of Oklahoma Press, 2009).

37. Fenno, *Home Style*, 168.

38. Matt Taibbi, "The Worst Congress Ever: How Our National Legislature Has Become a Stable of Thieves and Perverts—in Five Easy Steps," *Rolling Stone*, November 2, 2006, 46.

39. Woodrow Wilson, *Congressional Government* (1885; reprint, Baltimore: Johns Hopkins University Press, 1981), 210.

40. Thomas E. Mann and Norman J. Ornstein, *The Broken Branch: How Congress Is Failing America and How to Get It Back on Track* (New York: Oxford University Press, 2006), 141–191.

CHAPTER 2

1. Joseph J. Ellis, *His Excellency George Washington* (New York: Knopf, 2006), 184–186.

2. Alvin M. Josephy Jr., *On the Hill: A History of the American Congress* (New York: Simon and Schuster, 1980), 41–48.

3. Charles A. Beard and John P. Lewis, "Representative Government in Evolution," *American Political Science Review* (April 1932): 223–240.

4. Jack P. Green, ed., *Great Britain and the American Colonies, 1606–1763* (New York: Harper Torch Books, 1970), xxxix.

5. Edmund C. Burnett, *Continental Congress* (New York: Norton, 1964).

6. *Congressional Quarterly's Guide to Congress,* 5th ed., vol. 1 (Washington, DC: CQ Press, 2000), 9.

7. Burnett, *Continental Congress,* 171. The authors use modern capitalization when quoting the Declaration of Independence (as here) or the Constitution in this volume.

8. Jack N. Rakove, *The Beginnings of National Politics: An Interpretive History of the Continental Congress* (New York: Knopf, 1979), 43.

9. Charles C. Thach Jr., *The Creation of the Presidency, 1775–1789: A Study in Constitutional History* (Baltimore: Johns Hopkins University Press, 1969), 34.

10. James Sterling Young, "America's First Hundred Days," *Miller Center Journal* 1 (Winter 1994): 57.

11. On the Framers' general consensus on the need for a stronger national government, see Lance Banning, "The Constitutional Convention," in *The Framing and Ratification of the Constitution,* ed. Leonard W. Levy and Dennis J. Mahoney (New York: Macmillan, 1987); and John P. Roche, "The Founding Fathers: A Reform Caucus in Action," *American Political Science Review* 55 (1961): 799–816.

12. John Locke, *Two Tracts on Government,* ed. Philip Abrams (New York: Cambridge University Press, 1967), 374.

13. Alexander Hamilton, James Madison, and John Jay, *The Federalist Papers,* No. 48, ed. Clinton Rossiter (New York: Mentor, 1961), 308.

14. Joseph Story, *Commentaries on the Constitution of the United States,* 5th ed., vol. 1 (Boston: Little, Brown, 1905), 396. For Justice Robert Jackson's comments, see *Youngstown Sheet and Tube Co. v. Sawyer,* 343 U.S. 579, 635 (1952).

15. Mark A. Peterson, "The Three Branches of Government: Powers, Relationships and Checks," in *A Republic Divided,* ed. Annenberg Democracy Project (New York: Oxford University Press, 2007), 105.

16. William Howell and Jon Pevehouse, "When Congress Stops Wars," *Foreign Affairs,* September/October 2007.

17. In *Nixon v. United States,* 506 U.S. 224 (1993), the Supreme Court refused to review the Senate's procedures. A former federal judge, Walter L. Nixon Jr. objected that, although he had been convicted by a vote of the full Senate the evidence in his case had been taken by one of the chamber's committees.

18. *Federalist Papers,* No. 65, 396.

19. Emily Field, Van Tassel, and Paul Finkelman, *Impeachable Offenses: A Documentary History from 1787 to the Present* (Washington, DC: Congressional Quarterly, 1999). The only Senate impeachment trial since 1999 was that of Judge G. Thomas Porteous Jr. of the federal district court in Louisiana. See Jennifer Steinhauer, "Senate, for Just the 8th Time, Votes to Oust a Federal Judge," *New York Times,* December 8, 2010.

20. *U.S. v. Rayburn House Office Bldg., Room 2113,* Washington, DC, 20515, 497 F.3d 654 (D.C. Cir. 2007).

21. *Marbury v. Madison,* 1 Cranch 137 (1803).

22. *The Constitution of the United States of America: Analysis and Interpretation,* S. Doc. 92–80, 92d Cong., 2d sess., 1973, 1597–1619. Recent figures are courtesy of Kenneth Thomas, legislative attorney, American Law Division, Congressional Research Service.

23. The figures cited here are from J. Mitchell Pickerill, "Congressional Responses to Judicial Review," in *Congress and the Constitution,* ed. Neal Devins and Keith E. Whittington (Durham, NC, and London: Duke University Press, 2005), 159.

24. *Dred Scott v. Sandford,* 60 U.S. 393 (1856).

25. *Citizens United v. Federal Election Commission,* 130 S.Ct. 876 (2010).

26. *Immigration and Naturalization Service v. Chadha,* 463 U.S. 919 (1983).

27. William N. Eskridge Jr., "Overriding Supreme Court Statutory Interpretation Decisions," *Yale Law Journal* 101 (November 1991): 331–455. Also see R. Shep Melnick, *Between the Lines: Interpreting Welfare Rights* (Washington, DC: Brookings, 1994).

28. Louis Fisher, *Constitutional Dialogues: Interpretation as Political Process* (Princeton, N.J.: Princeton University Press, 1988), 275.

29. Quoted in Charles Warren, *The Making of the Constitution* (Boston: Little, Brown, 1928), 162.

30. Quoted in Charles Warren, *The Supreme Court in United States History* (Boston: Little, Brown, 1919), 195.

31. Wendy J. Schiller, "Building Careers and Courting Constituents: U.S. Senate Representation: 1889–1924," *Studies in American Political Development* 20 (Fall 2006): 185–197.

32. See Charles Stewart III, "Responsiveness in the Upper Chamber: The Constitution and the Institutional Development of the Senate," in *The Constitution and American Political Development,* ed. Peter F. Nardulli (Urbana: University of Illinois Press, 1992), 63–96; and Gregory J. Wawro and Eric Schickler, *Filibuster: Obstruction and Lawmaking in the U.S. Senate* (Princeton, N.J.: Princeton University Press, 2006).

33. Elaine K. Swift, *The Making of an American Senate* (Ann Arbor: University of Michigan Press, 1996), 5.

34. Joel H. Silbey, *The Partisan Imperative: The Dynamics of American Politics before the Civil War* (New York: Oxford University Press).

35. Sarah A. Binder, *Minority Rights, Majority Rule* (New York: Cambridge University Press, 1997), 49.

36. Norman J. Ornstein, Thomas E. Mann, and Michael J. Malbin, *Vital Statistics on Congress, 200*8 (Washington, DC: Brookings, 2002), 110–111.

37. See *Jefferson's Manual, and Rules of the House of Representatives,* Section XI, H. Doc. 105–358, 105th Cong., 2d sess., 1999, 145–148.

38. Nelson W. Polsby, "The Institutionalization of the House of Representatives," *American Political Science Review* 62 (March 1968): 146–147.

39. Norman J. Ornstein, Thomas E. Mann, and Michael J. Malbin, *Vital Statistics on Congress, 2001–2002* (Washington, DC: American Enterprise Institute Press, 2002), 149.

40. Eric Schickler, "Institutional Development of Congress," in *The Legislative Branch,* ed. Paul J. Quirk and Sarah A. Binder (New York: Oxford University Press), 40; Ornstein, Mann, and Malbin, *Vital Statistics on Congress, 2001–2002,* 149.

41. George B. Galloway, *History of the House of Representatives* (New York: Crowell, 1961), 67.

42. Joseph Cooper and Cheryl D. Young, "Bill Introduction in the Nineteenth Century: A Study of Institutional Change," *Legislative Studies Quarterly* 14: 67–105.

43. Barbara Sinclair, *Unorthodox Lawmaking: New Legislative Processes in the U.S. Congress* (Washington, DC: CQ Press, 2005).

44. Andrew J. Taylor, "Size, Power, and Electoral Determinants: Exogenous Determinants of Legislative Procedural Choice," *Legislative Studies Quarterly* 31 (August 2006): 338.

45. Schickler, "Institutional Development of Congress," 40.

46. Roger H. Davidson and Walter J. Oleszek, *Congress against Itself* (Bloomington: Indiana University Press, 1977), 14.

47. Quoted in Eric Schickler, *Disjointed Pluralism: Institutional Innovation and the Development of the U.S. Congress* (Princeton, N.J.: Princeton University Press, 2001), 142.

48. James L. Sundquist, *The Decline and Resurgence of Congress* (Washington, D.C.: Brookings, 1982).

49. Julian E. Zelizer, *On Capitol Hill: The Struggle to Reform Congress and Its Consequences, 1948–2000* (New York: Cambridge University Press, 2004), 153.

50. Roy Swanstrom, *The United States Senate, 1787–1801,* S. Doc. 99–19, 99th Cong., 1st sess., 1985, 283.

51. Gary W. Cox and Mathew McCubbins, *Setting the Agenda: Responsible Party Government in the U.S. House of Representatives* (Cambridge, UK: Cambridge University Press, 2005).

52. Binder, *Minority Rights, Majority Rule,* 17.

53. Ibid., 84.

54. David R. Mayhew, *Congress: The Electoral Connection* (New Haven, CT: Yale University Press, 1974), 95.

55. See David W. Rohde, *Parties and Leaders in the Postreform House* (Chicago: University of Chicago Press, 1991); and Nelson W. Polsby, *How Congress Evolves: Social Bases of Institutional Change* (New York: Oxford University Press, 2004).

56. See Sarah A. Binder and Steven S. Smith, *Politics or Principle? Filibustering in the United States Senate* (Washington, DC: Brookings, 1997); Gregory J. Wawro and Eric Schickler, *Filibuster: Obstruction and Lawmaking in the U.S. Senate* (Princeton, N.J.: Princeton University Press, 2006); and Sarah A. Binder, Anthony J. Madonna, and Steven S. Smith, "Going Nuclear, Senate Style," *Perspectives on Politics* 5 (4): 729–740

57. Schickler, *Disjointed Pluralism,* 13.

58. Ibid., 141–146.

59. Ibid., 213–217.

60. Ibid., 267.

61. Ibid., 267.

62. James Sterling Young, *The Washington Community, 1800–1828* (New York: Harcourt Brace Jovanovich, 1966), 89.

63. Noble Cunningham Jr., ed., *Circular Letters of Congressmen, 1789–1839,* 3 vols. (Chapel Hill: University of North Carolina Press, 1978), 57.

64. Swanstrom, *United States Senate,* 80.

65. Mildred Amer, "Average Years of Service for Members of the Senate and the House of Representatives, First–109th Congresses," Congressional Research Service Report RL32648, November 9, 2005. Earlier studies include Nelson W. Polsby, "The Institutionalization of the House of Representatives," *American Political Science Review* 62 (March 1968): 146–147; and Randall B. Ripley, *Power in the Senate* (New York: St. Martin's Press, 1969), 42–43.

66. Sam Goldfarb, "Term Limits Win Out in Chairmen Picks," *CQ Weekly,* December 13, 2010, 2868.

67. Joe Martin as told to Robert J. Donovan, *My First Fifty Years in Politics* (New York: McGraw-Hill, 1960), 49–50.

68. Ibid., 49.

69. U.S. Congress, House Commission on Administrative Review, *Administrative Reorganization and Legislative Management,* 2 vols., H. Doc. 95–232, 95th Cong., 1st sess., September 28, 1977, 2:17; and U.S. Congress, Senate Commission on the Operation of the Senate, *Senators: Offices, Ethics, and Pressures,* 94th Cong., 2d sess., 1977, Committee Print, xi.

70. Cunningham, *Circular Letters of Congressmen.*

71. Quoted in Galloway, *History of the House,* 122.

72. Quoted in Anthony Champagne, "John Nance Garner," in *Masters of the House: Congressional Leaders over Two Centuries,* ed. Roger H. Davidson, Susan Webb Hammond, and Raymond W. Smock (Boulder, CO: Westview Press, 1998), 148.

73. Martin, *My First Fifty Years,* 101.

74. Colleen J. Shogan, "Blackberries, Tweets, and YouTube: Technology and the Future of Communicating with Congress," *P.S.* 42 (April 2010): 231.

CHAPTER 3

1. *U.S. Term Limits v. Thornton,* 514 U.S. 779 (1995).
2. Arend Lijphart, *Democracies: Patterns of Majoritarian and Consensus Government in Twenty-one Countries* (New Haven, CT: Yale University Press, 1984), 174.
3. See Gary C. Jacobson, *The Politics of Congressional Elections,* 7th ed. (New York: Pearson Education, 2009), 16.
4. See Daniel H. Pink, "Givers and Takers," *New York Times,* January 30, 2004, A21.
5. John D. Griffin, "Senate Apportionment as a Source of Political Inequality," *Legislative Studies Quarterly* 31 (August 2006): 425.
6. Quoted in Judith Havemann, "Moynihan Poses Questions of Balance," *Washington Post,* August 14, 1995, A15.
7. The idea is that proportional differences in the number of persons per representative for any pair of states should be kept to a minimum. The first fifty House seats are taken because the Constitution ensures that each state has at least one representative. The question then becomes: which state deserves the fifty-first seat, the fifty-second, and so forth? The mathematical formula yields a priority value for each seat, up to any desired number. The bottom line is to ensure that states are "entitled to a percentage of representatives equal to [their] portion of the national population."
8. Jeffrey W Ladewig and Mathew P. Jasinski, "On the Causes and Consequences of and Remedies for Interstate Malapportionment of the U.S. House of Representatives," *Perspectives on Politics* 6 (2008): 90.
9. In 1960 the size of the House was temporarily increased from 435 to 437 members to accommodate the admission of Alaska and Hawaii as states. Three years later, after the 1960 census, the House reverted back to 435 members.
10. On the role of the Prohibition issue in the congressional failure to reapportion House seats in 1920, see Daniel Okrent, *Last Call: The Rise and Fall of Prohibition* (New York: Scribner, 2010), 239–241, 327–328.
11. *Congressional Quarterly's Guide to Congress,* vol. 2 (Washington, DC: CQ Press, 2000), 898.
12. Clark Bensen, "The Political Impact of Katrina: Apportionment in 2010," POLIDATA Press Release, December 22, 2006, 2.
13. Haya El Nasser, "For 2010 Census, the Counting Gets Tougher," *USA Today,* October 8, 2008, 1A.
14. Kathleen Hunter, "Minority Lawmakers to Ask Leadership to Address U.S. Census Undercounts," *CQ Today,* October 29, 2007, 6.
15. Sandy Hume, "GOP Fears 2000 Census Plan Will Overestimate Minorities," *The Hill,* May 7, 1997, 1.
16. *Department of Commerce et al. v. U.S. House of Representatives,* 525 U.S. 316 (1999).
17. Quoted in Charles Mathesian, "Dollars and Census," *Government Executive,* December 2007, 50.
18. For a more detailed discussion of districting than is provided here, see Thomas S. Arrington, "Redistricting in the U.S.: A Review of Scholarship and Plan for Future Research," *The Forum* 8 (2010): art. 7.
19. Arizona, Hawaii, Idaho, Montana, New Jersey, and Washington have established commissions for drawing congressional district lines. In the 2010 elections, California voters passed a proposition creating a Citizens Redistricting Commission to redraw its congressional districts. Iowa has a unique process in which the legislature's professional nonpartisan staff conducts the congressional line-drawing.
20. Aaron Blake, "GOP Can Draw Nearly Half of New House Districts," The Fix, *Washington Post* weblog, November 4, 2010, http://voices.washingtonpost.com/thefix/redistricting/gop-can-draw-nearly-half-of-ne.html.

21. Juliet Eilperin, "The Gerrymander That Ate America," *Slate* (online journal), April 17, 2006. Quoted from her book *Fight Club Politics: How Partisanship Is Poisoning the House of Representatives* (Lanham, MD: Rowman and Littlefield, 2006).

22. *Growe v. Emerson*, 507 U.S. 25 (1993). See Susan B. Glasser, "Supreme Court Voids Minnesota Redistricting," *Roll Call*, February 25, 1993, 1.

23. The classic study is still Gordon E. Baker, *The Reapportionment Revolution: Representation, Political Power, and the Supreme Court* (New York: Random House, 1966).

24. In 2001 Georgia Democrats produced a state legislature redistricting plan that tested the notion that a population deviation of plus or minus 5 percent would be acceptable at the state level. A circuit court panel invalidated the scheme and eventually drew up its own plan, which was ultimately affirmed by the Supreme Court. See *Larios v. Cox*, 300 F. Supp. 2d 1320 (N.D. Ga. 2004).

25. Alan Ehrenhalt, "Redistricting and the Erosion of Community," *Governing* (June 1992): 10.

26. The University of Southern California's Annenberg Center has created the ReDistricting Game, a Web application to illustrate how redistricting can be manipulated to achieve political goals; see www.redistrictinggame.org/.

27. *League of United Latin American Citizens v. Perry*, 548 U.S. 399 (2006).

28. *Davis v. Bandemer*, 478 U.S. 109 (1986).

29. See also *Vieth v. Jubelirer*, 541 U.S. 267 (2004), for another example of the Court grappling with issues of partisan gerrymandering but unable to articulate a definitive judicial standard to guide mapmakers.

30. *Congressional Record*, 110th Cong., 2d sess., July 29, 2008, H7285.

31. Sean M. Theriault, *Party Polarization in Congress* (New York: Cambridge University Press, 2008), 83.

32. Nolan McCarty, Keith T. Poole, and Howard Rosenthal, "Does Gerrymandering Cause Polarization?" *American Journal of Political Science* 53 (2009): 678.

33. Rhodes Cook, "Do the Math, and the Result Is: Not Much of a Contest," *Washington Post*, October 6, 2002, B3.

34. The sole incumbent defeated in California between 2002 and 2010 was Republican Richard Pombo, who served from 1993 to 2007.

35. Charles Backstrom, Samuel Krislov, and Leonard Robins, "Desperately Seeking Standards: The Court's Frustrating Attempts to Limit Political Gerrymandering," *PS* (July 2006): 409.

36. See Andrew Gelman and Gary King, "Enhancing Democracy through Legislative Redistricting," *American Political Science Review* 88 (1994): 541–559.

37. Steven Hill, "Schwarzenegger versus Gerrymander," *New York Times*, February 19, 2005, A29. See also Steve Lawrence, "Experts Question Redistricting Plan," *Santa Barbara News-Press*, February 20, 2005, A7.

38. Quoted in Bill Bishop, "You Can't Compete with Voters' Feet," *Washington Post*, May 15, 2005, B2. Also see James G. Gimpel and Jason E. Schucknect, *Patchwork Nation: Sectionalism and Political Change in American Politics* (Ann Arbor: University of Michigan Press, 2003); and Bill Bishop, *The Big Sort: Why the Clustering of Like-Minded America Is Tearing Us Apart* (Boston: Houghton Mifflin, 2008).

39. Quoted in Tricia Miller, "Redistricting Reform Is Tough Task Every Time," *Roll Call*, December 14, 2010.

40. Richard E. Cohen, "Seismic Change for California?" *Politico*, January 5, 2011, www.politico.com/news/stories/0111/47056.html.

41. Definition is from *Shaw v. Reno*, 509 U.S. 630 (1993), quoting *Davis v. Bandemer*, 478 U.S. 109 (1986).

42. Eric Foner, *Reconstruction: America's Unfinished Revolution, 1863–1877* (New York: Harper and Row, 1988), 590.

43. The "retrogression" standard was established in *Beer v. U.S.*, 425 U.S. 130 (1976). The 2006 amendments to the VRA clarified that the congressional intent behind Section 5 of the VRA were to "protect the ability of racial minorities to elect their candidates of choice" (P.L. 109–246).

44. National Conference of State Legislatures, *Redistricting Law 2010* (Washington, DC: National Conference of State Legislatures, 2009), 3.

45. *Shaw v. Reno*, 509 U.S. 630 (1993).

46. *Miller v. Johnson*, 515 U.S. 900 (1995).

47. Ibid.

48. The Court's interpretation of Section 2 of the VRA was laid out most clearly in *Thornburg v. Gingles*, 478 U.S. 30 (1986).

49. *Shaw v. Hunt,* 517 U.S. 899 (1996).

50. *Beer v. U.S.,* 425 U.S. 130 (1976). In *Shaw v. Reno* (509 U.S. 630, 655 [1993]), the Court stated, "A reapportionment plan would not be narrowly tailored to the goal of avoiding retrogression if the State went beyond what was reasonably necessary to avoid retrogression."

51. *Shaw v. Reno*, 509 U.S. 630 (1993); *Miller v. Johnson*, 515 U.S. 900 (1995); *Bush v. Vera,* 517 U.S. 952 (1996); *Shaw v. Hunt,* 517 U.S. 899 (1996).

52. *Miller v. Johnson*, 515 U.S. 900 (1995).

53. *Easley v. Cromartie*, 532 U.S. 234 (2001).

54. *Hunt v. Cromartie*, 526 U.S. 541 (1999).

55. Mara Caputo and Ragan Narash, "Despite Series of Court Rulings, State Officials Are Left Guessing," *CQ Weekly,* August 11, 2001, 1970.

56. Lani Guinier, "What Color Is Your Gerrymander?" *Washington Post,* March 27, 1994, C3.

57. David Lublin, Thomas L. Brunell, Bernard Grofman, and Lisa Handley, "Has the Voting Rights Act Outlived Its Usefulness? In a Word, 'No,'" *Legislative Studies Quarterly* 34 (2009): 547.

58. Ehrenhalt, "Redistricting and the Erosion of Community," 10.

59. Kevin A. Hill, "Does the Creation of Majority Black Districts Aid Republicans? An Analysis of the 1992 Congressional Elections in Eight Southern States," *Journal of Politics* 57 (1995): 384–401.

60. Carol M. Swain, *Black Faces, Black Interests: The Representation of African Americans in Congress* (Cambridge, MA: Harvard University Press, 1995), 205. But see Desmond S. King and Rogers S. Smith, "Strange Bedfellows? Polarized Politics? The Quest for Racial Equity in Contemporary America," *Political Research Quarterly* 64 (2008): 686–703. King and Smith argue, "Republicans benefited from the new districts but not via an unholy alliance" (p. 698).

61. David Lublin, *The Paradox of Representation: Racial Gerrymandering and Minority Interests in Congress* (Princeton, N.J.: Princeton University Press, 1997).

62. Carol M. Swain, "The Voting Rights Act: Some Unintended Consequences," *Brookings Review* 10 (Winter 1992): 51. See also Lublin, *Paradox of Representation.*

63. Alexander Bolton, "Dems Seek to 'Unpack' Minority Districts," *The Hill,* May 9, 2001, 4.

64. Louis Sandy Maisel, *From Obscurity to Oblivion: Running in the Congressional Primary* (Knoxville: University of Tennessee Press, 1982), 34.

65. Quoted in Jon Margolis, "The Disappearing Candidates," *American Prospect,* January 31, 2000, 32.

66. Alan Ehrenhalt, *The United States of Ambition* (New York: Random House, 1991), 17.

67. The four Capitol Hill campaign committees are the National Republican Senatorial Committee (NRSC), Democratic Senatorial Campaign Committee (DSCC), National Republican Congressional Committee (NRCC), and Democratic Congressional Campaign Committee (DCCC). See Paul S. Herrnson, *Congressional Elections: Campaigning at Home and in Washington,* 4th ed. (Washington, DC: CQ Press, 2004), 90–94.

68. Edward Walsh, "To Every Campaign, There Is a Recruiting Season," *Washington Post*, November 12, 1985, A1.

69. Alice A. Love, "Small Business Group Helps Grow Its Own Grassroots Candidates at Meeting Next Week," *Roll Call*, October 16, 1995, 22.

70. David T. Canon, *Actors, Athletes, and Astronauts: Political Amateurs in the United States Congress* (Chicago: University of Chicago Press, 1990), 2–3, 25–31.

71. David T. Canon, "The Year of the Outsider: Political Amateurs in the U.S. Congress," *The Forum* 8 (2010): art. 6, www.bepress.com/forum/v018/iss4/art6.

72. Michael Janofsky, "Two Congressional Candidates Know They'll Lose, But It's Still Fun," *New York Times*, October 31, 1992, 27.

73. Maisel, *From Obscurity to Oblivion*, 23.

74. William Claiborne, "In Neb., a Gridiron Hero Scores in Political Arena," *Washington Post*, June 14, 2000, A3.

75. This conceptualization is a combination of insights derived from a broad-based, pioneering study of House candidate recruitment by a team of scholars: Cherie D. Maestas, Sara Fulton, L. Sandy Maisel, and Walter J. Stone, "When to Risk It? Institutions, Ambitions, and the Decision to Run for the U.S. House," *American Political Science Review* 100 (May 2006): 195–208; and Stone and Maisel, "The Not-So-Simple Calculus of Winning: U.S. House Candidates' Nomination and General Election Prospects," *Journal of Politics* 65 (November 2003): 951–977.

76. The seminal work on strategic politician theory is Gary C. Jacobson and Samuel Kernell, *Strategy and Choice in Congressional Elections*, 2d ed. (New Haven, CT: Yale University Press, 1983).

77. Shira Toeplitz, "Ohio's Limits Tip Races," *Roll Call*, November 20, 2008, 15.

78. Jacobson and Kernell, *Strategy and Choice in Congressional Elections*, chap. 3.

79. L. Sandy Maisel, Cherie D. Maestas, and Walter J. Stone, "The Party Role in Congressional Competition," in *The Parties Respond*, ed. Paul S. Herrnson (Boulder, CO: Westview Press, 2002), 129.

80. Linda L. Fowler and Robert D. McClure, *Political Ambition: Who Decides to Run for Congress* (New Haven, CT: Yale University Press, 1989).

81. Quoted in Burt Solomon, "A Daunting Task: Running for House," *National Journal*, March 21, 1992, 712.

82. Jacobson, *Politics of Congressional Elections*, 23.

83. Quoted in Mark Binker, "Democrats Still Seeking Senate Candidates," *News and Record* (Greensboro, NC), November 17, 2009, A2.

84. Jacobson, *Politics of Congressional Elections*, 38.

85. See Walter J. Stone, Sarah A. Fulton, Cherie D. Maestas, and L. Sandy Maisel, "Incumbency Reconsidered: Prospects, Strategic Retirement, and Incumbent Quality in U.S. House Elections," *Journal of Politics* 72 (January 2010): 178–190.

86. Ibid.

87. Maisel, Maestas, and Stone, "Party Role in Congressional Competition," 129.

88. Cited in Robin Toner, "Willing Contenders at a Premium in Fierce Fight to Rule Congress," *New York Times*, January 3, 2000, A14.

89. Quoted in Sheryl Gay Stolberg, "Wooed for Congress, Fewer Will Say, 'I Do,'" *New York Times*, October 14, 2003, A22.

90. Jennifer L. Lawless and Richard L. Fox, *It Still Takes a Candidate: Why Women Don't Run for Office*, rev. ed. (New York: Cambridge University Press, 2010).

91. Gary C. Jacobson, *The Politics of Congressional Elections*, 7th ed. (New York: Pearson Education, 2009), 19.

92. Stephen Ansolabehere, John Mark Hansen, Shigeo Hirano, and James M. Snyder Jr., "The Decline of Competition in U.S. Primary Elections, 1908–2004," in *The Marketplace of Democracy,* ed. Michael P. McDonald and John Samples (Washington, DC: Cato Institute and Brookings, 2006), 74–101.

93. Harvey L. Schantz, "Contested and Uncontested Primaries for the U.S. House," *Legislative Studies Quarterly* 5 (November 1980): 559. The linkage between interparty and intraparty competition is sometimes referred to as Key's Law. See V. O. Key Jr., *Parties, Politics, and Pressure Groups,* 5th ed. (New York: Crowell, 1964), 438, 447.

94. Ansolabehere et al., "Decline of Competition in U.S. Primary Elections," 81.

95. L. Sandy Maisel, Cary T. Gibson, and Elizabeth J. Ivry, "The Continuing Importance of the Rules of the Game: Subpresidential Nominations in 1994 and 1996," in *The Parties Respond: Changes in American Parties and Campaigns,* 3d ed., ed. L. Sandy Maisel (Boulder, CO: Westview Press, 1998), 162–164.

96. Maisel, Maestas, and Stone, "Party Role in Congressional Competition," 130ff.

97. Ibid., 132.

98. Larry J. Sabato, "2010 By the Numbers," Center for Politics, University of Virginia, November 11, 2010, www.centerforpolitics.org/crystalball/articles/ljs2010111102/.

99. Raymond Hernandez, "Democrats Carrying Anti-Abortion Banner Put More Congressional Races in Play," *New York Times,* October 26, 2008, 26. See Greg Hitt, "The New Southern Strategy, Democrats Tap Conservative Candidates in GOP Bastions," *Wall Street Journal,* August 7, 2008, A1.

100. Ibid.

101. See Zachary Courser, "The Tea Party at the Election," *The Forum* 8 (2010): art. 5, www.bepress.com/forum/v018/iss4/art5.

102. Richard A. Oppel Jr., "Despite Big Issues, Primaries Prompted Only 17% to Vote," *New York Times,* September 28, 2002, A12.

103. Austin Ranney, "Parties in State Politics," in *Politics in the American States,* ed. Herbert Jacob and Kenneth Vines (Boston: Little, Brown, 1976), 61–99.

104. John F. Bibby, "State Party Organizations," in *The Parties Respond,* 3d ed., ed. L. Sandy Maisel (Boulder, CO: Westview Press, 1998), 20.

CHAPTER 4

1. Rob Ebert, "TEA Party Attendees Speak Out," *Northwestern* (Oshkosh, Wisconsin), October 11, 2009, A1.

2. Andrew Stiles, "Exclusive: Ron Johnson: The Reluctant Candidate (Part I)," Battle '10: Tracking the 2010 Midterm Elections, *National Review On-Line,* October 6, 2010, www.nationalreview.com/blogs/print/248951.

3. Jim Vandehei, "The Wisconsin Race That Says It All," *Politico,* October 12, 2010, www.politico.com/news/stories/1010/43444.html.

4. David Cantanese, "Johnson Balances GOP, Tea Party," *Politico,* July 6, 2010, www.politico.com/news/stories/0710/39408.html.

5. Vandehei, "Wisconsin Race."

6. Stiles, "Exclusive: Ron Johnson."

7. Clay Barbour, "Johnson GOP Nod a Shocker," *Wisconsin State Journal,* May 26, 2010, A1.

8. Ambreen Ali, "Feingold Held Most Town Halls in '10," Congress.org, January 19, 2011, www.congress.org/news/2011/01/19/feingold_held_most_town_halls_in_10.

9. Campaign finance information reported by the Center for Responsive Politics at OpenSecrets.org.

10. Katharine Q. Seelye, "Independent Voters Turned on One of Their Own," *New York Times,* November 4, 2010, A21.

11. Emily Heil, "Quiet Evening in a Building Some Love to Hate," *Roll Call,* November 4, 2010.

12. Scott Bauer, "Wis. Voters Look for Candidates to Create Jobs," Associated Press State and Local Wire, November 2, 2010.

13. Seelye, "Independent Voters." Campaign finance totals reported by the Center for Responsive Politics at OpenSecrets.org.

14. Clay Barbour and George Hesselberg, "Johnson Unseats Veteran Feingold," *Wisconsin State Journal* (Madison), November 3, 2010, A1.

15. Monica Davey, "A Battle of Plaid Shirts and Conflicting Visions," *New York Times,* November 1, 2010, A20.

16. Vandehei, "Wisconsin Race."

17. See Richard G. Niemi, Lynda W. Powell, and Patricia L. Bickell, "The Effects of Congruity between Community and District on Salience of U.S. House Candidates," *Legislative Studies Quarterly* 11 (May 1986): 187–201; and Dena Levy and Peverill Squire, "Television Markets and the Competitiveness of U.S. House Elections," *Legislative Studies Quarterly* 25 (May 2000): 313–325.

18. Theodore E. Jackson Jr., "Brand Marketing in Today's Cluttered Political Marketplace," *Campaigns and Elections* 24 (April 2003): 30.

19. Allison Stevens, "House Candidates in Maryland Striving to Hone Their Messages," *The Hill,* May 8, 2002, 31–32.

20. Quoted in Robin Toner, "In a Cynical Election Season, the Ads Tell an Angry Tale," *New York Times,* October 24, 1994, A1.

21. Parke Skelton, quoted in Mary Clare Jalonick, "How to 'Primary' an Incumbent," *Campaigns and Elections* 22 (May 2001): 35.

22. See Paul S. Herrnson, *Congressional Elections: Campaigning at Home and in Washington,* 5th ed. (Washington, DC: CQ Press, 2008), 166.

23. The figures cited in this chapter for the 2007–2008 cycle were taken from the website of the Center for Responsive Politics, www.opensecrets.org, and from reports issued by the Campaign Finance Institute, Washington, DC.

24. Norman J. Ornstein, Thomas E. Mann, and Michael J. Malbin, *Vital Statistics on Congress, 1999–2000* (Washington, DC: American Enterprise Institute, 2000), 87–88.

25. Quoted in Andy Plattner, "The High Cost of Holding—and Keeping—Public Office," *U.S. News & World Report,* June 22, 1997, 30.

26. *Buckley v. Valeo,* 424 U.S. 1 (1976).

27. Dave Levinthal, "Biggest Election Night Losers: Self-Funded Candidates," Center for Responsive Politics, Open Secrets Blog, November 3, 2010, www.opensecrets.org/news/2010/11/biggest-losers-on-election-night-se.html.

28. Campaign data are drawn from the Federal Elections Commission data compiled by the Center for Responsive Politics, www.opensecrets.org/overview/incumbs.php.

29. Gary C. Jacobson, *The Politics of Congressional Elections,* 7th ed. (New York: Pearson Education, 2009), 47.

30. Thomas B. Edsall, "In Tight Races, Early Cash Means Staying Competitive," *Washington Post,* July 14, 1998, A6.

31. Gary C. Jacobson, "The Effects of Campaign Spending on Congressional Elections," *American Political Science Review* 72 (June 1978): 469–491.

32. Gary C. Jacobson, "Money in the 1980 and 1982 Congressional Elections," In *Money and Politics in the United States: Financing Elections in the 1980s,* ed. Michael J. Malbin (Chatham, N.J.: Chatham House, 1984), 57.

33. Gary C. Jacobson, *The Politics of Congressional Elections,* 6th ed. (New York: Pearson Longman, 2004), 98.

34. Carl Hulse and Adam Nagourney, "Specter Switches Parties: More Heft for Democrats," *New York Times,* April 29, 2009, A1; Kathleen Hunder and Bart Jansen, "Specter's Defection Has Consequences for Balance of Power on Committees," *CQ Today,* April 30, 2009, 8, 12.

35. Herrnson, *Congressional Elections,* 5th ed., 222.

36. Robin Toner, "In Final Rounds, Both Sides Whip Out Bare-Knuckle Ads," *New York Times,* October 21, 1996, B7.

37. Reported in Aaron Blake, "Consultants Account for Half of Campaign Spending, Study Finds," *The Hill,* September 28, 2006, 27.

38. Pew Research Center for the People and the Press, "Internet Gains on Television as Public's Main News Source: More Young People Cite Internet than TV," survey report, January 4, 2011, http://people-press.org/report/689.

39. University of Southern California, Annenberg School of Communications, Norman Lear Center, "Local TV News Largely Ignores Local Political Races," press release, February 15, 2005.

40. Erika Franklin Fowler and Travis N. Ridout, "Advertising Trends in 2010," *The Forum* 8 (2010): art. 4.

41. Chris Cilizza, "The Best Campaign Ads of 2010," The Fix, *Washington Post* weblog, November 18, 2010, http://voices.washingtonpost.com/thefix/fix-notes/the-best-ads-of-2010.html.

42. David T. Canon, "The Wisconsin Second District: History in the Making," in *The Battle for Congress: Consultants, Candidates, and Voters,* ed. James A. Thurber (Washington, DC: Brookings, 2001), 230.

43. Larry J. Sabato and Glenn R. Simpson, *Dirty Little Secrets: The Persistence of Corruption in American Politics* (New York: Times Books, 1996), 156.

44. Quoted in Janet Hook, "Negative Ads a Positive in GOP Strategy," *Los Angeles Times,* September 26, 2006, A10.

45. Stephen Ansolabehere and Shanto Iyengar, *Going Negative: How Attack Ads Shrink and Polarize the Electorate* (New York: Free Press, 1996), 128.

46. Quoted in David S. Broder, "Death by Negative Ads," *Washington Post,* November 3, 2002, B7.

47. Richard R. Lau and Gerald M. Pomper, "Effects of Negative Campaigning on Turnout in U.S. Senate Elections, 1988–1998," *Journal of Politics* 63 (August 2001): 817.

48. Katharine Q. Seelye, "Kentucky G.O.P. Candidate, Livid over Opponent's Ad, Lashes Out," *New York Times,* October 22, 2010, www.nytimes.com/2010/10/23/us/politics/23kentucky .html.

49. Frank Newport, "State of the States: Importance of Religion," Gallup press release, January 28, 2009, www.gallup.com/poll/114022/State-States-Importance-Religion.aspx.

50. Manu Raju, "'Aqua Buddha' Ad Backfires on Jack Conway," *Politico,* October 26, 2010, www .politico.com/news/stories/1010/44222.html.

51. See Howard Kurtz, "Hearing 'Foul,' Stations Pull Political Ads," *Washington Post,* September 20, 2002, A14.

52. General Social Surveys (1972–2004), cited in Martin P. Wattenburg, *Is Voting for Young People?* (New York: Pearson Longman, 2007), 12–16.

53. Pew Research Center for the People and the Press, "Internet Now Major Source of Campaign News," press release, October 31, 2008, http://pewresearch.org/pubs/1017/internet-now-major-source-of-campaign-news.

54. Dan Morain, "Undercover Campaigning on the Web," *Los Angeles Times,* March 21, 2007, A11.

55. Ibid.

56. Quoted in Adam Nagourney, "Politicians Turn to Alternatives to TV Advertising," *New York Times,* October 5, 2002, A1.

57. Merle Miller, *Lyndon: An Oral Biography* (New York: Putnam, 1980), 120.

58. David S. Broder, "Shoe Leather Politicking," *Washington Post,* June 13, 2001, A29.

59. Donald P. Green and Alan S. Gerber, *Get Out the Vote!* (Washington, DC: Brookings, 2004), 40.

60. Dan Glickman, as told to Amy Zipkin, "Landing the Job He Wanted," *New York Times,* April 17, 2005, C10.

61. Paul Houston, "TV and High Tech Send Campaign Costs Soaring," *Los Angeles Times,* October 2, 1986, 121.

62. Jamie Stiehm, "Ben and Jerry's State Offers a Choice of Three Flavors," *The Hill,* November 22, 1995, 26.

63. Glenn R. Simpson, "In Rhode Island, Everyone Goes to Bristol Parade," *Roll Call,* July 9, 1990, 1; Glenn R. Simpson, "Judging from July 4th Bristol Parade in R.I., Chafee Looks Well-Positioned for November," *Roll Call,* July 11, 1994, 21.

64. Ron Faucheux, "Candidate Canvassing," *Campaigns and Elections* (May 1997): 43.

65. Green and Gerber, *Get Out the Vote!* 93–96.

66. Leslie Wayne, "Democrats Take Page from Their Rival's Playbook," *New York Times,* November 1, 2008, A15.

67. Jonathan E. Kaplan, "Large Voter Turnout Was Key to GOP Victory," *The Hill,* November 7, 2002, 17.

68. Emily Cadei and Karoun Demirjian, "Labor's High Hopes Matched by Money," *CQ Weekly Report,* September 29, 2008, 2556–2558.

69. Under the BCRA, individuals can donate $30,400 to national party committees per calendar year during the 2012 election cycle and $10,000 as a combined limit on contributions to state, district, and local party committees. These amounts are adjusted annually for inflation.

70. *Citizens United v.*, 558 U.S. __ (2010), slip op. at 44.

71. Ibid., at 55.

72. David G. Savage, "Corporate Campaign Ads Haven't Followed Supreme Court's Prediction," *Los Angeles Times,* October 27, 2010 (online edition).

73. Michael Luo and Stephanie Strom, "Donor Names Remain Secret as Rules Shift," *New York Times,* September 20, 2010 (online edition).

74. Andy Kroll, "The Billion-Dollar Batting Averages of 2010's Shadow Spenders," *Mother Jones,* http://motherjones.com/mojo/2010/11/american-crossroads-american-action-network-secret.

75. Ibid.

76. Savage, "Corporate Campaign Ads."

77. Quoted in Luo and Strom, "Donor Names Remain Secret as Rules Shift."

78. *Speechnow.org v. Federal Election Commission,* 99 F.3d 686 (2010).

79. Michael P. McDonald, "Voter Turnout in the 2010 Midterm Election," *The Forum* 8 (2010): art. 8.

80. Michael P. McDonald, "The Return of the Voter: Voter Turnout in the 2008 Presidential Election," *The Forum* 6 (2008): art. 4.

81. M. Margaret Conway, "Political Participation in Midterm Congressional Elections," *American Politics Quarterly* 9 (April 1981): 221–244.

82. International turnout figures from the Institute for Social Research, University of Michigan, reported in Pippa Norris, *Electoral Engineering: Voting Rules and Political Behavior* (Cambridge, U.K.: Cambridge University Press, 2004). A sensible review of the question is found in Martin P. Wattenberg, *Where Have All the Voters Gone?* (Cambridge, MA: Harvard University Press, 2002).

83. Pew Research Center for the People and the Press, "Who Votes, Who Doesn't, and Why," October 18, 2006, 4.

84. "Youth Turnout about 20%, Comparable to Recent Midterm Years," CIRCLE: The Center for Information and Research on Civic Learning and Engagement, Jonathan M. Tisch College of Citizenship and Public Service, Tufts University, November 3, 2010, www.civicyouth.org/youth-turnout-about-20-comparable-to-recent-midterm-years/.

85. Data on the results of the act are distressingly incomplete. See Raymond E. Wolfinger and Jonathan Hoffman, "Registering and Voting with Motor Voter," *PS* 34 (March 2001): 85–92.

86. Nina Totenberg, "Supreme Court Weighs Voter ID Requirements," *Morning Edition,* January 9, 2008, www.npr.org/templates/story/story.php?storyId=17942818.

87. Joseph D. Rich, "Playing Politics with Justice," *Los Angeles Times,* March 29, 2007, A23. Rich is former chief (1999–2005) of the voting section in the Department of Justice's Civil Rights Division.

88. *Crawford v. Marion County Election Board,* 553 U.S. ___ (2008).

89. Richard Morin and Claudia Deane, "As Turnout Falls, Apathy Emerges as Driving Force," *Washington Post,* November 4, 2000, A1; Michael Waldman and Justin Levin, "The Myth of Voter Fraud," *Washington Post,* March 29, 2007, A19.

90. Samuel L. Popkin and Michael P. McDonald, "Turnout's Not as Bad as You Think," *Washington Post,* November 5, 2000, B1.

91. Sidney Verba, Kay Lehman Schlozman, and Henry E. Brady, *Voice and Equality: Civic Voluntarism in American Politics* (Cambridge, MA: Harvard University Press, 1995).

92. Samuel L. Popkin, *The Reasoning Voter* (Chicago: University of Chicago Press, 1994), 7.

93. Exit polls, November 2, 2004, and November 7, 2006, reported in *New York Times,* November 9, 2006, P7; and by Ronald Brownstein, "Democrats' Losses Go Far beyond One Defeat," *Los Angeles Times,* November 4, 2004, A1, A17.

94. Alec MacGillis and Jon Cohen, "A Vote Decided by Big Turnout and Big Discontent with GOP," *Washington Post,* November 5, 2008, A5.

95. National House exit poll, Election Center, CNN Politics, November 24, 2010, www.cnn.com/ELECTION/2010/results/polls.main/.

96. Quoted in Richard Morin and Claudia Deane, "How Independent Are Independents?" *Washington Post,* August 2, 2002, A1.

97. Gary C. Jacobson, *The Politics of Congressional Elections,* 5th ed. (New York: Addison, Wesley, Longman, 2001), 108.

98. Martin P. Wattenberg, *The Rise of Candidate-Centered Politics* (Cambridge, MA: Harvard University Press, 1991), 36–39.

99. See Bernard Grofman, William Koetzle, Michael P. McDonald, and Thomas L. Brunell, "A New Look at Split-Ticket Outcomes for House and President: The Comparative Midpoints Model," *Journal of Politics* 62 (February 2000): 34–50.

100. Cited in Jeffrey McMurray, "Conservative Southern Dems Disappearing," *Washington Post,* April 25, 2005, A1.

101. Jacobson, *Politics of Congressional Elections,* 7th ed., 167.

102. Ibid., 167.

103. James E. Campbell, "The Midterm Landslide of 2010: A Triple Wave Election," *The Forum* 8 (2010): art. 3.

104. Angus Campbell, "Surge and Decline: A Study of Electoral Change," in *Elections and the Political Order,* ed. Angus Campbell, Phillip E. Converse, Warren E. Miller, and Donald E. Stokes (New York: Wiley, 1966), 40–62; Raymond E. Wolfinger, Steven J. Rosenstone, and Richard A. McIntosh, "Presidential and Congressional Voters Compared," *American Politics Quarterly* 9 (April 1981): 245–255.

105. Eric M. Uslaner and M. Margaret Conway, "The Responsible Electorate: Watergate, the Economy, and Vote Choice in 1974," *American Political Science Review* 79 (September 1985): 788–803; Samuel Kernell, "Presidential Popularity and Negative Voting: An Alternative Explanation of the Midterm Congressional Decline of the President's Party," *American Political Science Review* 71 (March 1977): 44–46.

106. Roberto Alesina and Howard Rosenthal, *Partisan Politics, Divided Government, and the Economy* (New York: Cambridge University Press, 1995).

107. Joseph Bafumi, Robert S. Erikson, and Christopher Wlezien, "Balancing, Generic Polls and Midterm Congressional Elections," *Journal of Politics* 72 (2010): 705–719.

108. Quoted in Dale Russakoff, "In Tight Arkansas Senate Race, Family Matters," *Washington Post*, August 3, 2002, A1.

109. Jacobson, *Politics of Congressional Elections*, 7th ed., 31.

110. Ibid., 27–28.

111. David R. Mayhew, *Congress: The Electoral Connection*, 2d ed. (New Haven, CT: Yale University Press, 2004).

112. National Election Studies (now called the American National Election Studies or ANES), 1980–2002, summarized in Jacobson, *Politics of Congressional Elections*, 122–126; Thomas E. Mann and Raymond E. Wolfinger, "Candidates and Parties in Congressional Elections," *American Political Science Review* 74 (September 1980): 623.

113. On the first view mentioned in this paragraph, see Morris P. Fiorina, *Congress: Keystone of the Washington Establishment*, 2d ed. (New Haven, CT: Yale University Press, 1989); and Bruce Cain, John Ferejohn, and Morris Fiorina, *The Personal Vote: Constituency Service and Electoral Independence* (Cambridge, MA: Harvard University Press, 1987), esp. chaps. 6–7. For more on the second view, see Glenn R. Parker and Roger H. Davidson, "Why Do Americans Love Their Congressmen So Much More Than Their Congress?" *Legislative Studies Quarterly* 4 (February 1979): 53–61. On the question of whether incumbents' resources are directly tied to votes, see John R. Johannes, *To Serve the People: Congress and Constituency Service* (Lincoln: University of Nebraska Press, 1984), esp. chap. 8.

114. Michael J. Robinson, "Three Faces of Congressional Media," in *The New Congress*, ed. Thomas E. Mann and Norman J. Ornstein (Washington, DC: American Enterprise Institute, 1981), 91.

115. Frances E. Lee and Bruce I. Oppenheimer, *Sizing Up the Senate: The Unequal Consequences of Equal Representation* (Chicago: University of Chicago Press, 1999), chap. 4.

116. Gary C. Jacobson, "Incumbents' Advantages in the 1978 U.S. Congressional Elections," *Legislative Studies Quarterly* 6 (May 1981): 198.

117. Owen G. Abbe, Jay Goodliffe, Paul S. Herrnson, and Kelly D. Patterson, "Agenda Setting in Congressional Elections: The Impact of Issues and Campaigns on Voting Behavior," *Political Research Quarterly* 56 (December 2003): 419.

118. John B. Bader, *Taking the Initiative: Leadership Agendas in Congress and the "Contract with America"* (Washington, DC: Georgetown University Press, 1996).

119. Edward Epstein, "The Search Is On for a Takeover Manifesto," *CQ Weekly*, February 8, 2010, 318.

120. Quoted in Judy Newman, "Do Women Vote for Women?" *Public Perspective* 7 (February–March 1996): 10.

121. Karen M. Kaufmann and John R. Petrocik, "The Changing Politics of American Men: Understanding the Sources of the Gender Gap," *American Journal of Political Science* 43 (July 1999): 864–887.

122. Quoted in Barbara Vobejda, "Fragmentation of Society Formidable Challenge to Candidates, Report Says," *Washington Post*, March 7, 1996, A15.

123. See Bruce I. Oppenheimer, James A. Stimson, and Richard W. Waterman, "Interpreting U.S. Congressional Elections: The Exposure Thesis," *Legislative Studies Quarterly* 11 (1986): 227–247.

124. Campbell, "Midterm Landslide of 2010."

125. See the symposium edited by James E. Campbell, "Forecasts of the 2010 Midterm Election," in *PS: Political Science and Politics* 43 (October 2010): 625–641.

126. For a discussion of these reversals, see Gary Miller and Norman Schofield, "Activists and Partisan Realignment in the United States," *American Political Science Review* 97 (May 2003): 245–260.

127. Jacobson, *Politics of Congressional Elections*, 6th ed., 249–253.

128. Delegates to the parties' national conventions were analyzed in a classic study by Herbert McCloskey, Paul Hoffman, and Rosemary O'Hara, "Issue Conflict and Consensus among Party Leaders and Followers," *American Political Science Review* 54 (1950): 406–427.

129. The "middlingness" of the citizenry is vigorously argued in Morris P. Fiorina, with Samuel J. Abrams and Jeremy C. Pope, *Culture War? The Myth of a Polarized America* (New York: Pearson-Longman, 2005).

130. Alan I. Abramowitz, *The Disappearing Center: Engaged Citizens, Polarization, and American Democracy* (New Haven, CT: Yale University Press, 2010). See also Pew Research Center for the People and the Press, "The 2004 Political Landscape: Evenly Divided and Increasingly Polarized," survey report, November 5, 2003, www.people-press.org/reports/.

131. David W. Brady, "Electoral Realignments in the U.S. House of Representatives," in *Congress and Policy Change,* ed. Gerald C. Wright Jr., Leroy N. Reiselbach, and Lawrence C. Dodd (New York: Agathon Press, 1986), 46–69.

132. Campbell, "Midterm Landslide of 2010."

133. Warren E. Miller and Donald E. Stokes, "Constituency Influence in Congress," *American Political Science Review* 57 (March 1963): 45–57.

134. Tracy Sulkin, *Issue Politics in Congress* (New York: Cambridge University Press, 2005), 2.

135. Ibid., 177.

CHAPTER 5

1. "Baucus Says He Will Lead Health-Care Overhaul," Associated Press State and Local Wire, October 18, 2008.

2. Ezra Klein, "The Sleeper of the Senate," *American Prospect,* November 6, 2008, 23.

3. Staff of Congressional Quarterly, *CQ's Politics in America 2008: The 110th Congress,* ed. Jackie Koszczuk and Martha Angle (Washington, DC: CQ Press, 2007), 597.

4. John K. Inglehart, "The New Medicare Prescription-Drug Benefit—A Pure Power Play," *New England Journal of Medicine* 350 (2004): 826–833.

5. *CQ's Politics in America 2008: The 110th Congress,* 598.

6. "High Plains Grifters: A Misguided Senate Plan Repackages Agricultural Welfare as Disaster Relief" (editorial), *Washington Post,* October 28, 2007, B6.

7. Rachel Van Dongen, "110th Senate Committees: Finance," *CQ Weekly,* November 13, 2006, 3029.

8. Amy Goldstein, "Hill Supports Medicare Boost to Rural Areas," *Washington Post,* October 20, 2003, A1.

9. Roger H. Davidson, *The Role of the Congressman* (Indianapolis: Bobbs-Merrill, 1969), 199.

10. Center for Responsive Politics, "Net Worth, 2009," November 17, 2010, www.opensecrets.org/pfds/index.php.

11. John Stuart Mill, *Considerations on Representative Government* (London: Longmans, Green, 1967 [1861]), quoted in Lisa Schwindt-Bayer and William Mishler, "An Integrated Model of Women's Representation," *Journal of Politics* 67 (2005): 413.

12. Hannah Finichel Pitkin, *The Concept of Representation* (Berkeley: University of California Press, 1967), 166.

13. Susan Welch and John R. Hibbing, "Hispanic Representation in the U.S. Congress," *Social Science Quarterly* 64 (June 1984): 328–335; Charles Tien and Dena Levy, "Asian-American and Hispanic Representation in the U.S. House of Representatives" (paper presented at the Midwest Political Science Association, Chicago, April 1998).

14. See David T. Canon, *Race, Redistricting, and Representation: The Unintended Consequences of Black Majority Districts* (Chicago: University of Chicago Press, 1999); Brinck Kerr and Will Miller, "Latino Representation, It's Direct and Indirect," *American Journal of Political Science* 41(1997): 1066–1071; Michele L. Swers, *The Difference Women Make* (Chicago: University of Chicago Press, 2002); and Sue Thomas, *How Women Legislate* (New York: Oxford University Press, 1994).

15. See Claudine Gay, "Spirals of Trust? The Effect of Descriptive Representation on the Relationship between Citizens and Their Government," *American Journal of Political Science* 46 (2002): 717–732; John D. Griffin and Michael Keane, "Descriptive Representation and the Composition of African American Turnout," *American Journal of Political Science* 50 (2006): 998–1012; and Katherine Tate, "The Political Representation of Blacks in Congress: Does Race Matter?" *Legislative Studies Quarterly* 26 (2001): 623–638.

16. Data on characteristics of members are found in Jennifer E. Manning, "Membership of the 112th Congress: A Profile," Congressional Research Service Report No. R41647, March 1, 2011.

17. Alan Ehrenhalt, *The United States of Ambition: Politicians, Power, and the Pursuit of Office* (New York: Times Books, 1992), 16.

18. William T. Bianco, "Last Post for 'The Greatest Generation': The Policy Implications of the Decline of Military Experience in the U.S. Congress," *Legislative Studies Quarterly* 30 (February 2005): 85–102.

19. Betsy Rothstein, "Congresswomen Press Women's Health Issues," *The Hill,* February 24, 1999, 19; Maureen Dowd, "Growing Sorority in Congress Edges into the Ol' Boys' Club," *New York Times,* March 5, 1993, A1, A18.

20. Kerry L. Haynie, "African Americans and the New Politics of Inclusion: A Representational Dilemma?" In *Congress Reconsidered,* 8th ed., ed. Lawrence C. Dodd and Bruce I. Oppenheimer (Washington, DC: CQ Press, 2005).

21. Thomas L. Brunell, Christopher J. Anderson, and Rachel K. Cremona, "Descriptive Representation, District Demography, and Attitudes toward Congress among African Americans," *Legislative Studies Quarterly* 33 (2008): 223–242.

22. Katherine Tate, "The Political Representation of Blacks in Congress: Does Race Matter?" *Legislative Studies Quarterly* 26 (November 2001): 631.

23. Janet M. Box-Steffensmeier, David C. Kimball, Scott R. Meinke, and Katherine Tate, "The Effects of Political Representation on the Electoral Advantages of Incumbents," *Political Research Quarterly* 56 (September 2003): 264.

24. See Canon, *Race, Redistricting, and Representation*; and Kerry L. Haynie, *African American Legislators in the American States* (New York: Columbia University Press, 2001).

25. Katrina L. Gamble, "Black Political Representation: An Examination of Legislative Activity within U.S. House Committees," *Legislative Studies Quarterly* 32 (2007): 421–448; Michael D. Minta, "Legislative Oversight and the Substantive Representation of Black and Latino Interests in Congress," *Legislative Studies Quarterly* 34 (2009): 193–218.

26. Inter-Parliamentary Union, "Women in National Parliaments," December 31, 2010, www.ipu .org/wmn-e/classif.htm.

27. The pioneering study of this subject is Irwin N. Gertzog, *Congressional Women: Their Recruitment, Treatment, and Behavior* (New York: Praeger, 1984). Two more recent studies are Barbara C. Burrell, *A Woman's Place Is in the House* (Ann Arbor: University of Michigan Press, 1994); and Richard Logan Fox, *Gender Dynamics in Congressional Elections* (Thousand Oaks, CA: Sage, 1997).

28. Quoted in Sheryl Gay Stolberg, "Working Mothers Swaying Senate Debate, as Senators," *New York Times,* June 7, 2003, A3.

29. Jamie Stiehm, "In Senate, Sisterhood Can Override Party," *The Hill,* November 22, 1995, 16.

30. Arturo Vega and Juanita Firestone, "The Effects of Gender on Congressional Behavior and the Substantive Representation of Women," *Legislative Studies Quarterly* 20 (May 1995): 213–222.

31. Quoted in Richard E. Cohen, "Member Moms," *National Journal,* April 7, 2007, 16.

32. Quoted in ibid., 19.

33. Kirk Victor, "Still an Old Boys' Club?" *National Journal,* March 12, 2005, 750, 752.

34. See Kathleen A. Dolan, *Voting for Women: How the Public Evaluates Women Candidates* (Boulder, CO: Westview Press, 2003); Leonie Huddy and Nayda Terkildsen, "Gender Stereotypes and the Perception of Male and Female Candidates," *American Journal of Political Science* 37 (1993): 119–147.

35. Michele Swers, "Building a Reputation on National Security: The Impact of Stereotypes Related to Gender and Military Experience," *Legislative Studies Quarterly* 32 (2007): 559–595.

36. "Cicilline Becomes 4th Openly Gay Congress Member," *Boston Globe,* January 5, 2011, www .boston.com/news/local/rhode_island/articles/2011/01/05/cicilline_to_become_4th_ openly_gay_congress_member/.

37. Donald P. Haider-Markel, Mark R. Joslyn, and Chad J. Kniss, "Minority Group Interests and Political Representation: Gay Elected Officials in the Policy Process," *Journal of Politics* 62 (2000): 568–577.

38. Quoted in Erika Niedowski, "Four Walk Out of the Closet and toward the House," *CQ Weekly,* April 25, 1998, 1051.

39. Pew Forum on Religion and Public Life, *U.S. Religious Landscapes Survey,* February 2008, http://religions.pewforum.org/reports.

40. Manning, "Membership of the 112th Congress," 1–2.

41. Ibid., 4–5. For tenure figures, see Table 2-1.

42. Charles S. Bullock and Burdett A. Loomis, "The Changing Congressional Career," in *Congress Reconsidered,* 3d ed., ed. Lawrence C. Dodd and Bruce I. Oppenheimer (Washington, DC: CQ Press, 1985), 66–69, 80–82.

43. Jennifer Wolak, "Strategic Retirements: The Influence of Public Preferences on Voluntary Departures from Congress," *Legislative Studies Quarterly* 32 (May 2007): 285–308.

44. Quoted in Shailagh Murray, "GOP Lawmakers Gird for Rowdy Tea Party," *Washington Post,* July 18, 2010, A3.

45. Frances E. Lee and Bruce I. Oppenheimer, *Sizing Up the Senate: The Unequal Consequences of Equal Representation* (Chicago: University of Chicago Press, 1999), 20–23. Also see Robert A. Dahl, *A Preface to Democratic Theory* (New Haven, CT: Yale University Press, 1956).

46. John D. Griffin, "Senate Apportionment as a Source of Political Inequality," *Legislative Studies Quarterly* 31 (2006): 405–432.

47. Bruce I. Oppenheimer, "The Representational Experience: The Effect of State Population on Senator-Constituency Linkages," *American Journal of Political Science* 40 (1996): 1280–1299.

48. Frances E. Lee, "Representation and Public Policy: The Consequences of Senate Apportionment for the Geographic Distribution of Federal Funds," *Journal of Politics* 60 (1998): 34–64. Also see Stephen Ansolabehere, Alan Gerber, and James M. Snyder Jr., "Equal Votes: Equal Money: Court-Ordered Redistricting and the Distribution of Public Expenditures in the American States," *American Political Science Review* 96 (2002): 767–777; Cary M. Atlas, Thomas W. Gilligan, Robert J. Hendershott, and Mark A. Zupan, "Slicing the Federal Government Net Spending Pie: Who Wins, Who Loses, and Why," *American Economic Review* 85 (1995): 624–629.

49. Robert Weissberg, "Collective vs. Dyadic Representation in Congress," *American Political Science Review* 72 (1978): 535–547.

50. Jane Mansbridge, "Rethinking Representation," *American Political Science Review* 97 (November 2003): 515–528.

51. Barry C. Burden, *Personal Roots of Representation* (Princeton, NJ: Princeton University Press, 2007).

52. Richard F. Fenno Jr., *The Making of a Senator: Dan Quayle* (Washington, DC: CQ Press, 1989), 119.

53. Quoted in Adam Nagourney, "Upbeat Schumer Battles Polls, Low Turnouts, and His Image," *New York Times,* May 16, 1998, A14.

54. Frank E. Smith, *Congressman from Mississippi* (New York: Pantheon, 1964), 129–130.

55. Donald R. Matthews, *U.S. Senators and Their World* (Chapel Hill: University of North Carolina Press, 1960), chap. 5; Ross K. Baker, *House and Senate,* 3d ed. (New York: Norton, 2001), chap. 2.

56. Barbara Sinclair, *The Transformation of the U.S. Senate* (Baltimore: Johns Hopkins University Press, 1989).

57. Herbert B. Asher, "The Learning of Legislative Norms," *American Political Science Review* 67 (June 1973): 499–513.

58. "Political Incivility: A Weekend of Ugly Discourse Preceded Historic Health Vote," *Cleveland Plain Dealer,* March 22, 2010, www.cleveland.com/nation/index.ssf/2010/03/political_incivility_a_weekend.html.

59. Quoted in Thomas E. Cavanagh, "The Two Arenas of Congress," in *The House at Work,* ed. Joseph Cooper and G. Calvin Mackenzie (Austin: University of Texas Press, 1981), 65.

60. David C. W. Parker and Craig Goodman, "Making a Good Impression: Resource Allocation, Home Styles, and Washington Work," *Legislative Studies Quarterly* 34 (November 2009): 493–524.

61. Box-Steffensmeier et al., "Effects of Political Representation," 266.

62. Kenneth M. Bickers and Robert M. Stein, "The Electoral Dynamics of the Federal Pork Barrel," *American Journal of Political Science* 40 (November 1996): 1300–1326.

63. Robert M. Stein and Kenneth M. Bickers, "Congressional Elections and the Pork Barrel," *Journal of Politics* 56 (May 1994): 377–399.

64. Quoted in Louis Jacobson, "For Arkansas, No Abundance of Clout," *National Journal,* February 20, 1999, 475.

65. Damon Chappie, "The New Look of Pork in the 104th," *Roll Call,* January 22, 1996, B19.

66. Quoted in Scott MacKay, "Chafee's New Book Is Tough on Pro-War Democrats, Republicans, President Bush," *Providence Journal,* January 27, 2008.

67. Marian Currinder, *Money in the House: Campaign Funds and Congressional Party Politics* (Boulder, CO: Westview Press, 2009); Eric S. Heberlig, "Congressional Parties, Fundraising, and Committee Ambition," *Political Research Quarterly* 56 (2003): 151–161; Anne H. Bedlington, and Michael J. Malbin, "The Party as Extended Network: Members Giving to Each Other and to Their Parties," in *Life after Reform,* ed. Michael J. Malbin (Lanham, MD: Rowman and Littlefield, 2003), 121–140.

68. Patrick Sellers, *Cycles of Spin: Strategic Communication in the U.S. Congress* (New York: Cambridge University Press, 2010).

69. Davidson, *Role of the Congressman*, 98; U.S. Congress, Senate Commission on the Operation of the Senate, *Toward a Modern Senate*, S. Doc. 94–278, 94th Cong., 2d sess., committee print, 1997, 27; U.S. Congress, House Commission on Administrative Review, *Final Report*, 2 vols., H. Doc. 95–272, 95th Cong., 1st sess., December 31, 1977, 2:874–875.

70. U.S. Congress, Joint Committee on the Organization of Congress, *Organization of Congress, Final Report*, H. Rept. 103–413, 103d Cong., 1st sess., December 1993, 2:231–232.

71. Quoted in Lyndsey Layton, "Capitol's Newcomers Try a Little Openness," *Washington Post*, February 4, 2007, A6. Then House freshman, now senator Kirsten Gillibrand, D-N.Y., identifies the lobbyists she meets and the issues discussed. See Raymond Hernandez, "The Frantic First Days of One of the Members of the Democratic Class of '06," *New York Times*, February 20, 2007, C14.

72. Richard L. Hall, *Participation in Congress* (New Haven, CT: Yale University Press, 1998).

73. Ross A. Webber, "U.S. Senators: See How They Run," *Wharton Magazine* (Winter 1980–1981): 38.

74. Quoted in Cohen, "Member Moms," 17, 21.

75. U.S. Congress, Senate Commission on the Operation of the Senate, *Toward a Modern Senate*.

76. Quoted in Lindsay Sobel, "Former Lawmakers Find Trade Association Gold," *The Hill*, November 26, 1997, 14.

77. Webber, "U.S. Senators," 37.

78. Center for Responsive Politics, *Congressional Operations: Congress Speaks—A Survey of the 100th Congress* (Washington, DC: Center for Responsive Politics, 1988), 47–49.

79. Quoted in *Washington Post*, October 18, 1994, B3.

80. Center for Responsive Politics, *Congressional Operations*, 62–64.

81. U.S. Congress, Joint Committee on the Organization of Congress, *Organization of Congress*, December 1993 2:281–287.

82. Quoted in Vernon Louviere, "For Retiring Congressmen, Enough Is Enough," *Nation's Business*, May 1980, 32.

83. John R. Hibbing, *Congressional Careers: Contours of Life in the U.S. House of Representatives* (Chapel Hill: University of North Carolina Press, 1991), 117 (italics in original).

84. Ibid., 126, 128.

85. Gerard Padro I. Miquel and James M. Snyder Jr., "Legislative Effectiveness and Legislative Careers," *Legislative Studies Quarterly* 31 (August 2006): 348.

86. Ibid.

87. Gary W. Cox and William C. Terry, "Legislative Productivity in the 93rd–105th Congresses," *Legislative Studies Quarterly* 33 (2008): 613.

88. William H. Riker, *The Theory of Political Coalitions* (New Haven, CT: Yale University Press, 1962), 24–38.

89. Pitkin, *Concept of Representation*, 166.

90. Steven Kull, *Expecting More Say: The American Public on Its Role in Government Decisionmaking* (Washington, DC: Center on Policy Attitudes, 1999), 13–14.

91. Henry J. Hyde, "Advice to Freshmen: 'There Are Things Worth Losing For,'" *Roll Call*, December 3, 1990, 5.

92. Quoted in Jamie Stiehm, "Ex-Rep Mike Synar, Who Fought Lobbyists, Succumbs to Brain Tumor," *The Hill*, January 10, 1996, 5.

93. Thomas E. Cavanagh, "The Calculus of Representation: A Congressional Perspective," *Western Political Quarterly* 35 (March 1982): 120–129.

94. John W. Kingdon, *Congressmen's Voting Decisions*, 3d ed. (Ann Arbor: University of Michigan Press, 1989), 47–54.

95. Lawrence N. Hansen, *Our Turn: Politicians Talk about Themselves, Politics, the Public, the Press, and Reform,* part 2 (Washington, DC: Centel Public Accountability Project, 1992), 9.

96. Richard F. Fenno Jr., *Home Style: House Members in Their Districts* (New York: Pearson Longman, 2003), 1.

97. See the discussion of senators' varied constituencies in Lee and Oppenheimer, *Sizing Up the Senate,* chap. 3.

98. Congressional Quarterly, *Congressional Districts in the 2000s* (Washington, DC: CQ Press, 2003), 1027–1028.

99. Fenno, *Home Style,* 4–8.

100. John F. Bibby and Thomas M. Holbrook, "Parties and Elections," in *Politics in the American States: A Comparative Analysis,* 7th ed., ed. Virginia Gray, Russell L. Hanson, and Herbert Jacob (Washington, DC: CQ Press, 1999), 66–112. Also see Thomas L. Brunell, *Redistricting and Representation: Why Competitive Elections Are Bad for America* (New York: Routledge, 2008).

101. Nate Silver, "Number of Competitive House Races Doubles from Recent Years," *Five Thirty Eight, New York Times* weblog, October 10, 2010, http://fivethirtyeight.blogs.nytimes .com/2010/10/10/number-of-competitive-house-races-doubles-from-recent-years/.

102. James L. Payne, "The Personal Electoral Advantage of House Incumbents, 1936–1976," *American Politics Quarterly* 8 (October 1980): 465–482; Robert S. Erikson, "Is There Such a Thing as a Safe Seat?" *Polity* 8 (Summer 1976): 623–632.

103. Thomas E. Mann, *Unsafe at Any Margin: Interpreting Congressional Elections* (Washington, DC: American Enterprise Institute, 1978).

104. Fenno, *Home Style,* 8–27.

105. Thomas P. O'Neill Jr., with William Novak, *Man of the House* (New York: St. Martin's Press, 1987), 25.

106. Nancy Bocskor, "Fundraising Lessons Candidates Can Learn from Tom Sawyer . . . and Other Great American Salesmen," *Campaigns and Elections* 24 (April 2003): 33.

107. Richard F. Fenno Jr., *Senators on the Campaign Trail* (Norman: University of Oklahoma Press, 1996), 131–132.

108. David E. Price, *The Congressional Experience,* 3d ed. (Boulder, CO: Westview Press, 2004), 10.

109. Fenno, *Home Style,* 153.

110. Ibid., 56.

111. Anthony Champagne, *Congressman Sam Rayburn* (New Brunswick, NJ: Rutgers University Press, 1984), 28.

112. Parker and Goodman, "Making a Good Impression," 517.

113. Kingdon, *Congressmen's Voting Decisions.*

114. Brian J. Fogarty, "The Strategy of the Story: Media Monitoring Legislative Activity," *Legislative Studies Quarterly* 33 (August 2008): 445–469.

115. Fenno, *Home Style,* 36, 209; E. Michael Myers, "Millions of Miles from Home," *The Hill,* June 14, 1995, 8.

116. Quoted in Jim Wright, *You and Your Congressman* (New York: Coward-McCann, 1965), 35.

117. Betsy Rothstein, "Hey, Congressman! Someone Is Blocking My Driveway!" *The Hill,* June 9, 2004, 18–19.

118. John R. Johannes, *To Serve the People: Congress and Constituency Service* (Lincoln: University of Nebraska Press, 1984), chap. 5.

119. U.S. Congress, House Commission on Administrative Review, *Final Report,* 1:655; Janet Breslin, "Constituent Service," in U.S. Senate, Senate Commission on the Operation of the Senate, *Senators: Offices, Ethics, and Pressures,* 94th Cong., 2d sess., committee print, 1977, 21.

120. Lee and Oppenheimer, *Sizing Up the Senate,* 56.

121. The National Election Study is now the American National Election Study (ANES). Warren E. Miller, Donald R. Kinder, Steven J. Rosenstone, and the National Election Study, *American National Election Study, 1990: Post-Election Survey,* 2d ed. (Ann Arbor, MI: Inter-University Consortium for Political and Social Research, January 1992), 166–170.

122. Ida A. Brudnick, "Congressional Salaries and Allowances," Congressional Research Service Report RL30064, January 4, 2011. Also see Congressional Management Foundation, *1999 Senate Staff Employment Study* (Washington, DC: Congressional Management Foundation, 1999), 82ff; and Congressional Management Foundation, *2000 House Staff Employment Study* (Washington, DC: Congressional Management Foundation, 2000), 48–49.

123. Congressional Management Foundation, *1999 Senate Staff Employment Study,* 88–89; and Congressional Management Foundation, *2000 House Staff Employment Study,* 1–2.

124. Cited in C. Simon Davidson, "Congressional Office Off-Limits for Members' Campaigns," *Roll Call,* April 16, 2007, 8.

125. Quoted in Charles R. Babcock, "Frankly, an Election-Year Avalanche," *Washington Post,* September 19, 1988, A19.

126. John Pontius, "Congressional Official Mail Costs," Congressional Research Service Report RL34188, August 16, 2010.

127. Quoted in David Burnham, "Congress's Computer Subsidy," *New York Times Magazine,* November 2, 1980, 98.

128. Brian Wingfield, "The Latest Initiative in Congress: Blogging," *New York Times,* February 24, 2005, E4; Jennifer Bendery, "Social Media Goes Viral on Capitol Hill," *Roll Call,* February 7, 2011, 1; Michael D. Shear, "G.O.P. to Open House to Electronic Devices," *New York Times,* December 25, 2010, A16.

129. E. Scott Adler, Chariti E. Gent, and Cary B. Overmeyer, "The Home Style Homepage: Legislator Use of the World Wide Web for Constituency Contact," *Legislative Studies Quarterly* 23 (November 1998): 585–595.

130. Dana Milbank, "A Tale of 140 Characters, Plus the Ones in Congress," *Washington Post,* February 25, 2009, A3.

131. Charles Bosley, "Senate Communications with the Public," in U.S. Senate, Commission on the Operation of the Senate, *Senate Communications with the Public,* 94th Cong., 2d sess., 1977, 17.

132. For descriptions of the studios, see Michael J. Robinson, "Three Faces of Congressional Media," in *The New Congress,* ed. Thomas E. Mann and Norman J. Ornstein (Washington, DC: American Enterprise Institute, 1981), 62–63; and Martin Tolchin, "TV Studio Serves Congress," *New York Times,* March 7, 1984, C22.

133. Tolchin, "TV Studio Serves Congress."

134. R. Douglas Arnold, *Congress, the Press, and Political Accountability* (Princeton, NJ: Princeton University Press, 2004).

135. Brian F. Schaffner, "Local News Coverage and the Incumbency Advantage in the U.S. House," *Legislative Studies Quarterly* 31 (November 2006): 491–511.

136. Robinson, "Three Faces of Congressional Media," 80–81.

137. Peter Clarke and Susan H. Evans, *Covering Campaigns: Journalism in Congressional Elections* (Stanford, CA: Stanford University Press, 1983). See also Charles M. Tidmarch and Brad S. Karp, "The Missing Beat: Press Coverage of Congressional Elections in Eight Metropolitan Areas," *Congress and the Presidency* 10 (Spring 1983): 47–61.

138. Robinson, "Three Faces of Congressional Media," 84.

139. Cokie Roberts, "Leadership and the Media in the 101st Congress," in *Leading Congress: New Styles, New Strategies,* ed. John J. Kornacki (Washington, DC: CQ Press, 1990), 94.

140. Markus Prior, "The Incumbent in the Living Room: The Rise of Television and the Incumbency Advantage in U.S. House Elections," *Journal of Politics* 68 (August 2006): 657–673.

141. Bob Benenson and Jonathan Allen, "It's Looking Like Blue Skies All Over Again," *CQ Weekly Report*, November 26, 2007, 3541.

142. Fenno, *Home Style*, 99.

CHAPTER 6

1. Quoted in David M. Herszenhorn, "Before Family and Friends, Passing a Gavel Heavy with Symbolism," *New York Times*, January 6, 2011, A16.

2. Peter J. Boyer, "House Rule: Will John Boehner Control the Tea Party Caucus?" *New Yorker*, December 13, 2010, 59.

3. Paul Kane, "The Rise, Fall, and Rise of John Boehner," *Washington Post*, October 27, 2010, A8.

4. Quoted in Boyer, "House Rule."

5. Lori Montgomery, "Rift over Spending Cuts Tests the GOP," *Washington Post*, February 11, 2011, A1.

6. Quoted in Jennifer Steinhauser, "Fervent G.O.P. Freshmen Ignite Clash on Funds," *New York Times*, February 18, 2011, A1.

7. Peter Roff, "The Republicans' New House Rules," *U.S. News and World Report*, December 23, 2010 (online edition).

8. Quoted in Boyer, "House Rule."

9. Howard Fineman, "The Man Who Would Be Speaker: John Boehner's Improbable Cool," *Newsweek*, September 6, 2010, 17.

10. Quoted in Boyer, "House Rule."

11. *Wall Street Journal*, January 30, 1985, 5.

12. The seminal work on the collective action problem is that by Mancur Olson, *The Logic of Collective Action, Public Goods, and the Theory of Groups* (Cambridge, MA: Harvard University Press, 1965).

13. Barbara Sinclair, *Legislators, Leaders, and Lawmaking* (Baltimore: Johns Hopkins University Press, 1995), 9.

14. Quoted in Carl Hulse, "Hastert, the Reticent Speaker, Suddenly Has Plenty to Say," *New York Times*, May 24, 2004, A17.

15. Quoted in Kerry Kantin, "Rep. Rob Portman," *The Hill*, April 10, 2002, 12.

16. For an excellent discussion of this era, see Gregory Koger, *Filibustering: A Political History of Obstruction in the House and Senate* (Chicago: University of Chicago Press, 2010).

17. Matthew N. Green, *The Speaker of the House: A Study of Leadership* (New Haven, CT: Yale University Press, 2010), 4.

18. Michael Teitelbaum, "You're Off to a Great Start, but Can You Keep It Up," *CQ Today*, February 2, 2007, 1.

19. See Graeme Browning, "The Steward," *National Journal*, August 5, 1995, 2004–2007.

20. Quoted in *U.S. News and World Report*, October 13, 1950, 30.

21. See, for example, Barbara Sinclair, *Majority Leadership in the U.S. House* (Baltimore: Johns Hopkins University Press, 1983).

22. Quoted in John M. Barry, *The Ambition and the Power: The Fall of Jim Wright* (New York: Viking Penguin, 1989), 4.

23. Tom Kenworthy, "House GOP Signals It's in a Fighting Mood," *Washington Post*, December 26, 1988, A8.

24. See Barbara Sinclair, *Unorthodox Lawmaking: New Legislative Processes in the U.S. Congress*, 3d ed. (Washington, DC: CQ Press, 2007), table 6.4, 123.

25. The GOP had wandered in the "wilderness of the minority" for forty years. A. B. Stoddard, "Rejuvenated Gingrich Mounts Media Offensive," *The Hill*, July 10, 1996, 24.

26. Ibid., 165–176.

27. Quoted in Cannon Centenary Conference, *The Changing Nature of the Speakership,* H. Doc. 108–204 (Washington, DC: Government Printing Office, 2004), 62.

28. Quoted in Eric Pianin and Helen Dewar, "GOP Leaders on Hill Find Unity Elusive," *Washington Post,* September 30, 2000, A10.

29. Ben Pershing, "Smith Spars with Leaders," *Roll Call,* March 26, 2003, 13.

30. Mark Leibovich, "Among His Official Duties, Keeping on Top of the 100-Hour Clock," *New York Times,* January 10, 2007, A18.

31. Quoted in Richard E. Cohen, "GOP's Dilemma: Substance Versus Spin," *National Journal,* March 7, 2009.

32. Rep. Jack Kingston, "When Is 100 Hours Not 100 Hours? When You're a Democrat," *Examiner,* January 19, 2007, 18.

33. Ibid.

34. Sarah A. Binder, Thomas E. Mann, Norman J. Ornstein, and Molly Reynolds, *Mending the Broken Branch: Assessing the 110th Congress, Anticipating the 111th,* Brookings Institution Report, January 2009, www.brookings.edu/papers/2009/0108_broken_branch_binder_mann.aspx.

35. Edward Epstein, "Boehner Cracks the Whip on Errant Colleagues," *CQ Weekly,* June 21, 2010, 14–89.

36. Major Garrett, "A Politician's Politician," *National Journal,* January 7, 2011.

37. Joseph J. Schatz, "The Trials Ahead for John Boehner," *CQ Weekly,* November 8, 2010, 2520.

38. John H. Aldrich and David Rohde, "The Logic of Conditional Party Government: Revisiting the Electoral Connection," in *Congress Reconsidered,* 7th ed., ed. Lawrence Dodd and Bruce Oppenheimer (Washington, DC: CQ Press, 2001), 275–276.

39. See "The House in Sam Rayburn's Time," in Nelson W. Polsby, *How Congress Evolves: Social Bases of Institutional Change* (New York: Oxford University Press, 2003).

40. Randall Strahan, Leading Representatives: *The Agency of Leaders in the Politics of the U.S. House* (Baltimore: Johns Hopkins University Press, 2007), xii.

41. See, for example, Green, *Speaker of the House;* Ronald M. Peters Jr., *The American Speakership: The Office in Historical Perspective,* 2d ed. (Baltimore: Johns Hopkins University Press, 1997); and D. B. Hardeman and Donald C. Bacon, *Rayburn: A Biography* (Austin: Texas Monthly Press, 1987).

42. Quoted in Randall Strahan and Daniel J. Palazzolo, "The Gingrich Effect," *Political Science Quarterly* (2004): 107.

43. Quoted in Jonathan Kaplan, "Hastert, DeLay: Political Pros Get Along to Go Along," *The Hill,* July 22, 2003, 8.

44. Alan K. Ota, "New Team Repackages the Right's Thinking," *CQ Weekly,* February 16, 2009, 340.

45. Sometimes exceptions are made to the general norm that top party leaders do not chair committees. During the 107th Congress (2001–2003), Majority Leader Dick Armey, R-Texas, chaired the Select Committee on Homeland Security, which reported the bill signed into law by President George W. Bush creating the Department of Homeland Security.

46. Christopher Madison, "Message Bearer," *National Journal,* December 1, 1990, 2906.

47. Floyd M. Riddick, *Congressional Procedure* (Boston: Chapman and Grimes, 1941), 345–346.

48. Philip Rucker and Paul Kane, "No Looking Back for Pelosi in House," *Washington Post,* December 22, 2010, A3.

49. Ibid., A3.

50. Carl Hulse, "Fractured Democrats Keep Pelosi as Leader," *New York Times,* November 18, 2010, A22.

51. Quoted in Cohen, "GOP's Dilemma."
52. See Charles O. Jones, *The Minority Party in Congress* (Boston: Little, Brown, 1970), 23.
53. Quoted in Jackie Kucinich, "New Whips Work in Tag Team," *Roll Call,* December 6, 2010.
54. Quoted in Jennifer Yachnin, "No 'Sharp Elbows' for Whip Clyburn," *Roll Call,* December 11, 2006, 36. Also see Richard Cohen, "A Different Kind of Whip," *National Journal,* January 20, 2007, 42–44.
55. Carl Hulse, "Democrats Reach Accord on Leadership in the House," *New York Times,* November 14, 2010, A28.
56. Eric Cantor, Paul Ryan, and Kevin McCarthy, *Young Guns: A New Generation of Conservative Leaders* (New York: Threshold Editions, 2010).
57. Quoted in Michelle Cottle, "McCarthyism," *New Republic,* October 26, 2010, 17.
58. Jonathan Kaplan, "New GOP Whip, Roy Blunt Offers Different Style," *The Hill,* November 20, 2002, 4.
59. Michael Doyle, "House GOP's Vote-Getter Off to a Rough Start," McClatchy Washington Bureau, February 11, 2011.
60. Woodrow Wilson, *Congressional Government* (Boston: Houghton Mifflin, 1885), 223.
61. David J. Rothman, *Politics and Power: The United States Senate, 1869–1901* (Cambridge, MA: Harvard University Press, 1966), 5–7.
62. Margaret Munk, "Origin and Development of the Party Floor Leadership in the United States Senate," *Capital Studies* 2 (Winter 1974): 23–41; Richard A. Baker and Roger H. Davidson, eds., *First among Equals: Outstanding Senate Leaders of the Twentieth Century* (Washington, DC: Congressional Quarterly, 1991).
63. See Robert Caro, *Master of the Senate* (New York: Random House, 2002).
64. Rowland Evans and Robert Novak, *Lyndon B. Johnson: The Exercise of Power* (New York: New American Library, 1966), 104.
65. See John G. Stewart, "Two Strategies of Leadership: Johnson and Mansfield," in *Congressional Behavior,* ed. Nelson W. Polsby (New York: Random House, 1971), 61–92; William S. White, *Citadel: The Story of the United States Senate* (New York: Harper and Bros., 1956); Joseph S. Clark, *The Senate Establishment* (New York: Hill and Wang, 1963); and Randall B. Ripley, *Power in the Senate* (New York: St. Martin's Press, 1969).
66. *Congressional Record,* 96th Cong., 2d sess., April 18, 1980, S3294.
67. Quoted in Kathleen Hunter, "Zen and the Art of Walking Softly," *CQ Weekly,* June 29, 2009, 1504.
68. David S. Broder, "Don't Bet on Bipartisan Niceties," *Washington Post,* January 1, 2003, A19.
69. Quoted in Kathy Kiely and Wendy Koch, "Committee Shaped by Party Ties," *USA Today,* October 5, 1998, 2A.
70. See Frances E. Lee, *Beyond Ideology: Politics, Principles and Partisanship in the U.S. Senate* (Chicago: University of Chicago Press, 2009).
71. Shawn Zeller, "2010 Vote Studies: Party Unity," *CQ Weekly,* January 3, 2011, 30.
72. Ibid.
73. Kirk Victor, "Deconstructing Daschle," *National Journal,* June 1, 2002, 610.
74. Quoted in William Welch, "In Reid, Bush Faces a Tenacious Force in the Senate," *USA Today,* December 12, 2006, 13A.
75. Quoted in Kirk Victor, "Getting to 60," *National Journal,* January 13, 2007, 37.
76. Kate Ackley and John Stanton, "Reid Keeps a Short List of Trusted Confidants," *Roll Call,* January 22, 2007, B-16.
77. Karen Tumulty, "Inside Man," *Time,* January 22, 2007, 29.
78. Quoted in ibid.

79. Quoted in Erin Billings, "McConnell Takes the Inside Track," *Roll Call,* January 31, 2007, 18.

80. Quoted in Carl Hulse, "Senate G.O.P. Leader Adapts to an Unexpected Role," *New York Times,* November 30, 2006, A20.

81. Quoted in Carl Hulse and Adam Nagourney, "Senate G.O.P. Leader Finds Weapon in Unity," *New York Times,* March 16, 2010.

82. Ibid.

83. Kirk Victor, "Short on Surprises," *National Journal,* October 28, 2006, 37.

84. Quoted in Jill Zuckman, "Dick Durbin's Passion Ignites Foes' Ire," *Chicago Tribune,* June 17, 2005 (online edition).

85. Massimo Calabresi and Perry Bacon Jr., "Jon Kyl: The Operator," *Time,* April 14, 2006.

86. Susan Davis, "'Draft Cantor' Move Pondered," *Roll Call,* November 14, 2006, 18.

87. *New York Times,* December 6, 1988, B13.

88. David Truman, *The Congressional Party* (New York: Wiley, 1959).

89. Stephen Jessee and Neil Malholtra, "Are Congressional Leaders Middlepersons or Extremists? Yes." *Legislative Studies Quarterly* 35 (2010): 361–392.

90. Sinclair, *Majority Leadership in the U.S. House.*

91. *Congressional Record,* 98th Cong., 1st sess., November 15, 1983, H9856.

92. Quoted in Thomas B. Rosenstiel and Edith Stanley, "For Gingrich, It's 'Mr. Speaker!'" *Los Angeles Times,* November 9, 1994, A2.

93. *Congressional Record,* 94th Cong., 1st sess., January 26, 1973, S2301.

94. Richard E. Cohen, Jake Sherman, and Simmi Aujla, "GOP Taps Freshmen for Prime Spots," *Politico,* December 9, 2010, www.politico.com/news/stories/1210/46216.html.

95. Kirk Victor, "Reid's Smooth Start," *National Journal,* December 9, 2006, 47.

96. Neil MacNeil, *Dirksen: Portrait of a Public Man* (New York: World, 1970), 168–169.

97. Mark Preston, "Daschle May Write Book Chronicling His Times as Leader," *Roll Call Daily Issue E-newsletter,* May 20, 2002, 3.

98. Sidney Waldman, "Majority Leadership in the House of Representatives," *Political Science Quarterly* 95 (Fall 1980): 377.

99. Patrick Sellers, *Cycles of Spin: Strategic Communication in the U.S. Congress* (New York: Cambridge University Press, 2010).

100. *New York Times,* June 7, 1984, B16.

101. Noelle Straub and Melanie Fonder, "GOP Shifts Strategy for New Minority Status," *The Hill,* July 18, 2001, 6.

102. Mark Preston, "Lott Showcases Senators Facing Re-election," *Roll Call,* March 15, 2001, 3.

103. Stephen Gettinger, "Potential Senate Leaders Flex Money Muscles," *Congressional Quarterly Weekly Report,* October 8, 1988, 2776.

104. Eric Heberlig, Marc Hetherington, and Bruce Larson, "The Price of Leadership: Campaign Money and the Polarization of Congressional Parties," *Journal of Politics* 68 (2006): 992–1005.

105. Sinclair, *Majority Leadership in the U.S. House, 96–97.*

106. Gail Russell Chaddock, "Two House Health Care Reform Votes," *Christian Science Monitor,* March 20, 2010.

107. House Democrats disbanded their policy committee at Pelosi's direction. In its place, she established a revamped Steering Committee, which has a policy component (headed by George Miller of California) and a committee assignment component (chaired by Rosa DeLauro of Connecticut). See Erin Billings, "Pelosi Revamps the Steering Committee," *Roll Call,* March 13, 2003, 3.

108. Sen. Byron Dorgan, "Senate's DPC Role Expands as It Begins New Decade," *Roll Call,* January 30, 2007, 4.

109. Quoted in Fred Barnes, "Raging Representatives," *New Republic,* June 3, 1985, 9.

110. Jim Hoagland, "The Price of Polarization," *Washington Post,* May 5, 2005, A25.

111. Gail Russell Chaddock, "Obama Wins His Economic Stimulus Package, but without the Bipartisanship He Sought," *Christian Science Monitor,* February 14, 2009.

112. Erin Billings, "All Together Now, Senate," *Roll Call,* January 4, 2007, 1.

113. Shailagh Murray and Jonathan Weisman, "Iraq Resolution Typifies Rift in Senate," *Washington Post,* February 11, 2007, A3.

114. Lyndsey Layton, "In Majority, Democrats Run Hill Much as GOP Did," *Washington Post,* February 18, 2007, A4.

115. Sean M. Theriault, *Party Polarization in Congress* (New York: Cambridge University Press, 2008).

116. Quoted in Elizabeth Shogren, "Will Welfare Go Way of Health Reform?" *Los Angeles Times,* August 10, 1995, A18.

117. See V. O. Key Jr., *Politics, Parties, and Pressure Groups,* 5th ed. (New York: Crowell, 1964); and Austin Ranney and Willmoore Kendall, *Democracy and the American Party System* (New York: Harcourt Brace, 1956).

118. See Harold W. Stanley and Richard G. Niemi, *Vital Statistics on American Politics, 2007–2008* (Washington, DC: CQ Press, 2007), tables 1–10 and 1–11.

119. Quoted in Jackie Kucinich and Anna Palmer, "House GOP Bulks Up Outreach Operation," *Roll Call,* January 7, 2009.

120. *Congressional Record,* 104th Cong., 1st sess., October 11, 1995, E1926. Rep. Lee H. Hamilton, D-Ind., who made the comment, strongly opposed the overuse of omnibus bills.

121. Lee H. Hamilton, with Jordan Tama, *A Creative Tension: The Foreign Policy Roles of the President and Congress* (Washington, DC: Woodrow Wilson Center Press, 2002), 33.

122. Nick Anderson, "In Shift, GOP Proposes Easing Immigration Rules," *Los Angeles Times,* October 26, 2000, A6.

123. Cantor, Ryan, and McCarthy, *Young Guns.*

124. Quoted in Erin Billings, "GOP Senators Stressing Reform," *Roll Call,* January 24, 2007, 25.

125. Quoted in Richard E. Cohen, "Byrd of West Virginia: A New Job, a New Image," *National Journal,* August 20, 1977, 1294.

CHAPTER 7

1. *Washington Post,* May 14, 1987, A23.

2. *Congressional Record,* 100th Cong., 1st sess., June 25, 1987, H5564.

3. Carl Hulse, "3 Republicans in Race to Lead Appropriations Committee," *New York Times,* December 7, 2010, A18.

4. Brian Faler, "Appropriations Loses Allure in Tight-Budget Congress," *Examiner,* January 31, 2011, 13.

5. Woodrow Wilson coined the term "little legislatures" in *Congressional Government* (Boston: Houghton Mifflin, 1885), 79.

6. The House has five delegates (District of Columbia, Virgin Islands, Guam, American Samoa, and Northern Mariana Islands) and one resident commissioner (Puerto Rico).

7. Quoted in *New York Times,* July 11, 1988, A14.

8. See, for example, Kenneth A. Shepsle and Barry R. Weingast, "The Institutional Foundations of Committee Power," *American Political Science Review* (March 1987): 85–104.

9. See Keith Krehbiel, *Information and Legislative Organization* (Ann Arbor: University of Michigan Press, 1991); and Bruce Bimber, "Information as a Factor in Congressional Politics," *Legislative Studies Quarterly* (1991): 585–606.

10. John W. Ellwood, "The Great Exception: The Congressional Budget Process in an Age of Decentralization," in *Congress Reconsidered*, 3d ed., ed. Lawrence C. Dodd and Bruce I. Oppenheimer (Washington, DC: CQ Press, 1985), 329. For the classic discussion of committee and member roles, see Richard F. Fenno Jr., *Congressmen in Committees* (Boston: Little, Brown, 1973).

11. Roy Swanstrom, *The United States Senate, 1787–1801*, S. Doc. 87–64, 87th Cong., 1st sess., 1962, 224.

12. Lauros G. McConachie, *Congressional Committees* (New York: Crowell, 1898), 124.

13. DeAlva Stanwood Alexander, *History and Procedure of the House* of Representatives (Boston: Houghton Mifflin, 1916), 228; George H. Haynes, *The Senate of the United States: Its History and Practice*, vol. 1 (Boston: Houghton Mifflin, 1938), 272; Ralph V. Harlow, *The History of Legislative Methods in the Period before 1825* (New Haven, CT: Yale University Press, 1917), 157–158.

14. *Cannon's Procedures in the House of Representatives*, H. Doc. 80–122, 80th Cong., 1st sess., 1959, 83.

15. Quoted in *Wall Street Journal*, May 3, 1979, 1.

16. Sam Goldfarb, "Trimming of House Panels Eliminates 73 Committee Slots," *CQ Today*, January 24, 2011, 6,

17. Jessica Brady, "Waxman Reduces Number of Subcommittees; Lineup Set," *National Journal's CongressDaily PM*, December 12, 2006, 10.

18. *Congressional Record*, 104th Cong., 1st sess., January 4, 1995, H33.

19. Theo Emery, "Controversial King Denied Top Immigration Slot," *CQ Today*, January 10, 2011, 5.

20. Sean Lengell, "Democrats Lament Demise of a Committee," *Washington Times*, December 6, 2010, A3.

21. Charles L. Clapp, *The Congressman: His Job as He Sees It* (Washington, DC: Brookings, 1963), 245.

22. Lawrence D. Longley and Walter J. Oleszek, *Bicameral Politics: Conference Committees in Congress* (New Haven, CT: Yale University Press, 1989), 196.

23. Keith Krehbiel, Kenneth A. Shepsle, and Barry R. Weingast, "Why Are Congressional Committees Powerful?" *American Political Science Review* 81 (September 1987): 935.

24. Roderick Kiewiet and Mathew McCubbins, *The Logic of Delegation: Congressional Parties and the Appropriations Process* (Chicago: University of Chicago Press, 1991).

25. Alex Isenstadt, "The Lucre of Landing a Key Committee," *Politico*, January 19, 2011, 20, www.politico.com.

26. James Bornemeier, "Berman Accepts Seat on House Ethics Panel," *Los Angeles Times*, February 5, 1997, B1; *CQ Daily Monitor*, December 11, 1999, 1.

27. Sonni Efron and Janet Hook, "Lugar Now the Man in the Middle," *Los Angeles Times*, December 23, 2002, A7. See Shailagh Murray, "Foreign Relations at Center Stage," *Washington Post*, March 28, 2007, A13.

28. Fenno, *Congressmen in Committees*. Also see Heinz Eulau, "Legislative Committee Assignments," *Legislative Studies Quarterly* (November 1984): 587–633.

29. Christopher J. Deering and Steven S. Smith, *Committees in Congress*, 3d ed. (Washington, DC: CQ Press, 1997), 61–62, 78.

30. Quoted in Nancy Roman, "Freshman Nets Prized Panel by Seeking Leader's Support," *Washington Times*, December 3, 1996, A4. Also see Greg Hitt, "Ways and Means: An Illinois Republican Staged Hard Campaign for Key House Panel," *Wall Street Journal*, January 3, 1997, A1.

31. Shirley Chisholm, *Unbought and Unbossed* (Boston: Houghton Mifflin, 1970), 84, 86.

32. Quoted in Ethan Wallison, "Freshman Democrats Get Panel Waivers," *Roll Call*, June 21, 1999, 20.

33. Reid Wilson, "McConnell Promises Boozman Ag Seat," *National Journal Hotline*, July 7, 2010 (online version).

34. Andrew Beadle, "First Lady's Résumé Won't Impress Seniority System," *CQ Daily Monitor*, November 20, 2000, 9.

35. Quoted in Peter Kaplan and David Mark, "With Election Day Over, the Campaigns Begin in the House," *CQ Daily Monitor*, November 20, 2000, 3.

36. Jim VandeHei, "Would-Be Chairmen Hit Money Trail," *Roll Call*, July 12, 1999, 1.

37. Kelsey Snell, "Caucus Selection of Levin Underscores Power of Seniority," *National Journal CongressDaily AM*, December 9, 2010, 11.

38. *Congressional Record*, 112th Cong., 1st sess., January 5, 2011, H5.

39. Paul Gigot, "Mack Uses Knife on Old Senate Order," *Wall Street Journal*, July 14, 1995, A12.

40. Margaret Kriz, "Gavels Turn Green," *National Journal*, November 18, 2006, 62.

41. Quoted in *Washington Post*, November 20, 1983, A9.

42. Amy Fagan, "Thomas Takes Reins on Social Security," *Washington Times*, February 6, 2005, A3.

43. Anna Palmer, "Cummings Bypasses Issa in Fight over Access to Letters," *Roll Call*, January 31, 2011 (online edition).

44. See David King, *Turf Wars* (Chicago: University of Chicago Press, 1997).

45. Allison Stevens, "No Ordinary Power Grab: Chairman Complains of 'Bold' Power Grab," *CQ Today*, June 23, 2004, 1, 9.

46. Darren Samuelsohn and Robin Bravender, "GOP Takeover Prompts Committee Turf Wars," *Politico*, November 11, 2010, 21, www.politico.com.

47. Rep. Fred Upton, "Don't Dilute Energy and Commerce Clout," *Roll Call*, November 3, 2010, 5.

48. Samuelsohn and Bravender, "GOP Takeover Prompts Committee Turf Wars," 21.

49. *CQ Today*, December 10, 2010, 10.

50. Quoted in Bob Pool, "Survivors Take Stock of Gains against Cancer," *Los Angeles Times*, May 30, 1997, B1.

51. Ralph Vartabedian, "Senate Panel Is Ready to Take IRS to Task," *Los Angeles Times*, September 22, 1997, A1.

52. "Dodd-Frank" refers to Sen. Christopher Dodd, D-Conn., who chaired the Banking, Housing, and Urban Affairs Committee and Rep. Barney Frank, D-Mass., who headed the Financial Services Committee. Senator Dodd retired at the end of the 111th Congress; Frank is the ranking member on Financial Services because of GOP control of the House in the 112th Congress.

53. Jane Norman, "Harkin Plans Hearings on Health Law to Counter GOP," *CQ Today*, January 7, 2011, 2.

54. Darlene Superville, "Congressional Panels Seek 'Real People,'" *Los Angeles Times*, March 25, 2007 (online edition).

55. Elizabeth Brotherton, "Webcasting Goes Mainstream among House Committees," *Roll Call*, March 7, 2007, 3.

56. Sean Piccoli, "Hill Samples 'Third Wave,'" *Washington Times*, June 13, 1995, A8.

57. Warren Leary, "When Astronauts Brief Congress, A Little Levity Goes a Long Way," *New York Times*, June 15, 2005, A16.

58. *Congressional Record*, 107th Cong., 2d sess., July 16, 2002, S6849.

59. Quoted in *Washington Post*, November 25, 1985, A4. Also see Richard L. Hall, *Participation in Congress* (New Haven, CT: Yale University Press, 1998).

60. Quoted in "CQ Midday Update Email," December 14, 2004, 1, www.cq.com.

61. Eric Redman, *The Dance of Legislation* (New York: Simon and Schuster, 1973), 140.

62. Hugh Heclo, "Issue Networks in the Executive Establishment," in *The New American Political System, ed.* Anthony King (Washington, DC: American Enterprise Institute, 1978), 87–124. Also see David E. Price, "Policy Making in Congressional Committees: The Impact of 'Environmental Factors,'" *American Political Science Review* (Fall 1978): 548–574.

63. Molly Hopper, "House Judiciary Committee Seeks Bipartisan Touch," *The Hill,* January 18, 2011, 8.

64. Meghan McCarthy, "Conservative Think Tanks Readying Overhaul Alternative," *National Journal CongressDaily PM,* January 24, 2011, 2.

65. Norris Cotton, *In the Senate* (New York: Dodd, Mead, 1978), 65.

66. *Washington Post,* March 20, 1977, E9.

67. David Whiteman, *Communication in Congress: Members, Staff, and the Search for Information* (Lawrence: University Press of Kansas, 1995).

68. Siobhan Gorman and Richard Cohen, "Hurtling toward an Intelligence Overhaul," *National Journal,* September 18, 2004, 2808.

69. Quoted in *Washington Post,* November 20, 1983, A13.

70. Brett Pulley, "Black Clerics Criticize Torricelli on Minority Hiring for His Staff," *New York Times,* March 21, 1997, A25.

71. Josephine Hearn, "House Staffers Follow Bosses' Footsteps on the Campaign Trail," *The Hill,* October 18, 2006, 4.

72. Quoted in Andrew Taylor, "Security Plan Changes Committee Name, Little Else," *CQ Today,* October 8, 2004, 1.

73. Ibid., 4.

74. *Congressional Record,* 109th Cong., 1st sess., January 4, 2005, H25–H26.

75. *CQ Weekly,* December 27, 2010, 2901.

76. All quotations in this paragraph all taken from Elana Shor, "Rockefeller Releases Deal on Intelligence Budgets," *The Hill,* March 7, 2007, 8.

77. Tim Starks, "Plan to Eliminate House Panel Raises Budgetary Oversight Questions," *CQ Today,* January 5, 2011, 9.

78. Chris Strohm, "House Dems Want Oversight Panel Reinstated," *National Journal CongressDaily PM,* January 19, 2011, 2.

79. Quoted in Roger H. Davidson and Walter J. Oleszek, *Congress against Itself* (Bloomington: Indiana University Press, 1977), 263.

80. E. Scott Adler, *Why Congressional Reforms Fail* (Chicago: University of Chicago Press, 2002), 11.

81. Richard Cohen and Marilyn Serfina, "Taxing Times," *National Journal,* December 23, 2000, 39–61.

82. David Firestone, "G.O.P.'s 'Cardinals of Spending' Are Reined In by House Leaders," *New York Times,* December 2, 2002, A16.

83. Alexander Bolton, "House GOP Puts Taylor on Warning," *The Hill,* February 15, 2005, 1.

84. Quoted in Josephine Hearn, "Pelosi Riles Old Guard Chairmen," *Politico,* January 23, 2007, 4, www.politico.com.

85. John Boehner, "What the Next Speaker Must Do," *Wall Street Journal,* November 5, 2010, A19.

86. Major Garrett, "A Politician's Politician," *National Journal,* January 8, 2011, 35.

87. Mike Lillis, "Speaker Boehner Says No to New Gun Controls," *The Hill,* January 12, 2011, 1; James Oliophant, "Gun Safety Hearings Rejected by Chairman of House Judiciary Committee," *Los Angeles Times,* January 28, 2011 (online edition).

88. Peter J. Boyer, "House Rule," *New Yorker,* December 13, 2010, 68.

89. Tim Starks, "Thornberry Starts with Outreach in Defining New Role as Cybersecurity Coordinator," *CQ Today,* January 12, 2011, 3.

90. Quoted in Kirk Victor, "Getting to 60," *National Journal,* January 13, 2007, 38.

91. David Drucker and Emily Pierce, "Reid to Baucus: Stop Chasing GOP Votes on Health Care," *Roll Call,* July 7, 2009 (online edition).

92. David Nather, "Daschle's Soft Touch Lost in Tough Senate Arena," *CQ Weekly,* July 20, 2002, 1922.

93. Noelle Straub, "Senate Finance Panel Faces July 15 Deadline," *The Hill,* July 3, 2002, 6.

94. Susan Davis, "Pelosi, Boehner Name Eight Members to Ethics Task Force," *Roll Call,* February 1, 2007, 3.

95. Jonathan Weisman, "House Creates New Panel on Ethics," *Washington Post,* March 12, 2008, A1.

96. Alan Ota, "Republicans Look for Input from House High-Tech Team," *CQ Today,* January 25, 2011, 1.

97. *National Journal's CongressDaily AM,* January 30, 2007, 15.

98. *Congressional Record,* 108th Cong., 2d sess., February 14, 2004, S1496.

99. *Congressional Record,* 112th Cong., 1st sess., January 5, 2011, S17.

100. Nather, "Daschle's Soft Touch Lost."

101. *Committee Structure,* Hearings before the Joint Committee on the Organization of Congress (Washington, DC: Government Printing Office, 1993), 779.

102. Curt Suplee, "The Science Chairman's Unpredictable Approach," *Washington Post,* October 15, 1991, A21.

CHAPTER 8

1. *Constitution, Jefferson's Manual, and Rules of the House of Representatives,* H. Doc. 110–162, 110th Cong., 2009, 127. The rules of the Senate are contained in *Senate Manual,* S. Doc. 107–1, 107th Cong., 2002.

2. Donald R. Matthews, *U.S. Senators and Their World* (Chapel Hill: University of North Carolina Press, 1960), chap. 5.

3. Chris Strohm, "Menendez to Introduce Overhaul before Election," *National Journal's CongressDaily PM,* September 1, 2010, 5.

4. See Barry C. Burden, *Personal Roots of Representation* (Princeton, NJ: Princeton University Press, 2007).

5. Quoted in John Solomon, "Family Crisis Shifts Politics," *USA Today,* August 16, 2001, 15A.

6. Deborah Sontag, "When Politics Is Personal," *New York Times Magazine,* September 15, 2002, 92.

7. *National Journal,* April 10, 1982, 632.

8. Reid Wilson, "Partisan Roles Don't Keep Van Hollen, Sessions from Reaching across the Aisle," *The Hill,* March 12, 2009, 3.

9. Quoted in Julie Rovner, "Senate Committee Approves Health Warnings on Alcohol," *Congressional Quarterly Weekly Report,* May 24, 1986, 1175.

10. Woodrow Wilson, *Congressional Government* (Boston: Houghton Mifflin, 1885), 320.

11. Theodore Sorensen, *Kennedy* (New York: Harper and Row, 1965), 184.

12. *Wall Street Journal,* June 2, 1988, 56.

13. *Congressional Record,* 95th Cong., 1st sess., May 17, 1977, E3076.

14. Quoted in Chuck Todd, "So Many Bills of Rights, So Little Time," *National Journal's CongressDaily PM,* August 1, 2001, 1.

15. Peter Baker, "White House Finds 'Fast Track' Too Slippery," *Washington Post,* September 14, 1997, A4. Also see *Congressional Record,* 105th Cong., 2d sess., September 29, 1998, S11133; *Congressional Record,* 106th Cong., 1st sess., January 25, 1999, S979; and Ceci Connolly, "Consultant Offers GOP a Language for the Future," *Washington Post,* September 4, 1997, A1.

16. For information on the drafting process, see Lawrence E. Filson, *The Legislative Drafter's Desk Reference* (Washington, DC: Congressional Quarterly, 1992).

17. *CQ Monitor,* July 24, 1998, 5.

18. Lawrence J. Haas, "Unauthorized Action," *National Journal,* January 2, 1988, 20.

19. Rep. John Boehner, "What the Next Speaker Must Do," *Wall Street Journal,* November 5, 2010, A19.

20. Alex Wayne, "Fight the Curse of the Big Bill," *CQ Weekly,* March 8, 2010, 558.

21. T. R. Reid, *Congressional Odyssey: The Saga of a Senate Bill* (San Francisco: W. H. Freeman, 1980), 17.

22. Paul Singer, "More Bills, More Lawyers for Leg. Offices," *Roll Call,* March 28, 2007, 22.

23. Carroll J. Doherty, "Lots of Inertia, Little Lawmaking as Election '98 Approaches," *CQ Weekly,* July 18, 1998, 1925.

24. Quoted in Margaret Kriz, "Still Charging," *National Journal,* December 6, 1997, 2462.

25. Jackie Kucinich, "GOP Surveys Itself on New Agenda," *Los Angeles Times,* July 6, 2010 (online edition).

26. Donald R. Wolfensberger, "Suspended Partisanship in the House: How Most Laws Are Really Made" (paper prepared for the annual meeting of the American Political Science Association, Boston, August 29–September 1, 2002), 11.

27. Martin Gold et al., *The Book on Congress* (Washington, DC: Big Eagle Publishing, 1992), 124.

28. Kathleen Hunter and Anna Palmer, "Boehner Faces First Defections," *Roll Call,* February 10, 2011 (online edition); Paul Kane and Karen Tumulty, "House GOP Trips over Another Vote," *Washington Post,* February 10, 2011, A3.

29. *Congressional Record,* 111th Cong., 2d sess., July 28, 2010, H6252.

30. *Congressional Record,* 112th Cong., 1st sess., January 5, 2011, H29.

31. Quoted in Jonathan Salant, "Under Open Rules, Discord Rules," *Congressional Quarterly Weekly Report,* January 28, 1995, 277.

32. *National Journal,* January 21, 1995, 183.

33. Lizette Alvarez, "Campaign Finance Measure Soundly Rejected by House," *New York Times,* June 18, 1998, A26.

34. Stanley Bach and Steven Smith, *Managing Uncertainty in the House of Representatives: Adaptation and Innovation in Special Rules* (Washington, DC: Brookings, 1988), 87.

35. *Congresssional Record,* 110th Cong., 1st sess., March 20, 2007, H2682.

36. Don Wolfensberger, "Leadership Control Is Faulted for House Ills," *Roll Call,* December 14, 2010, 15.

37. Quoted in S. A. Miller, "Democrats Hedge on Bipartisan Pledge," *Washington Times,* January 25, 2007, A9.

38. *Congressional Record,* 112th Cong., 1st sess., January 5, 2011, H5.

39. Mary Lynn F. Jones, "The Republican Railroad," *American Prospect,* April 2003, 16.

40. Lindsay Sobel, "Democrats Weigh Discharge Petition Barrage," *The Hill,* July 1, 1998, 2.

41. Emily Ethridge, "House GOP Leaders Join Effort to Force Vote on Repeal of Health Care Law," *CQ Today,* July 1, 2010, 13.

42. Alexander Bolton, "House Leaders Tighten Grip, Anger Centrists," *The Hill,* January 15, 2003, 23.

43. Information courtesy of Richard Beth, specialist in legislative process, Congressional Research Service, Library of Congress.

44. Molly Hooper, "Two Weeks On, One Week Off in 2011 House Schedule," *The Hill,* December 9, 2010, 6.

45. Sam Goldfarb, "House's Two-Weeks-On, One-Week-Off Plan Diverges from Senate, Tradition," *CQ Today*, December 9, 2010, 23.

46. *National Journal's CongressDaily PM*, January 13, 1995, 4.

47. Robert S. Walker, "Why House Republicans Need a Watchdog," *Roll Call*, January 19, 1987, 10.

48. John F. Bibby, ed., *Congress Off the Record* (Washington, DC: American Enterprise Institute, 1983), 2.

49. Erik Wasson, "Republicans to Hold Spending Vote before State of the Union," *The Hill*, January 20, 2011, 7.

50. *Congressional Record*, 111th Cong., 2d sess., May 20, 2010, H3683.

51. Norman Ornstein, "The Motion to Recommit, Hijacked by Politics," *Roll Call*, May 19, 2010, 31.

52. Kathleen Hunter, "Democrats Force Votes with Eye on Campaigns," *Roll Call*, January 31, 2011, 1.

53. Ibid., 6.

54. Sen. J. Bennett Johnston, D-La. (1972–1997), quoted in *New York Times*, November 22, 1985, B8.

55. Quoted in "Democrats to Forgo Control in Brief Edge," *Washington Times*, November 29, 2000, A4.

56. *Congressional Record*, 101st Cong., 2d sess., July 20, 1990, S10183.

57. Susan F. Rasky, "With Few Bills Passed or Ready for Action, Congress Seems Sluggish," *New York Times*, May 14, 1989, 24.

58. *Congressional Record*, 98th Cong., 2d sess., January 27, 1984, S328–S329.

59. Walter J. Oleszek, *Congressional Procedures and the Policy Process*, 8th ed. (Washington, DC: CQ Press, 2011), 245–250. Also see Lewis A. Froman Jr., *The Congressional Process* (Boston: Little, Brown, 1967); and Terry Sullivan, *Procedural Structure: Success and Influence in Congress* (New York: Praeger, 1984).

60. *Congressional Record*, 111th Cong., 2d sess., September 21, 2010, S7251.

61. Elizabeth Drew, *Senator* (New York: Simon and Schuster, 1979), 158.

62. *Congressional Record*, 97th Cong., 2d sess., May 20, 1982, S5648.

63. Mary Dalrymple, "Democrats Say They Are Unified in Opposition Platform," *CQ Today*, January 29, 2002, 5.

64. Major Garrett, "The Backseat," *National Journal*, February 5, 2011, 46.

65. Gail Russell Chaddock, "Limits on Filibusters Are Already Pervasive," *Christian Science Monitor*, May 24, 2005, 2.

66. *Congressional Record*, 107th Cong., 2d sess., April 17, 2002, S2850.

67. Helen Dewar, "'Hold' Likely for IRS Pick, Daschle Says," *Washington Post*, October 30, 1997, A11.

68. See comments by Alan Cranston of California, then Senate Democratic whip, in *New York Times*, July 17, 1986, A3.

69. Quoted in Sean Piccoli, "Byrd Still Senate Caesar Despite GOP Takeover," *Washington Times*, February 14, 1995, A11.

70. U.S. Congress, *Operations of the Congress: Testimony of House and Senate Leaders*, hearing before the Joint Committee on the Organization of Congress (Washington, DC: Government Printing Office, 1993), 50.

71. Doug Obey, "Alaska," *The Hill*, July 10, 1996, 27.

72. Sixteen additional cloture motions were filed but not voted upon. Two of the sixteen, however, were agreed to by unanimous consent. Information for the 109th Congress compiled by the U.S. Senate Library.

73. Eve Fairbanks, "Tough Reid," *The New Republic*, April 15, 2009, 14.

74. Josh Smith, "Majority Does Not Rule in Filibuster-Filled 111th Senate," *National Journal,* December 17, 2010, 4.

75. *Congressional Record,* 111th Cong., 2d sess., September 15, 2010, S7120.

76. *Congressional Record,* 112th Cong., 1st sess., January 27, 2011, S322.

77. Some analysts associate the nuclear option with a 2005 plan by Majority Leader Bill Frist, R-Tenn., to end filibusters on a specific matter—judicial nominations. As recounted by Senator Specter:

> In 2005, serious consideration was given by the Republican caucus to changing the long-standing Senate rule [requiring sixty votes to end a filibuster] by invoking the so-called nuclear or constitutional option. The plan called for Vice President Cheney to rule that 51 votes were sufficient to impose cloture for confirmation of a judge or executive nominee. His ruling, then to be challenged by Democrats, would be upheld by the traditional 51 votes to uphold the Chair's ruling.

The Senate's action upholding Cheney's ruling would establish an authoritative precedent ending judicial filibusters. Frist's plan, however, never materialized because a group of seven Democrats and seven Republicans (the "Gang of 14") refused to support the majority leader's parliamentary tactic. *Congressional Record,* 111st Cong., 2d sess., December 21, 2010, S10855.

78. Ibid., S325.

79. Testimony of Steven S. Smith, University of Minnesota, before the Joint Committee on the Organization of Congress, 103d Cong., 1st sess., May 20, 1993, 14.

80. *Congressional Record,* 106th Cong., 2d sess., October 13, 2000, S10520.

81. Jonathan Allen and John Cochran, "The Might of the Right," *CQ Weekly,* November 8, 2003, 2762.

82. Randall B. Ripley, *Power in the Senate* (New York: St. Martin's Press, 1969), 128.

83. Barbara Sinclair, *Unorthodox Lawmaking: New Legislative Processes in the U.S. Congress,* 3d ed. (Washington, DC: CQ Press, 2007).

84. Barber B. Conable, "Weaving Webs: Lobbying by Charities," *Tax Notes,* November 10, 1975, 27–28.

CHAPTER 9

1. David M. Herszenhorn, "In Senate, Republicans Block Spending Measure," *New York Times,* March 6, 2009, A16.

2. Quoted in ibid.

3. Humberto Sanchez and Christian Bourge, "Reid Sees Senate Action on Omnibus by March 6 Deadline," *National Journal CongressDaily PM,* February 24, 2009.

4. Gail Russell Chaddock, "Omnibus Bill's Hidden Item: A Democratic Rift," *Christian Science Monitor,* March 12, 2009.

5. Robert Pear, "House Passes Spending Bill, and Critics Are Quick to Point Out Pork," *New York Times,* February 26, 2009, A20.

6. Evan Bayh, "Deficits and Fiscal Credibility," *Wall Street Journal,* March 4, 2009.

7. Shailagh Murray, "Democrats Stung by Dissenters: Unity on Agenda Eludes Party Leaders," *Washington Post,* March 10, 2009, A1.

8. Quoted in Jill Smallen and Jason Dick, "The Week on the Hill: Obama Signs Omnibus Package," *National Journal,* March 14, 2009.

9. Dan Friedman, "Despite Threat, Appointed Senators Hold Firm against Vitter," *National Journal CongressDaily AM,* March 11, 2009.

10. Quoted in ibid.
11. Quoted in ibid.
12. Quoted in Emily Pierce, "Omnibus' Fate Not Accompli," *Roll Call*, March 5, 2009.
13. Quoted in ibid.
14. Emily Pierce, "Menendez Feels the Heat; Senators Fume over Omnibus," *Roll Call*, March 11, 2009 (online edition).
15. Quoted in ibid.
16. Paul Kane and Scott Wilson, "Obama Signs Spending Bill, Vowing to Battle Earmarks," *Washington Post*, March 12, 2009, A01.
17. Richard L. Hall, *Participation in Congress* (New Haven, CT: Yale University Press, 1998), 27–30.
18. Lauren Whittington, "Obscure Caucus: Members Allergic to the Spotlight Find a Home," *Roll Call*, September 10, 2007. The listing omits senators: "Senators are by definition not obscure, although there are several who seem to strive for it." To be listed in the Obscure Caucus, House members must have served at least two full terms.
19. Quoted in *The Hill*, November 15, 2000, 16.
20. David Price, *Who Makes the Laws?* (Cambridge, MA: Schenkman Publishing, 1972), 297; David E. Price, *The Congressional Experience*, 3d ed. (Boulder, CO: Westview Press, 2004), chap. 6.
21. Quoted in Bernard Asbell, *The Senate Nobody Knows* (Garden City, NY: Doubleday, 1978), 210.
22. Richard F. Fenno Jr., "Observation, Context, and Sequence in the Study of Politics," *American Political Science Review* 80 (March 1976): 3–15.
23. Lindsay Sobel, "Early Fast-Track Support Cost Members Leverage," *The Hill*, November 12, 1997, 33.
24. Matthew Daly, "Indians Benefited in 111th Congress," *Washington Times*, December 30, 2010, A4.
25. Cited in Philippe Shepnick, "Moynihan Is Champion Bill Writer," *The Hill*, March 10, 1999, 6.
26. Rick K. Wilson and Cheryl D. Young, "Cosponsorship in the U.S. Congress," *Legislative Studies Quarterly* 22 (February 1997): 25–43.
27. Jacob R. Straus, "Dear Colleague Letters in the House of Representatives: The Tracking of Internal House Communications" (paper presented at the annual meeting of the Midwest Political Science Association, Chicago, April 2–5, 2009), fig. 1.
28. T. R. Reid, *Congressional Odyssey: The Saga of a Senate Bill* (San Francisco: W. H. Freeman, 1980), 15.
29. Hall, *Participation in Congress*, 139; also see 119.
30. Ibid., 126–127.
31. Ibid., 102.
32. Gary Mucchiaroni and Paul J. Quirk, *Deliberative Choices: Debating Public Policy in Congress* (Chicago: University of Chicago Press, 2006), 197.
33. Andrew Taylor, "Democratic Leaders in House Keep Debate Short, Liability Low," *Washington Times*, July 17, 2009, A7.
34. Sarah Barr, "Senate Votes Down Repeal Proposal in Latest Battle over Health Reform Law," *Daily Report for Executives*, February 3, 2011, G-13.
35. Mary Beth Sheridan and Hamil R. Harris, "D.C. Voting Measure Clears the Senate: Added Gun Language Might Pose a Problem," *Washington Post*, February 27, 2009, A1.
36. *Congressional Record*, 103d Cong., 1st sess., June 23, 1993, H3941–H3973.
37. John D. Wilkerson, "'Killer' Amendments in Congress," *American Political Science Review* 93 (September 1999): 535–552.

38. Quoted in Peter Gosselin, "Paulson Will Have No Peer under Bailout Deal," *Los Angeles Times*, September 29, 2008 (online edition).

39. Dave Cook, "'Brutal Vote' Ahead on Whether to Raise the National Debt Ceiling," *Christian Science Monitor*, November 19, 2010 (online edition).

40. Quoted in Krissah Williams Thompson, "Those Up for Reelection Have Explaining to Do," *Washington Post*, October 1, 2008, A10.

41. John Cranford, "Showing Up Less," *CQ Weekly*, January 3, 2011, 42.

42. John B. Gilmour, *Strategic Disagreement: Stalemate in American Politics* (Pittsburgh: University of Pittsburgh Press, 1995), 41.

43. Quoted in Ramesh Ponnuru, "Division on the Right," *National Review*, November 21, 2003.

44. David C. King and Richard J. Zeckhauser, "Congressional Vote Options," *Legislative Studies Quarterly* 28 (August 2003): 400–401.

45. Quoted in Eric Schmitt, "House Votes to Bar Religious Abuse Abroad," *New York Times*, May 15, 1998, A1.

46. Albert R. Hunt, "Balanced-Budget Measure Is Likely to Pass Senate Next Week, Faces Battle in House," *Wall Street Journal*, July 30, 1982, 2.

47. Shawn Zeller, "The Staying Power of Partisanship," *CQ Weekly*, January 3, 2011, 32.

48. Norman J. Ornstein, Thomas E. Mann, and Michael J. Malbin, *Vital Statistics on Congress, 2008* (Washington, DC: Brookings, 2008), 148–149.

49. Zeller, "Staying Power of Partisanship," 32.

50. For an authoritative analysis of the decline and resurgence of congressional partisanship, see David W. Rohde, *Parties and Leaders in the Postreform House* (Chicago: University of Chicago Press, 1991), esp. 3–11.

51. Shankar Vedantam, "My Team vs. Your Team: The Political Arena Lives Up to Its Name," *Washington Post*, September 29, 2008, A6.

52. For an extended analysis of partisan interests as a source of party cohesion and conflict, see Frances E. Lee, *Beyond Ideology: Politics, Principles, and Partisanship in the U.S. Senate* (Chicago: University of Chicago Press, 2009).

53. Gary C. Jacobson, *The Politics of Congressional Elections,* 7th ed. (New York: Pearson Longman, 2009), 135–144.

54. Quoted in Randall B. Ripley, *Party Leaders in the House of Representatives* (Washington, DC: Brookings, 1967), 144.

55. John Breaux, "Congress's Lost Art of Compromise," *Roll Call*, April 19, 2005, 17.

56. Quoted in ibid.

57. Gary W. Cox and Mathew D. McCubbins, *Setting the Agenda: Responsible Party Government in the U.S. House of Representatives* (New York: Cambridge University Press, 2005), 18.

58. See John W. Kingdon, *Congressmen's Voting Decisions* (New York: Harper and Row, 1981); and Ripley, *Party Leaders in the House of Representatives,* 139–159.

59. Donald R. Matthews and James A. Stimson, *Yeas and Nays: Normal Decisionmaking in the U.S. House of Representatives* (New York: John Wiley, 1975), 95.

60. Quoted in Morton Kondracke, "Who's Running the House? GOP Freshmen or Newt?" *Roll Call*, December 18, 1995, 5.

61. See Gary W. Cox and Mathew D. McCubbins, *Legislative Leviathan: Party Government in the House* (Berkeley: University of California Press, 1993); Gary W. Cox and Keith T. Poole, "On Measuring Partisanship in Roll-Call Voting: The U.S. House of Representatives, 1877–1999," *American Journal of Political Science* 46 (3): 477–489; and Sean M. Theriault, *Party Polarization in Congress* (New York: Cambridge University Press, 2008).

62. *Congressional Record*, 100th Cong., 1st sess., June 23, 1987, S8438.

63. David W. Rohde, "Electoral Forces, Political Agendas, and Partisanship in the House and Senate," in *The Postreform Congress,* ed. Roger H. Davidson (New York: St. Martin's Press, 1992), 28.
64. David Fahrenthold, "In Political Gamble, Reid Holds Senate Votes He Knows He'll Lose," *Washington Post,* December 9, 2010, A3.
65. Helmut Norpoth, "Explaining Party Cohesion in Congress: The Case of Shared Policy Attitudes," *American Political Science Review* 70 (December 1976): 1171.
66. Alan K. Ota, "New Team Repackages the Right's Thinking," *CQ Weekly,* February 16, 2009, 340.
67. Major Garrett, "The $100 Billion Cave," *National Journal,* February 19, 2011, 48.
68. For discussion of the "creative class," see Richard Florida, "The Rise of the Creative Class," *Washington Monthly,* May 2002. For extended treatment of these different sources of electoral support for the Democratic Party, see John B. Judis and Ruy Teixeira, *The Emerging Democratic Majority* (New York: Simon and Schuster, 2004).
69. John F. Manley, "The Conservative Coalition in Congress," *American Behavioral Scientist* 17 (December 1973): 223–247; Barbara Sinclair, *Congressional Realignment: 1925–1978* (Austin: University of Texas Press, 1982); Mack C. Shelley, *The Permanent Majority: The Conservative Coalition in the United States Congress* (Tuscaloosa: University of Alabama Press, 1983).
70. William A. Galston, "Can a Polarized American Party System Be 'Healthy'?" *Issues in Governance Studies* (Brookings), April 20, 2010, 1.
71. Stephen Gettinger, "R.I.P. to a Conservative Force," *CQ Weekly,* January 9, 1999, 82–83.
72. Sarah A. Binder, "The Disappearing Political Center," *Brookings Review* 15 (Fall 1996): 36–39. An extended analysis of the problem and its results is found in Sarah A. Binder, *Stalemate: Causes and Consequences of Legislative Gridlock* (Washington, DC: Brookings, 2003).
73. Keith T. Poole and Howard Rosenthal, "Patterns of Congressional Voting," *American Journal of Political Science* 35 (February 1991): 228–278; Keith T. Poole and Howard Rosenthal, *Congress: A Political-Economic History of Roll-Call Voting* (New York: Oxford University Press, 1997). See Ornstein, Mann, and Malbin, *Vital Statistics on Congress, 2008,* 160–161.
74. Using different measures of similar data, the same point is made in Morris P. Fiorina, with Samuel J. Adams and Jeremy C. Pope, *Culture War? The Myth of a Polarized America,* 2d ed. (New York: Pearson Longman, 2006), 16–21 and fig. 2–2.
75. Sean M. Theriault, "The Case of the Vanishing Moderates: Party Polarization in the Modern Congress" (paper presented at the 2003 annual meeting of the Western Political Science Association, Denver), fig. 1. Ideology scores from similar years (1969–1970 and 1999–2000) yield virtually the same results. Binder, *Stalemate,* 23–26.
76. Quoted by E. J. Dionne Jr., "The Real Pelosi," *Washington Post,* April 9, 2009, A17.
77. Binder, "Disappearing Political Center," 37. Binder defines centrists as those members who are closer to the ideological midpoint between the two parties than to the ideological center of their own party.
78. These estimates are based on Prof. Keith Poole's DW-NOMINATE scores for senators and House members provided on his website, http://voteview.com/dwnomin.htm.
79. The South includes the eleven states of the Confederacy.
80. Rohde, "Electoral Forces," esp. 34–40.
81. Jeffrey M. Stonecash, Mark D. Brewer, and Mack Mariani, *Diverging Parties* (Boulder, CO: Westview Press, 2002).
82. Data on party loyalty in roll call voting in the 111th Congress is drawn from CQ's annual vote study, *CQ Weekly,* January 3, 2011, 33.
83. Zeller, "Staying Power of Partisanship," 31.
84. R. Douglas Arnold, *The Logic of Congressional Action* (New Haven, CT: Yale University Press, 1990).

85. Ibid., 68.

86. Ibid., 84.

87. It is worth noting that recent presidents have taken stands on fewer issues. See Ornstein, Mann, and Malbin, *Vital Statistics on Congress, 2008,* 144–145

88. Joseph Schatz, "Legislative Success, Political Peril," *CQ Weekly,* January 3, 2011 19.

89. David Nather, "Clinton's Floor Vote Victories Yielded Few Accomplishments," *CQ Weekly,* January 6, 2001, 52ff.

90. Roger H. Davidson, *The Role of the Congressman* (Indianapolis: Bobbs-Merrill, 1969), 22–23.

91. Robert L. Peabody, "Organization Theory and Legislative Behavior: Bargaining, Hierarchy, and Change in the U.S. House of Representatives" (paper presented at the 1963 annual meeting of the American Political Science Association, New York).

92. Carl J. Friedrich, *Constitutional Government and Democracy,* 4th ed. (Waltham, MA: Blaisdell Publishing, 1967), 269–270.

93. John W. Kingdon, *Congressmen's Voting Decisions,* 3d ed. (Ann Arbor: University of Michigan Press, 1989).

94. Quoted in John F. Bibby, ed., *Congress Off the Record* (Washington, DC: American Enterprise Institute, 1983), 22.

95. Quoted in Claudia Dreifus, "Exit Reasonable Right," *New York Times Magazine,* June 2, 1996, 26.

96. It is worth noting that a fall 2010 poll found that nearly "half of America—including nearly two-thirds of Republicans and 53 percent of independents—admires political leaders who refuse to compromise." But governing means bargaining. If half of Americans "admire political leaders who stick to their positions without compromising," then they are endorsing a formula for policy gridlock and polarized partisanship. Major Garrett, "Poll: Americans Want Their Leaders to Stand and Fight," *National Journal CongressDaily AM,* September 21, 2010, 1.

97. Edward J. Derwinski, "The Art of Negotiation within the Congress," in *International Negotiation: Art and Science,* ed. Diane B. Bendahmane and John W. McDonald Jr. (Washington, DC: U.S. Department of State, Foreign Service Institute, 1984), 11.

98. Elliott Abrams, "Unforgettable Scoop Jackson," *Reader's Digest,* February 1985. Quotation cited in *Congressional Record,* 99th Cong., 1st sess., February 20, 1985, E478.

99. Quoted in David E. Rosenbaum, "The Favors of Rostenkowski: Tax Revision's Quid Pro Quo," *New York Times,* November 27, 1985, B6.

100. Quoted in John Sawyer, "Prescription Drug Vote Came Down to Emerson, Push for Reimportation; Missouri Republican Believes Measure Could Save Billions in Drug Costs," *St. Louis Post-Dispatch,* June 29, 2003, A5.

101. Ibid.

102. Lynn Sweet, "House OKs Foreign Drug Imports," *Chicago Sun-Times,* July 26, 2003, 3.

103. Quotes from Jonathan Allen, "Effective House Leadership Makes the Most of Majority," *CQ Weekly,* March 29, 2003, 751.

104. See, for example, Chris Frates, "Payoffs for States Get Reid to 60," *Politico,* December 19, 2010, www.politico.com.

105. Gilmour, *Strategic Disagreement,* 4.

106. Gary W. Cox and Jonathan N. Katz, "Gerrymandering Roll Calls in Congress, 1879–2000," *American Journal of Political Science* 51 (January 2007): 117.

107. See William H. Riker, *The Theory of Political Coalitions* (New Haven, CT: Yale University Press, 1962), 32. Theorists define legislative bargaining situations formally as *n*-person, zero-sum games in which side payments are permitted— that is, a sizable number of participants

are involved; when some participants win, others must lose; and participants can trade items outside the substantive issues under consideration.

108. John G. Stewart, "Two Strategies of Leadership: Johnson and Mansfield," in *Congressional Behavior,* ed. Nelson W. Polsby (New York: Random House, 1971), 67.

109. Russell Hardin, "Hollow Victory: The Minimum Winning Coalition," *American Political Science Review* 79 (December 1976): 1202–1214.

110. Breaux, "Congress's Lost Art of Compromise," 17.

111. Binder, *Stalemate,* 127.

112. Robert J. Dole, quoting Dirksen, in remarks to the Senate, March 29, 2000. Dole quoted in *The Hill,* April 5, 2000, 32.

113. Clinton T. Brass, "Shutdown of the Federal Government: Causes, Processes, and Effects," Congressional Research Service Report RL34680, September 23, 2008. Note that "shutdowns" also include "funding gaps" that occur when there is a lag between the expiration of a continuing resolution (CR) and the enactment of a new one. In the absence of a CR, agencies begin their shutdown, even if it is only for a few days.

CHAPTER 10

1. Aaron Lorenzo, "Rep. Bachus Leads Assault on What GOP Labels Regulatory Overreach of Dodd-Frank," *Daily Report for Executives,* January 27, 2011, EE7.

2. Lori Montgomery and Paul Kane, "Congress on Course to Avert a Shutdown," *Washington Post,* February 26, 2011, A5.

3. Ross K. Baker, "Democrats, Not So Fast," *USA Today,* June 19, 2008, 11A.

4. Jim VandeHei and Mike Allen, "Lesson: Communication Is More Than Eloquence," *Politico,* March 20, 2009, 7.

5. See Stephen Wayne, *The Legislative Presidency* (New York: Harper and Row, 1978).

6. Charles O. Jones, *Separate but Equal Branches: Congress and the Presidency* (Chatham, NJ: Chatham House, 1995), 138–157.

7. Michael Nelson, "Evaluating the President," in *The Presidency and the Political System,* 7th ed., ed. Michael Nelson (Washington, DC: CQ Press, 2003), 21.

8. See Norman J. Ornstein, "Theories of the Presidency," in *Encyclopedia of the American Presidency,* vol. 4, ed. Leonard Levy and Louis Fisher (New York: Simon and Schuster, 1994), 1458–1462.

9. Richard E. Neustadt, *Presidential Power* (New York: John Wiley, 1960), 23.

10. Ibid., 16.

11. Leonard D. White, *The Federalists* (New York: Macmillan, 1948), 55.

12. Leonard D. White, *The Jeffersonians* (New York: Macmillan, 1951), 35.

13. Paul C. Light, *The President's Agenda* (Baltimore: Johns Hopkins University Press, 1982), 230–231.

14. John A. Farrell, *Tip O'Neill and the Democratic Century* (Boston: Little, Brown, 2001), 553.

15. Shawn Zeller, "Historic Success, At No Small Cost," *CQ Weekly,* January 11, 2010, 112.

16. Joseph J. Schatz, "Legislative Success, Political Peril," *CQ Weekly,* January 3, 2011, 19.

17. Susan Page and Mimi Hall, "Will Doing 'Big Things' Wind Up Costing Obama?" *USA Today,* May 12, 2010, 2A. Kohut's comment is also from this article.

18. Michael Scherer, "Mr. Unpopular," *Time,* September 13, 2010, 31.

19. Linda Feldmann, "Bold Moves, Then a Backlash," *Christian Science Monitor,* July 19, 2010, 17.

20. John B. Judis, "The Unnecessary Fall," *New Republic,* September 2, 2010, 15.

21. Chris Frates and Ben White, "Obama's Reforms to Change Future," *Politico,* July 12, 2010, 1.

22. Jennifer Steinhauer and Robert Pear, "G.O.P. Newcomers Set Out to Undo Obama Victories," *New York Times,* January 3, 2011, A1.

23. Lyndon B. Johnson, *The Vantage Point* (New York: Popular Library, 1971), 448.

24. Jack Valenti, "Some Advice on the Care and Feeding of Congressional Egos," *Los Angeles Times,* April 23, 1978, 3.

25. Richard Berke, "Courting Congress Nonstop, Clinton Looks for an Alliance," *New York Times,* March 8, 1993, A1.

26. Roy P. Basler, ed., *The Collected Works of Abraham Lincoln,* vol. 3 (New Brunswick: Rutgers University Press, 1953), 27.

27. Samuel Kernell, *Going Public: New Strategies of Presidential Leadership,* 3d ed. (Washington, DC: CQ Press, 1997), 2. Also see James Ceaser et al., "The Rise of the Rhetorical Presidency," *Presidential Studies Quarterly* 21 (Spring 1981): 158–171.

28. Richard M. Pious, *The American Presidency* (New York: Basic Books, 1979), 194. Also see George C. Edwards III, *The Public Presidency* (New York: St. Martin's Press, 1983).

29. Farrell, *Tip O'Neill and the Democratic Century,* 553.

30. *Wall Street Journal,* December 4, 1987, 8D.

31. George Hager, "For GOP, a New Song—Same Ending," *Congressional Quarterly Weekly Report,* June 14, 1997, 1406.

32. Paul Bedard, "Living, Dying by the Polls," *Washington Times,* April 30, 1993, A1.

33. David S. Broder, "The Reticent President," *Washington Post,* April 22, 2001, B7. Also see Mike Allen, "Bush on Stage: Deft or Just Lacking Depth?" *Washington Post,* February 19, 2001, A8–A9.

34. Ibid., A20.

35. Susan Page, "Bush's Job-Approval Rating Stuck Below 40%," *USA Today,* April 9, 2007, 8A.

36. James Oliphant, "Bush Never Recovered from Response to Katrina, Former Aides Say," *Los Angeles Times,* January 2, 2009 (online edition).

37. Quoted in Jeff Eller, "It's Time to Rewrite the Bully Pulpit," *Politico,* November 18, 2008, 29.

38. Peter Baker, "President Sticks to the Script, With a Little Help," *New York Times,* March 6, 2009, A16. President Obama uses a teleprompter regularly for both major addresses and routine announcements.

39. Christi Parsona and Mark Z. Barabak, "Obama to Sit Down with Leno on The Tonight Show," *Los Angeles Times,* March 17, 2009 (online edition).

40. Jonathan Martin, "Obama Wants Filter-Free News," *Politico,* March 24, 2009, 17.

41. Sheryl Gay Stolberg, "Obama Makes History in Live Internet Video Chat," *New York Times,* March 27, 2009, A15.

42. Michael Gerson, "The Lost Communicator," *Washington Post,* September 10, 2010, A27.

43. Jennifer Bendery, "Democrats Want White House Help on Messaging," *Roll Call,* September 30, 2010 (online edition).

44. John Harwood, "After 15 Months in Office, Policy vs. Politics for Obama," *New York Times,* April 26, 2010, A13.

45. Quoted in Walter Pincus, "More from Nixon the Political Scientist," *Washington Post,* January 26, 2010, A13.

46. See, for example, Richard P. Nathan, *The Administrative Presidency* (New York: John Wiley, 1983); and Robert R. Durant, *The Administrative Presidency Revisited* (Albany: State University of New York Press, 1992).

47. William G. Howell and David E. Lewis, "Agencies by Presidential Design," *Journal of Politics,* November 2002, 1096.

48. Ibid., 1100.

49. William G. Howell, *Power without Persuasion: The Politics of Direct Presidential Action* (Princeton, NJ: Princeton University Press, 2003). The Obama administration has abandoned the term *enemy combatant* for those held at Guantánamo Bay, Cuba. See David Savage, "No More 'Enemy Combatants' at Guantánamo Bay," *Los Angeles Times*, March 14, 2009 (online edition).

50. See Kenneth Mayer, *With the Stroke of a Pen: Executive Orders and Presidential Power* (Princeton, NJ: Princeton University Press, 2001).

51. Elizabeth Shogren, "President Plans Blitz of Executive Orders Soon," *Los Angeles Times*, July 5, 1998, A11.

52. Dana Milbank and Ellen Nakashima, "Bush Team Has 'Right' Credentials," *Washington Post*, March 25, 2001, A1.

53. Linda Feldmann, "Faith-Based Initiatives Quietly Lunge Forward," *Christian Science Monitor*, February 6, 2003, 2.

54. Gregg Carlstrom, "Midnight Rule-Making Bonanza," *Federal Times*, November 3, 2008, 19.

55. Cindy Skrzycki, "Democrats Eye Bush Midnight Regulations," *Washington Post*, November 11, 2009, D3.

56. Ceci Connolly and R. Jeffrey Smith, "Obama Positioned to Quickly Reverse Bush Actions," *Washington Post*, November 9, 2008, A16.

57. Andrew Noyes, "Obama's FOIA Directive Brings Praise, Bit of Skepticism," *National Journal CongressDaily AM*, January 22, 2009, 8. Also see Dan Eggen and Michael D. Shear, "The Effort to Roll Back Bush Policies Continues," *Washington Post*, January 27, 2009, A4.

58. See Wendy R. Ginsberg, "The Obama Administration's Open Government Initiative: Issues for Congress," Congressional Research Service Report R41361, August 17, 2010.

59. Aaron Wildavsky, "The Two Presidencies," in *The Beleaguered Presidency*, ed. Aaron Wildavsky (Brunswick, NJ: Transaction Publishers, 1991), 29. Wildavsky's article originally appeared in the December 1966 issue of *Transaction* magazine.

60. Aaron Wildavsky, "The Two Presidencies Thesis Revisited at a Time of Political Dissensus," in Wildavsky, *Beleaguered Presidency*, 47–65.

61. Dan Balz, "Bush Lays out Ambitious Plan for Long Term," *Washington Post*, May 6, 2001, A10.

62. Ronald Brownstein, "Strategies Shift as Bush Drops in Polls," *Los Angeles Times*, July 5, 2001, A9.

63. John Harwood and Jeanne Cummings, "Bush's Approval Rating Slips to 50%, a 5-Year Presidential Low," *Wall Street Journal*, June 28, 2001, A18.

64. Ron Faucheux, "Presidential Popularity: A History of Highs and Lows," *CQ Daily Monitor*, February 7, 2002, 14.

65. Editorial, "Bush's Big Regret," *Los Angeles Times*, December 4, 2008 (online edition).

66. Woodrow Wilson, *Congressional Government* (Boston: Houghton Mifflin, 1885), 52.

67. Kevin R. Kosar, "Regular Vetoes and Pocket Vetoes: An Overview," Congressional Research Service Report RS22188, January 26, 2009, 1.

68. Kara Rowland, "Obama's Veto Pen Likely to See More Action in 112th Congress," *Washington Times*, January 12, 2011, A4.

69. Alexis Simendinger, "The Veto-Free Zone," *National Journal*, December 17, 2005, 3888.

70. Ethan Wallison, "Can President Bush Stay Veto-Free for Four More Years?" *Roll Call*, January 24, 2005, 10.

71. Jill Barshay, "Popularity Not Required," *CQ Weekly*, January 1, 2007, 45.

72. Sheryl Gay Stolbert, "First Bush Veto Maintains Limits on Stem Cell Use," *New York Times*, July 20, 2006, A1.

73. Clea Benson, "The Power of No," *CQ Weekly*, January 14, 2008, 133.

74. Mike Allen, "Bush Signs Corporate Reforms into Law," *Washington Post,* July 31, 2002, A4. Also see Elizabeth Bumiller, "When Bush Picks up a Pen, He Drops Names," *New York Times,* December 2, 2002, A16.

75. Stephen Dinan, "Bloggers Will Join Bush in Bill-Signing Ceremony," *Washington Times,* September 26, 2006, A4.

76. See, for example, *The Hill,* December 19, 2007, 1; and *Washington Times,* December 19, 2007, A10, for photo coverage.

77. Nancy Ognanovich, "Obama Veto Threat Said to Doom Spending Earmarks for Next Two Years," *Daily Report for Executives,* January 27, 2011, A-22. Also see Sam Youngman, "Obama Promises That He'll Veto All Earmarks," *The Hill,* January 26, 2011, 1.

78. *Los Angeles Times,* March 18, 1988, part I, 4.

79. See T. J. Halstead, "Presidential Signing Statements: Constitutional and Institutional Implications," Congressional Research Service Report RL33667, April 13, 2007.

80. Ibid., 9.

81. Charles Savage, "Bush Challenges Hundreds of Laws; President Cites Powers of His Office," *Boston Globe,* April 30, 2006, A1. Also see Phillip J. Cooper, "George W. Bush, Edgar Allan Poe, and the Use and Abuse of Presidential Signing Statements," *Presidential Studies Quarterly* (September 2005): 515–532.

82. Dan Friedman, "On the Other Hand," *National Journal,* March 28, 2009, 54.

83. Michael D. Shear, "Obama Pledges to Limit Use of Signing Statements," *Washington Post,* March 10, 2009, A4.

84. Charlie Savage, "Obama Says He Can Ignore Some Parts of Spending Bill," *New York Times,* March 12, 2009, A18.

85. David Nather, "Grassley Blows Whistle on Obama for Signing Statement," *CQ Today,* March 16, 2009, 10.

86. Aaron Lorenzo, "Obama Review of Past Signing Statements Does Not Signal End of Presidential Practice," *Daily Report for Executives,* March 10, 2009, A-25.

87. Humberto Sanchez, "Obama Warned on Signing Statements," *National Journal Congress DailyPM,* July 21, 2009, 6–7.

88. *Congressional Record,* 110th Cong., 2d sess., October 2, 2008, E2197.

89. Louis Fisher, "The Pocket Veto: Its Current Status," Congressional Research Service Report RL30909, March 30, 2001, summary.

90. Erika Niedowski, "GOP to Skirt Line-Item Veto," *The Hill,* February 12, 1997, 24.

91. John Broder, "Clinton Vetoes Eight Projects, Two in States of Leadership," *New York Times,* October 18, 1997, A10.

92. Helen Dewar and Joan Biskupic, "Line-Item Vote Struck Down: Backers Push for Alternative," *Washington Post,* June 26, 1998, A1.

93. Neustadt, *Presidential Power,* 187.

94. Glenn Thrush, "With the 111th, the Age of Pelosi Dawns," *Politico,* January 6, 2009, 16.

95. Keith Koffler and Steven T. Dennis, "Obama Seeks Allies," *Roll Call,* March 12, 2009, 29.

96. Susan Davis, "The New Normal," *National Journal,* December 11, 2010, 43. Also see Carrie Budoff Brown, "Tax Deal Leaves Liberals Furious," *Politico,* December 7, 2010, 7.

97. Johnson, *Vantage Point,* 448.

98. See Emily Pierce and Jennifer Bendery, "Biden Expands Job Profile," *Washington Post,* December 9, 2010, 1; and Shailagh Murray and Lori Montgomery, "Obama Proposes Bipartisan Meeting to Hash Out Budget," *Washington Post,* March 3, 2011, A3.

99. Jonathan Alter, "What, Me Worry?" *Newsweek,* November 15, 2010, 28.

100. Naftali Bendavid, "GOP Aims to Tame Benefits Program," *Wall Street Journal,* March 4, 2011, A2.

101. Peter Baker, "Washington Worries about Its New Power Couple," *New York Times,* November 10, 2010, A18.
102. George C. Edwards III, *At the Margins* (New Haven, CT: Yale University Press, 1989).
103. See Joseph P. Harris, *The Advice and Consent of the Senate* (Berkeley: University of California Press, 1953); and G. Calvin Mackenzie, *The Politics of Presidential Appointments* (New York: Free Press, 1981).
104. James MacGregor Burns, *Presidential Government* (Boston: Houghton Mifflin, 1966), 284.
105. See, for example, Stephen J. Wayne, "Great Expectations: What People Want from Presidents," in *Rethinking the Presidency,* ed. Thomas E. Cronin (Boston: Little, Brown, 1982), 185–199.
106. Dean Scott, "Next President Likely to Have Limited Chance for Passage of Emission Caps, Senator Says," *Daily Report for Executives,* August 4, 2008, A-15.
107. Arthur M. Schlesinger Jr. and Alfred De Grazia, *Congress and the Presidency: Their Role in Modern Times* (Washington, DC: American Enterprise Institute, 1967), 1.
108. Wilson, *Congressional Government;* Burns, *Presidential Government.*
109. See Joseph S. Clark, *Congress: The Sapless Branch* (New York: Harper and Row, 1964); and Arthur Schlesinger Jr., *The Imperial Presidency* (Boston: Houghton Mifflin, 1973).
110. David Mayhew, *Divided We Govern* (New Haven, CT: Yale University Press, 1991), 198.
111. J. William Fulbright, "The Legislator as Educator," *Foreign Affairs* (Spring 1979): 726.

CHAPTER 11

1. David S. Broder, "So, Now Bigger Is Better?" *Washington Post,* January 12, 2003, B1.
2. Amy Goldstein, "Two Views on Rising Poverty," *Washington Post,* September 17, 2010, A16. Also see Erik Eckholm, "Recession Raises U.S. Poverty Rate to a 15-Year High," *New York Times,* September 17, 2010, A1.
3. Janet Hook, "Obama's Budget Is the End of an Era," *Los Angeles Times,* February 27, 2009 (online edition).
4. Donald F. Kettl, "Heading for Disaster," *Government Executive,* February 2009, 22.
5. Alan Fram, "'Tea Partiers Not on Same Page as Rest of Country," *Washington Times,* November 24, 2010, A4. This article points out that Tea Party supporters are generally white, male, and older and more affluent than others in the general populace.
6. "Transcript: Obama on Taxes, Economy, and START," interview, National Public Radio, December 10, 2010, 5.
7. Quoted in E. J. Dionne Jr., "Back from the Dead: Neoprogressivism in the 90s," *American Prospect,* September–October 1996, 25.
8. Kate Zerkike, "Proposed Amendment Would Enable States to Repeal Federal Law," *New York Times,* December 19, 2010, A13.
9. Sean Wilentz, "States of Anarchy," *New Republic,* April 29, 2010, 5.
10. Jonathan Walters, "Preempting Washington," *Governing,* September 2004, 12.
11. *Congressional Record,* 106th Cong., 1st sess., November 5, 1997, S11737.
12. Richard E. Neustadt, "Politicians and Bureaucrats," in *The Congress and America's Future,* 2d ed., ed. David B. Truman (Englewood Cliffs, NJ: Prentice-Hall, 1973), 199. See also Louis Fisher, *The Politics of Shared Power: Congress and the Executive,* 3d ed. (Washington, DC: CQ Press, 1993).
13. See Harold Relyea, "Executive Branch Reorganization and Management Initiatives: A Brief Overview," Congressional Research Service Report RL33441, May 30, 2006.
14. *Congressional Record,* 109th Cong., 1st sess., February 15, 2005, S1437.
15. Keith Koffler, "Confirmation Wars Could Be Thing of the Past," *Roll Call,* November 21, 2008, 10.

16. Steven V. Roberts, "In Confirmation Process, Hearings Offer a Stage," *New York Times*, February 8, 1989, B7.

17. See Al Kamen, "Recess Appointments Granted to 'Swift Boat' Donor, 2 Other Nominees," *Washington Post*, April 5, 2007, A6.

18. "Rationer-in-Chief," *Economist*, July 17, 2010, 32.

19. Sheryl Gay Stolberg, "Six Recess Appointments to Be Made, Obama Says," *New York Times*, December 30, 2010, A14.

20. *Congressional Record*, 111th Cong., 2d sess., July 12, 2010, S5722–S5723.

21. Such a move means further delay because committees must reconvene to report the same resubmitted nominations.

22. Brian Friel, "Senate to Block Recess Appointments," *CQ Today*, September 30, 2010, 20; Ezra Klein, "Same Old Senate Employs a New Maneuver," *Washington Post*, October 1, 2010, A15.

23. See Henry Hogue, *Temporarily Filling Presidentially Appointed, Senate-Confirmed Positions*, CRS Report RS21412, January 25, 2008.

24. See, for example, Will Englund, "Czar Wars," *National Journal*, February 14, 2009, 16–24.

25. Jim Puzzanghera and Peter Nicholas, "Obama Decision to Avoid Confirmation Battle for Elizabeth Warren Is Hailed and Criticized," *Los Angeles Times*, September 18, 2010 (online edition). Also see John Maggs, "Warring over Warren," *National Journal*, July 1, 2010, 41–42.

26. S. A. Miller, "Democrats Use Omnibus to Eviscerate Bush Policies," *Washington Times*, February 26, 2009, A17.

27. Bruce Ackerman, "A Role for Congress to Reclaim," *Washington Post*, March 11, 2009, A15.

28. Ibid.; William Schneider, "New Rules for the Game of Politics," *National Journal*, April 1, 1989, 830.

29. See Dennis Thompson, *Ethics in Congress* (Washington, DC: Brookings, 1995).

30. Anne Kornblut and Michael Shear, "Obama Says He Erred in Nominations," *Washington Post*, February 4, 2009, A1.

31. Norman Ornstein, "Confirmation Process Leaves Government in Serious Gridlock," *Roll Call*, March 25, 2009, 6.

32. Edward Luce and Krishna Guha, "Appointments Bottleneck at Treasury Tightens," *Financial Times*, March 19, 2009, 4.

33. Philip Rucker, "Potential Obama Appointees Face Extensive Vetting," *Washington Post*, November 18, 2008, A12.

34. Nancy Kassebaum Baker and Franklin Raines, "Uncle Sam Wants a Few Good Appointees," *Los Angeles Times*, April 5, 2001, A17. Baker and Raines were cochairs of the Presidential Appointee Initiative Advisory Board, a project of the Brookings Institution. Its basic goal was to propose improvements in the presidential appointment process. See *To Form A Government, A Bipartisan Plan to Improve the Presidential Appointments Process* (Washington, DC: Brookings, April 2001).

35. G. Calvin Mackenzie, "Hung Out to Dry," *Washington Post*, April 1, 2001, B5.

36. Paul Light, "The Glacial Pace of Presidential Appointments," *Wall Street Journal*, April 4, 2001, A20.

37. Al Kamen, "Confirmation Delays Hobble Administration," *Washington Post*, May 20, 2001, A1. See also Laurence McQuillan, "Complex Process Slows Hiring," *USA Today*, May 30, 2001, 10A.

38. Alan K. Ota, "A Capital's Empty Chairs," *CQ Weekly*, July 5, 2010, 1604.

39. Brady Dennis and Scott Wilson, "Warren Takes Post; Liberals Cheer," *Washington Post*, September 18, 2010, A8.

40. *Congressional Record*, 112th Cong., 1st sess., January 5, 2011, S14–S15.

41. Paul Kane, "Senate Leaders Agree on Changes in Filibuster, Confirmation Process," *Washington Post,* January 28, 2011, A5.

42. Carl Hulse, "Senate Approves Changes Intended to Ease Gridlock," *New York Times,* January 28, 2011, A16.

43. Light, "Glacial Pace of Presidential Appointments," A20.

44. See Senate Committee on Homeland Security and Governmental Affairs, *United States Government Policy and Supporting Positions* (Senate Print 110–36), November 12, 2008, Appendix No. 1, 197. This report is informally known as the "Plum Book" for its plum-colored title page. Another privately published report called *The Prune Book* identifies what are alleged to be the most difficult jobs in government. See John H. Trattner, *The Prune Book, Top Management Challenges for Presidential Appointees* (Washington, DC: Brookings, 2005).

45. Paul C. Light, *Thickening Government* (Washington, DC: Brookings and Governance Institute, 1995), esp. 111–116.

46. Paul C. Light, "Big Bureaucracy," *Washington Times,* May 10, 2001, A17.

47. Christopher Lee, "Agencies Getting Heavier on Top," *Washington Times,* July 23, 2004, A27.

48. Stephen Barr, "Title Creep Reported at Agencies," *Washington Post,* March 8, 1999, A17.

49. Fareed Zakaria, "Be More Like Ike," *Newsweek,* August 28 and 30, 2010, 18.

50. Paul C. Light, *A Government Ill Executed* (Cambridge, MA: Harvard University Press, 2008), 53.

51. Lee, "Agencies Getting Heavier on Top," A27.

52. G. Calvin Mackenzie, ed., *Innocent until Nominated* (Washington, DC: Brookings, 2001), 30.

53. Doyle McManus and Robert Shogun, "Acrid Tone Reflects Long-Term Trend for Nominations," *Los Angeles Times,* March 9, 1997, A6.

54. Peter Grier, "Why Senate Roughs Up Some Cabinet Nominees," *Christian Science Monitor,* March 19, 1997, 3.

55. Stephen Barr, "Plum Book Counts Political Jobs in Executive, Legislative Branches," *Washington Post,* December 15, 2004, B2.

56. See Henry Hogue, "Statutory Qualifications for Executive Branch Positions," Congressional Research Service Report RL33886, February 20, 2007.

57. *Congressional Record,* 105th Cong., 1st sess., September 12, 1996, S10367.

58. Shankar Vedantam, "Who Are the Better Managers—Political Appointees or Career Bureaucrats?" *Washington Post,* November 24, 2008, A6.

59. Alyssa Rosenberg, "Minding the Hatch Act," *Government Executive,* October 2008, 76.

60. Joe Davidson, "Guidelines on Hatch Act and Social Media Are 'Rules of the Road' for Upcoming Elections," *Washington Post,* August 24, 2010, B3.

61. Bart Jansen, "Details of the Lobbying Rules Law," *CQ Weekly,* September 17, 2007, 2693.

62. Zachary A. Goldfarb, "Regulators See Chance to Cash In," *Washington Post,* December 30, 2010, A11.

63. Kenneth P. Vogel, "Not Even Obama Can Halt the Hill's Revolving Door," *Politico,* January 18, 2011, 6.

64. Juliet Eilperin and Scott Higham, "Seeking Answers in MMS's Flawed Culture," *Washington Post,* August 25, 2010, A1.

65. See the three-part series on the post-9/11 explosion of the intelligence community in Dana Priest and William Arkin, "A Hidden World, Growing Beyond Control," *Washington Post,* July 19, 2010, A1; "National Security, Inc.," July 20, 2010, A1; and "The Secrets Next Door," July 21, 2010, A1.

66. Craig Whitlock, "Thousands of Defense Jobs to Be Eliminated," *Washington Post,* August 10, 2010, A4.

67. Ellen Nakashima, "Pentagon Hires Out More Than In," *Washington Post,* April 3, 2001, A19.

68. Ibid.

69. Paul C. Light, "The True Size of Government," *Government Executive,* January 1999, 20. Also see Light, *The True Size of Government* (Washington, DC: Brookings, 1990). Periodically, Light updates the number of contract workers. In his August 2006 revision, he compares the number of contract workers in 1999 (6.968 million) to 2005 (10.526 million), a 51.1 percent increase.

70. Joe Davidson, "Defining 'Inherently Governmental' and Role of Contractors in War," *Washington Post,* June 22, 2010, B3.

71. Bernard Wysocki Jr., "Is U.S. Government 'Outsourcing Its Brain'?" *Wall Street Journal,* March 30, 2007, A1.

72. *Congressional Record,* 96th Cong., 2d sess., July 1, 1980, E3320.

73. *Congressional Record,* 100th Cong., 1st sess., July 29, 1987, S10850.

74. See Curtis W. Copeland, "Regulations Pursuant to the Patient Protection and Affordable Care Act (PPACA)", CRS Report R41180, April 13, 2010.

75. David M. Drucker, "GOP Readies Assault on Health Care Law," *Roll Call,* December 27, 2010 (online edition).

76. N. C. Aizenman, "Win or Lose, GOP to Make Health-Care Law a Target," *Washington Post,* October 14, 2010, A3.

77. Noam Levy, "Republicans Are Spoiling for a Health Fight," *Los Angeles Times,* November 15, 2010 (online edition).

78. Marilyn Werber Serfina, "The Risk of Vow to 'Repeal and Replace,'" *Washington Post,* October 14, 2010, A21.

79. Seth McLaughlin, "Parties' Talking Points Spin Health Care Law," *Washington Times,* January 17, 2011, A11.

80. Under the expedited procedures that apply mainly to Senate consideration (the House employs its regular procedures for these measures), floor debate is limited to ten hours, thereby preventing filibusters. No amendments are allowed to the joint resolution of disapproval, and a simple majority is sufficient for passage. The CRA facilitates bicameral agreement by stipulating that if, for example, the House is considering a disapproval resolution and a companion disapproval measure is received from the Senate, the House will cast its final vote on the joint resolution sent to it by the other chamber. The continuing appropriations resolution for fiscal 2011 deleted a funding increase for a key health agency, the Center for Medicare and Medicaid Services. As one news article pointed out, "That omission complicates efforts by the administration to get the resources it needs to cope with the increased workload under the [health care] law." See John Reichard, "Updated Stopgap Bill Omits CMS Funding Increase Needed for Health Care Overhaul," *CQ Today,* December 22, 2010, 4.

81. Richard S. Beth, "The Congressional Review Act and Possible Consolidation into a Single Measure of Resolutions Disapproving Regulations," Congressional Research Service Report R40163, January 26, 2009, 8.

82. Rebecca Adams, "Republicans Dust Off a Little-Used Tool to Go after Overhaul Rules," *CQ Today,* November 29, 2010, 3.

83. Billy House, "House Republicans Are Dusting Off an Old Weapon to Target Obama Laws," *National Journal CongressDaily PM Update,* January 11, 2011, 12.

84. Stephen Losey, "Rule-Making's New Mass Appeal," *Federal Times,* June 15, 2009, 1, 22.

85. Matthew Wald, "Court Voids a Bush Move on Energy," *New York Times,* January 14, 2004, A12.

86. Cyril Zaneski, "Escape Artist," *Government Executive,* March 2001, 29.

87. Amy Goldstein, "Regulators Ordered to Leave Work Unfinished," *Washington Post,* January 21, 2009, A2.

88. See "New Regs Surge under Obama," *Federal Times,* September 27, 2010, 6; and Eric Lipton, "With Obama, Regulations Are Back in Fashion," *New York Times,* May 13, 2010, A13.

89. Jennifer Bendery, "Obama Grabs Reins on Regulation," *Roll Call,* January 19, 2011 (online edition).

90. Larry Margasak, "GOP Agenda: Major Impact May Be on 2012 Election," *Examiner,* January 3, 2011, 13.

91. Editorial, "A Coming Assault on the E.P.A.," *New York Times,* December 25, 2010, A20.

92. Amy Harder and Olga Belogolova, "Senators Weigh In on EPA Regulations," *National Journal Daily,* January 5, 2011, 4.

93. Frank Ackerman, Lisa Heinzerling, James K. Hammitt, and Milton C. Weinstein, "Balancing Lives against Lucre," *Los Angeles Times,* February 25, 2004, A17. Ackerman and Heinzerling are economists, and Hammitt and Weinstein are risk analysis experts.

94. Liz White, "Federal Regulations Cost Up to $12 Billion in Fiscal Year 2010, OMB Report Says," *Daily Report for Executives,* March 4, 2011, A-8.

95. *Congressional Record,* 104th Cong., 1st sess., July 11, 1995, S9705.

96. Ibid., S9697.

97. Joseph S. Clark, *Congress: The Sapless Branch* (New York: Harper and Row, 1964), 63–64.

98. David B. Frohnmayer, "The Separation of Powers: An Essay on the Vitality of a Constitutional Idea," *Oregon Law Review* (Spring 1973): 330.

99. David B. Truman, *The Governmental Process,* rev. ed. (New York: Knopf, 1971), 439.

100. Woodrow Wilson, *Congressional Government* (Boston: Houghton Mifflin, 1885), 297.

101. Lisa Rein, "Conversations: Gene L. Dorado," *Washington Post,* December 30, 2010, B3.

102. David Rogers, "Sen. Lott Becomes GOP's New Standard-bearer, But His Style Will Be Tested in the Next Congress," *Wall Street Journal,* November 15, 1996, A16.

103. Wilson, *Congressional Government,* 303.

104. Rochelle Stanfield, "Plotting Every Move," *National Journal,* March 26, 1988, 796.

105. *Watkins v. United States,* 354 U.S. 178 (1957). See also James Hamilton, *The Power to Probe* (New York: Vantage Books, 1976).

106. William S. Cohen and George J. Mitchell, *Men of Zeal: A Candid Inside Story of the Iran-Contra Hearings* (New York: Viking Penguin, 1988), 305.

107. *Immigration and Naturalization Service v. Chadha,* 462 U.S. 919 (1983).

108. Louis Fisher, in *Extensions* (Carl Albert Congressional Research and Studies Center newsletter), Spring 1984, 2.

109. John R. Johannes, "Study and Recommend: Statutory Reporting Requirements as a Technique of Legislative Initiative—A Research Note," *Western Political Quarterly* (December 1976): 589–596.

110. Guy Gugliotta, "Reporting on a Practice That's Ripe for Reform," *Washington Post,* February 11, 1997, A19.

111. John T. Bennett, "Fewer Reports to Congress? DoD Move Could Backfire, Experts Warn," *Federal Times,* October 18, 2010, 11.

112. Ibid.

113. Michael W. Kirst, *Government without Passing Laws* (Chapel Hill: University of North Carolina Press, 1969).

114. Joseph A. Davis, "War Declared over Report-Language Issue," *Congressional Quarterly Weekly Report,* June 25, 1988, 1752–1753; David Rapp, "OMB's Miller Backs Away from Report-Language Battle," *Congressional Quarterly Weekly Report,* July 9, 1988, 1928.

115. Sen. Chuck Grassley, "The Federal Government Needs an IG in Chief," *Politico,* July 22, 2009, 30. Also see Charles S. Clark, "Into the Limelight," *Government Executive,* March 2011, 17–24.

116. R. Jeffrey Smith, "Initiative on Worker Safety Gets Poor Marks," *Washington Post*, April 2, 2009, A6.

117. Otto Kreisher, "Pentagon IG Details Waste in Military Contractor Spending," *National Journal CongressDaily AM*, February 27, 2009, 8.

118. Jared Allen, "'Personal Pain' Is Teed Up for Head of HUD," *The Hill*, July 30, 2010, 8.

119. Greta Wodele, "DHS Facing Appropriators' Wrath for Missing Deadlines," *National Journal CongressDaily PM*, February 17, 2005, 2.

120. Slade Gorton and Larry Craig, "Congress's Call to Accounting," *Washington Post*, July 27, 1998, A23.

121. Jason A. MacDonald, "Limitation Riders and Congressional Influence over Bureaucratic Policy Decisions," *American Political Science Review*, November 2010, 781.

122. *Congressional Record*, 95th Cong., 1st sess., April 30, 1975, E2080.

123. Alan Baron and Michael Gerhardt, "Porteous Impeachment: A First," *National Law Journal*, January 17, 2011, 34.

124. See Peter Baker, *The Breach: Inside the Impeachment and Trial of William Jefferson Clinton* (New York: Scribner, 2000).

125. See Joel D. Aberbach, *Keeping a Watchful Eye: The Politics of Congressional Oversight* (Washington, DC: Brookings, 1990); and James Q. Wilson, *Bureaucracy: What Governmental Agencies Do and Why They Do It* (New York: Basic Books, 1991).

126. Major Garrett and Aamer Madhani, "Guerrilla War over Government," *National Journal*, December 18, 2010, 26.

127. Richard Cohen, "King of Oversight," *Government Executive*, September 1988, 17.

128. David Nather, "Congress as Watchdog: Asleep on the Job?" *CQ Weekly*, May 22, 2004, 1190.

129. *Congressional Record*, 111th Cong., 2d sess., September 29, 2010, S7705.

130. Larry Margasak, "Biden Makes Peace Offering to Rising House Republican," *Washington Times*, December 14, 2010, A4.

131. Susan Crabtree and Michael Gleeson, "Issa Surveys Broad Spectrum of Businesses on Obama Regs," *The Hill*, January 6, 2011, 4.

132. Joel D. Aberbach, "The Congressional Committee Intelligence System: Information, Oversight, and Change," *Congress and the Presidency* 14 (Spring 1987): 51–76; Mathew McCubbins and Thomas Schwartz, "Congressional Oversight Overlooked: Police Patrol versus Fire Alarm," *American Journal of Political Science* (February 1984): 165–177.

133. Bill Myers, "'Google Your Government' Database Bill Signed into Law," *Examiner*, September 29, 2006, 17.

134. Jennifer Martinez, "GOP to Public: We Want to Know What You'd Cut," *Politico*, January 20, 2011, 6.

135. Lyndsey Layton, "'Citizen Regulators' Take Toy Safety Testing into Their Own Hands," *Washington Post*, December 26, 2010, A3.

136. Louis Fisher, "Micromanagement by Congress: Reality and Mythology" (paper presented at a conference sponsored by the American Enterprise Institute, Washington, DC, April 8–9, 1988), 8. See also David S. Broder and Stephen Barr, "Hill's Micromanagement of Cabinet Blurs Separation of Powers," *Washington Post*, July 25, 1993, A1.

CHAPTER 12

1. Alexis de Tocqueville, *Democracy in America* (New York: American Library, 1956), 72.

2. *Marbury v. Madison*, 5 U.S. (1 Cranch) 137 (1803).

3. Quoted in Cliff Sloan and David McKean, "Why *Marbury v. Madison* Still Matters," *Newsweek*, March 2, 2009, 49.

4. Richard L. Pacelle Jr., *The Role of the Supreme Court in American Politics: The Least Dangerous Branch?* (Boulder, CO: Westview Press, 2001).

5. *United States v. Nixon,* 418 U.S. 683 (1974),

6. See Dexter Perkins and Glyndon Van Deusen, *The United States of America: A History,* vol. 2 (New York: Macmillan, 1962), 560–566.

7. Alexander Bickel, *The Least Dangerous Branch* (Indianapolis, IN: Bobbs-Merrill, 1962), 1.

8. Joan Biskupic, "Justices Defer to Congress' Power to Extend Copyright," *USA Today,* January 16, 2003, 4A.

9. Jamin Raskin, "Courts v. Citizens," *American Prospect* 14 (March 2003): A25.

10. Charles Gardner Geyh, *When Courts and Congress Collide: The Struggle for Control of America's Judicial System* (Ann Arbor: University of Michigan Press, 2006), 229.

11. *District of Columbia v. Heller,* 554 U.S. 570 (2008).

12. See, for example, Robert Schlesinger, "Sotomayor Hearings Remind Us the Republicans Can Be Judicial Activists, Too," *U.S. News and World Report,* July 22, 2009, www.usnews.com.

13. *Kelo v. City of New London,* 545 U.S. 469 (2005). See, for example, an editorial in the July 11, 2005, issue of the *New Republic* praising the *Kelo* decision as one that "defenders of judicial constraint, particularly liberals, should applaud" (p. 7).

14. For example, Sen. John McCain singled out *Kelo* as an example of judicial activism in a speech at Wake Forest University on May 6, 2008. Sen. Jeff Sessions made the same point in a *Washington Post* op-ed on May 7, 2010, A25.

15. Sandra Day O'Connor, "The Threat to Judicial Independence," *Wall Street Journal,* September 27, 2006, A18.

16. Linda Greenhouse, "High Court Faces Moment of Truth in Federalism Cases," *New York Times,* March 28, 1999, 3.

17. Louis Fisher, *American Constitutional Law,* 6th ed. (Durham, NC: Carolina Academic Press, 2005), 355.

18. Louis Fisher, "The Law: Litigating the War Power with *Campbell v. Clinton,*" *Presidential Studies Quarterly* (September 2000): 568.

19. The U.S. Supreme Court majority contended in this and similar rulings that the Eleventh Amendment granted states "sovereign immunity" from legal suits. But the amendment's plain language protects states only from suits by citizens of other states or foreign nations, *not* those from its own citizens. Moreover, it is hard to escape the supposition that, whatever the protections afforded by the Eleventh Amendment (ratified in 1798), they were super-seded—at least in the realm of civil rights—by the Fourteenth Amendment (ratified in 1868), which not only nationalized basic civil rights but also expressly granted Congress the power of enforcement. For a detailed critique of the Court's activism in such cases, see John T. Noonan Jr., *Narrowing the Nation's Power: The Supreme Court Sides with the States* (Berkeley: University of California Press, 2002).

20. See, for example, the House debate on the Lilly Ledbetter case, *Congressional Record,* 111th Cong., 1st sess., January 9, 2009, H113–H138.

21. See Robert A. Katzmann, ed., *Judges and Legislators* (Washington, DC: Brookings, 1988); and Robert A. Katzmann, *Courts and Congress* (Washington, DC: Brookings, 1997).

22. *New York Times,* May 12, 1983, B8.

23. Dan Eggen, "Record Shows Senators' 'Debate' That Wasn't," *Washington Post,* March 29, 2006, A6.

24. Emily Bazelon, "Invisible Men: Did Lindsay Graham and Jon Kyl Mislead the Supreme Court?" *Slate,* March 27, 2006.

25. Eggen, "Record Shows Senators' 'Debate' That Wasn't," A6.

26. See, for example, Antonin Scalia, *A Matter of Interpretation* (Princeton, NJ: Princeton University Press, 1997).

27. Quoted in Jonathan Kaplan, "High Court to Congress: Say What You Mean," *The Hill*, February 5, 2003, 21.

28. Ruth Marcus, "Lawmakers Override High Court," *Washington Post*, October 31, 1991, A1.

29. *Congressional Record*, 102d Cong., 1st sess., October 29, 1991, S15324–S15325.

30. Quoted in Joan Biskupic, "Scalia Sees No Justice in Trying to Judge Intent of Congress on a Law," *Washington Post*, May 11, 1993, A4.

31. Kaplan, "High Court to Congress," 21.

32. Stanley I. Kutler, *Judicial Power and Reconstruction Politics* (Chicago: University of Chicago Press, 1968).

33. Howard Gillman, "How Political Parties Can Use the Courts to Advance Their Agendas: Federal Courts in the United States, 1875–1891," *American Political Science Review* 96 (September 2002): 511–524.

34. Quoted in Stephen Dinan, "DeLay Threatens to Curb Courts' Jurisdiction," *Washington Times*, March 6, 2003, A4.

35. Tom S. Clark, "The Separation of Powers, Court Curbing, and Judicial Legitimacy," *American Journal of Political Science* 53 (October 2009): 971–989.

36. Joan Biskupic and Elder Witt, *Guide to the U.S. Supreme Court*, 3d ed., vol. 2 (Washington, DC: CQ Press, 1997), 720.

37. William H. Rehnquist, *Grand Inquests: The Historic Impeachment of Justice Samuel Chase and President Andrew Johnson* (New York: William Morrow, 1992), 132.

38. Russell R. Wheeler and Robert A. Katzmann, "A Primer on Interbranch Relations," *Georgetown Law Journal* (April 2007): 1172.

39. Rehnquist, *Grand Inquests*, 114.

40. "History of the Federal Judiciary: Impeachments of Federal Judges," Federal Judicial Center, www.fjc.gov/history/home.nsf/page/judges_impeachments.html.

41. Biskupic and Witt, *Guide to the U.S. Supreme Court*, 717.

42. Ibid., 718.

43. Carol Leonning, "New Rules for Judges Are Weaker, Critics Say," *Washington Post*, December 17, 2004, A31; David Von Drehle, "Scalia Rejects Pleas for Recusal in Cheney Case," *Washington Post*, February 12, 2004, A35; Eileen Sullivan, "Courts Order Review of Judges' Security," *Federal Times*, March 21, 2005, 12.

44. Tony Mauro, "Kennedy Talks Tough on Salaries, Cameras," *Legal Times*, February 19, 2007, 14.

45. Nathan Koppel, "Kagan Says 'Yes' to Cameras in the Courtroom," *WSJ Law Blog*, June 29, 2010, http://blogs.wsj.com/law/.

46. Joan Biskupic, "Judicial Panel Weighs Courtroom Cameras," *USA Today*, September 14, 2010.

47. Seth Stern, "A Career as Federal Judge Isn't What It Used to Be," *Christian Science Monitor*, January 22, 2002, 1.

48. American Bar Association, "Federal Judicial Pay, an Update on the Urgent Need for Action," May 2003, 4.

49. Mark Sherman, "Big Money Depletes Judges' Ranks," *Washington Times*, December 30, 2008, B3. Also see Adam Liptak, "The State of Courts, and a Plea for a Raise," *New York Times*, January 1, 2009, A13.

50. Greenhouse, "Chief Justice Advocates Higher Pay for Judiciary," A14. Also see editorial, "There Oughta Be a Law," *USA Today*, January 9, 2007, 12A.

51. Adam Liptak, "On the Subject of Judicial Salaries, a Sharp Difference of Opinion," *New York Times*, January 20, 2009, A14.

52. *Chisholm v. Georgia*, 2 U.S. 419 (1793).

53. *Dred Scott v. Sandford*, 60 U.S. 393 (1857).

54. See Fisher, *American Constitutional Law*, 1072.

55. Jennifer Dlouhy, "Congress Reluctant to Change Constitution," *CQ Today*, February 11, 2003, 9.

56. *Texas v. Johnson*, 491 U.S. 397 (1989).

57. Norman Ornstein, "To Break the Stalemate, Give Judges Less than Life," *Washington Post*, November 28, 2004, B3.

58. Tony Mauro, "Profs Pitch Plan for Limits on Supreme Court Service," *Legal Times*, January 3, 2005, 1. Also see Robert Barnes, "Legal Experts Propose Limiting Justices' Powers, Terms," *Washington Post*, February 23, 2009, A15.

59. From 1952 to 2001, every president consulted the Standing Committee on the Federal Judiciary of the American Bar Association (ABA) about judicial candidates prior to their formal nomination. President George W. Bush then curtailed the ABA's role in providing evaluations of prospective judicial candidates. However, the ABA still provides its evaluations to the Senate and the administration after the candidates' names have been made public. See Amy Goldstein, "Bush Curtails ABA Role in Selecting U.S. Judges," *Washington Post*, March 23, 2001, A1.

60. Jeff Zeleny, "A Premium on Secrecy in Vetting of Court Pick," *New York Times*, May 13, 2009.

61. Alpheus Thomas Mason, *Harlan Fiske Stone: Pillar of the Law* (New York: Viking, 1959), chap. 12.

62. Dennis Steven Rutkus and Lorraine H. Tong, "The Chief Justice of the United States: Responsibilities of the Office and Process for Appointment," Congressional Research Service Report RL32831, September 12, 2005, 30.

63. Ibid., 37.

64. Ibid., 34.

65. Brannon Denning, "The 'Blue Slip': Enforcing the Norms of the Judicial Confirmation Process," *William and Mary Bill of Rights Journal* 10 (December 2001): 92.

66. "GOP Move Would Help Nominees," *Washington Post*, January 24, 2003, A25.

67. Keith Perine, "Leahy Plans to Maintain 'Blue Slip' Policy," *CQ Today*, March 12, 2009, 17.

68. Stephen Dinan, "Strategy Shift on Nominations," *Washington Times*, March 17, 2009, B3.

69. Josiah Ryan, "Senate Ends Practice of Secret Holds," *The Hill*, January 27, 2011.

70. Ibid.

71. Quoted in Keith Perine, "As Judiciary Battles Loom, Leahy Revives Senate 'Blue Slip' Tradition," *CQ Today*, January 4, 2007, 3.

72. Ralph Neas, "United States Needs More Discussion of Judicial Philosophy," *Roll Call*, May 9, 2002, 10.

73. Seth Stern, "Senate Shows Supreme Decline in Deference," *CQ Weekly*, July 12, 2010, 1635.

74. Quoted in ibid.

75. Terri L. Peretti, "Where Have All the Politicians Gone? Recruiting for the Modern Supreme Court," *Judicature* (November–December 2007): 120. Also see Paul A. Sracic, "Politician on Court Isn't a Bad Thing," *USA Today*, March 30, 2005, 13A.

76. Charles E. Schumer, "Judging by Ideology," *New York Times*, June 26, 2001.

77. Lee Epstein, René Lindstädt, Jeffrey A. Segal, and Chad Westerland, "The Changing Dynamics of Senate Voting on Supreme Court Nominees," *Journal of Politics* 68 (May 2006): 306.

78. James Robertson, "A Cure for What Ails the Judiciary," *Washington Post*, May 27, 2003, A19.

79. Ronald Brownstein, "To End Battle over Judicial Picks, Each Side Must Lay Down Arms," *Los Angeles Times*, February 21, 2005, A8.

80. Linda Greenhouse, "Case of the Dwindling Docket Mystifies the Supreme Court," *New York Times*, December 7, 2006, A1.

81. Warren Richey, "Conservatives Near Lock on U.S. Courts," *Christian Science Monitor,* April 14, 2005, 10.

82. Elizabeth Palmer, "Appellate Courts at Center of Fight for Control of Judiciary," *CQ Weekly,* February 23, 2002, 534.

83. Ibid.

84. Sarah Binder, "Advice and Consent for Judicial Nominations: Can the President and Senate Do Better?" (Paper prepared for delivery at the seminar "Presidential Nominations and the Senate Confirmation Process," Woodrow Wilson International Center for Scholars, Washington, DC, March 16, 2009), 10–11.

85. *Congressional Record,* 110th Cong., 2d sess., April 15, 2008, S3012.

86. Binder, "Advice and Consent for Judicial Nominations," 16.

87. Neil A. Lewis, "New Democratic Majority Throws Bush's Judicial Nominations into Uncertainty," *New York Times,* November 12, 2006, 22.

88. R. Jeffrey Smith, "Judge's Fate Could Turn on 1994 Case," *Washington Post,* May 27, 2003, A8.

89. E. J. Dionne Jr., "They Started It," *Washington Post,* February 21, 2003, A27.

90. Jerry Markon and Shailagh Murray, "Federal Judicial Vacancies Reaching Crisis Point," *Washington Post,* February 8, 2011, A1.

91. Sarah A. Binder and Forrest Maltzman, *Advice and Dissent: The Struggle to Shape the Federal Judiciary* (Washington, DC: Brookings, 2009), 75.

92. Markon and Murray, "Federal Judicial Vacancies."

93. Louis Fisher, "Congressional Checks on the Judiciary," in *Congress Confronts the Court,* ed. Colton C. Campbell and John F. Stack Jr. (Lanham, MD: Rowman and Littlefield, 2001), 35.

CHAPTER 13

1. Peter Dreier, "Lessons from the Health-Care Wars," *American Prospect,* May 2010, 29.

2. Dan Eggen, "Interest Groups Rally for a Big Finish on Health-Care Reform," *Washington Post,* February 28, 2010, A3.

3. Michael D. Shear, "Health Bill Foes Solicit Funds for Economic Study," *Washington Post,* November 16, 2001, A1.

4. Bennett Roth and Alex Knott, "Medical Interests Spend $876 Million on Reform," *Roll Call,* May 3, 2010, 6. For an analysis of the battle over President Clinton's health care plan, see Haynes Johnson and David S. Broder, *The System* (Boston: Little, Brown, 1996).

5. Fredreka Schouten, "Special-Interest Spending Surges," *USA Today,* February 8, 2011, 5A.

6. See John R. Hibbing and Elizabeth Theiss-Morse, *Congress as Public Enemy: Public Attitudes toward American Political Institutions* (New York: Cambridge University Press, 1995).

7. Joel Jankowsky and Thomas Goldstein, "In Defense of Lobbying," *Wall Street Journal,* September 4, 2009, A15.

8. Kate Ackley, "'Kick the Lobbyist' Is Still a Favorite Pastime," *Roll Call,* May 10, 2010, 10.

9. Data are from James A. Thurber, American University.

10. Bill Swindell, "Industry's Increased D.C. Presence Reflects New Reality," *National Journal CongressDaily AM,* July 28, 2010, 1, 14. *CongressDaily* is published by *National Journal,* a Washington-based journal.

11. M. B. Pell and Joe Eaton, "K Street Cashes In on Bill," *Politico,* May 21, 2010, 1, www.politico .com.

12. Swindell, "Industry's Increased D.C. Presence Reflects New Reality," 14.

13. Baa Vaida, "Brisk Business for K Street in 2010," *National Journal,* July 24, 2010, 44. Many lobbying groups have their offices on K Street in the District of Columbia.

14. Kenneth P. Doyle, "Reported Spending on Federal Lobbying Up 5% in 2009 to $3.47 Billion, Study Finds," *Daily Report for Executives,* February 16, 2010, A-12.

15. Ibid.

16. Brody Mullins and Elizabeth Williamson, "Lobbyists Raise Stimulus Price Tag," *Wall Street Journal,* February 3, 2009.

17. Shawn Zeller, "K Street Remains an Easy Street in Hard Times," *CQ Weekly,* April 21, 2008, 995.

18. Alexis de Tocqueville, *Democracy in America,* ed. Phillips Bradley (New York: Knopf, 1951), 119. See also Richard A. Smith, "Interest Group Influence in the U.S. Congress," *Legislative Studies Quarterly* 20 (February 1995): 89–139.

19. Janny Scott, "Medicine's Big Dose of Politics," *Los Angeles Times,* September 25, 1991, A15.

20. Robert Putnam, "The Strange Disappearance of Civic America," *American Prospect,* Winter 1996, 35.

21. Quoted in Suzi Parker, "Civic Clubs: Elks, Lions May Go Way of the Dodo," *Christian Science Monitor,* August 24, 1998, 1.

22. Seth Stern, "No More Bowling Alone," *Christian Science Monitor,* September 4, 2003, 17.

23. Everett Carll Ladd, "The American Way—Civic Engagement—Thrives," *Christian Science Monitor,* March 1, 1999, 9. See Theda Skocpol, *Diminished Democracy: From Membership to Management in American Civic Life* (Norman: University of Oklahoma Press, 2003). Professor Skocpol argues that the decline of broad membership organizations such as the Elks or Moose, which encouraged civic and political participation, occurred in part because many middle-class citizens chose to rely on professionally run advocacy groups to speak on their behalf.

24. Ladd, "American Way."

25. Doyle McManus, "Great Recession's Psychological Fallout," *Los Angeles Times,* July 15, 2010 (online edition).

26. Mancur Olson Jr., *The Logic of Collective Action: Public Goods and the Theory of Groups* (Cambridge, MA: Harvard University Press, 1965).

27. Kay L. Schlozman and John T. Tierney, *Organized Interests and American Democracy* (New York: Harper and Row, 1986).

28. E. E. Schattschneider, *The Semi-Sovereign People* (New York: Holt, Rinehart and Winston, 1960), 35.

29. Melinda Burns, "K Street and the Status Quo," *Miller-McCune,* September–October 2010, 65. Also see Frank R. Baumgartner et al., *Lobbying and Policy Change: Who Wins, Who Loses and Why* (Chicago: University of Chicago Press, 2009).

30. Kristina C. Miler, "The View from the Hill: Legislative Perceptions of the District," *Legislative Studies Quarterly* 32 (November 2007): 597–628.

31. Sidney Verba, Kay Lehman Schlozman, and Henry Brady, "The Big Tilt: Participatory Inequality in America," *American Prospect,* May/June 1997, 78.

32. Elise D. Garcia, "Money in Politics," *Common Cause,* February 1981, 11.

33. Jeffrey H. Birnbaum, "Lobbyists: Why the Bad Rap?" *American Enterprise,* November/December 1992, 74. Also see also Jeffrey H. Birnbaum, *The Lobbyists* (New York: Times Books, 1992).

34. Norman J. Ornstein and Shirley Elder, *Interest Groups, Lobbying, and Policymaking* (Washington, DC: Congressional Quarterly, 1978), 224.

35. Tory Newmyer, "Majority Formalizes K St. Ties," *Roll Call,* February 15, 2007, 23.

36. Alexander Bolton, "Dems Enlist Help to Push Their Agenda," *The Hill,* February 14, 2007, 1.

37. Anna Palmer, "K Street Prepares for Televised Rendezvous with GOP Leaders," *Roll Call,* July 15, 2010 (online edition).

38. Jeffrey Birnbaum, "The Thursday Group," *Time,* March 27, 1995, 30–31.

39. Emily Pierce, "GOP Taps Thune to Get Cozy with K St.," *Roll Call,* January 22, 2009.

40. Quoted in Hedrick Smith, *The Power Game* (New York: Random House, 1988), 232.

41. Fredreka Schouten, "Private Citizens Take Troubles to Lobbyists," *USA Today,* June 1, 2010, 6A.

42. Quoted in Alan K. Ota, "Democratic Foot in Revolving Door," *CQ Weekly,* June 25, 2007, 1900.

43. Ronald J. Hrebenar and Ruth K. Scott, *Interest Group Politics in America* (Englewood Cliffs, NJ: Prentice-Hall, 1982), 63.

44. Bara Vaida, "Shutting the Revolving Door," *National Journal,* May 22, 2010, 52.

45. Jonathan D. Salant, "Obama's Spending Spurs Former U.S. Lawmakers to Join Lobbyists," *Bloomberg.com,* April 9, 2009.

46. Chris Frates, "Hill Experience Gives Lobbyists a Leg Up," *Politico,* May 17, 2007, 10, www .politico.com.

47. R. Jeffrey Smith and Dan Eggen, "More Former Lobbyists Flocking to Jobs on Hill," *Washington Post,* March 18, 2011, A1.

48. See, for example, David Ottaway and Dan Morgan, "Former Top U.S. Aides Seek Caspian Gusher," *Washington Post,* July 6, 1997, A1; and Chuck Neubauer and Ted Rohrlich, "Capitalizing on a Politician's Clout," *Los Angeles Times,* December 19, 2004, A1.

49. Mark Preston, "Ex-GOP Senators Get Special Access," *Roll Call,* April 3, 2003, 1, 24.

50. Quoted in Alan K. Ota, "Democratic Foot in the Revolving Door," *CQ Weekly,* June 25, 2007, 1900.

51. Sarah Pekkanen, "How Lobbyists Are Changing the Lobbying Game," *The Hill,* February 12, 1997, 21.

52. *National Journal CongressDaily PM,* May 30, 1997, 6.

53. Quoted in Sam Walker, "Who's In and Who's Out among Capitol Lobbyists," *Christian Science Monitor,* November 8, 1995, 3.

54. Quoted in *National Journal CongressDaily PM,* March 15, 2002, 8.

55. Steven Brill, "On Sale: Your Government," *Time,* July 12, 2010, 32.

56. Bertram J. Levine, *The Art of Lobbying: Building Trust and Selling Policy* (Washington, DC: CQ Press, 2008).

57. *New York Times,* January 20, 1981, B3.

58. Adam Graham-Silverman, "Travel Decreases as Ethics Rules Complicate Privately Funded Trips," *CQ Weekly,* December 1, 2008, 3178.

59. John Cochran and Martin Kady II, "The New Laws of the Lobby," *CQ Weekly,* February 26, 2007, 594.

60. Eliza Newlin Carney and Bara Vaida, "Shifting Ground," *National Journal,* March 31, 2007, 27.

61. Quoted in Cochran and Kady, "New Laws of the Lobby," 594.

62. Joseph Curl, "Big Money Buys Seats at Lawmakers' Dinner Tables," *Washington Times,* November 3, 2009, A1.

63. David Kirkpatrick, "Congress Finds Ways of Avoiding Lobbyist Limit," *New York Times,* February 11, 2007, 1.

64. Ibid.

65. Quoted in Editorial, "Wasn't There an Election Last November?" *Examiner,* March 9, 2007, 18.

66. Carol Matlack, "Getting around the Rules," *National Journal,* May 12, 1990, 1139.

67. Eric Lipton, "Congressional Charities Pulling in Corporate Cash," *New York Times,* September 5, 2010, A1.

68. Ibid., A10.

69. Eliza Newlin Carney, "Charitable Chicanery," *National Journal,* June 24, 2006, 20.

70. Bennett Roth and Alex Knott, "Gifts to Honor Members Are So 2008," *Roll Call,* February 24, 2010, 9.

71. Eric Lipton, "Lawmakers Linked to Centers Endowed by Corporate Money," *New York Times,* August 6, 2010, A3.

72. Ibid.

73. John Breaux, "Effective Coalitions for Coalitions," *The Hill,* March 21, 2007, 18.

74. Dan Eggen, "Investments Can Yield More on K Street, Study Indicates," *Washington Post,* April 12, 2009, A8.

75. Matthew Murray, "Tax Coalition to Target Members This Month," *Roll Call,* August 2, 2010 (online edition).

76. John Podesta and Robert Greenstein, "Bush Tax Cuts for the Rich Must Go," *Financial Times,* August 25, 2010, 7.

77. Ernest Wittenberg, "How Lobbying Helps Make Democracy Work," *Vital Speeches of the Day,* November 1, 1982, 47.

78. Robert Pear, "In Divide over Health Care Overhaul, 2 Major Unions Withdraw from a Coalition," *New York Times,* March 7, 2009, A12.

79. Jeff Patch, "Farm Bill Renewal Sows Fresh Alliances on Subsidies," *Politico,* May 8, 2007, www.politico.com.

80. Ellyn Ferguson, "An Unexpected Alliance Fights Ethanol Expansion," *CQ Today,* July 26, 2010, 7. Also see Anna Palmer, "Lobbying Coalition Calls for Congressional Hearing on Ethanol," *Roll Call,* August 25, 2010 (online edition).

81. Martin Kady II, "Keeping Grass-Roots Lobbying under Wraps," *CQ Weekly,* March 26, 2007, 877.

82. Shawn Zeller, "SEIU Spreads Its Wings, Ruffles Some Feathers," *CQ Weekly,* May 12, 2008, 1233.

83. John T. Tierney and Kay Lehman Schlozman, "Congress and Organized Interests," in *Congressional Politics,* ed. Christopher J. Deering (Chicago: Dorsey, 1989), 212.

84. *Washington Star,* December 31, 1980, C2.

85. Kady, "Keeping Grass-Roots Lobbying under Wraps," 877.

86. Ibid.

87. Juliet Eilperin, "Police Track Down Telecom Telegraphs," *Roll Call,* August 7, 1995, 1.

88. Lisa Caruso, "Turf Battle," *National Journal,* March 31, 2007, 34.

89. Cited in Jack Maskell, "Grassroots Lobbying: Constitutionality of Disclosure Requirements," Congressional Research Service Report RL33794, January 12, 2007, 3. Also see, for example, John Cochran, "A New Medium for the Message," *CQ Weekly,* March 13, 2006, 652–658; and Kady, "Keeping Grass-Roots Lobbying under Wraps," 877–878.

90. Alison Mitchell, "A New Form of Lobbying Puts Public Face on Private Interest," *New York Times,* September 30, 1998, A14. Also see Ken Kollman, *Outside Lobbying: Public Opinion and Interest Group Strategies* (Princeton, NJ: Princeton University Press, 1998).

91. Sara Fritz and Dan Morain, "Stealth Lobby Drives Fuel-Additive War," *Los Angeles Times,* June 16, 1997, A6.

92. Bennett Roth, "Interest Groups Log On for Fight over Kagan," *Roll Call,* May 24, 2010, 10.

93. Justin Cox, "Trading Bullhorns for Blog Posts," *The Hill,* June 23, 2010, 42.

94. Mitchell, "New Form of Lobbying Puts Public Face on Private Interest."

95. "Trends in Grassroots Lobbying: Consultant Q&A," *Campaigns and Elections,* February 1999, 22.

96. *New York Times,* January 24, 1980, A16.

97. Jackie Kucinich, "Tea Partiers Prepare for Washington Onslaught," *Roll Call*, August 25, 2010 (online edition). Also see Kathleen Hennessey, "Glen Beck and Fans to Rally on 'I Have a Dream' Anniversary," *Los Angeles Times*, August 25, 2010 (online edition).

98. Quoted in Jeffrey Birnbaum, "Advocacy Groups Blur Media Lines," *Washington Post*, December 6, 2004, A1.

99. Ibid., A7.

100. Eric Litchtblau, "Beyond Guns: N.R.A. Expands Political Agenda," *New York Times*, July 13, 2010, A3.

101. Jeffrey Birnbaum, "The Forces That Set the Agenda," *Washington Post*, April 24, 2005, B5.

102. Tom Hamburger, "U.S. Chamber of Commerce Grows into a Political Force," *Los Angeles Times*, March 8, 2010 (online edition).

103. Paul S. Herrnson, "Party Organizations, Party-Connected Committees, Party Allies, and the Financing of Federal Elections," *Journal of Politics* (November 2009).

104. Brody Mullins, "Growing Role for Lobbyists: Raising Funds for Lawmakers," *Wall Street Journal*, January 27, 2006, A1.

105. Philip M. Stern, "The Tin Cup Congress," *Washington Monthly*, May 1988, 24.

106. *Congressional Record*, 100th Cong., 1st sess., August 5, 1987, S11292.

107. "Fundamentals of Fund-raising," *Washington Post*, December 5, 1990, A23.

108. Fredreka Schouten, "Polled PAC Donations Add $33M Punch to Races," *USA Today*, August 17, 2010, 5A.

109. Manu Raju, "Members Get Bundles of Lobbyist Cash," *Politico*, February 16, 2010, 1, www.politico.com.

110. Jack Maskell, "Lobbying Law and Ethics Rules Changes in the 110th Congress," Congressional Research Service Report RL 33836, September 18, 2007.

111. Melanie Grottman, "Big Labor Groups to Pool Money for Fall Elections," *Wall Street Journal*, August 25, 2010, A4.

112. Tom Hamburger, "Corporate Campaign Fundraising Picks Up Speed," *Los Angeles Times*, August 2, 2010 (online edition).

113. John Brinkley, "Members of Congress Perform under Judging Eyes of Lobbyists," *Washington Times*, March 16, 1994, A16. See John Cochran, "Interest Groups Make Sure Lawmakers Know the 'Score,'" *CQ Weekly*, April 19, 2003, 924–929.

114. Bill Whalen, "Rating Lawmakers' Politics by Looking into Their Eyes," *Insight*, October 20, 1986, 21. See Cochran, "Interest Groups Make Sure Lawmakers Know the 'Score.'"

115. *New York Times*, May 13, 1986, A24.

116. *CQ Monitor*, April 13, 1998, 4.

117. "Environment," *National Journal CongressDaily PM*, February 21, 2006, 10.

118. Alan Gomez, "Tea Party Group Taps Bloggers to Keep Tabs on Lawmakers," *USA Today*, February 25, 2011, 4A.

119. Hibbing and Theiss-Morse, *Congress as Public Enemy*, 63–65.

120. Frank R. Baumgartner and Beth L. Leech, *Basic Interests: The Importance of Groups in Politics and in Political Science* (Princeton, NJ: Princeton University Press, 1998), 13.

121. Burns, "K Street and the Status Quo," 64. To be sure, some studies find that "corporations that poured money into Congress typically got the votes they wanted." See Leslie Wayne, "Lobbyists' Gift to Politicians Reap Benefits, Study Shows," *New York Times*, January 23, 1997, B11.

122. Interview with Prof. Marie Elizabeth Hojnacki, *CQ Weekly*, September 6, 2010, 2005.

123. Janet M. Gretzke, "PACs and the Congressional Supermarket: The Currency Is Complex," *American Journal of Political Science* 33 (1989): 1–24; Lawrence S. Rothenberg, *Linking Citizens to Government: Interest Group Politics at Common Cause* (New York: Cambridge

University Press, 1992); John R. Wright, "Contributions, Lobbying, and Committee Voting in the U.S. House of Representatives," *American Political Science Review* 84 (1990): 417–438.

124. Gary J. Andres, *Lobbying Reconsidered* (New York: Pearson Longman, 2009), 159. Worth noting is that the House Office of Congressional Ethics has investigated the "propriety of [lawmakers] using a vote as a fundraising opportunity by hosting events in close proximity to a major vote." See Edward Epstein, "Outside Panel in for Insider Criticism," *CQ Weekly*, August 9, 2010, 1911.

125. See the labor union profile at the Center for Responsive Politics, www.opensecrets.org/. The Center is a nonprofit research organization that tracks the role of money in politics.

126. See the oil and gas industry's profile at the Center for Responsive Politics, www.openscrets .org/industries/indus.php?ind-E01.

127. Richard L. Hall and Frank W. Wayman, "Buying Time: Moneyed Interests and the Mobilization of Bias in Congressional Committees," *American Political Science Review* 84 (September 1990): 800. See also their review of the literature on patterns in campaign contributions on pages 799–800.

128. Quoted in Claudia Dreifus, "And Then There Was Frank," *New York Times Magazine*, February 4, 1996, 25.

129. Don Van Natta Jr., "$250,000 Buys Donors 'Best Access to Congress,'" *New York Times*, January 27, 1997, A1.

130. See Richard A. Smith, "Advocacy, Interpretation, and Influence in the U.S. Congress," *American Political Science Review* 78 (1984): 44–63; and Hall and Wayman, "Buying Time."

131. Marie Hojnacki and David C. Kimball, "Organized Interests and the Decision of Whom to Lobby in Congress," *American Political Science Review* (December 1998): 775–790.

132. *Washington Star*, May 22, 1978, A1.

133. Elizabeth Brotherton, "A Recycled Idea," *Roll Call*, June 13, 2006, 3.

134. See Eric Lipton and Eric Lichtblau, "In Black Caucus, a Fund-Raising Powerhouse," *New York Times*, February 14, 2010, 1; Paul Singer, "The Tax-Payer-Funded Caucus Is Still Thriving," *Roll Call*, May 18, 2010, 4; Fredreka Schouten, "Lobbyists Get Power Access Via Caucuses," *USA Today*, July 24–26, 2009, 1A.

135. Richard L. Hall and Alan V. Deardorff, "Lobbying as Legislative Subsidy," *American Political Science Review* (February 2006): 69–84.

136. *Wall Street Journal*, October 5, 1987, 54.

137. Thomas Hale Boggs Jr., "All Interests Are Special," *New York Times*, February 16, 1993, A17.

138. Mary Lynn Jones, "Survey Says Lobbyists Find Information Rules the Hill," *The Hill*, November 18, 1998, 8. A recent study of congressional lobbying suggests that lobbyists' political connections to lawmakers are more important than their issue expertise. The president of the American League of Lobbyists, however, disputes this judgment. See Jeremy Hainsworth, "Study Finds Who You Know Counts Most Among Congressional Lobbyists," *Daily Report for Executives*, March 25, 2011, A-8.

139. Kirk Victor, "New Kids on the Block," *National Journal*, October 31, 1987, 2727.

140. Burns, "K Street and the Status Quo," 66. As an example, see Patrice Hill, "Facts Spin on Small-Business Tax," *Washington Times*, August 31, 2010, A1.

141. The "Guide to the Lobbying Disclosure Act" can be found on the website of the clerk of the U.S. House of Representatives, http://clerk.house.gov.

142. William Luneburg and Thomas Susman, *The Lobbying Manual*, 3d ed. (Washington, DC: American Bar Association, 2005), 7.

143. U.S. Congress, *Organization of the Congress*, H. Rept. 1675, 79th Cong., 2d sess., 1946, 26.

144. *United States v. Harriss*, 347 U.S. 612 (1954).

145. Francesca Contiguaglia, "GAO Finds That Lobbyist Registration Has Soared," *Roll Call*, May 14, 1998, 14.

146. Sam Fulwood, "Lobbying Reform Passes House on Unanimous Vote," *Los Angeles Times,* November 30, 1995, A9.

147. Alex Knott, *Special Report: Industry of Influence Nets Almost $13 Billion* (Washington, DC: Center for Public Integrity, 2005), 1–4.

148. Lee H. Hamilton, "Lobbying Murkiness Undermines Our Trust in Congress," Center on Congress at Indiana University, April 11, 2005, 2, http://congress.indiana.edu.

149. Deirdre Shesgreen, "Shining a Dim Light," *Legal Times,* December 21 and 28, 1998, 26, 27.

150. Editorial, "Scandal? What Scandal? Congress Ducks Ethics Reform," *USA Today,* September 6, 2006, 12A.

151. Michael Crowley and Jay Newton-Small, "Cleaning the People's House," *Time,* August 16, 2010, 24.

152. See John D. McKinnon and Brody Mullins, "Lawmakers Face Ethics Probe," *Wall Street Journal,* September 1, 2010, A4.

153. Dan Eggen, "Success of Lobbying Crackdown Questioned," *Washington Post,* February 14, 2010, A3.

154. Josh Rogin, "Committee Needs Waiver to Act on Lynn Nomination for Defense Deputy," *CQ Today,* January 23, 2009, 11.

155. Dan Eggen, "Lobbyists Push Off Advisory Panels," *Washington Post,* November 27, 2009, A13. For an overview of the Obama administration's restrictions on lobbyists, see Jacob R. Straus, "Lobbying the Executive Branch: Current Practices and Options for Change," Congressional Research Service Report R40947, December 1, 2009.

156. Kenneth Doyle, "Lobbyists Urged to Disclose Contributions after GAO Reported Thousands Fail to Do So," *Daily Report for Executives,* June 17, 2010, A-2.

157. David D. Kirkpatrick, "Intended to Rein In Lobbyists, Law Sends Them Underground," *New York Times,* January 18, 2010, A1.

158. Chris Frates, "When a Lobbyist Isn't a Lobbyist," *Politico,* July 26, 2010, 1, 12, www.politico .com; *Daily Report for Executives,* January 8, 2010, A-1.

159. Kevin Bogardus, "Korea Bulks Up on K Street as Obama Presses Trade Deal," *The Hill,* July 16, 2010, 9.

160. Dan Eggen, "Egypt Pushes Back against Senate Resolution," *Washington Post,* September 9, 2010, A19.

161. See Ken Silverstein, "Oil Adds Sheen to Kazakh Regime," *Los Angeles Times,* May 12, 2004, A1.

162. Ibid.

163. See Adam Hochschild, "Into the Light from the Heart of Darkness," *Los Angeles Times,* December 6, 1998, M1; and Katharine Seeyle, "National Rifle Association Is Turning to World Stage to Fight Gun Control," *New York Times,* April 2, 1997, A12.

164. Alan Ohnsman and Gopal Ratnam, "Toyota to Boost Lobbying Efforts as U.S. Operations Expand," *Examiner,* March 7, 2007, 21.

165. Edgar Lane, *Lobbying and the Law* (Berkeley: University of California Press, 1964), 18.

166. Brill, "On Sale: Your Government," 32.

CHAPTER 14

1. Peter Grier, "Bailout Tab: $3 Trillion So Far," *Christian Science Monitor,* March 31, 2009 (online edition).

2. John Stanton and Anna Palmer, "Spending Debate Cuts Both Ways," *Roll Call,* February 9, 2011 (online edition).

3. See *Washington Post,* February 20, 2011, A4.

4. Kathleen Hunter and Jessica Brady, "Republicans with 2012 Ambitions Score Points in CR Debate," *Roll Call*, February 19, 2011 (online edition).

5. Nancy Ognanovich, "Lawmakers under Pressure to Restart Talks after Senate Spending Plans Rejected," *Daily Report for Executives*, March 10, 2011, A-19.

6. Humberto Sanchez, "New CR Shows GOP's Strong Hand," *National Journal CongressDaily AM*, March 10, 2011 (online edition).

7. Janet Hook, "Three-Week Bill on Spending Seen," *Wall Street Journal*, March 11, 2011, A5.

8. Kerry Young and Sam Goldfarb, "Another Week, Another Stopgap," *CQ Today*, March 11, 2011, 1.

9. David Herszenhorn and Helene Cooper, "Concessions and Tension, Then a Deal," *New York Times*, April 10, 2011.

10. See David Easton, *The Political System* (New York: Knopf, 1963); Harold D. Lasswell, *Politics: Who Gets What, When, How* (New York: Meridian Books, 1958); and Randall B. Ripley and Grace A. Franklin, *Congress, the Bureaucracy, and Public Policy*, 5th ed. (Pacific Grove, CA: Brooks/Cole, 1991).

11. Theodore R. Marmor, *The Politics of Medicare* (Chicago: Aldine Publishing, 1973).

12. John W. Kingdon, *Agendas, Alternatives, and Public Policies* (Boston: Little, Brown, 1984), 3.

13. Ibid., 17–19.

14. Ibid., chap. 2.

15. Fareed Zakaria, "Free at Last," *Newsweek*, April 13, 2009, 42.

16. Steven Chu, "Pulling the Plug on Oil," *Newsweek*, April 13, 2009, 44.

17. Nelson W. Polsby, "Strengthening Congress in National Policymaking," *Yale Review* (Summer 1970): 481–497.

18. James L. Sundquist, *Politics and Policy: The Eisenhower, Kennedy, and Johnson Years* (Washington, DC: Brookings, 1968).

19. Elizabeth Wehr, "Numerous Factors Favoring Good Relationship between Reagan and New Congress," *Congressional Quarterly Weekly Report*, January 24, 1981, 173.

20. Kingdon, *Agendas, Alternatives, and Public Policies*, 148–149.

21. American Enterprise Institute, *The State of the Congress: Tomorrow's Challenges?* (Washington, DC: AEI, 1981), 8.

22. Theodore Lowi, "American Business, Public Policy, Case Studies, and Political Theory," *World Politics* (July 1964): 677–715; Theodore Lowi, "Four Systems of Policy, Politics, and Choice," *Public Administration Review* (July–August 1972): 298–310; Samuel P. Huntington, *The Common Defense* (New York: Columbia University Press, 1961); Ripley and Franklin, *Congress, the Bureaucracy, and Public Policy*.

23. Mary Russell, "'Park-Barrel Bill' Clears House Panel," *Washington Post*, June 22, 1978, A3.

24. George E. Condon Jr., "Bending Congress's Ear(marks)," *National Journal CongressDaily*, February 11, 2011, 5.

25. Stephen Dinan, "Earmarks End for One Year, but Perk Still Potent on Hill," *Washington Times*, February 10, 2011, A6.

26. Ibid.

27. *Congressional Record*, 111th Cong., 1st sess., May 6, 2009, H5279.

28. Frank Oliveri, "McKeon Lays Out Rules for Keeping Earmarks Out of Defense Authorization Bill," *CQ Today*, March 28, 2011, 2.

29. Raymond Hernandez, "A House District Liked Its Earmarks, and Then Elected Someone Who Didn't," *New York Times*, February 5, 2011, A16.

30. Humberto Sanchez, "Senators Line Up to Endorse Earmark Moratorium," *National Journal CongressDaily*, February 2, 2011, 7.

31. Eliza Newlin Carney, "The Earmarks Paradox," *National Journal CongressDaily*, February 14, 2011, 5.

32. Humberto Sanchez, "Senators Want to Clarify What Makes an Earmark," *National Journal CongressDaily,* March 3, 2011, 11.

33. Ron Nixon, "Earmarks Ban May Loom, but Lawmakers Find Ways to Finance Pet Projects," *New York Times,* December 28, 2010, A11.

34. Kevin Bogardus, "Keep the Earmark Requests Coming, Says Some Lawmakers to Constituents," *The Hill,* March 17, 2011, 12.

35. Condon, "Bending Congress's Ear(marks)," 5.

36. See, for example, Margaret Kriz, "Heavy Breathing," *National Journal,* January 4, 1997, 8–12.

37. Joby Warrick, "White House Taking a Hands-on Role in Writing New Clean Air Standards," *Washington Post,* May 22, 1997, A10.

38. Chris Frates, "Rule-Writing a Second Stimulus for K Street," *Politico,* March 17, 2011, 1.

39. Alan Charles Raul, "Obama Review of Regulatory Burden to Be Weighed in Cost-Benefit Analysis", *Daily Report for Executives,* February 9, 2011, B-1.

40. See, for example, Kenneth A. Shepsle, Robert P. Van Houweling, Samuel J. Abrams, and Peter C. Hanson, "The Senate Electoral Cycle and Bicameral Appropriation Politics," *American Journal of Political Science* 53 (2009): 343–359; Jeffrey Lazarus and Amy Steigerwalt, "Different Houses: The Distribution of Earmarks in the U.S. House and Senate," *Legislative Studies Quarterly* 34 (2009): 347–373; and Robert A. Bernstein, Gerald C. Wright Jr., and Michael B. Berkman, "Do U.S. Senators Moderate Strategically?" *American Political Science Review* 82 (1988): 237–245.

41. Donald Lambro, "Steady GOP Rebound Strategy," *Washington Times,* June 7, 2001, A17.

42. Benjamin I. Page, "Cooling the Legislative Tea," in *American Politics and Public Policy,* ed. Walter Dean Burnham and Martha Wagner Weinberg (Cambridge, MA: MIT Press, 1978), 171–187.

43. Judy Sarasohn, "Money for Lat. 40 N, Long. 73 W," *Congressional Quarterly Weekly Report,* May 12, 1979, 916.

44. Paula Drummond, "Unfunded Mandates Bill Becomes Law," *Kansas Government Journal,* May 1995, 122.

45. "Don't Just Do Something, Sit There," *Economist,* December 23, 1995–January 5, 1996, 11–12.

46. Barber Conable, "Government Is Working," *Roll Call,* April 19, 1984, 3. Congress has initiated change many times. A classic example is the Thirty-seventh Congress (1861–1863), which drafted "the blueprint for modern America" by enacting measures to finance the Civil War, build the transcontinental railroad, eradicate slavery, promote the land-grant college movement, provide settlers with homestead land, and create the Department of Agriculture. See James M. McPherson, *Battle Cry of Freedom: The Civil War Era* (New York: Ballantine, 1988), 452.

47. *Congressional Record,* 110th Cong., 2d sess., September 22, 2008, S9173.

48. Robert Luce, *Legislative Problems* (Boston: Houghton Mifflin, 1935), 426. Also see Louis Fisher, "The Authorization-Appropriation Process in Congress: Formal Rules and Informal Practices," *Catholic University Law Review* (Fall 1979): 51–105; Richard F. Fenno Jr., *The Power of the Purse* (Boston: Little, Brown, 1966).

49. John Cranford, "Just Say Maybe," *CQ Weekly,* March 7, 2011, 542.

50. Richard Munson, *The Cardinals of Capitol Hill* (New York: Grove Press, 1993), 6.

51. See Louis Fisher, "Annual Authorizations: Durable Roadblocks to Biennial Budgeting," *Public Budgeting and Finance* (Spring 1983): 23–40.

52. Chris Strohm, "Tensions Arise over Revised Intel Measure," *National Journal CongressDaily,* March 16, 2011, 16.

53. Quoted in Alan Ota, "Spending Bills May Be Democrats' Plan B," *CQ Today,* April 27, 2007, 8.

54. *Congressional Record,* 109th Cong., 1st sess., May 10, 2005, S4847.

55. See Elana Shor and Jackie Kucinich, "GOP Plots Blue-Slip Attack," *The Hill,* May 30, 2007, 1.

56. See Robert Keith, "Duration of Continuing Resolutions in Recent Years," Congressional Research Service Report RL32614, March 9, 2009.

57. Major Garrett, "Extreme Makeover," *National Journal,* March 12, 2011, 20.

58. Ibid., 18.

59. Susan Davis, "Yellow Lights," *National Journal,* February 5, 2011, 47.

60. Sarah Barr, "House Republicans Plan Legislation to Make Defunding Reform Law Easier," *Daily Report for Executives,* March 4, 2011, A-15.

61. Jason DeParle, "U.S. Welfare System Dies as State Programs Emerge," *New York Times,* June 30, 1997, A1.

62. Quoted in Jonathan Weisman and Michael Fletcher, "GOP May Be Splintering on Social Security," *Washington Post,* April 27, 2005, A4.

63. Robert Bixby, Stuart Butler, and Isabel Sawhill, "Entitlement Reform Options," *Washington Times,* November 18, 2008, A19; Robert Pear, "Recession Erodes 2 Largest Funds in U.S. Safety Net," *New York Times,* May 13, 2009, A1.

64. Damian Paleta, "Democrats Split on Social Security," *Wall Street Journal,* March 21, 2011, A4. The Congressional Budget Office (CBO) projects that in 2039 Social Security will be unable to pay full benefits under current law. See Jonathan Nicholson, "CBO Says Social Security Funds Will Run Out in 2039, Two Years Later than SSA [Social Security Administration] Estimate," *Daily Report for Executives,* July 2, 2010, A-23.

65. *Congressional Record,* 109th Cong., 1st sess., February 28, 2005, S1784.

66. David R. Francis, "Social Security: A Contrarian View," *Christian Science Monitor,* February 26, 2007, 17.

67. Billy House, "Dems Ramp Up Criticism of GOP on Social Security Cuts," *National Journal CongressDaily,* March 10, 2011, 12.

68. Neil King Jr. and Scott Greenberg, "Poll Shows Budget-Cuts Dilemma," *Wall Street Journal,* March 3, 2011, A5.

69. Alex Roarty, "Senior Moment," *National Journal,* February 26, 2001, 76.

70. David Cook, "Rising Healthcare Costs Pose Fundamental Risk to U.S.," *Christian Science Monitor,* September 18, 2007 (online edition).

71. Tim Fernholz, "Mind the Gap," *National Journal,* February 19, 2011, 50.

72. William Welch, "Medicare: The Next Riddle for the Ages," *USA Today,* March 17, 2005, 10A.

73. Quoted in Julie Rovner, "The Real Budget Buster," *National Journal's CongressDaily AM,* April 5, 2001, 5.

74. Donald Kettl, "Looking for a Real Crisis: Try Medicaid," *Governing,* April 2005, 20.

75. Matthew Miller, "The Big Federal Freeze," *New York Times Magazine,* October 15, 2000, 94.

76. Jonathan Nicholson, "Do Tax Expenditures Really Work? Experts Say Not Enough Data to Tell," *Daily Report for Executives,* October 25, 2010, J-1.

77. Ibid.

78. Paleta, "Democrats Split on Social Security," A4.

79. N. Gregory Mankiw, "The Blur between Spending and Taxes," *New York Times,* November 21, 2010, B5. Also see Nicholson, "Do Tax Expenditures Really Work?" J-1.

80. Gregory Rodriguez, "Hidden Federal Benefits," *Los Angeles Times,* February 28, 2011 (online edition). See Suzanne Mettler, *The Submerged State: How Invisible Government Policies Undermine American Democracy* (Chicago: University of Chicago Press, 2011); and

Christopher Howard, *The Hidden Welfare State: Tax Expenditures and Social Policy in the United States* (Princeton, NJ: Princeton University Press, 1997).

81. Mark Trumbull, "Does Crisis Loom over 'Debt Ceiling'?" *Christian Science Monitor*, March 14, 2011, 18–19.

82. Patrice Hill, "Debt-Ceiling Debate Stirs Up Speculation," *Washington Times*, February 11, 2011, A6.

83. "Failure to Raise Debt Ceiling 'Catastrophey,' Adviser Says," *USA Today*, January 3, 2011, 2A.

84. Paul Krawzak, "GOP Senators Push Obama on Entitlement Reform," *CQ Today*, March 17, 2011, 9.

85. Gerald F. Seib, "As Budget Battle Rages On, a Quiet Cancer Grows," *Wall Street Journal*, March 8, 2011, A4.

86. Steven Mufson, "On National Debt, Interest Is the Monster," *Washington Post*, February 17, 2011, A1.

87. David Clarke, "The 2 Percent Dissolution," *CQ Weekly*, May 28, 2007, 1576–1583.

88. *Congressional Record*, 106th Cong., 2d sess., March 2, 2000, S1050.

89. Stephanie Kirchgaessner, "Republicans' Rising Start Takes Risk on Medicare," *Financial Times*, April 6, 2011, 4. See Paul D. Ryan, "The GOP Path to Prosperity," *Wall Street Journal*, April 5, 2011, A15.

90. Mark Preston, "'Vote-a-Rama' Keeps Wearing Senate Down," *Roll Call*, March 26, 2003, 1.

91. *Congressional Record*, 107th Cong., 1st sess., February 15, 2001, S1532.

92. John Ellwood, "Budget Control in a Redistributive Environment," in *Making Economic Policy in Congress*, ed. Allen Schick (Washington, DC: American Enterprise Institute, 1983), 93. Data on the number of times reconciliation has been employed were provided by budget expert Robert Keith, Congressional Research Service.

93. Testimony of Sen. Robert C. Byrd, Senate Budget Committee, *Senate Procedures for Consideration of the Budget Resolution/Reconciliation*, February 12, 2009, 3.

94. David Rosenbaum, "Democratic Filibuster Hopes Fade," *New York Times*, November 18, 2002, A15; David Baumann, "The Octopus That Might Eat Congress," *National Journal*, May 14, 2005, 1470–1475.

95. Peter Cohn, "Hill Veteran Sees Pitfalls in Using Budget Reconciliation," *National Journal CongressDaily PM*, March 6, 2009, 3.

96. William Dauster, "Budget Process Issues for 1993," *Journal of Law and Politics* 9 (1992): 26.

97. Quoted in ibid., 27.

98. *Congressional Record*, 107th Cong., 1st sess., January 4, 2001, S19.

99. Lori Montgomery, "House GOP Passes New Rules on Tax and Spending Legislation," *Washington Post*, January 6, 2011, A7.

100. Paul Krawzak, "House Conservatives Seek Big Cuts," *CQ Weekly*, January 24, 2011, 211.

101. John Maggs, "The Trillion-Dollar Deficit," *National Journal*, November 1, 2008, 34.

102. Gail Russell Chaddock, "GOP's Family Feud over Spending," *Christian Science Monitor*, May 22, 2006, 10.

103. Matt Bai, "Sure Recipe for Decline: Neglect and Gluttony," *New York Times*, February 17, 2011, A17.

104. *Congressional Record*, 107th Cong., 2d sess., July 16, 2002, H4749.

CHAPTER 15

1. Mark Mazzetti and Eric Schmitt, "C.I.A. Spies Aiding Airstrikes and Assessing Quaddafi's Foes," *New York Times*, March 31, 2011, A1.

2. Philip Ewing, "Partisan Battle Lines Blur on Libya," *Politico*, March 31, 2011, 13.

3. Quoted in Samuel Eliot Morison, *The Oxford History of the American People* (New York: Oxford University Press, 1965), 346.

4. Edward S. Corwin, *The President: Office and Powers, 1787–1957,* 4th ed. (New York: New York University Press, 1957), 171. Also see Cecil V. Crabb Jr. and Pat M. Holt, *Invitation to Struggle: Congress, the President, and Foreign Policy,* 4th ed. (Washington, DC: CQ Press, 1992).

5. Corwin, *President,* 171 (emphasis in the original).

6. Alexander Hamilton, James Madison, and John Jay, *The Federalist Papers,* ed. Clinton Rossiter (New York: Mentor Books, 1961), 391–393.

7. Jonathan Mahler, "After the Imperial Presidency," *New York Times Magazine,* November 9, 2008, 45.

8. Jonathan Broder and Emily Cadei, "A Question of Authority," *CQ Weekly,* March 28, 2011, 670. Obama did consult with a small number of congressional leaders before the air war campaign began.

9. Testimony before the House International Relations Committee, January 12, 1995. Reported by Maureen Dowd, *New York Times,* January 13, 1995, A1.

10. Corwin, *President,* 171 (emphasis in the original).

11. Sen. Dick Lugar, "Congress Must Have a Say in Libya War," *The Hill,* March 29, 2011, 24.

12. Rajiv Chandrasekaran, "Battle Looms over Pace of Afghanistan Pullout," *Washington Post,* March 31, 2011, A11.

13. *Youngstown Sheet and Tube Co. v. Sawyer,* 343 U.S. 636 (1952).

14. Cecil V. Crabb Jr., Glenn J. Antizzo, and Leila E. Sarieddine, *Congress and the Foreign Policy Process* (Baton Rouge: Louisiana State University Press, 2000), 4.

15. Ibid., 163.

16. Bryan Bender, "Kerry Poised to Cap Long Journey," *Boston Globe,* November 20, 2008 (online edition).

17. Ibid.

18. Holbert N. Carroll, *The House of Representatives and Foreign Affairs,* rev. ed. (Boston: Little, Brown, 1966), 20.

19. Amy B. Zegart, "The Domestic Politics of Irrational Intelligence Oversight, *Political Science Quarterly* (Spring 2011): 25.

20. National Commission on Terrorist Attacks upon the United States, *The 9/11 Report* (New York: St. Martin's Paperbacks, 2004), 596–599.

21. *Congressional Record,* 110th Cong., 2d sess., September 23, 2008, S9268.

22. By law, the sixteen intelligence agencies are the CIA, Bureau of Intelligence and Research (State Department), Defense Intelligence Agency, National Security Agency, National Reconnaissance Office, National Geospatial-Intelligence Agency, FBI, Army Intelligence, Navy Intelligence, Air Force Intelligence, Marine Corps Intelligence, Department of Homeland Security, Coast Guard, Treasury Department, Department of Energy, and Drug Enforcement Agency. See Richard A. Best Jr., *Intelligence Issues for Congress,* Congressional Research Service Report RL33539, January 9, 2009.

23. Mark Mazzetti, "Report Faults Spy Chief for Inaction on Turf Wars," *New York Times,* April 2, 2009, A15.

24. Henry A. Kissinger, "Implementing Bush's Vision," *Washington Post,* May 16, 2005, A17.

25. *Congressional Record,* 105th Cong., 2d sess., March 2, 1998, E252.

26. Ibid.

27. Chris Strohm, "A Secure Role," *National Journal CongressDaily,* February 28, 2011, 3.

28. Information provided by Congressional Research Service defense expert Pat Towell.

29. Christopher J. Deering, "Congress, the President, and Military Policy," in *Congress and the Presidency: Invitation to Struggle,* ed. Roger H. Davidson, *The Annals* 499 (September 1988): 136–147.

30. Stephen Daggett, "Costs of Major U.S. Wars," Congressional Research Service Report RS2296, June 29, 2010, 2.

31. Shaun Waterman, "Lawmakers Grill Gates on Price of 'Illegal War,'" *Washington Times,* April 1, 2011, A1.

32. Quoted in Matt Richtel, "Trade Investors Cull Start-Ups for Pentagon," *New York Times,* May 7, 2007, C8.

33. *Budget of the United States Government, Fiscal Year 2006,* Historical Tables (Washington, DC: Government Printing Office, 2005), table 3.2.

34. Quoted in Thomas Shanker, "Defense Secretary Urges More Spending for U.S. Diplomacy," *New York Times,* November 27, 2007, A6.

35. Leslie Wayne, "Pentagon Spends without Bids, a Study Finds," *New York Times,* September 30, 2004, C1.

36. Christopher Dickey, "The Surveillance-Industrial Complex," *New York Times Book Review,* January 11, 2009, 11.

37. Tim Smart, "Getting the F-22 off the Ground," *Washington Post,* April 20, 1998, 12; Tim Weiner, "Air Superiority at $258 Million a Pop," *New York Times,* October 27, 2004, C1.

38. Julian E. Barnes, "Pentagon Chief Takes Aim at Big Weapons Systems," *Los Angeles Times,* April 7, 2009 (online edition).

39. Gordon Lubold, "Gates Axes Some Costly Weapons, Emphasizes 'Irregular' Warfare," *Christian Science Monitor,* April 6, 2009 (online edition).

40. Both quotes are from William Matthews and John T. Bennett, "Outlook for Gates' Plan Good, Despite Opposition," *Federal Times,* April 13, 2009, 8.

41. "Skelton Statement on Defense Budget Proposals," press release, House Armed Services Committee, April 6, 2009.

42. Fredreka Schouten, "The Challenge of Belt-Tightening," *USA Today,* February 14, 2011, 4A.

43. Tim Weiner, "For Military Plane in Crash, a History of Political Conflict," *New York Times,* April 11, 2000, A1.

44. Quoted in Roxana Tiron, "Marines, Weldon Score Victory on Osprey," *The Hill,* October 6, 2005, 16.

45. Christopher Bolkcom, "V-22 Osprey Tilt-Rotor Aircraft," Congressional Research Service Report RL31384, January 2, 2009, 11.

46. Quoted in Vernon Loeb, "Weapon Systems Die Hard, Especially on Capitol Hill," *Washington Post,* May 6, 2002, A4.

47. Quoted in Kevin Sack, "For the South, GOP Secures Defense Bounty," *New York Times,* November 18, 1997, A1.

48. *Congressional Record,* 100th Cong., 2d sess., July 7, 1988, 17072.

49. Karl Viox, "It's Closing Time for Base Commission," *Washington Post,* December 29, 1995, A21. Scholars regard this as an intriguing example of blame-avoidance politics. See, for example, Christopher J. Deering, "Congress, the President, and Automatic Government: The Case of Military Base Closures," in *Rivals for Power: Presidential-Congressional Relations,* ed. James A. Thurber (Washington, DC: CQ Press, 1996).

50. William H. Cooper, "The Future of U.S. Trade Policy: An Analysis of Issues and Options for the 112th Congress," Congressional Research Service Report R41145, January 4, 2011.

51. U.S. Trade Representative Ron Kirk, "The Monitor Breakfast," *Christian Science Monitor,* March 28, 2011, 19.

52. Rep. David Dreier, "Parties Can Work Together to Revive Trade Agenda," *Politico,* January 5, 2011, 35.

53. Joseph J. Schartz, "Trade Pacts No Longer an Easy Sell in GOP," *CQ Weekly,* December 13, 2010, 2848.

54. Quoted in John Stanton, "Sessions Continues Blockade of Trade Bill over Sleeping Bags," *Roll Call*, February 9, 2011 (online edition).

55. *Congressional Record*, 102d Cong., 2d sess., August 6, 1992, H7701–H7703.

56. Keith Bradsher, "NAFTA: Something to Offend Everyone," *New York Times*, November 14, 1993. Also see I. M. Destler, "Protecting Congress or Protecting Trade?" *Foreign Policy* 62 (Spring 1986): 96–107.

57. Elizabeth Becker, "Free Trade Pact Faces Trouble in Congress," *New York Times*, May 10, 2005, C1.

58. John E. Yang, "House Backs Clinton on China Trade Privileges," *Washington Post*, June 25, 1997, A1.

59. Sander Levin, "Derailing a Consensus on Trade," *Washington Post*, December 5, 2001, A29.

60. Barack Obama, "Making the World Work Again," *Los Angeles Times*, March 24, 2009 (online edition).

61. Richard Simon and Nancy Cleeland, "Senate OKs Fast-Track Trade Bill," *Los Angeles Times*, August 2, 2002, A1.

62. Ian Swanson, "Senator to Return Focus to 'Fast-Track' Trade Authority," *The Hill*, January 25, 2011, 18.

63. Leslie Wayne, "Foreign Sales by U.S. Arms Makers Doubled in a Year," *New York Times*, November 11, 2006, B3.

64. Charles McC. Mathias Jr., "Ethnic Groups and Foreign Policy," *Foreign Affairs* 59 (Summer 1981): 975–998.

65. Megan Scully, "Gates Warns against Big Cuts in Future Defense Spending," *National Journal's CongressDaily PM*, April 17, 2009, 4.

66. Joseph J. Schatz, "Has Congress Given Bush Too Free a Spending Hand?" *CQ Weekly*, April 12, 2002, 859.

67. Richard McGregor, "A Question of Sale," *Financial Times*, March 7, 2011, 7.

68. "Threatening a Sacred Cow," *The Economist*, February 12, 2011, 33. See Frank Oliveri and John M. Donnelly, "A Fiscally Offensive Forecast for Defense," *CQ Weekly*, July 19, 2010, 1740–1746; and Jamie Fly and John Noonan, "In Defense of the Pentagon's Budget," *Politico*, February 14, 2011, 21.

69. James Kitfield, "The Indispensable, Unaffordable Nation," *National Journal*, September 11, 2010, 35.

70. Micah Zenko and Rebecca R. Friedman, "A Soft Power Bargain," *Los Angeles Times*, February 16, 2011 (online edition).

71. T. Christian Miller, *Blood Money: Wasted Billions, Lost Lives, and Corporate Greed in Iraq* (New York: Little, Brown, 2006).

72. Zenko and Friedman, "Soft Power Bargain."

73. Robin Wright, "Don't Just Fund the War, Shell Out for Peace," *Washington Post*, March 10, 2001, B5; and Stephen Kinzer, "Why They Don't Know Us," *New York Times*, November 11, 2001, D5.

74. Ibid.

75. Josh Smith, "Global Reach," *National Journal Daily*, March 2, 2011, 5. Also see Sen. Dick Durbin, "Tyrants Can Use Facebook, Too," *Politico*, March 7, 2011, 21; and Mark Preifle, "Web's Identity Crisis: Tool of Freedom or Repression," *Christian Science Monitor*, March 14, 2011, 34.

76. David P. Auerswald, "Advice and Consent: The Forgotten Power," in *Congress and the Politics of Foreign Policy*, ed. Colton C. Campbell, Nicol C. Rae, and John Stack (Upper Saddle River, NJ: Prentice Hall, 2003), 47–48.

77. Loch Johnson and James M. McCormick, "Foreign Policy by Executive Fiat," *Foreign Policy* 28 (Fall 1977): 118–124.

78. Roger H. Davidson, "Senate Floor Deliberation: A Preliminary Inquiry," in *The Contentious Senate,* ed. Colton C. Campbell and Nicol C. Rae (Lanham, MD: Rowman and Littlefield, 2001), 22–29.

79. David Silverberg, "Nasty, Brutish and Short: The CTBT Debates," *The Hill,* December 8, 1999, 16.

80. Ibid.

81. Peter Baker, "Gamble by Obama Pays Off with Final Approval of Arms Control Pact," *New York Times,* December 23, 2010, A6.

82. Quoted in Gail Russell Chaddock, "Off-Radar Tax Breaks Draw New Scrutiny," *Christian Science Monitor,* March 9, 2005, 11.

83. Michael John Garcia, "International Law and Agreements: Their Effect Upon U.S. Law," Congressional Research Service Report RL32528, January 26, 2010, 3.

84. Ibid., 21.

85. Glen S. Krutz and Jeffrey S. Peake, *Treaty Politics and the Rise of Executive Agreements: International Commitments in a System of Shared Powers* (Ann Arbor: University of Michigan Press, 2009), 10.

86. Jeanne J. Grimmett, "Why Certain Trade Agreements Are Approved as Congressional-Executive Agreements Rather Than as Treaties," Congressional Research Service Report 97–896, February 17, 2009, 5.

87. This section draws on the invaluable summary of congressional policy initiation in Ellen C. Collier, "Foreign Policy Roles of the President and Congress," Congressional Research Service Report 93–20F, January 6, 1993, 11–17.

88. The classic account of this incident is Chalmers M. Roberts, "The Day We Didn't Go to War," *Reporter,* September 14, 1954, 31–35.

89. Alexander Bolton, "Dems Want Clearer Benchmarks from Obama on Afghanistan," *The Hill,* April 15, 2009, 3.

90. William G. Howell and Jon C. Pevehouse, *When Danger Lurks: Congressional Checks on Presidential War Powers* (Princeton, NJ: Princeton University Press, 2007), 223.

91. Ellen C. Collier, "Foreign Policy by Reporting Requirement," *Washington Quarterly* 11 (Winter 1988): 75.

92. Bruce J. Schulman, "Congress' Wartime Quandary," *Los Angeles Times,* April 27, 2003, M2.

93. Cited in Frederick A. O. Schwarz Jr. and Aziz Huq, "Where's Congress in This Power Play?" *Washington Post,* April 1, 2007, B1.

94. Ibid.

95. Thomas E. Mann and Norman J. Ornstein, *The Broken Branch* (New York: Oxford University Press, 2006), 151–152.

96. Richard Sobel, "Contra Aid Fundamentals: Exploring the Intricacies and the Issues," *Political Science Quarterly* 110 (Summer 1995): 287–306.

97. James M. Lindsay, "Congress, Foreign Policy, and the New Institutionalism," *International Studies Quarterly* 38 (June 1994): 281–304.

98. An early influential analysis of this phenomenon is John E. Mueller, *War, Presidents, and Public Opinion* (New York: Wiley, 1973), 208–213.

99. Richard F. Grimmett, "Instances of Use of United States Armed Forces Abroad, 1798–2006," Congressional Research Service Report RL32170, January 8, 2007.

100. Andrew J. Bacevich, "War Powers in the Age of Terror," *New York Times,* October 31, 2005, A21.

101. Quotes from Helen Dewar, "Congress's Reaction to TV Coverage Shows Ambivalence on Foreign Policy," *Washington Post,* October 9, 1993, A14; and Dewar, "Clinton, Congress at Brink of Foreign Policy Dispute," A1.

102. Douglas L. Kriner, *After the Rubicon: Congress, Presidents, and the Politics of Waging War* (Chicago: University of Chicago Press, 2010).
103. Richard F. Grimmett, "War Powers Resolution: Presidential Compliance," Congressional Research Service Report RL33532, March 25, 2011. Also see Grimmett, "The War Powers Resolution: After Thirty-Six Years," Congressional Research Service Report R4119, April 22, 2010.
104. Ivo H. Daalder and James M. Lindsay, *America Unbound: The Bush Revolution in Foreign Policy* (New York: Brookings, 2003), 90.
105. Caroline Heldman, "Presidential Persuasion and Press Coverage of the War in Iraq," in *Understanding the Presidency,* 4th ed., ed. James P. Pfiffner and Roger H. Davidson (New York: Pearson Longman, 2007), 199–200.
106. Gary C. Jacobson, *A Divider, Not a Uniter* (New York: Pearson Longman, 2007), 108.
107. *Congressional Record,* 107th Cong., 2d sess., October 10, 2002, S10247.
108. Editorial, "Iraq's Ticking Clock," *Washington Post,* April 3, 2011, A20.
109. Rajiv Chandrasekaran, "Battle Looms over Pace of Afghanistan Pullout," *Washington Post,* March 31, 2011, A1.
110. Ibid.
111. Editorial, "War, What Is It Meant For?" *Los Angeles Times,* March 12, 2011 (online edition). The two types of war are attributed to Richard Haas, the president of the Council on Foreign Relations.
112. Jonathan Broder, "Divided over a Stealth War," *CQ Weekly,* April 4, 2011, 751.
113. Ibid., 752.
114. Editorial, "War, What Is It Meant For?"
115. Quoted in Stephen Daggett, "Quadrennial Defense Review 2010: Overview and Implications for National Security Planning," Congressional Research Service Report R41250, May 17, 2010, 2–3.
116. Ian Morris, "The Fragile State of Nation States," *Washington Post,* April 3, 2011, B7.
117. Michael Abramowitz, "Bush, Congress Could Face Confrontation on Issue of War Powers," *Washington Post,* February 16, 2007, A5.
118. Bacevich, "War Powers in the Age of Terror," A21.
119. John E. Reilly, *Public Opinion and Foreign Policy* (Chicago: Chicago Council on Foreign Relations, 1999).
120. James M. Lindsay, "Congress and Foreign Policy: Why the Hill Matters," *Political Science Quarterly* 107 (Winter 1992–1993): 626–627.
121. Robert C. Byrd, *Losing America* (New York: Norton, 2005), 23

CHAPTER 16

1. Quoted in Carl Hulse and David M. Herszenhorn, "Behind Closed Doors, Warnings of Calamity," *New York Times,* September 20, 2008, C5.
2. Jonathan Weisman, David Cho, and Paul Kane, "With No Plan B, House Reluctantly Passes Politically Risky Measure," *Washington Post,* October 4, 2008, A1.
3. Quoted in ibid.
4. David M. Herszenhorn, "Administration Is Seeking $700 Billion for Wall Street in Possible Record Bailout," *New York Times,* September 21, 2008, A1.
5. Quoted in Hulse and Herszenhorn, "Behind Closed Doors," C5.
6. Quoted in Joe Nocera, "36 Hours of Alarm and Action as Crisis Spread," *New York Times,* October 2, 2008, A1.
7. Jackie Calmes, "Dazed Capital Feels Its Way, Eyes on Nov. 4," *Washington Post,* September 20, 2008, A1.

8. Quoted in Lori Montgomery, Paul Kane, and Neil Irwin, "Bailout Proposal Meets Bipartisan Outrage; Lawmakers Balk as Officials Press Case for Quick Action," *Washington Post,* September 24, 2008, A1.

9. David M Herszenhorn, "Word Reaches Congress. As the Market Goes Down, So Goes the Electorate," *New York Times,* October 2, 2008, C10.

10. Jonathan Weisman, "House Rejects Financial Rescue, Sending Stocks Plummeting," *Washington Post,* September 30, 2008, A1.

11. Editorial, "Bailout Breakdown," *New York Times,* September 25, 2008, A18; David S. Broder, "Credibility Test for Congress," September 25, 2008, A19.

12. Sarah A. Binder, Thomas E. Mann, Norman J. Ornstein, and Molly Reynolds, "Mending the Broken Branch: Assessing the 110th Congress, Anticipating the 111th," Brookings Institution Report, January 2009, www.brookings.edu/papers/2009/0108_broken_branch_binder_ mann.aspx, 33.

13. Andrew Kohut, "Pessimistic Public Doubts Effectiveness of Stimulus, TARP," Pew Research Center for the People and the Press, April 28, 2010, http://people-press.org/reports/pdf/608 .pdf.

14. Editorial, "Surprise! The Hated Bank Bailout Is About to Turn a Profit," *USA Today,* February 9, 2011, 8A.

15. Steven Pearlstein, "Unfairly Rewarding Greedy Bankers, and Why It Works," *Washington Post,* January 14, 2009, D1.

16. See Charles O. Jones, *The Presidency in a Separated System* (Washington, DC: Brookings, 1994).

17. *Congressional Record,* 105th Cong., 1st sess., May 21, 1997, H3072.

18. Glenn R. Parker and Roger H. Davidson, "Why Do Americans Love Their Congressmen So Much More Than Their Congress?" *Legislative Studies Quarterly* 4 (February 1979): 53–61.

19. See Roger H. Davidson, "The House of Representatives: Managing Legislative Complexity," in *Workways of Governance: Monitoring Our Government's Health,* ed. Roger H. Davidson (Washington, DC: Governance Institute and Brookings, 2003), 24–46; and Sarah A. Binder, "The Senate: Does It Deliberate? Can It Act?" in Davidson, *Workways of Governance,* 47–64.

20. Michael Leahy, "House Rules: Freshman Congressman Joe Courtney, Elected by a Margin of 83 Votes, Is Learning that the First Requirement of Power Is Self-Preservation," *Washington Post Magazine,* June 10, 2007, W12.

21. Quoted in Mary Lynn F. Jones, "Family Concerns Prompt Early Hill Retirements," *The Hill,* March 20, 2002, 12.

22. Quoted in ibid.

23. Quoted in Leahy, "House Rules," W12.

24. Frank Newport, "Congressional Approval at 17% after Elections," Gallup, Inc., News Release, November 11, 2010, www.gallup.com/poll/144419/Congressional-Approval-Elections.aspx.

25. Frank Newport, "Re-Election Measures Continue to Predict Major House Shakeup," Gallup, Inc., News Release, October 22, 2010, www.gallup.com/poll/143960/election-measures-continue-predict-major-house-shakeup.aspx?version=print.

26. Jeffrey M. Jones, "Congress' Job Approval Rating Worst in Gallup History," Gallup, Inc., News Release, December 15, 2010, www.gallup.com/poll/145238/congress-job-approval-rating-worst-gallup-history.aspx.

27. Quoted in Leahy, "House Rules," W12.

28. Bob Benenson, "Savvy 'Stars' Making Local TV a Potent Tool," *Congressional Quarterly Weekly Report,* July 18, 1987, 1551–1555.

29. Timothy Cook, *Making Laws and Making News: Media Strategies in the U.S. House of Representatives* (Washington, DC: Brookings, 1989), 82–83.

30. Quoted by Jonathan Kaplan, "Not on Speaking Terms," *The Hill*, June 3, 2004, 8.

31. Jeffrey M. Jones, "Nurses Top Honesty and Ethics List for 11th Year: Lobbyists, Car Salespeople, Members of Congress Get the Lowest Ratings," Gallup, Inc., News Release, December 3, 2010, www.gallup.com/poll/145043/nurses-top-honesty-ethics-list-11-year .aspx.

32. Ibid.

33. Lee H. Hamilton, "Ten Things I Wish Political Scientists Would Teach about Congress," Pi Sigma Alpha Lecture, American Political Science Association, August 31, 2000, 7. Also see Hamilton's thoughtful book, *How Congress Works and Why You Should Care* (Bloomington: Indiana University Press, 2004).

34. Norman J. Ornstein, "Prosecutors Must End Their Big Game Hunt of Politicians," *Roll Call*, April 26, 1993, 16.

35. Quoted in T. R. Goldman, "The Influence Industry's Senior Class," *Legal Times*, June 16, 1997, 4.

36. John Bresnehan and Jonathan Allen, "House Censures a Defiant Charles Rangel by Overwhelming Vote," *Politico*, December 2, 2010, www,politico.com/news/stories/1210/ 45883.html.

37. Jack Tripper, Avery Miller, and Katie Hinman, "The 2006 Election: The Year of the Scandal," ABC News, October 6, 2006, http://abcnews.com.

38. Norman J. Ornstein, "The Abramoff Saga: The Worst Hill Scandal in Our Lifetime?" *Roll Call*, October 19, 2005, 5–6.

39. Susan Schmidt and James V. Grimaldi, "Abramoff Pleads Guilty to 3 Counts," *Washington Post*, January 4, 2006, A1.

40. Paul Blumenthal, "Abramoff Investigation Continues Apace," Sunlight Foundation weblog, February 2, 2009, http://sunlightfoundation.com/blog/2009/02/02/abramoff-investigation- continues-apace/.

41. Norman J. Ornstein, "Lax Ethics Enforcement Created Culture of Carelessness in House," *Roll Call*, May 11, 2005, 6.

42. Bob Cusack, "Speaker Nancy Pelosi Did Not Drain Swamp, Key Voters Believe," *The Hill*, October 7, 2010.

43. Cass R. Sunstein, "Unchecked and Unbalanced," *American Prospect* 38 (May–June 1998): 23. Sunstein currently serves as the head of the Office of Information and Regulatory Affairs in the Office of Management and Budget.

44. David Catanese, "John Ensign, Citing 'Consequences to Sin,' Announces Retirement," *Politico*, March 7, 2011, www.politico.com/news/stories/0311/50799.html.

45. David A. Fahrenthold and Aaron Blake, "Rep. Chris Lee Resigns after Reports of Craigslist Flirtation," *Washington Post*, February 10, 2011.

46. This list includes would-be Speaker Bob Livingston, R-La. (1977–1999), Rep. Gary A. Condit, D-Calif. (1989–2003), Rep. Mark Foley, R-Fla. (1995–2006), and Rep. Tim Mahoney, D-Fla. (2007–2008).

47. Edward Epstein, "GOP Makes Much Ado about the Size of Pelosi's Plane; the House Speaker Has Had the Use of a Government Jet since the September 11 Attacks," *San Francisco Chronicle*, February 8, 2007, A3.

48. G. Calvin Mackenzie with Michael Hafken, *Scandal Proof: Do Ethics Laws Make Government Ethical?* (Washington, DC: Brookings, 2002), 158.

49. Benjamin Ginsberg and Martin Shefter, *Politics by Other Means: Politicians, Prosecutors, and the Press from Watergate to Whitewater*, 3d ed. (New York: Norton, 2002).

50. Paul C. Light, "Measuring the Health of the Public Service," in Davidson, *Workways of Governance*, 96–97.

51. Jennifer L. Lawless and Richard Logan Fox, *It Still Takes a Candidate: Why Women Don't Run For Office* (New York: Cambridge University Press, 2010).

52. John Hibbing and Christopher Larimer, "What the American Public Wants Congress to Be," in *Congress Reconsidered,* 8th ed., ed. Lawrence C. Dodd and Bruce I. Oppenheimer (Washington, DC: CQ Press, 2005), 55.

53. Gary C. Jacobson, "The Misallocation of Resources in House Campaigns," *Congress Reconsidered,* 5th ed., ed. Lawrence C. Dodd and Bruce I. Oppenheimer (Washington, DC: CQ Press, 1993), 153–182.

54. Woodrow Wilson, *Constitutional Government in the United States* (New York: Columbia University Press, 1908), 79–80.

55. Diane Hollern Harvey, "Who Should Govern? Public Preferences for Congressional and Presidential Power," Ph.D. dissertation, University of Maryland, 1998.

56. Hamilton, "Ten Things I Wish Political Scientists Would Teach about Congress," 3.

57. Center on Congress, Indiana University, "The Public's Opinions on Congress," March 18, 2011, 2.

58. Paul C. Light, *Government's Greatest Achievements: From Civil Rights to Homeland Security* (Washington, DC: Brookings, 2002).

59. Ibid., 63.

60. Devlin Barrett, "Most in U.S. Say Congress Short-Sighted," *Washington Post,* September 29, 2006.

61. Richard Hall, *Participation in Congress* (New Haven, CT: Yale University Press, 1996), 2.

62. Binder et al., "Mending the Broken Branch," 7.

63. Barbara Sinclair, *Unorthodox Lawmaking: New Legislative Processes in the U.S. Congress,* 3d ed. (Washington, DC: CQ Press, 2007).

64. Ibid.

65. Norman J. Ornstein, Thomas E. Mann, and Michael J. Malbin, *Vital Statistics on Congress, 2008* (Washington, DC: Brookings, 2008), 110.

66. Thomas E. Mann and Norman J. Ornstein, *The Broken Branch: How Congress Is Failing America and How to Get It Back on Track* (New York: Oxford University Press, 2006), 216.

67. Lee Hamilton, "We Can't Wait Much Longer to Fix Congress," *Comments on Congress,* December 15, 2005.

68. "Efficiency Up against Precedent," *CQ Weekly,* December 13, 2010: 2841.

69. Paul Bedard, "House to Work Just 32 Weeks in 2011," *U.S. News and World Report,* Weblog, December 8, 2010, www.usnews.com/news/washington-whispers/articles/2010/12/08/house-to-work-just-32-weeks-in-2011.

70. Nelson W. Polsby, *How Congress Evolves: Social Bases of Institutional Change* (New York: Oxford University Press, 2004), 130–137.

71. Binder et al., "Mending the Broken Branch," 7.

72. Quoted by David S. Broder, "Role Models, Now More than Ever," *Washington Post,* July 13, 2003, B7.

73. Ibid.

74. Mickey Edwards, "Wanted: A Congress with a Backbone," *Los Angeles Times,* August 29, 2006, B13.

75. Mark D. Ramirez, "The Dynamics of Partisan Conflict on Congressional Approval," *American Journal of Political Science* 53 (July 2009): 681–694.

76. Ibid., 683.

77. Sinclair, *Unorthodox Lawmaking,* 127.

78. Ibid.

79. *Congressional Record,* 110th Cong., 1st sess., December 17, 2007, H15508.

80. Sinclair, *Unorthodox Lawmaking,* 282.

81. Ian Millhiser, "The Tyranny of the Timepiece: Senate Rules Obstruct Voting to a Degree that Wounds Our Government," Center for American Progress Report, September 28, 2010, www.americanprogress.org/issues/2010/09/tyranny_of_the_timepiece.html.

82. For an extended analysis of these dilemmas, see John B. Gilmour, *Strategic Disagreement: Stalemate in American Politics* (Pittsburgh: University of Pittsburgh Press, 1995).

83. C-SPAN began gavel-to-gavel telecasting of House proceedings in 1979 and Senate proceedings in 1986.

84. Joseph J. Schatz, "Tune a New Channel into the Senate," *CQ Weekly,* April 19, 2010, 956.

85. E. Scott Adler, *Why Congressional Reforms Fail: Reelection and the House Committee System* (Chicago: University of Chicago Press, 2002), 11.

86. Eric Schickler, *Disjointed Pluralism: Institutional Innovation and the Development of the U.S. Congress* (Princeton, NJ: Princeton University Press, 2001), 268.

87. Ibid., 267.

88. Bob Schieffer, *This Just In: What I Couldn't Tell You on TV* (New York: Putnam, 2003).

89. See Martin P. Wattenburg, *Is Voting for Young People?* 2d ed. (New York: Pearson Longman, 2007), esp. chaps. 1–2.

90. Bill Moyers, "Journalism and Democracy," *Nation,* May 7, 2001, 12.

91. Media critic Neal Gabler's commentaries are especially incisive. See "The Media Bias Myth," *Los Angeles Times,* December 22, 2002, M1.

92. John R. Hibbing and Elizabeth Theiss-Morse, *Congress as Public Enemy* (Cambridge: Cambridge University Press, 1995), 147.

93. Ibid., 158.

94. Alan K. Ota, "Finding Solutions to Secure Events," *CQ Weekly,* January 17, 2011, 164.

95. Christopher Lee, "An Amendment to Be Recommended on Continuity of Congress," *Washington Post,* May 25, 2003, A11.

96. Norman Ornstein, "Government in Denial; No Branch Is Prepared for a Decapitating Strike," *Washington Post,* July 12, 2007, A23.

97. See Louis Fisher, *Presidential War Power,* 2d ed. (Lawrence: University Press of Kansas, 2004).

98. Josh Rogin, "How Obama Turned on a Dime toward War," The Cable, *Foreign Policy* Weblog, March 18, 2011, http://thecable.foreignpolicy.com/posts/2011/03/18/how_obama_turned_on_a_dime_toward_war.

99. Quoted in Kirk Victor, "Congress in Eclipse," *National Journal,* April 5, 2003, 1068.

100. Ibid., 1069.

101. *Congressional Record,* 107th Cong., 2d sess., February 12, 2002, S2268, S2271.

102. Hamilton, "We Can't Wait Much Longer to Fix Congress."

103. David Nather, "Congress as Watchdog: Asleep on the Job?" *CQ Weekly,* May 22, 2004, 1190.

104. According to data available from the Federal Judicial Center (www.fjc.gov/history/home.nsf/page/research_categories.html), as of March 21, 2011, 433 active federal district and appeals court judges were appointed by Republican presidents and 327 were appointed by Democratic presidents. If senior-status judges are included, 738 federal judges were appointed by Republican presidents and 524 were appointed by Democratic presidents.

105. John T. Noonan Jr., *Narrowing the Nation's Power* (Berkeley: University of California Press, 2002), 11.

106. Ibid., 139.

107. James L. Sundquist, *The Decline and Resurgence of Congress* (Washington, DC: Brookings, 1981), 482–483.

108. Ibid., 483.

109. Andrew Rudalevige, *The New Imperial Presidency: Renewing Presidential Power after Watergate* (Ann Arbor: University of Michigan Press, 2005), 261.

110. Hamilton, "Ten Things I Wish Political Scientists Would Teach about Congress," 10.

Boxes, figures, tables and notes are indicated by *b, f, t, and n* following the page number. Appendix page numbers start with A, and note page numbers start with N.

Photo Credits

CQ Press, a division of SAGE, is a leading publisher of books, directories, periodicals, and electronic products on American government and politics, with an expanding list in international affairs, history, and journalism. CQ Press consistently ranks among the top commercial publishers in terms of quality, as evidenced by the numerous awards its products have won over the years. CQ Press owes its existence to Nelson Poynter, former publisher of the *St. Petersburg Times,* and his wife Henrietta, with whom he founded Congressional Quarterly in 1945. Poynter established CQ with the mission of promoting democracy through education and in 1975 founded the Modern Media Institute, renamed The Poynter Institute for Media Studies after his death. The Poynter Institute (*www.poynter.org*) is a nonprofit organization dedicated to training journalists and media leaders.

In 2008, CQ Press was acquired by SAGE, a leading international publisher of journals, books, and electronic media for academic, educational, and professional markets. Since 1965, SAGE has helped inform and educate a global community of scholars, practitioners, researchers, and students spanning a wide range of subject areas, including business, humanities, social sciences, and science, technology, and medicine. A privately owned corporation, SAGE has offices in Los Angeles, London, New Delhi, and Singapore, in addition to the Washington DC office of CQ Press.

CONGRESSIONAL TIME LINE: **1789–1932**

	1790		1810		1830		1850	
Size of House of Representatives	65	142	186	213	242	232	237	
Size of Senate	26	34	36	48	48	52	62	

Parties
Federalist Era (1789–1800) — Jeffersonian Era (1800–1828) — Jacksonian Era (1828–1856) — GOP formed (1856)

Presidents

Washington (1789–1797) — Jefferson (1801–1809) — "Jeffersonians" Madison, Monroe (1809–1825) — Jackson (1829–1837) — Polk (1845–1849) — "Doughfaces" (Fillmore, Pierce, Buchanan) (1849–1861)

Internal

Capitol cornerstone (1793)

Capitol burned by British (1814)

Restored Capitol (1818–1826)

Printed election ballots (1829)

Speaker Henry Clay (1811)

Senate oratory (Webster, Clay, Calhoun) (1830s, 1840s)

Procedural rules, standing committees (1790s)

Congressional Nominating Caucus (1804–1828)

Committees control legislation (1820s)

Congress convenes; Ways and Means Committee (1789)

Jefferson's *Manual* (1801)

Unlimited debate in Senate (1828)

Major Laws/ Investigations

Louisiana Purchase (1803)

Rivers and Harbors Act (1823)

Judicial review *Marbury v. Madison* (1803)

McCulloch v. Maryland (1819)

Dred Scott v. Sandford (1857)

Judiciary Act (1789)

Slave importation halted (1807)

St. Clair investigation (1792)

Alien and Sedition Acts (1798)

Missouri Compromise (1820)

Compromise of 1850

Bill of Rights (1791)

Wars and Alarms

Barbary pirates (1801–1805)

War of 1812 (1812–1814)

Mexican War (1846–1848)

| 1790 | 1810 | 1830 | 1850 |